# PSYCHOMETRIC THEORY

# McGraw-Hill Series in Psychology

*Consulting Editors*
Norman Garmezy
Lyle V. Jones

**Adams:** *Human Memory*
**Berlyne:** *Conflict, Arousal, and Curiosity*
**Blum:** *Psychoanalytic Theories of Personality*
**Bock:** *Multivariate Statistical Methods in Behavioral Research*
**Brown:** *The Motivation of Behavior*
**Butcher:** *MMPI: Research Developments and Clinical Applications*
**Campbell, Dunnette, Lawler, and Weick:** *Managerial Behavior, Performance, and Effectiveness*
**Crites:** *Vocational Psychology*
**D'Amato:** *Experimental Psychology: Methodology, Psychophysics, and Learning*
**Dollard and Miller:** *Personality and Psychotherapy*
**Ferguson:** *Statistical Analysis in Psychology and Education*
**Fodor, Bever, and Garrett:** *The Psychology of Language; An Introduction to Psycholinguistics and Generative Grammar*
**Forgus and Melamed:** *Perception: A Cognitive-Stage Approach*
**Franks:** *Behavior Therapy: Appraisal and Status*
**Gilmer and Deci:** *Industrial and Organizational Psychology*
**Guilford:** *Psychometric Methods*
**Guilford:** *The Nature of Human Intelligence*
**Guilford and Fruchter:** *Fundamental Statistics in Psychology and Education*
**Guilford and Hoepfner:** *The Analysis of Intelligence*
**Guion:** *Personnel Testing*
**Hetherington and Parke:** *Child Psychology: A Contemporary Viewpoint*
**Hirsh:** *The Measurement of Hearing*
**Hjelle and Ziegler:** *Personality Theories: Basic Assumptions, Research, and Applications*
**Horowitz:** *Elements of Statistics for Psychology and Education*
**Hulse, Deese, and Egeth:** *The Psychology of Learning*
**Hurlock:** *Adolescent Development*
**Hurlock:** *Child Development*
**Hurlock:** *Developmental Psychology*
**Krech, Crutchfield, and Ballachey:** *Individual in Society*
**Lakin:** *Interpersonal Encounter: Theory and Practice in Sensitivity Training*
**Lawler:** *Pay and Organizational Effectiveness: A Psychological View*
**Lazarus, A.:** *Behavior Therapy and Beyond*
**Lazarus, R.:** *Patterns of Adjustment*
**Lewin:** *A Dynamic Theory of Personality*

# PSYCHOMETRIC THEORY

## Second Edition

**Jum C. Nunnally**
**Professor of Psychology**
**Vanderbilt University**

**McGraw-Hill Book Company**

New York  St. Louis  San Francisco  Auckland  Bogotá  Düsseldorf
Johannesburg  London  Madrid  Mexico  Montreal  New Delhi
Panama  Paris  São Paulo  Singapore  Sydney  Tokyo  Toronto

**PSYCHOMETRIC THEORY**

890 DODO 8987654

Library of Congress Cataloging in Publication Data

Nunnally, Jum C
    Psychometric theory.

    (McGraw-Hill series in psychology)
    Bibliography:  p.
    Includes index.
    1.  Psychometrics.  I.  Title.
BF39.N8 1978       152.8      77-23950
ISBN 0-07-047465-6

This book was set in Times Roman by A Graphic Method Inc.
The editors were Richard R. Wright and Michael Gardner;
the production supervisor was Dennis J. Conroy
New drawings were done by J & R Services, Inc.
R. R. Donnelley & Sons Company was printer and binder.

To my parents

# CONTENTS

Ad-lib factoring. Higher-order factors. Comparison of factors in different analyses. How to fool yourself with factor analysis. An outlook on factor analysis. Suggested additional readings.

# PREFACE

The first edition of *Psychometric Theory* was far too warmly received for the author to markedly change the content, style, or fundamental principles of measurement. Mainly the book has been modernized. Ten years ago I was writing the first edition, and today's readers need to be brought up to date regarding developments since that time. In looking back over the first edition, I can see that most of the general principles of psychological measurement stated there remain valid, but there are many modern developments and points of view that should be discussed.

In order to introduce modern developments, it was necessary to omit some topics that are no longer very important and in other cases to abbreviate sections that were discussed in more detail than necessary. Some examples of topics that are either added or discussed more fully because of developments during the last 10 years are new methods of unidimensional scaling in Chapter 2, additional points of view about validity in Chapter 3, computerized approaches to multiple correlation in Chapter 5, a new chapter on test construction (Chapter 9) to take account of some special new approaches and to more extensively discuss methods that were only mentioned in Chapter 8 of the first edition, new approaches to factor analysis in Chapters 10 and 11, a much more extensive discussion of multidimensional scaling in Chapter 12 than was given in Chapter 11 of the first edition, and a general updating of "the content areas" in Part Four.

This book is intended to serve primarily as a comprehensive text for graduate-level courses in psychology and education which are designated variously as psychological measurement, test theory, or psychometric theory. In addition, I hope that the book will be useful as a handbook to professionals in the behavioral sciences.

It should be pointed out quite firmly that the book is not intended for any special group, such as students in clinical psychology or students who intend to concentrate on psychological and educational measurement in their careers. It aims to present an understandable account of what every good behavioral scientist should know about psychometric theory. The book is as important for persons interested in basic research in the behavioral sciences as for the person interested in applied research; and it is as important for the person interested in experiments as for the person interested in studies of individual differences. Psychometric theory is a pertinent issue for all behavioral sciences, and any graduate students who do not receive good grounding in that topic will miss a very important part of their education. For this reason, in writing this book, I tried to keep in mind the needs of students interested in physiological psychology, learning, perception, personality, education, clinical psychology, and other areas. Some sections in Part Four are particularly relevant to students interested in studies of individual differences, but even there much of the discussion is relevant to all fields of behavioral science.

I purposely named the book *Psychometric Theory* rather than *Psychometric Methods*, because the book is intended to discuss *principles* rather than to go into great detail on all the many technical matters that underlie such principles. Whole books are written on many of the particular methods that underlie principles of psychometric theory, such as books on predictive validity, test construction, reliability, factor analysis, multidimensional scaling, measurement of abilities, measurement of personality traits, and others. Not only would it have been impossible to cover the major technical details regarding all these particular issues in one book, but that was not my desire. I wanted to formulate and state in an understandable manner what I considered to be the major principles that underlie all aspects of psychometric theory. The reader will be supplied with copious references to detailed accounts of the major psychometric techniques subsumed under these principles, and the reader who has a special interest in psychometric theory will even be provided with sources for searching out the "museum pieces" generated by the superspecialists in psychometric theory.

When students first hear the term *psychometric theory*, they probably think of complex mathematical and statistical developments, and many students who are not well grounded in mathematics will be fearful of treading this ground. It is true that many of the principles of psychometric theory have mathematical implications, but that does not mean that the important *ideas* must be expressed in equations. Indeed, some of the most abstract principles pertaining to even very complex matters in psychometrics (e.g., in factor analysis) can be stated in simple words, even though these words may be laden with implications that would keep the gifted mathematician busy for a long time in developing specific mathematical techniques. Only the most essential mathematical developments are directly presented in this book. Most are simply talked out, and large numbers of specific mathematical techniques are pinpointed in references. I have included a special section, Suggested Additional Readings, at the end of each chapter as general sources for the reader who would like to learn more about a topic, and up-to-date references are given for computational routines and computerized procedures for all the major analytic techniques.

A consistent theme throughout the book is an emphasis on *scientific generalization*. Whereas the search for general principles was discussed at various points in the first edition, in the second edition it is shown that almost every topic in psychometric theory relates in one way or another to the scientist's search for general statements regarding reality. This is true of measurement itself, reliability, validity, psychological scaling, complex methods of multivariate analysis, and research in all substantive areas.

At this point it is common to thank all the people that have helped one write a book. I want to thank Barbara Bryant for her invaluable assistance and advice in all phases of writing the book. I want to thank my wife, Kay, for tolerating my absent-minded neglect on many occasions while my mind wandered off to some issue associated with this book. She believed that the venture was important and encouraged me to work on the book even at times when we wanted to enjoy life together. My old friend Henry Kaiser was kind enough to read and advise me about Part Three. With his reputation in psychometrics, it could go without saying that any unwise statements in that section are not his fault. Mainly, however, I would like to thank my colleagues, friends, relatives, and students for the rare occasions on which they left me alone to think and write.

*Jum C. Nunnally*

# PSYCHOMETRIC THEORY

## BASIC PRINCIPLES

# INTRODUCTION

## MEASUREMENT IN SCIENCE

Although tomes have been written on the nature of measurement, in the end it boils down to something rather simple: *measurement consists of rules for assigning numbers to objects in such a way as to represent quantities of attributes.* The term *rules* indicates that the procedures for assigning numbers must be explicitly stated. In some instances the rules are so obvious that detailed formulations are not required. This is the case when a yardstick is employed to measure lengths of lumber. What should be done is intuitively obvious, and consequently it is not necessary to study a thick manual of rules before undertaking the measurement. Such examples are, however, the exception rather than the usual in science. For instance, measuring the amounts of various components in chemical compounds often requires complex procedures that are not intuitively obvious. Certainly the rules for measuring most psychological attributes are not intuitively obvious. Examples are the measurement of intelligence in school children, amount of retention in the study of paired-associate learning, drive level in a study of rats, attitudes toward minority groups, degree of cooperation in social situations, and so on.

The definition above speaks of the use of *rules* as an important aspect of measurement, which relates to the matter of *standardization.* A measure is not well standardized if the rules are unclear and impractical to apply or if they require different kinds and amounts of skills by persons who use the measurement procedure. One of the primary aspects of standardization requires that different people who employ the measuring instrument, or supposedly alternative measures of the same attribute, should obtain similar results. Thus a measure of the surface temperature of planets in the solar system is well standardized if different astronomers who employ the methods obtain very similar numerical results for particular planets on particular occasions. Similarly, an intelligence test is well standardized if different examiners give approximately the same scores to the same children. Formulating explicit rules for the assignment of numbers is a major aspect of the standardization of measures. Other aspects of standardization will be discussed throughout this book.

In the definition above, the term *attribute* indicates that measurement always concerns some particular feature of objects. Strictly speaking, one does not measure objects—one measures their attributes. Thus one measures not the child, but rather the intelligence of the child. Although the distinction may sound like mere hairsplitting, it is important. First, it demonstrates that measurement requires a process of abstraction. An attribute concerns relations among objects on a particular dimension, e.g., weight or intelligence. A red rock and a white rock may weigh the same, and two white rocks may have different weights. Thus the attribute of weight is an abstraction which must not be confounded with all the particular features of objects. The point should be obvious to the sophisticated reader of this book, but it is not obvious, for example, to children or to adults in many primitive societies. With the latter sometimes there is confusion between a particular attribute of objects and all the recognizable attributes of objects. The failure to abstract a particular attribute makes concepts of measurement difficult to grasp. To some extent this confusion resides in the minds of civilized adults. For example, it is difficult for some people to understand that a criminal and a well-behaved member of society can have the same level of intelligence (as measured by intelligence tests).

A second reason for emphasizing that measurement always concerns a particular attribute is that it forces us to carefully consider the nature of the attribute before attempting to measure it. One possibility is that the attribute does not exist. For example, the many negative results obtained in the efforts to measure an overall attribute of "rigidity" in people make it doubtful that there is such an attribute. It is not necessarily the case that all the terms used to describe people are matched by measurable attributes, e.g., ego strength, extrasensory perception, and dogmatism. Another possibility is that a measurement method may concern a mixture of attributes rather than only one attribute. Frequently this occurs in questionnaire measures of "adjustment," which tend to contain items relating to a number of separable attributes. Although such conglomerate measures sometimes are partly justifiable on practical grounds, the use of such conglomerate measures offers a poor foundation for psychological science. As this book will show in detail, each measure should concern some one *thing,* some distinct, unitary attribute. To the extent that unitary attributes should be combined to form an overall appraisal, e.g., of adjustment, they should be rationally combined from different measures rather than haphazardly combined within one measure.

Still looking at the definition of measurement, it is emphasized that *numbers* are used to represent *quantities.* Quantification concerns how much of an attribute is present in an object; numbers are used to communicate the amount. Quantification is so intimately interwoven with the concept of measurement that the two terms are often used interchangeably.

In the definition it is said that numbers are assigned to *objects*. The objects in psychology usually involve people or lower animals, such as, with people, numbers of words correctly spelled, geometrical forms recognized in perception, or correct responses in a study of learning. In some instances, however, the objects are material objects. For example, when people rate the pleasantness of each word in a list, the words are measured and the people act as part of the measurement process. There are many other instances in which people serve essentially as the measurement method for objects, such as in measuring (1) the attention-getting properties of different works of art in terms of how long people look at them, (2) the difficulty of spelling words in terms of the percent of students who make errors on each, and (3) the meaningfulness of complex geometrical designs in terms of the number of names that subjects can give to each.

Although the definition emphasizes that *rules* for quantification are at the heart of measurement, it does not specify the nature of such rules or place any limit on the "allowable" kinds of rules. This is because a clear distinction should be made between the standards of measurement, qua the measurement process, and standards for validating measures, or determining their usefuless, once they are in existence. Numerous standards can be applied to obtain the usefulness of a measurement method, including (1) the extent to which data obtained from the method fit a mathematical model, (2) reliability of measurement, (3) validity in various senses, and (4) the extent to which the measurement method produces interesting relationships with other scientific measures. Such standards will be discussed throughout this book. Thus some psychologists might establish a set of rules for the measurement of dogmatism which seems quite illogical to their colleagues, but the usefulness of the measure could not be dismissed a priori. The usefulness of the measurement method would have to be determined by the procedures that will be discussed in this book.

In establishing rules for the employment of a particular measure, the crucial consideration is that the set of rules must be unambiguous. The rules may be developed from an elaborate deductive model, they may be based on much previous experience, they may flow from common sense, or they may spring from only hunches; but the proof of the pudding is in how well the measurement method serves to explain important phenomena. Consequently *any* set of rules that unambiguously quantifies properties of objects constitutes a *legitimate* measurement method and has a right to compete with other measures for scientific usefulness.

## ADVANTAGES OF STANDARDIZED MEASURES

Although probably the reader already has a healthy respect for the importance of measurement in science, it might be useful to look at some particular advantages which measurement provides. To note the advantages of standardized measures, it is necessary to compare them with what would be left if they were not available—for example, if there were no measures of temperature or intelligence. What would be left would be subjective appraisals, personal judgments, or whatever one would want to call the intuitive processes involved. Some of the advantages of standardized measures over personal judgments are as follows:

**Objectivity** The major advantage of measurement is that it takes the guesswork out of scientific observation. A key principle of science is that any statement of fact made by one scientist should be independently verifiable by other scientists. The principle is violated if there is room for disagreement among scientists about the observation of empirical events. For example, since we have no standardized measure of "ego strength," two psychologists could disagree widely about the ego strength of a particular person. Obviously then, it is not possible to make scientific tests of theories concerning ego strength until satisfactory measurement methods are developed. Thus theories concerning atomic particles, hardness of rocks, temperature of stars, intelligence of children, emotions in adults, drive level in rats, and so on are testable to the extent to which there exist unambiguous procedures for documenting empirical events. Standardized measurement methods provide such procedures.

A case could be made that the major problem in psychology is that of measurement. There is no end of theories, but most theories are populated to some extent with terms (hypothesized attributes) which presently cannot be adequately measured; consequently the theories cannot be properly tested. This is the problem with Freudian theory. There are no agreed-on procedures for observing and quantifying such attributes as ego strength, libidinal energy, narcissism, and others. In fact, it seems that major advances in psychology, and probably in all sciences, are preceded by breakthroughs in measurement methods. This is attested to by the flood of research following the development of intelligence tests. Recent advances in techniques for measuring the electrical activity of individual nerve cells in the brain provide another example of how the development of measurement methods spurs research. Scientific results inevitably are reported in terms of functional relations among measured variables, and the science of psychology will progress neither slower nor faster than it becomes possible to measure important variables.

**Quantification** The numerical results provided by standardized measures have two advantages. First, numerical indices make it possible to report results in finer detail than would be the case with personal judgments. Thus the availability of thermometers makes it possible to report the exact increase in temperature when two chemicals are mixed, rather than for the investigator to intuitively judge only that "the temperature increases." Similarly, whereas teachers may be able to reliably assign children to broad categories of intelligence such as "bright," "average," and "below normal," intelligence tests provide finer differentiations. The same precision can be obtained for many types of variables studied in the behavioral sciences.

A second advantage of quantification is that it permits the use of powerful methods of mathematical analysis. Thus, the numbers obtained from measurement methods can be "plugged into" powerful mathematical systems of algebra, geometry, calculus, and other extremely useful mathematical tools. This is essential in the elaboration of theories and in the analysis of experiments. Although it may occur far in the future for some (but not all) types of investigations in psychology, it is reasonable to believe that all theories eventually will be expressed in mathematical form. When theories are in mathematical form, it is possible to make precise deductions for experimental investigation. Also, after experiments are completed, powerful methods of mathematical analysis, such as the use of factor analysis and analysis of variance, are needed in order to analyze the results. Without the availability of such powerful methods of mathematical and statistical analysis, it would not be possible to precisely and thoroughly analyze the results of research.

**Communication** Science is a highly public enterprise in which efficient communication among scientists is essential. Each scientist builds on what has been learned in the past, and day by day his or her findings must be compared with those of other scientists working on the same types of problems. Communication is greatly facilitated when standardized measures are available. Suppose, for example, in an experiment concerning the effects of stress on anxiety reaction, it is reported that a particular treatment made the subjects "appear anxious." This would leave many questions as to what the experimenter meant by "appear anxious," and consequently it would be very difficult for other experimenters to investigate the same effects. Much better communication would be achieved if standardized measures of anxiety were available. If the means and standard deviations of scores for the different treatment groups were reported, very efficient and precise communication with other scientists would be possible. Even if subjective evaluations of experimental results are very carefully done, they are much more difficult to communicate than are statistical analyses of standardized measures. The rate of scientific progress in a particular area is limited by the efficiency and fidelity with which scientists can communicate their results to one another.

**Economy** Although it frequently requires a great deal of work to develop standardized measures, once developed, they generally are much more economical of time and money than are subjective evaluations. For example, even being a good judge of intelligence, a teacher probably would need to observe a child for some months to make a good judgment. A better appraisal usually could be obtained from one of the group measures of intelligence, which would take no more than an hour to administer and might cost less than 50 cents per child. Rather than have clinical psychologists individually interview each recruit for the armed services, a printed test can be administered to a large group of recruits. In a study of the effect of a particular drug on amount of activity of white rats, it would be far more economical to employ standardized measures (e.g., the activity wheel) than to have trained observers sit for hours noting the amount of activity.

Besides saving time and money, standardized measures often free highly trained professionals for more important work. A great saving is obtained in many instances when time-consuming observations by professionals are replaced by standardized measures. Of course, sometimes it is difficult to disentangle the scientist from the measurement process, which, for example, is the case in employing individually administered tests of intelligence. Although some individual tests of intelligence are highly standardized, they still require much time for administration and scoring. The direction of progress, however, is always toward developing measures that either require very little effort to employ or are so simple to administer and score that semiskilled workers can do the job. Standardized measures are in most cases, although not always, more economical of the scientist's time than are subjective observations; consequently they give scientists more time for the scholarly and creative aspects of their work.

**Scientific Generalization** As will be mentioned with respect to many topics in this book, *scientific generalization* is at the very heart of scientific work. Most observations in daily life are of particular events—a "falling" star, a baby crying, a feeling of pain from a pin scratch, and a friend remarking about the weather. The intention in science is to try to find some underlying order in all the particular events that occur in nature. This is done by the formulation of hypotheses which, if they "pan out" in the crucible of experimentation, are referred to as *laws*. Of course, the most widely known examples are the simple laws in physics pertaining to gravitation, heat, and states of gases. Regarding the last, one principle is that the temperature of a gas is directly related to how highly the gas is compressed. Laws such as these in physics, and in all other areas of science including the behavioral sciences, are intended to be general, in the sense that they explain a large number of phenomena with a simple set of principles. For example, the law relating the compression of a gas to temperature explains why the expanding gas in an air-conditioning system results in cooling.

Many generalizations in all areas of science, and particularly in the behavioral sciences, must be stated in statistical terms, with respect to the probability of an event occurring, rather than specified with more exactness. However, statistical principles also are intended to be generalizations, to explain as much as possible with simple statements regarding the real world. The development and use of standarized measurement methods are essential for formulating such generalizations in all areas of science. A simple illustration of this point is depicted in Fig. 1-1, which shows the relationship between the complexity of randomly generated geometrical forms and the amount of time that subjects

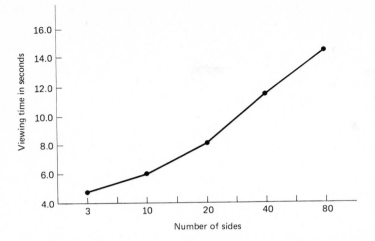

**Figure 1-1** Relationship between complexity of geometric forms varying from 3 to 80 sides and amount of looking time.

spend looking at the forms in studies of voluntary visual attention. The graph shows the average responses for a group of subjects, which of course presents a much more regular trend than if relationships were shown for individual subjects. However, with these types of stimulus materials and many others, there is a general law at work: the more complex the figure, the longer people tend to look at it. Of course, experiments on this topic would have been rather pointless, and the lawful relationship depicted in Fig. 1-1 could not have been determined without the availability of well-standardized, precise measures of both the complexity of geometrical forms and the amount of voluntary visual attention. Generalizations such as that illustrated in Fig. 1-1 are the very meat of science, and scientists can reach their objectives only if standardized measures are available.

## MEASUREMENT AND MATHEMATICS

It is important to make a clear distinction between measurement, which is directly concerned with the real world, and mathematics, which is purely an abstract enterprise that need have nothing to do with the real world. Perhaps the two would not be so readily confused if they did not both frequently involve quantification. Mathematical systems are purely deductive, being sets of rules for the manipulation of symbols. Symbols for quantities constitute only one type of symbol found in mathematics, and much of modern mathematics concerns deductive systems whose symbols do not relate to numbers. Any set of rules for manipulating a group of symbols can be a legitimate branch of mathematics as long as the rules are internally consistent. Thus the statement *iggle wug drang flous* could be a legitimate mathematical statement in a set of rules stating that when any *iggle* is *wugged* it *drang* a *flous*. An elaborate mathematical system could be constructed in which both the objects and the operations were symbolized by nonsense words. Of course, the system might not be of any practical use, but the legitimacy of the system would depend entirely on the internal consistency of the rules. Thus if the system of rules left it in doubt whether the *iggle drang* a *flous* or *drang* a *squiegle,* there would be a flaw in the system.

In contrast to mathematics, measurement always concerns numbers, and the legitimacy of any system of measurement is determined by empirical data (facts from the real world). Measurement always concerns *how much* of an attribute is present, which requires a numerical statement of the amount. Although it may seem to be an exception to the rule, most specialists in psychological measurement would include categorical data at least as a prelude to quantified data, e.g., the presence or absence of brain damage or whether a person is a farmer or in some other profession. This type of prelude to quantitative measurement will be discussed more fully later.

Measurement concerns the real world in terms of purposes, operations, and validity. The purpose is to quantify the attributes of real objects and persons; the operations concern doing something (according to a set of rules) to obtain measurements. The validity, or usefulness, of a measure always depends on the character of empirical data. If a measure is intended to fit a set of axioms for measurement (a model), the closeness of the fit can be determined only by the extent to which relations in empirical data meet the requirements of the model. Regardless of the character of the model or even if there is no formal model, the eventual and crucial test of any measure is the extent to which it has explanatory power in its relations with other variables. As will be discussed in Chap. 3, the various types of validity for psychological measures all depend on some type of data from the real world rather than on purely mathematical deductions.

Scientists *develop* measures by stating rules for the quantification of attributes of real objects; they *borrow* mathematical systems for examining the internal relations of the data obtained with a measure and for relating different measures to one another. Although past experience, common sense, and rational argument may make a good case for one method of measurement or mathematical analysis over another, the final justification requires finding a rich set of lawful relations among variables in the real world. Fortunately measurement methods that prove to be scientifically useful usually can be associated with many powerful systems of mathematics.

**Measurement and statistics** Because the term *statistics* is used so broadly, it is necessary to make distinctions among different uses of the term in order to see their implications for psychometric theory. First, it is important to make a distinction between *inferential statistics* and other mathematical methods of analysis. Inferential statistics concern probability statements relating observed sample values to population parameters. Thus, obtaining the arithmetic mean of the scores on one test or the correlation between scores on two tests would constitute mathematical analyses which need not involve inferential statistics. Since the purpose of performing mathematical analyses of central tendency, dispersion, and correlation is to describe various aspects of empirical data, these and related methods of analysis are said to form *descriptive statistics,* in contrast to inferential statistics. Employment of inferential statistics, as in setting confidence zones or in "testing for significance," would constitute additional steps. Because very little will be said in this book about probability statements relating sample values to population parameters, the quantitative methods would be better spoken of as methods of analysis or descriptive statistics rather than as inferential statistics. Thus correlational analysis, factor analysis, discriminatory analysis, and others can be discussed and employed without necessarily resorting to inferential statistics, which is not meant to imply that inferential statistics per se are not useful adjuncts to the development and use of psychological measures.

This book emphasizes powerful descriptive statistics rather than inferential statistics for two reasons. First, psychometric theory mainly is a *large-sample* theory, in which it is assumed that a large number of people are used in the development, validation, and other studies of psychological measurement methods. Second, this book covers enough ground without going off into a somewhat ancillary topic, and there are excellent books on the relevant inferential statistics for psychometric theory which will be referenced at the appropriate places.

A second important distinction is that between statistics concerning the sampling of people and statistics concerning the sampling of content (test items). After measures are developed and then employed in empirical investigations, it is important to employ inferential statistics concerning the sampling of people. Before measures are developed, however, the theory that guides such measurement is related much more to the sampling of content than to the sampling of people. As will be described in detail later, it is useful to think of the items on a particular test as being a sample from a hypothetical infinite population or universe of items measuring the same trait. Thus a spelling test for fourth-grade students can be thought of as a sample of all possible words that would be appropriate. Measurement theory, then, would concern statistical relations between the scores actually made on the test and the hypothetical scores that would be made if all items in the universe had been administered.

Thus there is a two-way sampling problem in all psychology, one concerned with the sampling of people and the other with the sampling of content. The former concerns the generality of findings over populations of persons, and the latter concerns the generality of findings over populations of test items. In performing statistical analyses it is virtually impossible to simultaneously take account of both dimensions of sampling. One dimension of sampling is difficult enough to consider in any particular analysis. Typically what is done in practice is to explicitly take account of one dimension of sampling and simply keep the other dimension in mind as a possible influence on the results of the experiment. Thus in a study of the influence of a particular type of training on achievement in mathematics, explicit account would be taken of the sampling of subjects, but it would be kept in mind that somewhat different results might have been obtained with a different measure of achievement. Similarly, in a study of reliability, where the major concern would be with the sampling of content, it would be kept in mind that the results might have been somewhat different in a larger sample of persons or in a sample drawn from another source.

The practical necessity in particular studies of making explicit statistical analyses of only one of two dimensions of sampling does not spoil the game. What is required is that the generality of findings, either over people or over content, be investigated in subsequent studies. An even safer approach, if feasible, is to sample so extensively on one dimension that only sampling error with respect to the other dimension need be a serious concern. This is the recommended approach in the development of psychological measures. Enough subjects should be used in developing psychological measures that sampling error with respect to persons is a minor consideration. At least hundreds, and where possible thousands, of subjects should be used in the development of a new measure. In the remainder of this book it will be assumed that all mathematical analyses are based on large numbers of subjects; consequently the text will consider only the sampling of content. Even if it were feasible to work with statistics that simultaneously considered both dimensions of sampling, studies conducted on relatively small numbers of subjects would not be sufficient. For example, in a study of the reliability of a new measure, the need is to determine what the reliability *is;* a statement only that the reliability coefficient is significantly different from zero is nearly worthless.

Apparently it is difficult for some persons to comprehend that in the development of psychological measures the major concern is with the sampling of content rather than with the sampling of people. For example, graduate students in psychology frequently fall into the trap of assuming that the reliability of a test increases with the number of *people* used in the study of reliability. Any reader who does not already know will learn later that the reliability estimate obtained in any particular study is independent of the number of persons in the study, but in any study the reliability is related directly to the number of *items* on the test.

## MEASUREMENT SCALES

In psychology and other behavioral sciences, there has been much talk about the different possible types of measurement scales, and there has been much soul-searching about the types of scales which characterize psychological measures. Although these discussions represent a healthy self-consciousness about scientific methods, they have led to some unfortunate confusions. Essentially the issues concern what sorts of "interpretations" can be made of the numbers obtained from psychological measures. More precisely, the issues concern the legitimacy of employing particular classes of mathematical procedures with measures of psychological attributes. Does a measure of intelligence have the same mathematical status as a yardstick? Does a measure of learning rate in paired-associate learning have the same mathematical status as a measure of electrical resistance? In this section a simplified, conventional classification of measurement scales will be presented. The next section will contain a more probing discussion about the nature of psychological measurement.

Measurement scales concern different uses made of numbers. Following is a classification of some of these uses.

**Labels** Frequently numbers are used as a way of keeping track of things, without any suggestion that the numbers can be subjected to mathematical analyses. For example, a geologist working in the field might choose to number the specimens of rocks 1, 2, 3, etc., in which case the numbers would be used purely as labels and would have no implications for mathematical analyses. It would make no sense to add the numbers representing the first and second rock and equate that in any way with the 3 relating to the third rock. Other examples of numbers used as labels are the numbers on the backs of football players, numbers on highway signs, and the numbers of atomic elements.

It must be emphasized that any measurement scale concerns an *intended use* of numbers. One intended use of numbers is labeling. In this instance there is no intention of performing mathematical analyses of the numbers, and the numbers are not considered to represent quantities of attributes. It may be the case, however, that numbers used as labels happen to correlate with quantities of attributes. Thus in the example of the geologist's rocks it may be that, as the sack of rocks grows heavier, the geologist discerningly picks smaller and smaller specimens; consequently the numbers used as labels would incidentally relate to the weights of the rocks. Similarly, high-numbered highways may in some way be quantitatively different from low-numbered highways, and atomic elements further along in the numbering scheme may be quantitatively different from earlier-positioned elements. The crucial point is that, in discussing the nature of measurement scales in particular instances, one must justify the *use* of the numbers. Whether or not there are incidental quantitative correlates of a particular set of numbers is not relevant to a discussion of the legitimacy of the intended use of the numbers. Since labels are not intended to imply quantities of attributes, no justification is required for employing numbers as labels; but numerical labels are not measures.

**Categories** Categories consist of groupings of objects or people without any specified quantitative relationships among the categories. For example, the geologist might classify each rock into one of the categories—sedimentary, igneous, or metamorphic. Other classification schemes include different professions, the two sexes, and brain-damaged and normal people. There are three essential features of categories. First, in any particular scheme of categorization, the categories must be designated before persons are classified, and the number of categories so designated usually is greater than one. Second, except in rare circumstances, more than one person will end up in each category. Third, all persons assigned to the same category are alike with respect to some attribute.

Although by definition categories are not formed specifically with respect to any quantitative relationship among them, as with labels, there may be many incidental quantitative correlates of categories. Thus, males differ from females in height, certain types of athletic ability, and many other attributes; but that is entirely unrelated to justifying this two-fold classification of people. People in different professions tend to make different incomes on the average, but again such incidental quantitative correlates are not essential to the formulation of a set of categories. Later we will discuss a hybrid type of measurement scale, in which categories are purposely ordered quantitatively in terms of an attribute; but these are spoken of as *ordered categories* specifically, and they are not to be confused with the normal use of the term categories.

Whereas categorization itself does not explicitly concern quantitative relations, numerical results in employing categories are very important in many types of research. Thus the geologist might categorize 22 specimens as being igneous rocks. In such instances it is sometimes said that one "measures" the number of cases in different categories, but according to the definition of measurement given earlier, this would be an improper use of the term. It would be more proper to say that one "enumerates," or counts, the objects in categories. Very often, the primary results of experiments are expressed in terms of frequencies of persons who perform in one way or another with respect to different types of experimental treatments. A simple example would be the administering of three different drugs to 150 hospitalized mental patients who were randomly placed in three treatment groups (each a category relating to the drug) of 50 patients each. One measure of the effectiveness of the drug (among other possible ones) would be the number of patients in each category who improved sufficiently to leave the hospital after three months of treatment with the drug. One could give many more examples of actual experiments in which the treatment groups are categories and the primary data consist of frequencies of response.

**Ordinal scales** An *ordinal scale* (a set of ranks) is one in which (1) a set of objects or people is ordered from "most" to "least" with respect to an attribute, (2) there is no indication of "how much," in an absolute sense, any of the objects possess the attribute, and (3) there is no indication of how far apart the objects are with respect to the attribute. Rank-ordering is the most primitive form of measurement (excluding labels and considering categories as an important prelude to quantitative measurement)—primitive in that it is basic to all higher forms of measurement and it conveys only meager information.

An ordinal scale is obtained, for example, when a group of boys is ranked from tallest to shortest. This scale would give no indication of the average height: as a group the boys might be relatively tall or relatively short. The scale would supply no information about how much the boys varied in terms of height. They might be very close to one another in terms of height, or they might vary from extremely tall to extremely short. With respect to methods of analysis, it is meaningless to interpret the mean and the standard deviation of a set of ranks. These indices are the cornerstone of most of the powerful methods of mathematics and statistics needed in psychology, methods without which it would be all but impossible to advance the science.

Frequently it is not understood that the numbers employed with ordinal scales provide only a convenient shorthand for designating relative positions of persons. A rank-order scale is obtained when, for any $N$ persons ($S$'s), it is known that $S_i > S_j > S_k > S_n$ with respect to an attribute.

There are numerous examples in psychology and other behavioral sciences in which data obviously are ranked and thus should not be analyzed by any mathematical methods that assume scales higher than ordinal scales (unless subsequently a sensible scaling model is employed which converts ranks to a higher-order scale). One example is when three clinical psychologists each rank a dozen patients in terms of amount of improvement after a number of sessions of group psychotherapy. Another example is any type of contest that is reported in terms of who makes the highest score, the second highest score, etc., as in a spelling bee, a beauty contest, or a horse race.

In some cases where measures actually are obtained on one of the two higher forms of scales to be discussed subsequently, either the investigators choose to degrade such scores into ranks (which frequently is a bad mistake), or they report their results in professional journals only in the form of ranks. In all the instances mentioned above where the data inherently are in the form of ranks or one has information about ranks only, clearly ordinal measurement is the scale type under consideration.

Some have claimed that most psychological scales, e.g., intelligence tests or scores in an experiment on learning, should be considered as providing only a rank-ordering of people rather than any higher form of measurement. In a later section strong issue will be taken with that point of view.

Two specific cases need to be considered to clarify the meaning of ordinal scales. The first was mentioned previously, that of ordered categories. Such ordered categories are present when the researcher has more precise information available from a measurement method, but chooses to lump scores into a number of successively ordered categories. A simple example would be on a test concerning 99 items, which potentially could measure people on 100 points varying from 0 correct responses to 99 correct responses. Rather than show the scores of each subject, for simplicity's sake the researcher might decide to group them in steps in categories of 10 items correct each, with the lowest category being from 0 to 9 items correct, the next one from 10 to 19 items correct, and up at the top of the scale from 90 to 99 items correct. If the number of ordered categories is relatively large, e.g., at least 10, not a great deal of information is lost; but if the number of categories is made considerably smaller than that, much valuable information may be thrown away. In other instances the data themselves come from subjects in the form of ordered categories; then the experimenter uses various scaling models to try to obtain more precise measurement. This is the case when subjects rate various objects on a seven-step scale ranging from very pleasant to very unpleasant. In this case, many experimenters would consider this as constituting seven ordered categories. With either of these two approaches to obtaining ordered categories, naturally one ends up with many tied scores of subjects, which can cause problems for some types of statistical analysis.

A second special case with respect to ordinal scales, which frequently is misleadingly referred to as constituting categorization, is *pass-fail*. An example would be on a multiple-choice test concerning any type of ability. On each item the subject is scored as having passed or failed, and usually a pass is designated "1" and a failure is designated "0." This definately is not categorization; rather it is the most gross form of ordered categories that can be obtained. The people who pass score higher on the attribute measured by the particular item than those who failed, and thus each item is a mini ordinal scale. Of course, when there are only two ordered categories, there are many tied scores. If 30 people pass an item and 50 people fail the item, then obviously there are 80 tied scores. Of course, it is nearly always the case that such 1's and 0's are summed to obtain total test scores, which then represent relatively continuous measurement rather than gross ordered categories.

**Interval scales** An interval scale is one in which (1) the rank-ordering of objects is known with respect to an attribute and (2) it is known how far apart the objects are from one another with respect to the attribute, but (3) no information is available about the *absolute* magnitude of the attribute for any object. An interval scale would be obtained for the heights of a group of boys if, instead of being measured directly, the height of each boy were measured with respect to the shortest boy in the group. Thus the shortest boy would obtain a score of 0, a boy 2 inches taller than the shortest boy would obtain a score of 2, a boy 3 inches taller would obtain a score of 3, and so on. More directly related to what is done with most psychological measures would be to specify intervals in terms of the distance of each boy from the arithmetic mean of heights of the boys. Thus a boy whose height is 2 inches above the mean would receive a score of $+2$, and a boy who is 2 inches below the mean would receive a score of $-2$. Intervals about the mean height, or such intervals for any other attribute, can be calculated without actually knowing how far any of the persons are from the zero point (for example, zero height or zero intelligence).

A potentially important item of information not supplied by interval scales is the absolute magnitude of the attribute for any particular person or object. Thus even though the tallest boy may have an interval score above the mean of $+6$ (6 inches above the average), this would not tell us how tall he is in an absolute sense. He might be the tallest boy in a group of pygmies. This is the distinguishing characteristic of the interval scale from the ratio scale (to be discussed subsequently): whereas the intervals are known on an interval scale, there is no knowlege of a zero point on the measurement continuum.

Because interval scales are sometimes spoken of as "equal interval" scales, it is easy to make the mistake of assuming that such scales require an equal number of persons or objects at each point on a continuum—a rectangular distribution of scores. What actually is meant by "equal" is that intervals on the scale are equal regardless of the number of persons or objects at different points on the scale. Thus on an interval scale for measurement of intelligence, the *difference* between IQs of 100 and 105 would be assumed equal to the *difference* between IQs of 120 and 125. Of course, the practical implications of such equal differences on the scale might be most unequal, but strictly speaking that has nothing to do with the interval character of the scale. Similarly, if three automobiles are traveling 30, 60, and 90 miles per hour, respectively, the interval between the first two is equal to the interval between the second and third, but of course these two intervals might have very different implications for traffic safety, gas mileage, and wear and tear on the automobiles. Thus it is necessary to draw a careful distinction between the character of a measurement scale—interval scale or otherwise—and the practical implications of the scale points.

The author strongly believes that it is permissible to treat most of the measurement methods in psychology and other behavioral sciences as leading to interval scales (and in some instances, ratio scales). Whereas the logic of determining measurement scales in any area of science is a highly controversial matter and logically very involved, it will be argued that usually no harm is done in most studies in the behavioral sciences by employing methods of mathematical and statistical analysis which take intervals seriously. This is true for the measurements used in experiments, such as experiments in learning, physiological responses of rats to stress, detectability of rapidly projected geometrical forms on a screen, and differences in average test scores of groups with different types of educational experiences. Similarly, it is argued that one has a right to take seriously the intervals among scores in performing analyses of correlations among various sources of individual differences on tests of ability, achievement, attitude, interest, personality, and so on.

**Ratio scales** A ratio scale is obtained when (1) the rank-order of persons with respect to an attribute is known, (2) the intervals between persons are known, and (3) in addition, the distance from a rational zero is known for at least one of the persons. In other words, a ratio scale is a particular type of interval scale in which distances are stated with respect to a rational zero rather than with respect to, for example, the height of the tallest boy or the shortest boy or the mean height. Obviously, if an interval scale of height is available and in addition the absolute height (distance from zero) of any boy in the group is known, the absolute heights of all the other boys can be calculated.

There are some, but not many, instances in which it makes sense to consider psychological measurements as constituting ratio scales. This is the case when scores are expressed in terms of such simple physical properties as time and length. For example, in the study of reaction time, the zero point (no time at all) is known, and it makes sense to form ratios of the amounts of time taken to respond in different treatment situations. In a study of motor skills involved in using a pencil to track a randomly wavering line rolling past the subject on a piece of paper, the result can be scored in terms of the average distance of the pencil mark from the line. Here also there is a rational zero, and it makes sense to form ratios among such distances from the line. Primarily, ratio scales are sensibly used to describe research results when experiments concern very simple functions in some aspect of skilled performance. In Chap. 2 some efforts to apply particular mathematical models to the problem of converting interval scales into ratio scales will be discussed.

Actually, in nearly all research in the behavioral sciences, one does not need ratio scales to state theories in precise form or to conduct the necessary types of analyses of experimental results. However, the assumption of interval scales is crucial and justifiable with most measurement methods in the behavioral sciences that obviously are not in the form of ranks or categories.

**Other scales** Ordinal, interval, and ratio scales are the basic scales of measurement. There are, however, many possible variants and combinations of these (for discussion of some of the possibilities see Coombs, 1964, and Coombs, Dawes, and Tversky, 1970). For example, one could have an *ordered metric* scale in which (1) the rank-order of persons is known, (2) the rank-order of intervals is known, but (3) the magnitudes of the intervals are not known. In such a scale it would be possible to say that the largest interval is between persons $A$ and $B$ and the smallest interval is between persons $C$ and $D$, but it would not be possible to say that the former interval is twice as large as the latter.

Stevens (1958) has proposed a *logarithmic interval scale,* where if the successive points on the scale are designated $a,b,c,$ etc., the successive ratios of magnitudes corresponding to those points would be $a/b = b/c = c/d$, etc. Then

$$\log a - \log b = \log b - \log c = \log c - \log d$$

etc. Many other variants of the three basic types of measurement scales can be postulated, but they have been of little importance in psychometric theory or application.

**Permissible arithmetic operations** The relative importance of discussing different measurement scales is that some types of scales are open to many more forms of mathematical treatments than are others. The ratio scale is susceptible to the fundamental operations of algebra: addition, subtraction, division, and multiplication. Thus it makes sense to apply these operations to the height of boys, e.g., to say that Tom is seven-eighths as tall as Bob. All the usual operations of arithmetic can be applied with those psychological measurements that are sensibly construed as constituting ratio scales, e.g., those mentioned previously in this chapter. With these operations come all the power of mathematics, including algebra, analytic geometry, calculus, and all the more powerful statistical methods. Without such mathematical tools the scientist is almost out of business.

An important consideration with regard to measurement scales is that of the circumstances over which a particular type of scale remains *invariant*. Any ratio scale remains invariant over all transformations where the scale is multiplied by a constant:

$$X' = cX$$

If $X$ symbolizes all possible points on a ratio scale and all such points are multiplied by a constant $c$, the resulting scale $X'$ is a ratio scale. The resulting scale will meet all the requirements of a ratio scale, because (1) the rank-order of points will remain the same, (2) the ratios of points will remain the same, and (3) the zero point will remain the same. An example of such a transformation is when one changes a scale of inches to a scale of feet by dividing all the points in the scale of inches by 12.

Two examples of invariant transformations of a ratio scale are shown in Fig. 1-2. An invariant transformation is represented by any straight line passing

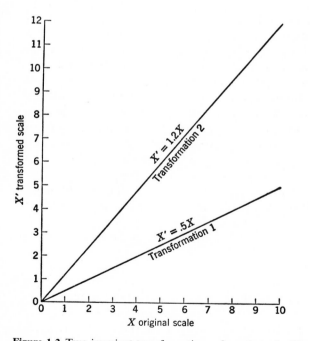

**Figure 1-2** Two invariant transformations of a ratio scale ($X$) to a new ratio scale ($X'$).

through the origin. If the line curves or does not go through the origin, the transformation is not invariant. In those cases if $X$ is a ratio scale, then $X'$ is not a ratio scale.

The importance of invariance is that it determines the generality of scientific statements regarding a scale. It is easy to imagine the chaos that would result if some measures of physical quantities lacked the invariance of ratio scales. Without invariance, it might be found that one stick is twice as long as another when measured in feet but three times as long when measured in inches. The range of invariance of a scale determines the extent to which natural laws remain essentially the same when the scale is expressed in different units, e.g., feet rather than inches. Suppose that a natural law has the following form:

$$X = 2Y^2 + 4Y + 6$$

Let $Y$ be any variable of scientific interest—monthly rainfall, speed of atomic particles, reaction of humans to stress, or whatever. Let $X$ be any other variable that would be of scientific interest to relate to $Y$. If $X$ is a ratio scale, any invariant transformation of a ratio scale will produce another scale which will preserve the general form of the relationship with $Y$. Thus if $X' = cX$ and $c = 2$, the above relation with $Y$ would be

$$X' = 4Y^2 + 8Y + 12$$

An invariant transformation of a ratio scale alters proportionally the coefficients of any equation relating that measure to any other measure, but otherwise has no effect on the form of the relationship; e.g., it does not alter any of the exponents. Thus, for all pratical purposes, any invariant transformation of a scale produces the *same* scale—same in the sense that it will manifest the same general form of relationship with any other variable.

The potential disadvantage of having only an interval scale of measurement rather than a ratio scale is that with the former some limitations are placed on application of the fundamental operations of algebra. For example, if on an intelligence test Sarah gets 80 items correct and Bill gets 40 items correct, it makes no sense to say that Sarah is twice as intelligent as Bill. Multiplication and division with interval scales are permissible only with respect to the *intervals* and not with respect to the scale values. With ratio scales, it is permissible to employ addition and subtraction on the scale values as well as on the intervals.

If $a, b, c, \ldots, k$ are points on a scale, an interval scale is defined by two statements:

1. $a > b > c > \cdots > k$
2. $a - b = b - c = c - d = \cdots = j - k$

Since an interval scale is defined in terms of algebraic differences between points, it follows that subtraction and addition of the scale points are permissible operations. Thus since $a - b = b - c$, the sum of the two intervals equals $(a - b) + (b - c) = a - c$, which logically it should. The difference of the two intervals should equal zero:

$$(a - b) - (b - c) = a - 2b + c$$

The expression equals zero because $a + c = 2b$:

$$a - b = b - c$$

$$a + c = 2b$$

These calculations demonstrate the reason for permitting addition and subtraction of the scale values on interval scales.

Since by definition the points are assumed to be equidistant on an interval scale, it follows that

$$\frac{a - b}{b - c} = 1$$

which illustrates the legitimacy of forming ratios of *intervals* on interval scales. As another example of the legitimate employment of multiplication and division with the intervals, the distance from $a$ to $c$ should equal twice the distance from $a$ to $b$ when calculated from the equalities stated in the definition of the scale, which of course it does.

The permissible mathematical operations with interval scales relate to the circumstances under which invariance is obtained. Whereas a ratio scale is invariant under transformations of the form

$$X' = cX$$

an interval scale is invariant under any linear transformation:

$$X' = cX + b$$

In transforming one interval scale for measuring an attribute to any other interval scale for measuring the same attribute, invariance will be obtained not only if the points on the first scale are multiplied by any constant, but also if a constant amount $b$ is added to each point. This is because the absolute magnitudes on an interval scale are irrelevant. Adding such a constant will not change the ordinal positions of points or the equality of intervals. After the transformation is made, intervals separating persons at different points on the scale will be a constant proportion of the same intervals on the original scale. Take the case where on the original scale person $S_1$ is at 20 (a point on the interval scale), $S_2$ is 30, $S_3$ is 40, and $S_4$ is 45. The interval between the first two persons is 10, and the interval between the latter two persons is 5. The first interval is twice as large as the second. Any transformation that maintains such proportions is invariant. Suppose that we transform the scale by multiplying all the points by 2 and then adding 10 to each of the resulting points. Now $S_1$ and $S_2$ are 50 and 70, respectively, and $S_3$ and $S_4$ are 90 and 100, respectively. The proportionality of intervals is maintained, and thus the transformation is invariant. Because the $b$ term is the same for all points, it "falls out" when the intervals are calculated; consequently the proportionality is maintained regardless of what $b$ is.

Whereas the conditions of invariance demonstrate why it is permissible to form ratios of the *intervals* (multiply and divide by one another), they also demonstrate why it is not permissible to form ratios among the *scale points* on an interval scale. Conditions of invariance permit the addition of an arbitrary constant to each of the scale points on an interval scale, but the arbitrary constant could markedly change the ratios among the scale points. Consider the invariant transformation

$$X' = X + 50$$

and consider persons at points 2 and 4 on $X$. The ratio of the second person to the first person is 2, but the ratio of the transformed scores is 54:52. This illustrates why it is not permissible to multiply scale points by one another or divide them into one another.

As is true of invariant transformations of ratio scales, invariant transformations of any interval scale do not change the general form of the relationship of that scale with any other variable. Thus if there is a linear relationship between $X$ and $Y$ and an invariant (linear) transformation is made of $X$, then $X'$ also will have a linear relationship with $Y$. The importance of this point is that any natural laws stated with respect to an interval scale will remain essentially the same when invariant transformations are made of the scale. Some invariant transformations of an interval scale are shown in Fig. 1-3.

With ordinal scales, none of the fundamental operations of algebra may be applied. In the use of descriptive statistics, it makes no sense to add, subtract, divide, or multiply ranks. Since an ordinal scale is defined entirely in terms of inequalities, only the algebra of inequalities can be used to analyze measures made on such scales—which is awkward, weak algebra. Ordinal scales are invariant over any *monotonic* transformation. Some invariant transformations of an ordinal scale are shown in Fig. 1-4. In the figure, $X$ is either an interval or ratio scale on which the scores of individuals are to be ranked; $X'$ is any monotonic transformation of $X$ on which individuals also are to be ranked. It might be helpful to think of $X$ as a measure of overall problem-solving ability in terms of the number of problems that are correctly solved. Transformation 1 shown in Fig. 1-4 could be obtained by a weighting scheme for the 10 problems, in which getting some items correct is given more weight than getting others correct. Similarly, transformation 2 can be thought of as the result of applying another weighting scheme to the 10 items, resulting in another monotonic transformation of the original scale $X$. If students are ranked on $X$, the order will be preserved when they are ranked on the two monotonic transformations $X'$.

Functional relations among ordinal scales provide only meager information about what the relations would be if interval or ratio scales were available. Sup-

monotonic – having the property of never increasing or of never decreasing as the 'independent variable' increases

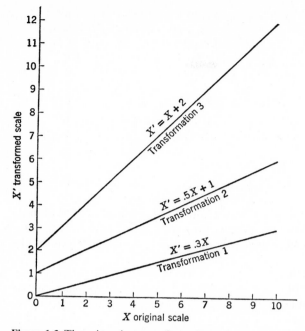

**Figure 1-3** Three invariant transformations of an interval scale ($X$) to a new interval scale ($X'$).

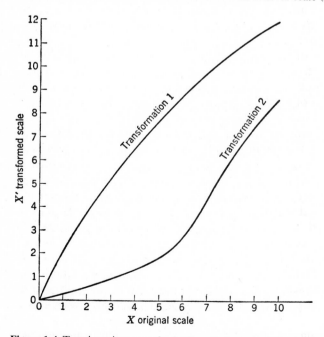

**Figure 1-4** Two invariant transformations that preserve the rank-order of points from $X$ to points on $X'$.

pose that with ratio scales the following monotonic relations are known between positive values of $X$ and positive values of two other variables, $Y$ and $Z$:

$$Y = aX + b$$
$$Z = X^3 + X^2 + X + b$$

If all three scales were transformed to ordinal scales (ranks), the expressions would change to

$$Y = X$$
$$Z = X$$

Since both $Y$ and $Z$ are monotonic functions of $X$, the ordinal scales are unable to "detect" the very different forms of relationship, which illustrates the amount of information that is lost when only ordinal scales are available. This is why much effort has been spent in psychometrics to develop methods for transforming ordinal data into interval scales or ratio scales. These matters will be discussed in Chap. 2.

## DECISIONS ABOUT MEASUREMENT SCALES

The previous section presented the "fundamentalist" point of view about measurement scales, which, to summarize, holds that (1) there are distinct types of measurement scales into which all possible measures of attributes can be classified, (2) each measure has some "real" characteristics that permit its proper classification, and (3) once a measure is classified, the classification specifies the types of mathematical analyses that can be employed with the measure. In this section it will be argued that this is a narrow point of view that needs to be severely modified before it can meet the actualities of scientific inquiry.

The fundamentalist point of view has caused much consternation among psychologists about proper methods of analysis. Take, for example, the psychologists who want to study the relations among tests involving a variety of human abilities. What type of scales do they have? They do not need to claim that the scales are ratio scales, because the powerful methods of analysis needed in this situation, such as factor analysis, require only interval scales. But how do they know if they have interval scales? Maybe there are only ordinal scales, or maybe no legitimate scales of any kind. Although the fundamentalist point of view forces these questions upon the investigator, it does not provide methods for answering the questions. One result of this dilemma was a flight into nonparametric statistics (those appropriate to ordinal scales and categories) during the early 1950s. In many cases these methods are so weak that they simply cannot do the job at hand. Partly as a consequence, psychologists apparently have gone back mainly to those powerful methods of analysis that take the interval seriously; but still there is a lingering feeling of guilt among some that such methods of analysis are not really justified. Here it will be argued that it is only the guilt, rather than the use of the methods of analysis, that is unjustified.

Those who accept the fundamentalist point of view hold that (1) measurement scales have empirical reality in addition to being theoretical constructions and (2) the investigator must show evidence of the scale properties of particular measures before employing certain methods of analysis. The first will be severely questioned in a later section. Even if one accepts the first point, no one has made it clear with respect to the second point what types of evidence would justify unequivocally the assumption of a particular type of scale. In the following sections, these issues will be clarified.

**Ostensive characteristics** One way to judge the scale characteristics of a particular measure is in terms of the physical characteristics of the measurement operations. The best example of this, and perhaps the only pure one, is the measurement of length with a yardstick. To prove that the attribute in question is measured on a ratio scale requires (1) a proof of equal intervals and (2) the demonstration of an axiomatically unquestionable zero point. Anyone can see the zero point—it is where the yardstick starts. Back of that point is open space; in front of it is the wooden beginning of the measuring instrument. Who could argue that a more meaningful zero point could be located elsewhere on the yardstick? The equality of intervals is also easy to demonstrate. One way would be to saw the yardstick inch by inch and then compare the pieces two at a time to ensure that they are all equal. (Actually, one could make science fiction–type arguments that there are alternative zero points and alternative ways of establishing equal intervals in the measurement of length, but for the sake of the discussion here it will be assumed that the scale properties of yardsticks are intuitively obvious.)

The yardstick exemplifies the two ostensive characteristics supposedly required for a ratio scale: visually (or palpably otherwise) discernible zero and fractionation into visually equal intervals. No other measure so obviously passes the tests. The closest is the measurement of weight with a balance. If two objects keep the scale in balance even when the right-left placements on the scale are alternated, it is intuitively obvious that they are of the same weight. Then either of the two weights can be compared with other weights to find one that is equal to the first two. Continuing in this way, a collection of equal units can be obtained, e.g., of 1-pound size, to form an interval scale for the measurement of weight. This would provide an obvious physical fractionation into equal intervals of weight. The rational zero also is intuitively obvious—nothing on the scale.

No other measures have the palpable qualities that allow the scale properties to be determined by ostensive characteristics. To a lesser or greater extent, all other measures consist of inspecting the physical states of variables that correlate (perfectly or only in a statistical sense) with the variable to be measured. In other words, all other measures are indirect. When measuring length, one is actually seeing the attribute directly rather than seeing some correlate of length. Any two pieces of twine can be directly compared in length; thus one sees length itself and not just a correlate of length. With the measuring of weight, this is only partially so, because the attribute itself is the pull of gravity on the object, which is correlated with the influence of the object on the balance (or other devices for the measurement of weight). Thus one cannot see weight directly. Though it may be argued that one can *feel* weight directly (by lifting), such judgments are not nearly reliable enough to serve as evidence that weight has the ostensive characteristics required for a ratio scale.

When measures of length and weight are set aside, it becomes obvious that almost all attributes are measured indirectly, and consequently one cannot look to the ostensive characteristics of the *correlate* to determine the scale characteristics by which the attribute itself is manifested in the correlate. Even the measurement of such a basic attribute as time is done quite indirectly. Time has no ostensive characteristics that specify the equality of intervals as measured by clocks and other devices. Intervals of time are *defined* in terms of the regularity of certain events. Thus the clock ticks, the pendulum swings, and the earth turns, and these are defined as measures of time (which, of course, is not completely in keeping with the Einsteinian concept of time).

For other measures of physical attributes, it is even more obvious that the measure itself is only a correlate of the actual attribute. Thus to observe the height of the column of mercury in a thermometer is to observe not temperature itself, but a correlate of temperature. Most measures of physical attributes are ostensive only with respect to the gauges and meters by which the correlated variable is indexed. For example, a meter for the measurement of steam pressure in a boiler might entail springs, weights, magnets, and various electrical devices to produce the movement of a pointer on a gauge, in which case we would be observing correlates of correlates of correlates of the actual variable involved. In all sciences, and certainly in psychology, the observations required in the operations of measurement usually are not the same as observations of the attributes themselves. Thus in a measure of intelligence, one is observing not intelligence directly, but rather its supposed by-products. A body-sway test of suggestibility is, of course, only an indirect measure of the attribute.

Although perhaps none have said it directly, those who take the fundamentalist point of view imply that scale properties can be judged only by ostensive characteristics. Since, for example, there are no ostensive properties to guarantee the equality of intervals in the measurement of intelligence, it has been argued that tests of intelligence constitute ordinal scales at best. It is hoped the previous paragraphs have shown that by the same standards there would be few measures in all science that could be considered more than ordinal scales; the following sections will show that proper standards for judging the scale properties of a measure are not necessarily dependent on observing the ostensive characteristics of the attribute to be measured.

**Scaling models** Another approach to the discussion of scale characteristics concerns the use of various models for the construction of measures. Each such model constitutes a set of axioms concerning how the data should appear when the measure is put to use. For example, a sensible axiom in any model for the development of interval scales is that of *transitivity*. If a model leads to independent scorings of intervals among persons on a scale of measurement and it is found that the score for person $A$ is 5 points above that for person $B$ and the score for person $B$ is 5 points above that for person $C$, then it should also be found that the score for person $A$ is 10 points above that for person $C$. This extremely simple and commonsense assumption is mentioned only to illustrate the axioms that appear in different measurement models. The details of some of the most prominent measurement models will be described in Chap. 2.

If the data obtained from applying a measurement scale fit the axioms of the particular model under consideration and the axioms (assumptions) of the model are correct, then the measure has scale properties specified by the model. An example may help to clarify this important point. In Chap. 2 a model proposed by Louis Guttman for the construction of ordinal scales will be described. It makes a set of assumptions about patterns of people's responses to test items. After the items are administered to samples of persons, mathematical analyses can be made to determine how well the actual patterns of scores fit the patterns of scores predicted by the model. If the fit is good, the model stipulates that an ordinal scale of measurement has been obtained; if the fit is poor, the hypothesis of an ordinal scale is rejected.

There are three important points to be made about the place of scaling models in discussions of scale properties. First, this type of standard is based on empirical data, in contrast to standards concerning ostensive characteristics. In the former, one studies the results from applying a measure to objects in the real world; in the latter, one "studies" the observable characteristics of the measurement tool itself. For example, instead of determining the scale properties of yardsticks merely by looking at them, one could establish a model concerning the properties of ratio scales and then see if the data obtained from employing the yardstick to measure many objects fit the model. One could derive the scale properties of the yardstick from the model even if one had never seen a yardstick. (Actually, data obtained from applying the yardstick to, say, sticks of different lengths would beautifully fit a number of the models that have been proposed for the scaling of psychological attributes. The data would, for example, fit the assumption of transitivity mentioned previously.) This is what psychological scaling is about: It is an attempt to work backward from empirical data to test the fit to a model. In this way an attempt is made to develop ratio, interval, and ordinal scales for psychological attributes, many of which attributes cannot be seen directly.

The second point is that the use of scaling models is a healthy trend in the development of measurement methods. Many of the models are intuitively quite appealing; and because they specify characteristics that should be found in actual data, they are subject to refutation. Also, some of the scaling models have produced scales that led to interesting scientific findings in subsequent studies.

A third important point about the place of scaling models in discussing the properties of measurement scales is that a model is no better and no worse than its assumptions (axioms). There is ample room for disagreement, and there is plenty of it, about the *fruitfulness* of different models. For example, later it will be argued that certain measures should be analyzed with methods that assume interval scales even though data obtained with the measures would not even fit the assumptions of one of the models for ordinal scaling. If psychologists are "allowed" to disagree about the correctness of different scaling models, then how are the scale characteristics of measures ever determined? If, for example, models for the development of interval scales are being tried on a particular type of data, e.g., responses to statements concerning attitudes toward abortion, the failure of the data to fit one model does not automatically prevent the measure from being considered as an interval scale; and if the data fit all the models under consideration, this does not automatically indicate that the measure should be considered as an interval scale. The final decision in this matter should be made with respect to standards that will be discussed in the following sections.

**Consequences of assumptions** Even if one believes that there is a "real" scale for each attribute, which is either mirrored directly in a particular measure or mirrored as some monotonic transformation, an important question is, "What difference does it make if the measure does not have the same zero point or proportionally equal intervals as the 'real' scale?" If the scientist assumes, for example, that the scale is an interval scale when it "really" is not, something should go wrong in the daily work of the scientist. What would go wrong? How would the difficulty be detected? All that could go wrong would be that the scientist would make misstatements about the specific form of the relationship between the attribute and other variables. For example, using an imperfect interval scale, the scientist might report a linear relationship between the attribute and some other variable; whereas if the "real" interval scale had been employed, a power function would have been found instead.

How seriously are such misassumptions about scale properties likely to influence the reported results of scientific experiments? In psychology at the present time, the answer in most cases is "very little." The results of most studies are reported in the form of either correlations between scores of individuals on different measures or differences in mean scores of differently treated groups. Regarding the former, correlations are affected very little by monotonic transformations of variables. Suppose that (1) a product-moment correlation is computed between a measure and another variable, (2) the measure is only an imperfect representation of the "real" scale, the intervals on the "real" scale being obtainable by a square root transformation of the measure, and (3) the correlation is found to be .50. Would the correlation have been very different if the "real" scale rather than the imperfect scale had been correlated with the other variable? Usually the correlation would change very little. It might, for example, go down to .45 or up to .55.

Within very broad limits, the correlation between two variables is affected very little by monotonic transformations of the variables. (This principle will be discussed more extensively and properly qualified in Chap. 4.) Product-moment correlation mainly is sensitive to the rank-order of individuals on two measures. As long as that rank-order is not disturbed, changes in the shapes of distributions make only very small changes in the correlation. Since the correlation coefficient is basic to all more complex methods of multivariate analysis, e.g., factor analysis, it follows that these more complex methods also are affected very little by transformations of measures. Consequently a strong argument can be made that the analysis of results would be very much the same whether the "real" scales had been employed or only approximate ones had been used. Then even if one accepted the fundamentalist point of view about measurement scales, what sense would it make to sacrifice powerful methods of analysis just because there is no way of proving the claimed scale properties of the measures?

In analyzing differences between means in differently treated groups, of major concern are the ratios of variances among different sources of variation. For example, an important ratio is the estimate of the population variance obtained from the differences among treatment means divided by the variance estimate obtained within the treatment groups. This and other important ratios among sources of variation are affected very little by monotonic transformations of the dependent measure. Then if it is granted that the measure used in the experiment is at least monotonically related to the "real" scale, it usually will make little difference which is used in the analysis.

After analyzing the results of investigations (obtaining correlations and ratios of variance components), it often is important to make probability statements about the results—in other words, to apply inferential statistics. Thus it may be important to set confidence zones for a correlation coefficient or to test the "significance" of a particular ratio among components of variance. Such statistical methods are completely indifferent to the zero point on a scale, and consequently ratio scales are not required. However, since such methods are based on ratios of variation and covariation, they operate directly on the interval properties of the measures. Following from this has been the mistaken assumption by some that such methods of analysis, e.g., analysis of variance, can be performed only on interval scales of measurement. Statistical methods are completely blind to any meaning in the real world of the numbers involved. All that is required for the use of such methods is a definable population of numbers that meets the assumptions in the particular statistical method, e.g., normality of the population distribution. For example, it would be perfectly permissible to employ analysis of variance to test hypotheses about the average size of the numbers on the backs of football players on different teams. Taking a more extreme example, if one suspected that different methods of obtaining tables of random numbers led to different results, analysis of variance could be used to compare different tables.

The important question in relation to inferential statistics concerns whether the indices of relationship, e.g., ratio of variance, should be computed and whether they can be meaningfully interpreted. After it is decided that such indices should be computed, there is no question of whether it is permissible to take the next step and apply inferential statistics. In dealing with measures of attributes, the computation of such indices requires assumptions about the interval character of the data; however, as was said above, violations of the assumptions usually have very little effect on the indices or on inferential statistics applied to the indices.

**Convention** So far in this section it has been necessary to take seriously the fundamentalist point of view that it is meaningful to think in terms of "real" scales and to think of actual measures as approximations of such "real" scales. These assumptions were tolerated up to this point to show that (1) they lead to unanswerable questions and (2) even if they were good assumptions, violations of them usually would not be harmful. As must be clear by this point, the author opposes the concept of "real" scales and deplores the confusion which this conception has wrought. It is much more appropriate to think of any measurement scale as a convention—an agreement among scientists that a particular scaling of an attribute is a "good" scaling.

In saying that scales are established by convention (rather than being God-given), it is not meant to imply that such conventions should be arbitrary. Before measures of particular attributes are constructed, all manner of wisdom should be brought to bear on the nature of the attribute. With some types of measures, the nature of a "good" scaling is so readily agreed on by all that a convention is easily established. Thus it is with length and weight: no one opposes the ways of setting the zero point and establishing the intervals. In exasperation about the confusion in theories of measurement, it is tempting to wish that there were no yardsticks and no balances for the measurement of weight. Then all scientists might see that measurement is a matter of convention rather than of discovering the "real" measure.

In some instances a convention of measurement is established by one person, and since many scientists do not realize that they do, or should, participate in establishing such conventions, the particular scale is accepted by the scientific community as *the* scale. Thus for some time the Fahrenheit thermometer was taken as *the* scale for measuring temperature. Later, with the discovery of "absolute zero," a new scaling was developed, one which scientists in general will agree is a more proper scale for the assertion of natural laws. Another example is that of the use of "age scales" for intelligence tests, in which the IQ is a ratio of mental age to chronological age. This convention was established for many years, until it gradually became apparent that the approach to scaling had enormous practical difficulties. Now the convention is changing to the use of "normative scores," in which IQs are expressed normatively within each age group. In both these instances it would be wrong to think that the "real" scales had been discovered. It would be more proper to say that conventions changed, and in both examples it may be that better conventions will be established in the future.

After all available wisdom has been applied to the problem, in the actual construction of measurement scales it is good to apply some type of formal scaling model. Although any set of rules for the assignment of numbers constitutes measurement, if the rules seem silly and/or ad hoc, they probably will not result in a measure that will eventually be agreed on as a good scaling of the attribute in question. It might be useful to think of a model as an internally consistent plan for seeking a good scaling of an attribute. When the plan is put to use, it may result in a measure that eventually proves unsatisfactory to the scientific community, but having a plan increases the probability of finding an acceptable measure. The situation is much like that in which two persons are searching for gold—one has a definite plan based on known facts about the location of gold, and the other person simply wanders around aimlessly hoping to discover the stuff. If the first person finds no gold and the second stumbles onto a bonanza, there is no question of who obtained the best result *in that particular instance.* Most persons will agree, however, that explicit plans based on common sense and past experience improve the probabilities of finding gold or finding a measurement scale that eventually will be accepted as a useful convention.

Even if some of the models disagree with one another about the scaling of particular attributes, those who advocate and deal with formal models for the scaling of attributes are to be praised. Even if the data fit a number of the models for forming a particular scale, however, there is no guarantee that the obtained measure will serve as a useful convention. It may be that a relatively planless scale will win out in the end, but the odds are in favor of the more systematic approaches.

A convention establishes the scale properties of a measure. If it is established as a ratio scale, then the zero point can be taken seriously and the intervals may be treated as equal in any form of analysis. If it is established as an interval scale, the intervals may be treated as equal in all forms of analysis. This is not meant to imply that such conventions are, or should be, established quickly or until much evidence is in, but in the end they are conventions, not discoveries of "real" scales.

Certain conventions are not established because they make no sense to scientists. For example, it made no sense to scientists to adopt the zero point on the Fahrenheit thermometer as a rational zero. Similarly, it makes little sense to establish zero points on scales for many, but not all, psychological attributes. What would be zero intelligence? Only that of a dead person or a stone would qualify, and compared to either, all living persons could be scored only as infinitely intelligent. Psychologists do seek to develop interval scales for many attributes, because it is reasonable to think not only in terms of the ordering of persons, but also in terms of how far apart they are on the scale.

Even those scaling procedures that do make sense to scientists may not produce scales that *work well in practice*. The last four words are the key to establishing a measurement convention—a good measure is one that mathematically fits well in a system of lawful relationships. In Chap. 3 it will be emphasized that the usefulness (validity) of a measure is in the extent to which it relates to other variables in a domain of interest. The "best" scaling of any particular attribute is that which will produce the *simplest* forms of relationship with other variables. In an increasing hierarchy of simplicity would be (1) a random relationship, which is the most complex of all possible relationships, (2) a nonrandom pattern, but one which fits no particular line of relationship, (3) an unevenly ascending or descending monotonic relationship, (4) a smooth monotonic relationship, (5) a straight line, and (6) a straight line passing through the origin. Whereas the only way to completely describe a random relationship is to describe every point on the graph, a straight line passing through the origin is completely described by $Y = aX$. Since the task of the scientist is to translate the complexity of events in the universe into a relative simplicity of lawful relationships, the simpler those relationships, the better.

One way to make relationships simpler is to change the scaling of one or more of the variables. Thus a nonsmooth monotonic relationship can be smoothed by stretching some of the intervals. A monotonic curve can be transformed to a straight line with the proper equation. A straight line can be made to pass through the origin by changing the origin (zero point) on one of the scales. Of course, the conventions regarding a particular attribute should not be altered because of the relationships found with only one or two other measures; but in the long run if it is found that many relationships would be simplified by a particular transformation of that scale, logically the new scale would be a better scale. Actually such transformations are made quite frequently. For example, logarithmic transformations have been made of many scales to simplify relations with other variables.

Following this point of view to the extreme, there is no reason that all the variables known to science could not be rescaled so as to simplify all natural laws. If this could be done, it would be a wise move. The new scales would be as "real" as the old ones, and there would be every reason to take seriously the zero points and the intervals on the new scales.

There are two major problems with considering scaling as a matter of convention. First, it is disquieting to those who think in terms of "real" scales and who wish for, but cannot find, some infallible test for the relationship between a particular measure and the "real" scale. Also, looking at measurement scaling as a matter of convention seems to make the problem "messy." How well a particular scaling of an attribute "fits in" with other variables is an open-ended question. Which variables? How good is a particular "fit"? To avoid such questions, however, is to blind oneself to the realities of scientific enterprise. To seek shelter in the apparent neatness of conceptions regarding "real" scales is not to provide answers about the properties of measurement scales but to ask logically unanswerable questions.

A second, and more serious, problem with considering scaling as a matter of convention is that there often are two or more conventions strongly competing with one another. For example, there has been much dispute about which of two methods of scaling certain dimensions of sensation—Thurstone's law of comparative judgment or the magnitude-estimation methods—is *the* correct method. (The methods are described in Chap. 2.) When these methods are used to scale judgments about the loudness of tones, different scales are obtained: one is logarithmically related to the other. More appropriate than asking which is "correct" would be asking which in the long run will "fit in" better in a system of natural laws. For example, there is already evidence that scalings based on methods of magnitude estimation have a broad generality over different modalities of sensation—which is the kind of evidence required to establish a convention for the use of one method rather than others.

For two reasons, having competing conventions regarding the scaling of attributes is not as bad as it may sound. First, if the two scalings are monotonically related to each other, as is usually the case, then if one has a monotonic relationship with a third variable, so will the other. Thus the laws established with one scaling will show the same variables functionally related as would be found in employing the alternative scaling, although the specific forms of the relationships could differ. Actually, at the present time in psychology, there are few problems in which the *specific form* of a relationship is the major issue. In correlational analysis, the major issue is the regression of one variable on another. Correlations greater than .60 are the exception rather than the rule, and, as was said previously, such correlations are largely insensitive to transformations of the variables involved. Consequently if there are two competing conventions for scaling which are monotonically related, both would correlate much the same with any other variable. In analyzing the results of experiments, the major considerations are whether there are mean differences among treatment groups and whether, in some problems, the means are monotonically or nonmonotonically related to levels of a treatment parameter. In these problems, transformations of the scale of the dependent measure make little difference in the findings. Consequently it would make little difference which of two monotonically related scalings of the dependent measure was employed.

There are some problems in which the specific form of a relationship is very important: (1) the previously mentioned problem of determining the specific form of relationship for judging the loudness of tones, (2) determining the shape of a learning curve, and (3) determining the shape of the curve relating intelligence to age. The specific forms of relationship in such studies can be settled only when there are firm conventions for scaling the variables involved. The specific form of a relationship is relative to the measurement convention; to hope to find *the* relationship is either to continue to search in vain for "real" scales or to assume that one measurement convention eventually will win out over others.

## SUGGESTED ADDITIONAL READINGS

Coombs, C. H. *A theory of data.* New York: Wiley, 1964.

Coombs, C. H., Dawes, R. M., and Tversky, A. *Mathematical psychology: An elementary introduction.* Englewood Cliffs, N.J.: Prentice-Hall, 1970.

Jones, L. V. The nature of measurement. In R. L. Thorndike (ed.), *Educational measurement* (2nd ed.). Washington, D.C.: American Council on Education, 1971.

Stevens, S. S. Problems and methods of psychophysics. *Psychological Bulletin,* 1958, *55,* 177–196.

Torgerson, W. S. *Theory and methods of scaling.* New York: Wiley, 1958, chaps. 1 and 2.

# CHAPTER TWO

## SCALING MODELS

In the previous chapter it was said that measurement concerns the assignment of numbers to objects to represent quantities of attributes. Although any system of operations that will so assign numbers can be spoken of as measurement, it helps to have some internally consistent plan for the development of a new measure. The plan is spoken of as a *scaling model*, and the measure which results from exercising the plan is spoken of as a *scale* (*scale* being another word for *measurement method*). The simplest example is that of the ruler as a scale of length. The methods for constructing and applying rulers constitute the scaling model in that case. The purpose of any scaling model is to generate one or more continua on which persons or objects are located. In the following example, persons $P_1$, $P_2$, $P_3$, and $P_4$ are located on such a continuum:

The attribute could be thought of as anxiety, spelling ability, attitude toward abortion, or any other trait. Because it is an interval scale, the distances between persons are taken seriously. Thus $P_1$ is considerably higher in the attribute than the other persons, $P_2$ and $P_3$ are close together, and $P_4$ is far below the others.

In most measurement problems, scaling concerns a data matrix (table) such as that in Fig. 2-1. On the front face of the cube, rows represent stimuli and columns represent responses to the stimuli. The "slices" of the cube going from front to back represent the responses of each person to each of the stimuli. The words *stimuli* and *responses* represent anything that the experimenter does to the subjects and anything the subjects do in return. Typical things (stimuli) the experimenter does to the subjects are to have them lift weights, to present them

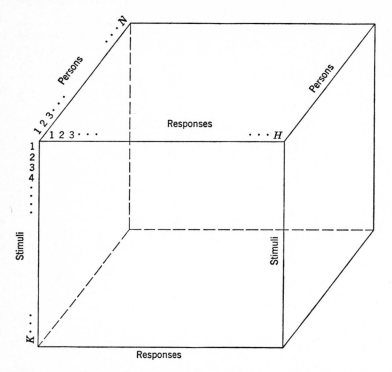

**Figure 2-1** A data matrix for *H* responses of *N* persons to *K* stimuli.

with spelling words, or to show them a list of foods. Typical responses required for these types of stimuli would be judging which of two weights is heavier, indicating whether or not each word is correctly spelled, and rating how much each food is liked.

The data matrix illustrated in Fig. 2-1 presents a very complex problem for scaling. The problem is much simpler when there is only a two-dimensional table, as when only one person is studied at a time. This also would be the case if only one type of response were made to each stimulus, e.g., agreeing or disagreeing with each of a list of statements (stimuli). Also, there would be a two-dimensional table of data if each person made a number of different types of responses to the same stimulus, e.g., rating the United Nations on different rating scales anchored by pairs of adjectives such as "effective-ineffective," "valuable-worthless," and "strong-weak." If in the problem there are more than one person, more than one stimulus, and more than one type of response required for each stimulus, there are many ways in which one of the three could be scaled. Usually an effort is made to simplify the problem by making the elements in one dimension "replicates" of one another, or at least assuming them to be so.

Some methods of scaling assume that persons are replicates of one another.

For example, the percentage of persons in a *group* that says one weight is heavier than another is assumed to be the same as the percentage of times an ideal *modal individual* would say that one weight is heavier than another on different occasions. The assumption that individuals are replicates is frequently made in scaling stimuli. In scaling persons, it frequently is assumed that responses are replicates of one another. Thus in the previous example of rating stimuli on scales anchored by bipolar adjectives, an overall "favorableness" rating can be obtained by adding responses over the separate rating scales.

In looking carefully at the different methods for scaling, in most cases it is clear that either one of the dimensions of the data matrix is not present (e.g., only one person, or one stimulus, or one type of response made to each stimulus) or an assumption is made that allows at least one of the dimensions to be dispensed with. When the latter is the case, there usually are ways of testing the correctness of the assumption. For example, if a different scale concerning the judgment of weights is constructed for each person and it is found that there are systematic differences in those scales, this would violate the assumption that persons are replicates in that particular situation. If it is found that the bipolar rating scales either do not correlate with one another or evolve into a number of different factors, it would be wrong to assume that the scales are replicates. When such assumptions are found to be incorrect, it is necessary to develop more than one scale for stimuli or for persons. Methods for developing multiple scales from data matrices, such as that in Fig. 2-1, concern multivariate analysis, which will be the subject of Part Three of this book. In this chapter we will discuss unidimensional scaling—those situations in which the data under consideration can be summarized satisfactorily with only one "yardstick."

Starting with a two-dimensional table of data, the usual strategy in the development of a measurement method is to test for the presence of a unidimensional scale. Essentially this consists of trying to "do away with" one of the two dimensions by employing some sensible procedure for combining the information from the "unwanted" dimension. An example would be where each individual has been required to rank a number of weights from heaviest to lightest. Then the data matrix would consist of the ranks of weights for each person—a two-dimensional table of data. One way to do away with the person dimension would be to average the ranks over persons, which would provide a scaling of the weights. Then one could place the average ranks in rank-order, which would provide an ordinal scaling of the weights for the group of people as a whole. Later, methods will be described whereby one could combine different sets of ranks from people in such a way as to achieve higher forms of measurement than ordinal scales only. Another example would be in having individuals either agree or disagree with statements concerning the United Nations. Agreement with each statement is thought to represent a positive attitude; disagreement, a negative attitude. Since there is only one object being rated, a two-dimensional table of data is obtained. By summing the number of agreements for each person, one collapses the response dimension of the table. Then sums of agreements would constitute an ordering of the persons with respect to their attitudes, and one might want to take the intervals between persons seriously.

Before one turns a two-dimensional table of data into a one-dimensional scale, first a set of assumptions should be stated regarding how the attribute in question is manifested in actual data. Then one must test how well the assumptions hold in the data. Each set of assumptions is a *model*. This chapter is primarily concerned with the models that are employed most frequently for turning two-dimensional tables of data into unidimensional scales. If the data do not fit the assumptions of a particular model for unidimensional scaling, the investigator has three choices: (1) try one of the other models for unidimensional scaling, (2) try methods of multivariate analysis, or (3) try some other scientific problem. If methods of multivariate analysis are applied, it might be found that more than one unidimensional scale is required to account for the data. For example, with statements concerning attitudes toward the United Nations, factor analysis might indicate that the statements relate to two different dimensions of attitude. It might be found that some statements relate to a factor concerning the effectiveness of the United Nations in settling diplomatic disputes among nations and other statements relate to a factor concerning activities of the United Nations in economic matters. Then two scales of attitudes, rather than only one, would be developed. Such methods of multivariate analysis will be treated in Chaps. 10 to 12. This chapter will be concerned only with models that are used for developing unidimensional scales.

**Evaluation of models** Often different models can be used for the development of particular scales, and sometimes the models lead to different conclusions about the scale properties of the data. One model might lead to a scale that failed to have a linear relationship with a scale derived from another model applied to the same data. One model might reject the data as conforming to an ordinal scale, whereas another model would accept the data as conforming to an interval scale. How, then, does one know which model is appropriate for a particular problem? As was said in the previous chapter, there is no sure way to know this in advance. The ultimate test is how well the scales which are derived fit in a nexus of lawful relations with other variables. Before time and effort are spent on such investigations, however, there are some criteria of "good sense" that can be applied.

Part of "good sense" concerns the intuitive appeal of a scaling model. Although the data of science must be objective, the scientist must rely on his intuition for research ideas. Looked at in one way, a measurement model is nothing more than an explicitly defined hunch, a hunch that particular operations on data will lead to an important measurement method. If the author's observations are correct, psychologists tend to find intuitively appealing those measurement models that are analogous to the measurement of simple physical attributes such as length and weight.

Another aspect of "good sense" in selecting scaling models concerns the evaluation of assumptions in the models in terms of what is already known about the type of data involved. For example, one of the models that will be discussed subsequently assumes that responses to individual test items are highly reliable; yet there is a wealth of evidence to show that such items usually are not highly reliable.

After a model is used to derive a scale and before strenuous efforts are made to find lawful relations with other variables, there are some preliminary forms of evidence regarding the usefulness of the scale. If the scale values for objects or persons are markedly affected by slightly different ways of gathering data, probably the scale will not work well in practice. There are, for example, numerous ways in which one can have subjects make judgments of weight. If two approaches that seem much the same lead to very different intervals of judged weight, one would be quite suspicious of the interval scales obtained by both approaches. An even more important type of preliminary evidence concerns the amount of measurement error involved in using a particular type of scale, a matter which will be discussed in detail in Chaps. 6 and 7. A scale that occasions a great deal of measurement error cannot possibly be useful for any purpose. Beyond the standards of good sense, however, the ultimate test of any model is the extent to which it produces scales with a high degree of explanatory power with respect to other variables in an area of scientific interest.

**Stimuli and people** Previously it was stated that scaling problems concern a three-dimensional matrix of persons, stimuli, and types of responses. In unidimensional scaling, usually each person makes only one type of response to each stimulus; or if each person makes more than one type of response, it is sensible to combine responses in some manner. (If there is doubt about the sensibility of combining responses, methods of multivariate analysis can be employed.) In either situation, a scaling model is applied to a two-dimensional matrix of data. What has not been made explicit so far is that usually methods of scaling employed for scaling *stimuli* are different from those for scaling *people*. Also, which of the two is to be scaled has a strong influence on the way responses are obtained.

It is probably easier to think of measurement problems in terms of the scaling of people. In a simple example, the data matrix is bordered by spelling words on the side and by people on the top. The required response is to indicate whether each word is correctly spelled (a single response to each stimulus). With the use of a 1 for correct spellings and a 0 for incorrect spellings, the data matrix would be filled with 1s and 0s. The dimension concerning stimuli (spelling words) would be collapsed by summing the number of 1s for each person. If it were not thought necessary to apply a more elaborate model to the data, the simple sums of correct responses would serve to scale people on the attribute of spelling ability.

Something more subtle is at issue when the purpose is to scale stimuli rather than people. For example, when subjects are asked to judge the loudness of tones by one method or another, the object is to generate a continuum of *perceived* loudness. In this instance the tones are quantified with respect to the attribute, and people are part of the measurement process. In another example of scaling stimuli, preferences for foods can be scaled by having a group of people rate each food on a like-dislike rating scale. One method of scaling in this instance would be to let the average rating of each food be its scale value.

When one seeks a unidimensional scale of stimuli, the hope is to find a scaling that fits the modal individual. Thus a scale developed in this way would be typical of persons as a group, even though it might not perfectly represent the scale that would be obtained by an intensive investigation of any one person. The long-range research purpose in scaling stimuli (rather than persons) is to relate scalings of the same stimuli with respect to different attributes. Thus after a unidimensional scale is developed for the perceived loudness of tones, another scaling of the same tones could be made against a background of noise. Another scaling could be made when each tone is accompanied by a light whose intensity is correlated with the intensity of the tone. Scaling of the tones could be made in various applied problems, such as in employing the tones as communication signals. At issue would be mathematical relations between the different scalings of the tones. The same would be true of scaling foods in terms of preferences. Rated preferences could be compared with what recruits in the Armed Forces choose to eat or with what homemakers would purchase. In each instance the object is to relate a scaling of stimuli on one attribute with the scaling of stimuli on a related attribute.

Important as it is to scale stimuli, this usually is not so large an issue in psychology as is the scaling of people with respect to attributes. It is probably true that if one searched through numerous journal articles and textbooks in psychology, one would find that most of the studies are primarily concerned with variables involving the scaling of people (or lower animals) rather than the scaling of stimuli. Prominently appearing in the literature are studies of learning rate, anxiety, decision time, intelligence, and strength of conditioned responses—all definitely concerned with the scaling of people. The issue is the same regardless of whether the scaling of people is for studies of individual differences or for controlled experiments. Although, for example, approaches to measurement employed for studies of individual differences concerning typical levels of anxiety might be different from those for controlled experiments on anxiety, in both types of studies it would be necessary to scale persons with respect to the attribute of anxiety.

It is important to make a distinction between the scaling of stimuli and the scaling of persons, because there are more severe problems with the former. In the scaling of stimuli, research issues frequently concern the exact nature of functional relations between scalings of the stimuli in different circumstances. Thus in the scaling of tones under different conditions, a careful study would be made of the exact "curves" between different scalings. Then it would make quite a difference if a particular relation were linear rather than logarithmic. As was stated in Chap. 1, in most studies concerning the scaling of people, exact forms of relationship between different scalings are not important—at least, not at the present stage of development of psychological science. The major requirement is that different scalings of people be monotonically related to one another, i.e., that they rank-order people in the same way. Thus if there are two different methods for scaling people for the attribute of anxiety and the two are monotonically related, research results will be much the same regardless of which scale is employed.

Because there are more serious problems with the scaling of stimuli than with the scaling of persons, most of the issues concerning scaling, and most of the models for scaling, have arisen in the context of problems concerning the scaling of stimuli. This can be seen, for example, in the comprehensive treatments of scaling methods by Guilford (1954) and by Torgerson (1958). In both books, most of the scaling models are illustrated with the scaling of stimuli (tones, weights, foods), and most of the models are more appropriate for the scaling of stimuli than for the scaling of persons. This difference has had an influence on the language used to describe psychological research. When one speaks of "scaling" and "scaling methods," usually one is discussing a problem concerning the scaling of stimuli. When one is discussing a problem concerning the scaling of persons with respect to an attribute, one is more likely to use terms like *measurement* and *test construction.*

## TYPES OF RESPONSES REQUIRED OF SUBJECTS

Before scaling models are discussed, it is necessary to review some of the different types of responses required of subjects. The type of response tends to correlate with the type of stimuli being studied; e.g., different types of responses would be required for the study of tones than for the study of food names. Different types of responses usually are required for the scaling of stimuli and for the scaling of persons. Also, different scaling models often require different types of responses. Endless distinctions could be made regarding all the kinds of responses that are possible in different studies. The three most important types of distinctions are discussed in the following sections.

**Judgments and sentiments** Although there are no two words that perfectly symbolize the distinction, one of the most important distinctions in measurement theory is that between responses concerning *judgments* and those concerning *sentiments.* The word *judgment* is used to cover all those types of responses where there is a *correct* response. This would be the case, for example, when a child is asked, "How much is two plus two?" This would also be the case when subjects are required to judge which of two tones is louder or which of two weights is heavier. In all these instances there is some *veridical comparison* for the subject's response, and it is possible to determine whether each response is correct or incorrect. With some types of judgments, it is also possible to determine the degree of correctness and thus the relative accuracy. For example, when a subject is required to adjust one light to the apparent brightness of another light, it is possible to measure how accurate the subject is in units of illumination.

The word *sentiment* is used to cover all responses concerning personal reactions, preferences, interests, attitudes, values, and likes and dislikes. One makes responses concerning sentiments when one (1) rates boiled cabbage on a seven-step, like-dislike rating scale, (2) answers the question, "Which would you rather do, organize a club or work on a stamp collection?" and (3) rank-orders 10 actors in terms of one's preferences. The important difference between judgments and sentiments is that with sentiments there is no veridical comparison. Thus if an individual says, "I like chocolate ice cream better than vanilla ice cream," it makes no sense to say, "You are incorrect." We may abhor another person's tastes for food or sentiments in any other sphere, but sentiments do not require veridical justification. Of course, it may be that the subject is incorrect in the sense that he or she lies or actually behaves in daily life in a manner different from that implied by the stated sentiments. The important point, however, concerns *what the subject is asked to do* in the experimental setting. When expressing a sentiment, the subject is asked to give a personal reaction to a stimulus, and there is no external standard of "accuracy" that makes sense.

In the study of judgments, an important problem is to relate *perceived* intensity of some attribute to the *physical* intensity of the attribute. For example, in a study where subjects are asked to adjust one light so that it appears twice as bright as another light, the ratio of perceived brightness can be compared with the ratio of physical magnitudes of illumination. Whenever subjects make judgments, there is a veridical comparison either actually available or at least potentially so. The latter possibility is illustrated in the problem where astronomers are asked to estimate the temperature of a number of stars. At the present there might be considerable controversy about the correct answers, but *conceivably* there are correct answers that one day can be used to determine the accuracy of present judgments. Such veridical comparisons are not conceivable with sentiments.

In the scaling of stimuli, the logic for validating models for the scaling of judgments is clearer than that for the scaling of sentiments. This is because the scale of judgments, after it is developed, can be compared with the scale of physical magnitudes. Then, intuitively, one would expect certain types of relations between the scale of judgments and the scale of physical magnitudes. If, for example, an interval scale of the judged loudness of tones does not have a smooth, monotonic relationship with the scale of physical magnitudes, probably one would reject the model used for developing the scale. Probably one would expect not a straight line of relationship, but some type of smooth, monotonic curve. If this expectation is borne out, it provides no guarantee that the model is correct, but it does provide intuitive support for continued use of the model. Since with sentiments there is no physical scale, there is no way of comparing a scale of sentiments with "actuality." What typically is done then is to explore new scaling models on data concerning judgments, and if they apparently work well there, to extend them to studies of sentiments. It is even more apparent with sentiments than with judgments that the usefulness of any scale is determined in the long run by how well it fits into a system of lawful relations with other variables in a particular area of scientific interest.

In the scaling of people, all tests of ability concern judgments, in a broad sense of the term. This is true in tests of mathematics, vocabulary, and reasoning ability. The subject either exercises judgment in supplying a correct answer for each item or judges which of a number of alternative responses is most correct. Tests of interests concern sentiments: the subject indicates the activities that are liked and those that are disliked. Measures of attitudes and personality can require either judgments or expressions of sentiment, and it is with these types of measures that frequently the distinction is obscure. On a personality inventory, when responding to the item "Do you like to be the center of attention at parties?" the subject is asked to express a sentiment. When responding to the item "Do you usually lead the discussion in group situations?" the subject is asked to make a judgment about her or his actual behavior in group situations. When responding to the item "Do most people like you?" the subject is asked to make a judgment about other peoples' sentiments.

Frequently other terms are employed to refer to these two broad categories of responses. The word *choice* frequently is used in place of the word *sentiments*. The term *cognitive* frequently refers to judgmental responses; and sentiments are frequently referred to as *affects*. One can make a good argument for referring to judgment as concerning "knowing" and sentiments as concerning "feeling." By whatever names they go, judgments and sentiments present different types of problems in some cases for the scaling of stimuli and the scaling of people.

## CHARACTERISTICS OF STIMULUS SCALING

As mentioned previously, the technical issues are more complex in the development of scales for stimuli than of those for people. Later in the chapter we will discuss the technical aspects of developing scales ("tests") for measuring individual differences among people with respect to abilities, personality characteristics, and other aspects of judgments and sentiments. Prior to that discussion of the scaling of people, we will discuss some of the major principles and methods for the scaling of stimuli.

**Comparative and absolute responses** An important distinction concerns whether the subject is required to make an absolute response to each stimulus separately or to make comparative judgments or expressions of sentiment among the stimuli. An example of an absolute response would be to the question, "How long is this line in inches?" Another example is when the subject is required to rate boiled cabbage on a seven-step, like-dislike scale. In both instances the subject responds to each stimulus separately and indicates the amount of the attribute in an absolute sense.

With comparative judgments and sentiments, stimuli are presented in groups of two or more, and the subject responds to the "more" and "less" of some property. A comparative response is required when the subject is asked to indicate a preference for boiled cabbage or boiled turnips or which of two weights is heavier. All items on multiple-choice tests of ability and personality concern comparative responses—the individual picks one answer from a number of alternative answers. In some tests of ability and personality, the individual is required to rank alternative answers to test items in terms of correctness, degree of agreement, pleasantness, or some other attribute.

There are few instances in which it makes sense to require absolute judgments of subjects, as, for example, in asking the subject, "How long is this line in inches?" People are notoriously poor at making many types of absolute judgments of length, weight, and other physical properties of stimuli. In many cases the subject has no way of communicating absolute judgment of such physical properties. How would the subject respond if asked simply, "How bright is this light?" or "How loud is this tone?"

People are not accustomed to making absolute judgments in daily life, since most judgments are inherently comparative. Thus subjects can respond with a high degree of confidence when asked which of two lights is brighter or which of two tones is louder. Whereas people are notoriously inaccurate in judging the absolute magnitudes of stimuli, e.g., the length of a line in inches, they are notoriously accurate in making comparative judgments. If the subject is within 20 feet of the stimuli and is asked to judge which of two lines is longer, the subject will be accurate almost every time unless the lines differ by less than $\frac{1}{2}$ inch.

As is true of most judgments in daily life, to a lesser extent most sentiments are partly comparative. The individual has some feeling regarding the absolute liking for an object or activity, but such sentiments are influenced by the range of objects or activities available. Thus an individual required to rate boiled cabbage on a like-dislike rating scale (an absolute response) must surely say, "What else would there be to eat?" If women are required to rate the photograph of a man on a rating scale anchored by the adjectives "handsome" and "ugly," how can they make such responses unless they subjectively compare the features of the man with those of the many men that they have seen previously?

Even when subjects are requested to make absolute responses to each stimulus in a set, there is considerable evidence that their responses sometimes are comparative. This would be found when weights are to be rated on a scale ranging from "very heavy" to "very light." If subjects actually were responding to each weight separately, the rating given any weight would remain the same regardless of the sizes of the other weights in the set. But as anyone would guess, the rating of a particular weight shifts markedly when it is placed in the context of heavier or lighter weights. The same is true to a lesser extent of sentiments. If women are asked to make ratings of the handsomeness of men shown in 20 photographs, the rating of the man in any particular photograph can be shifted somewhat by placing it in the context of all relatively ugly men. When giving absolute judgments and expressions of sentiment, subjects tend to anchor their responses in terms of (1) stimuli of the same kinds that they have experienced in the past and (2) the range of stimuli in the set presented. However, the difficulties of obtaining absolute rather than comparative responses are usually much more serious with judgments than with sentiments.

Potentially, the major advantage of absolute responses is with sentiments rather than with judgments. The comparative methods are sufficient for most studies of judgments and are useful in studies of sentiments; but in some studies of sentiments, it is important to learn the absolute level of responses to stimuli. This is the case in most studies of attitudes, e.g., in studies of attitudes toward different national groups. This information could not be obtained from comparative responses, as where the subject is required to rank the names of 10 national groups from "most prefer" to "least prefer." The individual may dislike all the national groups or like them all, but there would be no hint of that from the rankings (comparative responses). Absolute responses are important in those studies of sentiments where it is necessary to obtain an approximate indication of the "neutral" point either for the scaling of persons or for the scaling of stimuli. For example, in studies of attitudes, it has been hypothesized that people near the neutral point (e.g., of attitudes toward the United Nations) are more susceptible to change than are people who are far from the neutral point in either direction. By requiring absolute responses from subjects, one would be able to approximately determine the neutral point.

Even when absolute responses are required of subjects, the experimenter sometimes makes comparative analyses and interpretations of those responses. This is done because absolute responses frequently are much easier and faster to obtain than comparative responses. For example, in a study of preferences for 95 foods, probably the investigator would be interested mainly in which foods are liked more and which are liked less. A direct way to obtain this information would be to have each subject rank all the foods from "most prefer" to "least prefer," but that probably would take each subject an hour or more. Approximately the same information could be obtained in a much shorter time from absolute responses. Each subject would rate each food on a like-dislike scale. An average rating of each food over subjects would be obtained. Then the experimenter could rank the foods in terms of average ratings, and some of the comparative models for scaling could be used to estimate intervals between foods on the continuum of sentiment. Thus in many cases where subjects are asked to make absolute responses, the experimenter takes seriously only the comparative information in those responses.

**Scale for response** Another important distinction among types of responses concerns the scale on which the subject is required to respond. In most types of responses, subjects are required to respond to stimuli in terms of an ordinal, interval, or ratio scale; that is, each subject is required to generate a scale having the properties of one of these three basic types of scales. There are many ways in which responses can be obtained with respect to the three types of scales, each way being referred to as a *psychophysical method*. Historically, the term *psychophysical methods* was applied to studies of judgments and not to both judgments and sentiments. Thus the intention was to obtain psychological counterparts of physical stimulation, e.g., the psychological response to lifted weights. However, since the same methods that are employed to scale judgments are frequently employed to scale sentiments, the term *psychophysical methods* is now applied to techniques for scaling both types of responses.

Frequently subjects are required to operate on an ordinal scale. All the particular methods that can be applied for that purpose are called methods of *ordinal estimation*. The most straightforward way to do this is by the method of *rank-order*, which, as the name implies, requires the subject to rank stimuli from "most" to "least" with respect to some attribute of judgment or sentiment. A more thorough approach is with the method of *paired comparisons,* in which the subject is required to rank stimuli two at a time in all possible pairs. For example, eight weights would be presented two at a time in all possible pairs, and for each comparison the subject would be required to indicate which is heavier. Another example which will be illustrated later is when the individual is given the names of a number of criminal offenses, two at a time, and asked to indicate which is the more serious crime. Even though on each response a comparison is made between only two stimuli, in essence the subject is required to rank the stimuli "one" and "two" on each comparison. From these responses, the experimenter deduces ordinal and interval scales for the full set of stimuli, by methods which will be described in a later section.

Another ordinal method is the method of *constant stimuli.* This method is similar to paired comparisons, except that a standard stimulus is successively paired with each member of a constant set of stimuli. An example would be in a study of lifted weights where the standard stimulus is a weight of 200 grams and the six constant comparisons are weights of 185, 190, 195, 205, 210, and 215 grams, respectively. Constant stimuli would be paired in a random order with the standard stimulus, and on each comparison the subject would be required to indicate which is heavier. (Of course, on each comparison only the experimenter would know which is the standard stimulus.) To obtain reliable data, it usually is necessary to present numerous random orderings of the constant stimuli in comparison with the standard stimulus. Typical results obtained from applying the method of constant stimuli are shown in Fig. 2-2.

Another ordinal method is that of *successive categories,* in which the subject is asked to sort a collection of stimuli into a number of distinct "piles," or categories, which are ordered with respect to a specified attribute. For example, subjects could be required to sort 100 statements concerning their favorableness toward the United Nations. The subject would be given 10 categories, with the first category defined as "very favorable," the tenth category

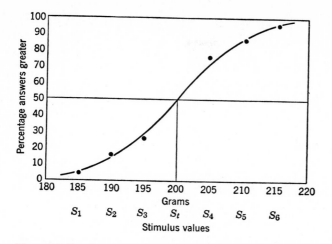

**Figure 2-2** Psychometric function for the application of the method of constant stimuli to a study of lifted weights.

defined as "very unfavorable," and categories between being anchored with verbal labels representing intermediate levels of favorableness. Usually this type of information is obtained more simply by having the individual mark one of 10 steps on a rating scale placed on a printed form.

There are many variants of the method of successive categories, depending on the type of information that the experimenter hopes to obtain. When the experimenter is seeking only ordinal information, usually the subject is allowed to operate as he chooses in assigning stimuli to categories. A variant is to require subjects to place an equal number of stimuli in each category, e.g., the top 10 stimuli in category 1 and the bottom 10 stimuli in category 10. Another variant is to require subjects to sort the stimuli into an approximate normal distribution, with it being specified how many stimuli are to be placed in each category (this variant is called the "Q sort").

These approaches to the method of successive categories can be used to obtain ordinal information about the stimuli. The method can be thought of as requiring the subject to rank a set of stimuli in a situation where tied ranks are mandatory. Thus if it is required to place 10 stimuli in each of 10 categories, those placed in category 1 can be thought of as tied for the top rank, and those placed in category 10 as tied for the bottom rank. Then, by averaging the tied ranks over subjects, one can obtain a rather complete ranking of the stimuli, in which there would be few tied ranks. Although there are numerous variants of these methods, the basic approaches to obtaining ordinal judgments and expressions of sentiment are with rank-order, paired comparisons, constant stimuli, and successive categories.

The method of successive categories also can be employed to obtain *inter-val* responses from subjects. As in the example given previously of a 10-step rating scale of successive rating categories, experimenters frequently take those numbers as corresponding to equal intervals on whatever scale of response is being investigated. Often the experimenter instructs the subject to use the scale as though the distances between successive categories were the same; e.g., the difference between a rating of 2 and 4 is equal to the difference between a rating of 6 and 8. Also, to help obtain interval responses from subjects with rating scales, verbal labels frequently are employed. For example, in a scale concerning relative amounts of pleasantness, the scale could be anchored with adjectives ranging in pleasantness from "extremely pleasant" to "extremely unpleasant." Often rating scales can be expressed in terms of percentages, which further serve to ensure that interval responses are being given. For example, subjects could be asked to rate various statements in terms of their judgment of what percent of the general population would agree with each statement. When rating scales are used to obtain interval responses of judgment or sentiment, they are said to constitute the method of *equal-appearing intervals*.

Another approach to obtaining interval responses involves a broad category of techniques which will be referred to as methods of *interval estimation*. The most frequently used method in this group is the method of *bisection*. For example, the subject is given two lights of different intensity and asked to adjust a third light to a point halfway between the other two lights in terms of apparent brightness. Or the subject is given two statements differing in favorableness toward the United Nations and asked to select a statement that is halfway between the two in favorableness. Rather than having the distance between the two stimuli bisected, another approach has intervals estimated in terms of some other ratio. For example, with two fixed stimuli, the subjects can be asked to select a third stimulus such that the interval between one of the fixed stimuli and the third is twice as great as the distance between the other fixed stimulus and the third. Another approach presents the subjects with two stimuli that are extreme with respect to the attribute and has them judge the ratio of intervals formed when each of a number of stimuli are inserted between.

It must be kept in mind that with all the methods of interval estimation, the subject responds in terms of *intervals* of judgment or sentiment. Though the subject may be forming ratios, e.g., a 1:1 ratio in the method of bisection, responses are with respect to intervals among the stimuli and not with respect to the absolute intensities of the stimuli. The experimenter might seek to deduce absolute intensities for the stimuli according to a model, but it is important to make a clear distinction between what the subject is required to do and interpretations that the experimenter makes of what is done. With the interval-estimation methods, the subject is required to estimate the comparative sizes of intervals among stimuli.

The *ratio-estimation* methods require subjects to respond to the absolute magnitudes of stimuli. As is true of the interval-estimation methods, there are numerous particular forms of ratio estimation. In a simple example, the subject is given a light at one intensity and asked to adjust another light until it appears twice as bright as the first. Or a subject is given the name of a food that is thought to be liked moderately well by most persons and asked to rate each food in a list on a scale ranging from "like only one-tenth as much" to "like 10 times as much."

In those cases where the zero point can be taken seriously, percentage scales, as described previously, also can be employed for ratio estimation. An example would be subjects rating the complexity of 100 geometrical forms that vary from extremely simple to extremely complex. From previous studies, the experimenter knows which form is rated clearly more complex than the others. This geometrical form is either placed in front of the individual on a card or printed in a booklet. The subject is then shown all the other geometrical forms. one at a time, and asked to rate percentagewise how complex each geometrical form is in relation to the most complex one used as a standard. If a group of people rate the least complex form as 20 percent, one can argue that it is 20 percentage points above zero complexity. Although one might argue about the legitimacy of developing ratio scales from such ratings of percentages or other numerical values, it is surprising how closely they resemble the scales obtained from more direct methods of ratio estimation (see discussion in Stevens 1960).

Superficially, some of the methods of interval estimation appear similar to some of the methods of ratio estimation. For example, choosing a stimulus that is halfway between two others is apparently similar to choosing a stimulus that is twice as great as another with respect to some attribute. There are, however, very important differences between methods of interval estimation and methods of ratio estimation. In both examples above, the subject forms two equal-appearing intervals. When a stimulus halfway between two others is chosen, two equal-appearing intervals are formed. When a stimulus is chosen that is twice as intense as another with respect to an attribute, again two equal-appearing intervals are formed. The important difference is that in the latter case the lower interval is bounded by a *phenomenal zero*. In that case the subject essentially is required to form an interval between two stimuli that is equal to the interval between the less intense stimulus and zero. Regardless of whether the subject can perform the task, this must be what the experimenter wants the subject to do. In other words, in methods of ratio estimation, the experimenter seeks to obtain responses from subjects with respect to a ratio scale of judgment or sentiment.

The purpose of this section has been to discuss three broad categories of stimulus scaling methods depending on the scaling tasks required of subjects: ordinal estimation, interval estimation, and ratio estimation. There are many variants of each of these, many of which have their own names and many of which are called by different names. These are the so-called psychophysical methods, and if one wants to give a different name to each shade and hue of difference in procedure, there are literally hundreds of psychophysical methods. The reader who has a special interest in these methods should consult the excellent books by Guilford (1954), Torgerson (1958), and the other citations in

Suggested Additional Readings at the end of this chapter. More important for most readers, however, is to understand the three major classes of scaling tasks described in this section.

**Specification of an attribute** With all the methods discussed so far in this section, judgments or sentiments are expressed with respect to a *stated attribute*. Thus weights are judged with respect to heaviness, and men are rated with respect to handsomeness. In most studies it is possible for the experimenter to specify the attribute involved, but in some studies this is not the case. The latter occurs when it is known in advance, or suspected, that the stimuli differ with respect to more than one dimension or attribute. This would be the case where responses are made to colored chips that vary in terms of hue, saturation, and brightness. It would occur when subjects respond to the names of United States senators, the senators varying on a number of dimensions of political belief and practice. When the attribute cannot be stated in advance and/or the stimuli vary with respect to a number of attributes, the methods discussed so far cannot be used. The experimenter must obtain *similarity estimates* from the subjects. A frequently used method is to present the subject with three stimuli at a time and ask which two are more similar. In this way, the experimenter does not have to specify the attribute(s), but relies instead on the rather global notion of similarity. Although similarity estimates can be used in place of some of the methods discussed in this chapter for obtaining unidimensional scales, they are mainly useful in multidimensional scaling, which will be discussed in some detail in Chap. 12.

# METHODS FOR CONVERTING RESPONSES TO STIMULUS SCALES

After responses have been obtained by one of the psychophysical methods discussed above, the next step is to generate an ordinal, interval, or ratio scale. In the scaling of stimuli, usually complex models are not required for deriving ordinal scales, and the different models used for that purpose usually arrive at the same ordering of stimuli. Some examples will serve to show how ordinal scales are obtained. With the method of rank-order, the average ranks would be obtained over subjects, and these would be converted to ranks. The final set of ranks would constitute an ordinal scaling of the stimuli for the typical subject. In a study where men in photographs are rated for handsomeness, the average ratings would be obtained over subjects, and these would be converted to ranks. With a method of paired comparisons, the first step in converting data from a group of subjects is to determine the percent of subjects that rated each stimulus as being higher on the particular response dimension than each of the other stimuli. Thus, if there were 10 stimuli, there would be 9 percentages for each stimulus in comparing it with the others one at a time. The full data from the group of subjects could then be summarized in a square table showing all possible percentages of the paired comparisons. These percentages could be summed for each stimulus, and then it would be a simple matter to rank these sums from highest to lowest. So it is with all the methods discussed in the previous section—methods for obtaining ordinal scales usually are intuitively obvious.

Scaling models become important in constructing either an interval or a ratio scale for stimuli. Usually the effort is to construct an interval scale, but in some cases efforts are made to construct ratio scales. The remainder of this section will consider models that are used for these purposes. The two classes of models that are used in the majority of cases will be discussed and illustrated in detail, mention will be made of some other possibilities, and references will be given to a wide variety of specialized methods for developing stimulus scales. Computational procedures are described by Guilford (1954), Torgerson (1958), and in other sources that will be referenced in appropriate places.

**Scaling models based on subjective estimates** In the previous section psychophysical methods were discussed in terms of the *scale of responses.* It was said that most methods require the subject to respond in terms of an ordinal, interval, or ratio scale. Even though the subject might be instructed to respond in terms of one type of scale, the experimenter might take the responses as representing another type of scale; e.g., although the subject responded in terms of interval estimates, the experimenter might take seriously only the ordinal information obtained.

With some models for scaling stimuli, the experimenter *does* take seriously the scaling task required of the subject. This is usually the case when the experimenter employs one of the particular psychophysical methods discussed previously for interval estimation or ratio estimation. In those instances it is easy to obtain interval or ratio scales. What the experimenter does is to average such responses over repeated measurements of one individual to obtain a scale for that person, or more commonly the experimenter averages responses over subjects in a group to obtain a scale that characterizes the group as a whole. Some examples of this process follow. The subject is required to sort 100 shades of gray paper into 10 categories ranging from "darkest" to "lightest." The subject is instructed to treat the 10 numbered categories as though they constituted equal intervals with respect to the attribute in question.The experimenter assumes that the subjective processes of the individual are capable of generating an interval scale of perceived brightness. It is admitted that there is some error in the judgments made by one person on one occasion, but efforts are made to reduce the error by averaging judgments over subjects. Thus if a particular shade of gray is rated 9, 9, 8, and 8 by four subjects, the average rating of 8.5 is considered the measurement of that shade of gray on an interval scale. In the same way, measurements would be obtained for all the shades of gray. Then the scale would be used in other investigations concerning discrimination of shades of gray.

A second example of the development of an interval scale based on subjective estimates follows. The individual is shown two lights that vary greatly in luminance—one is very bright and the other is very weak. The subject is asked to adjust a third light to a point halfway between the two extremes. Next the subject is asked to pick a fourth light which is halfway between the middle light and the upper light. On the next trial, the subject is asked to choose a light that subjectively divides the interval of brightness between the two lower lights. Continuing this process through numerous trials, one could obtain many equal-appearing intervals of brightness between the two extremes. After the physical measures of luminance corresponding to these different perceived levels of brightness are averaged, one obtains an interval scale for brightness based on subjective estimates.

There are numerous other approaches to obtaining interval scales directly from subjective estimates. Such scales can be developed for sentiments as well as for judgments. For example, rather than employ 100 shades of gray in the illustration given above in the use of rating methods, one could have employed 100 girls' names and asked male subjects to rate them in terms of preference.

There are various approaches to obtaining ratio scales from subjective estimates. These are based on the psychophysical methods concerning ratio estimation discussed previously. For example, a subject can be shown a bright light and in a random order pair that light with lights of lower levels of luminance ranging down to very dim lights. On each such comparison, the subject can be asked to rate on a percentage scale the percent of brightness of the weaker light to the standard stimulus. Of course, a sensible zero point is when the light is turned off or the current is so weak that no illumination is evident. This provides a ratio scale for any one subject, and such ratios can be averaged over subjects to obtain a ratio scale for a group as a whole.

Subjective estimates also could be used to develop ratio scales for sentiments of various kinds. A simple example is developing a ratio scale for the prestige of various professional groups, such as doctors, dentists, lawyers, professors, engineers, and others. With a collection of such names of professions, any of the psychophysical methods of ratio estimation could be employed to obtain responses, some methods being more sensible in this regard than others. The most direct approach is to have each subject first pick out the most prestigious profession and then employ percentage scales comparing that profession with all the others, as illustrated above in developing ratio scales of judgment. Another approach is to have the subject compare the professions two at a time and then verbalize a ratio of the perceived more prestigious profession to the less prestigious profession, e.g., one-and-half times as much, twice as much, etc. After such ratios are obtained among all pairs of names of professions, these ratios can be averaged over subjects to obtain a ratio scale for the professions.

There are numerous other models for developing interval and ratio scales based on subjective estimates. In essence subjects are assumed capable of producing such scales directly. After this fundamental assumption is made and appropriate methods of gathering responses (particularly those of interval estimation and ratio estimation) are employed, it is a rather straightforward matter to derive the final interval and ratio scale. In most cases, the responses of subjects simply are averaged as shown in the examples above. In other cases, some assumptions are made, and the average responses are altered appropriately. In either case, the actual models and computational procedures for this purpose tend to be simpler than models based on other fundamental assumptions. The various approaches to ratio scaling are discussed in detail by Stevens (1960) and at various places in the Suggested Additional Readings.

**Discriminant models for developing stimulus scales** The second major class of models (there are only two that are used widely in empirical research) differs in a number of important ways from the class based on subjective estimates. In discriminant models, one does not take very seriously the subject's ability to generate interval and ratio scales directly; rather, one assumes that this is something the scientist has to do after the data are collected. Discriminant models place primary emphasis on the variability of response to each stimulus—the variability of responses by different persons to the same stimulus and the potential variability of responses by the same person to the same stimulus on different occasions. Although with models based on subjective estimates it is admitted that such variability is present, most models take no formal account of the variability. Whereas models based on subjective estimates typically require responses by various methods of interval estimation and ratio estimation, discriminant models typically require responses by methods of ordinal estimation, e.g., rank-order and paired comparisons.

The foundation for all discriminant models for scaling stimuli was laid by L. L. Thurstone. For any individual confronted with any stimulus, there is assumed to be a *discriminal process* with respect to a specified attribute. A discriminal process is simply a broadly defined *reaction* of some kind which correlates with the intensity of the stimulus on an interval scale for an attribute. Because of fluctuations of many different kinds within the individual, there is a *discriminal distribution* for each stimulus. That is, if the individual responds to the same stimulus on numerous occasions, the discriminal processes will be somewhat different. Since these differences are thought to represent random errors, it is expected that reactions would be normally distributed. Such distributions for three stimuli are illustrated in Fig. 2-3. The reader should keep in

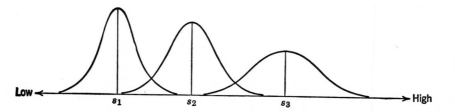

**Figure 2-3** Discriminal distributions with respect to three stimuli.

mind that the attribute continuum on which the distributions are shown and the distributions themselves are entirely hypothetical. There is no way that the experimenter can measure the stimuli directly on the attribute. Of course, if there were some way to measure the attribute directly, then there would be no need to develop special mathematical models for that purpose. Only after the experimenter makes a series of assumptions about what is going on "in the head" of the subject and the relationship of such covert reactions in a statistical sense to a hypothetical continuum is it possible to derive an actual measurement method for obtaining an interval scale.

The mean discriminal process (reaction) to each stimulus is the best estimate of the scale value for that stimulus (best in the sense of least squares). If the means were known for all stimuli, an interval scale would be obtained and the scaling problem would be complete. According to the discriminant class of models, there is no way to obtain these means directly; they must be deduced from the subject's responses. In doing this, each of the different models makes somewhat different assumptions about the nature of the discriminal distributions. In the general model, it is not assumed that the standard deviations are equal (unequal standard deviations are illustrated in Fig. 2-3). This allows for the possibility that a subject would vary more in responses to some stimuli than in responses to others.

Crucial to all discriminant models is that there be overlapping distributions of discriminal processes. If, for example, the discriminal distribution of one stimulus is so high on the attribute that the lower tail of the distribution does not overlap somewhat with the distribution of the stimulus immediately below, then there is no way to determine the position of that stimulus on an interval scale. Because it is crucial to have overlapping discriminal distributions, it is said that discriminant models are based on *confusions.*

In a practical sense, the discriminant models are useful only when stimuli are close together; consequently, it is somewhat difficult for the subjects to make up their mind regarding judgments or sentiments between pairs of stimuli. The discriminant models would not work, for example, if in the study of preferences employing the method of paired comparisons the subject were asked to choose among having a pencil, a transistor radio, a color television set, or a new automobile. There simply would be no overlap in such preferences, and thus nothing to investigate with respect to discriminant models for the development of interval scales. The following presentation of discriminant models is based on the assumption that there is a sufficient amount of overlap to permit the discriminant models to be employed effectively

A series of brilliant simplifying assumptions and deductions by Thurstone (1927) led to the now famous law of comparative judgment. Actually there are numerous forms of the "law," depending on the assumptions made in particular cases. Complete discussions of numerous models and research techniques following from the law of comparative judgment are given by Bock and Jones (1968), Guilford (1954), Torgerson (1958), and at various places in the other citations in Suggested Additional Readings at the end of this chapter. Here we consider only the basic ideas and the particular model which has been used most widely. Although the same computational procedures can be applied to testing one individual on many occasions as to combining the responses of numerous individuals tested on only one occasion, here we will illustrate the logic with the classic example of how the subjective reactions of one individual could be "brought out into the open" in the form of an interval scale. The major assumptions and deductions are as follows:

1. Let covert discriminal responses of one person to stimulus $j$ be denoted $r_j$ and covert discriminal responses to stimulus $k$ be denoted $r_k$.
2. Let the mean discriminal responses to two stimuli, $\bar{r}_j$ and $\bar{r}_k$, be the best estimates of scale positions for those stimuli. That is, if there were some objective way of determining the many responses of the one subject to each stimulus, the mean (the arithmetic average) of these would constitute the best estimate of the typical reaction. Similarly, the means of all the covert processes would represent the best scale positions for the one person on the interval scale of judgment or sentiment.
3. If the discriminal distributions overlap, on some occasions the difference in response to the two stimuli, $r_j - r_k$, will be positive and on other occasions negative; i.e., the subject will "change his or her mind" from one occasion to another about which is higher on the attribute. Understanding such distributions of difference scores is absolutely crucial to understanding how the discriminant models work. An analogy is in comparing two athletes who frequently run the 100-yard dash. The running times over different occasions could be shown as distributions analogous to the three distributions shown in Fig. 2-3. Although on the average one runner is faster than the other, they are sufficiently close together that their distributions overlap. On some occasions, the runner who is slower on the average actually runs the 100-yard dash faster than the runner who usually has the faster time. On any particular day, one could subtract the running time of the slower runner from that of the faster runner. Most of these differences would be positive, but some would be negative. For example, some of the differences would be of the order of 1.0 second, 0.7 second, 0.5 second, −0.2 second, and −0.3 second. Such difference scores are perfectly "good" numbers and can be cast into a frequency distribution which then summarizes the overlap of two separate distributions.
4. If the discriminal processes for two stimuli are normally distributed, as most errors of this type tend to be for many different phenomena, the distribution of differences in discriminal processes will be normally distributed. That is, on each occasion, if $r_k$ were subtracted from $r_j$, the distribution of such differences over many occasions would be normal. This follows from a mathematical proof which is presented in many statistics books and need not be repeated here. A distribution of discriminal differences is illustrated in Fig. 2-4. The shaded area is proportional to the percentage of times stimulus $j$ is judged greater than stimulus $k$, and vice versa for the unshaded

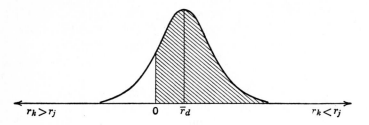

**Figure 2-4** Distribution of discriminal differences for two stimuli.

area. Note that the zero point is not at the middle of the distribution but is noticeably to the left of the mean ($\bar{r}_d$). This is because the average discriminal response to stimulus $r_j$ is higher on the attribute than the average response to $r_k$; consequently, the majority of the differences (those indicated by the shaded portion of the curve) are positive rather than negative.

5. The mean of the differences between responses to the two stimuli on numerous occasions, $\bar{r}_d$, equals the best estimate of the interval separating the two stimuli on an interval scale. This would be equal to $\bar{r}_j - \bar{r}_k$. There is no way to obtain this quantity directly, because it is entirely hypothetical, "something in the head" that can be estimated only from a set of assumptions and mathematical techniques. By employing Thurstone's law of comparative judgment, the difference between mean discriminal processes can be estimated as follows.

6. On numerous occasions ask a subject to state whether stimulus $j$ is greater or less than stimulus $k$ with respect to an attribute. (For the sake of exploring this model, assume at this point that such an approach is feasible.) This porportion is denoted $p_{j>k}$.

7. Next, make the preliminary assumption that discriminal differences are normally distributed with a standard deviation of 1.0. The mean of the distribution would be $\bar{r}_d$ rather than zero. The zero point would be either to the left or to the right of the mean, depending on which of the two stimuli is more frequently judged to be greater with respect to the attribute. Then the zero point could be expressed in terms of the number of standard deviations it is below or above the mean $\bar{r}_d$ (or $\bar{r}_j - \bar{r}_k$). This is done by looking in a table of areas under the normal curve for the normal deviate corresponding to $p_{j>k}$. If, for example, $j$ is judged greater than $k$ 92 percent of the time, this corresponds to a normal deviate $z_{jk}$ of approximately 1.4. Thus the zero point on the scale of discriminal differences is 1.4 standard deviations below the mean. More importantly, *the mean is 1.4 standard deviations above the zero point* (and this is the fact that gets us close to a solution).

8. With the size of $\bar{r}_d$ (or $\bar{r}_j - \bar{r}_k$) found in terms of standard deviations on the unit normal curve $z_{jk}$, all that is left is to express $\bar{r}_d$ in terms of the actual standard deviation of the dispersion of discriminal differences. This is necessary to account for the possibility that the standard deviations of discrim-

inal differences might be different for different pairs of stimuli. This would tend to be the case if the discriminal dispersions for two stimuli were larger than those for two other stimuli. If that occurred, even if two pairs of stimuli were separated by a function of the same normal deviate, they could be separated by very different intervals on an interval scale. Thus even if $z_{fl}$ and $z_{jk}$ are the same, when the standard deviations of distributions of discriminal differences are taken into account in the two cases, the two intervals might be very different. Account needs to be taken of these standard deviations to place intervals back on the same unit of measurement as that of the discriminal continuum, which, of course, is hypothetical rather than directly observable.

9. The standard deviation of the dispersion of discriminal differences can be expressed in the same way as it is with the standard deviation of any set of difference scores. In this case it would be as follows:

$$\sigma_d = \sqrt{\sigma_j^2 + \sigma_k^2 - 2rjk\sigma_j\sigma_k} \tag{2-1}$$

where $\sigma_d$ = standard deviation of discriminal differences
$\sigma_j$ and $\sigma_k$ = standard deviations of discriminal distributions for stimuli $j$ and $k$
$r_{jk}$ = correlation between discriminal processes for the two stimuli

The standard deviation of the distribution of discriminal differences involves the standard deviations of the two discriminal distributions and the correlation between them. If the correlation is different from zero, it means that there are correlated "errors" in the fluctuations in discriminal processes from one occasion to another. A positive correlation could be obtained easily in studying the average responses of a group of individuals in terms of judgments or sentiments. People might differ consistently from one another in how high they place *all* the stimuli on the covert continuum. Thus, all the stimuli in a set might be more pleasant to one person than to a second, and more pleasant to the second than to a third, and so on for all persons. This could force a substantial positive correlation between the two discriminal distributions, which could be calculated in the usual way if there were any means of measuring such covert responses directly.

10. If the standard deviation of the distribution of discriminal differences is known, the interval separating two stimuli is obtained as follows:

$$\bar{r}_d = \bar{r}_j - \bar{r}_k = z_{jk}\sigma_d \tag{2-2}$$

$$\bar{r}_j - \bar{r}_k = z_{jk}\sqrt{\sigma_j^2 + \sigma_k^2 - 2r_{jk}\sigma_j\sigma_k}$$

All that is done in Eq. (2-2) is to multiply the normal deviate by the standard deviation of the distribution of discriminal differences between the two stimuli so that the proper interval can be found on the underlying hypothetical measurement scale. Equation (2-2) is called the "complete law of comparative judgment." To use it requires knowledge of (1) the proportion of times each stimulus is judged greater than another with respect to an attribute, (2) the standard deviations of discriminal distributions for the two stimuli, and (3) the correlation between the two discriminal distributions. Rarely is information obtained about all three of these statistics; consequently some simplifying assumptions usually are made. (For some methods of learning about these statistics see Bock and Jones 1968; Guilford 1954; and Torgerson 1958.) Most frequently, two assumptions are made: (1) that the correlations between discriminal distributions are zero (responses are independent) and (2) that standard deviations of discriminal distributions are all equal. Then Eq. (2-2) reduces to the following:

$$\bar{r}_j - \bar{r}_k = z_{jk} \sqrt{\sigma_j^2 + \sigma_k^2} \tag{2-3}$$

$$\bar{r}_j - \bar{r}_k = z_{jk}\sigma\sqrt{2} \tag{2-4}$$

Since all dispersions (standard deviations) of discriminal processes are assumed to be the same, the term under the radical can be reduced to the square root of 2 multiplied by any of the standard deviations. Since that term would be constant for all pairs of stimuli and since the intervals on an interval scale remain proportionately the same when all scale values are multiplied by a constant, the formula can be reduced to

$$\bar{r}_j - \bar{r}_k = z_{jk} \tag{2-5}$$

Thus, with these assumptions, the normal deviate itself serves as the interval separating two stimuli. By far the most frequent use of the law of comparative judgment has been with this formula.

To actually apply the law of comparative judgment, further simplifying assumptions are made. In its most general form, the model is based on the distributions of responses for one subject on numerous occasions. For three reasons, this is seldom done. First, with most types of judgments and sentiments it would be impractical to have the same subject respond to the same stimuli on numerous occasions. It would be hard to find subjects who would devote the time. Second, with most types of stimuli it would not be possible to obtain independent responses. Subjects would remember some of their responses on previous occasions and would tend to repeat them. Third, these difficulties notwithstanding, the usual purpose in scaling stimuli is to obtain a scale that applies to people in general or at least to some definable class of persons. Although some approaches are possible, the scientific problem is made extremely difficult if it is necessary to develop a different scale for each person and difficult to a lesser extent if it is necessary to develop scales for definable groups of persons. For these reasons, the law of comparative judgment is usually applied to the responses of a group of persons rather than to numerous responses by only one person.

Although any method of ordinal estimation can be employed with the law of comparative judgment, the method of paired comparisons is the most obvious approach. Each subject is given all possible pairs of stimuli in a set (the number of stimuli in the set usually ranges from 10 to 20). For each pair, the

**Table 2-1 Proportions of subjects that preferred each vegetable in comparison to each of the other vegetables**

| Vegetable | 1 | 2 | 3 | 4 | 5 | 6 | 7 | 8 | 9 |
|---|---|---|---|---|---|---|---|---|---|
| 1. Turnips | .500 | .818 | .770 | .811 | .878 | .892 | .899 | .892 | .926 |
| 2. Cabbage | .182 | .500 | .601 | .723 | .743 | .736 | .811 | .845 | .858 |
| 3. Beets | .230 | .399 | .500 | .561 | .736 | .676 | .845 | .797 | .818 |
| 4. Asparagus | .189 | .277 | .439 | .500 | .561 | .588 | .676 | .601 | .730 |
| 5. Carrots | .122 | .257 | .264 | .439 | .500 | .493 | .574 | .709 | .764 |
| 6. Spinach | .108 | .264 | .324 | .412 | .507 | .500 | .628 | .682 | .628 |
| 7. String beans | .101 | .189 | .155 | .324 | .426 | .372 | .500 | .527 | .642 |
| 8. Peas | .108 | .155 | .203 | .399 | .291 | .318 | .473 | .500 | .628 |
| 9. Corn | .074 | .142 | .182 | .270 | .236 | .372 | .358 | .372 | .500 |

*Source:* Adapted from Guilford (1954) by permission of the author and publisher.

subject indicates which is greater along a stated dimension of judgment or sentiment. A table is formed showing the proportion of persons in a group who indicate that each stimulus is greater than the others. Typical results from a study of food preferences are shown in Table 2-1. It is assumed that each stimulus would be judged greater than itself half of the time, so .5 goes in each diagonal of the table. The next step is to convert each proportion into a normal deviate $z_{jk}$, which is done in Table 2-2.

If the assumptions are correct for Eq. (2-5), each of the normal deviates in Table 2-2 can be considered an interval between the two stimuli involved. However, since there is likely to be some error in the normal deviate between any two stimuli, the error can be reduced as follows. The sum of normal deviates in each column is obtained, and these are averaged. The logic for doing this is discussed in Torgerson (1958). These are then normal deviates expressed about the average stimulus in the set. To prevent having negative

**Table 2-2 Derivations of an interval scale from normal deviates among stimuli**

| Vegetable | 1 | 2 | 3 | 4 | 5 | 6 | 7 | 8 | 9 |
|---|---|---|---|---|---|---|---|---|---|
| 1. Turnips | .000 | .908 | .739 | .882 | 1.165 | 1.237 | 1.276 | 1.237 | 1.447 |
| 2. Cabbage | −.908 | .000 | .256 | .592 | .653 | .631 | .882 | 1.015 | 1.071 |
| 3. Beets | −.739 | −.256 | .000 | .154 | .631 | .456 | 1.015 | .831 | .908 |
| 4. Asparagus | −.882 | −.592 | −.154 | .000 | .154 | .222 | .456 | .256 | .613 |
| 5. Carrots | −1.165 | −.653 | −.631 | −.154 | .000 | −.018 | .187 | .550 | .719 |
| 6. Spinach | −1.237 | −.631 | −.456 | −.222 | .018 | .000 | .327 | .473 | .327 |
| 7. String beans | −1.276 | −.882 | −1.015 | −.456 | −.187 | −.327 | .000 | .068 | .364 |
| 8. Peas | −1.237 | −1.015 | −.831 | −.256 | −.550 | −.473 | −.068 | .000 | .327 |
| 9. Corn | −1.447 | −1.071 | −.908 | −.613 | −.719 | −.327 | −.364 | −.327 | .000 |
| Sum | −8.891 | −4.192 | −3.000 | −.073 | 1.165 | 1.401 | 3.711 | 4.103 | 5.776 |
| Average | −.988 | −.465 | −.333 | −.008 | +.129 | +.156 | +.412 | +.456 | +.642 |
| Final scale | .000 | .523 | .655 | .980 | 1.117 | 1.144 | 1.400 | 1.444 | 1.630 |

*Source:* Adapted from Guilford (1954) by permission of the author and publisher.

values on the final scale, the positive amount of the largest negative value is added to each of the values. This produces the final scale, which, in the example in Table 2-2, is presumed to be an interval scale of preference for the foods involved. On this scale, corn is liked most and turnips are liked least, the latter being arbitrarily designated as zero on the interval scale.

An interesting illustration of the law of comparative judgment is given in Table 2-3, which shows interval scales for paired-comparison ratings of the seriousness of various crimes. The crimes are numbered and listed on the right-hand side of the table, and two different scalings of the crimes are shown. The scale on the left was obtained by Thurstone in 1927 from 266 students at the University of Chicago. The scale on the right was obtained in 1966 by Coombs from 369 students at the University of Michigan. In addition to the information contained in each scale, it is interesting to see the changes that transpired over the period of time in which the two studies were conducted (using identical methods of data collection and analysis). Note, for example, the relative shifts in the positions for rape and homicide. Because this is an interval scale, it was arbitrarily indexed from 0.0 through 100 for the sake of convenience, but of course this is not intended to be a rational zero. Notice that on both scales vagrancy is by far the lowest in terms of seriousness and homicide is near the top of both.

Although the law of comparative judgment has its most obvious and direct application to data obtained from the psychophysical method of paired comparisons, it can be applied to any method of ordinal estimation such as rank-order or the method of successive categories. In rank-ordering stimuli, in essence one must make paired comparisons among them in order to properly perform the task. On an operational level, one can directly count the number of times that one individual ranks one stimulus above another on a number of different testings or, as is usually done, count the number of people in a group who rank one stimulus above another. In employing the method of successive categories, it is also possible to convert data to a form that provides percentages like those shown in Table 2-1 (see discussion in Bock and Jones, 1968).

Because of the historical and continuing importance of the law of comparative judgment in models for scaling stimuli, it is important to end this discussion with some firm statements. The author had the privilege of sitting in Thurstone's classroom when he stated in effect that the law of comparative judgment was his proudest achievement—this coming from a man for whom the word *genius* would not be inappropriate. Hundreds of journal articles and numerous books (e.g., Bock and Jones 1968) have been written in large measure about empirical studies employing the law of comparative judgment or about theoretical issues relating to it. Derivations relating to the law are difficult for some students to understand, and the law is held almost in a sanctum of reverence by some specialists in psychometrics. In the end, however, the law is very simple. It consists of converting percentages of responses "greater than" into corresponding deviates on the normal curve. The mass of material that has been written about the topic concerns the underlying logic of making

**Table 2-3 Interval scalings of seriousness of crimes by Thurstone (1927) and Coombs (1966)**

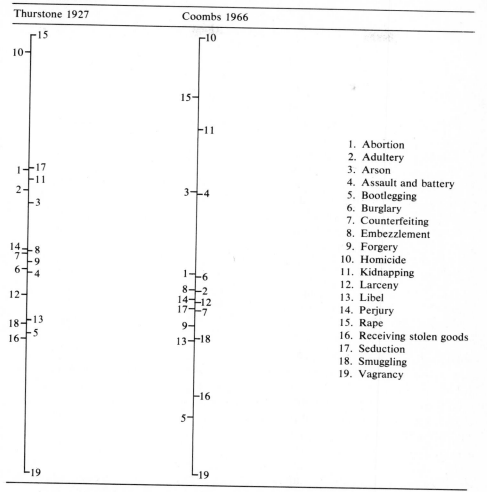

| Thurstone 1927 | Coombs 1966 |
| --- | --- |

1. Abortion
2. Adultery
3. Arson
4. Assault and battery
5. Bootlegging
6. Burglary
7. Counterfeiting
8. Embezzlement
9. Forgery
10. Homicide
11. Kidnapping
12. Larceny
13. Libel
14. Perjury
15. Rape
16. Receiving stolen goods
17. Seduction
18. Smuggling
19. Vagrancy

*Source:* Adapted from Coombs et al. (1970) by permission of authors and Prentice-Hall, Inc.

this transformation, the psychophysical methods that can be employed for gathering data, the mathematical techniques that can be applied to hundreds of special cases, and applications to very unusual situations. This transformation is illustrated in Fig. 2-5. The horizontal axis of the figure is indexed in percentage of times that one stimulus is judged greater than another, either by one individual on many occasions or by many individuals on one occasion. The vertical axis is indexed in standard-score deviates for the normal curve. The curve in the graph is nothing more than the cumulative normal curve or, as it is called, the normal ogive. The interval between any two stimuli is found quite simply by

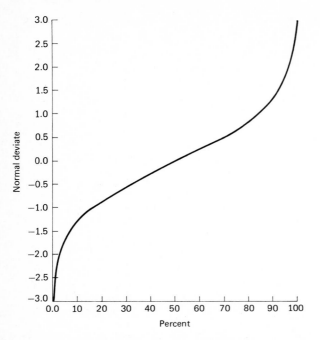

**Figure 2-5** Transformation of percent of responses "greater than" in paired comparisons to interval scale values based on the law of comparative judgment.

looking up the percentage "greater than" on the percentage axis and finding the corresponding normal deviate. Then this is done for all pairs of stimuli. Although all intervals could be obtained directly in this way, the normal deviates usually are averaged as indicated in Table 2-2 to obtain more consistent and reliable results. The underlying logic, however, is not changed. The law of comparative judgment consists purely and simply of making a normal-ogive transformation of percentages of "greater than" responses. Then arguments about the wisdom of employing the law of comparative judgment reduce to whether the normal-ogive transformation or some other transformation is more scientifically fruitful in the long run.

**Other models for converting responses to scales** Although the two general approaches to converting responses to scales of stimuli are used in the majority of cases, numerous scaling models are employed for special purposes. Either these are special versions of models based on subjective estimates, discriminant models, or they have an underlying logic of their own. The reader who is interested in such specialized approaches to scaling will find them amply discussed throughout the Suggested Additional Readings. To illustrate the possibilities, several approaches will be mentioned briefly.

One approach to scaling is quite old. It was developed by Gustav Fechner (see discussion in Falmagne 1974) and is concerned with the *just noticeable difference* (JND). Quite simply, the JND is the difference in physical magnitude between two stimuli when the subject first notices there is a difference. An overly simplified example would be where the subject is shown two light bulbs, of which one remains at a fixed degree of luminance and the other is varied by the experimenter by remote-control mechanisms. In the simplest use of the method, the subject would be asked on each trial whether the variable stimulus was greater or the same as the standard stimulus. In this way, one can measure a *threshold,* which is the point of difference in physical intensity that makes a JND. The amount of difference where the subject correctly identifies the stimuli as being different 75 percent of the time often is used as the threshold value. This is 50 percent better than chance—the threshold on which the subject recognizes the difference correctly half of the time and misses identifying the difference half of the time. The physical difference in amount of illumination between the two light bulbs would constitute the physical measure of JND in that overly simplified situation.

Another approach to obtaining the JND is the method of *constant stimuli,* which was discussed previously and illustrated in Fig. 2-2. In that figure, one can draw a horizontal line from the 75 percent point on the vertical percentage axis and then drop a line vertically to the horizontal axis to determine the JND. In that case, it can be seen that the hypothetical value for the JND is approximately 206 grams, only slightly above the actual value for stimulus $S_4$, which is 205 grams. This means that the JND for a stimulus of 200 grams is $\frac{6}{100}$ gram.

Although it is laborious to do so, one can work out JNDs for all members of sets of stimuli, e.g., eight weights, luminance levels of lights, loudness of tones, or any other stimuli that can be varied on some physical continuum. Then, if there are 10 stimuli, there are 9 JNDs for the stimuli which could be found either from the repeated testing of one person or, more frequently in practice, from the testing of numerous people. Either one could take the JNDs themselves as constituting a sensible interval scale, or more often transformations of these JNDs are taken as the proper intervals. One such transformation is to take the logarithmic value of each such JND and employ this as an interval scale for subsequent investigation in relation to other scalings of the same variable or in relation to measures of other variables. Scaling models based on the JND are not used more frequently because (1) they are restricted to only certain types of judgments, (2) such investigations are extremely laborious to conduct, (3) assumptions relating the JND to scale intervals are controversial, and (4) the two major classes of scaling methods discussed previously are found to be more widely useful.

Paradoxical as it may sound, another approach to unidimensional scaling of stimuli for both judgments and sentiments is with methods of multidimensional scaling. Previously in this chapter it was mentioned that in some types of scaling problems the experimenter either cannot specify the attribute of judgment or sentiment along which stimuli are to be given responses or simply would like to explore the stimulus attributes that underlie such judgments and sentiments. Examples were given with respect to color chips that varied on dimensions and U.S. senators used as stimuli. It was said that prior to employing multidimensional scaling, most frequently one obtains responses relating to the similarity of the stimuli to one another. An example would be as follows. The stimuli consist of adjectives such as good, fair, kind, friendly, pleasant, dependable, efficient, and others. The experimenter uses paired comparisons, but different from the way it was illustrated previously. Each subject rates each pair on a percentage scale concerning the percent of times that the adjectives could replace one another in the same sentence without materially changing the meaning. Then this would yield a square table of data showing the paired-comparison ratings of similarity for each subject. As is typically done, one would average these values over subjects in a group. These average percentage ratings could then be subjected to procedures of multidimensional scaling (which will be discussed in Chap. 12). Although in such instances of multidimensional scaling the experimenter usually expects to find a number of different scales underlying judgments of similarity, quite frequently it turns out that only one scale is needed to explain the data well in a statistical sense. Thus, with the adjectives above, one would find an underlying dimension of *evaluation,* because they vary considerably in terms of pleasantness.

Although in multidimensional scaling one often finds a number of underlying scales, frequently the first scale which is derived goes a very long way toward explaining all the statistical relationships, thus showing that the additional scales obtained are not highly necessary. In this roundabout way, methods of multidimensional scaling often produce only one scale, which the other methods discussed in this chapter are expressly intended to do. Of course, if there really are a number of important scales underlying ratings of similarity or other responses that can be employed in multidimensional scaling, then what one obtains is a number of scales, each of which is, by itself, a univariate scale.

Another approach to scaling that can be employed in some special circumstances concerns reaction time in making responses of various kinds to paired comparisons of stimuli in a set. This type of scaling is based on the commonsense observation that the more difficult decisions are, the longer it takes individuals to make up their minds. An example of employing reaction time would be in scaling the 50 states in this country in terms of the individuals' preferences of where to live. Individuals could be shown the pairs of state names on a screen and asked to push a button on the right if they preferred the state appearing on the right or a button on the left if they preferred the state appearing on the left. To the extent to which they much preferred living in one state rather than another, they would be expected to respond rapidly; conversely, if they preferred the states about equally, they would be expected to take a relatively longer amount of time in responding. If subjects had been requested previously to rank-order the states from 1 to 50 in terms of preferences, the reaction times could then be used to form intervals between the states so as to obtain an interval scale. Either this could be done by accepting the amounts of time themselves as constituting intervals, or some reasonable transformation could be made, e.g., square roots or logarithmic transformations of the time.

There still are many other highly specialized approaches to obtaining univariate stimulus scales for judgment and preference. The reader who has a special interest in the topic will find these rather unusual methods scattered throughout the Suggested Additional Readings. However, the methods discussed so far in this chapter for the univariate scaling of stimuli surely cover 90 percent or more of those actually employed in research in the behavioral sciences. Many of the highly specialized techniques of both univariate scaling and multivariate scaling are used almost exclusively by specialists on that topic; and although they are useful for theorizing about basic problems of measurement, they seldom result in usable "hardware" for the empirical scientist.

**Checks and balances** So far in this chapter numerous assumptions have been discussed regarding the use of various models for scaling stimuli. How does one know if the assumptions are correct? First, for any model, there are standards of *internal consistency* that the data must meet. (For detailed discussions of these standards see Torgerson 1958 and other citations in Suggested Additional Readings.) Some examples will show how such standards are applied. If a rank-order scale is developed by averaging the ranks given to the same stimuli by different people, the data are internally consistent to the extent that subjects give much the same ranks to the stimuli. Internal consistency for the method of bisection can be tested as follows. First, the subject is required to adjust a light to the point halfway between two others in perceived brightness. Second, the subject obtains two intensities that bisect the two intervals obtained in the first step. Finally, the subject bisects the intensities obtained in the second step. If the data are internally consistent, the subject should arrive back at the first intensity used to bisect the first two stimuli. Data obtained from pair comparisons can be tested for internal consistency by examining the transitivity of scale values. If, for example, stimulus $j$ is found to be 1.0 greater than stimulus $k$, and stimulus $k$ is 0.5 greater than stimulus $i$, and if the data are internally consistent, stimulus $j$ should be 1.5 greater than stimulus $i$. For all the scaling models, there are standards of internal consistency that apply. If the internal consistency is low when a scale is developed from a particular model, one would be very suspicious of the scale. If scales typically fail the test of internal consistency in various uses of the model, one should become very suspicious of the model itself.

In addition to internal consistency, another important standard concerns the extent to which scale values can be replicated in studies that differ slightly in procedures. This applies when a new study is undertaken using only some of the stimuli employed in an earlier study. If, for example, the study of vegetables illustrated in Table 2-2 were redone and five new vegetables were added, the relative sizes of the intervals between turnips, cabbage, and beets should remain much the same. If the relative sizes of these intervals change markedly, it would provide little confidence in any scaling of vegetables by that method. Another example would be in the ratio scaling of brightness of lights. Either a percentage scale could be used to compare each level of brightness of a variable light with a standard, or subjects could be asked to provide their own numerical ratios for pairs of lights at different levels of intensity. Unless one obtained similar scales from these two approaches, one would be suspicious of the underlying logic for developing ratio scales from subjective estimates. In all other uses of scaling models, one expects to find essentially the same rank-order, intervals, and ratios when methods of gathering responses or methods of analysis are slightly different.

## MODELS FOR SCALING PEOPLE

Early in the chapter it was stated that problems of scaling potentially concern a three-dimensional table of data, with the dimensions representing persons, stimuli, and responses. (This was illustrated in Fig. 2-1.) In the development of unidimensional scales for either persons or stimuli, it is usually possible to "collapse" the dimension concerning different types of responses. Either it is known from previous studies that all the types of responses concern the same attribute, e.g., by a factor analysis of rating scales bounded by different pairs of adjectives, or only one type of response is required to each stimulus. The latter would be the case, for example, if the subject were required only to agree or disagree with each statement in a list or to indicate whether each statement in a list is correct or incorrect. After the three-dimensional table is reduced to a two-dimensional table, models for developing unidimensional scales concern ways for collapsing one of the two remaining dimensions. The previous section discussed ways of collapsing the person dimension to scale stimuli. This section will treat ways of collapsing the stimulus dimension to scale persons.

**Multi-item measures** Prior to a discussion of models for collapsing the stimulus dimension of a two-dimensional table of data, it might be wise to reflect on the need for more than one stimulus in psychological measures. The word *items* will be used in a broad sense to stand for any stimuli used in measurement methods. Thus items may be words on a spelling test, comparisons between weights, statements concerning attitudes toward the United Nations, correct choices of a rat in a maze, and reactions in a study of reaction time. What is presented to the subject is the item (stimulus), and in each of the examples above, the subject is required to make only one type of response to each item.

There are a number of important reasons for requiring more than one item in nearly all measures of psychological attributes. First, individual items usually have only a low degree of relationship with the particular attribute in question. That is, each item tends to have only a low correlation with the attribute being measured; also, each item tends to relate to attributes other than the one to be measured. On a spelling test, for example, whether children could correctly spell *umpire* would depend in part on their interest in baseball. A child who spent much time reading baseball stories might spell the word correctly even though she or he was a poor speller in general. Another example of the specificity of individual items with respect to a particular trait is in rating the following statement: "We give more to the United Nations than we get in return." Supposedly that is a negative statement about the United Nations, and people who agree with the statement *tend* to have negative attitudes. Even though one might have an overall positive attitude, however, one might agree with the statement because one is not happy with the share of financing borne by our country.

In both examples above, it can be seen that each item relates only in a statistical sense with the attribute being measured. Each item tends to correlate with the attribute in question, but also correlates with attributes other than the one being measured. In addition, each item has a considerable *specificity;* that is, it has a type of individuality that is not correlated with any general attribute or factor. These several components of variance in individual test items will become clearer when factor analysis is discussed in Chaps. 10 and 11.

Even if individual items did not relate to factors other than the one being measured and had a considerable amount of specificity, there are other reasons why measures require more than one item. One reason is that most items attempt to categorize people into either two groups or only a relatively small number of groups. Thus an item requiring dichotomous responses (e.g., pass or fail) can distinguish between at most two levels of the attribute. A seven-step rating scale can distinguish between at most seven levels of an attribute. In most measurement problems it is desirable to make fine differentiations among people, and this can seldom be done with a one-item measure.

Even if there were no specificity in items and items were capable of making very fine distinctions among people, still there would be an important reason why one-item measures would not suffice. Individual items have considerable measurement error; in other words, they are unreliable. Each item, in addition to its specificity, occasions a considerable amount of random error. This is seen when people are required to repeat a set of ratings after a period of time. The person who gave a rating of 3 on one occasion is likely to give a rating of 5 on another, and many other changes of this kind are expected. Another example would be the solving of arithmetic problems on two occasions. The child who got the correct answer on one occasion might not get the correct answer to the same problem on another occasion, and vice versa. Thus there is some randomness related to any item, and consequently the individual item cannot be trusted to give reliable measurement of an attribute. This unreliability averages out when scores on numerous items are summed to obtain a total score, which then frequently is highly reliable.

All three difficulties that have been discussed can be diminished by the use of multi-item measures. The tendency of items to relate to factors other than the attribute being investigated usually averages out when items are combined. By combining items, one can make relatively fine distinctions among people. For reasons which will be discussed in Chaps. 6 and 7, the reliability tends to increase (measurement error reduces) as the number of items in a combination increases. Thus nearly all measures of psychological attributes are multi-item measures. This is true both for measures used in studies of individual differences and for measures used in controlled experiments. The problem of scaling people with respect to attributes is then one of combining responses to a number of items so as to obtain one score (measurement) for each person.

**The trace line** Nearly all models for scaling people can be depicted by different types of curves relating an attribute to the probability of responding in one way to items versus another. Such trace lines frequently are referred to as *item characteristic curves.* Four different types of trace lines are depicted in Figs. 2-6 to 2-9. Dichotomous items are depicted in these figures. For each item, there are two types of responses, alpha and beta. Alpha would variously consist of passing rather than failing an item, agreeing rather than disagreeing with a statement, and a rat making the correct rather than the incorrect turn in a maze.

In Figs. 2-6 to 2-9, the attribute is the particular thing being measured. In this connection, it is important to make a distinction between the particular attribute being measured and some more general attribute of interest. Thus the responses of a rat in a maze constitute a particular attribute. It is hoped that this attribute relates to the more general attribute of habit strength. On vocabulary tests, identifying correct synonyms for words is a particular attribute, and it is hoped that this particular attribute relates to the general attribute of intelligence. The particular attribute will be referred to as an "attribute." More general attributes will be referred to as "constructs." (The measurement of constructs is discussed in Chap. 3.) The measurement problem itself concerns the relations between particular attributes and the probability of responding in one way rather than another. It is only after measures of particular attributes are constructed that they can be combined to measure more general attributes (constructs).

In the remainder of this chapter, the abscissa for models concerning trace lines will concern particular attributes. Attributes are defined in a circular sense in terms of whatever a number of items tend to measure in common. Thus a list of spelling words would tend to measure spelling ability, and the number of correct turns of a rat in a maze would tend to measure amount learned. The word *tend* is used because it must be recognized that no attribute is perfectly mirrored in any set of items. Perfect measurement would be available, for example, if children were administered a spelling test containing all words in the English language or if rats were capable of running an infinitely long maze. When there is a limited number of items, as there always is, there is some unreliability of measuring the particular attribute. Completely reliable measures of the attribute are called *true scores,* and the approximations to true scores obtained from any collection of items are called *fallible scores.* In all the figures showing item trace lines, the abscissa concerns true scores on the particular attribute. Of course, one does not know exactly what the true scores are, but they can be approximated by scores obtained from some combination of the available items. For this reason, after some way has been formulated for combining items, an approximate test can be made for the actual trace line of any

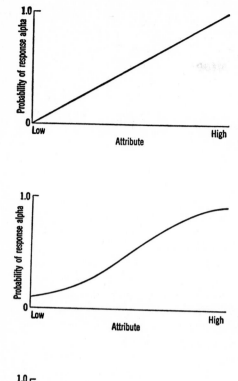

Figure 2-6 An ascending linear trace line for an item.

Figure 2-7 An ascending monotonic trace line for an item.

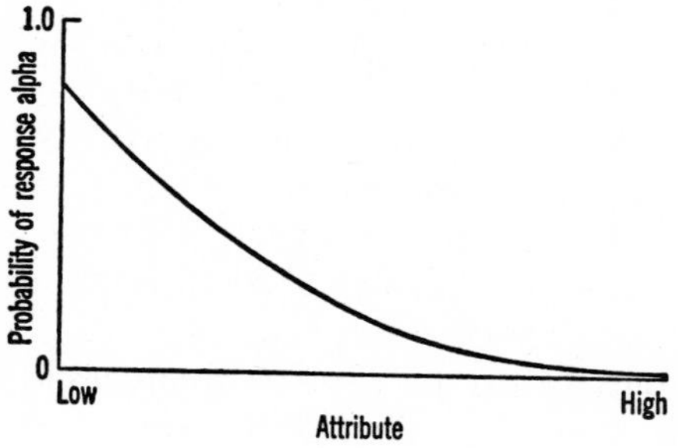

Figure 2-8 A descending monotonic trace line for an item.

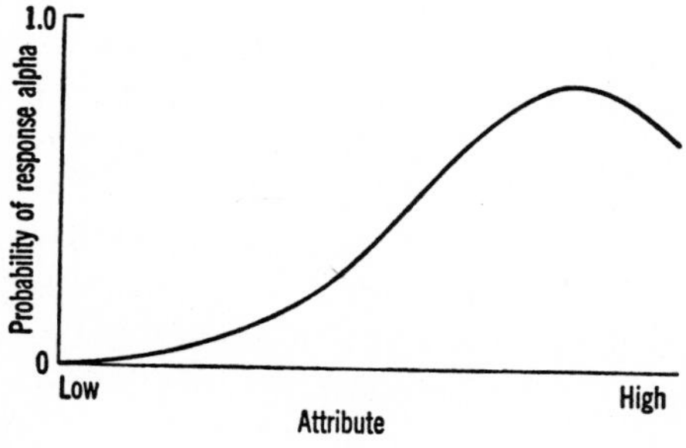

Figure 2-9 A nonmonotonic trace line for an item.

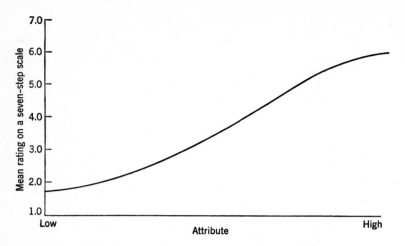

**Figure 2-10** Trace line of average scores on a seven-step rating scale.

particular item; e.g., the trace line for a spelling item can be computed as a function of the number of words correctly spelled on a long, reliable test.

The concept of trace lines also applies to multipoint items (items that are scorable on more than two points), an example of which is shown in Fig. 2-10. Instead of depicting the probability of response alpha, the ordinate depicts the average score on the item. In Fig. 2-10 are shown the average scores on a seven-step rating scale for persons at different levels of an attribute. Other multipoint items whose trace lines could be depicted in that way are scores on essay questions in a classroom examination, number of words correctly recalled in a study of memory, and amount of time in responding to a signal in studies of reaction time. It should be recalled that an average score is an *expected score,* and consequently Fig. 2-10 depicts the expected score as a function of levels of an attribute.

In discussing trace lines it is useful to think of the attribute as being completely continuous—i.e., it is theoretically possible to make infinitely fine discriminations among people. Also, it is useful to think of there being a large number of persons at each of the infinite number of points on the attribute. In this hypothetical circumstance, the trace line shows the expected response for people at each level of the attribute, the expectation being expressed either as a probability of response alpha for dichotomous items or as an average score for multipoint items. By their nature, expectations are accompanied by some error. On dichotomous items, there is a probability of response alpha at each point, but there is no certainty as to *which* persons at a point will respond alpha and which persons will respond beta. On multipoint items, there is a band of error surrounding the expected average score. Thus although the expected score for a particular point on an attribute might be 3.0, the actual scores of people at that point might range from 1.0 to 5.0.

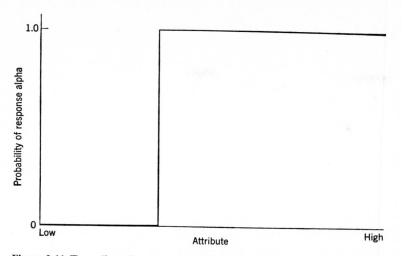

**Figure 2-11** Trace line of an item that discriminates perfectly at one point on an attribute.

## DETERMINISTIC MODELS FOR SCALING PEOPLE

Deterministic models are so called because they assume that there is *no error* in item trace lines. For dichotomous items, at each point of the attribute it is assumed that the probability of response alpha is either 1.0 or 0. The particular deterministic model employed most frequently is one which assumes that up to a point on the attribute the probability of response alpha is 0 (probability of response beta is 1.0), and beyond that point the probability of response alpha is 1.0. An item of this type is shown in Fig. 2-11, and a family of such items is shown in Fig. 2-12. Each item has a biserial correlation (see Chap. 4) of 1.0

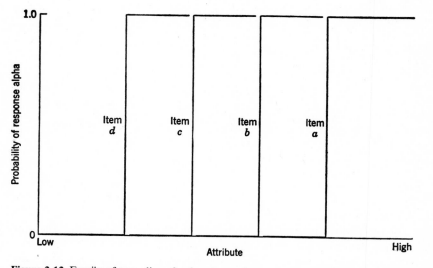

**Figure 2-12** Family of trace lines for four items that meet the requirements of a monotone deterministic model.

**Table 2-4 Triangular pattern of responses that would fit requirements of a monotone, deterministic scaling model**

| Item | Person | | | | |
|------|--------|--------|--------|--------|--------|
|      | 1      | 2      | 3      | 4      | 5      |
| a    | X      |        |        |        |        |
| b    | X      | X      |        |        |        |
| c    | X      | X      | X      |        |        |
| d    | X      | X      | X      | X      |        |
| e    | X      | X      | X      | X      | X      |

with the attribute, and consequently each item perfectly discriminates at a particular point of the attribute. Intuitively, this is a very appealing model, because it is exactly what one expects to obtain in measurements of length. Thus one would expect to obtain a family of trace lines like that in Fig. 2-12 for the following items:

|  | YES | NO |
|--|-----|-----|
| (a) Are you above 6 feet 6 inches in height? | _____ | _____ |
| (b) Are you above 6 feet 3 inches in height? | _____ | _____ |
| (c) Are you above 6 feet in height? | _____ | _____ |
| (d) Are you above 5 feet 9 inches in height? | _____ | _____ |
| (e) Are you above 5 feet 6 inches in height? | _____ | _____ |

Answering *yes* can be considered response alpha. Any person who answered *yes* to question (*a*) would answer *yes* to the others. Any person who did not answer yes to (*a*) but did answer *yes* to (*b*) would also answer *yes* to questions (*c*) through (*e*). For five people with different patterns of responses, a triangular pattern of data would be found like that in Table 2-4. An *X* symbolizes an answer of *yes* (response alpha).

**Guttman scale** Although one never knows the exact nature of trace lines, one can look at data and see if they evolve into a triangular pattern like that in Table 2-4. (In so doing, however, one is making a subtle logical assumption—a point which will be discussed later.) Some types of items tend to produce a pattern of data like that in Table 2-4. The following is an example:

|  | YES | NO |
|--|-----|-----|
| (a) The United Nations is the savior of all people. | _____ | _____ |
| (b) The United Nations is our best hope for peace. | _____ | _____ |
| (c) The United Nations is a constructive force in the world. | _____ | _____ |

(*d*) We should continue to participate in the
United Nations. _____    _____

For any person who answers *yes* to (*a*), there is a high probability that the person will answer *yes* to the other items. Any person who does not answer *yes* to (*a*) but does answer *yes* to (*b*) has a high probability of answering *yes* to the other items.

Any set of items that produces a pattern of responses approximately like that in Table 2-4 is called a "Guttman scale." In developing such a scale, one administers a collection of items to a group of people and then attempts to arrange the responses so as to produce the required triangular pattern. (Since in actual data there would be more than one person at each level of the attribute, the data would appear in the form of a solid staircase, with the width of each step being proportional to the number of persons at each level.) There are numerous cut-and-try methods for doing this (see Torgerson 1958). The methods for attempting the development of Guttman's scales are referred to as "scalogram analysis."

Of course, obtaining the triangular pattern exactly is very unlikely; therefore it is necessary (1) to discard some items and (2) to find the best possible ordering of items and people. Regarding the latter, the *reproducibility* of score patterns is of primary concern. If the triangular pattern is perfectly obtained, a knowledge of the *number* of responses of *yes* allows one to reproduce all the person's responses. When the triangular pattern is approximately obtained, a knowledge of the number of *yeses* by a person allows one to approximately reproduce all that person's responses. For all people and all items, one can investigate the percentage of reproducibility, and it is this percentage which is all-important in the development of Guttman scales.

Conceivably, Guttman scales could be developed for all types of items requiring dichotomous responses. This can be illustrated with a spelling test where there are 40 items. The teacher reads each item, and the students attempt to correctly spell each word. Subsequently, the teacher scores each item as being correct or incorrect. If the items had trace lines like those in Fig. 2-12, a triangular pattern of data would be obtained. In this instance an $X$ would stand for a correct response to the spelling of the word. If one person has a score of 35 and another a score of 34, this would necessarily mean that the former person got the *same* 34 items correct as the latter person, plus one additional item. If one knew how many words an individual passed, one would know exactly which items that person passed.

**Evaluation of the Guttman scale** In spite of the intuitive appeal of the Guttman scale, it is highly impractical. First, it is highly unrealistic to think that items could have trace lines like those in Fig. 2-12. No item correlates perfectly with any attribute. Although there is no way to obtain the trace lines directly, some good approximations are available. For example, with items concerning spelling, the number of words correctly spelled can be used as an approximation of the attribute (true scores in spelling). When the trace line is obtained in such instances, not only is it not perpendicular at a point, but it typically tends to have a relatively flat, approximately linear form. Typically, individual items correlate no higher than .40 with total scores. Consequently it is very unreasonable to work with a model that assumes perfect biserial correlations between items and an attribute.

Second, having the triangular pattern of data is no guarantee that items have trace lines like those in Fig. 2-12. If items are spaced far enough apart in difficulty (in popularity on nonability items), the triangular pattern can be obtained even if the trace lines are largely flat rather than vertical. This is illustrated with the following four items:

(a) Solve for $x$: $x^2 + 2x + 9 = 16$.
(b) What is the meaning of the word *severe*?
(c) How much is $10 \times 38$?
(d) When do you use an umbrella? (given orally)

Although the author has not performed the experiment, the above four items administered to persons ranging in age from 4 to 16 probably would form an excellent Guttman scale. Any person who got the first item correct probably could get the others correct. Any person who failed the first item but got the second correct would probably get the other two correct. Those four items would produce the required triangular pattern of data even though there is good evidence that they do not all belong to the same attribute ("factor," in the language of factor analysis). The reason they apparently fit the model for a unidimensional scale is that they are administered to an extremely diverse population. Consequently, as was suggested earlier, it is not entirely logical to assume that having a triangular pattern of data like that in Table 2-4 is *sufficient* evidence for the presence of a unidimensional scale.

Because the triangular pattern of data can be approximated in any study where items vary greatly in difficulty, in practice this results in scales with very few items (seldom more than eight). To take an extreme case, if there are three items that respectively are passed by 10, 50, and 90 percent of the people, the triangular pattern will be obtained almost perfectly regardless of what the items concern. This applies to personality tests as well as tests of ability. With personality tests "item difficulty" consists of the percent of persons who agree with an item rather than disagree with it. The difficulties of items can be dispersed in this way only if the final scale contains a small number of items. Usually this is done by starting with a relatively large number of items (say, 20) and discarding all items but a few that vary widely in difficulty. This is only a way of fooling oneself into believing that a unidimensional scale has been obtained when it really has not. Also, since such scales seldom have more than eight items, they can make only rather gross distinctions among people.

A third criticism of the Guttman scale is that it seeks to obtain only an ordinal measurement of human attributes. As was argued in the previous chapter, there are good reasons for believing that it is possible to measure human attributes on interval scales, if not usually on ratio scales. If psychology were to settle only for ordinal measurement, it would so limit the usable methods of mathematics that the science would be nearly crippled.

A fourth criticism of the Guttman scale concerns its intuitive appeal. It would be more appropriate to think of items not as yardsticks being applied to the heights of people, but rather as rubber yardsticks applied by half-blind investigators. Also, to complete the analogy, one should think of each item as a different rubber yardstick which has been copied from a real yardstick by a 5-year-old child. On some of the yardsticks, the zero point starts at 4 inches, and the child has made numerous, large random errors in copying intervals (widths of 1 inch). If 20 such rubber yardsticks were applied to a group of people, any yardstick (item) would have only a rather flat trace line with respect to the actual heights. However, with the methods that will be discussed in subsequent sections, one could combine many different measurements of people with such rubber yardsticks to obtain an approximate linear relationship with the real scale of heights, and thus one could obtain an interval scale.

In summary, the deterministic model underlying the Guttman scale is thoroughly illogical for most psychological measurement because (1) almost no items exist that fit the model, (2) the presence of a triangular pattern is a necessary but not sufficient condition for the fit of the model in particular instances, (3) the triangular pattern can be (and usually is) artificially forced by dealing with a small number of items that vary greatly in difficulty, (4) the model aspires only to develop ordinal scales, and (5) there are better intuitive bases for developing models for psychological attributes. Considering this heavy weight of criticism, it is surprising that some people still consider this deterministic model a good basis for developing measures of psychological attributes. However, as will be mentioned with respect to some other models, often a model or statistical method of analysis that is impractical for use in actual research is very important in theories concerning mathematical models themselves. Practicable models for actual use in research frequently grow out of idealized models such as that underlying the Guttman scale, and it is useful to make comparisons between such practicable methods of analysis and idealized models.

**Nonmonotone deterministic models** There are other deterministic models in addition to the Guttman scale (see Coombs et al. 1970; Torgerson 1958; and relevant sections in the other citations in Suggested Additional Readings). One of these makes the following assumptions. Each item is responded to in manner alpha by all the people at one level, and each person responds in manner alpha to only one item. Trace lines for three such items are shown in Fig. 2-13. The pattern of data produced by such a model is shown in Table 2-5. In contrast to

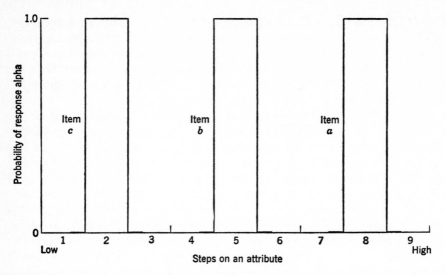

**Figure 2-13** Trace lines for three items that meet the requirements of a nonmonotone, deterministic scaling model.

the Guttman scale, in this deterministic model each item has a nonmonotone trace line; i.e., the line goes up and then comes down. The following four items would fit this model:

|  | YES | NO |
|---|---|---|
| (*a*) Are you between 6 feet 3 inches tall and 6 feet 6 inches? | _____ | _____ |
| (*b*) Are you between 6 feet tall and 6 feet 3 inches? | _____ | _____ |
| (*c*) Are you between 5 feet 9 inches tall and 6 feet? | _____ | _____ |
| (*d*) Are you between 5 feet 6 inches tall and 5 feet 9 inches? | _____ | _____ |

In using the word *items* in the broadest sense, it would be very rare to find any items on psychological measures that would fit this model. All the criticisms

**Table 2-5  Pattern of responses to four items that meets requirements of a monotone, deterministic scaling model**

| Item | Person | | | |
|---|---|---|---|---|
|  | 1 | 2 | 3 | 4 |
| *a* | X |  |  |  |
| *b* |  | X |  |  |
| *c* |  |  | X |  |
| *d* |  |  |  | X |

that apply to the Guttman scale apply with added force to this nonmonotone deterministic model.

Deterministic models are of use mainly to specialists in the theory of psychological measurement. Such models frequently represent "limiting cases" of models that are actually used to develop measures of psychological attributes. Other than for this use, they are only interesting museum pieces. Only by working with some type of nondeterministic probability model can one develop the measures that are needed in research.

## PROBABILITY MODELS FOR SCALING PEOPLE

If trace lines (item characteristic curves) are not assumed to have perpendicular ascents and descents, one is working with some type of probability model. There are numerous types of probability models, depending on the type of curve assumed for the trace lines. The most prominent models are discussed in the following sections.

**Nonmonotone models** Analogous to nonmonotone deterministic models, such as the one discussed above, are nonmonotone probability models. Any type of curve that changes slope at some point from positive to negative or vice versa is nonmonotone. Some examples are shown in Fig. 2-14. The only nonmonotone model that has been used frequently assumes that (1) the attribute is continuous and (2) each item has a trace line that approximates the normal distribution. The probability of responding in manner alpha is highest at a particular point on the attribute, and from that point the probability of responding in manner alpha falls off in both directions in general resemblance to the normal curve. Three such items are shown in Fig. 2-15.

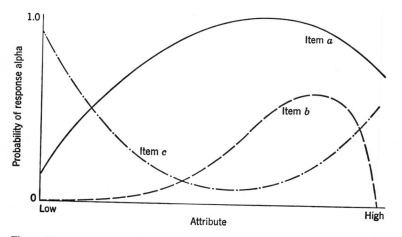

**Figure 2-14** Three items with nonmonotone trace lines.

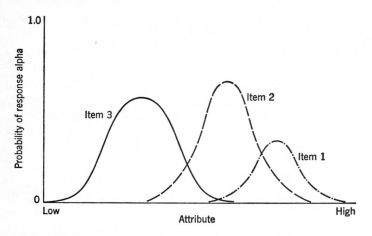

**Figure 2-15** Nonmonotone, normal trace lines for three items.

Trace lines need not be exactly normal, and standard deviations of trace lines need not be identical. This model has been used for only one purpose: the development of certain types of attitude scales. Since the scaling procedure was developed by Thurstone, the type of scale is referred to as a "Thurstone scale of attitudes" (which has nothing to do with, and should not be confused with, Thurstone's law of comparative judgment discussed previously in this chapter). Items at three points on such a scale are as follows:

|  | AGREE | DISAGREE |
|---|---|---|
| 1. I believe that the church is the greatest institution in America today. | _____ | _____ |
| 2. When I go to church, I enjoy a fine ritual service with good music. | _____ | _____ |
| 3. The paternal and benevolent attitude of the church is quite distasteful to me. | _____ | _____ |

The first step in obtaining a Thurstone scale is to have a large number of attitude statements rated by about 100 judges (see Edwards 1957 for a complete discussion of procedures). Each statement is usually rated on an 11-step scale ranging from "strongly favorable statement" to "strongly unfavorable statement." From the larger collection of items, 10 to 20 are selected according to the following two standards: (1) items that have small standard deviations of ratings over judges, i.e., agreement is good among judges about where the items belong on the scale, and (2) items that range evenly from one extreme to the other.

The essence of the Thurstone nonmonotone model is that each item should tend to receive agreement (response alpha) at only one zone of the attribute. To assume an approximately normal distribution for the trace line is to admit that each item occasions some error. If there were no error and the model applied strictly, a person should respond in manner alpha to only one item, and then the scale value of this item found from the prior ratings of judges mentioned previously would serve as the scale score for the subject. However, since the subjects usually do respond in manner alpha (e.g., agree with statements) on a number of items, a frequent practice is to take the average scale score for these items as the overall score for the subject. Another approach is to take the scale score of the highest item on the scale with which the person agrees as being his or her score.

The major fault of the Thurstone scale and of other nonmonotone probability models is that it is very difficult to find any items that fit. The model obviously would not fit any type of item relating to ability. For example, how could one find spelling words such that each would be correctly spelled only by persons in a narrow band of the attribute of spelling ability? An item that "peaked" at the lower end of the scale would be one that is spelled correctly only by rather poor spellers. For an item that peaked in the middle of the scale, very few people with superior ability in spelling would give a correct response. This type of scale clearly does not apply to any items requiring judgments.

Even with responses concerning sentiments, the Thurstone model would seem to apply only to certain types of statements relating to attitudes, and even there the model is in logical trouble. Attitude statements tend to fit this model only if they are "double-barreled"—only if they say two things, of which one is good and the other bad. This can be seen by a careful analysis of the three attitude statements given earlier. In item 2, the subject is asked to agree simultaneously with two hidden statements:

I sometimes go to church.
I probably would not go to church if it were not for a fine ritual service with
    good music.

Item 3 is "triple-barreled." To agree with it, the subject must agree that the church is paternal, benevolent, and distasteful. The three modifiers add up to a moderately negative attitude toward the church. It is possible to construct such items only by subtly building two or more statements into what is ostensibly one statement. This type of item not only is very difficult to construct, but tends to be ambiguous to subjects. Some subjects respond to one of the hidden statements and some subjects to another. In a more exaggerated form, this ambiguity is evidenced in the following double-barreled statement:

The church is a wonderful, horrible institution.

Another important criticism of nonmonotone probability models is that it is very difficult to think of items for the ends of the scale that would fit. This is illustrated with item 1 in the previous example. Who could have so *positive* an attitude toward the church as to *disagree* with the statement, "I believe the church is the greatest institution in America today"? Such items necessarily are monotone, continuing to rise as one reaches higher and higher levels of the attribute.

In summary, nonmonotone probability models conceivably apply to only certain types of items for the measurement of attitudes, and there are better ways to construct attitude scales (see Chap. 15).

**Monotone models with specified distribution forms** In some of the models that assume monotone trace lines, it is assumed that the trace lines fit a particular statistical function. Most frequently it has been assumed that the function is a *normal ogive*. (A normal ogive is a cumulative normal distribution.) In Fig. 2-16 three items are shown having normal-ogive trace lines. The important feature of a normal-ogive trace line is that it is much more discriminating at certain levels of the attribute than it is at neighboring levels. The zone where discrimination is good is that below the steeply ascending parts of the curve. The steeper that section of the curve, the higher is the biserial correlation of that item with the attribute. If that section were vertical, the "tails" would disappear, the item would correlate perfectly with the attribute, and a collection of such items would form a Guttman scale. As items correlate less and less with the attribute, the S shape tends to flatten toward a straight line and the slope approaches the horizontal.

The normal-ogive model is appealing for two reasons. First, it makes good sense intuitively. Thus, for each item, one can think of a critical zone on the attribute where there is considerable uncertainty concerning how people will respond. As one moves away from that zone in either direction, the uncertainty is markedly reduced. Persons below that zone will predominately fail the item, and persons above it will predominately pass. An increasing slope of the trace

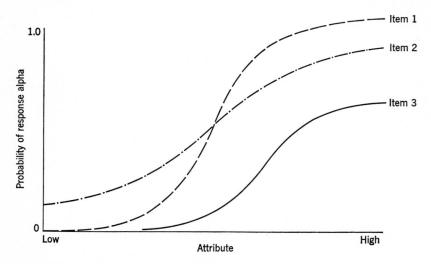

**Figure 2-16** Three items with normal-ogive trace lines.

line over some zone is more to be expected than, say, a straight line. Other intuitive support for the normal ogive comes from studies concerning the scaling of stimuli. There it is found, for example, that judgments of weights by the method of constant stimuli usually fit a normal ogive (see Fig. 2-2).

The second reason for the appeal of this model is that it has very useful mathematical properties that permit the deduction of many important principles (Lord 1974). For example, the sum of any number of normal ogives is also a normal ogive, and the exact shape and slope of the latter can be predicted from the ogives which are summed. Then if one obtains a scale by summing scores on individual items (e.g., enumerating the number correct), the average scores or sums of scores form a normal-ogive relationship with the attribute. (The sum of probabilities for any number of normal ogives over a point on an attribute would be the expected sum of scores on the test as a whole for persons at that point.) This means that summing scores on items to obtain total scores (which is the usual approach) produces a scale that is *not* linearly related to the attribute. However, in practice this is a very slight danger, because even if trace lines do form normal ogives, the curves are so flat that they are hard to distinguish from straight lines. Also, when items are combined that vary considerably in difficulty, combined normal ogives look less S-shaped than if all items are equally difficult. For these two reasons, even if one accepts the normal-ogive model, it is reasonable to assume that total test scores have an approximately linear relationship with the attribute.

There are many other interesting deductions from the normal-ogive model. The most discriminating collection of items for any particular point on the attribute would be those items whose sum of ogives is as steep as possible over that point. This fact permits some interesting deductions about the relations among discrimination at a point, difficulty of items, and correlations of items with total scores. Other interesting deductions from this model concern the amount of measurement error (unreliability) for a test corresponding to different points on the attribute (discussed in Chap. 9).

In addition to the normal ogive, other statistical functions have been proposed for trace lines. The function which has achieved most use in this respect is the logistic curve. To the naked eye the logistic curve and the normal ogive are very much the same. The advantage of the logistic curve is that it is much easier to work with mathematically. Very much the same deductions are made from both types of curves.

Still other types of curve forms have been hypothesized as appropriate as trace lines for certain types of tests. Typically these require some type of restrictive assumption, such as the assumption that the items all correlate the same with one another or correlate highly with one another or that the underlying distribution of scores on the attribute is "normal." These special assumptions about the nature of the exact mathematical form of the trace line lead to additional interesting deductions that would apply if the assumptions hold. For example, one could mathematically deduce the score that individuals would make on a second test that they have not taken from the score that they made on an easier test that they actually had taken. The use of these and other mathematical models based on assumptions regarding the specific character of trace lines gives some promise of developing interesting types of tests in the future, and considerable research is being done on those possibilities now (see Lord 1952b, 1974; Lord and Novick 1968; and Wright and Douglas 1975). Some psychological principles that follow from these assumptions regarding mathematical shapes of trace lines and some experimental new tests that have been developed on the basis of them will be discussed in Chap. 9.

An important point to grasp in discussing monotone models with specified distribution forms is that, at least so far, they have not supplanted the conventional approach to the scaling of persons with respect to attributes, which is to sum scores on items. Thus, if one is scaling spelling ability, the conventional approach is simply to sum the number of words correctly spelled. This conventional approach is employed with nearly all other methods for scaling people with respect to hypothesized attributes. Scaling models based on the assumption of specific mathematical forms of trace lines have led to some suggestions for modifications of this conventional approach; for example, in using a computerized procedure in which the individual is given items one at a time, depending upon whether he passes or fails each item, the computer selects a more or less difficult item to administer next. However, these and other modifications of the conventional approach to administering and scoring tests are largely experimental; and they have not shown significant enough advantages over the conventional approach to be adopted for practical use. Rather, some new types of tests have been developed on an experimental basis, some of which may be of practical value in the years ahead. The mathematical models based on various assumptions regarding the exact form of the trace line have had two major impacts on psychometric issues regarding the scaling of people with respect to judgments and sentiments. First, as mentioned, the use of such models has led to some very interesting theorizing and research on new types of experimental tests. Second, these mathematical models permit some important deductions about the psychometric characteristics of measures that are obtained by summing item scores, and for both these purposes they have proved very useful.

**Monotone models with unspecified distribution forms** Finally we arrive at the model that underlies most efforts to scale people (and lower animals) with respect to most types of judgments and sentiments. The model makes three major assumptions. First, it is assumed only that each item has a monotonic trace line. It is not assumed that all items have the same type of monotonic curve. Second, it is assumed that the sum of the trace lines for a particular set of items (the trace line for total test scores) is approximately linear. That is, even if items do not all have the same type of monotonic trace line, it is assumed that departures from linearity tend to average out as items are combined. A family of such trace lines is shown in Fig. 2-17. The sum of these trace lines is shown in Fig. 2-18, which is the trace line of expected scores on a four-item test.

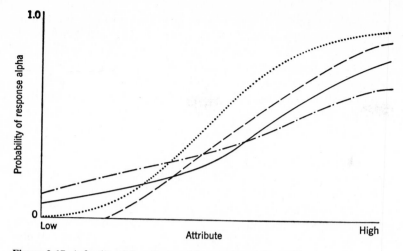

**Figure 2-17** A family of four items with monotone trace lines.

The third assumption is that the items as a whole tend to measure only the attribute in question. This is the same as saying that the items have only one factor in common, a point which will be discussed in detail in later chapters. The implication is that total scores on the particular collection of items summarize all the important information about psychological attributes that is inherent in the item scores.

The three assumptions discussed above constitute the *linear model* or, as it is frequently called, the *summative model*. It is said to be "linear" for two reasons. First, it is assumed that the sum of item scores has an approximately

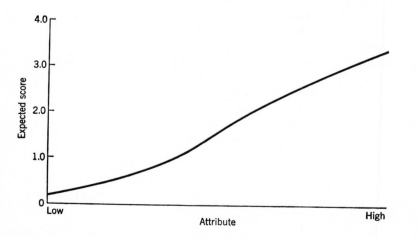

**Figure 2-18** Expected scores on a four-item test—the sum of trace lines in Fig. 2-17.

linear relationship with the attribute in question. Second, and more important for the sake of the name, the model leads to a *linear combination* of items. A simple sum of variables is a linear combination of variables, and a simple sum of item scores is a linear combination of those scores.

If one looks carefully at psychological measures, in nearly all cases they consist of summing scores over items. Spelling ability is measured by summing scores over items, i.e., by simply counting the number of words correctly spelled. In paired-associate learning, the amount learned by each person is measured by counting the number of pairs correctly recalled. In a study of rat learning in a T maze, the level of learning is measured by the number of correct choices in a block of trials. In a measure of attitudes toward the United Nations, a total score is obtained by summing the number of agreements to positive statements and the number of disagreements with negative statements.

The linear or summative model applies to multipoint items as well as to items which are scored dichotomously. Reaction time in a particular experiment would be determined by summing and then by averaging the reaction times for a subject in a block of trials. Total scores on an essay examination in history would be obtained by summing scores on individual questions. Attitudes toward the United Nations would be obtained by summing the ratings of 10 statements on a seven-step scale of agreement-disagreement.

It is not difficult to think of psychological measures that fit the linear model—rather, it is difficult to think of measures that do not fit the model. In this chapter we have come a long way around to the conclusion that the most sensible way to measure psychological attributes of people is to sum scores on items. The essence of the summative model is that it does not take individual items very seriously. It recognizes that the individual item has considerable specificity and measurement error. It does not make stringent assumptions about the trace line. The only assumption made is that each item has some form of monotonic trace line, and even that is not a strict assumption, since some of the items could have slightly curvilinear trace lines and a linear relationship of total scores with the attribute would still be obtainable.

The remainder of the book is mostly based on the linear model. This model makes sense and works well in practice. Previously we mentioned some uses of models concerning monotone items with specified distribution forms to deduce interesting new scales for judgments and sentiments of people; these and other new approaches to the scaling of people (test construction) will be mentioned in Chap. 9. However, at the present time there is no serious challenge to the summative (or linear) model for the scaling of people and lower animals with respect to psychological attributes.

## SUGGESTED ADDITIONAL READINGS

Bock, R. D., and Jones, L. V. *The measurement and prediction of judgment and choice.* San Francisco: Holden-Day, 1968.

Coombs, C. H. *A theory of data*. New York: Wiley, 1964.

Coombs, C. H., Dawes, R. M., and Tversky, A. *Mathematical psychology: An elementary introduction*. Englewood Cliffs, N.J.: Prentice-Hall, 1970, chaps. 1 and 2.

Guilford, J. P. *Psychometric methods*. New York: McGraw-Hill, 1954, chaps. 2 and 10.

Gulliksen, H., and Messick S. (eds.). *Psychological scaling: Theory and applications*. New York: Wiley, 1960.

Krantz, D. H., Atkinson, R. C., Luce, R. D., and Suppes, P. (eds.). *Contemporary developments in mathematical psychology*. Vol. 2: *Measurement, psychophysics, and neural information processing*. San Francisco: W. H. Freeman, 1974.

Torgerson, W. S. *Theory and methods of scaling*. New York: Wiley, 1958.

# THREE

## VALIDITY

After a model has been chosen for the construction of a measuring instrument and the instrument has been constructed, it is necessary to inquire whether the instrument is useful scientifically. This is usually spoken of as determining the *validity* of an instrument. Unfortunately, the term has considerable "surplus meaning," in that it implies all things good about a measuring instrument rather than explicitly indicating the standards by which measuring instruments must be judged. Because the word *validity* is so well ingrained in the literature, it will be employed here also; however, special efforts will be made to sharply distinguish the different meanings which validity can have in working with psychological measurement methods.

In a very general sense, a measuring instrument is valid if it does what it is intended to do. Proper performance of some instruments is rather easily verified, e.g., of the yardstick as a measure of length. It takes very little "research" with this instrument to find that resulting measurements (1) fit in perfectly with axiomatic concepts of the nature of length and (2) relate in a lawful way with many other variables. If all measures met these standards so perfectly, there would be little need to consider the validation of measuring instruments; but such is not the case. For example, whereas it might seem highly sensible to develop measures of emotions from physiological indices such as heart rate, muscle tonus, brain waves, and palmar sweat, it has proved very difficult to find combinations of such indices to measure various emotions. So it is with many proposed measures in the physical, biological, and behavioral sciences: what seem to be good approaches to measurement on an intuitive basis prove not to be valid by the standards and methods of investigation that will be discussed in this chapter.

Validation always requires empirical investigations, with the nature of the evidence required depending on the type of validity. With one type of validity which will be discussed, the empirical evidence depends mainly on gathering opinions of people regarding the reasonableness of various aspects of developing and employing a measuring instrument, but this still concerns evidence from the real world. To state the principle in reverse: there is no way to prove the validity of an instrument purely by appeal to authority, deduction from a psychological theory, or any type of mathematical proof. Validity usually is a matter of degree rather than an all-or-none property, and validation is an unending process. Whereas measures of length and of some other simple physical attributes may have proved their merits so well that no one seriously considers changing to other measures, most measures should be kept under constant surveillance to see if they are behaving as they should. New evidence may suggest modifications of an existing measure or the development of a new and better approach to measuring the attribute in question, e.g., the measurement of anxiety, intelligence, the temperature of stars, or the effects of a blood disorder.

Strictly speaking, one validates not a measuring instrument but rather some use to which the instrument is put. For example, a test used to select first-year college students must be valid for that purpose, but it would not necessarily be valid for other purposes, such as measuring how well students have mastered the curriculum in high school. Whereas an achievement test in spelling ability in the fifth grade might be valid for that purpose, it might be nearly worthless for other purposes, such as forecasting success in high school. Similarly, a valid measure of the response to stressful experimental treatments would not necessarily be a valid measure of neuroticism or anything else. Although a measure may be valid for many different purposes, e.g., as intelligence tests are, the validity with which each class of functions is served must be supported by evidence.

Psychological measures serve three major functions: (1) establishment of a statistical relationship with a particular variable, (2) representation of a specified universe of content, and (3) measurement of psychological traits. Corresponding to these are three types of validity: (1) predictive validity, (2) content validity, and (3) construct validity. At a number of places so far in this book, it has been mentioned that the concept of *scientific generalization* is at the very heart of many issues in psychometrics; and that certainly is the case in discussing the validity of measurement methods. It will become evident that the three types of validity discussed above constitute different issues concerning scientific generalization. Examples of measures intended to have these three types of validity are a test for selecting first-year college students, a test for measuring spelling ability in the fifth grade, and a measure of anxiety. Each of the types of validity will be discussed in turn.

## PREDICTIVE VALIDITY

Predictive validity is at issue when the purpose is to use an instrument to estimate some important form of behavior that is external to the measuring instrument itself, the latter being referred to as the *criterion*. The example given above was that of a test employed to select first-year college students. The test, whatever it is like, is useful in that situation only if it accurately estimates successful performance in college. The criterion in this case probably would be grade-point average obtained over four years of college. After the criterion is obtained, the validity of a prediction function is straightforwardly, and rather easily, determined. Primarily it consists of correlating scores on the predictor test with scores on the criterion variable. The size of the correlation is a direct indication of the amount of validity.

The term *prediction* will be used in a general (and ungrammatical) sense to refer to functional relations between an instrument and events occurring before, during, and after the instrument is applied. Thus a test administered to adults could be used to make "predictions" about events occurring in their childhood. A test intended to "predict" brain damage is, of course, intended not to forecast who will suffer brain damage at some time in the future, but rather to "predict" who does and who does not have brain damage at the time the test is administered. When a test is used to predict success in college, prediction properly means forecasting. Others have referred to predictive validity at those three points in time, respectively, as *postdiction, concurrent validity,* and *prediction.* Using different terms, however, suggests that the logic and procedures of validation are different, which is not true. In each case a predictor measure is related to a criterion measure, and after the data are available, it does not matter when they were obtained. The nature of the problem dictates when the two sets of measurements are obtained. Thus to forecast success in college, it is necessary to administer the predictor instrument before students go to college; and to obtain the criterion of success in college, it is necessary to wait four years. (Some persons refer to predictive validity as constituting *criterion-related* validity, which has some merit to it in referring to the three subprocesses involved; however, this use would tend to conflict with some other hyphenated terms involving the word *criterion* which one frequently encounters in special problems of testing.)

Predictive validity is determined by, and only by, the degree of correspondence between the two measures involved. If the correlation is high, no other standards are necessary. Thus if it were found that accuracy in horseshoe pitching correlated highly with success in college, horseshoe pitching would be a valid measure for predicting success in college. This is not meant to imply that sound theory and common sense are not useful in selecting predictor instruments for investigation; but after the investigations are done, the proof of the pudding is in the correlations. This does not mean, however, that in the actual use of tests to serve a prediction function there are not additional considerations that determine usefulness in particular applied situations. For example, as will be illustrated subsequently, there are applications in which a test is useful in forecasting performance even if it has only a modest correlation with the criterion. Such usefulness depends on the size of the available pool of persons, the percent of persons that must be selected, the difficulty of the performance situation, and other matters. The overall strategy for employing predictor tests is discussed by Cronbach and Gleser (1965), Ghiselli (1966), Guion

(1965), Hills (1971), and Horst (1966). Aside from technical considerations of how validity coefficients actually are employed in selection problems, a predictor test cannot be valid unless it has a significant correlation with the criterion; in any circumstance the higher that correlation, the better. Similarly, if only one test is being employed for selection, the test with the highest correlation with the criterion is most valid in that particular instance.

Perhaps because of the simplicity of the ideas and the related methods of research, up to about 1950 frequently it was said that the validity of a measure is indicated by the correlation between the measure and its criterion; but this is quite an oversimplification. Predictive validity is mainly important for making decisions in certain types of applied problems in the behavioral sciences; but the two types of validity that will be discussed subsequently are equally, or more, important in research as a whole. This is particularly the case in evaluating effects of any type of training program on people and in determining the results of basic research. Predictive validity is very important in making decisions related to applied problems in psychology and education, such as in using tests to select office clerks, officer candidates for the Armed Forces, and students for medical school and in making many different kinds of decisions about the management of people. Regarding this last consideration, predictive validity is at issue when tests are employed in making *decisions*, for example, in choosing among different methods of treating mental patients, in placing students in special classes for "slow learners," and in deciding about the proper grade placement of a transfer student. The word *decision* should be kept in mind, because this is what predictor tests are all about. If the statistical results (usually correlation coefficients) lead to wise decisions, then those tests have predictive validity.

In no other area is predictive validity more important than in using tests to make decisions about schooling—in elementary school, high school, college, graduate training, and the many forms of schooling that occur in industry, the military, government agencies, and other places. In schools, predictive validity is at issue in measures of "readiness." Thus, for under-age children, a test of readiness for the first grade is valid only to the extent that it predicts how well children will perform in the first grade. A test used to divide children into different ability levels is valid only to the extent that it predicts how well children will do in their different levels of instruction. A test used to select students for special programs of study in high school is valid only to the extent that it actually predicts performance in those programs. And so it is with all other tests used for the selection and placement of students—they are valid only to the extent that they serve prediction functions well.

Clear as the difference may seem, some people confuse predictor instruments with the criteria they are meant to predict. A story (a true one) will help to illustrate this confusion. A college graduate applied for entrance to a graduate training program to work toward a master's degree. She failed to score sufficiently high on an entrance examination (a predictor test) but was given special permission to enter on a trial basis. Once in training, she performed very well, doing better than most of her fellow students. Near completion of the student's training, the dean of the college insisted that the student would need to retake the entrance examination and make a satisfactory grade before her degree could be granted! Many other equally foolish examples could be given to show how predictor tests are confused with the criteria they are meant to predict.

Whereas it is easy to talk about correlating a predictor test with its criterion, in actuality obtaining a good criterion may be more difficult than obtaining a predictor test. In many cases either no criterion is available or the criteria that are available suffer from various faults. The logic of the problem is discussed by Cronbach (1971); many examples and some possible solutions to the problem are discussed by Ghiselli (1966) and Hills (1971).

Predictive validity represents a very direct, simple issue in scientific generalization that concerns the extent to which one can generalize from scores on one variable to scores on another variable. The correlation between the predictor test and the criterion variable specifies the degree of validity of that generalization.

**Validity coefficients**  Techniques for employing predictor tests and for validating such usages are part of the applied psychology of personnel selection. In personnel selection, there are numerous decision strategies and numerous statistical designs that relate to the employment of different types of predictor measures for different types of jobs with respect to different types of criterion variables. The technical details are discussed in Ghiselli (1964), Hills (1971), and Horst (1966). Although these matters are of considerable practical importance, for several reasons they need not be discussed in detail here. First, this book is intended for behavioral scientists and future behavioral scientists in general rather than only for future specialists in personnel selection. Second, as was mentioned previously, predictive validity constitutes only one of the three types of validity that are required of measuring instruments, and in many ways predictive validity is the most simple of the three. Third, even though some of the details of employing and validating predictor instruments are technically complex, the *logic* of validating prediction functions is relatively simple.

The validity of individual predictor instruments and combinations of predictor instruments is determined by correlational analysis and extensions of correlational analysis to multivariate analysis (methods of analysis to be discussed in later chapters). The simplest example of a validity coefficient is the correlation of an individual predictor test with an individual criterion, e.g., the correlation of a test of scholastic aptitude with average grades over four years of college training. In evaluating the worth of predictor tests, it is a mistake to think in terms of perfect correlations in any case or even of high correlations in most cases.

In most prediction problems, it is reasonable to expect only modest correlations between a criterion and either an individual predictor test or a combination of predictor tests. People are far too complex to permit a highly accurate estimate of their proficiency in most performance-related situations from any practicable collection of test materials. Equally complex are the situations in which criterion data are obtained, e.g., the immense complexity of all the variables involved in determining the average grades of students over four years of college or the total amounts of sales of an insurance agent over a period of several years. If we consider the immense complexities of the problem, it is remarkable that some predictor tests correlate as highly as they do with criterion variables. For example, scholastic aptitude tests are as predictive of grades in college four years hence as meteorologists' predictions are of the weather in Chicago 10 days in advance.

The proper way to interpret a validity coefficient is in terms of the extent to which it indicates a *possible improvement in the average quality of persons* that would be obtained by employing the instrument in question. Tests that have only modest correlations with their criteria (e.g., correlations of .30 and .40) often are capable of markedly improving the *average* performance of personnel in some situations. Of course, many mistakes would be made in predicting the performance of individuals, but on the average, persons who score high on the test perform considerably better than persons who score low on the test. Such differences in mean performance frequently are highly important in applied settings. As a simple example, suppose that a test is being validated for the selection of vacuum cleaner sales agents, and it is found that the test correlates .30 with the dollar volume of sales each year by sales agents. On examination of the scatter plot of the relationship between the two variables, it is seen that the average sales of persons who score very highly on the test is 10 percent greater than the average sales of all persons combined. Then, by using the test to select future sales agents, the company increases gross sales by 10 percent, which might make the difference between going into bankruptcy and becoming a very profitable enterprise. In a similar way, tests that have only modest correlations with their criteria often can make highly important improvements in the average performance of groups in educational institutions, industry, government services, and other activities.

## CONTENT VALIDITY

For some instruments, validity depends primarily on the adequacy with which a specified domain of content is sampled. A prime example would be a final examination for a course in introductory psychology. Obviously, the test could not be validated in terms of predictive validity, because the purpose of the test is not to predict something else but to *directly measure* performance in a unit of instruction. The test must stand by itself as an adequate measure of what it is supposed to measure. Validity cannot be determined by correlating the test with a criterion, because the test itself *is* the criterion of performance.

Even if one argued that course examinations should be validated in terms of correlations with other behaviors, what behaviors would serve as adequate criteria? A student might, by any standard, deserve an A in the course but never take another course in astronomy or ever work in a position where knowledge from the course would be evidenced. Of course, one would expect the test to correlate with some other variables, and the size of such correlations would provide hints about the adequacy of the test. For example, one would expect to find a substantial correlation between scores on the final examination in introductory psychology and scores on the final examination in abnormal psychology (for those students who took both courses). If the correlation were zero, it would make us suspect that something were wrong with one or both of the examinations (or with one or both of the units of instruction). However, such correlations would offer only hints about the validity of the examinations, with the final proof resting on the adequacy with which content had been sampled.

There are many other examples of measures that require content validity. Such is the case with all course examinations in all types of training programs and at all levels of training. All commercially distributed achievement tests require content validity, as would be the case, for example, with a comprehensive measure of progress in school up to the end of the fourth grade or a comprehensive measure of the extent to which men had performed well in a school for electronics technicians in the Armed Forces.

Rather than test the validity of measures after they are constructed, one should *ensure* validity by the plan and procedures of construction. To take a very simple example, an achievement test in spelling for fourth-grade students could obtain its content from a random sampling of words occurring in widely used readers. The plan is to randomly sample from a specified domain of content, and most potential users of the test should agree that this procedure ensures a reasonably representative collection of words. In addition, a sensible procedure would be required for transforming the words into a test. For example, it might be decided to compose items by putting each correctly spelled word in with three misspellings and requiring the student to circle the correct one. Other decisions would need to be made about ordering the items in the test and about the oral or written instructions to students. These and other details are part of the plan for selecting content and for test construction. The validity of the measure is judged by the character of the plan and by the apparent skill with which the plan has been carried out. If it is agreed by most potential users of the test, or at least by persons in positions of responsibility, that the plan was sound and well carried out, the test has a high degree of content validity. How test plans are formulated and converted into content-valid instruments is discussed in detail in Nunnally (1972) and in Thorndike (1971).

The simple example above illustrates the two major standards for ensuring content validity: (1) a representative collection of items and (2) "sensible" methods of test construction. Of course, in most instances these standards are not so easy to judge as the spelling test. Often, it is logically impossible or unfeasible to actually sample content. For example, how would one sample (in a strict sense of the word) items for an achievement test in geography? Neither the sampling unit nor the domain is well specified. One could sample sentences from textbooks and turn them into true-false items, but for obvious reasons such a test would not be adequate. Rather, in such instances one *formulates* a collection of items that broadly represents the unit of instruction. To ensure that the items actually represent the unit of instruction, it is necessary to have a detailed outline, or blueprint, of the kinds of questions and problems that will be included. In such cases, judging the quality of the outline is an important part of assessing content validity.

The simple example of a random sampling of content is unrealistic in most situations for a second reason: the selection of content usually involves questions of values. Thus, for the spelling test, one might decide that it is more important to measure performance on nouns, adjectives, and verbs than on other parts of speech; consequently one would restrict sampling to those types of words. In an achievement test for arithmetic, one might decide that it is more important to stress questions concerning quantitative concepts than those on numerical computations. And so it is with nearly all measures based on content validity: values determine the relative stress on different types of content. Of course, where values are important, there are differences in values among people; consequently, usually there is some disagreement about the proper content coverage of particular tests. The values behind the construction of a measure should be made explicit, e.g., in test manuals, and it should be indicated how those values guided formulation of the test outline and the construction of items (see discussion in Krathwohl and Payne 1971).

A second point at which content validity becomes somewhat complex is in ensuring that "sensible" methods of test construction are employed. This is not much of a problem with spelling tests, because it is relatively easy to construct items that most people will agree are satisfactory. It requires much more skill, however, to construct items in some other domains of content, e.g., geography, history, and sales training; and often there is controversy about the employment of different types of items (using the word *item* to refer broadly to questions, problems, work samples, and other evidence of accomplishment). The construction of test items is discussed in detail by Wesman (1971).

Even though there are problems with ensuring content validity, inevitably content validity rests mainly on appeals to reason regarding the adequacy with which important content has been sampled and on the adequacy with which the content has been cast in the form of test items. In addition, there are various methods of analyzing data obtained from the test which will provide important circumstantial evidence (see the discussion in Henryssen 1971).

For example, at least a moderate level of internal consistency among the items within a test would be expected; i.e., the items should tend to measure something in common. (Methods for performing such analyses will be described in Chap. 8.) This is not an infallible guide, however, because with some subject matter it is reasonable to include materials that tap somewhat different abilities. For example, abilities for numerical computation are not entirely the same as those for grasping some of the essential ideas about quantification, but a good argument could be made for mixing these two types of content to measure overall progress in arithmetic.

Another type of circumstantial evidence for content validity is obtained by comparing performance on a test before and after a period of training. If the test is intended to measure progress in training, scores should increase from before to after; and the improvement in scores on individual items can be considered evidence for the validity of those items. There are, however, numerous flaws in this reasoning. An item can be obviously trivial yet show marked changes from the beginning to the end of the course, e.g., spelling of the teacher's name. Conversely, on some very important items there may be little change from before to after; but that may be because of inadequate texts, unskilled teachers, or lazy students.

Another type of evidence for content validity is obtained from correlating scores on different tests purporting to measure much the same thing, e.g., two tests by different commercial firms for the measurement of achievement in reading. It is comforting to find high correlations in such instances, but this does not guarantee content validity. Both tests may measure the same wrong things.

In spite of some efforts to settle every issue about psychological measurement by a flight into statistics, content validity is mainly settled in other ways. Although helpful hints are obtained from analyses of statistical findings, content validity primarily rests upon an appeal to the propriety of content and the way that it is presented.

Content validity also relates to a rather direct issue in scientific generalization—the extent to which one can generalize from a particular collection of items to all possible items that would be representative of a specified domain of items. This type of scientific generalization is obviously at issue in developing an achievement test for spelling. The intention is to sample words in such a way as to obtain a collection that is representative of those in the learning environment as a whole for students at a particular grade level. Although in testing spelling ability and other types of achievement (e.g., knowlege of law enforcement practices for a civil service examination for promoting police officers) usually the collection of items is formulated rather than actually sampled in a statistical sense, still the intention is to obtain a broad collection of item material that is as representative as possible of relevant content. Also, a method of testing is selected that tends to produce very similar results as sensible alternative approaches. This permits one to generalize from the content of the test not only to the wider domain of possible content but also to similar methods of testing for the same attribute. Predictive validity and content validity simply represent different types of issues regarding the fidelity of scientific generalizations.

## CONSTRUCT VALIDITY

Whereas up to about 1950 most textbooks on measurement spoke only of predictive validity and content validity, with many different names being used to refer to the two, there is a third important type of validity which is particularly relevant to measurement problems in basic research in the behavioral sciences. Like all basic science, psychological science is concerned with establishing functional relations among important variables. Of course, variables must be measured before they can be related to one another in experiments; and for statements of relationship to have any meaning, each measure must, in some sense, validly measure what it is purported to measure. Examples of important variables in psychology are reaction time, habit strength, intelligence, anxiety, drive level, and degree of frustration. How does one validate measures of such variables? Take, for example, an experiment where a particular treatment is hypothesized to raise anxiety. Can the measure of anxiety be validated purely as a predictor of some specific variable? No, it cannot, because the purpose is to measure the amount of anxiety then and there, not to estimate scores on any other variable obtained in the past, present, or future. Also, the measure cannot be validated purely in terms of content validity. There is no obvious body of "content" (behaviors) corresponding to anxiety reactions, and if there were, how to measure such content would be far more of a puzzle than it is with performance in arithmetic. Although both predictive validity and content validity add some supporting evidence for the measurement of traits studied in basic research, those two types of validity are by no means sufficient.

As another illustration of why predictive validity and content validity do not suffice in many basic science problems, consider a study investigating the effects of heredity and environment on intelligence. After an intelligence test is administered, correlations are obtained between spouses, between identical twins, between nonidentical twins, and between nontwin siblings. Analyses of the correlations indicate the different contributions of heredity and environment to intelligence. The intelligence test cannot be validated by correlating it with a "criterion," because there is no better measure known. (If there were, why not use it in the study?) Although the test can be validated in part through content validity, that is by no means sufficient. Although most intelligence tests were constructed in such a way as to broadly "sample" behaviors that most people would consider as fitting the term *intelligence,* current methods of measuring intelligence frequently are disputed. Thus whereas all may agree that "problem solving" is an important aspect of intelligence, this still leaves many questions about how problem solving should be measured. What types of problems should be considered? How should the problems be presented? How should the results be scored? Many more question marks could be expended in illustrating why it is not feasible to employ content validity as the only standard for the usefulness of intelligence tests employed in this instance and for measures of many other traits that are employed in basic research.

The degree to which it is necessary and difficult to validate measures of psychological variables is proportional to the degree to which the variable is concrete or abstract. A highly concrete variable would be reaction time, which would be measured, say, by the length of time taken to press a button on a given signal. How quickly subjects press the button *is* the variable of interest, and how to measure the variable is rather obvious. Specialists in studies of reaction time might quibble over microscopically fine differences in measurement techniques, but such slight differences in measurement methods would have scant effects on experimental results. In this case the operations of measurement are of direct interest, and there is no need to "validate" the measure; consequently the researcher can go about the business of finding interesting relations between that measure and other variables. There are, however, very few variables that are so obviously manifested in simple operations. In most instances the particular operations are meant to measure a variable which extends well beyond the operations in question. Consider the use of an activity wheel for investigations with rats. How rapidly the rat treads the wheel really is of little interest in itself, except to the extent that it represents a general level of activity that logically should be manifested in many ways, e.g., in the amount of movement around the floor of a box. Thus the intention is to measure a somewhat abstract variable of activity level, and consequently the validity of any particular measure is open to question. So it is with most measurement methods: they represent efforts to index relatively abstract variables, ones that are thought to be evidenced in a variety of forms of behavior and not perfectly so in any one of them.

To the extent that a variable is abstract rather than concrete, we speak of it as being a *construct*. Such a variable is literally a construct in that it is something that scientists put together from their own imaginations, something that does not exist as an isolated, observable dimension of behavior. A construct represents a hypothesis (usually only half-formed) that a variety of behaviors will correlate with one another in studies of individual differences and/or will be similarly affected by experimental treatments.

It is important to realize that all theories in science concern statements mainly about constructs rather than about specific, observable variables. A prime example of confusion in this regard comes from the final oral examination for a Ph.D. candidate who had investigated the effects of different drugs on how rapidly mice would swim through a water maze filled with cold water. The dependent measure was time taken to traverse the maze. The candidate spoke of the dependent measure as representing "reaction to stress," the cold water supposedly being stressful to the mice. A member of the examining committee objected to speaking of the dependent measure as representing reaction to stress and took the student to task for not sticking to a description of the experimental results purely in terms of the observables, i.e., mice swimming in cold water. Both the student and the committee member were partly right and partly wrong. By speaking of the dependent measure as representing reaction to stress, the student assumed that the measure had a generality far beyond the actual observables. By suggesting that science is concerned only with the particular observables in an experiment, the committee member was painting a very faulty picture. No one really cares how rapidly mice swim in cold water. The particular measure is of interest only to the extent that it partly mirrors performance in a variety of situations that all concern "stress" or some other construct.

Scientists cannot do without constructs. Their theories are populated with them, and even in informal conversation scientists find it all but impossible to discuss their work without using words relating to constructs. It is important to keep in mind not only that proposed measures of constructs need to be validated for that purpose, but also that science is primarily concerned with developing measures of constructs and finding functional relations between measures of different constructs.

Construct validation is an obvious issue in scientific generalization. The effort in studying constructs is to employ one or several measures whose results are intended to be general to a broader class of measures which all go by the same name, e.g., anxiety, intelligence, learning rate, aggressiveness, and many other trait names. However, the logical issues relating construct validity to scientific generalization are considerably more complex than those in predictive validity and content validity. That is why the issues relating to construct validity are discussed here in detail and from a number of complementary points of view.

Constructs vary widely in the extent to which the domain of related observable variables is (1) large or small and (2) specifically or loosely defined. Regarding point 1, in some cases the domain of related variables is so small that any one of the few observable variables in the domain will suffice to measure the construct. This is true of reaction time, where, as mentioned previously, the alternative methods of measuring are so few and so closely related that any one of them can be spoken of as measuring reaction time without doing much injustice to the "construct." At a higher level of complexity, activity level in the rat logically should be manifested in at least a half-dozen observables, and as it turns out, some of these do not correlate well with others. At the extreme of complexity are constructs like anxiety, frustration, empathy, and intelligence, where the domains of related observables are vast indeed.

Considerations in point 1 above tend to correlate with considerations in point 2: the larger the domain of observables related to a construct, the more difficult it tends to be to define which variables do or do not belong in the domain. Thus it might be relatively easy for psychologists to agree whether a particular observable should be related to "activation level" in humans, e.g., a measure of pupillary dilation. The boundaries of this domain are relatively well prescribed. In contrast, for many constructs the domain of related observables has "fuzzy edges," and scientists are not sure of the full meanings of their own constructs. Typically, scientists hold a firm belief about some of the more prominent observables related to the construct, but beyond that they can only hypothesize how far the construct extends. In measuring the construct of intelligence, for example, all would agree that the construct should be evidenced to some extent in various types of problems involving reasoning abilities; but it is a matter of dispute as to what extent some measures of perceptual and memory abilities should be considered part of the construct. Such is the case with most constructs (e.g., anxiety and rigidity): the boundaries of the domain of related observables are not entirely clear.

Because constructs concern domains of observables, logically a better measure of any construct would be obtained by combining the results from a number of measures of such observables than by taking any one of them individually. However, since the work is often tedious enough with one measure, let alone a handful, sometimes it is asking too much to expect the scientist to employ more than one or several measures in a particular investigation. Thus any particular measure can be thought of as having a degree of construct validity depending on the extent to which results obtained from using the measure would be much the same if some other measure, or hypothetically all the measures, in the domain had been employed in the experiment. Similarly, the combined scores from a number of measures of observables in the domain can be thought of as having a higher degree of construct validity for the domain as a whole. Thus by combining the information from a number of particular measures relating to a construct, one can increase the validity of the scientific generalization over that which would be obtained from employing only one measure.

The logical status of constructs in psychology concerning individual differences is the same as that for constructs concerning the results of controlled experiments. Thus, whereas the construct of intelligence is discussed more frequently with respect to studies of individual differences and the construct of habit strength is discussed more frequently with respect to controlled experiments, problems of construct validity are essentially the same for both.

If the measurement of constructs is a vital part of scientific activity, then how are such measures developed and validated? This is not a simple question, and there are legitimate arguments about the correct answer. First the most widely accepted point of view will be presented; then more formal logical analyses will be made of construct validity. In the end it will be seen that the different points of view are complementary rather than contradictory. The most prevalent point of view is as follows. There are three major aspects of construct validation: (1) specifying the domain of observables related to the construct; (2) from empirical research and statistical analyses, determining the extent to which the observables tend to measure the same thing, several different things, or many different things; and (3) subsequently performing studies of individual differences and/or controlled experiments to determine the extent to which supposed measures of the construct produce results which are predictable from highly accepted theoretical hypotheses concerning the construct. Aspect 3 consists of determining whether a supposed measure of a construct correlates in expected ways with measures of other constructs or is affected in expected ways by particular experimental treatments. These steps are seldom, if ever, purposefully planned and undertaken by any investigator or group of investigators. Also, although it could be argued that the aspects should be undertaken in the order 1, 2, and then 3, this order is seldom, if ever, followed. More likely, psychologists will develop a particular measure that is thought to partake of a construct; then they will leap directly to aspect 3 and perform a study relating the supposed measure of the construct to measures of other constructs, e.g., correlating a particular measure of anxiety with a particular measure of response to frustration. Typically, other investigators will develop other particular measures of the same construct, and skipping aspects 1 and 2, they will move directly to aspect 3 and try to find interesting relations between their measures and measures of other constructs. As the number of proposed measures of the same construct grows and suspicion grows that they might not all measure the same thing, one or more investigators seek to outline in writing the domain of observables related to the construct, which is aspect 1. All, or parts, of one or more such outlines of the domain are subjected to investigation to determine the extent to which variables in the domain tend to measure the same thing, which is aspect 2. The impact of theorizing with respect to aspect 1 and the research results from aspect 2 tend to influence which particular variables are studied in aspect 3.

Since most scientists work as individuals rather than being tied to some overall plan of attack on a problem, each scientist does much as he or she pleases, and consequently there is seldom a planned, concentrated effort to develop valid measures of constructs according to a step-by-step procedure. Instead of the domain of observables for any construct being tightly defined initially (aspect 1), more likely the nature of the domain will be *suggested* by numerous attempts to develop particular measures relating to the construct; and subsequently, some investigators will attempt to more explicitly outline the domain of content. Instead of a planned, frontal attack on the empirical investigations required in aspects 2 and 3, more likely evidence *accrues* from many studies of different proposed measures of the construct; and subsequently, the available evidence is accumulated and evaluated. Hopefully the end product of this complex process is a construct (1) that is well defined in terms of a variety of observables, (2) for which there are one or several variables that well represent the domain of observables, and (3) that eventually proves to relate strongly with other constructs of interest. Some of the methods required to reach those goals are described in the following sections.

**Domain of observables** Whereas, on the face of it, one might think that the scientist should outline the domain of observables before assuming that any one observable relates to a construct, this is seldom done. More frequently, scientists investigate only one observable and assume that it is related to the construct, at least for the time being. For example, there have been many studies relating the Taylor manifest anxiety scale (Taylor 1953) to supposed measures of other constructs. The test is intended to relate strongly to other variables in a domain of behaviors constituting anxiety. Many studies were undertaken before the domain of the construct was well outlined (but fortunately this particular test did tend to relate well to other hypothesized measures of the same construct).

Scientists should not be criticized for provisionally assuming that particular observables relate to a construct even though the domain of the construct is only vaguely understood. In one lifetime each scientist can perform only a relatively small number of major studies, and consequently there is no time to do all that is required to specify the domain of a construct, develop measures of the construct, and relate those measures to other variables of interest. As the evidence accrues from the work of different scientists interested in a particular construct, however, it is fruitful to attempt a specification of the domain of related variables.

No precise method can be stated for properly outlining the domain of variables for a construct. The outline essentially constitutes a theory regarding how variables will relate to one another; and though theories themselves should be objectively testable, the theorizing process is necessarily intuitive. Outlining a construct consists essentially of stating what one means by the use of particular words—words such as *anxiety, habit strength,* and *intelligence.* In the early attempts to outline a domain, the outline usually consists of only a definition in which the word denoting the construct is related to words at a lower level of abstraction. An example is the early attempt by Binet and Simon (1905) to define *intelligence*: "The tendency to take and maintain a definite direction; the capacity to make adaptations for the purpose of attaining a desired end; and the power of auto-criticism." Brave as such attempts are, when they define a construct with words that are far removed from specific observable variables, they do little to specify the domain in question. An example of a more clearly specified domain is that by Hull (1952) for the construct of "net reaction potential," where the specification is in terms of the observables of probability of response, latency of response, amplitude of response, and number of responses to extinction. Further specifications are made of the observables in each of the four classes of observables.

Whether or not a well-specified domain for a construct actually leads to adequate measurement of the construct is a matter for empirical investigation; but until there is a well-specified domain, there is no way to know exactly which studies should be done to test the adequacy with which a construct is measured. In other words, the importance of aspect 1 (outlining the domain) is that it tells you what to do in aspect 2 (investigating relations among different proposed measures of a construct).

**Relations among observables** The way to test the adequacy of the outline of a domain relating to a construct is to determine how well the measures of observables "go together" in empirical investigations. In studies of individual differences, the first step is to obtain scores for a sample of individuals on some of the measures; next, each measure is correlated with all other measures. An analysis of the resulting correlations provides evidence about the extent to which all the measures relate to the same thing. (Essentially this is a problem in factor analysis, which will be discussed briefly later in this chapter and in detail in Chaps. 10 and 11.)

In investigations of construct validity in controlled experiments, the logic is much the same as that in studies of individual differences. One investigates the extent to which treatment conditions have similar effects on some of the measures of observables in the domain. A hypothetical example is given in Fig. 3-1 which shows the effects of five levels of stress (the independent variable) on four supposed measures of the constuct of fear. Measures *A* and *B* are monotonically related to levels of stress, which means that they are affected in much the same way by the experimental treatments. Measure *C* is monotonically related to treatment levels up to level 4, but falls off sharply at level 5, and consequently measures something that is not entirely the same as that in *A* and *B*. Measure *D* is not related in any systematic manner to the treatment levels, and thus logically it could not measure the same thing as measured by *A*, *B*, and *C*. To fully determine the extent to which these and other measures of fear "go together," it would be necessary to see how similarly they behaved with respect to other experimental treatments, e.g., different levels of electrical stimulation of "fear areas" in the brains of rats.

The test of how well different supposed measures of a construct "go together" is the extent to which they have similar curves of relationship with a variety of treatment variables. It does not matter what the form of the relationship is with a paricular treatment variable as long as the supposed measures of the construct behave similarly. Thus, for two supposed measures of a construct, the relationship with one treatment variable could be monotonically increasing, the relationship with another curvilinear, and the relationship with another a flat line; but in all three instances the two measures of the construct should be affected much the same. If two measures were affected in exactly the

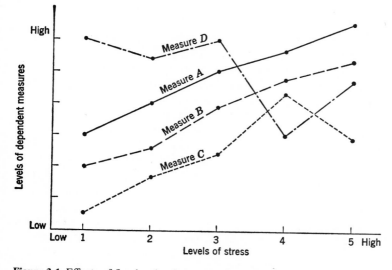

**Figure 3-1** Effects of five levels of stress on four dependent measures.

same way by all possible experimental treatments, it would not matter which one were used in a particular experiment, and consequently one could speak of them as measuring the same thing. To the *degree* to which two measures are affected similarly by a variety of experimental treatments, they can be spoken of as measuring much the same thing. When a variety of measures behave similarly in this way over a variety of experimental treatments, it becomes meaningful to speak of them as measuring a construct. The measures that most consistently behave as the majority of measures do can be said to have the most construct validity.

Methods of investigating construct validity both in studies of individual differences and in controlled experiments involve correlations. Actual correlations are computed among measures of individual differences. A comparison of two curves is, in essence, a correlating of two curves, even though correlational methods might not be applied. Regardless of whether correlations are over individual differences or over levels of treatment effects, such correlations provide evidence about the structure of a domain of observables relating to a construct.

The results of investigations like those described above would lead to one of three conclusions. If all the proposed measures correlate highly with one another, it can be concluded that they all measure much the same thing. If the measures tend to split up into clusters such that the members of a cluster correlate highly with one another and correlate much less with the members of other clusters, it can be concluded that a number of *different* things are being measured. For example, in studying different supposed measures of anxiety, one might find that measures concerning bodily harm tend to go together and those concerning social embarrassment tend to go together. As a third possibility, if correlations among the measures all are near zero, they measure different things. Of course, the evidence is seldom so clear-cut as to enable one to unequivocally reach one of these three conclusions; rather, there usually is room for dispute as to which conclusion should be reached.

Evidence of the kind described above should affect subsequent efforts to specify the domain of observables for a construct and should affect theories relating the construct to other constructs. If all the measures supposedly related to a construct correlate highly, this should encourage investigators to keep working with the specified domain of observables and should encourage continued investigation of theories relating that construct to others. If the evidence is that more than one thing is being measured, the old construct should be abandoned for two or more new ones, and theories that assume only one construct should be modified to take account of the multiplicity of constructs. If none of the variables correlates substantially with the others, the scientist has an unhappy state of affairs. Of course, it is possible that one of the measures is highly related to the construct and the others are unrelated to the construct, but it is much more likely that none of them relate well to the construct. The investigator can postulate an entirely new domain of observables for a construct, as would be the case, for example, if questionnaire measures of anxiety were abandoned in favor of physiological measures. The alternative is to abandon the construct altogether.

**Relations among constructs** In the previous section, means were discussed for studying construct validity in terms of the *internal consistency* with which different measures in a domain tend to supply the same information (tend to correlate highly with one another and be similarly affected by experimental treatments). To the extent that the elements of such a domain show this consistency, it can be said that *some* construct may be employed to account for the data, but it is by no means sure that it is legitimate to employ the construct name which motivated the research. In other words, consistency is a *necessary* but not *sufficient* condition for construct validity. A discussion of how one can, if ever, obtain sufficient evidence that a domain of observables relates to a construct requires an analysis of some of the deepest innards of scientific explanation.

First, we shall accept the assumption that it is possible to find immutable proof that a particular set of variables measures a particular construct, and we shall see what forms of evidence would be required. Later that assumption will be challenged, and different perspectives will be advocated for interpreting evidence regarding construct validity. If the assumption is accepted, sufficient evidence for construct validity is that the supposed measures of the construct (either a single measure of observables or a combination of such measures) *behave as expected.* If, for example, a particular measure is thought to relate to the construct of anxiety, common sense would suggest many findings that should be obtained with the measure. Higher scores (higher anxiety) should be found for (1) patients classified as anxiety neurotics than for unselected nonpatients, (2) subjects in an experiment who are kept threatened with a painful electric shock than for subjects not so threatened, and (3) graduate students waiting to undergo a final oral examination for the Ph.D. than for the same students after passing the examination. As another example, if a particular measure is thought to relate to the construct of intelligence, one would expect it to correlate at least moderately with grades in school, teachers' ratings of intelligence, and levels of professional attainment. So it is with all constructs: there are expected correlations with other variables and expected effects in controlled experiments.

If, according to the assumption above, it is possible to obtain immutable proof of the extent to which measures of observables measure a construct, the proof would come from determining the extent to which the measures "fit" in a lawful way into a network of relationships that would be expected on the basis of sensible theories. First would come the test of internal consistency of elements in the domain; then many correlational studies and many controlled experiments would need to be performed. To the extent to which the measures met expectations in those regards, there would be proof of construct validity.

One could argue that there is a logical fallacy in claiming evidence such as that discussed previously as "proof" of construct validity. To determine construct validity, a measure must fit a theory about the construct; but to use this as evidence it is necessary to *assume* the theory is true. The circularity in this logic can be illustrated by the following four hypotheses:

1. Constructs $A$ and $B$ correlate positively.
2. $X$ is a measure of construct $A$.
3. $Y$ is a measure of construct $B$.
4. $X$ and $Y$ correlate positively.

To give meat to the bones of the example, assume that $A$ is the construct of anxiety, $B$ is the construct of stress, $X$ is a questionnaire thought to measure anxiety, and $Y$ is a parameter of experimental treatments that is thought to induce stress. Even though the four hypotheses are not independent, it should be obvious that one experiment cannot test them all simultaneously. All that can be tested directly by the experiment is hypothesis 4, that X correlates positively with $Y$. From this one finding, it would be necessary to *infer* the truth or falsity of the other hypotheses; but look at the many possibilities among the four hypotheses. Hypothesis 1 may be correct, but even if hypothesis 4 is correct, that would offer no direct proof for the truth of either or both hypotheses 2 and 3. Obviously $X$ and $Y$ could correlate positively, not because they relate to constructs $A$ and $B$, respectively, but rather because they relate to still other constructs. As another possibility, hypothesis 2 could be correct, but if hypothesis 3 is incorrect, there would be no necessity for $X$ to correlate with $Y$.

From the standpoint of inductive logic, it is apparent that the above paradigm for determining construct validity will not hold water. In the illustrative experiment, the experimenter hoped to obtain some evidence for hypothesis 2, that $X$ is a measure of anxiety. All that can be validly tested by the experiment is whether hypothesis 4 is correct, whether $X$ correlates with $Y$.

One who wanted to defend the above paradigm for testing construct validity could point out that the situation is not nearly as bleak as it has been painted. What is done in practice is to *assume* that two of the hypotheses 1 through 3 are correct, and by performing an empirical test of hypothesis 4, to allow a valid inference regarding the remaining hypothesis. Thus, for the example above, it would be assumed that hypothesis 1 is correct, that stress does relate to anxiety. Also, it would be assumed that hypothesis 3 is correct, that the threat of painful electric shock does induce stress. If these assumptions are correct, the actual correlation between $X$ and $Y$ permits a valid inference regarding the truth of hypothesis 2, that $X$ is a measure of the construct of anxiety.

One could further argue that making such assumptions in the modified paradigm above is not really so dangerous. The danger can be lessened by restricting investigations of construct validity to those situations in which the truth of some of the hypotheses is very evident. The evidence of such truth could be based either on other experiments involving the variables, e.g., prior investigations of the construct validity of electric shock as an inducer of stress, or on strong appeals to common sense. Thus in performing studies of construct validity, one relates variables in situations where the assumptions are very safe. For example, nearly everyone will agree that increases in stress should be accompanied by increases in anxiety and that the threat of painful electric shock is a form of stress. Such assumptions are made even safer by correlating a supposed measure of one construct with the supposed measure of another where the domain of the latter is both well defined and highly restricted. Thus if a supposed measure of anxiety is correlated with a supposed measure of reaction time, it is rather safe to assume that the particular measure of reaction time validly represents the construct of reaction time.

In the limiting case, construct validity concerns a hypothesized relationship between a supposed measure of a construct and a particular, observable variable. Thus it would be hypothesized that tests of intelligence should correlate positively with grades in school, teachers' rating of intelligence, and level of professional accomplishment. Such "other" variables are constructs only in the sense that there are slight variations possible in the measurement of each of these, which would probably have little effect on empirical correlations. In this way one can reduce the number of hypotheses in the above paradigm from four to three. The hypothesis "$Y$ is related to $B$" becomes the assumption "$Y$ is $B$." Then if the assumption is very safe that $A$ *relates to $B$*, e.g., intelligence relates to progress in school, an empirical correlation of $X$ with $Y$ provides a safe basis of inference regarding the construct validity for the measurement of $A$ with $X$. According to this point of view, studies of construct validity are safe when, and should be undertaken only when, (1) the domain of the "other" construct is well defined and (2) the assumption of a relationship between the two constructs is unarguable.

## EXPLICATION OF CONSTRUCTS

The foregoing explanation of construct validation is the one currently accepted by many leading theorists, although perhaps the related procedures were specified in more detail than has been done by some authors. This is a workable set of standards, which provides a basis for the measurement of psychological constructs. If, however, the reader wants to go a step further in thinking about the measurement of psychological constructs, there is a more defensible logic. Rather than referring to this logic as relating to construct validation, it would be more correct to refer to it as concerning *construct explication*, by which is meant the process of making an abstract word explicit in terms of observable variables.

A potential problem with the logic described above for determining construct validity is that it might permit the unwary individual to slip into the mistaken notion that a construct has *objective reality* beyond that of the particular variables used to measure the construct. Thus we speak of anxiety as though it were a real variable, one to be *discovered* in the course of empirical studies.

The evidence supplies support for arguments as to whether or not *it* has been measured. One hears arguments such as, "This is not really a measure of anxiety." Inherent in these and other words used to discuss the measurement of constructs is the implicit assumption that constructs have objective reality. It is more defensible to make no claims for the objective reality of a construct name, e.g., anxiety, and instead to think of the construct name as being a useful way to label a particular set of observable variables. Then the name is "valid" only to the extent that it accurately communicates to other scientists the kinds of observables being studied.

A more airtight set of standards for construct validity starts with the definition of a set of measures concerning observables. Thus set $A$ would be said to consist of measures of particular observables $X_1$, $X_2$, $X_3$, etc., and set $B$ would be said to consist of the particular observables $Y_1$, $Y_2$, $Y_3$, etc. (The $X$'s could be thought of as different measures of anxiety and the $Y$'s as different measures of learning.) Construct validation (later the term will be modified), then, consists of the following steps. Through a series of empirical studies, a network of probability statements is formed among the different measures in set $A$, and the same is done for $B$. There are many ways to do this, depending on the types of empirical studies undertaken and the types of probability statements thought to be most meaningful. The most straightforward example is where individual differences on the different measures within a set are correlated with one another. Thus it might be found that $X_1$ correlates .50 with $X_2$ and .45 with $X_3$, and that $X_2$ correlates .55 with $X_3$. Knowing these correlations, one could make probability statements concerning scores on the three measures. If, for example, it is known that a person has a score of 20 on measure $X_1$, the odds can be established as to whether that person has a score between 40 and 60 on $X_2$. Although it seldom is necessary to explicitly make such probability statements about correspondences between scores on different measures, correlations among the measures directly specify the extent to which such probability statements are possible.

After correlations among the individual observables have been obtained, it is then possible to deduce correlations between different combinations of variables in the set (by methods that will be described in Chap. 5). Thus it would be possible to deduce the correlation between the sum of any three of the measures and the sum of any other three measures in the set. More importantly, it would be possible to deduce the correlation between any particular measure in the set and the sum of all measures that had been investigated in the set.

Gradually, in the course of many studies, more and more is learned about correlations among the measures of observables in a particular set. The total information in this regard can be spoken of as forming an *internal structure* for the elements of a set. The structure may indicate that all the variables tend to measure much the same thing, which would be support for retaining the set as it originally was defined; or the structure may indicate that two or more things are being measured by members of the set, e.g., two types of anxiety. If the latter is the case, it would be appropriate to break the original set $A$ into two sets $A_1$ and $A_2$ corresponding to those variables that actually correlate well with one another. If all the correlations among members of the set are very low, it is illogical to continue speaking of the variables as constituting a set, and the investigator should focus on other sets of variables. Regardless of which of these three conclusions is required by the evidence, eventually the evidence leads to a probability structure for the full set or for subdivisions of the set. Factor analysis is invaluable for studying such internal structures of variables hypothesized to be related to a construct.

When the above has been accomplished, the internal consistency is known for the elements of a set $A$. Similarly, the internal consistency is determined for another set $B$. Taking the argument a step further, assume that a particular variable $X_1$ in $A$ is correlated with a particular variable $Y_1$ in set $B$. Depending on the size of the correlation, it would then be possible to make many types of probability statements regarding unknown correlations between any other member of $A$ and any other member of $B$. For example, if $X_1$ and $X_2$ are known to correlate highly and if $Y_1$ and $Y_2$ are known to correlate highly, finding a high correlation between $X_1$ and $Y_1$ permits a prediction of what the correlation would be between $X_2$ and $Y_2$. As another example, if the sum of all variables in $A$ is known to correlate highly with the sum of all variables in $B$, it is possible to estimate the correlation between any particular variable from $A$ and $B$ or the correlation between any two combinations of variables from $A$ and $B$. Thus there are *internal structures* for the variables in sets $A$ and $B$ separately and a *cross structure* between variables in the two sets. If the internal structure of any set is satisfactory, it permits the scientist to explore cross structures of that set with other sets. As the simplest of examples, the average score over the variables in one set could be correlated with the average score over variables in the other set. If such cross structures are satisfactory, scientific progress is being made: either theories are being tested or interesting discoveries are being made.

Whereas, in the ultimate analysis, the "measurement" and "validation" of constructs can consist of nothing more than the determination of internal structures and cross structures, that way of looking at it is disquieting to both the layperson and the scientist. There is a need to put more meaning into the system. The scientist, not content to say only that members of set $A$ relate to something else, wants to say that anxiety, or a construct by another name, relates to something else. As was mentioned previously, words denoting constructs are essential to the scientist in thinking about problems, formulating theories, and communicating the results of experiments. This need for names pushes the scientist, and the layperson even more, into assuming that corresponding to the name is some *real* variable which will be discovered some day. For example, some psychologists talk as though there is some real counterpart to the word anxiety that eventually will be found. The problem is not that of searching for a needle in the haystack, but that of searching for a needle that is not in the haystack.

The words that scientists use to denote constructs, e.g., *anxiety* and *intelligence,* have no real counterparts in the world of observables; they are only heuristic devices for exploring observables. Whereas, for example, the scientist might find it more comfortable to speak of anxiety than set $A$, only set $A$ objectively exists, empirical research concerns only set $A$, and in the final analysis only relations between members of set $A$ and members of other sets can be unquestionably determined.

Although words relating to constructs are undeniably helpful to the scientist, they also can be real trouble. Such words are only symbols for collections of observables. Thus the word *fear* is a symbol for many possible forms of behavior. The difficulty is that the individual scientist is not sure of all the observables that should relate to such a word, and scientists frequently disagree about the related observables. The denotations of a word can be no more exact than the extent to which (1) all possible related observables are specified and (2) all who use the word agree on the specification. Dictionary definitions of words concerning constructs help very little; they serve only to relate one unspecified term to other unspecified terms.

In considering the inexactness of denotations of words relating to constructs, it is not possible to *prove* that any collection of observables measures a construct. It would be much like an expedition starting out to catch a rare bird, the awrk. All scientists agree that the awrk has red wings, a curved bill, and only two toes, but everything else about the awrk is either unknown or a matter of dispute. How, then, would the expedition ever know for sure whether it had found an awrk? The analogy really is not farfetched; the same inconsistency is apparent in efforts to "find" measures of some constructs, e.g., "ego strength."

Although in a very strict sense one can never prove that any set of measurement methods precisely fits a construct name, there are forms of proof that amount to essentially the same thing. The scientist starts with a word, e.g., *anxiety* and from that hypothesizes a set of related observables. Proof can be obtained for the internal structure of those observables by methods described previously. If some combination of the members of this set of variables relates strongly to some combination of the members of another, this is proof that the first set has explanatory power. If it is useful to refer to these two steps as "construct validation," probably no harm is done, but it is important to understand what is being proved and how the related evidence is gathered.

Whereas it would be good if words denoting constructs were altered as evidence is obtained regarding sets of observables said to be related to the constructs, unfortunately this is not done as frequently as it should be. Ideally, one could envision a process whereby gradual refinements of a set of observables would be matched by gradual refinements of the words used to denote the set. Thus relatively inexact terms like *anxiety* and *intelligence* would be successively replaced by terms that were more denotatively exact for a set of observables, the set itself being continually refined in terms of an internal structure and a cross structure with other sets of variables. It is doubtful, though, that any terms in common parlance will ever suffice to serve this purpose, and consequently only impartial designations such as "set $A$" can ever meet the full test of denotative explicitness.

Strictly speaking, scientists can never be sure that a construct has been measured or that a theory regarding that construct has been tested, even though it may be useful to speak as though such were the case. A construct is only a word, and although the word may suggest explorations of the internal structure of an interesting set of variables, there is no way to prove that any combination of those variables actually "measures" the word. Theories consist of collections of words (statements about natural events), and though such theories may suggest interesting investigations of cross structures among sets of observables, the evidence obtained is not so much proof of the *truth* of the theories as it is proof of their *usefulness* as guides to empirical reality. Call it the "measurement" and "validation" of constructs if you like, but, at least as far as science takes us, there are only (1) words denoting constructs, (2) sets of variables specified for such constructs, (3) evidence concerning internal structures of such sets, (4) words concerning relations among constructs (theories), (5) which suggest cross structures among different sets of observables, (6) evidence regarding such cross structures, and (7) beyond that, nothing.

**A commonsense point of view** After the reader has mastered the logical intricacies of construct validity, as discussed previously, in this final section on the topic let us come back down to earth and look at a commonsense point of view. Although there is nothing wrong with the logical analysis that was presented, one could rightly argue that all this fuss and bother about construct validity really boils down to something rather homespun—namely, *circumstantial evidence* for the usefulness of a new measurement method. New measurement methods, like most new ways of doing things, should not be trusted until they have proved themselves in many applications. If over the course of numerous investigations a measuring instrument produces interesting findings and tends to fit the construct name applied to the instrument, then investigators are encouraged to continue using the instrument in research and to use the name to refer to the instrument. On the other hand, if the evidence is dismal in this regard, it discourages scientists from investing in additional research with the instrument, and it makes them wonder if the instrument really fits the trait name that had been employed to describe it. From the standpoint of the work-a-day world of the behavioral scientist, essentially this is what construct validity is about.

## OTHER ISSUES CONCERNING VALIDITY

**Relations among the three types of validity** Whereas the three types of validity were discussed separately in order to emphasize their differences, actually they tend to complement one another in practice. There are obvious ways in which construct validity is supported by predictive validity and content validity. It was mentioned that in many cases instruments which essentially are intended to measure constructs sometimes are used as specific predictors. This is the case with intelligence tests. Although in some uses of an intelligence test (e.g., basic research on inheritance) measurement functions must be largely in terms of construct validity, intelligence tests are also used in many specific prediction problems such as in predicting success in college and in various occupations. To the extent to which the test serves these prediction functions well, this adds to the overall construct validity of the instrument. Content validity also is supportive of construct validity, in that the same procedures required to ensure content validity are intimately related to defining the domain of observables in construct validity. Also, to the extent that each instrument investigated with respect to construct validity can be shown to be representative of a specified domain of content, this adds additional circumstantial evidence to construct validity.

Whereas content validity mainly depends on a rational appeal to the carefulness with which a domain of content has been sampled and placed in the form of a good test, both predictive validity and construct validity provide important auxiliary information. Although achievement tests and other instruments that rely mainly on content validity are not specifically constructed for the purpose, in many cases they prove to be excellent predictors of specific criteria, such as success in higher education or in various career choices.

Although ideally predictive validity should be determined simply and directly from a correlation of a test with its criterion, in many cases one must rely heavily on both content validity and construct validity to support the usage of a particular test in a particular applied problem of personnel selection or placement. If a predictor test also has content validity in the sense that it follows from a good outline of a domain of content, the items broadly sample that domain, and the method of testing is sensible, then there is circumstantial evidence for the usefulness of the predictor test beyond the sheer correlation with the criterion. Construct validity also is helpful with predictor tests. If it is known that the predictor test correlates well with measures of a construct, which logically should be important for the criterion variable, this is important circumstantial evidence regarding the usefulness of the predictor test. Even though a test that is used specifically for a prediction function should be validated as such, in many cases the only recourse is to rely heavily on content validity and construct validity instead. The reason is that in some cases a test must be selected for use before there is an opportunity to perform studies in which it is correlated with a criterion. In many performance situations, the criterion measure might not be available for years after it is necessary to start employing the predictor instrument. In other cases, either there is no sensible criterion available, or the ones that are available are obviously biased in one way or another or are very unreliable. In such instances, only by falling back on evidence relating to content validity and construct validity can one make a sensible argument for employing the predictor test in lieu of direct evidence of predictive validity.

**Other names** Other authors have called the three types of validity discussed in this chapter by different names. Predictive validity has been referred to as "empirical validity," "statistical validity," and more frequently "criterion-related validity"; content validity has been referred to as "intrinsic validity," "circular validity," "relevance," and "representativeness"; and construct validity has been spoken of as "trait validity" and "factorial validity."

One frequently sees the term *"face validity,"* which concerns the extent to which an instrument "looks like" it measures what it is intended to measure. For example, an achievement test for fourth-grade arithmetic would be said to have face validity if potential users of the test liked the types of items which were employed. Any instrument that is intended to have content validity should meet that standard, but the standard is far from complete. Face validity concerns judgments about an instrument *after* it is constructed. As was discussed previously, content validity more properly is ensured by the plan of content and the plan for constructing items. Thus face validity can be considered as one aspect of content validity, which concerns an inspection of the final product to make sure that nothing went wrong in transforming plans into a completed instrument.

When an instrument is intended to perform a prediction function, validity depends entirely on how well the instrument correlates with what it is intended to predict (a criterion), and consequently face validity is irrelevant. There are many instances in which an instrument looks as though it should correlate well with a criterion although the correlation is close to zero. Also, there are many instruments that bear no obvious relationship to a criterion but actually correlate well with the criterion. With prediction functions, face validity is important only in formulating hypotheses about instruments that will correlate well with their criteria. Thus even though the correlations tell the full story, it is not wise to select predictors at random. Before research is done on a prediction problem, there must be some hope that a particular instrument will work. Such hope is fostered when the instrument looks as if it should predict the criterion. Also, tests usually are more predictive of a criterion if their item content is phrased in the language and the terms of the objects actually encountered in the particular type of performance. For example, if an arithmetic test is being constructed for the prediction of performance in the operation of particular types of machines, the test probably would be more predictive if problems were phrased in terms of numbers of nuts and bolts rather than numbers of apples and oranges. For these two reasons, face validity plays a part in decisions about types of tests to be used as predictors and in the construction of items for those tests.

In applied settings, face validity is to some extent related to public relations. For example, teachers would be reluctant to use an achievement test unless the items "looked good." Less logical is the reluctance of some administrators in applied settings, e.g., industry, to permit the use of predictor instruments which lack face validity. Conceivably, a good predictor of a particular criterion might consist of preferences among drawings of differently shaped and differently colored butterflies, but it would be difficult to convince administrators that the test actually could do a good job of selecting employees.

**Place of factor analysis** Methods of factor analysis and their use in the development of measures will be discussed in Chaps. 10 and 11 and at other points in the book; but since factor analysis is intimately involved with questions of validity, it would be helpful to place some of the related issues in perspective. For those who are not already familiar with factor analysis, it should be noted that it essentially consists of methods for finding clusters of related variables. Each such cluster, or factor, is denoted by a group of variables whose members correlate more highly among themselves than they do with variables not included in the cluster. Each factor is thought of as a unitary attribute (a yardstick) which is measured to greater and lesser degrees by particular instruments, depending on the extent to which they correlate with the factor. Such correlations have been spoken of as representing the *factorial validity* of measures. It would be better to speak of such correlations as representing the *factorial composition* of measures, because the word *validity* is somewhat misleading.

The factorial composition of measures plays a part in all three types of validity discussed in this chapter. Factor analysis is important in the selection of instruments to be tried as predictors. Instead of constructing a new test for each applied problem as it arises, one selects a predictor instrument from a "storehouse" of available instruments. Factor analysis can construct such a storehouse of measures with known factorial composition. Then it is much easier to formulate hypotheses about the possible predictive power in particular instances of factors rather than to formulate hypotheses about the predictive power of instruments developed ad hoc for the problem. (In Chap. 8 it will be argued that in prediction problems, developing measures ad hoc for applied problems as they arise is not only highly wasteful of energy, but also leads to some illogical methods of test construction.)

Factor analysis provides helpful evidence regarding measures that are intended to have content validity. For example, a factor analysis of a battery of achievement tests might show that a test intended to measure mathematics correlates rather highly with a factor of verbal comprehension. This would suggest that the words and sentences used to phrase problems were sufficiently difficult to introduce an unwanted factor in the test, which would lead to revisions of the test for mathematics.

Factor analysis is at the heart of the measurement of psychological constructs. As was said previously, the explication of constructs mainly consists of determining (1) the internal statistical structure of a set of variables said to measure a construct and (2) the statistical cross structures between the different measures of one construct and those of other constructs. Factor analysis is used directly to determine item 1, and procedures related to factor analysis are important in determining item 2. To take the simplest case, if all the elements of set *A* correlate highly with one another and all the elements of set *B* correlate highly with one another, then the members of each set have high correlations with a factor defined by that set. This would be evidence that the two sets, corresponding to two supposed constructs, meet the test of a "strong" internal structure. If, in addition, the two factors correlate substantially, this would provide evidence regarding the cross structure of the two sets of measures.

Factor analysis plays important parts with respect to all three types of validity, but it plays somewhat different parts with each. Regarding predictive validity, factor analysis mainly is important in suggesting predictors that will work well in practice. With content validity, factor analysis is important in suggesting ways to revise instruments for the better. With construct validity, factor analysis provides some of the tools that are most useful for determining internal structures and cross structures for sets of variables.

## SUGGESTED ADDITIONAL READINGS

American Psychological Association. *Standards for educational and psychological tests.* Washington, D.C.: American Psychological Association, 1974.

Bechtoldt, H.P. Construct validity: A critique. *American Psychologist,* 1959, *14*, 619–629.

Campbell, D. T. Recommendations for APA test standards regarding construct, trait, and discriminant validity. *American Psychologist,* 1960, *15*, 546–553.

Cronbach, L. J. Test validation. In R. L. Thorndike (ed.), *Educational measurement* (2nd ed.). Washington, D.C.: American Council on Education, 1971.

Cronbach, L. J., and Meehl, P. E. Construct validity in psychological tests. *Psychological Bulletin,* 1955, *52,* 281–302.

Hills, J. R. Use of measurement in selection and placement. In R. L. Thorndike (ed.), *Educational measurement* (2nd ed.). Washington, D.C.: American Council on Education, 1971.

Loevinger, J. Objective tests as instruments of psychological theory. *Psychological Reports* (Monograph No. 9), 1957, *3,* 635–694.

# INTERNAL STRUCTURE OF MEASURES

# FOUR

## VARIANCE AND COVARIANCE

A person who thoroughly understands some elementary concepts concerning the variance of measurements and covariance among different measures will have little difficulty in understanding the theory of measurement error, measurement of reliability, test construction, and multivariate analysis. Although most readers of this book already have been introduced to these topics, some reminders might prove helpful. Also, an effort will be made in this chapter to relate issues regarding variance and covariance to more complex issues to be discussed throughout the remainder of the book.

It might be said that scientific issues are posed only to the extent that objects or people *vary* with respect to particular attributes. For example, since the speed of light is a constant, there is little to investigate. Also, except for a few unfortunate persons, the number of fingers is constant, which leaves nothing of interest to investigate in that regard. Once a constant is found in nature, it may prove useful in many equations specifying relations among attributes that do vary; but otherwise there is little to investigate about a constant per se. Thus there would be little to study if all stars had the same temperature or if all people had the same level of intelligence. To stir the interest of scientists, variation is as important in controlled experiments as it is in studies of individual differences. For example, if different groups of people are subjected to different levels of stress and the effects of such treatments are tested by a measure of anxiety, the results are of interest only to the extent that mean scores on the measure of anxiety are different for the differently treated groups. In studies of individual differences, variance of an attribute among people is of interest; in controlled experiments, variance among means for differently treated groups is of interest. Scientists look for attributes that vary considerably, develop measures of those attributes, and attempt to "explain" such sources of variation with theories and experimentation.

The purpose of a scientific theory is to "explain" as much variation of interrelated variables as possible. That is, a theory is intended to have a high level of generalizability as evidenced in its explanatory power. Variance is "explained" by studying covariance among measures of different attributes. The scientist hopes to find a relatively small number of basic variables that will explain the variation in many other variables. The variance of one variable is "explained" by another to the extent that the variables covary or correlate. Thus if performance in school correlates highly with measures of intelligence, social background, motivation, and others, then performance in school is "explained" by the other variables. To the extent that the rate of memorizing pairs of words in paired-associate learning correlates with familiarity with the words, familiarity serves to "explain" rate of memorization.

## VARIANCE

Although there are many possible measures of variation, or dispersion, one has proved to be the most fruitful by far:

$$\sigma^2 = \frac{\Sigma x^2}{N} \tag{4-1}$$

where $\sigma^2$ = variance

    $x$ = deviation scores on a measure

    $N$ = number of measurements

Each $x$ value is the deviation score for a particular person, obtained by subtracting the mean of a set of scores from each of the raw scores $(X - M_x)$. Since in most studies the grand mean of raw scores is of little interest, analyses of both studies of individual differences and controlled experiments can begin by converting all raw scores to deviation scores. The variance is the average squared deviation score. Squared deviations are worked with because they lend themselves very neatly to algebraic manipulations. A measure of variation cannot be developed from the deviations themselves, because by definition these sum to zero for any distribution. A possibility would be to develop measures of variation from the absolute deviations, disregarding signs, but such absolute deviations prove very awkward for mathematical developments. By working with squared deviations, one is able to apply a very wide variety of *least-squares* statistics which are very useful in numerous mathematical proofs required for the development of statistical methods.

Although the variance is easy to work with mathematically, the square root of the variance (the standard deviation) has useful descriptive properties. The standard deviation is expressed in the same units as the measure involved. Thus if a standard deviation of 5 is found on a 40-item test, it permits an easy interpretation of the amount of variability of the particular group of scores. It is somewhat more difficult to think in terms of variances. In the example above, the variance would be 25, which would be difficult to interpret with respect to scores on a 40-item test. The variance is used more frequently in mathematical developments, and the standard deviation is used more often in "making sense" out of the amount of variation. Since one is directly convertible to the other, which one is used in a particular instance is a matter of convenience.

It will be noted that the variance and the standard deviation are expressed in terms of the Greek letter $\sigma$ rather than as $s$. The former is employed typically to signify the standard deviation of the population as a whole, and the latter is used to signify an estimate of sigma from a sample. The difference, of course, is that in Eq. (4-1) one would employ $N - 1$ rather than $N$ in the denominator in order to obtain $s$. In general, one employs degrees of freedom rather than numbers of observations to develop sample estimates of population parameters. As was mentioned previously in this book, however, psychometric theory mainly is a "large-sample" theory, which assumes that major topics such as reliability, validity, factor analysis, and others are undertaken with large numbers of subjects; consequently the basic principles can be stated without resorting to small-sample statistics. Although small-sample statistics do prove useful in some aspects of psychometric theory (but not many), in this book psychometric theory will be presented mainly as a large-sample topic.

In most methods of analysis, not only is the grand mean of raw scores unimportant, but the absolute sizes of deviations about the mean are unimportant. What are important are the *relative* sizes of deviations about the mean. The absolute sizes of deviations depend on artifacts of measurement. For example, a deviation of 2.5 about the mean might be a relatively large deviation if the test contained only 10 items, but it might be a relatively small deviation if the test contained 100 items. A good way to "relativize" deviation scores is to divide each by the standard deviation, which results in *standard scores*. Thus a particular individual who has a deviation score of 20 points above the mean, where the standard deviation of scores in the group is 10, has a standard score $z$ of 2. Similarly, a person in that group with a deviation score of $-10$ would have a standard score of $-1$.

Standard scores are very easy to interpret—each specifies how many standard deviations an individual is above or below the mean. If a distribution of scores is approximately normal, standard scores can be easily interpreted in terms of the percentage of individuals above and below particular points on the score continuum. Since standard scores have such useful descriptive properties, it is important to think in terms of standard scores in discussing various methods of mathematical analysis. As will be discussed later, the correlation between any two measures would be exactly the same whether the analysis started with raw scores, deviation scores, or standard scores. Similarly, the results of a particular analysis of variance would be the same whether the analysis started with raw scores, deviation scores about the grand mean, or standard scores about the grand mean. The different ratios of variance would be the same regardless of which type of scoring were used.

That is, the results of such analyses are invariant with respect to any linear transformation, such as

$$X' = bX + a$$

where $X'$ = set of transformed scores
$\quad\quad b$ = any constant multiplier of $X$
$\quad\quad a$ = any constant added to $bX$

Of particular interest is the case in which the variance is computed for a variable that can have values of 1 and 0 only, e.g., for a test item that is scorable only as pass or fail. In this example the variance can be expressed in terms of the proportion of persons who pass the item, $p$, and the proportion of persons who fail the item, $q$ (which equals $1 - p$):

$$\sigma^2 = pq \tag{4-2}$$

It should be apparent that all dichotomous distributions can be scored as 1 or 0 whether they represent quantitative or qualitative dichotomies. Thus, persons with IQs at or above average could be scored 1, and those below average could be scored 0. In the comparison of a new method of instruction with a traditional method of instruction, members of the new treatment group could be given a score of 1 and members of the old treatment group could be given a score of 0. It is obvious from Eq. (4-2) that the variance of a dichotomous distribution is at a maximum when $p$ and $q$ are .5 and becomes less and less as $p$ and $q$ deviate from that point. Since $q = 1 - p$, the variance is entirely determined by the size of either of the two values. Thus two items have the same variance if 80 percent of the persons pass one item and only 20 percent of the persons pass the other item.

Some people find it odd to think of a dichotomous distribution as having "variance." Not only is it mathematically sound to speak of the variance of a dichotomous item, but also a moment's reflection will show that it makes intuitive sense. Variance is closely related to the concept of uncertainty. Thus if a test has a large variance, there is more uncertainty as to the actual score of any person. Similarly, the nearer the $p$ value is to .5, the more uncertainty there is about the scores of individuals. In that situation, if nothing were known about the individuals and it were required to make bets as to whether particular individuals passed or failed the item, the accuracy of such bets would be only 50 percent and thus no better than flipping a coin. In contrast, if it is known that 90 percent of the individuals pass an item, the variance is smaller, and there is much less uncertainty. By betting "pass" for each person in turn, 90 percent accuracy would be achieved.

**Transformations of distributions** The formula for the variance [Eq. (4-1)] employs deviation scores ($x$). This is because the variance is computed about the mean score, the size of the mean being of no consequence in determining amount of score variability. Thus the variance is left unchanged if any arbitrary constant is added to, or subtracted from, all the scores in a distribution. Whatever the mean of the original distribution, adding a constant to all scores increases the mean by the amount of the constant; but it has no effect on the standard deviation.

If all the scores in a distribution are multiplied by a constant, the variance is multiplied by the square of the constant, and the standard deviation is multiplied by the constant. For example, if all scores are multiplied by $c$,

$$\sigma_{cx}^2 = \frac{\Sigma (cx)^2}{N}$$

$$= \frac{\Sigma c^2 x^2}{N} \tag{4-3}$$

$$= c^2 \frac{\Sigma x^2}{N}$$

$$= c^2 \sigma_x^2$$

Frequently it is useful to transform a distribution of scores to a distribution having a particular mean and standard deviation. For example, it might be found that the mean of obtained scores is 40 and the standard deviation is 5. To compare scores on the test with scores on another test or to place scores in an easily interpretable form, it might be desirable to transform the original distribution to one having a mean of 50 and a standard deviation of 10. The principles stated above permit the derivation of a formula for that purpose:

$$X_t = \frac{\sigma_t}{\sigma_o} (X_o - M_o) + M_t \tag{4-4}$$

where $X_t$ = scores on transformed scale
$\quad\quad X_o$ = scores on original scale
$M_o, M_t$ = means of $X_o$ and $X_t$, respectively
$\quad \sigma_o, \sigma_t$ = standard deviations of $X_o$ and $X_t$, respectively
In the foregoing example, a score of 40 would be transformed to a score of 50, and a score of 25 to a score of 20. Because Eq. (4-4) provides a linear transformation, it does not change the shape of the score distribution.

## CORRELATION AND COVARIANCE

Because correlational analysis is so intimately related to the development of measures and to the analysis of data obtained from research, a thorough understanding of some basic principles of correlational analysis is essential for the understanding of more advanced topics in this book. There are different indices of correlation, but they all have one thing in common: they describe the *degree* of relationship between two variables. Although it is fine to hope for the day when variables, or combinations of variables, will be found that correlate perfectly, such a day is a long way off for most scientific problems. Thus whereas the temperature of an enclosed gas may lawfully relate to the *average* molecular motion, that temperature relates only in a statistical sense to the activity of individual molecules. Whereas the density of different stars may correlate with their chemical compositions, such correlations are far from perfect. And whereas the number of mutations of genes would correlate with the amount of irradiation, the correlation would be far from perfect. So it is in most investigations of psychological variables—the most that the experimenter can hope for is a *trend* of correspondence between two variables, and experience has taught that in many cases the degree of correspondence between variables will not be high. For example, it is unreasonable to expect a very high relationship between predictor tests and success in college. Similarly, in controlled experiments, there usually is considerable dispersion on dependent measures for the various subjects in a treatment group, and distributions of different treatment groups usually overlap considerably. Correlational analysis is useful in specifying the form and degree of imperfect functional relationships.

The choice of a measure of correlation between two variables depends upon assumptions about permissible mathematical operations with the measurement methods involved (assumptions about scale properties). It will be recalled from Chap. 1 that numbers may be used with respect to ratio scales, interval scales, ordinal scales, categories, and as labels. Since psychologists seldom claim to have sensible ratio scales and correlational results with ratio scales are the same as those with interval scales, there is no problem regarding claims about ratio scales. Since numbers used as labels are not meant to imply quantities of attributes, such numbers can be excluded as possibilities for correlational analysis. The issues then concern assumptions regarding interval scales, ordinal scales, and categories. First will be described methods of correlational analyses that assume permissible operations relating to interval scales. Later will be described correlational methods appropriate to ordinal scales and categories.

## PRODUCT-MOMENT CORRELATION

This section deals with *product-moment* (PM) correlation of two relatively continuous distributions. Complete continuity of distributions is only a mathematical abstraction that never occurs in the actual measurement of attributes. For complete continuity, infinitely precise measurement would be required. More specifically, a distribution is continuous if no matter how close two possible points are on a scale, there is a possible point lying between the two. In actual measurement, all scales have discrete steps rather than infinitely fine gradations. Thus an instrument for measuring minute lengths would still be able to measure only to the nearest thousandth of an inch or less, and there would be a limit to which finer gradations would be possible. On a 40-item test where correct scores are counted 1 and incorrect scores 0, only 41 possible points are measurable (0 to 40). On a seven-step rating scale, measurement is made of only seven discrete levels.

When a variable in psychology is reliably measurable on about 11 levels or more, then little information is lost relative to when more continuous measurement is possible. In many cases, correlational analysis must be performed with fewer levels of measurement (as low as 2 in some problems), in which case there is less information than if more continuous measurement were made.

Product-moment correlation is used to specify the degree of relationship between two variables expressed in the form of standard scores. The problem begins with standard scores, because in this type of analysis the means and standard deviations of raw scores are irrelevant. For illustration, the scores for nine persons on two tests, $z_1$ and $z_2$, are shown below:

| Person | Test $z_1$ | Test $z_2$ | $z_1 \times z_2$ |
|--------|------------|------------|------------------|
| $a$ | 1.55 | 1.18 | 1.83 |
| $b$ | 1.16 | 1.77 | 2.05 |
| $c$ | .77 | .59 | .45 |
| $d$ | .39 | −1.18 | −.46 |
| $e$ | .00 | .59 | .00 |
| $f$ | −.39 | −.59 | .23 |
| $g$ | −.77 | −.59 | .45 |
| $h$ | −1.16 | −.59 | .68 |
| $i$ | −1.55 | −1.18 | 1.83 |

$$r = \frac{\Sigma z_1 z_2}{N}$$

$$= \frac{7.06}{9}$$

$$r = .78$$

A scatter diagram of the above pairs of scores is shown in Fig. 4-1.

The problem in PM correlational analysis is to determine the straight line that best summarizes the trend of correspondence between two sets of standard scores. A straight line has only two parameters: the slope, which will be symbolized as $r$, and the point of intercept with the $z_2$ axis, which will be symbolized as $a$. The problem can be phrased as that of obtaining a straight line that will "best estimate" scores on $z_2$ from scores on $z_1$ as follows:

$$z_2' = rz_1 + a \tag{4-5}$$

where $z_2'$ = estimates of scores on $z_2$. The quality of the estimates would be gauged by some function of the differences between the estimated scores for $z_2$

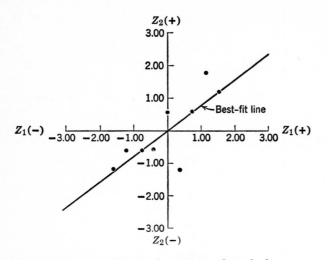

**Figure 4-1** A scatter diagram for two sets of standard scores.

and the actual scores on $z_2$:

$$z_2 - z_2'$$

This is the same as

$$z_2 - rz_1 - a$$

Various ways could be used to obtain $r$ and $a$, depending on what function of the foregoing differences was to be minimized. Thus one could try to derive $r$ and $a$ in such a way that the sum of absolute differences between $z_2$ and $z_2'$ would be a minimum. Various other functions of the differences could be employed as a standard, each such function being referred to as a "loss function." The loss function that has proved most useful for this problem is that of *least squares*: $r$ and $a$ are determined so that the sum of squared differences between actual scores on $z_2$ and estimated scores $z_2'$ is a minimum. Thus the problem is to minimize the following expression by the proper choice of $r$ and $a$:

$$\Sigma(z_2 - z_2')^2 = \Sigma(z_2 - rz_1 - a)^2$$

Whether or not the foregoing expression has a unique minimum and, if it does, how to determine $r$ and $a$ are simple problems in calculus. Solving by the method of partial derivatives tells us three things. First, $a = 0$ for any comparison of sets of standard scores. Thus the line must go through the origin, as indicated in Fig. 4-1. The problem then can be rephrased as finding an $r$ that will minimize the expression

$$\Sigma(z_2 - rz_1)^2$$

Second, calculus tells us that $r$ is unique in any problem, which means that there is only one value of $r$ that minimizes the loss function. Third, calculus tells us that $r$ is obtained as follows:

$$r = \frac{\Sigma z_1 z_2}{N} \tag{4-6}$$

The proper value of $r$ is obtained by multiplying pairs of standard scores on the two measures, summing these, and dividing the sum by the number of pairs (persons). These calculations were performed in the previous example of scores for persons on two tests. Once $r$ is obtained, the line of best fit can be drawn, as was done in Fig. 4-1. The best estimate of $z_2$ is obtained by multiplying each standard score on $z_1$ by $r$ (which gives $z_2'$). Such estimates can be made from any particular score on $z_1$ either by using Eq. (4-6) or by reading off from the line of best fit to any point on $z_2$ corresponding to a point on $z_1$.

Because $r$ is such a useful index, it is given a special name, the *product-moment correlation coefficient*. It is used so much more frequently than any other index that, unless some other index of correlation is specified, the word *correlation* is usually assumed to stand for the PM correlation. The reason for calling it the product-moment coefficient is as follows. Deviations about a mean are spoken of as "moments" of a distribution. The deviates themselves are spoken of as the first moments of a distribution; squared deviates are second moments; cubed deviates are third moments; and so on. Since standard scores are deviates about a mean of zero, they are first moments of a distribution. Because the first step in obtaining $r$ is to multiply corresponding standard scores on two measures, this can be spoken of as multiplying corresponding moments on two measures. Then $r$ is the average product of first moments of two distributions, hence the name *product-moment correlation coefficient*.

The usefulness of $r$ extends far beyond that of determining the best-fit line. Because $r$ ranges from $+1.00$ to $-1.00$, its sign and size provide a very understandable indication of the direction and degree of relationship between two variables. Why $r$ cannot be greater than 1.00 requires no elaborate proof. In the case where each person had the *same* standard score on two variables, then the equation for $r$ would equal the result obtained from the equation for the variance of any set of standard scores, which is 1.00. The maximum negative correlation would be when the standard scores of each person were the same but opposite in sign, which would produce an average of cross products of $-1.00$. As will be discussed more fully in subsequent sections, other advantages of the PM coefficient are that it (1) permits a partitioning of the variance of each of the two measures into meaningful components and (2) serves as a foundation for many complex methods of analysis, such as multiple correlation and factor analysis.

In discussing $r$, it makes no difference whether one phrases the problem as that of predicting $z_2$ from $z_1$ or vice versa. In either case the same numerical value would be found for $r$. This is not necessarily the case with some correlational methods applied to nonlinear relationships, which will be discussed later.

**Different formulas** Although in a sense there is only one way to compute $r$, which is done by averaging the product of standard scores, the same numerical value can be obtained from many differently appearing formulas. These formulas vary in terms of ease of computation and the facility with which they permit more complex derivations. Regarding the former, Eq. (4-6) is almost never used in the actual computation of $r$, because it requires a tedious derivation of standard scores. Regarding the latter, it sometimes is easier to visualize the derivation of statistics based on $r$ when one formula rather than another is used as a starting point. Some formulas for computing $r$ are obtained from Eq. (4-6):

$$r = \frac{\Sigma z_1 z_2}{N}$$

Since any standard score equals a deviation score divided by the standard deviation of the distribution of deviation scores, the foregoing expression can be phrased in the following different ways:

$$r = \frac{\Sigma (x_1/\sigma_1)(x_2/\sigma_2)}{N}$$

$$= \frac{\Sigma x_1 x_2}{N \sigma_1 \sigma_2} \tag{4-7}$$

$$= \frac{\Sigma x_1 x_2}{\sqrt{\Sigma x_1^2} \sqrt{\Sigma x_2^2}}$$

The above equation is the most convenient approach to computing $r$ when deviation scores are available at the start of the problem. Since any deviation score equals a raw score minus the mean of the raw scores in a distribution, Eq. (4-7) can be rephrased as follows:

$$r = \frac{\Sigma (X_1 - M_1)(X_2 - M_2)}{\sqrt{\Sigma(X_1 - M_1)^2} \sqrt{\Sigma(X_2 - M_2)^2}}$$

This can be transformed to the raw-score formula that appears most frequently in textbooks:

$$r = \frac{N\Sigma X_1 X_2 - \Sigma X_1 \Sigma X_2}{\sqrt{N\Sigma X_1^2 - (\Sigma X_1)^2} \sqrt{N\Sigma X_2^2 - (\Sigma X_2)^2}} \tag{4-8}$$

Many other formulas can be derived for actually computing $r$. The important point, however, is that $r$ always specifies the degree of relationship between two sets of standard scores. Either standard scores are used directly for the computation of $r$ or other formulas essentially convert raw scores or deviation scores to standard scores in the process of computation.

**Covariance** The covariance $\sigma_{12}$ is defined as the average cross product of two sets of deviation scores:

$$\sigma_{12} = \frac{\Sigma x_1 x_2}{N} \tag{4-9}$$

where $x_1$ = deviation scores on one measure

$x_2$ = corresponding deviation scores on another measure

$N$ = number of pairs (persons)

$\sigma_{12}$ = covariance

The covariance is not derived in such a way as to have any optimum property such as $r$ does. For example, it is not restricted to the range of $-1.00$ to $+1.00$, and unless one knows more about the standard deviations of the variables, the covariance is not directly interpretable. Rather than being derived in terms of some optimum property, the covariance is simply defined as in Eq. (4-9). The importance of the covariance is that it proves very useful in the development of many complex statistics relating to correlational analysis. This is amply illustrated by seeing what happens when both the numerator and denominator of Eq. (4-7) are divided by $N$:

$$r_{12} = \frac{\sigma_{12}}{\sigma_1 \sigma_2} \tag{4-10}$$

The correlation between two measures can be thought of as the covariance of the two measures divided by the product of the standard deviations of the two measures. This way of phrasing $r$ provides a very helpful starting point for understanding more complex forms of correlational analysis. At numerous places in the pages ahead, it will be shown that *combinations* of variables can be placed in Eq. (4-10) rather than individual variables. Another useful way of expressing Eq. (4-10) is as follows:

$$\sigma_{12} = r_{12} \sigma_1 \sigma_2$$

**Partitioning of variance** As was mentioned previously, one of the reasons $r$ is so useful is that it permits a partitioning of variance into meaningful components. Let us take the case where $z_1$ is being used to estimate $z_2$; but keep in mind that as long as both variables are in standard-score form, it makes no difference which direction the predictions go. Before correlational analysis is undertaken, there are two variables, $z_1$ and $z_2$. After correlational analysis is completed, there are two additional variables. One is $z_2'$, which is a set of estimates of $z_2$. The other is a set of error scores, obtained by subtracting the estimates of $z_2$ from the actual scores on $z_2$, which will be symbolized as $z_{2-1}$. It is extremely important to consider the means and variances of these four variables and the correlations among them. Throughout the book it will be shown that many important principles rest on some simple facts regarding these four sets of scores.

It should be apparent that the means of all four variables above are zero.

The means of $z_1$ and $z_2$ are zero by definition. Since $z_2'$ is obtained by multiplying $z_1$ by a constant $r$, the mean is left at zero. Since $z_{2-1}$ is obtained by subtracting scores on $z_2'$ from actual scores on $z_2$, the mean of $z_{2-1}$ is zero. This is because of the simple principle in algebra that the mean of differences equals the difference of the means.

By definition, the variances of $z_1$ and $z_2$ are 1. Snce $z_2' = rz_1$ and multiplying all the scores in a distribution by a constant multiplies the variance by the square of that constant, the variance of $z_2'$ is $r^2$. The variance of $z_{2-1}$ is obtained as follows:

$$\sigma_{2-1}^2 = \frac{\Sigma z_{2-1}^2}{N}$$

$$= \frac{1}{N} \Sigma (z_2 - z_2')^2$$

$$= \frac{1}{N} \Sigma (z_2 - rz_1)^2$$

$$= \frac{1}{N} \Sigma (z_2^2 - 2rz_1z_2 + r^2z_1^2) \tag{4-11}$$

$$= \frac{\Sigma z_2^2}{N} - 2r \frac{\Sigma z_1 Z_2}{N} + r^2 \frac{\Sigma z_1^2}{N}$$

$$= 1 - 2r^2 + r^2$$

$$= 1 - r^2$$

Multiplying a variable by a constant does not change the correlation of that variable with any other variable. Consequently since $z_2' = rz_1$ and the correlation of $z_1$ and $z_2$ is $r$, the correlation of $z_2'$ and $z_2$ likewise is $r$. The correlation of $z_{2-1}$ with $z_1$ is obtained as follows:

$$r_{z_1 z_{2-1}} = \frac{(1/N) \Sigma z_1 z_{2-1}}{\sigma_{2-1}}$$

The above equation is a form of Eq. (4-10). The numerator is the covariance of $z_1$ with $z_{2-1}$. The "missing" standard deviation in the denominator is for $z_1$, which is 1.00, and thus does not appear. It will be sufficient to examine only the numerator of the expression to prove that $z_1$ and $z_{2-1}$ correlate precisely to zero:

$$\frac{1}{N} \Sigma z_1 z_{2-1} = \frac{1}{N} \Sigma z_1 (z_2 - rz_1)$$

$$= \frac{1}{N} (\Sigma z_1 z_2 - r \Sigma z_1^2)$$

$$= r - r$$

$$= 0$$

Since $z_2'$ correlates 1.0 with $z_1$, the above is also proof that $z_2'$ correlates 0 with error scores $z_{2-1}$.

The correlation of $z_2$ with error scores $z_{2-1}$ is as follows:

$$r_{z_2 z_{2-1}} = \frac{(1/N) \, \Sigma \, z_2 z_{2-1}}{\sigma_{2-1}}$$

This is another application of Eq. (4-10). This time $\sigma_2$ is "missing" from the denominator. The denominator of the equation is the standard deviation of the errors of prediction. Previously the variance of the errors of prediction was shown to be $1 - r^2$; consequently the square root of that quantity is the denominator. The numerator can be expanded as follows:

$$\frac{1}{N} \Sigma z_2 z_{2-1} = \frac{1}{N} \Sigma z_2 (z_2 - r z_1)$$

$$= \frac{1}{N} \Sigma (z_2^2 - r z_1 z_2)$$

$$= \frac{\Sigma z_2^2}{N} - r \frac{\Sigma z_1 z_2}{N}$$

$$= 1 - r^2$$

Placing numerator and denominator back in the original equation gives

$$r_{z_2 z_{2-1}} = \frac{1 - r^2}{\sqrt{1 - r^2}}$$

$$= \sqrt{1 - r^2} \qquad (4\text{-}12)$$

The above relationships among means, variances, and correlations are summarized in Table 4-1. You should derive these simple principles on your own; then the results should be burnt into your brain. These simple principles are the foundation stones for more complex methods of multivariate analysis.

**Table 4-1 Means, variances, standard deviations, and correlations among scores involved in correlational analysis**

| Measure | $Z_1$ | $Z_2$ | $Z_2'$ | $Z_{2-1}$ |
|---|---|---|---|---|
| Mean | .0 | .0 | .0 | .0 |
| $\sigma^2$ | 1.0 | 1.0 | $r_{12}^2$ | $1 - r_{12}^2$ |
| $\sigma$ | 1.0 | 1.0 | $r_{12}$ | $\sqrt{1 - r_{12}^2}$ |
| $r$ with $Z_1$ | 1.0 | $r_{12}$ | 1.0 | .0 |
| $r$ with $Z_2$ | $r_{12}$ | 1.0 | $r_{12}$ | $\sqrt{1 - r_{12}^2}$ |
| $r$ with $Z_2'$ | 1.0 | $r_{12}$ | 1.0 | .0 |

(Column header "Score" spans $Z_1$, $Z_2$, $Z_2'$, $Z_{2-1}$.)

A number of important points should be understood from the foregoing discussion. Product-moment correlational analysis serves to summarize the relationship between two variables. The correlation coefficient $r$ defines a line of best fit between one variable and another. For each score on one variable, there is a corresponding predicted score on the other variable. Unless the correlation is perfect, the variance of such predictions is less than that of the variable being predicted. Error scores are uncorrelated with predicted scores and uncorrelated with scores on the variable used as a basis of prediction. Correlational analysis then serves to partition the variance of a particular variable into two independent, or *orthogonal*, sources—one source which can be explained by another variable and a second source which cannot be explained by that other variable. For the variable being predicted, $z_2$, the variance is partitioned into two additive components, and the sum of squared correlations with these two components is 1.00. This is why it is meaningful to speak of the squared correlation as equaling a percent (really a fraction) of variance and why it is meaningful to speak of correlational analysis as decomposing the variance of one variable into parts attributable to different sources. In factor analysis, this logic is expanded to permit the partitioning of one variable into sources of variance that can, and cannot, be accounted for by *combinations* of other variables. Unless you thoroughly understand everything that has been said so far in this chapter about fundamental principles of correlational analysis, you should go back to the first page and read this material carefully again. Most of the complex methods of analysis required in psychometric theory grow from these simple statistical roots.

**Error of estimate**  In addition to viewing PM correlation in terms of obtaining a best-fit straight line for the relationship between two sets of standard scores, it is also useful to think of correlation in terms of the errors of estimate. Previously the variance of the errors of estimate was symbolized as $\sigma^2_{2-1}$, which will now be abbreviated as $\sigma^2_e$. If both variables are expressed as standard scores, then

$$\sigma^2_e = 1 - r^2 \tag{4-13}$$

and

$$\sigma_e = \sqrt{1 - r^2} \tag{4-14}$$

The latter, being the standard deviation of the errors of estimate, is referred to as the *standard error of estimate* (in the special case where the dependent variable is expressed as standard scores). If both variables are expressed as raw scores or deviation scores rather than as standard scores, Eqs. (4-13) and (4-14) would be modified as follows:

$$\sigma^2_e = \sigma^2_y(1 - r^2) \tag{4-15}$$

$$\sigma_e = \sigma_y \sqrt{1 - r^2} \tag{4-16}$$

In Eqs. (4-15) and (4-16), $\sigma^2_y$ is the variance of the variable being estimated, the so-called dependent variable. Equation (4-16) is the general form of the standard error of estimate. In the special case of standard scores for the dependent variable, $\sigma_y$ "falls out" of the equation. The variance and standard deviation of errors of estimate depend only on the correlation between the two variables and the variance of the dependent variable. The standard-score formulas are special cases of Eqs. (4-15) and (4-16). Since for standard scores $\sigma_y$ is 1.0, it "falls out" of the standard-score formulas.

Several points should be clear from an examination of the formulas regarding the variance and standard deviation of errors of estimate and from prior discussions of the nature of errors of estimate. First, there is an inverse relationship between the squared correlation and the variance of the errors of estimate. The more the points tend to scatter about the best-fit line, the less the correlation. Second, $\sigma_e$ is useful in certain situations for setting confidence intervals for estimating scores on one variable from scores on another variable. Thus if it is known that an aptitude test correlates .50 with college grade-point averages, confidence intervals could be set for predictions of the dependent variable. It might be found, for example, that for students scoring 85 or higher on the aptitude test, the odds are less than 5 in 100 that a grade-point average of less than 1.0 (C average) would be obtained in college.

The third, and most important, point about the variance of errors of estimate is that it offers an approach to the development of many indices of relationship between variables. The formula for $\sigma_e^2$ can be rearranged as follows:

$$\sigma_e^2 = \sigma_y^2(1 - r^2)$$

$$r^2 = 1 - \frac{\sigma_e^2}{\sigma_y^2} \tag{4-17}$$

Thus the correlation is inversely related to the ratio of $\sigma_e^2$ to $\sigma_y^2$. When $\sigma_e^2$ is as large as $\sigma_y^2$, the correlation is zero; when $\sigma_e^2$ is very small relative to $\sigma_y^2$, the correlation is very high. This very important ratio will be spoken of as the *relative amount of error* (RE) in estimating any dependent variable. Also, it will be useful to talk about RE as a percentage. Thus if $\sigma_e^2$ is 5 and $\sigma_y^2$ is 10, it will be said that the RE is 50 percent. Whereas RE has been discussed with respect to a linear relationship between two variables, the concept extends to (1) any number of variables used to estimate a dependent variable and (2) any form of relationship, linear or otherwise. In addition, the RE is directly related to various ratios of sums of squares obtained in analysis of variance of controlled experiments. The RE is a direct measure of the *strength of relationship* both in correlational investigations and in the analysis of experiments. These extensions will be discussed in later sections.

## OTHER USES OF PM CORRELATION

In this section three indices of relationship will be discussed: phi, point-biserial, and rho. There apparently is some confusion in the minds of nonspecialists about these coefficients. Frequently it is assumed that these coefficients are dif-

ferent from one another and that they are all different from the PM formula
[Eq. (4-1)]. Both assumptions are incorrect. All three of these "other" coefficients are the same, and they are all the same as the "regular" PM coefficient.
Such "other" coefficients are sometimes thought to be different because the
computations "look" different, but this is entirely because of the type of data to
which they are applied rather than a different mathematical rationale. Some
shortcut formulas have been developed for cases where one or both of the variables are not continuous, e.g., for correlating two dichotomous variables. These
are only special cases of the PM formula, and aside from the convenience of
working with such shortcut formulas when computers are not available, the PM
formula could be used to obtain exactly the same result that would be obtained
from phi, point-biserial, or rho.

**Phi** When both distributions are dichotomous, a shortcut version of the PM coefficient is available which is called "phi." Phi can be illustrated in the situation
where two test items are being correlated:

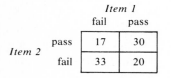

The above diagram shows the scores for 100 students on two items. It indicates,
for example, that 30 students pass both items and 33 fail both items. It is convenient to symbolize the four quadrants as follows:

*Item 1*

| | |
|---|---|
| b | a |
| c | d |

*Item 2*

A shortcut version of the PM coefficient is obtained as follows:

$$\text{phi} = \frac{ac - bd}{\sqrt{(a + b)(c + d)(b + c)(a + d)}} \tag{4-18}$$

There is a very useful relationship between phi and chi-square:

$$\text{chi-square} = N\,(\text{phi})^2 \tag{4-19}$$

Chi-square is obtained by squaring phi and multiplying by the number of persons involved in the correlation. A test of the null hypothesis for zero correlation can then be made by referring the obtained value to a table of chi-square
with one degree of freedom.

　　As was mentioned previously, although the formula for phi looks different
from the PM formula, the former is only a special case of the latter. When
correlating two dichotomous distributions, exactly the same results as obtained

from phi would be obtained by standardizing scores and placing these in the PM formula. If half the persons pass one item and passes are scored 1 and failures scored 0, all persons passing would have a standard score of $+1$ and all failing would have a standard score of $-1$. Such standard scores may look rather strange, but that does not disturb the mathematics of the PM correlation.

Before the advent of high-speed computers, phi was frequently applied to artificially dichotomized variables. For example, in item analysis, dichotomous item scores can be correlated with artificially dichotomized total scores on the test. One way to dichotomize total scores is to make all scores below the median 0 and all scores at or above the median 1. Phi could then be used to correlate each item with total test scores. Unless computational labor is a very important consideration (it seldom is these days), it is unwise to artificially dichotomize one or both of the variables being investigated. If both variables are continuous, it is best to apply the regular PM formula. If one variable is inherently dichotomous (e.g., pass-fail on test items) and one is continuous, it is best to apply point-biserial, which will be discussed in the next section. Information is always lost when a continuous variable is artificially dichotomized. As a shortcut version of the PM coefficient, phi is the preferred measure of relationship when variables are inherently dichotomous.

**Point-biserial** When one dichotomous variable is to be correlated with a continuous variable, a shortcut version of the PM formula called *point-biserial* ($r_{pb}$) is available. The most frequent occasion for employing this formula is in correlating a dichotomous test item (e.g., pass-fail) with total scores on a test. The shortcut formula is as follows:

$$r_{pb} = \frac{M_s - M_u}{\sigma} \sqrt{pq} \qquad (4\text{-}20)$$

where $M_s$ = mean score on continuous variable of "successful" group on dichotomous variable

$M_u$ = mean score on continuous variable of "unsuccessful" group on dichotomous variable

$\sigma$ = standard deviation on continuous variable for total group

$p$ = proportion of persons falling in "successful" group on dichotomous variable

$q = 1 - p$

Point-biserial can be applied in any situation where one of the two variables is dichotomous, in addition to that in which the dichotomy consists of being successful rather than unsuccessful in a particular task. For example, the formula could be applied to agreeing or disagreeing with a statement concerning attitudes toward abortion. It does not matter how the two means are designated by subscripts, and it is irrelevant which category of the dichotomy is represented by $p$ and which is represented by $q$.

As was true of phi, $r_{pb}$ was sometimes employed in the past where one of two continuous variables was artificially dichotomized. For example, rather than employ the regular PM formula to the continuous scores on two tests, scores on one of the two tests were dichotomized, the "cut" most frequently being done at the median. Then the shortcut formula was applied. This is very poor practice, however. The saving in computational time is not great, and fuller information would be obtained by correlating the two continuous variables. Point-biserial is the preferred measure of correlation when one variable is continuous and the other is inherently dichotomous, e.g., pass-fail or male-female. As was mentioned previously, the numerical result obtained by applying the regular PM formula is exactly the same as that which would be obtained from the shortcut version $r_{pb}$.

**Rho** For correlating two sets of ranks, a shortcut version of the PM formula called "rho" is available. The formula could be used, for example, to correlate the rankings of two judges on the extent to which 20 patients had improved in the course of psychotherapy. The formula is as follows:

$$\text{rho} = 1 - \frac{6\Sigma d^2}{N(N^2 - 1)} \tag{4-21}$$

where $N$ = number of objects or persons ranked
$d$ = algebraic difference in ranks for each object or person in two distributions of ranks

Although rho is sometimes spoken of as a "nonparametric" index of relationship, this certainly is not the case. Rho is only a shortcut version of the regular PM formula. Results obtained by applying rho are exactly the same as those obtained by applying the regular PM formula to two sets of ranks.

There are three possible reasons for employing rho. First, two continuous distributions can be converted to ranks and rho applied to save computational labor. This is a poor reason, though, because the savings in computational time is not great with a desk calculator, and there is no savings in time at all if high-speed computers are available. In this instance, rho applied to the ranks would usually be very close to the regular PM formula applied to the continuous variables, particularly if both continuous variables are approximately normally distributed. A second reason for applying rho is to estimate what the PM correlation would be between two distributions which are markedly different in shape if the two were rescaled to have approximately the same shape. If, for example, one distribution is highly skewed to the left and the other is highly skewed to the right, the PM correlation will be less than it would be if both distributions had the same shape (for reasons that will be discussed in a later section). If both distributions were transformed to have the same shape, say, both were normalized, the correlation would increase somewhat. Before one goes to the labor of transforming the two distributions, it might be useful to estimate how much the variables would correlate after the transformation. This can be done with rho. By ranking scores on the two variables and applying rho, one will obtain a correlation that closely approximates the correlation that would be obtained from the two normalized variables. However, this approach usually takes as much time as is required to make the necessary transformations initially.

The third, and best, reason for employing rho is to correlate two distributions that are inherently expressed as ranks. This would be the case for the example mentioned earlier where 20 patients were ranked with respect to improvement during the course of therapy. When measurement is in the form of rank-order, rho provides a useful index of correlation. Because rho is a PM formula and PM formulas are often said to "require" interval scales, some would call this an "illegitimate" use of rho. It is hard to see much sense in such arguments. Since rho ranges between $+1$ and $-1$, it describes the degree of relationship between two sets of ranks. The direction and size of the coefficient have the same meaning as they do with variables that are more sensibly construed as interval scales. Tests of statistical significance are available (Guilford and Fruchter 1973; and McNemar 1962) when both variables are inherently in the form of rank-order. The use of the PM coefficient allows one to get ranked data into various complex forms of multivariate analysis. Although special coefficients have been developed specifically for ranked data, none of these has the advantages of rho. As a shortcut version of the regular PM formula, rho is the preferred measure of relationship when both variables are inherently in the form of ranks.

## ESTIMATES OF PM COEFFICIENTS

Although they are not PM coefficients themselves, two coefficients have been used to estimate results that would, under special circumstances, be obtained from the PM formula. It will be recommended that these coefficients not be used in most cases, but they are spoken of so frequently in the literature relating to measurement theory that a brief discussion of them is required.

**Biserial** When one variable is dichotomous and the other continuous, the biserial correlation $r_{bis}$ can be used in place of the point-biserial correlation. The formula for $r_{bis}$ is as follows:

$$r_{bis} = \frac{M_s - M_u}{\sigma} \left( \frac{pq}{z} \right) \qquad (4\text{-}22)$$

where $M_s$ = mean score on continuous variable of "successful" group on dichotomous variable

$M_u$ = mean score on continuous variable of "unsuccessful" group on continuous variable

$\sigma$ = standard deviation on continuous variable for total group

$p$ = proportion falling in "successful" group on dichotomous variable

$q = 1 - p$

$z$ = ordinate of normal curve corresponding to $p$

Biserial can be used to estimate the PM correlation that would be obtained from two continuous distributions if the dichotomized variable were normally distributed. The biserial correlation can be used in all the circumstances mentioned previously for the point-biserial correlation. In the past, $r_{bis}$ has been used to save computational time over that required for the PM coefficient. This could be done by "cutting" one distribution at the median and then computing $r_{bis}$ rather than $r$ (but with high-speed computers available these days, no time at all is saved). Another use of $r_{bis}$ is to correlate scores on an inherently dichotomous variable with those on a continuous variable. For example, a preliminary form of a questionnaire might employ dichotomous items, e.g., agree-disagree. If the preliminary form is successful, it is planned to construct a form in which each item will be rated on an 11-point scale of agreement. The success of each item is the extent to which it correlates with performance in a learning experiment. The biserial correlation of each dichotomous item with the criterion (success in the learning experiment) would be an estimate of the PM correlation that would be obtained by correlating the 11-point scale with the criterion.

**Tetrachoric correlation** If we take the logic of biserial correlation a step further, the tetrachoric correlation coefficient $r_t$ is used to estimate the PM correlation of two continuous, normally distributed variables from dichotomized versions of those variables. One use of $r_t$ would be with two continuous variables that have been artificially dichotomized, such as two continuous variables each of which has been "cut" at the median. Another use of $r_t$ is with two variables which are inherently dichotomous at the time of the analysis. The purpose here would be to estimate what the PM coefficient would be *if* the two variables were continuous, e.g., the correlation between two questionnaire items scored on 11-point scales rather than in terms of dichotomous responses.

Exact computing formulas for $r_t$ are extremely complex, and even some of the approximate formulas are rather involved. Instead of employing the formulas, it is better to use the computing diagrams available for the purpose (discussed in Guilford and Fruchter 1973).

**Use of $r_{bis}$ and $r_t$** There are very strong reasons for *not* using $r_{bis}$ and $r_t$ in most of the ways that they have been used in the past. If continuous scores are available for both variables, any savings in computational labor over the regular PM coefficient is not worth the dangers involved. If high-speed computers are available, as they are in so many research settings these days, then hundreds of PM correlations can be obtained almost literally in the blink of an eye. First, if one variable or both are inherently dichotomous, usually it is illogical to estimate what the PM coefficient would be if both variables were continuous. Unless subsequent steps are made to turn the dichotomous variables into continuous variables, such estimates only fool one into thinking that the variables have explanatory power beyond that which they actually have. It is tempting to employ

$r_{bis}$ and $r_t$ rather than phi and $r_{pb}$, because the former usually are larger—further from zero in either the negative or positive direction except in the special case where either of the two coefficients is actually zero. Unless the $p$ values of both dichotomous variables are the same, phi will be less than $r_t$. Point-biserial is always less than $r_{bis}$, and if the $p$ value of the dichotomous variable is considerably different from .50 in either direction, $r_{bis}$ will be much larger than $r_{pb}$. Then to use $r_{bis}$ is to paint a faulty picture of the actual size of correlations obtainable from existing data.

A second reason for *not* employing $r_{bis}$ and $r_t$ is that, even if it were sensible to make such estimates of the PM coefficient between two continuous variables, they frequently are very poor estimates. Both these coefficients very much depend on a strict assumption of the normality of the continuous variables, either of the variables that have been artificially dichotomized or of continuous variables that are to be generated later. When the assumption of normality is not met, the estimates can be off by more than 20 points of correlation. The author once had occasion to compare a biserial correlation between two continuous variables (one being dichotomized at the median for the analysis) with the regular PM coefficient applied to the continuous variables. The former was .71 and the latter was .52! The amount of error that often is found by employing biserial and other such estimates of the regular PM coefficient shows that these estimates generally should not be employed.

If the foregoing are not reasons enough for generally avoiding use of $r_{bis}$ and $r_t$, there is another important reason. Whereas it was said that one of the great virtues of PM correlation is that it opens the door to many powerful methods of analysis, this is not true for the two estimates of PM correlation. After one obtains $r_{bis}$ and $r_t$, there is very little that can be done with them mathematically. It should be strongly emphasized that, strictly speaking, it is illegitimate to use such estimates in partial correlation, multiple correlation, or in any other form of multivariate analysis. For example, one still sees instances of $r_t$ employed in factor analysis. In employing $r_{bis}$ and $r_t$ in multivariate analysis, the experimenter can claim that these are estimates of the PM formula and thus can be used like PM coefficients. In a strict sense this is not mathematically proper and should be tolerated only in the study of mathematical models relating to psychometric theory and not in analyzing the results of actual research on people.

After this scathing denunciation of $r_{bis}$ and $r_t$, it should be pointed out that there is one important, legitimate use for these coefficients. The use is in the development of mathematical models relating to measurement theory. It might be necessary, for example, in one mathematical model concerning test construction to assume that all the items have the same biserial correlation with total test scores or the same tetrachoric correlation with one another. This might permit the development of some useful principles which could be tested in empirical studies. There is nothing wrong with using $r_{bis}$ and $r_t$ in mathematical models, but they definitely should not be used to determine the correlation between sets of empirical data.

# OTHER MEASURES OF CORRELATION

In addition to the measures of correlation discussed in the previous section, many other measures of the degree of relationship between two variables have been developed. (See the discussion in Guilford and Fruchter 1973.) None of these has achieved the prominence of the PM coefficient, because none fits as neatly into the mathematical developments required for psychometric theory in general, e.g., test construction, determining reliability, factor analysis, and many other areas where methods of multivariate analysis are needed.

In this discussion of the value of different approaches to correlational analysis, it should become clear why it was stated in Chap. 1 that it is essential to employ methods of analysis appropriate to interval scales. (In the case of the rank-order correlation coefficient rho, it was even argued that in some cases methods that depend upon interval scales should be employed with ranks.) It was shown that the PM coefficient is a function of the ratio of two variances, the variance of the errors of estimate divided by the variance of the dependent measure [Eq. (4-17)]. The variance is a sensible index of dispersion only when the intervals of the scale are taken seriously. To forsake the interval would be to forsake the variance, and to forsake the variance would be to forsake all the powerful methods of analysis that are needed.

What is lost when the assumption of an interval scale is forsaken is illustrated by the attempt to develop nonparametric correlation coefficients for ranked data. (Previously it was pointed out that rho is not a nonparametric index of relationship.) The only index that has achieved prominence is Kendall's tau (Kendall 1948). Although tau is an index of the extent to which persons or objects are ordered alike on two variables, and the sampling distribution of the index is known, it has been used very little in research. The reason is that, like so many other non-PM measures, it is very difficult to extend tau to problems of multivariate analysis.

# FACTORS THAT INFLUENCE THE PM CORRELATION

**Assumptions** It is frequently said that there are certain assumptions that must be met in employing the *PM* coefficient for two continuous distributions. First, it is said that there must be a linear relationship; that is, a straight line must do a good job of describing the trend, regardless of how much points may scatter above and below the line. If the trend of correspondence is highly irregular or there is a definite curve in the trend line, the assumption of linearity would not be met. (Methods of analysis for these situations will be mentioned later in the chapter.) Second, it is said that each of the variables must be normally distributed. Third, it is said that the relationship must be *homoscedastic* rather than heteroscedastic. In the former case, the spread about the best-fitting straight line is approximately the same at all levels of the two variables. In the latter case, the spread is much more at certain levels of the variables than at others. For the latter case, it might, for example, be found in correlating an aptitude test with college grades that the spread of grades about the best-fit line is considerably larger for persons who score high on the test than it is for persons who score low on the test.

There has been considerable controversy as to whether the above three characteristics should be considered "assumptions" in correlational analysis. Strictly speaking, these three assumptions are important for two purposes, the first of which is employing inferential statistics relating to correlational analysis. When these three characteristics are present, the relationship is said to be *bivariate normal*. The bivariate-normal distribution is an assumption in developing inferential statistics relating to PM correlations, e.g., "tests of significance" of the departure of a particular correlation from zero, and, much more importantly, in the many inferential statistics employed with complex methods of multivariate analysis. To the extent to which any of the three assumptions is not met and consequently bivariate-normality is not precisely obtained, probability statements about the correlations might not be exactly correct. However, this is not a great problem. Unless one of the assumptions were seriously violated, inferential statistics would not be highly erroneous. An example of a "serious" violation would be to correlate a normally distributed variable with scores from a *J* curve. Also, if there is some evidence of departure from the assumptions, a safe procedure is to use a higher level of "significance" than ordinarily would be required, e.g., to require that differences be significant at the .001 level rather than at the .01 level.

The second reason for considering normality of distributions, linearity of relationships, and homoscedasticity is that these are assumptions not so much for *using* the PM coefficient as for *interpreting* the results. Thus there is nothing to prevent the use of PM correlation even if one of the distributions is markedly different from the other in shape, if the relationship is far from linear, and if the spread of points is different at different places along the line. Unless these assumptions are seriously violated, no real problem in interpretation is involved. For example, if there is a moderate departure from linearity (say, the trend of correspondence tends to "flatten out" over the high end of the independent variable), no great damage is done in using the regular PM coefficient. It might be slightly more appropriate to employ a nonlinear measure (which will be discussed later), but the difference would not be large. Unless there is a marked curve in the relationship, the linear measure gives much the same results as does the curvilinear measure.

If the relationship were strongly heteroscedastic, the PM correlation would fail to reveal some important information. It would not reveal that the relationship was much stronger at certain levels of the variables than at others. This would be important in testing a theory or in using a test to select first-year college students. If the two variables have very differently shaped distributions, that is important, because it artificially forces a degree of nonlinearity and a degree of heteroscedasticity in the relationship.

**Restriction of range** Previously it was shown that the correlation is inversely related to the relative error (RE) $\sigma_e^2/\sigma_y^2$. It should be obvious that the correlation is a function of the variance of the dependent variable. Thus if a broader range of subjects is studied, the correlation will increase; if a narrower range of subjects is studied, the correlation will decrease. If the assumption of homoscedasticity is justifiable, then $\sigma_e$ should be approximately the same for the different sizes of $\sigma_y$ that would be obtained in different samples. Thus, in sampling broader or more narrow groups of persons, $\sigma_e$ would tend to remain a constant, but $\sigma_y$ would vary over the different groups being sampled. The change in variance must be a *real* change arising from differences in sampling methods. The correlation is not affected by *artificial* changes in the variance, as would be the case if all the scores on the dependent variable were multiplied by 5. In that case $\sigma_y$ and $\sigma_e$ would increase proportionally, and consequently the correlation would remain the same.

Whereas the effect of variance on correlation was illustrated with respect to the variance of the dependent variable, the effect is the same regardless of which of the two variances is altered. If a change in sampling doubles the variance of $y$, the effect on the correlation would be the same as if a change in sampling had doubled the variance of $x$. As mentioned previously, which variable in correlational analysis is called the dependent variable and which is called the independent variable is only a matter of convenience. The correlation is the same either way. Rather than obtain a standard error for estimating $y$ from $x$, it would be just as sensible to obtain a standard error for estimating $x$ from $y$. This could be done by substituting $\sigma_x$ for $\sigma_y$ in Eq. (4-16). In Eq. (4-16) it can be seen that $\sigma_e$ for predicting $y$ is the same as $\sigma_e$ for predicting $x$ when both variables are expressed as standard scores, because in both cases the standard deviations are 1.00 and thus drop out of the equation. However, in predicting one variable from another when both are expressed as deviation scores or raw scores, the standard deviations of the variables would be 1.00 only by the sheerest chance. The standard deviations may be much smaller or much larger than 1.00. Also, usually the standard deviations are different in size, e.g., one could be based on a test with only 20 items and another could be based on a test with 100 items, which would probably lead to very different-sized standard deviations. (It should be remembered that the standard deviation of a set of deviation scores is always exactly the same as the standard deviation of the set of raw scores from which the deviation scores were obtained.) Thus, in predicting deviation scores or raw scores, usually $\sigma_e$ is different depending on which variable is used to predict the other. However, in the case where $x$ is being estimated from $y$ rather than vice versa, the correlation is inversely related to the squared standard error of estimating $x$ from $y$ divided by $\sigma_x^2$. RE is the same either way. Also, when the correlation is expressed in this way, it can be seen that variations in the standard deviation of $x$ caused by different approaches to sampling subjects have a predictable effect on $r$ in the same way as such variations in $\sigma_y$ have from different approaches to sampling.

The usual concern in correlational analysis is with sampling methods that *restrict* the variances, and consequently the problem is referred to as that of *restriction in range*. A restriction occurs when sampling procedures are biased with respect to one of the two variables. Suppose, for example, that an aptitude test is being validated for the selection of first-year college students. The test is administered to all students applying for admission to a particular college. Only the top 50 percent of the students on the aptitude test are selected for admission. Later, scores on the aptitude test of those admitted to college are correlated with grade-point averages. In this case there has been a restriction of range on the aptitude test. The variance of scores on the test would have been much larger had *all* the applicants been admitted to college. Since the test will be used with all applicants, the validity manifested in the restricted sample is spuriously low.

Although the problem has been posed as one of restriction in variance, it is no different when there has been an inflation of variance. Of course, if the variance of either variable is spuriously inflated by the approach to sampling, then the correlation coefficient will be falsely higher than it would be if more appropriate sampling methods had been employed. In any study, what is important to consider is the *appropriate* variance for each variable. What is appropriate depends on the types of scientific statements (generalizations) that are made about data. If the results are to be discussed with respect to people in general, the appropriate variance is found by investigating an unbiased sample of the population in general. If the results are to be discussed with respect to boys between the ages of 7 and 10, the appropriate variance is found in an unbiased sample of that group. If an aptitude test is to be used for the selection of college students only after certain preliminary hurdles are successfully passed, e.g., B average in high school, the appropriate variance is found for all applicants who have B averages in high school.

In any correlational study, if variances are known for the appropriate populations, these variances can be compared with the variances employed to compute a correlation. If the two sets of variances differ appreciably, estimates can be made of what the correlation would be if there were no restriction or elevation of range. Formulas for this purpose are discussed in Guilford and Fruchter (1973).

**Distribution form** Regardless of the shape of either distribution, normal or otherwise, if one is shaped differently from the other, the size of the correlation is restricted. The most obvious evidence of this principle is found in the fact that it is not possible to obtain a perfect correlation between two variables unless they have exactly the same distribution form (normal or otherwise). This is illustrated in Fig. 4-2. The variable $X$ is highly skewed toward the low end, and the variable $Y$ is highly skewed toward the high end. This difference in skewness could be seen by plotting separately the frequency distributions for $X$ and for $Y$. The author tried to depict the highest correlation he could by pairing high scores on $X$ with high scores on $Y$ and vice versa for low scores. Why a

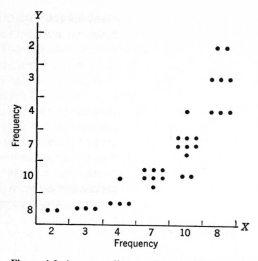

**Figure 4-2** A scatter diagram for two differently shaped distributions of scores.

perfect correlation is not possible is obvious when one tries to place the top eight people on $X$. For there to be a perfect correlation, all eight would have to lie at the highest point on $Y$. But since there are only two persons at the highest point on $Y$, it is necessary to place six of eight persons at lower points on $Y$. Not only is the correlation less than 1.00, but also the relationship is curvilinear, which is the usual accompaniment of correlating differently shaped distributions.

The restriction of the correlation depends on (1) how high the correlation would be if the distributions had the same shape and (2) how different in shape the distributions are. Regarding point 1, whereas the effect was demonstrated with the attempt to obtain a perfect correlation, differences in shapes of distributions have an effect regardless of the size of the correlation. Suppose, for example, two variables have the same-shaped distributions and the correlation is found to be .50. Also assume that the relationship is linear. Then if the form of one distribution is artificially altered, the correlation tends to be less than .50. How much the correlation is lowered depends on the size of the correlation when the distributions are of the same shape. For a correlation of 1.00, a change in shape of one distribution might lower the correlation by 10 or 20 points. As the correlation between the same-shaped distributions becomes less and less, altering the shape of one distribution has less effect. Although no formulas are available for forecasting the amount of change, experience indicates that changes in the shape of one distribution seldom alter a correlation of .50 by more than five points. For correlations of .30 or lower, even drastic changes in the shape of one distribution (e.g., changing a normal distribution to one that is extremely skewed) tend to have very little effect. Thus the results of correlating two continuous variables in most studies in psychology would be about the same whether the distributions were shaped the same or somewhat differently. Correlations as high as .70 are rare, and the average of all correlations reported in the literature probably is less than .40.

The previous statements regarding the insensitivity of differences in distribution shape on moderate-sized correlations are based on the assumption that a relatively large sample of subjects is being investigated, e.g., of at least 100. When correlational studies concern relatively small numbers of subjects, such as 30 or less, *any* changes in the scores, including a mathematical transformation of one or both of the score distributions, can have effects on the correlation that are quite unpredictable. This is one of the many reasons that have been given in this book for basing psychometric theory on a large-sample logic.

Although differences in shapes of distributions tend to have slight effects in studies of *continuous* variables, the effect can be quite large when one or both of the variables is *dichotomous*. At first thought, it might seem odd to speak of a dichotomous distribution as having a "shape," but it is useful to think in that way. All distributions can be thought of as containing a standard area. One can think of pulling and squeezing the area under a normal distribution to form differently shaped distributions, all of which would cover the same area. For a dichotomous distribution, the total area available could be divided into two rectangles proportional to the percentage of persons in each half of the dichotomy. Then it is meaningful to talk about the similarity in shape of two dichotomous distributions or the similarity in shape of a dichotomous distribution to a continuous distribution.

The PM correlation between two dichotomous variables (phi) is restricted by the extent to which the percentage of persons in the "pass" group on one variable is different from the percentage of persons in the "pass" group on the other variable. An example should suffice to show why this is so. Suppose that on item *a* 70 percent pass and 30 percent fail and on item *b* 50 percent pass and 50 percent fail. In Table 4-2 an effort is made to achieve the highest correlation possible in that case. It is quite evident that a perfect correlation cannot be obtained: it would require that all who passed item *a* would have to pass item *b*, but this obviously is not possible. Because 70 percent passed *a* and only 50 percent passed *b*, 20 percent must be failing *b*.

In correlating two dichotomous variables, a perfect positive correlation

**Table 4-2 Correlation table for two items with different *p* values**

|  |  | Percentage of persons Item a | |
|---|---|---|---|
|  |  | fail (30) | pass (70) |
| Percentage of persons Item b | pass (50) | 0 | 50 |
|  | fail (50) | 30 | 20 |

cannot be obtained unless the $p$ values are the same for both variables. To the extent to which they are different, a ceiling is placed on the possible size of a positive correlation. The ceiling on negative correlations is proportional to the extent to which the $p$ value on one item is different from the $q$ value on the other item, and vice versa. Thus if 30 percent pass one item and 70 percent pass another item, it is possible to obtain a correlation of $-1.00$ but not one of $+1.00$. The reverse would be true if 70 percent had *failed* the second item. Figure 4-3 illustrates the degree to which correlations are restricted by differences in $p$ values for the two variables. The figure shows, for example, that if the $p$ value of one item is .5 and the $p$ value of the other item differs by as much as .3 (being either .2 or .8), the correlation cannot be greater than .50. It should be emphasized that the restriction on phi is because of the *difference* in $p$ values for the two variables. A perfect correlation can be found when two variables both have $p$ values of .90 as well as it can for two variables that both have $p$ values of .50.

What was said about the effects of differences in $p$ values on the restriction of phi holds when any two dichotomous variables are correlated, of which a special case is correlating pass or fail on two test items. An example would be correlating responses of males versus females to answers of *yes* or *no* to the question, "Should abortion be legal?" If about equal numbers of male and female subjects are studied, and if the number of *yes* responses is consider-

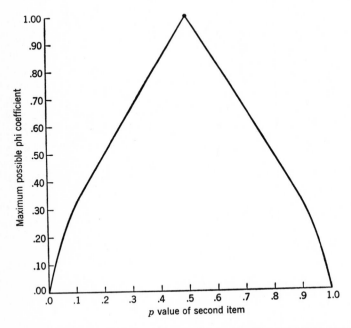

**Figure 4-3** Maximum possible value of the phi coefficient between two test items when the $p$ value of the first item is .5 and the $p$ value of the second item varies from .0 to 1.0.

ably greater than the number of *no* responses, or vice versa, then the size of the possible phi value will be restricted in the manner indicated in Fig. 4-3.

Whereas it is possible to obtain a perfect correlation between two dichotomous variables (phi), it is not possible to obtain a perfect correlation between one dichotomous variable and one continuous variable $r_{pb}$. The reason is that, whereas the distribution shapes can be the same for two dichotomous variables, it is not possible for a dichotomous variable and a continuous variable to have the same shape. Why there cannot be a perfect relationship between a dichotomous variable and a continuous variable is illustrated in Fig. 4-4. For the dichotomous variable, all the scores are on two points. To have a perfect correlation, it would be necessary for all the scores at those two points to fall exactly on two points on the other variable. But since the other variable is continuous, this is not possible. Consequently scores at either of the two points on the dichotomous variable must correspond to a range of points on the continuous variable.

The maximum size of $r_{pb}$ between a dichotomous variable and a normally distributed variable is about .80, which occurs when the *p* value of the dichotomous variable is .50. The further the *p* value deviates from .50 in either direction, the lower the ceiling on $r_{pb}$. This is because the shape of a dichotomous distribution is most similar to that of a normal distribution when *p* is .50.

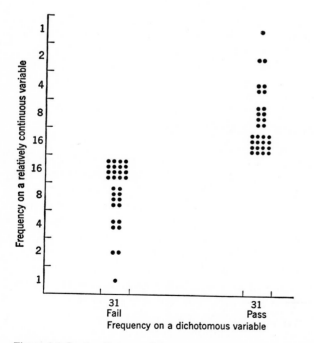

**Figure 4-4** Scatter diagram of the maximum possible correlation between a dichotomous variable that has a *p* value of .5 and a variable that is relatively continuous.

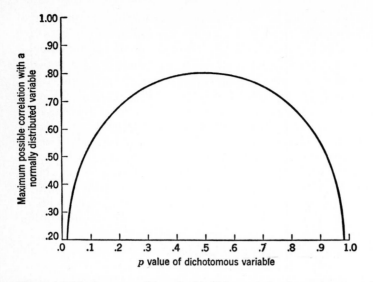

**Figure 4-5** Maximum possible point-biserial correlation between a normally distributed variable and dichotomous variables ranging in *p* values from .0 to 1.0.

When *p* departs from .50, the shape of the dichotomous distribution becomes less and less like that of the normally distributed variable. The ceiling on the correlation between a dichotomous variable and a normally distributed variable $r_{pb}$ as a function of the *p* value of the dichotomous variable is shown in Fig. 4-5. There it is seen, for example, that when *p* is as high as .90 or as low as .10, the maximum possible correlation is about .58.

## A UNIVERSAL MEASURE OF RELATIONSHIP

Correlational analysis has been discussed in this chapter in terms of the best-fitting straight line, but it is entirely possible that relationships in particular studies will not be linear. Linear methods are used wherever possible because they are easily extended to more complex forms of analysis, e.g., factor analysis. Even if there is some departure from linearity in particular comparisons, a best-fitting straight line often does a reasonably good job of describing the degree of relationship. In those instances where the relationship is markedly nonlinear, however, the PM correlation is inappropriate.

Previously it was shown that the PM coefficient is inversely related to the relative error (RE) about the best-fitting straight line, the variance about the line divided by the variance of the dependent measure. The same logic can be used to develop a universal measure of relationship, one that can be used regardless of the form of the relationship. The universal measure is called "eta" or the "correlation ratio." The logic for using eta and the computational procedures are discussed in Kennedy (1970). He provides references to other discussions of the correlation ratio eta.

The first step in obtaining eta is to compute the variance about *any* curve of relationship. This is then divided by the variance of the dependent variable to obtain an RE. When this is subtracted from 1, the result is eta squared. The equation for eta is as follows:

$$(eta)^2 = 1 - RE \tag{4-23}$$

How eta is used is illustrated in Fig. 4-6, which shows a hypothetical relationship between scores on a measure of anxiety and scores on a learning task. Since the relationship is distinctly nonlinear, the PM coefficient would not do a good job of summarizing the trend. What one can do is compute the correlation about the best-fitting smooth curve. The sum of squared deviates in learning scores above and below the curve is divided by the number of points (persons) to obtain the error variance. This is divided by the variance of learning scores to obtain an RE. The RE is subtracted from 1, and the square root of that quantity is eta.

Eta is said to be a "universal" measure of relationship because (1) it can be applied regardless of the form of the relationship, (2) either it can be applied to a predicted curve of relationship or the best-fitting curve can be sought after the data are in hand, and (3) it applies equally well when independent variables are continuous measures and when they are only categorical in nature. It already has been demonstrated why point 1 holds: the RE is as meaningful about a complex curve as it is about a straight line. Regarding point 2, the form of a relationship might be predictable from a theory. Thus the form of the relationship between two variables might be predicted as parabolic or hyperbolic. Curves of these forms could be tried on the data, and eta

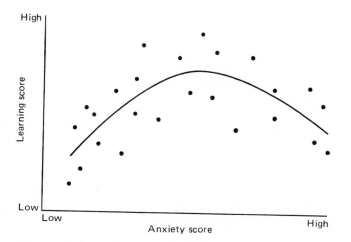

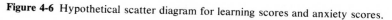

**Figure 4-6** Hypothetical scatter diagram for learning scores and anxiety scores.

would tell how well the curves explained scores in the dependent measure. (The mechanics of fitting curves and obtaining eta in different problems are presented in Lewis 1960.) If no particular curve is predicted for the data, a variety of curves can be tried. The one with the largest eta provides the best fit (in the sense of least squares). At many computer centers, programs are available for automatically fitting the best least-squares curve to any set of points and for directly giving eta as parts of the printout of results. Thus, many computer routines will provide the best-fitting straight line and eta (which is $r$ in that case), the best-fitting quadratic trend line and eta for that circumstance, the best-fitting cubic trend line and eta for that circumstance, and so on for more complex equations for fitting a curve to the observed relationship.

Regarding point 3 above, eta can be applied when the independent variable is a set of categories rather than a continuous variable. This is illustrated in Fig. 4-7, which shows the effect of four different drugs on bar pressing (in a Skinner box) by rats. The independent variable consists of different drugs, and consequently it is arbitrary which drug is listed as $A$ and which is listed as $D$. In this instance it is not meaningful to talk about the "form" of the relationship. There would be nothing wrong with reordering the drugs on the graph, which would drastically change the visible "form" of relationship. Eta can be applied in this case, however, in the same way that it is applied when both variables are continuous. The sum of squared departures can be calculated from the mean score on the dependent measure for each drug. These can be pooled and divided by the total number of rats, which

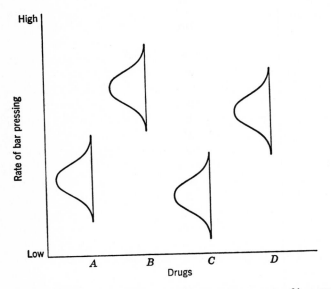

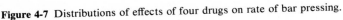

**Figure 4-7** Distributions of effects of four drugs on rate of bar pressing.

provides a measure of error variance. This can be divided by the variance of all scores on the dependent measure to provide an RE, which can, in turn, be converted to eta.

Eta can be applied in any study where the *dependent* measure is continuous, or at least relatively so. The logic extends to all forms of analysis of variance. Customarily one thinks in terms of the $F$ ratio, in which the variance estimate from any systematic source (e.g., different drugs) is divided by an appropriate error term (e.g., pooled "within" variance of scores on the dependent measure). Although the $F$ ratio is useful in applying inferential statistics, eta indicates *how strong* the relationship is. Eta measures the *explanatory power* of an independent variable. The statistical significance of the $F$ ratio depends on the number of subjects, but eta is independent of the number of subjects. If a large number of subjects is involved in the study, it is possible for the $F$ ratio to be "highly significant"; but when the $F$ ratio is converted to eta, it might be found that only a small portion of the variance of the dependent measure is explained by the independent measure. Whereas it is important to employ inferential statistics, it also is important to determine the strength of relationships, which can be done with eta.

The correlation ratio, eta, provides a direct tie-in between the correlational statistics that most frequently are employed with psychometric theory and the statistics based on analysis of variance that are employed most often with controlled experiments. Previously a use of eta was illustrated in an analysis of variance-type design concerning one treatment factor, that of four drugs in Fig. 4-7. It was shown there that the RE and eta apply to experimental designs as well as they do to correlational analysis such as in correlating two tests. The concept of RE and eta can be extended to complex correlational problems and complex experimental designs in analysis of variance. In analysis of variance designs where there is more than one factor, an eta can be obtained for each treatment factor. For example, with respect to the experiment depicted in Fig. 4-7, one could have added a second factor concerning three levels of amounts of each drug. Then one could have obtained not only a significance test for the drugs overall, but also a significance test for dosage levels and for the interaction of dosage levels and drugs. Then this would have led to three correlation ratios, one for drugs as a main effect, one for dosage levels as a main effect, and one for interaction. One approach is to divide the sums of squares attributable to any systematic source, including sources due to interaction, by the total sum of squares, which produces the squared correlation ratio, eta square, for that source of variance. For alternative approaches, see Kennedy (1970). When one looks carefully at the complex statistics based on correlational analysis that are usually employed in psychometric theory and compares these with the complex methods of analysis of variance that are employed most frequently in psychological experiments, one will see that basically they are the same statistics in different-appearing forms.

The PM coefficient can be thought of as a special case of eta. When both variables are continuous and the RE is computed with respect to the best-fitting straight line, eta reduces to the PM coefficient. What has been intended in this section is to show that the logic behind the PM coefficient is very general. The concept of relative error, and the correlation ratio more generally, can be used to measure the degree of relationship regardless of whether or not (1) the investigation is of correlations among sets of individual differences or concerned with the effects of experimental treatments; (2) the relationship is linear or of some other form; (3) the form of the relationship is hypothesized before the study is undertaken or sought after the data are in hand; (4) the independent variables are in the form of ratio scales, interval scales, ordinal scales, or only categories; and (5) there are only two variables involved or numerous variables involved in the analysis.

## SUGGESTED ADDITIONAL READINGS

Baggley, A. R. *Intermediate correlational methods.* New York: Wiley, 1964, chaps. 1 to 3.

Guilford, J. P., and Fruchter, B. *Fundamental statistics in psychology and education* (5th ed.). New York: McGraw-Hill, 1973, chaps. 5, 6, 12, and 15.

McNemar, Q. *Psychological statistics.* New York: Wiley, 1962, chaps. 8, 12.

# CHAPTER FIVE

# MULTIVARIATE CORRELATIONAL ANALYSIS

As was mentioned in the previous chapter, one of the benefits of working with PM correlation formulas is that they are easily extended to problems of multivariate analysis. Multivariate analysis is possible with nonlinear counterparts (eta) of the PM coefficient, but such methods are tedious to apply. Probably for some time to come most forms of multivariate correlational analysis will be outgrowths of linear PM correlation. As was stated previously, even in cases where relations are not strictly linear, linear measures often do a satisfactory job of describing the trends. Also, if a variable typically has monotonic, but nonlinear, relations with other variables, frequently it can be rescaled to achieve relations more nearly linear. As some have suggested, until the *data* in psychology are generally better than they are, it would be unwise in most cases to abandon linear methods of multivariate correlational analysis for more cumbersome methods that take account of nonlinear relations.

Multivariate analysis will be treated more extensively in Chaps. 10 through 12. In this chapter it will be necessary to discuss some of the foundations of multivariate analysis to make meaningful the material in Chaps. 6 to 9. Also to be discussed in this chapter are the variance of linear combinations (sums) of variables, characteristics of score distributions, the correlation of sums, multiple correlation, and partial correlation. They are important in the development, validation, and use of measurement methods in research.

## VARIANCE OF LINEAR COMBINATIONS

Usually distributions of scores being studied are obtained by summing other distributions of scores. In the simplest case, the total scores on a test usually are obtained by summing item scores. Then the total-score distribution is a linear combination, or sum, of the dichotomous distributions of item scores. As another example, an attitude scale might consist of 20 statements, half of them favorable toward the United Nations and half unfavorable. Each statement would be rated on a seven-step scale of agreement-disagreement. A total scale score could be obtained by adding all the ratings of positive statements and subtracting ratings of negative statements. The total score would then be a linear combination of the item scores. As another example, if standard scores on three tests are added (with or without weights) for assigning grades in introductory psychology, the total distribution is a linear combination of the three distributions of test scores.

There are some very important relations between the characteristics of score distributions and linear combinations of such distributions. Once these are thoroughly understood, more complex methods of multivariate analysis are easily developed. A simple linear combination ($y$) of three variables is as follows:

$$y = x_1 + x_2 + x_3 \tag{5-1}$$

Because the results from most multivariate analyses are the same regardless of whether one starts with raw scores or deviation scores, it will be more convenient to develop methods from equations employing deviation scores, like that above. In Eq. (5-1), each person's score on $y$ is obtained by summing the score on the three $x$ measures. (The principles which will be developed are the same if some of the variables in the linear combination are subtracted rather than added.) It should be obvious that the mean of $y$ is zero; $y$ is in deviation-score form. A typical nonlinear measure would be one in which some of the $x$ variables are multiplicatively combined, as follows:

$$y = x_1 + x_2 + x_3 + x_1x_2 + x_1x_3 + x_2x_3$$

A very useful principle in studying linear combinations of variables is that many of the mathematical properties of linear combinations can be learned by substituting the linear combination in the equations that hold for individual distributions. Thus the variance of the previously given linear combination is obtained as follows:

$$\sigma_y^2 = \frac{\Sigma y^2}{N}$$

$$= \frac{\Sigma (x_1 + x_2 + x_3)^2}{N} \tag{5-2}$$

$$= \frac{1}{N} \Sigma(x_1^2 + x_2^2 + x_3^2 + 2x_1x_2 + 2x_1x_3 + 2x_2x_3)$$

$$= \sigma_1^2 + \sigma_2^2 + \sigma_3^2 + 2\sigma_{12} + 2\sigma_{13} + 2\sigma_{23}$$

In the general case, the variance of any sum of variables $\sigma_\Sigma^2$ is obtained as follows:

$$\sigma_\Sigma^2 = \Sigma\sigma_i^2 + 2\Sigma\sigma_{ij} \qquad i \neq j \qquad (5\text{-}3)$$

The variance of a sum of variables equals the sum of the variances of the variables plus twice the sum of all possible covariances among variables. Because of the relationship between $r_{ij}$ and $\sigma_{ij}$, Eq. (5-3) also can be expressed as

$$\sigma_\Sigma^2 = \Sigma\sigma_i^2 + 2\Sigma r_{ij}\sigma_i\sigma_j \qquad i \neq j$$

There is a very useful method for depicting the variance of a linear combination, one that will make it easier to understand more complex matters regarding multivariate analysis. One way to expand the terms in the variance of a linear combination is as follows. First, the terms are placed along the top and side of a table, as follows:

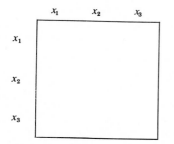

Corresponding elements are multiplied as follows:

|       | $x_1$     | $x_2$     | $x_3$     |
|-------|-----------|-----------|-----------|
| $x_1$ | $x_1^2$   | $x_1 x_2$ | $x_1 x_3$ |
| $x_2$ | $x_1 x_2$ | $x_2^2$   | $x_2 x_3$ |
| $x_3$ | $x_1 x_3$ | $x_2 x_3$ | $x_3^2$   |

If some of the variables have negative signs, then these signs would appear on the top and sides of the table and would be shown in appropriate combinations within the table. To obtain the elements in the variance of a linear combination of the three variables above [Eq. (5-3)], a summation sign is placed in front of each of the nine elements in the table, and each resulting sum is divided by the number of persons in the study $N$. This results in the following table:

|  | $x_1$ | $x_2$ | $x_3$ |
|---|---|---|---|
| $x_1$ | $\sigma_1^2$ | $\sigma_{12}$ | $\sigma_{13}$ |
| $x_2$ | $\sigma_{12}$ | $\sigma_2^2$ | $\sigma_{23}$ |
| $x_3$ | $\sigma_{13}$ | $\sigma_{23}$ | $\sigma_3^2$ |

A look back at Eq. (5-2) will show that the above table contains all the elements in the variance of a sum of three variables. The sum of the elements in the table is then the variance of the sum of the variables ($y$). Any rectangular table of variables such as the one above is called a *matrix*. The matrix above is called a *covariance matrix*. This is often spoken of as a variance-covariance matrix, because the diagonal elements actually are variances rather than covariances; however, because of the many places in which the term will be used, it is much simpler to refer to it as a covariance matrix. In going down from left to right, the diagonal elements of the matrix are the covariances of the variables with themselves, which are the variances of the variables. Off of the diagonal are the covariances of the variables with one another. All possible covariances (three in this instance) are shown above the diagonal and again below the diagonal. What has been shown is that the variance of the linear combination of $k$ variables is equal to the sum of all the elements in the covariance matrix for those $k$ variables.

A covariance matrix will be symbolized as $C$. The covariance matrix is the same for a set of raw scores as for a set of corresponding deviation scores, and consequently the elements of $C$ would be identical in both. Later, subscripts will be used to distinguish different covariance matrices in particular problems. The symbol $\bar{C}$ will be used to symbolize "the sum of all the elements in the covariance matrix $C$." (The use of a bar over $C$ in this way to indicate summing is an unusual symbolism that the reader is not likely to encounter in other books, but the present author finds this a very convenient symbolism in this case.) Then the variance of a sum of variables is $\bar{C}$.

**Variance of a weighted sum** Often weights are applied to each variable before they are summed, as follows:

$$y = b_1 x_1 + b_2 x_2 + b_3 x_3$$

Such weights might be determined either on some a priori basis to give greater importance to some of the variables or a posteriori so as to maximize some characteristic of the variables. (Some weights might be negative and others positive, depending on the nature of the problem.) An example of the former would be when a theory predicts that one variable should be twice as important as another variable in explaining individual differences in some attribute. An example of the latter is multiple regression, where weights are derived in such a way that the weighted sum will correlate as highly as possible with some variable not included in the sum. The variance of a weighted sum is obtained by an extension of the matrix approach for obtaining the variance of an unweighted sum. The only difference is that weights for the variables are shown with the variables on the top and side of the covariance matrix, as follows:

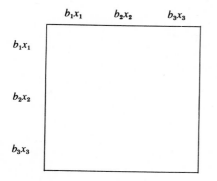

Corresponding elements are multiplied, summation signs are placed before each product, and each such sum is divided by $N$. Each element in the resulting matrix will be a covariance multiplied by the product of the two weights for the two variables. The resulting matrix is as follows:

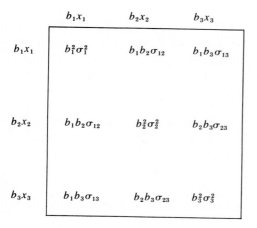

The variance of a weighted sum equals the sum of the elements in the weighted covariance matrix, as shown above. The variances of both weighted and unweighted sums will be said to equal $\bar{C}$. Where there is any likelihood of confusion in a particular instance, it will be stated whether or not weights are involved.

**Variance of a sum of standard scores** The simplest case is that in which the variables to be summed are each expressed as standard scores, as in the following linear combination:

$$y = z_1 + z_2 + z_3$$

In terms of the matrix arrangement for the calculation of the variance of a sum, it is easy to see what results. There are no weights, so no $b$ terms appear in the matrix. The variance of any set of standard scores is 1; consequently 1s will appear in the diagonal spaces. Since the covariance of any two sets of standard scores is the PM correlation between them, $r$'s will appear in the off-diagonal spaces. The result is a correlation matrix, illustrated as follows:

|       | $z_1$    | $z_2$    | $z_3$    |
|-------|----------|----------|----------|
| $z_1$ | 1.00     | $r_{12}$ | $r_{13}$ |
| $z_2$ | $r_{12}$ | 1.00     | $r_{23}$ |
| $z_3$ | $r_{13}$ | $r_{23}$ | 1.00     |

Correlation matrices will be symbolized as $R$. The variance of the sum of $k$ sets of standard scores equals the sum of all the elements in the correlation matrix of those sets of scores. The sum will be symbolized as $\bar{R}$. If variables expressed as standard scores are weighted before they are summed, products of the weights will appear in the correlation matrix in the same way as was shown for a covariance matrix. Because the diagonal 1.00s are variances, they will be positive in all cases. However, the off-diagonal correlation coefficients might be either negative or positive depending upon (1) the natural correlations among the variables or (2) the choice of negative rather than positive weights for some of the variables.

**Variance of sums of dichotomous distributions** One of the most important cases for measurement theory is when the variance of a sum is obtained for $k$ dichotomous variables, as when the total-score variance for $k$ dichotomous items is studied. Where one response is scored 1 and the other 0, the matrix representation shows that the variance of total test scores for a three-item test would be as follows:

|       | $x_1$       | $x_2$       | $x_3$       |
|-------|-------------|-------------|-------------|
| $x_1$ | $p_1 q_1$   | $\sigma_{12}$ | $\sigma_{13}$ |
| $x_2$ | $\sigma_{12}$ | $p_2 q_2$   | $\sigma_{23}$ |
| $x_3$ | $\sigma_{13}$ | $\sigma_{23}$ | $p_3 q_3$   |

The off-diagonal elements would be covariances. Since the variance of a dichotomous item scorable only as 1 and 0 is $pq$, the diagonal is populated with $pq$ values for the items. It will be remembered that the covariance between any two variables equals the PM correlation of the variables multiplied by the product of the standard deviations of the two variables. Consequently the covariance between any two items, say, between items 1 and 2, would be as follows:

$$\sigma_{12} = r_{12} \sqrt{(p_1 q_1)\,(p_2 q_2)} \tag{5-4}$$

The correlation between the two items could be computed by the shortcut formula phi. Since $pq$ grows smaller as $p$ departs from .5 in either direction, the term under the radical will be relatively large when both $p$ values are near .5 and relatively small when both $p$ values are well removed from .5. Also, the diagonal elements will tend to be larger when the $p$ value is close to .5 rather than removed in either direction from that point. These considerations will prove very important in discussing the variance of score distributions and test reliability.

The variance of the sum of $k$ dichotomous items equals the sum of the elements in the covariance matrix for those items, which also will be symbolized as $\bar{C}$. (Only for the sum of the elements in a correlation matrix will the special symbol $\bar{R}$ be employed.) With dichotomous items, $\bar{C}$ equals the sum of $pq$ values plus the sum of all off-diagonal covariances in the matrix.

## CHARACTERISTICS OF SCORE DISTRIBUTIONS

The principles discussed in the previous section, plus some other principles that will be discussed in this section, permit the development of numerous other useful principles concerning the mean, variance, and shape of distributions of test scores. The principles will be developed with respect to test scores obtained by summing scores on dichotomous items, but these principles also hold when items are scorable on more than two points.

**The mean** The mean of raw scores $Y$ on any test composed of dichotomous items scored as 1 or 0 can be developed as follows:

$$M_y = \frac{\Sigma Y}{N}$$

where $Y = X_1 + X_2 + \cdots + X_k$. The distribution of raw scores on the total test $Y$ is a linear combination of scores on the dichotomous items. The mean of $Y$ can be expressed in terms of item scores as follows:

$$M_y = \frac{\Sigma(X_1 + X_2 + \cdots + X_k)}{N}$$

$$= \frac{\Sigma X_1}{N} + \frac{\Sigma X_2}{N} + \cdots + \frac{\Sigma X_k}{N}$$

$$= M_1 + M_2 + \cdots + M_k$$

The sum of scores on any item is simply the number of persons who passed the item. The mean score on the item equals the number who passed divided by the total number of persons, $N$, which equals $p$. In other words, $p$ is the mean of an item scorable only as 1 or 0. Then the mean of total scores on a test composed of such items can be expressed as follows:

$$M_y = p_1 + p_2 + \cdots + p_k \tag{5-5}$$

$$= \Sigma p_i$$

The mean equals the sum of the $p$ values. This holds not only for pass-fail items, but also for any type of dichotomous item that is scored 1 or 0. It would be the case, for example, on an attitude scale containing dichotomous, agree-disagree items. Agreement with positive statements would be scored 1, and *disagreement* with *negative* statements would be scored 1. Other responses would be scored 0. The $p$ value of each positive item would equal the number of persons agreeing divided by the number of persons in the study; the $p$ value of each negative item would equal the number of persons disagreeing divided by the total number of persons. The mean score on the total scale would then equal the sum of the $p$ values.

**Variances** Since the variance of a sum equals the sum of the variances plus twice the sum of the covariances, the variance of any set of test scores is dependent on these two factors. Where the sum of the covariances is zero, the variance of total scores will equal the sum of the item variances. If the items are scored only as 1 or 0 (which will be assumed to be the case throughout this section), the variance of test scores will equal the sum of $pq$ values. The sum of covariances will be zero if all correlations between items are zero or if there is a balance of negative and positive covariances among items. If the sum of covariances is close to zero, this is usually because the correlations among items tend to be quite small, and there is a balance of negative and positive coefficients.

An interesting case is that where the sum of covariances among items is zero and all items have the same $p$ value. In this case the sum of $pq$ would reduce to $k(pq)$, with $k$ standing for the number of items. Thus on a 10-item test, if all items had a $p$ value of .5, the variance of total scores would be 2.5; if all items had a $p$ value of .2 (or .8), the variance of total scores would be 1.6.

In the special case where the sum of the covariance terms is zero and all items have the same $p$ value, the variance of total test scores is the same as that of the *binomial distribution*. An example of the binomial distribution is presented in Fig. 5-1, which shows the expected number of heads obtained when 10 pennies are tossed 1,024 times. The variance of that distribution is precisely $k(pq)$, where $k$ is 10 and $p$ is .5. This tie-in with the binomial distribution permits the development of some very useful principles concerning the properties of score distributions. In the coin-toss example, each coin is analogous to a dichotomous test item. A head can be thought of as passing, receiving a score of 1, and a tail can be thought of as failing, receiving a score of 0. A toss of 10 coins is analogous to the performance of one person on a 10-item test, the number of heads being the person's score.

Several principles should be clear from the foregoing discussion. First, the variance of score distributions tends to be less as the $p$ values of the items are removed from .5. This is so even if the *average $p$* value is .5 but the individual $p$ values vary widely about that point. Second, the average size of correlations (and thus covariances) among items is directly related to the variance of total scores. High positive correlations among items make for a large variance among test scores, and vice versa for low correlations. Because, as will be shown in Chap. 6, high test reliability depends upon positive average correla-

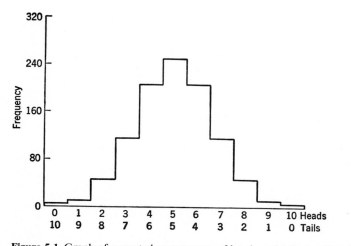

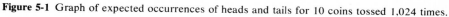

**Figure 5-1** Graph of expected occurrences of heads and tails for 10 coins tossed 1,024 times.

tions among items, a highly reliable test has a larger variance than a less reliable test.

**Distribution shape**  The shape of the test-score distribution is determined by the $p$ values, the covariances among items, and the number of items. As the number of items increases, the distribution becomes less and less jagged and more like a smooth curve. The binomial distribution in Fig. 5-1 is a series of discrete steps rather than a smooth curve, and the same would be true of scores on a 10-item test. The binomial distribution approaches the smooth normal distribution as the number of coins is increased, and a similar smoothing of the curve comes as the number of test items is increased. Of course, this smooth appearance depends upon maintaining approximately the same extension for the horizontal axis of the graph, as in Fig. 5-1. If the horizontal axis were made longer and longer as the number of coins was increased or the number of test items was increased, the stair-step appearance would remain. However, since horizontal axes are not stretched out in that way but retained on the page as in Fig. 5-1, the increase of number of coins or number of test items would lead to an appearance of smoothing.

Strictly speaking, test scores are seldom normally distributed, even if the number of items is large. Because of the positive correlations among items, a normal distribution would not be obtained. In a coin-toss experiment the "items" are expected to be uncorrelated: the probability of one coin turning up heads would be independent of (uncorrelated with) what occurred for the other coins. But it certainly is not expected that the items on psychological measures will be uncorrelated. If they are, they have nothing in common; there is no central "theme," or factor, in their content. If items are uncorrelated, they all measure different things. Then it would not be sensible to give the total score a name or to assume that the total score measures any trait, or even to add scores on the items to obtain a total score.

Most measures of psychological attributes are obtained by adding scores over a collection of responses, of which test items are a special example. The principle applies equally well in studies of the learning rate in rats where the total error score is obtained by adding the number of errors at different points in a maze, and the principle applies in studies of human perception where the total score consists of the number of correct identifications of alphabetical letters that are rapidly presented on a screen one at a time. Reflection will indicate that most measures are comprised of "items." Seldom is a trait measured by only one response.

A precisely normal distribution of test scores, or a binomial distribution, usually would represent *dead data*. Because the items must correlate positively with one another for the measurement method to make any sense, the variance of total scores usually would be larger than that obtained from a binomial distribution. The correlations also serve to flatten the distribution of test scores over that expected in a normal distribution, which is illustrated in Fig. 5-2. What is meant by "flattening" is that, as shown in Fig. 5-2, the tails of the distribution

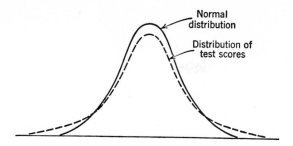

**Figure 5-2** Comparison of a normal distribution with a distribution of test scores.

stretch out more widely in each direction relative to the height at the mean than is the case with a normal distribution. When the average correlation among items is small, as is typically the case, the flattening will be slight. Average correlations as high as .40 would tend to produce a distribution that was markedly flatter than the normal distribution. Further increases in the size of correlations would tend to produce a bimodal distribution. In the limiting case where all correlations among items were 1.00, a person who passed one item would pass all items, and a person who failed one item would fail all items. In that case the total test scores would be distributed over only two points. (In the above cases the shapes of distributions would depend both on the correlations among items and on the $p$ values, but the rules above are approximately correct for widely different sets of $p$ values.)

The typical variation between the distribution of test scores and the normal distribution has been exaggerated somewhat in Fig. 5-2 to show the difference. In most actual research with summative scores obtained from items, the distribution shape is sufficiently similar to the normal distribution so that many of the very useful statistical properties of the normal distribution can be justifiably borrowed.

Whether a distribution is symmetrical or skewed (lopsided) mainly depends on the average $p$ value and the number of items. The influence of $p$ values can be illustrated with a 10-item test in which all $p$ values are .1 (only 10 percent of the subjects pass each item). Since the mean equals $kp$, in this case the mean is 1.0. Then there is practically no room for scores to occur below the mean but considerable room for scores to occur above it. A typical distribution for this case is shown in Fig. 5-3. The nearer $p$ values are to .5, the more symmetrical distributions tend to be. Whenever the average $p$ value departs from .5, there is a tendency for the distribution to be skewed. Average $p$ values below .5 tend to produce distributions that are skewed toward the high end of the scale (said to be "skewed to the right"), and the opposite occurs for average $p$ values above .5. Typical distributions for these cases are shown in Fig. 5-4.

In cases where the $p$ values of items have not been determined, one can simply look at the shape of a score distribution and tell if the average $p$ value is far removed from .5. Thus, if the distribution of total scores is markedly

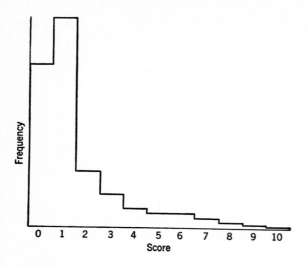

**Figure 5-3** A skewed distribution of test scores where the $p$ value of each item is .1.

skewed to the right, the average item must be rather difficult, and vice versa if the skew is to the left.

If a distribution with a particular number of items is skewed, a very important principle is that the skewness tends to *decrease* as the *number of items* is *increased*. This occurs regardless of the average $p$ value of items. Previously it was shown that a very nonsymmetrical distribution would be obtained for a 10-item test whose items all had $p$ values of .1. If the number of items were increased to 100, the distribution would tend to be more symmetrical. For 1,000 items the distribution would not be skewed in a way that could be seen. In the limiting case where a hypothetical infinity of items was involved, all distributions would be symmetrical regardless of the $p$ values of the items. The reason this is so is that, even if the average $p$ value is extreme in one direction or the other, with a large number of items there is still ample room for scores to spread out above and below the mean.

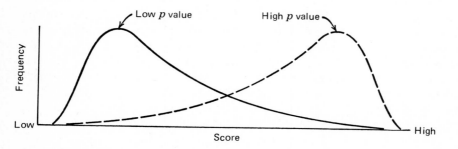

**Figure 5-4** Skewed distributions of scores when the average $p$ value is high and when the average $p$ value is low.

The analogy of the coin-toss experiment with results from psychological measures provides other ways of visualizing how the symmetry of distributions is determined by $p$ values and numbers of items. For this purpose, it will be useful to think of a coin-toss experiment in which 10 biased coins are used. For each coin, the probability of a head is .2, and thus the probability of a tail is .8. The average number of heads for many tosses of the 10 coins would be 2.0. The distribution would be skewed to the right, i.e., the tail of the distribution would be stretched out over the higher numbers of heads. With only 10 coins on each toss, the skewness of the distribution would be marked. As the number of coins on each toss was increased above 10, the skewness would become less and less. In the hypothetical limiting case of an infinite number of such biased coins, the distribution would be precisely normal. A more elaborate proof of this principle follows from the *central limit theorem*, which is a rather complex proof in mathematical statistics. It must be firmly kept in mind that the relative symmetry of the distribution is a function of the number of test items or the number of coins. It is not systematically related to the number of *people* taking a test or, in a coin-toss experiment, the number of times the collection of coins is tossed.

## COVARIANCE OF LINEAR COMBINATIONS

In the previous section it was shown that by "looking inside" the variance of a linear combination, one can generate some useful principles regarding the characteristics of score distributions. In this section some principles concerning the covariance between linear combinations of variables will be discussed. The principles will be illustrated with two linear combinations, each having three variables, but the principles hold regardless of the number of variables in each combination. Following are two linear combinations:

$$y = x_1 + x_2 + x_3$$
$$w = x_4 + x_5 + x_6$$

The $x$'s could relate to dichotomous items, items scorable on more than two points, or total scores on tests. In the previous section it was shown that the variance of $y$ equals the sum of all the elements in the covariance matrix for the variables entering into the linear combination. This sum will be symbolized as $\bar{C}_y$. Similarly, the variance of $w$ would equal $\bar{C}_w$. The covariance of the two linear combinations would be obtained as follows:

$$\sigma_{wy} = \frac{\Sigma wy}{N}$$

$$= \frac{1}{N} \Sigma (x_1 + x_2 + x_3)(x_4 + x_5 + x_6) \tag{5-6}$$

$$= \sigma_{14} + \sigma_{15} + \sigma_{16} + \sigma_{24} + \sigma_{25} + \sigma_{26} + \sigma_{34} + \sigma_{35} + \sigma_{36}$$

The covariance of $y$ and $w$ equals the sum of all covariances *between* members of the two linear combinations. Note that none of the variances is involved and none of the covariances of members *within* each of the two linear combinations is involved. Just as it was useful to display the variance of a linear combination in terms of a matrix of variance and covariance terms, it also is useful to display the covariance of two linear combinations in matrix form. (If some of the variables have negative signs in their linear combinations, these signs would be shown at the appropriate places on the sides of the matrix.) This is done by placing the variables in one linear combination on the top of the matrix and the variables in the other linear combination on the side, as follows:

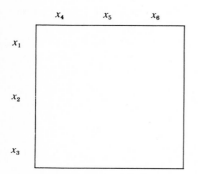

Corresponding terms are multiplied, summed over people, and divided by the number of people. The resulting matrix contains all covariances *between* the two sets of variables, as follows:

|       | $x_4$       | $x_5$       | $x_6$       |
|-------|-------------|-------------|-------------|
| $x_1$ | $\sigma_{14}$ | $\sigma_{15}$ | $\sigma_{16}$ |
| $x_2$ | $\sigma_{24}$ | $\sigma_{25}$ | $\sigma_{26}$ |
| $x_3$ | $\sigma_{34}$ | $\sigma_{35}$ | $\sigma_{36}$ |

The sum of the elements in the above matrix is equal to the covariance of $w$ and $y$. It will be useful to speak of such a matrix as a matrix of "between" covariances to distinguish it from the matrix of "within" covariances involved in the variance of a linear combination. A between matrix will be symbolized as $C_{wy}$, with different sets of double subscripts used where necessary to indicate which linear combinations are involved. The covariance of two linear combinations then is equal to $\bar{C}_{wy}$.

If weights were applied to the terms in each linear combination before they were summed, the weights would appear on the top and side of the matrix and would be appropriately multiplied as follows:

|  | $b_4x_4$ | $b_5x_5$ | $b_6x_6$ |
|---|---|---|---|
| $b_1x_1$ | $b_1b_4\sigma_{14}$ | $b_1b_5\sigma_{15}$ | $b_1b_6\sigma_{16}$ |
| $b_2x_2$ | $b_2b_4\sigma_{24}$ | $b_2b_5\sigma_{25}$ | $b_2b_6\sigma_{26}$ |
| $b_3x_3$ | $b_3b_4\sigma_{34}$ | $b_3b_5\sigma_{35}$ | $b_3b_6\sigma_{36}$ |

In the study of the variance and covariance of linear combinations, it is helpful to think in terms of the total matrix of covariances, which is illustrated in Table 5-1 for two linear combinations with three variables in each. Lines are drawn in

**Table 5-1 Total covariance matrix for two linear combinations $y$ and $w$**

|  |  | $y$ set | | | $w$ set | | |
|---|---|---|---|---|---|---|---|
|  |  | $x_1$ | $x_2$ | $x_3$ | $x_4$ | $x_5$ | $x_6$ |
| $y$ set | $x_1$ | $\sigma_1^2$ | $\sigma_{12}$ | $\sigma_{13}$ | $\sigma_{14}$ | $\sigma_{15}$ | $\sigma_{16}$ |
|  | $x_2$ | $\sigma_{12}$ | $\sigma_2^2$ | $\sigma_{23}$ | $\sigma_{24}$ | $\sigma_{25}$ | $\sigma_{26}$ |
|  | $x_3$ | $\sigma_{13}$ | $\sigma_{23}$ | $\sigma_3^2$ | $\sigma_{34}$ | $\sigma_{35}$ | $\sigma_{36}$ |
| $w$ set | $x_4$ | $\sigma_{14}$ | $\sigma_{24}$ | $\sigma_{34}$ | $\sigma_4^2$ | $\sigma_{45}$ | $\sigma_{46}$ |
|  | $x_5$ | $\sigma_{15}$ | $\sigma_{25}$ | $\sigma_{35}$ | $\sigma_{45}$ | $\sigma_5^2$ | $\sigma_{56}$ |
|  | $x_6$ | $\sigma_{16}$ | $\sigma_{26}$ | $\sigma_{36}$ | $\sigma_{46}$ | $\sigma_{56}$ | $\sigma_6^2$ |

the table to show elements respectively concerning the variance of $y$, the variance of $w$, and the covariance of $y$ and $w$. These can be symbolized as follows:

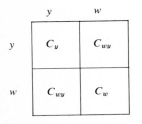

The variances of the two linear combinations, and the covariance between them, can be obtained by summing the elements in the appropriate sections of the matrix. If all variables were expressed as standard scores, the appropriate sections of the correlation matrix would enter into these computations.

**Correlation of linear combinations** The correlation of the two linear combinations $w$ and $y$ can be obtained as follows:

$$r_{wy} = \frac{\sigma_{wy}}{\sigma_w \sigma_y}$$

It should be obvious by this point that the correlation between two linear combinations of variables can be written in terms of the separate variables as follows:

$$r_{wy} = \frac{\bar{C}_{wy}}{\sqrt{\bar{C}_w}\sqrt{\bar{C}_y}} \tag{5-7}$$

The numerator is the covariance of $w$ and $y$ expressed in terms of the elements of $w$ and $y$. The denominator equals the product of the standard deviations of $w$ and $y$ expressed in terms of their respective elements. It should be strongly emphasized that there is no limit to the number of variables that can appear in $C_w$ or $C_y$, and the formulas work equally well regardless of whether the number of variables in each linear combination is the same or different. Regarding the latter consideration, if there were only two variables in one linear combination and 400 in the other, then all the formulas throughout this chapter concerning variances, covariances, and correlations among linear combinations would be valid.

If all variables are standardized, Eq. (5-7) reduces to:

$$r_{wy} = \frac{\bar{R}_{wy}}{\sqrt{\bar{R}_w}\sqrt{\bar{R}_y}} \tag{5-8}$$

In the case of Eq. (5-8), the elements of Table 5-1 would contain $z$ scores on the top and side, 1.00s in the diagonal spaces, and correlations in the off-diagonal spaces. Thus, the sum of all the elements within a correlation matrix has meaning: it is the variance of the sum of a set of standard scores. Likewise, the sum of the elements in a "between" correlation matrix is the covariance of two sets of summed standard scores. If variables were weighted, the elements of the covariance matrix or correlation matrix would be appropriately weighted.

An important special case is where a linear combination of variables is correlated with a single variable, one that is not a linear combination of other variables. The elements relating to the correlation are schematized as follows:

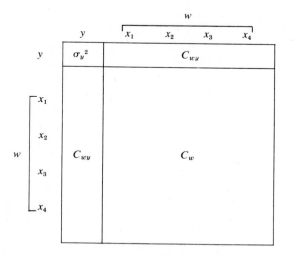

In the above case, $\bar{C}_y$ reduces to $\sigma_y^2$, there being only one variable in the "linear combination." The sum of between covariances $\bar{C}_{wy}$ equals the sum of all the elements in the first row or first column of the matrix excluding the diagonal term for $y$, $\sigma_y^2$. Then the correlation will be as follows:

$$r_{wy} = \frac{\bar{C}_{wy}}{\sigma_y \sqrt{\bar{C}_w}} \qquad (5\text{-}9)$$

If all variables are expressed as standard scores, Eq. (5-9) reduces to

$$r_{wy} = \frac{\bar{R}_{wy}}{\sqrt{\bar{R}_w}} \qquad (5\text{-}10)$$

In that case, since $\sigma_y = 1.0$, it will "fall out" of the denominator of Eq. (5-9).

The equations in this section hold equally well when the elements in linear combinations are dichotomous items scored as 1 or 0. On the diagonals of the total covariance matrix would be $pq$ values. The off-diagonal elements would consist of phi coefficients multiplied by the square root of the product of the two respective $pq$ values. Equation (5-7) would give the correlation between total scores on two tests composed of dichotomous items. Equation (5-9) would, for example, give the correlation between one test item and the sum of scores on the remaining items of the test.

The principles developed so far in this chapter are the basis of linear, multivariate correlational analysis. Once they are thoroughly understood, it will be relatively easy to understand such extensions as multiple correlation, factor analysis, and discriminatory analysis. If the reader does not understand these principles thoroughly, the material should be read again, because otherwise much of what lies ahead in this book will be difficult to understand.

## PARTIAL CORRELATION

The effort in science is to find a relatively small set of variables which will suffice to "explain" all other variables. A small set of variables "explains" a larger set if some combination of the smaller set correlates highly with each member of the larger set. For example, in the study of factors of human ability, it has been found that about six factors do a relatively good job of explaining much of the variance in most tests of human ability. When the six are combined in multiple-correlation analysis, the combined scores correlate highly with most tests of human ability. To achieve such a small set of "explainer" variables is the essence of scientific parsimony.

Before a new variable is added to the set of "explainers," it should be demonstrated to actually add something to the existing explainers. In this connection, the concept of "partialing" is very important. An example would be the development of a new measure of anxiety. After the test is developed, scores are correlated with speed of solving simple problems in arithmetic, and a positive correlation is found. This is taken as evidence that the measure of anxiety is a useful "explainer" of speed of solving simple problems. Later it is found that both measures correlate positively with scores on an intelligence test. Since IQ has proved to be an important explainer, it must be determined whether the new measure of anxiety *adds* something to the prediction of problem solving. For this purpose, scores on the intelligence test could be partialed from scores on the other two measures. If the partialed scores on the anxiety test still correlate with partialed scores on the measure of problem solving, the measure of anxiety actually adds something to what could be explained by the intelligence test alone; but if not, there is no evidence from the study to demonstrate that the anxiety test is an important new explainer.

A partialed score is simply the error score when the PM correlation is used to estimate one variable from another. (At this point, the reader might review some very important points in this connection by looking back at Table 4-1.) Using the example above, the partialed score for the anxiety test would be as follows:

$$z_{1-3} = z_1 - r_{13} z_3 \tag{5-11}$$

where $z_1$ = standard scores on anxiety test

$z_3$ = standard scores on intelligence test

$r_{13}$ = PM correlation between 1 and 3

$z_{1-3}$ = partialed score on anxiety test after variance explainable by intelligence test is removed

Similarly, the partialed score for the problem-solving test, holding intelligence constant, would be

$$z_{2-3} = z_2 - r_{23} z_3 \qquad (5\text{-}11)$$

where $z_2$ = standard scores in problem solving. It will be remembered that partialed scores correlate precisely zero with the variable used for the estimation ($z_3$ in this case). Consequently any correlation between $z_{1-3}$ and $z_{2-3}$ is independent of scores on the intelligence test. Such a correlation is called a *partial correlation*, symbolized as $r_{12.3}$. The formula is developed as follows. The correlation between any two variables can be stated as

$$r_{xy} = \frac{\sigma_{xy}}{\sigma_x \sigma_y} \qquad (5\text{-}12)$$

For partial correlation the symbols are

$$r_{12.3} = \frac{\sigma_{(1-3)(2-3)}}{\sigma_{1-3} \sigma_{2-3}} \qquad (5\text{-}13)$$

The denominator is the product of the standard deviations of the two sets of partialed scores. Previously it was shown (Table 4-1) that the variance of any set of partialed scores is 1 minus the squared correlation between the two variables. Thus the equation can be transformed to

$$r_{12.3} = \frac{\sigma_{(1-3)(2-3)}}{\sqrt{1 - r_{13}^2} \; \sqrt{1 - r_{23}^2}} \qquad (5\text{-}14)$$

In the numerator, the covariance equals the sum of cross products of the two sets of partialed scores divided by $N$. The numerator can be expanded as follows:

$$\sigma_{(1-3)(2-3)} = \frac{1}{N} \Sigma (z_1 - r_{13} z_3)(z_2 - r_{23} z_3)$$

$$= \frac{1}{N} \Sigma (z_1 z_2 - r_{23} z_1 z_3 - r_{13} z_2 z_3 + r_{13} r_{23} z_3^2)$$

$$= r_{12} - r_{23} r_{13} - r_{13} r_{23} + r_{13} r_{23}$$

$$= r_{12} - r_{13} r_{23}$$

Reassembling numerator and denominator gives the following formula for the partial correlation:

$$r_{12.3} = \frac{r_{12} - r_{13} r_{23}}{\sqrt{1 - r_{13}^2} \; \sqrt{1 - r_{23}^2}} \qquad (5\text{-}15)$$

It will be important to remember that the numerator in Eq. (5-15) is the covariance of two sets of partialed scores with variable 3 being partialed from variables 1 and 2, and the denominator is the product of the standard deviations of the two sets of partialed scores.

A number of points should be understood about partial correlation. First, partial correlation is the correlation expected between two variables when a third variable is held constant. Thus in the example above, if subjects who all had the *same* intelligence test score had been selected, the raw correlation between anxiety and problem solving would be expected to equal the partial correlation obtained when intelligence was allowed to vary. Unless there were homoscedastic relations between intelligence and the other two variables, however, the exact correlation between anxiety and problem solving for all subjects at the same level of intelligence would depend somewhat on *which* level of intelligence. For example, the partial-correlation coefficient might underestimate the raw correlation between anxiety and problem solving if all subjects had high intelligence and overestimate for subjects who were average in intelligence; but in practice, the partial correlation is usually a good estimate of the correlation found between two variables when a third variable is actually held constant. This provides very useful information in testing theories or in exploratory studies of correlations among variables.

The second important point is that the size of the partial correlation depends on the signs of the three correlations involved. If $r_{12}$ is positive, $r_{12.3}$ usually is *smaller* than $r_{12}$ when $r_{13}$ and $r_{23}$ have the same sign, regardless of whether the sign is positive or negative. It usually is larger than $r_{12}$ when the signs for the other two correlations are different. The reverse usually is true in both instances when $r_{12}$ is negative. The word *usually* is an essential part of the foregoing three rules, because there are instances in which the rules are incorrect. This occurs, for example, in computing $r_{12.3}$ when $r_{12} = .30$, $r_{13} = .10$, and $r_{23} = .80$. In this instance $r_{12.3}$ is .37, which is larger than $r_{12}$, rather than smaller as would be predicted from the first rule given above.

A third important point is that the amount of change frequently expected in partialing a third variable is an overestimate. For example, when anxiety and problem solving correlate .60 and each variable correlates .40 with intelligence, it might be thought that partialing intelligence will markedly reduce the correlation of .60. In fact, what occurs is as follows:

$$r_{12.3} = \frac{r_{12} - r_{13}r_{23}}{\sqrt{1 - r_{13}^2}\ \sqrt{1 - r_{23}^2}}$$

$$= \frac{.6 - (.4 \times .4)}{\sqrt{1 - .16}\ \sqrt{1 - .16}}$$

$$= \frac{.6 - .16}{.84}$$

$$= \frac{.44}{.84}$$

$$r_{12.3} = .52$$

The partial correlation is only eight points less than the simple correlation, which might not matter a great deal. This and other examples show that it is easy to be fooled about the size of a partial correlation before the statistics are actually applied.

A fourth important point is that the variable which is partialed from the relationship between two other variables may itself be a linear combination of other variables. Thus if $y$ is a linear combination of variables $x_1$ through $x_5$, there is nothing wrong with partialing $y$ from variables $x_6$ and $x_7$. Saying it another way, there is nothing to prevent partialing the variance of a linear combination of variables from the correlation between two particular variables. This point will prove important in the discussion of factor analysis, which consists essentially of successively partialing linear combinations of variables from the correlations among the variables.

**Semipartial correlation**  In partial correlation, variable 3 is held constant in *both* variables 1 and 2. A possibility not previously mentioned is to hold variable 3 constant in one of the other two variables but not in both of them. In the previous example, scores on the intelligence test could have been partialed from the anxiety test only, and not partialed from scores in problem solving. This could be justified on the grounds that intelligence is a "natural" part of problem solving and therefore the variance because of intelligence should be left in the latter variable. Then the task would be to determine the correlation of problem solving with the anxiety test after intelligence is partialed from anxiety scores but not from problem solving. This could be done with the *semipartial* correlation coefficient, which is very similar to the partial correlation. If problem solving is variable 1, anxiety is variable 2, and intelligence is variable 3, the problem is to correlate $z_1$ with $z_{2-3}$. These scores can be placed in the regular PM formula, and after terms are expanded in a manner similar to that done previously in developing the formula for the partial correlation, the following formula is developed for the semipartial correlation $r_{1(2.3)}$:

$$r_{1(2.3)} = \frac{r_{12} - r_{13}r_{23}}{\sqrt{1 - r_{23}^2}} \tag{5-16}$$

A comparison of Eq. (5-15) with Eq. (5-16) shows that in the former an additional term is included in the denominator, namely the square root of $1 - r_{13}^2$. For this reason, the relative size of the semipartial and partial correlations depends on the sign of $r_{13}$. If the correlation between the criterion (here variable 1) and the non-partialed predictor (here variable 3) is positive, then the semipartial correlation necessarily will be larger than the counterpart in terms of full partial correlation. The opposite would be the case if $r_{13}$ in the example above were negative. By "larger" is meant more in either a positive or negative direction depending on the sign of the numerator.

In most practical problems, it makes more sense to employ the partial correlation than to employ the semipartial correlation. Semipartial correlation proves important in the development of methods of multivariate analysis such as multiple correlation and factor analysis. Some of these uses will be shown later in this chapter in the section on multiple correlation. What is referred to here as the "semipartial correlation" is called the "part correlation" by some authors.

**A general approach to partialing** Whereas the partial-correlation coefficient has been developed above for only three variables, a more general approach is available which will not only facilitate computations but provide the basis for some other methods of multivariate analysis. Steps in the method are shown in Table 5-2. The more general approach starts with a matrix of correlations, the number of variables being irrelevant. Starting with such a matrix, it is possible to first partial the variance of variable 1 from the relations between the remaining variables, then partial variable 2, and so on, as far as one wants to go. (For the sake of convenience, it is good to line up the variables in the order in which partialing will be done, but the method which will be described can be employed regardless of the order in which variables appear in the matrix.)

The first step in partialing variable 1 is to take the correlations from the first row of the correlation matrix and place them at the top and side of an empty matrix. Appropriate correlations are then multiplied as indicated in Table 5-2. Element by element this matrix of products is then subtracted from the original matrix of correlations. This is spoken of as a matrix of residual coefficients, more specifically, in this case, the *first residual matrix*. A careful inspection of this matrix will show that (1) the diagonal elements are partial variances, where variable 1 is partialed from the other variables, and (2) the off-diagonal elements are partial covariances for that case. Thus to obtain the partial correlation between any two variables, variable 1 being partialed, all that is required is to divide the element in the residual matrix corresponding to the intersection of the two variables by the product of the square roots of the diagonal elements for the two variables. For example, when variable 1 is to be partialed from variables 2 and 3, the partial correlation for the latter two variables will be

$$r_{23.1} = \frac{r_{23} - r_{12}r_{13}}{\sqrt{1 - r_{12}^2}\ \sqrt{1 - r_{13}^2}} \tag{5-17}$$

Note that the numerator is the term appearing at the intersection of variables 2 and 3 in the first residual matrix, and the denominator consists of the product of square roots of the diagonal elements for 2 and 3. The whole residual matrix can be converted to a matrix of partial correlations, variable 1 being partialed, by dividing all the elements in each row of the residual matrix by the square root of the diagonal element in that row and then dividing each element in each column of the matrix by the square root of the diagonal element in that column. The result is illustrated in Table 5-2.

In the matrix of first-order partial correlations in Table 5-2, the column and row corresponding to variable 1 are filled with zeros. This is to be expected, because when variable 1 is partialed from variable 1, there are no scores left to correlate with other scores. Since the matrix of first-order partial correlations shows the correlations between variables when the variance because of variable 1 is removed, one can then proceed to partial another variable from the

## Table 5-2 Computational steps in a general approach to obtaining partial correlations

*Correlation Matrix*

|   | 1 | 2 | 3 | 4 |
|---|---|---|---|---|
| 1 | 1.00 | $r_{12}$ | $r_{13}$ | $r_{14}$ |
| 2 | $r_{12}$ | 1.00 | $r_{23}$ | $r_{24}$ |
| 3 | $r_{13}$ | $r_{23}$ | 1.00 | $r_{34}$ |
| 4 | $r_{14}$ | $r_{24}$ | $r_{34}$ | 1.00 |

*First Matrix of Products*

|  |  | 1 | 2 | 3 | 4 |
|---|---|---|---|---|---|
|  |  | 1.00 | $r_{12}$ | $r_{13}$ | $r_{14}$ |
| 1 | 1.00 | 1.00 | $r_{12}$ | $r_{13}$ | $r_{14}$ |
| 2 | $r_{12}$ | $r_{12}$ | $r_{12}^2$ | $r_{12}r_{13}$ | $r_{12}r_{14}$ |
| 3 | $r_{13}$ | $r_{13}$ | $r_{12}r_{13}$ | $r_{13}^2$ | $r_{13}r_{14}$ |
| 4 | $r_{14}$ | $r_{14}$ | $r_{12}r_{14}$ | $r_{13}r_{14}$ | $r_{14}^2$ |

*First Matrix of Residuals*

|   | 1 | 2 | 3 | 4 |
|---|---|---|---|---|
| 1 | .00 | .00 | .00 | .00 |
| 2 | .00 | $1.00 - r_{12}^2$ | $r_{23} - r_{12}r_{13}$ | $r_{24} - r_{12}r_{14}$ |
| 3 | .00 | $r_{23} - r_{12}r_{13}$ | $1.00 - r_{13}^2$ | $r_{34} - r_{13}r_{14}$ |
| 4 | .00 | $r_{24} - r_{12}r_{14}$ | $r_{34} - r_{13}r_{14}$ | $1.00 - r_{14}^2$ |

*Computation of Partial Correlations*

$$r_{23.1} = \frac{r_{23} - r_{12}r_{13}}{\sqrt{1 - r_{12}^2}\ \sqrt{1 - r_{13}^2}}$$

$$r_{24.1} = \frac{r_{24} - r_{12}r_{14}}{\sqrt{1 - r_{12}^2}\ \sqrt{1 - r_{14}^2}}$$

$$r_{34.1} = \frac{r_{34} - r_{13}r_{14}}{\sqrt{1 - r_{13}^2}\ \sqrt{1 - r_{14}^2}}$$

*First-order Partial Correlations*

|   | 1 | 2 | 3 | 4 |
|---|---|---|---|---|
| 1 | .00 | .00 | .00 | .00 |
| 2 | .00 | 1.00 | $r_{23.1}$ | $r_{24.1}$ |
| 3 | .00 | $r_{23.1}$ | 1.00 | $r_{34.1}$ |
| 4 | .00 | $r_{24.1}$ | $r_{34.1}$ | 1.00 |

remaining ones. This can be done by employing the first-order partial correlations from Table 5-2 in the formula for the partial correlation. For example, if after variable 1 is partialed, it is desired to partial variable 2 from the correlation between variables 3 and 4, the formula would be as follows:

$$r_{34.12} = \frac{r_{34.1} - r_{23.1}r_{24.1}}{\sqrt{1 - r_{23.1}^2}\ \sqrt{1 - r_{24.1}^2}} \tag{5-18}$$

Note the similarity of Eqs. (5-18) and (5-17), the only difference being that in the former each coefficient is a partial correlation rather than a raw correlation. The raw correlations are called "zero-order coefficients"; when one variable is partialed, they are called "first-order partial correlations"; and so on for any order of partial correlation, depending on the number of variables appearing after the decimal point.

The second-order partial correlations can be obtained in the same way that the first-order partial correlations were. Partial correlations for variable 2 (variable 1 being previously partialed) are placed on the top and side of an empty table. Corresponding elements are multiplied to form a second matrix of cross products. This matrix of cross products is subtracted, element by element, from the table of first-order partial correlations. The square root of the diagonal element in each row is divided into each element in the row, and the same is done for each column. The result is a matrix of second-order partial correlations. By repeating this procedure, one can partial any number of variables from any other number of variables. Computational procedures for this method are illustrated in Table 5-3.

**Table 5-3  A worked-out example of a general approach to the computation of partial correlations**

*Correlation Matrix*

|   | 1 | 2 | 3 | 4 | 5 |
|---|---|---|---|---|---|
| 1 | 1.00 | .43 | −.23 | .45 | .39 |
| 2 | .43 | 1.00 | −.34 | .36 | .09 |
| 3 | −.23 | −.34 | 1.00 | −.23 | .26 |
| 4 | .45 | .36 | −.23 | 1.00 | .32 |
| 5 | .39 | .09 | .26 | .32 | 1.00 |

*First Product Matrix*

|   |   | 1 | 2 | 3 | 4 | 5 |
|---|---|---|---|---|---|---|
|   |   | 1.00 | .43 | −.23 | .45 | .39 |
| 1 | 1.00 | 1.00 | .43 | −.23 | .45 | .39 |
| 2 | .43 | .43 | .18 | −.10 | .19 | .17 |
| 3 | −.23 | −.23 | −.10 | .05 | −.10 | −.09 |
| 4 | .45 | .45 | .19 | −.10 | .20 | .18 |
| 5 | .39 | .39 | .17 | −.09 | .18 | .15 |

*First Residual Matrix*

|   | 1 | 2 | 3 | 4 | 5 |
|---|---|---|---|---|---|
| 1 | 0 | 0 | 0 | 0 | 0 |
| 2 | 0 | .82 | −.24 | .17 | −.08 |
| 3 | 0 | −.24 | .95 | −.13 | .35 |
| 4 | 0 | .17 | −.13 | .80 | .14 |
| 5 | 0 | −.08 | .35 | .14 | .85 |
| *Square root of diagonal* |   | .9055 | .9747 | .8944 | .9220 |

## Table 5-3  A worked-out example of a general approach to the computation of partial correlations (Continued)

### First-order Partial Correlations

|   | 1 | 2 | 3 | 4 | 5 |
|---|---|---|---|---|---|
| 1 | 0 | 0 | 0 | 0 | 0 |
| 2 | 0 | 1.00 | −.27 | .21 | −.10 |
| 3 | 0 | −.27 | 1.00 | −.15 | .39 |
| 4 | 0 | .21 | −.15 | 1.00 | .17 |
| 5 | 0 | −.10 | .39 | .17 | 1.00 |

### Second Product Matrix

|   |   |   | 1 | 2 | 3 | 4 | 5 |
|---|---|---|---|---|---|---|---|
|   |   |   | 0 | 1.00 | −.27 | .21 | −.10 |
| 1 | 0 |   | 0 | 0 | 0 | 0 | 0 |
| 2 | 1.00 |   | 0 | 1.00 | −.27 | .21 | −.10 |
| 3 | −.27 |   | 0 | −.27 | .07 | −.06 | .03 |
| 4 | .21 |   | 0 | .21 | −.06 | .04 | −.02 |
| 5 | −.10 |   | 0 | −.10 | .03 | −.02 | .01 |

### Second Residual Matrix

|   | 1 | 2 | 3 | 4 | 5 |
|---|---|---|---|---|---|
| 1 | 0 | 0 | 0 | 0 | 0 |
| 2 | 0 | 0 | 0 | 0 | 0 |
| 3 | 0 | 0 | .93 | −.09 | .36 |
| 4 | 0 | 0 | −.09 | .96 | .19 |
| 5 | 0 | 0 | .36 | .19 | .99 |
| Square root of diagonal |  |  | .9644 | .9798 | .9950 |

### Second-order Partial Correlations

|   | 1 | 2 | 3 | 4 | 5 |
|---|---|---|---|---|---|
| 1 | 0 | 0 | 0 | 0 | 0 |
| 2 | 0 | 0 | 0 | 0 | 0 |
| 3 | 0 | 0 | 1.00 | −.10 | .38 |
| 4 | 0 | 0 | −.10 | 1.00 | .20 |
| 5 | 0 | 0 | .38 | .20 | 1.00 |

The procedure described above is very useful for "taking apart" relations among variables. The zero-order correlations show relationships among variables when none is held constant. First-order partial correlations show what remains when the influence of one variable is removed. One can remove any number of variables to see if there is any remaining correlation between two variables. For that purpose, the result is the same regardless of the order in which variables are partialed, e.g., $r_{12.345} = r_{12.543}$. Whereas previously it was shown that the first-order partial correlation frequently is not very different from the zero-order coefficient, the zero-order coefficient often is drastically altered when a number of variables are partialed.

## MULTIPLE CORRELATION

Previously it was stated that the problem in simple (zero-order) correlation is to find the line of best fit between two sets of standard scores. "Best fit" was defined in terms of the minimization of the sum of squared errors of estimation—the principle of least squares. The logic and method are easily extended to the problem of estimating a dependent variable from some combination of a number of independent variables. Let the dependent variable be designated $z_y$ and the independent variables be designated $z_1, z_2, \ldots, z_k$. Let any combination of the independent variables which is used to estimate the dependent variable be designated $z_y'$. Although many different kinds of combinations of the independent variables could be used to estimate $z_y$, most frequently a linear combination is used:

$$z_y' = \beta_1 z_1 + \beta_2 z_2 + \beta_3 z_3 \qquad (5\text{-}19)$$

where $z_y' =$ estimates of $z_y$
$z_1, z_2, z_3 =$ independent variables
$\beta_1, \beta_2, \beta_3 =$ weights for independent variables
The $\beta$'s are called *beta weights,* and the problem is to find a set of beta weights such that

$$\Sigma(z_y - z_y')^2 = \text{a minimum}$$

$$\Sigma(z_y - \beta_1 z_1 - \beta_2 z_2 - \beta_3 z_3)^2 = \text{a minimum}$$

After the last expression is squared and summed, a solution for the beta weights can be sought through calculus. What is learned is that a unique set of beta weights is obtainable for any problem. The weights are found by the solution of a set of simultaneous equations. When only two independent variables are involved, the solution is very simple:

$$\beta_1 = \frac{r_{y1} - r_{y2} r_{12}}{1 - r_{12}^2}$$

$$\beta_2 = \frac{r_{y2} - r_{y1} r_{12}}{1 - r_{12}^2} \qquad (5\text{-}20)$$

When more than two independent variables are involved, the computations are straightforward but complex. Proofs for the derivation of beta weights in the general case are presented throughout the Suggested Additional Readings. In particular see the book by Kerlinger and Pedhazur (1973) for an extensive discussion of all aspects of multiple correlation and regression.

Once the beta weights are computed, they are applied to the independent variables to obtain $z_y'$, least-squares estimates of $z_y$. One could then correlate $z_y'$ with $z_y$ using the regular PM formula. This would be referred to as the *multiple correlation,* which would be symbolized as $R_{y.12}$ for two independent variables and as $R_{y.1\ldots k}$ in the general case. Rather than actually compute $z_y'$ and then calculate the correlation with $z_y$, one can obtain the multiple correlation directly from the zero-order correlations and beta weights as follows:

$$R^2_{y.1\cdots k} = \beta_1 r_{y1} + \beta_2 r_{y2} + \cdots + \beta_k r_{yk} \tag{5-21}$$

In most problems concerning multiple correlation, the investigator is interested not in the beta weights but in the correlation itself. Later, a comprehensive method will be discussed for obtaining the multiple correlation from the correlations with the criterion and correlations among variables. In the case of only two predictor variables this is done as follows:

$$R^2_{y.12} = \frac{r^2_{y1} + r^2_{y2} - 2r_{y1}r_{y2}r_{12}}{1 - r^2_{12}} \tag{5-22}$$

A number of important principles should be understood about multiple correlation. First, $R$ tends to be high when the independent variables have high correlations with the dependent variable. If all the independent variables correlate zero with the dependent variable, the multiple correlation must be zero also. If some of the independent variables have high correlations with the dependent variable, the multiple correlation will be high. Second, the multiple correlation cannot be less than the highest correlation of any one of the independent variables with the dependent variable. If, for example, one of the independent variables correlates .50 with the dependent variable, no matter what the other correlations are, $R$ cannot be less than .50. The multiple correlation cannot be negative. The statistical procedures for deriving the multiple correlation force the resulting $R$ to be zero or positive. However, one can observe the trend of correspondence of the individual variables with the criterion by looking at the simple correlations before they are placed in the formula for multiple correlation.

Third, $R$ is larger when the independent variables have relatively *low* correlations among themselves. When correlations among independent variables are low, each *adds* something to the predictive power obtainable from the others. When correlations among independent variables are high, each is highly redundant of the others, and consequently they tend to add little predictive power to one another. When all correlations among independent variables are zero, the squared multiple correlation equals the sum of the squared correlations with the dependent variable.(This is a very important fact that can be easily proved from the correlation of sums. This principle will be used many times in discussing multivariate statistics.) For example, if two independent variables correlated zero and each correlated .50 with the dependent variable, the squared multiple correlation would be .50 ($R = .71$). In that case, if the two independent variables correlated .50, $R$ would be only .58. Further increases in the correlation between the independent variables would further reduce $R$. In the case of a perfect correlation between the two independent variables, $R$ would be .50.

A fourth important principle is that the multiple correlation often produces results that would be hard to estimate when looking at the zero-order correlations. This is particularly so when there are numerous independent variables and a mixture of positive and negative correlations. An outstanding example is where a *suppressor variable* is present among the independent variables, as follows:

$$r_{y1} = .60$$

$$r_{y2} = .00$$

$$r_{12} = .50$$

$$\beta_1 = \frac{.6 - (.0 \times .5)}{1 - .5^2} = .8$$

$$\beta_2 = \frac{.0 - (.5 \times .6)}{1 - .5^2} = -.4$$

$$R^2 = (.8 \times .6) + (-.4 \times .0)$$

$$R = .69$$

Even though the second independent variable correlates zero with the dependent variable, when it is included in the multiple correlation with the first independent variable, the multiple correlation is substantially higher than the correlation between the first independent variable and the dependent variable. Even though variable 2 has a zero correlation with the dependent variable, the high correlation with variable 1 supplies important information. This correlation between the two independent variables necessarily concerns variance that is not related to the dependent variable. Consequently when this component of variance is subtracted from the first independent variable (note that the beta weight for variable 2 is negative), the predictive power of the first variable is increased. Actually, such suppressor variables are rarely found in practice, but when found, they serve to illustrate the distinct surprises that sometimes come from multiple correlation.

A fifth important principle is that in applied problems of prediction the multiple correlation usually does not increase dramatically as the number of independent variables is made larger and larger. For example, where 10 tests are being investigated for their ability to predict performance in college, a typical finding is that (1) one of the tests has a moderately high correlation with the criterion, (2) when that test is combined with another test that also has a high correlation with the criterion, the multiple correlation is considerably higher than any of the zero-order correlations, (3) adding a third test provides a small increment to the multiple correlation, and (4) beyond that, adding additional tests produces only very small increases in the multiple correlation. There is no necessary reason why adding tests beyond three, four, or five does not continue to produce substantial increases in multiple correlation in applied problems of prediction. Typically it does not continue to increase because of the redundancy among the independent variables, as manifested in the correlations among them. After a point, the redundancy begins to catch up with the possible information that can be obtained from adding more and more independent variables to the prediction equation. Of course, there is always the hope and possibility of finding a new independent variable that will be less redundant of existing variables and will considerably increase the multiple correlation. For example, in the development of tests for creativity, it was hoped that they would add to conventional tests in predicting successful performance in high-level scientific work. The search for important new "explainers" that will add to multiple correlations also continues in basic research on human abilities and personality characteristics.

A sixth important principle is that the multiple correlation tends to be systematically biased "upward"; that is, it tends to be larger than the population parameter. The first of two major reasons for the bias is that there is a preselection of independent variables from a larger set. This would be the case, for example, if 10 tests were correlated with a criterion and then the 3 tests having the highest correlation with the criterion were placed in the multiple correlation formula. Preselecting in this way would be "taking advantage of chance." Some of the variables preselected would have relatively high correlations with the criterion because of sampling error, and consequently their correlations would tend to be lower in another sample. Even more advantage is taken of chance when numerous combinations of variables are placed in the formula for multiple correlation. For example, if there are 10 independent variables, many different sets of 3 each could be placed in the formula, many different sets of 4 variables each could be tried, and so on for sets of different sizes. Then advantage is taken of chance not only in terms of the correlations with the criterion, but also in terms of the many different patterns of correlations among independent variables.

The extent to which it is possible to take advantage of chance depends inversely on the number of persons being studied and directly on the size of the total collection of variables from which a smaller set is to be selected. For example, if there are only 100 persons in the sample and a set of 3 variables is to be selected from a total group of 20, the multiple correlation will be so spuriously high as to be worthless. In contrast, if 1,000 persons are sampled and 3 variables are to be selected from a total of 6, the bias in the multiple correlation will be so small that it can be ignored. Whereas in the former case the multiple correlation might be as much as 40 points higher than the population value, in the latter it might be only several points higher.

Even when there is no preselection among independent variables, there is a second reason why the multiple correlation is still biased upward. This would be the case, for example, when only three tests were being tried as predictors of a criterion and all three were placed in the formula for multiple correlation. There would be no possibility of taking advantage of chance through preselection, but advantage would be taken of chance in another way. Whenever a set of weights is chosen to minimize or maximize some function, there is an opportunity to take advantage of chance. This is the case with the beta weights in multiple correlation. They are selected in such a way as to wring the last ounce of predictive power out of a set of variables. In so doing they will capitalize on sampling error among correlations. The test that "happens" to have a high correlation because of sampling error will receive a large beta weight, and a test which happens to have a relatively small correlation will receive a small beta weight. Consequently the multiple correlation obtained in a relatively small sample of persons will tend to be smaller in a larger sample of persons. This tendency for the multiple correlation to decrease as the sample grows larger (even when no preselection occurs) is called *shrinkage*. The following formula can be used to estimate the shrinkage in going from a sample of any particular size to an infinitely large sample:

$$\hat{R}^2 = 1 - (1 - R^2)\left(\frac{N-1}{N-k}\right) \qquad (5\text{-}23)$$

where $\hat{R}$ = unbiased estimate of population multiple correlation
$\quad R$ = multiple correlation found in sample of size $N$
$\quad k$ = number of independent variables

Equation (5-23) can be illustrated in the situation where a multiple correlation of .50 is found with 100 persons and eight independent variables. The unbiased estimate of the population multiple correlation would be .44. From Eq. (5-23), one can see that the amount of bias is directly related to the number of independent variables divided by the number of persons sampled. When that ratio is 100:1, the bias is insignificant. When it is 10:1, the bias is important. When the ratio is as high as 3:1, the multiple correlation in the sample is highly biased upward. When the number of independent variables is as large as the number of people, a perfect multiple correlation will always be found. In that case there would be complete opportunity to take advantage of chance. This result would hold even if the dependent variable consisted of social security numbers and the independent variables were drawn from tables of random numbers. When there are as many unknowns (here, beta weights) as persons in the study, the equations can be solved so as to obtain a perfect multiple correlation. Of course, the multiple correlation would not "hold up" when other samples were employed.

As is true of most other problems in psychological measurement, in dealing with multiple correlations nothing helps so much as to have a large sample of subjects. If there are only 2 or 3 independent variables and no preselection is made among them, 100 or more subjects will provide a multiple correlation with little bias. In that case, if the number of independent variables is as large as 9 or 10, it will be necessary to have from 300 to 400 subjects to prevent substantial bias. When there is no preselection among variables, the shrinkage formula can be used to obtain an unbiased estimate of the multiple correlation. But if, as usually happens, there is some preselection among variables, the shrinkage formula may not "shrink" as much as is needed. If there are as many as 10 variables from which the several best are to be selected, it will be wise to employ 500 or more persons in the study. Whatever the sample size and amount of preselection among predictor variables, it is wise to look for information in subsequent studies that serves to cross-validate both the beta weights and the multiple correlation obtained in the initial investigation. Methods for doing this are discussed in Kerlinger and Pedhazur (1973).

**A general approach to multiple correlation** Previously it was stated that if the independent variables correlate precisely zero with one another, the squared multiple correlation will be as follows:

$$R^2_{y.123} = r^2_{y1} + r^2_{y2} + r^2_{y3} \tag{5-24}$$

The reader can easily derive this formula by reinspecting the logic of Eq. (5-10). Of course, independent variables will almost never all correlate precisely zero with one another, and consequently methods are required to "untangle" the correlations among variables before the multiple correlation can be obtained. Equation (5-22) showed how the untangling is done when there are only two independent variables. Here a general approach to multiple correlation will be presented; it can be used with any number of variables and should provide some insights into methods for obtaining multiple correlations. (The method looks different from the computational routines that will be found in many textbooks, but it will produce exactly the same multiple correlation; and the method to be discussed here is by far the most understandable approach to multiple $R$.) The method is based on the semipartial correlation, which can be used to untangle correlations among independent variables. The method will be illustrated with three independent variables, but can be generalized to any number of independent variables. Regardless of the size and sign of correlations among the variables, the multiple correlation can be obtained as follows:

$$R^2_{y.123} = r^2_{y1} + r^2_{y(2.1)} + r^2_{y(3.12)} \tag{5-25}$$

where $r_{y1}$ = raw correlation between $y$ and 1

$r_{y(2.1)}$ = semipartial correlation between $y$ and 2, with 1 partialed from 2

$r_{y(3.12)}$ = semipartial correlation between $y$ and 3, with both 1 and 2 partialed from 3

In using Eq. (5-25), it does not matter which independent variable is designated 1, 2, and so on. The formula works equally well for any ordering of the variables. The same multiple correlation would have been obtained if the first term on the right-hand side of the equation were $r^2_{y2}$ and the second term were $r^2_{y(1.2)}$. However, later it will be discussed how the order of selecting variables is determined by the need either to obtain an optimal group of predictor tests for some applied problem or to determine the explanatory power of a theory regarding the independent variables.

The first step in computing $R$ is to square any one of the correlations between the dependent variable and the independent variables. Next, take any one of the remaining independent variables and obtain the semipartial correlation between that variable and the dependent variable, holding constant the variable in the first term. This is squared and entered as the second term in the equation. Next, take any variable from the remaining independent variables and compute the semipartial correlation with $y$, holding constant the variables in the first two terms. This is squared and entered as the third term. This process can be carried on for any number of independent variables. Successive terms in the equation are successively higher orders of squared semipartial correlations. The first term is the square of a zero-order (raw) correlation, the second term is the square of a first-order semipartial correlation, the third term is the square of a second-order semipartial correlation, and so on.

It might not be obvious why semipartial correlations rather than partial correlations are used in the formula. The reason is that what is needed is to partial the independent variables from one another but not to partial their variances from the dependent variable. The partial-correlation coefficient answers a hypothetical question: What would the correlation be for two variables if one or more other variables were held constant? This would be the same as the result that, hypothetically, would be obtained if such "other variables" really were constants rather than variables, in which case all persons would have exactly the same score on each variable. In multiple correlation, one asks another hypothetical question: What would be the sum of squared correlations with $y$ if the independent variables correlated zero with one another? In this instance, however, the question is hypothetical only with respect to the independent variables, not with respect to the dependent variable. In multiple correlation, one wants to leave the dependent variable *intact* and not partial any variance attributable to the independent variables. The problem is one of determining how much an *actual* variable $y$ correlates with a linear combination of independent variables which have been *orthogonalized* (made to correlate zero with one another).

**A computational approach to multiple correlation**  In this section a method will be presented for easily obtaining the semipartial correlations required for the multiple-correlation formula. The method will be explained in detail because it is a very useful approach to multiple correlation, and it will be very useful later in the discussion of factor analysis. Also, the method is easily programmed for computers.

The method is similar to that for successive partialing discussed in a previous section. Steps in the method are shown in Table 5-4. The first step is the computation of a matrix of zero-order correlations, showing all correlations among independent variables and all correlations with the dependent variable $y$. Correlations for $y$ are placed in the last row and last column of the matrix. The derivation of semipartial correlations will be done in the order of 1 through 4 for the independent variables. In looking back at Eq. (5-25) for the multiple correlation in terms of semipartial correlations, one will see that the first term is the square of one of the zero-order correlations with the dependent variable. Consequently the first term is "computed" merely by picking out $r_{1y}$, the correlation of the first variable with $y$.

The first row (or column) of the correlation matrix shows the correlations of variable 1 with the other variables. This is then set aside and labeled $F_1$. The next problem is to obtain first-order semipartial correlations with $y$, in which case variable 1 will be partialed from the independent variables but not from $y$. The first step in doing this is to place the elements of $F_1$ along the top and side of an empty table. Corresponding elements are then multiplied, which produces

## Table 5-4 Computational procedures for obtaining multiple correlations

|  | 1 | 2 | 3 | 4 | y |
|---|---|---|---|---|---|
| 1 | 1.0 | $r_{12}$ | $r_{13}$ | $r_{14}$ | $r_{1y}$ |
| 2 | $r_{12}$ | 1.0 | $r_{23}$ | $r_{24}$ | $r_{2y}$ |
| 3 | $r_{13}$ | $r_{23}$ | 1.0 | $r_{34}$ | $r_{3y}$ |
| 4 | $r_{14}$ | $r_{24}$ | $r_{34}$ | 1.0 | $r_{4y}$ |
| y | $r_{1y}$ | $r_{2y}$ | $r_{3y}$ | $r_{4y}$ | 1.0 |

### Zero-order Correlations with Variable 1

|  | 1 | 2 | 3 | 4 | 5 |
|---|---|---|---|---|---|
| $F_1$ | 1.0 | $r_{12}$ | $r_{13}$ | $r_{14}$ | $r_{1y}$ |

### First Matrix of Cross Products

|  | 1.0 | $r_{12}$ | $r_{13}$ | $r_{14}$ | $r_{1y}$ |
|---|---|---|---|---|---|
| 1.0 | 1.0 | $r_{12}$ | $r_{13}$ | $r_{14}$ | $r_{1y}$ |
| $r_{12}$ | $r_{12}$ | $r^2_{12}$ | $r_{12}r_{13}$ | $r_{12}r_{14}$ | $r_{12}r_{1y}$ |
| $r_{13}$ | $r_{13}$ | $r_{12}r_{13}$ | $r^2_{13}$ | $r_{13}r_{14}$ | $r_{13}r_{1y}$ |
| $r_{14}$ | $r_{14}$ | $r_{12}r_{14}$ | $r_{13}r_{14}$ | $r^2_{14}$ | $r_{14}r_{1y}$ |
| $r_{1y}$ | $r_{1y}$ | $r_{12}r_{1y}$ | $r_{13}r_{1y}$ | $r_{14}r_{1y}$ | $r^2_{1y}$ |

### First Matrix of Residuals

|  | 1 | 2 | 3 | 4 | y |
|---|---|---|---|---|---|
| 1 | .0 | .0 | .0 | .0 | .0 |
| 2 | .0 | $1 - r^2_{12}$ | $r_{23} - r_{12}r_{13}$ | $r_{24} - r_{12}r_{14}$ | $r_{2y} - r_{12}r_{1y}$ |
| 3 | .0 | $r_{23} - r_{12}r_{13}$ | $1 - r^2_{13}$ | $r_{34} - r_{13}r_{14}$ | $r_{3y} - r_{13}r_{1y}$ |
| 4 | .0 | $r_{24} - r_{12}r_{14}$ | $r_{34} - r_{13}r_{14}$ | $1 - r^2_{14}$ | $r_{4y} - r_{14}r_{1y}$ |
| y | .0 | $r_{2y} - r_{12}r_{1y}$ | $r_{3y} - r_{13}r_{1y}$ | $r_{4y} - r_{14}r_{1y}$ | $1 - r^2_{1y}$ |

$F_2$

1   $\dfrac{0}{\sqrt{1 - r^2_{12}}} = 0$

2   $\dfrac{1 - r^2_{12}}{\sqrt{1 - r^2_{12}}} = \sqrt{1 - r^2_{12}} = r_{2(2.1)}$

3   $\dfrac{r_{23} - r_{12}r_{13}}{\sqrt{1 - r^2_{12}}} = r_{3(2.1)}$

4   $\dfrac{r_{24} - r_{12}r_{14}}{\sqrt{1 - r^2_{12}}} = r_{4(2.1)}$

y   $\dfrac{r_{2y} - r_{12}r_{1y}}{\sqrt{1 - r^2_{12}}} = r_{y(2.1)}$

### F

|  | $F_1$ | $F_2$ | $F_3$ | $F_4$ |
|---|---|---|---|---|
| 1 | 1.0 | .0 | .0 | .0 |
| 2 | $r_{12}$ | $r_{2(2.1)}$ | .0 | .0 |
| 3 | $r_{13}$ | $r_{3(2.1)}$ | $r_{3(3.12)}$ | .0 |
| 4 | $r_{14}$ | $r_{4(2.1)}$ | $r_{4(3.12)}$ | $r_{4(4.123)}$ |
| y | $r_{1y}$ | $r_{y(2.1)}$ | $r_{y(3.12)}$ | $r_{y(4.123)}$ |

the *first matrix of cross products*. Elements in this matrix are subtracted from corresponding elements in the original matrix of correlations, and this results in the *first matrix of residuals*. The diagonal elements of that matrix are partial variances, variable 1 being held constant, and the off-diagonal terms are partial covariances. As was shown in a previous section, the first residual matrix can be converted to a matrix of first-order partial correlations by dividing each off-diagonal element by the product of the square roots of the two corresponding diagonal elements. This can be done because the partial correlation equals the partial covariance divided by the product of the square roots of the two partial variances.

Since the formula for semipartial correlation is only slightly different from that for partial correlation, it is easy to turn the first matrix of residuals into a matrix of first-order semipartial correlations. The only difference between the two formulas is that, in obtaining the semipartial correlation, one divides the partial covariance of any two variables by the square root of only one of the two variances. Since in the residual matrix the only interest is in the variable to be used next in obtaining semipartial coefficients, the major concern in the first residual matrix is with the elements in column 2. By dividing each element in that column by the square root of the diagonal element, one obtains first-order semipartial correlations, where variable 1 is partialed from variable 2 but not from the other variables. One can see how this works by looking at the formula for the semipartial correlation for variables 2 and 3, with variable 1 held constant only in 2:

$$r_{3(2.1)} = \frac{r_{23} - r_{12}r_{13}}{\sqrt{1 - r_{12}^2}} \qquad (5\text{-}26)$$

The above is precisely what one would obtain by dividing the element in the first residual matrix corresponding to variables 2 and 3 by the square root of the diagonal element corresponding to variable 2. All the semipartial correlations are listed as $F_2$. Naturally the semipartial correlation for variable 1 is zero, since when variable 1 is held constant in variable 1, there is nothing left to correlate with any other variable. The semipartial correlation for variable 2 is the square root of the variance of scores on 2 after 1 has been partialed. The most important correlation in $F_2$ is that of $y$ with 2 when 1 is held constant in 2, which is $r_{y(2.1)}$. When squared, this serves as the second term in the formula for the squared multiple correlation [see Eq. (5-25)]. If one wanted the multiple correlation for variables 1 and 2 with $y$, $R_{y.12}^2$ could be obtained by squaring $r_{y1}$ and adding that to the square of $r_{y(2.1)}$.

The above process of obtaining multiple correlations for different numbers of variables can be repeated as many times as necessary. These steps are not shown in Table 5-4, because they are only repetitions of the steps required to obtain $F_2$. If a third independent variable is to be added to the multiple correlation, the first step is to obtain a second matrix of cross products. The elements in $F_2$ are placed on the top and side of an empty table, and corresponding elements are multiplied. This matrix is then subtracted, element by element, from the first matrix of residuals. If variable 3 were next to be added to the prediction of $y$, each element in column 3 would be divided by the square root of the diagonal element for variable 3. This would produce semipartial correlations where variables 1 and 2 were held constant in variable 3, which would be $F_3$. The square of $r_{y(3.12)}$ could be added to $r_{y1}^2$ and $r_{y(2.1)}^2$ to obtain $R_{y.123}^2$.

The fourth variable could be added to the multiple correlation in the same way that variables 2 and 3 were added. A third matrix of cross products would be obtained by appropriately multiplying the elements of $F_3$. That matrix would be subtracted from the second matrix of residuals, which would give the third matrix of residuals. All the elements would be zero in columns and rows for variables 1, 2, and 3. The square root of the diagonal element for variable 4 would be divided into the element corresponding to 4 and $y$. This would give $r_{y(4.123)}$, which when squared could be added to the other terms in the squared multiple correlation.

The final results of the analysis are shown in the last part of Table 5-4 under the label $F$. The sum of the squares of the elements in the bottom row of $F$ would be the squared multiple correlation with $y$. This procedure offers a very useful way of "picking apart" the relative contributions of variables to a multiple correlation.

**Selection of variables** So far in this section it has been assumed that the intention in a particular study is to find the multiple correlation of *all* independent variables with $y$, but this usually is not the case. Variables are selected (1) to find a parsimonious set of predictor tests that do a good job of estimating scores on a criterion or (2) in an order that fits a psychological theory regarding the importance of various concepts in explaining some type of individual differences.

An example of the latter consideration is when a theory leads to the prediction of individual differences in scores on a self-report measure of anxiety as a function of various measures of physiological processes. The theory leads to the formation of a hierarchy of physiological variables in terms of ability to explain anxiety. The multiple correlation would be obtained in the same order as the hierarchy. This would permit a statistical picture of the explanatory power of each independent variable and of the hierarchy as a whole. Also, the result obtained from such a theoretical approach to multiple correlation could be compared to a purely statistical approach.

An example of the former consideration is when the researcher is seeking a relatively small number of variables that will do an adequate job of predicting a criterion variable. This circumstance arises much more frequently in obtaining multiple correlations than does that of testing a theoretical position as illustrated previously. In applied situations, the effort usually is to wring the last possible ounce of predictive power out of the smallest number of test variables. For example, in predicting success on a particular job ($y$), as many as 10 or more tests might be applied. If in practice it will not be possible to use more than, say, 3 or 4 of the tests, the problem is to find a small set of variables that has a higher multiple correlation with $y$ than any other set with the same number of variables. The only foolproof way to solve that problem is to try the variables in all possible combinations two at a time, three at a time, and so on, but this would be prohibitively time-consuming and would provide many opportunities for taking advantage of chance. Some other complex approaches to obtaining the best set of predictors for multiple correlations are discussed by Kerlinger and Pedhazur (1973). However, the method that will be discussed subsequently is much more understandable than any other approach, and it usually results in the best possible selection of variables in applied prediction problems.

The previous method for computing the terms required for multiple correlation can be adapted to the problem of selecting a smaller set of independent variables from a larger set. In this case imagine that the problem is that of picking the best set of 4 variables from a total collection of 10. First obtain a matrix of correlations for all 10 independent variables and for correlations with $y$. The independent variable that has the highest correlation with $y$ is selected as the first variable in the multiple-correlation equation. Next compute the matrix of first residuals. (In doing this it is not necessary to place the variable which has the highest correlation with $y$ on the first row and column of the correlation matrix or to place the second variable to be partialed on the second row and column of the first residual matrix. The operations can be carried out regardless of where variables are in the matrix of correlations and in the successive matrices of residual coefficients.) In the first residual matrix, divide each element in the row for $y$ by the square root of the diagonal element in the column for the element. This would give all possible semipartial correlations with $y$. The variable with the highest coefficient would add the most to the first variable in the multiple-regression formula for predicting $y$.

After the second variable is found, the next step is to convert all the elements in the column for that variable into semipartial correlations, by the method shown in Table 5-4. These are then used to compute a second matrix of residual coefficients. Elements in the row for $y$ are divided by the square roots of corresponding diagonal elements. The variable with the largest value is selected as the third variable for the set. A fourth variable is obtained by the same method.

A test can be applied to determine the "statistical significance" of the increment in multiple correlation supplied by each variable (Kerlinger and Pedhazur 1973). One would stop adding variables when the next variable to be added failed to have a "significant" semipartial correlation with $y$.

There is no guarantee that the method described above for obtaining a set of independent variables will always obtain the most predictive set. This is because the method selects variables one at a time. It is possible to obtain a more predictive set of variables by trying all possible combinations of variables. For example, this might occur if the most predictive set does not contain the variable which has the highest zero-order correlation with the dependent variable, but the method described above always employs that variable as the first member of the set. In practice, however, this method usually does pick the most predictive set of variables. In those instances where some other combination of variables is more predictive than the set chosen by the method, the difference usually is small. Also, since more advantage is taken of chance by trying variables in all possible combinations and other complex approaches than by the method described above, the latter tends to shrink less when larger numbers of persons are studied.

## ADDITIONAL CONSIDERATIONS

Before we leave this chapter on multivariate correlational analysis, a number of issues need to be mentioned that have not been discussed in detail. First, nearly all large problems in multivariate correlational analysis as well as all the complex statistical methods that will be discussed throughout this book are carried out on high-speed computers these days rather than by hand or with desk calculators. The reader will find ready-made programs for such computations (e.g., multiple correlation and regression) at almost any major computing facility in university settings and in many settings in industry, the military, and governmental bureaus. The mathematical equations employed for such computer analyses look very different from the simple-appearing approaches that have been adopted in this chapter. The reason is that the equations which are most useful for explaining various types of multivariate correlational analysis and most easily understood by the reader are not the most economical approaches to actually computing results. The equations that are employed in computer calculations are based on solutions of complex equations concerning raw scores; but even if these are economical to employ with computers, they would be rather unintelligible to the individual being introduced to the statistical issues. Exactly the same results would be obtained by the simple-appearing formulas presented and discussed in this chapter as by the more elaborate-appearing versions. Even though it is good that complex multivariate correlational statistics can be computed very rapidly on present-day computers, merely reading the printout from such electronic monsters does not provide one with an understanding of the statistical methods involved. To understand such methods, not only is it useful to take them apart in simple terms, such as was done in this chapter, but also it helps to actually compute such statistics by hand on concrete examples. It would be helpful to the reader if this were done on some small problems that are available.

A second consideration relating to this chapter is that actual estimation equations relating to partial and multiple correlation were only mentioned and not concretely illustrated. Analogous to the use of the simple correlation coefficient (for example, $r_{12}$) to estimate one variable from another, the independent variables involved in both partial and multiple correlation can be used to predict the dependent variable $y$. These are derived from the same logic as that for the multiple and partial correlation. They are referred to as regression equations, because in most circumstances predictions are less than perfect, and thus one can speak of estimated scores on the dependent variable $z_y'$ as regressing toward the mean in comparison to actual scores on $z_y$. Such regression equations can be formed for standard scores, deviation scores, or raw scores. These are discussed in detail throughout the Suggested Additional Readings; see in particular the extensive discussion by Kerlinger and Pedhazur (1973).

Regression equations have not been discussed in detail for simple correlation or extensions to multiple and partial correlation because they are useful mainly for two rather specialized functions that are not highly important to behavioral scientists in general. The first function involves the actual mechanics of employing predictor tests in applied situations to estimate performance on some type of criterion variable, e.g., dollar amounts of sales of persons being selected as insurance agents. The second function is that of being employed as an adjunct to various types of statistics relating to analysis of variance. For example, all analysis of variance can be reduced to a special type of problem in multiple-regression analysis (see discussion in Kerlinger and Pedhazur 1973), and analysis of covariance involves partial regression analysis in some instances. However, even though the experimenter may be aware that partial- and multiple-regression analyses are intrinsic to the overall use of the statistical methods, the actual regression equations usually are "hidden" in the overall computational routines and thus need not be dealt with more directly.

The third and final issue that should be mentioned here is that of inferential statistics relating to multivariate correlational analysis. Whereas earlier it was said that psychometric theory will be discussed mainly as a large-sample theory and consequently that little mention would be made of inferential statistics, which is important mainly when samples are relatively small, there are some instances in multivariate correlational analysis where inferential statistics is helpful. Such uses of inferential statistics are discussed throughout the works cited in Suggested Additional Readings. The simplest case would be in testing the null hypothesis for a simple correlation, a partial correlation, or a multiple correlation. Although statistical significance in this regard provides only relatively meager information in psychometric theory, it is important to know that correlational values at least meet such minimal hurdles as are set by inferential statistics. More complex tests of hypotheses can be made concerning differences among simple, partial, and multiple correlations. More important is to employ confidence bands regarding the exactness with which correlational results obtained from research can be trusted. For example, it would be useful to know in a particular instance that the odds are less than 1 in 100 that the multiple correlation in a particular instance is less than .50 or greater than .60. Inferential statistics relating to the establishment of such confidence bands is a useful adjunct to psychometric theory and methodology.

# SUGGESTED ADDITIONAL READINGS

Guilford, J. P., and Fruchter, B. *Fundamental statistics in psychology and education* (5th ed.). New York: McGraw-Hill, 1973, chaps. 14 to 16.

Kerlinger, F. N. *Foundations of behavioral research* (2d ed.). New York: Holt, Rinehart, and Winston, 1973, chap. 35.

Kerlinger, F. N., and Pedhazur, E. J. *Multiple regression in behavioral research.* New York: Holt, Rinehart, and Winston, 1973, chaps. 1 to 4.

McNemar, Q. *Psychological statistics.* New York: Wiley, 1962, chaps. 10 and 11.

Van de Geer, J. P. *Introduction to multivariate analysis for the social sciences.* San Francisco: W. H. Freeman, 1971, chaps. 9 to 11.

# CHAPTER SIX

# THEORY OF MEASUREMENT ERROR

Some error is involved in any type of measurement, whether it is the measurement of the temperature of liquids, blood pressure, or intelligence. Measurement error can be in the form of either a systematic bias or random errors. The former would be the case if a chemist had only one thermometer, and although it was read precisely, the thermometer always registered two degrees higher than it should. Random error would be at work if the thermometer were accurate but the chemist nearsightedly misread it while making different measurements. Because of blurred vision, on some occasions the chemist would record the temperature as being slightly higher and on other occasions as slightly lower than it actually was. Over many such measurements, one would find a distribution of errors. One can envision a normal distribution of such errors by the nearsighted chemist attempting over and over again to employ the thermometer. Although systematic biases in psychological measures are important to learn about, they will not be considered in this chapter. (Systematic biases will be discussed in Chap. 16.) This chapter is concerned with random errors. Systematic biases contribute to the mean score of all subjects being studied, and as has been pointed out previously, the mean score of all subjects is not very important in studies of individual differences and in most psychological experiments. Random errors are important in all studies, because to the extent they are present, limits are placed on the degree of lawfulness that can be found in nature. Why this is so can be illustrated with the nearsighted chemist. Suppose that when no measurement error is present, there is a smooth curve relating temperature to the ratio of one chemical to another in a compound. To the extent to which random errors of measurement occur, the smooth curve will not be found, and instead the curve will appear somewhat jagged. In all areas of science, random errors of measurement tend to jumble up any form of lawfulness that exists in nature.

There are many ways that random errors can influence measurements in the behavioral sciences. If a test in introductory psychology contains only a small number of items, how well students perform will depend to some extent on their luck in knowing the correct answers. If a test is given on a day when a student is not feeling well, he or she might perform more poorly than ordinarily. If required to rate 10 patients in terms of amount of improvement in psychotherapy, a clinical psychologist probably is not exactly sure of the ratings and might give somewhat different ratings on another occasion. On a true-false test, a student could get approximately half the answers correct by flipping a coin. When the student actually knows the answer to half the questions and guesses at the other half, such guessing adds an element of randomness or unreliability to the overall test results. Later, numerous ways will be discussed in which random error can influence the results of measurement methods in the behavioral sciences.

Random errors of measurement are never completely eliminated; but to portray nature in its ultimate lawfulness, efforts are made to reduce errors as much as possible. To the extent to which measurement error is slight, a measure is said to be *reliable*. Reliability concerns the extent to which measurements are *repeatable*—when different persons make the measurements, on different occasions, with supposedly alternative instruments for measuring the same thing and when there are small variations in circumstances for making measurements that are not intended to influence results. In other words, measurements are intended to be *stable* over a variety of conditions in which essentially the same results should be obtained. Science is concerned with repeatable experiments; and for experiments to be repeatable, any particular object in any particular circumstance must have a set quantity of any particular attribute. If the data obtained from experiments are influenced by random errors of measurement, then results are not exactly repeatable. Thus science is limited by the reliability of measuring instruments and/or the reliability with which scientists use them.

Measurement reliability represents a classic issue in scientific generalization. In the effort to measure any particular attribute, numerous sources of error might be introduced by variations in alternative forms of a test, approaches used by different examiners, subtle factors that influence the behavior of subjects in the testing situation, and many other factors that might lead to variation in the measurements made on each person. To the extent to which an approach to measurement provides very much the same result regardless of these opportunities for variations to occur, then it is reliable; and one can generalize from any particular use of the measurement method to a wide variety of other circumstances in which it might be employed. The close tie-in between the theory of reliability and scientific generalization will become even more apparent when specific models for studying measurement error are discussed.

Of course, high reliability does not necessarily mean high validity. One could, for example, seek to measure intelligence by having children throw stones as far as they could. How far stones were tossed on one occasion might correlate highly with how far they were tossed on another occasion, and thus, being repeatable, the measure would be highly reliable; but obviously the tossing of stones would not constitute a *valid* measure of intelligence. The amount of measurement error places a limit on the amount of validity that an instrument can have, but even in the complete absence of measurement error, there is no guarantee of validity. Reliability is a *necessary* but not *sufficient* condition for validity.

It is interesting that the theory of measurement error has been developed largely in the context of psychology, and largely by psychologists. One might imagine that this is because psychological measures are plagued by measurement error, but this is only a partial explanation. Measures in other areas of science often are accompanied by as much, or more, random error as in psychology. For example, the measurement of blood pressure in physiological studies is far less reliable than many psychological measures, and similar examples could be drawn from the physical and social sciences. The development of the theory of measurement error by psychologists can be attributed either to an accident of history or to the fact that, being self-conscious about problems of measurement, psychologists have developed the theory of measurement error along with other advances in the methodology of measurement. Among his many other contributions to psychological measurement, Charles Spearman (1904) laid the foundation for the theory of measurement error.

For two reasons, it is easy to overstate the importance of the theory of measurement error in psychological measurement. First, as will be shown later, measurement error frequently does not harm most investigations as much as might be thought. Second, there are numerous topics regarding psychological measurement that are equally or more important than the theory of measurement error, as evidenced throughout this book. A large proportion of journal articles on psychological measurement and a major portion of some books on the topic have been devoted to measurement error. This is probably because the theory of measurement error is so neatly expressible in mathematical terms, in contrast to some other important issues, e.g., validity, where grounds for argument are not so straightforward. The theory of measurement error is *one* important topic in psychological measurement, and consequently this and the next chapter will be devoted to it.

The theory of measurement error which will be presented is surely one of the most workable sets of mathematical models in psychology. The theory can be derived with few assumptions about the nature of data, and the same formulas can be derived from quite different sets of assumptions. The theory is very "robust," in the sense that it tends to hold well even when the assumptions of various models are markedly violated. This and the following chapter will develop the theory of reliability from some simple principles that have been with us since near the turn of the century. Although mention will be made of some rather sophisticated, complex mathematical models that also concern measurement error, it is surprising how well the major conclusions from these more complex models agree with many of the major principles that can be derived from the simple, conventional theory which will be emphasized here.

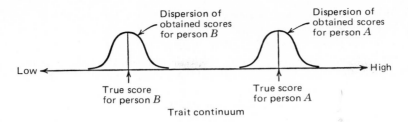

**Figure 6-1** True scores and distributions of obtained scores for two persons.

The classical theory for the discussion of measurement error is illustrated in Fig. 6-1 (this theory will be modified subsequently). It is assumed that each person has a *true score*, one that would be obtained if there were no errors of measurement. In the figure, person *A* has a relatively high true score and person *B* has a relatively low true score. Since there is some random error in the score obtained for a person on a particular occasion, obtained scores would differ from true scores on a random basis. If it were possible to give many alternative forms of a test, e.g., many different spelling tests constructed by the same procedures, the average score on the tests would closely approximate true scores. Scores obtained from the alternative forms would be distributed symmetrically above and below the true scores. Since such distributions of random errors are expected to be normally distributed, it is expected that distributions of obtained scores will be normally distributed about true scores.

The wider the spread of obtained scores about true scores, the more error there is in employing the type of instrument. The standard deviation of the distribution of errors for each person would be an index of the amount of error. If the standard deviation of errors were much the same for all persons, which usually is assumed to be the case, one standard deviation of errors could typify the amount of error to be expected. This typical standard deviation of errors is called the *standard error of measurement*, $\sigma_{meas}$. The size of $\sigma_{meas}$ is a direct indication of the amount of error involved in using a particular type of instrument. The issues, as illustrated in Fig. 6-1, could be carried on to a more extensive discussion of measurement error, but first we will look at a very general model for the discussion of test reliability.

## THE DOMAIN-SAMPLING MODEL

The most useful model for the discussion of measurement error is that which considers any particular measure as being composed of *a random sample of items from a hypothetical domain of items*. An example would be a particular spelling test for fourth-grade students, which could be thought of as constituting a random sample of spelling words from all possible words appropriate to that age group. Another example would be a measure of anxiety containing 10 positive and 10 negative statements, in which case the items could be thought of as a random sample of the many possible items that could be composed for that measurement problem. Measures used in controlled experiments also can be thought of as concerning random samples of items, as well as those used primarily in studies of individual differences. An example would be the study of recognition memory for complex geometrical forms. The experimenter first shows to the subject 100 geometrical forms one at a time. Subsequently, the 100 forms that were to be remembered are mixed with another 100 forms that have not been seen previously, and the task of the subject is to decide which forms were in the first set. The geometrical forms employed in the study can be thought of as a sample of the many possible geometrical forms that could have been constructed for the experiment. Many other examples could be given of how it is reasonable to think of particular measures as representing samples of items from hypothetical domains of items. Instead of using the word *domain* to refer to the hypothetical, very large collection of items, this is referred to by many authors as a *universe*, or *population*, of items. (The danger in employing the latter term is that it is likely to be confused with issues relating to the sampling of populations of persons.)

Of course, at the outset it is obvious that the model is not true to life, because, strictly speaking, items are almost never sampled randomly; rather items are *composed* for particular measures. However, the model usually does lead to accurate predictions in practice. This is because the test constructor usually develops a wide variety of items for a test (e.g., of arithmetic), and this variety has much the same effect as actual random sampling. First it is stated that the purpose of any particular measurement is to estimate the measurement that would be obtained if *all* the items in the domain were employed, e.g., all possible spelling words. The score that any subject would obtain over the whole domain is spoken of as the *true score*. It is equally meaningful to speak of this as a domain score, and other authors frequently call this a universe score. To the extent to which any sample of items correlated highly with true scores, the sample would be highly reliable.

Later the model will be augmented to consider the possibility that the items in the domain vary in terms of circumstances of many kinds, such as the physical condition of the subject, the skill of the test examiner, the testing environment, and many other possible contributors to measurement error. However, rather than complicate the model at this point, it would be better to simply concentrate on the problem of sampling items from a domain. Later, it will be shown that it is a very simple conceptual step to include factors that influence measurement error other than the sampling of items per se.

The domain-sampling model can be developed without consideration of the number of items sampled for particular measures. Each sample could contain many items or, at the lower extreme, only one item. Also, the model can be developed without concern for the type of item employed or the factorial composition of items.

The domain-sampling model will be developed initially on the basis of standard scores for items and for tests composed of sums of standard scores on items. This development in terms of standard scores rather than deviation scores or raw scores will permit the use of statistics based on the correlation coefficient $r$ rather than on variances and covariances. Of course, usually one does not standardize items before they are summed to obtain total test scores (sums of 0 and 1 for dichotomous items). However, the assumption of standard scores does very little to violate the overall results that can be obtained in the domain-sampling model, and basing statistical derivations on standard scores will make it much easier for the reader to understand the theory of reliability that follows from the model. Later, it will prove useful to switch from derivations based on correlations to derivations based on variances and covariances for the development of some statistics relating to measurement error; but for the present we will assume that all scores relating to the domain-sampling model are standardized.

Basic to the model is the concept of an infinitely large correlation matrix showing all correlations among items in the domain. The average correlation in the matrix, $\bar{r}_{ij}$, would indicate the extent to which some common core existed in the items. The dispersion of correlations about the average would indicate the extent to which items varied in sharing the common core. If the assumption is made that all items have an equal amount of the common core, the average correlation in each column of the hypothetical matrix would be the same, which would be the same as the average correlation in the whole matrix. Keep in mind that the assumption is not necessarily that all correlations in the matrix are the same, but rather that the sum of correlations, or average, of each item with all the others is the same for all items. The latter is a much less restrictive assumption than the former.

If the above assumption holds, it is possible to directly compute (not just estimate) the correlation of any particular item with the sum of all items in the domain as follows. If all items are expressed as standard scores, the formula for the correlation of item 1 with the sum of scores on $k$ items is

$$r_{1(1\,\ldots\,k)} = \frac{1/N\;\Sigma z_1(z_1 + z_2 + z_3 + \ldots + z_k)}{\sqrt{\Sigma z_1^2/N}\;\sqrt{1/N\,\Sigma\,(z_1 + z_2 + z_3 + \ldots + z_k)^2}} \tag{6-1}$$

Equation (6-1) is simply the formula for the correlation of one variable with the sum of $k$ variables. It is important to note that variable 1, being an item in the domain, is included in the sum of variables 1 through $k$. The numerator of the equation could be transformed as follows:

$$\frac{1}{N}\,\Sigma z_1(z_1 + z_2 + z_3 + \cdots + z_k) = \frac{1}{N}\,\Sigma(z_1^2 + z_1 z_2 + z_1 z_3 + \cdots + z_1 z_k)$$

$$= \frac{1}{N}\,(\Sigma z_1^2 + \Sigma z_1 z_2 + \Sigma z_1 z_3 + \cdots + \Sigma z_1 z_k)$$

$$= 1 + r_{12} + r_{13} + \cdots + r_{1k}$$

$$= 1 + (k - 1)\,\bar{r}_{1j}$$

$$= 1 + (k - 1)\bar{r}_{ij}$$

After the summation sign is "run through" terms (the third expression above), in parentheses is the product of sets of standard scores for variable 1 with all other variables. When these are divided by the number of people $N$, the fourth expression results. Each element in the sum is the correlation of variable 1 with one of the other variables. Since the first term is the correlation of variable 1 with itself, that term equals 1. Thus the equation can be transformed to 1 added to $k - 1$ multiplied by the average correlation of variable 1 with each of the other variables. If the assumption holds that the average correlation of each item with the others is the same (remember that this is a crucial assumption) and thus the same as the average correlation in the matrix, then the sum of the correlations of item 1 with the remaining $k - 1$ items (excluding item 1) would equal $(k - 1) \bar{r}_{ij}$.

In the denominator of Eq. (6-1), the term on the left is the standard deviation of standard scores on variable 1. Being 1, this "falls out" of the denominator. In the denominator, under the radical in the term on the right is the variance of the sum of $k$ sets of standard scores. Note that variable 1 is included in the sum. Previously it was shown that the variance of the sum of $k$ sets of standard scores equals the sum of all the elements in the correlation matrix for those scores (see discussion in Chap. 5). There are $k^2$ elements in any symmetric matrix of correlations. Of these, $k$ are diagonal elements and consequently $k^2 - k$ are off-diagonal elements. Since in a correlation matrix each diagonal element is 1, the sum of the diagonal elements equals $k$. Rather than the sum of off-diagonal elements, one could obtain the same value by multiplying the average off-diagonal element by $k^2 - k$. Unlike the crucial assumption that had to be made in the derivation of the numerator, the denominator can be derived without making any assumptions about the nature of the correlations in the domain. With these considerations in mind, it should be understandable why the denominator of Eq. (6-1) can be phrased as follows:

$$\sqrt{k + (k^2 - k)\bar{r}_{ij}}$$

Reassembling numerator and denominator gives the following formula for the correlation of item 1 with the sum of the $k$ items in the domain.

$$
\begin{aligned}
r_{1(1 \cdots k)} &= \frac{1 + (k - 1)\bar{r}_{ij}}{\sqrt{k + (k^2 - k)\bar{r}_{ij}}} \\
&= \frac{1 + k\bar{r}_{ij} - \bar{r}_{ij}}{\sqrt{k + k^2\bar{r}_{ij} - k\bar{r}_{ij}}}
\end{aligned}
\tag{6-2}
$$

If, as the model assumes, the domain of items is infinitely large, we can see what happens as $k$ approaches infinity. (Of course, in this case $\bar{r}_{ij}$ would equal the average of an infinite number of correlations in a domain rather than only the average correlation in a finite $k$-by-$k$ matrix.) The first step is to divide each term in the numerator and denominator by $k$. Since the elements in the denominator are under the radical, this would require dividing each term by $k^2$. The result is as follows:

$$r_{1(1\cdots k)} = \frac{1/k + \bar{r}_{ij} - \bar{r}_{ij}/k}{\sqrt{1/k + \bar{r}_{ij} - \bar{r}_{ij}/k}} \tag{6-3}$$

$$k \to \infty$$

As $k$ approaches infinity, any term divided by $k$ approaches zero. Since there are only two terms in Eq. (6-3) that are not divided by $k$, the equation reduces to

$$r_{1(1\cdots k)} = \frac{\bar{r}_{ij}}{\sqrt{\bar{r}_{ij}}} = \sqrt{\bar{r}_{ij}} \tag{6-4}$$

$$k \to \infty$$

The correlation of item 1 with the sum of an infinite number of items in a domain would equal the square root of the average correlation among items in the domain. The same could be proved for item 2 or item 3 or any other item. This holds only under the assumption that all items have the same average correlation with other items. Since in that case the average correlation of item 1 with other items would equal $\bar{r}_{ij}$, Eq. (6-4) can be written as

$$r_{1(1\cdots k)} = \sqrt{\bar{r}_{1j}} \tag{6-5}$$

$$k \to \infty$$

where $\bar{r}_{1j}$ is the average correlation of item 1 with all other items in the domain. Since when $k$ approaches infinity, the correlation of item 1 with the $k$ items approaches the correlation of item 1 with *true scores*, it will be meaningful to use the following abbreviation of symbols:

$$r_{1(1\cdots k)} = r_{1t} = \sqrt{\bar{r}_{1j}} \tag{6-6}$$

$$k \to \infty$$

The correlation $r_{1t}$ of variable 1 with true scores in the domain (the sum of all items in the domain) would equal the square root of the average correlation of item 1 with all other items.

If the reader feels that some trick is being pulled by invoking the ghostly concept of infinity in order to derive these equations, then think in terms of any big number instead. If, for example, the number 1,000 were used rather than infinity, one would arrive at a result so close to that found in Eq. (6-6) that there would be no practical difference at all. Even if one thought in terms of a domain that contained only 100 items, the derivations up to this point would be very close to those obtained in employing the concept of infinity.

The formulas derived so far are the foundations of the theory of measurement error, and if they are properly understood, it will prove easy to develop many principles from them.

**Multi-item measures** In the previous section, the basic formulas for measurement error were developed with respect to a hypothetical domain of *items*, but in nearly all measurement problems, measures are composed of a number of items. The model can be easily extended to take care of this. The infinitely large matrix of correlations among items can be thought of as divided into groups, each containing $h$ items. The sum of scores on each group of items would constitute a test. If items were randomly sampled to compose the tests, correlations among different tests would tend to be the same. Such randomly sampled collections of items are said to constitute *randomly parallel* tests, since their means, standard deviations, and correlations with true scores differ only by chance. If it is assumed that the average correlation of each test with the sum of all other tests is the same for all tests, one can start back with Eq. (6-1) and insert standard scores for whole tests rather than for individual items. The successive steps are the same for proving that

$$r_{1t} = \sqrt{\bar{r}_{1j}} \qquad (6\text{-}7)$$

where $1$ = scores on test 1

$t$ = true scores in domain

$\bar{r}_{1j}$ = average correlation of test 1 with all tests in domain

The same formula results whether one is considering individual items or whole tests and no matter how many items are in each of the whole tests. Of course, the crucial assumption of equal correlations of scoring units with all other scoring units is much more sensible when one is talking about correlations among whole tests rather than correlations among individual test items. (It should be kept in mind that the average correlation among whole tests will be larger than the average correlation among items, and consequently correlations with true scores will be higher for the whole tests.)

By convention, the average correlation of one test, or one item, with all tests, or items, in the domain is called the *reliability coefficient*, which will be symbolized as $\bar{r}_{11}$ for variable 1, $\bar{r}_{22}$ for variable 2, and so on. Then the square root of $\bar{r}_{11}$ equals the correlation of item 1 or test 1 with true scores in the domain, $\bar{r}_{22}$ equals the squared correlation of test 2 with true scores, and so on for all other randomly parallel tests in the domain.

**Estimate of reliability** If the assumption made previously regarding correlations among elements of a domain is correct, the correlation of any test with true scores is precisely equal to the square root of $\bar{r}_{11}$, which is not an estimate, but an actual determination. Of course, in practice one never knows $\bar{r}_{11}$ exactly, because it is not possible to generate an infinite number of tests. Also, one almost never has even large numbers of tests that can be construed as randomly parallel. Consequently $\bar{r}_{11}$, and thus $r_{1t}$, can be only *estimated* in practice. An estimate of $\bar{r}_{11}$ will be symbolized as $r_{11}$, which is the conventional symbol for the reliability coefficient.

Obviously $r_{11}$ is a better estimate of $\bar{r}_{11}$ when the former is obtained by averaging the correlations of test 1 with a large, rather than a small, number of tests from the domain. If the tests were obtained actually by randomly drawing items from the domain, the key assumption regarding correlations among tests would be approximately correct. The average correlation of test 1 with a number of other tests would then be an estimate of the average correlation of test 1 with all tests in the domain. For example, the average correlation between one spelling test and five other spelling tests with the same number of items would be an estimate of $\bar{r}_{11}$, and the square root of that would be an estimate of the correlation between test 1 and hypothetical true scores in spelling. Usually, in practice, test 1 is correlated with only one other test (test 2), and the correlation is symbolized as $r_{11}$, which is taken as an estimate of $\bar{r}_{11}$. (It could be symbolized equally well as $r_{22}$ and taken as an estimate of the squared correlation of test 2 with true scores in the particular domain.) When only one correlation is taken as an estimate of a hypothetical infinite number of correlations, however, it is right to question how efficient such estimates are; this will be considered in a later section.

**The importance of the reliability coefficient** Care has been taken to show that it follows that $r_{1t}$ is equal to the square root of $\bar{r}_{11}$ and to show how $r_{1t}$ is estimated by the square root of $r_{11}$ (the average of any number of correlations between test 1 and other tests from the domain, including the "average" of only one such correlation). Once a good estimate of $\bar{r}_{11}$, and thus a good estimate of $r_{1t}$, is obtained, many important principles can be developed about measurement error. In this section it will be assumed that a precise method of estimating $\bar{r}_{11}$ is being used in particular problems; in later sections the precision of such estimates in different circumstances will be discussed. If we assume, then, that $r_{11} = \bar{r}_{11}$, $r_{1t}$ equals the square root of $r_{11}$.

The scores on a particular test are often spoken of as *fallible scores*—fallible because there is a degree of measurement error involved. In contrast, true scores are, in that sense, infallible. Although $r_{1t}$ is the correlation between an existing variable and a hypothetical variable rather than between two existing variables, it can be used in mathematical derivations in the same way that any correlation can. One can visualize a scatter diagram showing the relationship between the fallible scores on any test and true scores. This is illustrated in Fig. 6-2. Then, according to what has been learned about correlational analysis, the line of best fit for estimating true scores $z_t$ from fallible scores $z_1$ would be obtained as follows:

$$z_t' = r_{1t}z_1 = \sqrt{r_{11}}z_1 \tag{6-8}$$

where $z_t'$ = estimates of true standard scores

$z_1$ = standard scores on fallible measure

$r_{1t}$ = correlation of fallible scores with true scores

$r_{11}$ = reliability coefficient for variable 1

More about the estimation of true scores will be given in a later section. The important point here is that $r_{1t}$ can be placed in the usual equations for correlational analysis. It is particularly important to realize that, since the square of any correlation equals the variance in one variable explainable by variance in another variable, $r_{1t}^2$ equals the percentage of true-score variance explainable by

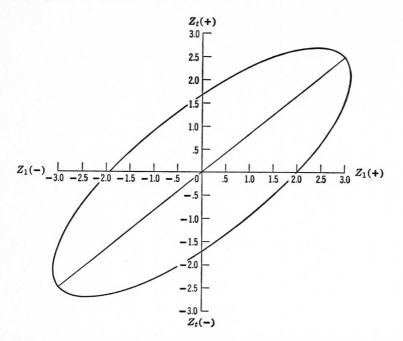

**Figure 6-2** Regression line and scatter contour for hypothetical relationship between obtained scores and true scores.

a fallible measure and vice versa. Then it can also be said that $r_{11}$ equals the same percentage of true-score variance in the fallible measure. This percentage takes on even more meaning when the fallible measure is expressed as deviation scores or raw scores rather than as standard scores. In the former two instances, the reliability coefficient could be expressed as follows:

$$r_{11} = \frac{\sigma_t^2}{\sigma_1^2} \tag{6-9}$$

where $\sigma_1^2$ = variance of variable 1

$\sigma_t^2$ = variance of variable 1 explainable by true scores

What Eq. (6-9) shows is that $r_{11}$ equals the amount of true-score variance in a measure divided by the actual variance of the measure. This way of viewing the reliability coefficient opens the door to the development of many principles concerning measurement error, but before those principles are developed, another model will be described for deriving the same principles.

## THE MODEL OF PARALLEL TESTS

The model discussed in the previous section concerned *randomly parallel* tests, which differ somewhat from one another in means, standard deviations, and correlations because of random factors in the sampling of items. It was stated that the best way to estimate the reliability is to correlate one test with a number of other tests from the same domain of content. Since in practice that is impractical, usually one test is correlated with only one other test to estimate the reliability. But since, on the face of it, there may be much inaccuracy in letting one correlation stand for the average of many unknown correlations, it rightly could be questioned whether the correlation between only two tests can be considered a precise estimate of the reliability of either test. The precision of such estimates will be discussed later.

If it is assumed that two tests actually are parallel, rather than just tending to be so on a sampling basis, the reliability coefficient and related measures can be directly derived without need for considering the precision of estimates. Two tests are parallel if (1) they have the same standard deviation, (2) they correlate the same with a set of true scores, and (3) the variance in each test which is not explainable by true scores is due to purely random error. (For some purposes, it also is useful to assume that the two tests have the same mean, but that assumption will not be necessary for developments here. Some of the other assumptions usually made about the characteristics of parallel tests will be shown to be derivable from the assumptions above.)

The deviation scores on two parallel tests can be broken down as follows:

$$x_1 = t + e_1$$

$$x_2 = t + e_2$$

where $x_1$ = obtained deviation scores on test 1

$\quad\quad x_2$ = obtained deviation scores on test 2

$\quad\quad t$ = true scores in domain

$\quad\quad e_1$ = errors on test 1

$\quad\quad e_2$ = errors on test 2

Since only the fallible scores on the two tests would actually be open to observation, the only way to learn about the true and error scores would be through the correlation of obtained scores on the two tests. Above it was assumed that the two tests correlate the same with true scores. If that correlation were known, it could then be used in a regression equation to estimate scores on the two fallible variables. From simple principles of correlation, much can be deduced about components of true and error variance.

In addition to principles incorporated in the above three basic assumptions for parallel tests, other principles can easily be deduced from the third assumption, that the portion of variance in each test not explainable by true scores is because of purely random error. First, by definition, random errors tend to balance one another, and consequently the mean of the errors on each test is expected to be zero. Second, since purely random errors do not correlate with any variable except by chance, (1) errors on one test are expected to correlate zero with errors on the other test, and (2) errors on either test are expected to correlate zero with true scores.

With this model, the following principles have been assumed or deduced:

$$\sigma_1 = \sigma_2$$

$$r_{1t} = r_{2t}$$

$$r_{te_1} = 0$$

$$r_{te_2} = 0$$

$$r_{e_1 e_2} = 0$$

$$M_{e_1} = 0$$

$$M_{e_2} = 0$$

Since error scores are uncorrelated with true scores, it follows that

$$\sigma_1^2 = \sigma_t^2 + \sigma_{e_1}^2 \tag{6-10}$$

and

$$\sigma_2^2 = \sigma_t^2 + \sigma_{e_2}^2 \tag{6-11}$$

Because variances of obtained scores are equal on the two tests and variances of true scores are equal, it follows that variances of error scores also are equal.

It is important to examine the correlation between the two parallel tests, as follows:

$$r_{12} = \frac{(1/N) \, \Sigma x_1 x_2}{\sigma_1 \sigma_2}$$

Since $x_1$ and $x_2$ can be expressed as the sum of true and error scores, and in the denominator the two standard deviations are equal, the correlation can be written as

$$r_{12} = \frac{(1/N) \, \Sigma \, (t + e_1) \, (t + e_2)}{\sigma_1^2}$$

$$= \frac{(1/N) \, (\Sigma t^2 + \Sigma t e_1 + \Sigma t e_2 + \Sigma e_1 e_2)}{\sigma_1^2}$$

$$= \frac{\sigma_t^2 + \sigma_{te_1} + \sigma_{te_2} + \sigma_{e_1 e_2}}{\sigma_1^2}$$

Because errors on the two parallel tests are uncorrelated with true scores and uncorrelated with each other, the three covariance terms in the numerator drop out, leaving

$$r_{12} = \frac{\sigma_t^2}{\sigma_1^2} = r_{11} \tag{6-12}$$

The correlation between two parallel tests equals the true-score variance in either test divided by the variance of either test. The same ratio was derived from the domain-sampling model. Since the ratio is the same for both tests, it is symbolized as $r_{11}$, $r_{22}$, or $r_{xx}$ in the general case, rather than as $r_{12}$.

A number of different methods could be used to prove that the correlation of test 1 with true scores equals the square root of the correlation between the two parallel forms. One method for showing this will prove useful later in discussing the assumptions of the model. It is implicit in the assumptions and derivations so far in this section that, when true scores are partialed from the two parallel tests, the residual scores on the two tests correlate zero. The error scores on the two tests would be the residuals after true scores were partialed, and these errors are uncorrelated. Thus the partial correlation would have to be zero, in which case the numerator of the partial correlation would have to be zero, as follows:

$$r_{11} - r_{1t}r_{2t} = 0$$

Since the model assumes that both tests correlate the same with true scores, the foregoing equation could be transformed to

$$r_{11} = r_{1t}^2 \qquad or \qquad r_{1t} = \sqrt{r_{11}}$$

With the correlation of obtained scores with true scores derived, it is possible to develop many principles concerning measurement error, but first it would be wise to look carefully at some relations between the two models that have been presented.

## PERSPECTIVES ON THE TWO MODELS

It may seem paradoxical that two such different-appearing models reach the same conclusions about measurement error. Many other identical formulas can be derived from the two models. Actually, though, as can be seen on careful inspection, they are not different models—the parallel-test model is a special case of the more general domain-sampling model. If in the latter all sample tests have the same standard deviation and correlation with total scores in the domain (true scores), and when true scores are partialed from all sample tests the partial correlations among sample tests are zero, the domain will be populated with parallel tests rather than randomly parallel tests. In this case the correlation between any two tests will be the same as the average of all correlations among tests, and the square root of that correlation will be the correlation of each test with true scores.

In making the three assumptions necessary for the parallel-test model, one primarily ignores the actual problem involved in estimating the correlation of obtained scores with true scores. The assumptions in that model are tantamount to assuming that the correlation between any two tests in a domain is a completely precise determination of the reliability coefficient, rather than only an estimate. The domain-sampling model frankly faces the fact that there is a problem regarding the precision of estimation.

The parallel-test model offers a conceptual dead end for the development of theories of measurement error. Since true scores are defined by only two tests, one naturally wonders, "True scores on what attribute?" It is easier to think in terms of a domain of possible items and of any test being a sample, random or otherwise, of those items. If there are three supposedly parallel tests rather than two and the three correlations among them are different, what then is the reliability? Since the model explicitly assumes that all parallel tests have the same reliability, one is in a quandary. This is no problem for the domain-sampling model, where this possibility is admitted and an estimate of the reliability of any one test is the average of its correlations with the other two tests.

Although the parallel-test model involves three assumptions, only one of these assumptions, the equality of variances, can be empirically determined. That, however, is the least important of the assumptions. A more crucial assumption is that the two tests have the same correlation with true scores, and there is no direct way to determine from the parallel-test model if this assumption is correct. Equally crucial is the assumption that errors on the two tests are uncorrelated, which was shown to be tantamount to the assumption that, when true scores are partialed from scores on the two tests, the partial correlation is zero. There is no direct way in the parallel-test model to determine whether that assumption is correct.

The parallel-test model probably has achieved its popularity because of its simplicity and because it ignores problems regarding the precision of reliability estimation. An important principle is that any formula obtained from the parallel-test model which *specifies* a characteristic of measurement error is matched by a formula from the domain-sampling model that *estimates* the same characteristic. For example, in the former model the correlation between two tests supposedly specifies the reliability, whereas in the latter model the correlation is considered only an estimate. The same is found true for all formulas that have been derived from the parallel-test model: an identical formula, albeit an estimate rather than a specification, can be found in the domain-sampling model. However, the reverse of the principle does not hold. There are many principles and formulas that can be derived from the domain-sampling model which cannot be matched by the parallel-test model. An example was mentioned previously of unequal correlations among three tests. Another example is that the domain-sampling model permits deductions about the precision of the estimate of reliability obtained with different numbers of items and with different distributions of correlations among them. The parallel-test model precludes even asking questions about such issues. The only way that the latter model can handle any questions regarding relations among numerous tests is to postulate numerous parallel tests. Inevitably, thinking in this way encourages one to relax the assumptions regarding parallel tests, and what starts as a parallel-test model soon evolves into a domain-sampling model.

The author is strongly in favor of the domain-sampling model as a theoretical framework for discussing and investigating reliability. Actually, the basic idea of randomly sampling items from a domain leads to many different models for measurement error. (Some useful auxiliary models will be discussed later in this chapter.) The one developed previously was the simplest of all these, its only assumption being that the average correlation of each item with the others is the same for all items.

**Factorial composition** It sometimes is said that both models which have been described for considering measurement error assume that all items measure one factor only. Strictly speaking, this is not correct. Both models would hold if items were equally divided between two factors, e.g., if half the items in the domain concerned spelling and the other half concerned arithmetic. In the domain-sampling model, random samples of items from this two-factor domain would tend to correlate the same with one another. True scores would consist of combined ability in spelling and arithmetic. The square root of average correlations among sample tests would approximate the correlation of individual tests with true scores, which is the key deduction from the model. All other formulas for measurement error could be derived for this two-factor domain. The model would hold as well if instead of two kinds of items relating to two factors, all items were compounded in equal proportions of a number of factors. For example, if each item simultaneously measured anxiety, reaction time, and muscle coordination, all items would tend to correlate much the same with one another, and consequently the average correlation among 20 or more of them would well represent the average correlation that would be obtained among much larger numbers of them.

The domain-sampling model concerns the extent to which one "anything" correlates with an infinite number of other "anythings." This correlation is estimated by taking the square root of the average correlation of one anything with a number of other anythings or the square root of the correlation with only one other anything. All the mathematical properties of the models, particularly the domain-sampling model, hold regardless of the factorial composition of the items.

The factorial composition of items is important in two ways. First, to the extent that the items diversely measure a number of factors rather than only one factor, correlations among items are likely to be rather heterogeneous in size. As will be discussed more fully in the next section, the more homogeneous the correlations in the domain, the more precise are estimates of correlations with true scores. Consequently even though the domain-sampling model leads to *unbiased* estimates of correlations with true scores when the domain is factorially complex, such estimates might be accompanied by a considerable amount of *content-sampling error.*

The second important consideration regarding factorial composition is that, in actual investigations, the *intention* is to investigate a domain of items that principally concerns one factor. No one is, or should be, interested in studying the internal consistency of a polyglot domain of test materials. As has been mentioned previously and will be stressed in future chapters, the purpose in the development of a new measure is to tap a unitary attribute. Even though the model holds when items concern more than one factor, the problem is more meaningful and estimates of reliability are more precise when items are dominated by only one factor.

## PRECISION OF RELIABILITY ESTIMATES

At a number of places so far the question has arisen as to the precision of reliability estimates from the domain-sampling model. Such estimates are precise to the extent that different random samples of items correlate the same with true scores. If an item correlated exactly the same with all other items in the domain, the correlation with any other item would be a precise indication of reliability. If all items in the domain correlated exactly the same with one another, then all items would have exactly the same correlation with true scores, which would equal the square root of the typical correlation. To the extent that correlations among items in the domain vary, there is some random error connected with the average correlation found in any particular sampling of items. For example, if item 1 had correlations with other items in the domain ranging from .10 to .30, the average correlation of item 1 with a number of other items randomly selected from the domain would provide a relatively precise estimate of the reliability of item 1. In contrast, if such correlations ranged between −.30 and .60, the average correlation of item 1 with the other items might give only a rough approximation of the reliability.

Related to the precision of estimates of reliability is a double problem of sampling—that concerned with the sampling of people and that concerned with the sampling of items. As was mentioned previously, it is very difficult to consider both problems of sampling simultaneously, and to do so would lead us into statistical complexities beyond the scope of this book. Earlier it was said that measurement theory is mainly a large-sample theory, in which it is assumed that sufficient numbers of persons are studied so that this source of sampling error is a minor consideration. This is necessary not only to simplify measurement theory, but also because the precision required in measurement theory usually cannot tolerate large doses of sampling error because of the small number of subjects. Consequently, in this discussion it will be assumed that a representative sample of 300 or more persons is employed in studies of measurement error, in which case the sampling error because of the sampling of people will be a minor consideration. In the theory of measurement error, the primary concern is with the *sampling of items*.

A domain of items is of interest only if the average correlation among items is positive. If the average correlation is zero or near zero, the items as a group have no common core, and it is not sensible to consider them as measuring a unitary attribute. Assuming that the average correlation is positive and sufficiently higher than zero to encourage further investigation, the next point of interest is the relative homogeneity of correlations. As was mentioned previously, it is hoped that the correlations will be relatively homogeneous.

Whatever the case, there will be a distribution of correlations about the average value. An approximate statistical model will help to evaluate the influence of that distribution on the precision of estimates of reliability. The model assumes that correlations are normally distributed about the average value and statistically independent of one another, and both assumptions are known to be at least slightly incorrect. If the average correlation is positive, a random distribution of correlations about that average tends to be negatively skewed rather than strictly normal. Also, correlations in a matrix are not independent of one another. For example, the correlation of item 1 and item 2 is not independent of the correlation of item 2 and item 3. However, when correlations are as low as they usually are among test items (typically ranging between .10 and .30), those assumptions are violated only slightly, and consequently the model probably will hold well in practice.

As will be explained more fully in a later section, regardless of the number of items sampled from a domain to obtain a test, the reliability of the test is directly related to the average correlation among those items. Longer tests have higher reliability coefficients than shorter tests, but in both cases the reliabilities of the tests are deducible from the average correlations among their items. This being so, the precision with which the reliability is estimated for any test is a direct function of the precision with which the average correlation of items in a test estimates the average correlation of all items in the domain. If such correlations are normally distributed in the domain, an approximate standard error for the estimation of $\bar{r}_{ij}$ is obtained as follows:

$$\sigma_{\bar{r}_{ij}} = \frac{\sigma_{r_{ij}}}{\sqrt{\frac{1}{2}k(k-1) - 1}} \qquad (6\text{-}13)$$

where

$\sigma_{\bar{r}_{ij}} =$ standard error of estimating $r_{ij}$ in whole domain

$\sigma_{r_{ij}} =$ standard deviation of distribution of actual correlations within a test

$k =$ number of test items

Equation (6-13) is merely an adaptation of the customary formula for the standard error of the mean, in which case people would be sampled rather than test items. In that instance the standard error of average scores for people would equal the standard deviation of scores divided by the number of persons minus 1. In Eq. (6-13), each correlation is considered analogous to a score made by one person. The standard deviation of correlations within a test is taken as an estimate of the standard deviation of correlations in the whole domain. At first glance, the denominator of Eq. (6-13) may look complicated, but it is only the square root of the number of possible correlations among $k$ items minus 1, the 1 being subtracted to obtain the proper "degrees of freedom."

What is immediately apparent from the formula is that the error of estimating $\bar{r}_{11}$ is directly related to the standard deviation of correlations among items. Also apparent from an inspection of the denominator is that the precision (the inverse of the standard error) of estimating $\bar{r}_{11}$ is directly related to the number of test items. Thus an important principle is deduced: Not only are longer tests more reliable (which will be proved later), but also their estimates of reliability are more precise than those of shorter tests.

In a typical situation the average correlation among items is .20 and the standard deviation of correlations is .10. Then the standard error for estimating $\bar{r}_{ij}$ from a 10-item test is obtained as follows:

$$\sigma_{\bar{r}_{ij}} = \frac{.10}{\sqrt{(5 \times 9) - 1}}$$

$$= \frac{.10}{\sqrt{44}}$$

$$= \frac{.10}{6.63}$$

$$\sigma_{\bar{r}_{ij}} = .015$$

In any sampling problem, the expectation is that 95 percent of sample means will lie in a band stretching from approximately two standard errors below the population mean to two standard errors above it. The analogous expectation here is that, for random samples of items, the average correlation among items will be distributed in a like manner. By using this logic, if the average correlation among items in a domain is .20 and the standard deviation of correlations is .10, the standard error for average correlations obtained from 10-item tests is only .015. Then the expectation is that 95 percent of the sample values lie between approximately .17 and .23. If in this instance there were 40 items on each test, the standard error would be only .0036!

What is illustrated in the above example is that, even when tests have as few as 10 items, reliability estimates are rather precise. When there are as many items as appear on most tests, the sampling error because of the selection of items is vanishingly small. The reason for this precision is that as the number of items is increased, the number of correlations among items increases at a rapid rate, the factor being that appearing in the denominator of Eq. (6-13). For example, there are 780 possible correlations among 40 items. One then obtains approximately the same precision for estimating the average correlation that would be obtained in sampling people if 780 subjects were used in estimating the population mean score for a variable. Thus, in most measurement problems, there is very little error in the estimation of reliability that could be attributed to random error in the selection of items. A very important point is that if two tests supposedly from the same domain correlate less with one another than would be predicted from the average correlation among items within each test, the difference usually is caused not by random errors in the selection of items, but either by sampling error because of the numbers of persons or by systematic differences in the way items are obtained for the two tests. In other words, when this occurs in a large sample of persons, the indication is that the two tests are representative of somewhat different domains of content, a point which will be discussed more fully later.

It should be kept in mind that if, for example, the average correlation in a sample of 40 items is .20, the estimated correlation of total scores on the test with true scores will not be .20, but considerably higher than that (exactly how much will be discussed later). A confidence zone for the reliability of the whole test can be obtained by extrapolating the upper and lower bounds of the confidence zone for the average correlation among items on the test. This can be done with Eq. (6-18), which will be discussed later. First, the lower bound of the confidence zone for the average correlation among items is placed in the formula, which provides a lower bound of the confidence zone for the reliability $r_{11}$ of the whole test. Next, the upper bound of the confidence zone for the average correlation among items is placed in the formula, which provides an estimate of the upper bound of the confidence zone for the reliability of the whole test. Although confidence zones are larger for whole tests than for individual items, if the test has as many as 40 items, the confidence zone usually is surprisingly small.

It should be reiterated that the foregoing principles concerning the precision of reliability estimates are based on an approximate model which does some injustice to actuality by assuming that correlations among items in a domain are normally distributed and statistically independent of one another. As was mentioned previously, however, these assumptions hold reasonably well for the usual correlations among test items; consequently formulas based on those assumptions should provide useful information about the amount of error to be expected in estimating the reliability coefficient in particular investigations.

**Variances of items** In this chapter the basic formulas for reliability were derived on the assumption that all items are expressed as standard scores, but in practice items are rarely standardized before they are summed to obtain test scores. One might wonder if such differences in variances that exist among items would disturb the principles that have been developed so far. For example, since dichotomous items will not all have the same $p$ value and thus will not all have the same variance, this might introduce difficulties for the domain-sampling model. In fact, it does not. The model could have been developed from the covariances among items as well as from the correlations among items, and the same principles would have resulted. Also, it is clear that differences in $p$ values of items usually have very little effect on the precision of reliability estimates, particularly if the number of items is 20 or more. This was made quite clear in a study by Cronbach and Azuma (1962), in which they randomly sampled artificial items having a range of $p$ values. They found that such random variation in $p$ values had very little effect on the reliability estimates.

## DEDUCTIONS FROM THE DOMAIN-SAMPLING MODEL

When the domain-sampling model is accepted as a useful foundation, it is possible to deduce many principles regarding measurement error. These principles are useful both for the development of measurement theory and for handling everyday problems of measurement error in research.

**Test Length** As was mentioned previously, the reliability of scores obtained on a sample of items from a domain increases with the number of items sampled. Thus the individual item would be expected to have only a small correlation with true scores; a 10-item test might correlate .50 with true scores, and a 100-item test might correlate above .90 with true scores. The rate at which the reliability increases as a function of the number of items can be deduced in the following way. The matrix below depicts the correlations of items with true scores and with one another:

The first column and first row of the matrix would contain correlations of true scores with all variables. The first diagonal element would contain the correlation of true scores with themselves, which would be 1.0. Also, all the other diagonal elements would equal 1.0. The remaining portions of the matrix would contain all possible correlations of items with one another. From what was learned previously about the correlation of sums, one can develop the correlation of the $k$ items with true scores in the following steps:

$$r_{t(1 \ldots k)} = \frac{\Sigma r_{it}}{\sqrt{r_{tt}} \sqrt{k + 2\Sigma r_{ij}}} \tag{6-14}$$

Equation (6-14) is simply the correlation of the sum of $k$ variables with one variable $t$. The numerator can be expressed as $k$ times the average correlation of items with true scores. In the denominator, the term on the left is 1.0; thus it drops out of the equation. The remaining term of the denominator is the square root of the sum of the elements in that part of the matrix showing correlations among the $k$ items. There would, of course, be $k$ diagonal elements. Instead of having 2 times the sum of correlations among items, one can place in the denominator 2 times the average correlation multiplied by the number of correlations. With these considerations in mind, Eq. (6-14) can be transformed as follows:

$$r_{t(1 \ldots k)} = \frac{k \bar{r}_{it}}{\sqrt{k + k^2 \bar{r}_{ij} - k \bar{r}_{ij}}} \tag{6-15}$$

The formula is theoretically correct, but since the numerator contains the average hypothetical correlation of items with true scores, as it stands it is of no practical use. It is instructive to see what happens when both sides of the equation are squared ($r^2_{t(1 \cdots k)}$ will be symbolized as $r_{kk}$):

$$r_{kk} = \frac{k^2 \bar{r}^2_{it}}{k + k^2 \bar{r}_{ij} - k\bar{r}_{ij}} \tag{6-16}$$

Then numerator and denominator are divided by $k$:

$$r_{kk} = \frac{k\bar{r}^2_{it}}{1 + (k-1)\bar{r}_{ij}} \tag{6-17}$$

Since the correlation of any item with true scores is *estimated* by the square root of the average correlation of that item with other items, in the numerator $k\bar{r}_{ij}$ can be substituted for $k\bar{r}^2_{it}$, resulting in

$$r_{kk} = \frac{k\bar{r}_{ij}}{1 + (k-1)\bar{r}_{ij}} \tag{6-18}$$

It is hard to overestimate the importance of Eq. (6-18) for the theory of measurement error. On behalf of the originators, it is called the *general form of the Spearman-Brown Prophecy Formula*. An example will show what can be learned from applying the formula. If, in a 20-item test, the average correlation among items is .25, these values could be substituted in Eq. (6-18) as follows:

$$r_{kk} = \frac{20 \times .25}{1 + (19 \times .25)}$$

$$= \frac{5.00}{1 + 4.75}$$

$$= \frac{5.00}{5.75}$$

$$r_{kk} = .87$$

Previously it was shown that $r_{kk}$ is the estimated square of the correlation of scores on a collection of items with true scores. Consequently, in the above example, the estimated correlation with true scores would equal the square root of .87, which is .93. In the equation, $r_{kk}$ is the reliability coefficient, which in this case is .87. Thus can be seen how a highly reliable total test score can be obtained from items that correlate only .25 with one another on the average.

Although $r_{kk}$ was introduced as a way of obtaining the correlation of a collection of items with true scores, it has considerable meaning in its own right. It is the expected correlation of one $k$-item test with other $k$-item tests drawn from the same domain. Thus $r_{kk}$ is the *reliability coefficient* for a $k$-item test determined from the *intercorrelations of items* on the test. As will be discussed more fully in the next chapter, in many ways this is a highly meaningful measure of reliability in actual research.

Equation (6-18) holds regardless of the size of units that are added. All one needs to know is the average correlation among the units. Thus the formula would hold if the $k$ units being combined were pairs of items, groups with 10 items in each, or groups with 1,000 items in each. If the assumptions of the domain-sampling model hold, one will come to approximately the same conclusion about the reliability of a test with a particular number of items regardless of the number of items in each unit which is combined to obtain the final test. (This assumes that each collection of items, regardless of size, represents a random sample from the domain, which means that all tests are randomly parallel.) For example, for a 40-item test, rather than estimate the reliability by placing the average correlation among items in Eq. (6-18), a different approach would be to randomly divide the 40 items into four groups of 10 each. The average correlation among the four groups of items would be inserted in Eq. (6-18), with $k$ equaling 4 rather than 40. The estimated reliability of the 40-item test would be approximately the same by the two approaches.

One of the most frequent uses of Eq. (6-18) is with respect to the split-half measure of reliability, which will be discussed more fully in the next chapter. For this, the items of a test are divided in half, and the two half-tests are correlated. Then the question is what the reliability of the whole test would be. When only two samples of items from the domain are being added, Eq. (6-18) reduces to

$$r_{kk} = \frac{2r_{12}}{1 + r_{12}} \tag{6-19}$$

where $r_{12}$ = correlation between two half-tests
$\quad\ \ r_{kk}$ = reliability of whole test

**Reliability of an item sample** The logic developed in the previous section for determining the effect of test length on reliability can be extended to determine the reliability of any particular sample of items. It was shown that the reliability depends entirely on the average correlation among items and the number of items. These values could be substituted in Eq. (6-18) to obtain the reliability for any particular test. In practice, however, it is tedious to compute all correlations among items or other units being summed. There is a much easier way to obtain the same result. Looking back at Eq. (6-16), one can see that in the numerator $\bar{r}_{ij}$ could be used instead of $\bar{r}^2_{it}$. Equation (6-16) then would be

$$r_{kk} = \frac{k^2\bar{r}_{ij}}{k + k^2\bar{r}_{ij} - k\bar{r}_{ij}} \tag{6-20}$$

If one can assume that the average correlation in a collection of items is a good estimate of the hypothetical average correlation of all items in a domain, $\bar{r}_{ij}$, then some very useful formulas can be deduced. Rather than introduce new terminology, a precise estimate of $\bar{r}_{ij}$ will be symbolized as the actual average correlation in the domain. Under these conditions, the denominator of Eq. (6-20) equals the sum of all elements in the matrix of correlations of the $k$ variables.

Thus Eq. (6-20) could be rewritten as

$$r_{kk} = \frac{k^2 \bar{r}_{ij}}{\bar{R}}$$ (6-21)

The numerator equals the sum of all the elements in a square table of correlations where the average element is $\bar{r}_{ij}$. This is almost the same as the sum of elements in the matrix of correlations among items (or sums of items used as scoring units), except for two important differences. First, the former matrix would not have variances on the diagonal (unities, in this case, with standardized scores). Consequently the sum of variances $(k)$ would have to be subtracted from $R$ to give a first approximation of the numerator. It would be only an approximation, because the sum of elements with zeros in the diagonal would equal $(k^2 - k)\bar{r}_{ij}$ rather than $k^2\bar{r}_{ij}$. In other words, after the sum of variances is subtracted from $R$, the result would need to be inflated by the following ratio to obtain $k^2\bar{r}_{ij}$:

$$\frac{k^2}{k^2 - k} = \frac{k}{k - 1}$$

With these considerations in mind, it is possible to write the formula for the reliability of a $k$-item test as

$$r_{kk} = \frac{[k/(k - 1)] \, (\bar{R} - \Sigma \sigma_i^2)}{\bar{R}}$$

$$= \frac{k}{k - 1} \left( \frac{\bar{R} - \Sigma \sigma_i^2}{\bar{R}} \right)$$ (6-22)

Since variables are expressed as standard scores, Eq. (6-22) would reduce to

$$r_{kk} = \frac{k}{k - 1} \left( \frac{\bar{R} - k}{\bar{R}} \right)$$ (6-23)

Whereas up to this point it has proved convenient to work with standardized scores, in actual computations it is more convenient to work with the covariances among items than with their correlations. Also, as was mentioned previously, the assumption that all items have the same variance (same $p$ value for dichotomous items) is a potential source of imprecision in the estimation of reliability. All the formulas and principles that have been developed could have been developed on the basis of the average covariance among items. In that case Eq. (6-22) would change to

$$r_{kk} = \frac{k}{k - 1} \left( \frac{\bar{C} - \Sigma \sigma_i^2}{\bar{C}} \right)$$ (6-24)

It will be remembered that $\bar{C}$ is the sum of the elements in a covariance matrix, in this case the square matrix showing all variances of items and all covariances among them.

Equation (6-24) could actually be used to estimate the reliability of a $k$-item test. After the covariance matrix was obtained, the proper sums of elements could be placed in the formula. But what was learned previously about the variance of sums points to a much simpler approach. Since the variance of a sum of items $\sigma_y^2$ equals the sum of the elements in the covariance matrix for the items entering the sum, $\bar{C} = \sigma_y^2$. Thus Eq. (6-24) may be rewritten as

$$r_{kk} = \frac{k}{k-1}\left(\frac{\sigma_y^2 - \Sigma\sigma_i^2}{\sigma_y^2}\right) \tag{6-25}$$

It also can be written as

$$r_{kk} = \frac{k}{k-1}\left(1 - \frac{\Sigma\sigma_i^2}{\sigma_y^2}\right) \tag{6-26}$$

Equation (6-26) is one of the most important deductions from the domain-sampling theory of measurement error. In that form it is referred to as *coefficient alpha*. The same formula is derivable from the parallel-test model, and very similar formulas are derivable from other mathematical models for measurement error. Although it may look very different, coefficient alpha is identical to Eq. (6-18) for estimating the reliability of a $k$-item test when (1) the average covariance among items is employed in the latter rather than the average correlation among items and (2) the average of the item variances ($pq$ values for dichotomous items) is substituted for 1 as the first item in the denominator of Eq. (6-18). All these considerations justify the statement that coefficient alpha is a very important formula in the theory of reliability. It represents the expected correlation of one test with an alternative form containing the same number of items. The square root of coefficient alpha is the estimated correlation of a test with errorless true scores. It is so pregnant with meaning that it should routinely be applied to all new tests.

When, as is frequently the case, an investigation is being made of the reliability of a test composed of dichotomous items, coefficient alpha takes on the following special form:

$$r_{kk} = \frac{k}{k-1}\left(1 - \frac{\Sigma pq}{\sigma_y^2}\right) \tag{6-27}$$

Equation (6-27) follows from Eq. (6-26) because, in the latter, $\Sigma pq$ is equal to $\Sigma\sigma_i^2$. The first step in determining the reliability of a test composed of dichotomous items is to find the $p$ value for each item, which is then multiplied by $1 - p$. These products are then summed. The second step is to compute the variance of scores on the total test, which is then divided into the sum of $pq$ values. After this is subtracted from 1, the result is multiplied by the ratio of the number of test items to the number of test items minus 1. This version of coefficient alpha is referred to as "Kuder-Richardson Formula 20" (KR-20). It is easy to compute, and there is no excuse for not computing it for any new measure consisting of items scored 1 or 0.

Another way of looking at coefficient alpha will serve to further indicate its importance. It will be remembered that the reliability coefficient of any test is the estimated average correlation of that test with all possible tests with the same number of items which are obtainable from sampling a domain. Thus coefficient alpha is the expected correlation of one test with another test of the same length when the two tests purport to measure the same thing. Coefficient alpha can also be derived as the expected correlation between an actual test and a *hypothetical* alternative form, one that may never be constructed. If the actual test is called $x$ and the hypothetical test is called $y$, then the total covariance matrix for all items on the two tests can be schematized as follows:

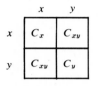

From the domain-sampling model, it is expected that the average diagonal term in $C_x$ is the same as that in $C_y$, and the average off-diagonal elements in the two matrices are the same. Also, it is expected that the average element throughout $C_{xy}$ equals the average off-diagonal element in $C_x$. Thus coefficient alpha can be derived from the correlation of sums as follows:

$$r_{xy} = \frac{\bar{C}_{xy}}{\sqrt{\bar{C}_x}\,\sqrt{\bar{C}_y}}$$

According to the model, $\bar{C}_x$ approximately equals $\bar{C}_y$, so the equation can be rewritten as

$$r_{xy} = \frac{\bar{C}_{xy}}{\bar{C}_x}$$

According to the model, the average coefficient in $C_{xy}$ (and thus the sum of coefficients) is derivable from $C_x$. First, it would be necessary to subtract from $C_x$ the variances of items lying on the diagonal. Then it would be necessary to inflate the result by the factor developed previously, that is, $k/(k-1)$. This then brings one right back to coefficient alpha. It is at the heart of the theory of measurement error.

**Variance of true and error scores** Previously it was shown that the reliability coefficient can be expressed as follows:

$$r_{11} = \frac{\sigma_t^2}{\sigma_x^2}$$

The reliability coefficient equals the estimated ratio of true-score variance to the actual variance of the measure. Then it is apparent that

$$\sigma_t^2 = r_{11}\sigma_x^2 \qquad (6\text{-}28)$$

and that

$$\sigma_t = \sqrt{r_{11}}\,\sigma_x$$

Whenever one sees the symbol for true scores, $t$, as in $\sigma_t$ shown in Eq. (6-28), it should be kept in mind that true scores are always hypothetical and can be estimated only in practice. Unless $x$ is perfectly reliable, the variance of true deviation scores will be less than the variance of obtained deviation scores by a factor of $r_{11}$. Since error scores are uncorrelated with true scores, it follows that

$$\sigma_x^2 = \sigma_t^2 + \sigma_e^2 \qquad (6\text{-}29)$$

These facts might lead one to the erroneous conclusion that, generally speaking, reliable tests tend to have smaller standard deviations than unreliable tests. Just the reverse is true. A look back at coefficient alpha [Eq. (6-26)] will show why this is so. The larger the average covariance among items, the more reliable is the test. When the sum of covariance terms is zero, the reliability is zero. It will be remembered that the variance of a sum equals the sum of variances *plus* the sum of all covariances in the covariance matrix. The variance of a totally unreliable test equals the sum of variances only. Consequently the more reliable the test, the larger is the variance of test scores. If, for example, two 20-item tests have the same average *pq* value, then the one with the larger variance is more reliable.

It is true that the error variance adds to *whatever reliable variance is present*, but it also is true that the reliable variance adds to whatever error variance is present. Since, in a completely unreliable measure, the variance of scores equals the sum of the variance of items, this places a lower limit on the size of the variance. As the test becomes reliable, the covariance terms become positive; and as the covariance terms become larger, the variance of test scores becomes larger. Whereas there is a severe limit on the size of the variance of errors, there is a much less severe limit on the sum of covariance terms. For example, in the typical 30-item test with moderately high reliability, the covariances among items contribute at least three times as much to the variance of test scores as do the item variances. Thus it is seen that reliable tests tend to have large variances of total scores relative to that found on unreliable tests of the same length.

**Estimation of true scores** Since the square root of $r_{11}$ is the estimated correlation of obtained scores with true scores ($r_{1t}$), it can be used to estimate true scores from obtained scores. It will be remembered that when variables are expressed as deviation scores, the regression equation for estimating one variable from the other is as follows:

$$y' = \frac{\sigma_y}{\sigma_x}\,r_{xy}x$$

The problem to be considered is the estimation of true deviation scores $t'$ from obtained deviation scores $x$. Previously it was shown that the standard deviation of true scores equals $\sqrt{r_{xx}}\,\sigma_x$ ($r_{xx}$ being the reliability of $x$). Then estimates of true scores can be obtained as follows:

$$t' = \frac{\sigma_t}{\sigma_x}\,(r_{xt})x$$

$$= \frac{\sqrt{r_{xx}}\,\sigma_x}{\sigma_x}\,(r_{xt})x \qquad\qquad (6\text{-}30)$$

$$= \sqrt{r_{xx}}\,(r_{xt})x$$

Since $r_{xt}$ equals the square root of $r_{xx}$,

$$t' = \sqrt{r_{xx}}\,\sqrt{r_{xx}}\,x$$

$$= r_{xx}x \qquad\qquad (6\text{-}31)$$

Estimates of true deviation scores $t'$ are computed by multiplying obtained deviation scores by the reliability coefficient.

Although Eq. (6-31) is the best least-squares estimate of true scores from *linear* regression, it was not assumed in the domain-sampling model that tests in the domain necessarily have linear regressions with true scores. The assumption of linear regression of true scores on obtained scores is not crucial for most of the principles derivable from the domain-sampling model, e.g., the effect of test length on reliability, but it is crucial for the development of any relatively simple methods for the estimation of true scores. In this section it will be assumed that the relationship of obtained scores to true scores is essentially linear, and then this assumption will be discussed more fully later.

As is true in any correlational analysis, obtained scores must be *regressed* to obtain a best least-squares estimate of true scores. Hidden in this fact is an important principle: *Obtained scores are biased estimates of true scores.* Scores above the mean are biased upward, and scores below the mean are biased downward. The farther scores are in either direction from the mean of obtained scores, the more, in an absolute sense, scores are biased. As a group, people with high obtained scores have a preponderance of positive errors of measurement, and the opposite is true for people who have low obtained scores. In one sense this fact makes little difference, because estimated true scores correlate perfectly with obtained scores. For this reason, in most investigations there is nothing to be gained by estimating true scores, which is a point that will be considered more fully in the next chapter. The only practical importance in most research of estimating true scores is in setting confidence zones for the effects of measurement error on obtained scores, which will be discussed in the next section.

The fact that obtained scores are biased raises an important theoretical point. If one actually had true scores, these could be used in the usual regression equation for estimating obtained scores. To simplify the problem, imagine that both true scores and obtained scores were standardized, in which case the regression equation would be given as

$$z'_x = r_{xt} z_t \qquad (6\text{-}32)$$

where $z'_x$ = estimates of obtained standard scores for $x$

$\quad z_t$ = true scores

$\quad r_{xt}$ = correlation of true and obtained scores

Subtracting values of $z'_x$ from the actual values of $z_x$ would provide the errors of estimation, which are the errors because of unreliability. It will be remembered that such errors of estimation correlate zero with the variable used to make the estimates (true scores), which is another way of stating the assumption that error scores are uncorrelated with true scores. But it also should be remembered that errors of estimate do correlate with the variable being estimated, in this case with obtained scores. The amount would be as follows:

$$\begin{aligned} r_{xe} &= \sqrt{1 - r_{xt}^2} \\ &= \sqrt{1 - r_{xx}} \end{aligned} \qquad (6\text{-}33)$$

Thus it would be found, for example, that if $x$ had a reliability of .64, obtained scores would correlate .60 with error scores. The correlation would be positive, because high obtained scores are biased upward and low obtained scores are biased downward. In spite of the obvious conclusion that errors must correlate positively with obtained scores, it is surprising how often this point is either overlooked or misunderstood.

**Standard error of measurement** The standard error of estimating obtained scores from true scores is computed as it is in all correlational problems. In the general case, the standard error of estimating one variable in deviation-score form ($x$) from another variable in deviation-score form ($y$) is

$$\sigma_{\text{est}} = \sigma_x \sqrt{1 - r_{xy}^2}$$

If $x$ is a set of obtained scores and $y$ is a set of true scores, the formula is

$$\begin{aligned} \sigma_{\text{est}} &= \sigma_x \sqrt{1 - r_{xt}^2} \\ &= \sigma_x \sqrt{1 - r_{xx}} = \sigma_{\text{meas}} \end{aligned} \qquad (6\text{-}34)$$

The standard error of estimating obtained scores from true scores is called the *standard error of measurement* and is given the special symbol $\sigma_{\text{meas}}$.

The standard error of measurement is the expected standard deviation of scores for any person taking a large number of randomly parallel tests. One can use it to set confidence zones for obtained scores, but in so doing one must understand that such confidence zones *are not symmetrical about the obtained score*. Thus, although it usually is done in practice, it is incorrect to set the 95 percent confidence zone as equaling two standard errors of measurement below and two above the obtained score. The confidence zone is symmetrical about the estimated true score $t'$, as will be discussed more fully in the next chapter.

The use of $\sigma_{\text{meas}}$ implicitly assumes that the distribution of errors has the same shape and size for people at different points on the continuum of true scores. These assumptions are not made by the domain-sampling model, and they are not needed for the most important deductions from the model. They are required, however, if one is to set confidence zones for estimated true scores; but there are reasons to believe that both assumptions are somewhat incorrect in most empirical problems. This matter will be discussed more fully subsequently.

**Attenuation**   At the start of this chapter it was said that measurement error is "bad," because it tends to obscure—or, as it is called, "attenuate"—any lawfulness in nature. This means that it makes correlations less than they would be if measurement error were not present. From the theory of measurement error, it is possible to estimate how much effect measurement error has on particular correlations or, conversely, how much correlations between true scores would be higher than those between fallible scores. The proper formulas could be developed in a number of ways. A simple approach is as follows. Any two tests from two different domains would be expected to have uncorrelated errors, and errors on either test would be uncorrelated with true scores on either test. Then the correlation between fallible scores on the two tests can be "taken apart" as follows:

$$r_{12} = \frac{\sigma_{12}}{\sigma_1 \sigma_2}$$

$$= \frac{(1/N) \, \Sigma (t_1 + e_1)(t_2 + e_2)}{\sigma_1 \sigma_2}$$

$$= \frac{(1/N) \, \Sigma (t_1 t_2 + t_1 e_2 + t_2 e_1 + e_1 e_2)}{\sigma_1 \sigma_2}$$

$$= \frac{(1/N) \, (\Sigma t_1 t_2 + \Sigma t_1 e_2 + \Sigma t_2 e_1 + \Sigma e_1 e_2)}{\sigma_1 \sigma_2}$$

All but the first term in the numerator are zero, so the formula can be written as

$$r_{12} = \frac{\sigma_{t_1 t_2}}{\sigma_1 \sigma_2} \tag{6-35}$$

This transformation of the numerator shows that *the covariance of obtained scores is equal to the covariance of true scores.* If there were no error present, the covariance term in the numerator would remain the same, but the standard deviations in the denominator would shrink by the amount derived previously. Thus if there were no error present, the correlation $\hat{r}_{12}$ between the two sets of scores would be as follows:

$$\hat{r}_{12} = \frac{\sigma_{12}}{(\sqrt{r_{11}}\,\sigma_1)\,(\sqrt{r_{22}}\,\sigma_2)}$$

$$= \frac{\sigma_{12}/(\sigma_1\sigma_2)}{\sqrt{r_{11}}\,\sqrt{r_{22}}}$$

$$= \frac{r_{12}}{\sqrt{r_{11}}\,\sqrt{r_{22}}} \qquad (6\text{-}36)$$

Equation (6-36) is spoken of as the "correction" for attenuation, but it is really an estimate rather than a correction—an estimate of how much the correlation would be if two variables were made perfectly reliable. In other words, Eq. (6-36) estimates the limiting value of the correlation between samples of items from two domains when the number of items from each domain is made larger and larger.

Equation (6-36) also applies to samples of items drawn from the *same* domain, but in this case the result is trivial. The correlation between two such tests would be expected to equal the product of terms in the denominator, and consequently $\hat{r}_{12}$ would equal 1.0.

One important principle derivable from Eq. (6-36) concerns the maximum correlation that any set of fallible scores can have with any other set of scores. If $\hat{r}_{12}$ were 1.0, $r_{12}$ would be limited only by the reliabilities of the two tests:

$$1.00 = \frac{r_{12}}{\sqrt{r_{11}}\,\sqrt{r_{22}}}$$

$$r_{12} = \sqrt{r_{11}}\,\sqrt{r_{22}} \qquad (6\text{-}37)$$

Thus it can be seen that it is possible for one test to have a correlation with another test which is higher than its own reliability coefficient. In the limiting case, if the second test were perfectly reliable, the first test could correlate with the second test as high as the square root of its reliability coefficient. Since the square root of the reliability is the correlation of a test with true scores, this naturally places a limit on the extent to which a sample of items from one domain can correlate with a sample of items from another. Had any other conclusion been reached, the utility of the domain-sampling model would have been seriously questioned. In the next chapter various uses of formulas concerning attenuation will be discussed and illustrated.

## ALTERNATIVE MODELS

Major emphasis in this chapter has been placed on the domain-sampling model because (1) it is easy for most persons to understand, (2) it permits simple derivations of many important principles, and (3) deductions from the model have a high degree of internal consistency. Regarding this last point, it was seen in numerous places that there are several different approaches to deriving the same formulas, and formulas serving quite different purposes were shown to be derivable from one another.

Other models are available to "compete" with the domain-sampling model. For example, one of these is the parallel-test model, which some authors prefer. It was shown that this model is only a special case of the domain-sampling model, and any advantages it supposedly has are illusory. Actually this and other possible models discussed in this section are complementary to rather than competitive with the domain-sampling model. They supply useful information supplementary to what could be obtained from the domain-sampling model alone in the simple form in which it was presented.

**Factorial domain-sampling model** As it was presented, the domain-sampling model concerned a hypothetical infinite number of test items or other scoring units in which all items were intended to be measures of the same trait of ability or personality. No distinctions were made between possible subgroups of items within the domain, and the major problem for the development of statistical formulas for measurement error concerned the average correlation among items in the domain and the dispersion of correlations about that average. This is the simplest form of possibly more complex models which do classify the items in various ways within the overall domain in a way similar to what is done in analysis of variance designs for controlled experiments. Each such method of classifying the content within a domain is called a *factor*, and there can be as many factors as types of measurement error that one wants to investigate. For example, the problem might concern ratings by clinical psychologists of the improvement of patients in psychotherapy. If ratings were to be averaged over five clinical psychologists, then clinical psychologists could be considered one factor in the design of the domain. If ratings of patients are made on a number of different occasions, then occasions could be another factor in the domain. If the measuring instrument contained five rating scales which were intended to measure the same trait of adjustment, then scales would constitute another factor of the domain. In this case, one can think of a three-factor design for structuring the content of the domain of measurements.

The logic of the domain-sampling model would be applied to this factorial structure for the domain. If one can think in terms of an infinite number of possible items for the domain, one can also think of an infinite number of possible measurements in each category of the factorial design for the domain. Correlations can be deduced between different cells of such factorial designs by the correlation of sums in an analogous way to the methods shown in this chapter for computing the reliability coefficient in the domain-sampling model. Potentially, many different reliability coefficients could be deduced depending upon the number of factors used to structure the domain and the sources of measurement error that the experimenter wishes to investigate. Such factorial designs for structuring domains of content are useful to consider in performing particular studies of reliability, and they provide an important theoretical framework for psychometric theory relating to measurement error. However, such complex factorial designs are more interesting theoretically than directly applicable in most actual research. The problems concerning measurement error encountered in nearly all everyday research activity can be adequately handled by the relatively simple approaches provided by the straightforward domain-sampling model. For an extensive discussion of factorial designs for the study of measurement error, see Cronbach et al. (1971).

**The binomial model** A mathematical model that provides useful supplementary information to the domain-sampling model is the *binomial model*. The model is based on the assumption that errors have a binomial distribution about true scores. The model can be illustrated in the special case where all items in a domain would have $p$ values of .5 if they were administered to a large group of people. Then a person with an average true score would have a probability of .5 of correctly answering any item selected at random from the domain. The expected score on any random sample of items would be half the number of items, but this would vary from sample to sample in terms of the binomial distribution. Since errors are random, for any person the scores obtained on one sample of items would be statistically independent of scores obtained on other samples, and consequently a binomial distribution of obtained scores would be found for each person. As was mentioned previously, the shape of the binomial distribution and its standard deviation depend on $p$ values and the number of test items. For this hypothetical person, one would expect to find a symmetrical distribution, approximating the normal distribution as the number of items in different tests were made larger and larger.

With this model, it is interesting to see what deductions would be made about a person who had a very high true score. That person would have a high probability of correctly answering items drawn at random from the domain. Consequently the distribution of scores on different samples of items would not be symmetrical, but would tend to be skewed to the left, toward the lower end of the continuum of obtained scores. Also, the standard deviation of obtained scores would be *less* than that for a person with an average true score. For a person with a very low true score, the distribution of obtained scores would be skewed to the right, and she or he also would have a smaller standard deviation of such scores than would a person with an average true score. The amount of skewness for persons at either extreme of the true-score continuum would be inversely related to the number of test items. With no more than 20 items, the skewness might be quite marked; with as many as 100 items, the skewness might be unnoticeable.

Since the binomial model is a very sensible model for determining the shape and distribution of obtained scores, it forces one to reconsider the simple model depicted in Fig. 6-1. The situation illustrated in Fig. 6-3 is more realistic than that of depicting the standard error of measurement as the same

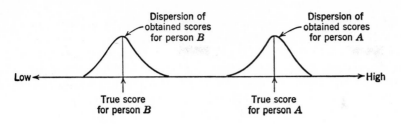

**Figure 6-3** True scores and skewed distributions of obtained scores for two persons.

at all points on the continuum of true scores and the distribution of such errors as normal. In Fig. 6-3, it is indicated that as true scores depart from the average, distributions of obtained scores tend to have smaller standard deviations and tend to be skewed toward the opposite end of the continuum. This means that the relationship between obtained scores and true scores is somewhat heteroscedastic or, in other words, that the standard error of measurement is not quite the same on the extremes as it is near the middle of the distribution. Also, when this is the case, the relationship between two variables tends to be slightly nonlinear. From this model and from models to be mentioned subsequently, one can deduce that the relationship between obtained scores and true scores actually is slightly S-shaped rather than strictly linear. What is important to realize, however, is that these potential modifications of statistics obtained from the domain-sampling model are so slight in most cases as to be of interest to only the specialist in psychometric theory. The binomial model is discussed in Lord and Novick (1968).

**Item-characteristic curves** In Chap. 2 it was stated that the most widely used model for discussing psychological measurement and for actually obtaining scores is the linear or summative model. All it assumes is that the item trace lines monotonically relate the underlying attribute to the probability of one type of response rather than another on a dichotomous item. It is not assumed that the trace lines have any particular mathematical form in general. However, in Chap. 2 it also was said that some mathematical models for measurement theory do assume that the trace lines have specific mathematical forms. The two mathematical forms that have been hypothesized for this purpose are the normal ogive and logistic curves, which are almost indistinguishable in appearance. The reader might want to glance back at Figs. 2-16 through 2-18 to recall these relationships.

Complex mathematical models have been developed for combining item-characteristic curves to form overall measures of ability (referred to as ICC theory). ICC theory is conceptually and mathematically very complex and is of much more interest to the specialist in psychometrics than to the average reader of this book. This theory supplies some supplementary information to that obtained from the much simpler domain-sampling model for the study of measurement error. Like the binomial model, the theory leads to the conclusion that the relationship between obtained scores and true scores on the trait is slightly S-shaped and that the standard error of measurement is not precisely the same at all points on the ability continuum. Regarding the tendency for the relationship with true scores on the ability continuum to be slightly S-shaped, in most cases this departure from strict linearity is small. When scores developed by ICC theory can be correlated with those obtained by the more usual approach to simply sum item scores, typically it is found that the two sets of scores correlate .90 or higher; thus it is really hair splitting to argue about any difference between the two approaches or any marked departure from linearity of the measurements obtained from the two approaches. Of more interest and more importance are deductions from ICC theory regarding the reliability at various points on the underlying trait. For example, ICC theory allows one to deduce in a rather precise way the reliability at different points on the continuum of ability, the effects of guessing, and some other effects of measurement error that would be hard to evaluate by any other approach. ICC theory will be discussed at various points in subsequent chapters where it is relevant. However, the supplementary information that can be obtained by these complex mathematical models should be viewed from two perspectives. First, ICC theory makes definite assumptions about relationships between obtained scores and underlying traits of ability or personality; and in many cases these assumptions are open to question. Second, in those situations where ICC theory operates on a reasonable base of assumptions, it does not drastically alter nor seriously impair the validity and practicability of the many statistics that are based on the domain-sampling model. ICC theory is discussed in detail in Lord (1974), Lord and Novick (1968), and Weiss (1975).

## SUGGESTED ADDITIONAL READINGS

Cronbach, L. J. Coefficient alpha and the internal structure of tests. *Psychometrika*, 1951, *16*, 297–334.

Cronbach, L. J., Gleser, G. C., Nanda, H., and Rajaratnam, N. *The dependability of behavioral measurements.* New York: Wiley, 1971.

Guilford, J. P. *Psychometric methods.* New York: McGraw-Hill, 1954, chaps. 13 and 14.

Guilliksen, H. *Theory of mental tests.* New York: Wiley, 1950, chaps. 1 to 8.

Horst, P. *Psychological measurement and prediction.* Belmont, Calif.: Wadsworth, 1966, chaps. 16 to 19.

Lord, F. M. Individualized testing and item characteristic curve theory. In D. H. Krantz, R. C. Atkinson, R. D. Luce, and P. Suppes (eds.), *Contemporary developments in mathematical psychology.* (Vol. 2) *Measurement, psychophysics, and neural information processing.* San Francisco: W. H. Freeman, 1974.

Lord, F. M., & Novick, M. R. *Statistical theories of mental tests.* Reading, Mass.: Addison-Wesley, 1968, chaps. 5 to 11.

Stanley, J. C. Reliability. In R. L. Thorndike (ed.), *Educational measurement* (2d ed.). Washington, D.C.: American Council on Education, 1971.

# CHAPTER SEVEN

# ASSESSMENT OF RELIABILITY

Whereas the previous chapter presented the theory of reliability, this chapter will discuss principles for employing the theory in applied uses of tests and in basic research. Also, some additional formulas will be developed for problems that frequently occur in the investigation of the effects of measurement error on research results. Previously it was said that measurements are reliable to the extent that they are repeatable and that any random influence which tends to make measurements different from occasion to occasion or circumstance to circumstance is a source of measurement error. The domain-sampling model was offered as a way of investigating such random sources of error. Each test is considered as a random sample of items from a domain, and measurement error is present only to the extent that samples are limited in size. Thus if the average correlation among items is positive, a very long test is always a highly reliable test, the degree of reliability being estimated by Eq. (6-18). This line of argument assumes that all measurement error is because of content sampling. But is content sampling the only factor that prevents measurements from being exactly the same on two occasions? First we shall look at some of the factors that reduce the repeatability of measurements, and then we shall see if these can be adequately handled by the domain-sampling model.

## SOURCES OF ERROR

In practice there are many factors that prevent measurements from being exactly repeatable, the number and kind of factors depending on the nature of the test and how the test is used. Some of the principal sources of measurement error are described in the following sections. (A very detailed list is presented in Stanley 1971.)

**Variation within a test** It is important to make a distinction between errors of measurement that cause variation in performance from item to item within a test and errors that are manifested only in variation in performance on different forms of a test given at the same or different times. Errors of the former kind can easily be handled by the domain-sampling model, but a conceptual extension of the model is necessary to handle errors of the second kind.

The major source of error within a test is due to the sampling of items. According to the domain-sampling model, each person has a particular probability of correctly answering each item, depending on the person's true score and the difficulty of the item. In the simplest case, if a person has an average true score in a sample of subjects and all the items have $p$ values of .5, that person has a probability of .5 of correctly answering any item chosen at random from the domain. The person would be expected to correctly answer half the items on any test drawn from the domain, but that expectation would be accompanied by some error. The more items in each test, the less would be the error. The same logic can be extended to items that have no "correct" responses, e.g., to items concerning agreement and disagreement with statements. Each person can be thought of as having a set probability of agreeing with each statement, which in turn would lead to an expected number of agreements with a sample of items. Depending on the number of items in each sample, there would be some variability in scores from test to test.

The error because of the sampling of items is entirely predictable from the average correlation. Consequently, coefficient alpha would be the correct measure of reliability for any type of item, and the special version of that formula, KR-20, would be used with dichotomous items.

On multiple-choice tests, guessing is a source of measurement error. For example, not really knowing the answer to two questions, an individual might pass one and fail the other purely because of guessing. (Effects of guessing will be discussed more fully in Chap. 16.) Guessing causes some variation in performance from item to item, which lowers the test reliability. Guessing is easily handled by the domain-sampling model. The domain can be thought of as consisting of multiple-choice items. The typical correlation among such items would allow an estimate of the reliability of any sample of items. Guessing would serve to lower the typical correlation, but once that typical correlation were estimated from the correlations within a test, it could be used to estimate reliability.

In addition to guessing, many other factors produce variation in scores from item to item within a test. Halfway through a test, one might get a headache, and this would tend to lower the scores on the remaining items. One might intend to mark alternative $a$ for a particular item but, purely as a clerical error, mark alternative $b$ instead. Someone else might inadvertently skip an item which she or he could have answered correctly. Halfway through a test, one might realize that he or she misinterpreted the test instructions regarding how to respond to items, and not having time to go back to earlier items, one would do better on the remaining items than on the earlier items. Even if one actually knew the answer to a question, one might give the wrong answer because one accidentally misread "is not an example of" as "is an example of." There are many other factors that produce errors within tests.

To some extent errors of scoring can be assessed within a test. On objective tests, errors of scoring are purely mechanical, but since they tend to lower correlations among items, they are within the scope of the domain-sampling model. On some tests the scoring is largely subjective, as in essay examinations or in most projective tests. The element of chance in the scores given on such tests provides a source of measurement error. Measurement error is caused by fluctuations in standards by the individual grader and by differences in standards of different graders. For the individual grader, such errors are manifested within a test if each item is graded *independently* of other items. For example, on an essay examination the instructor might grade all responses to question 1, then grade all responses to question 2, and so on. If such scores are independent, the average correlation among the items can be used to obtain an accurate estimate of reliability. Although it occurs infrequently, if half the items are scored by one person and the other half are independently scored by another person, the correlation between the two half-tests will provide an estimate of the reliability.

All the errors that occur *within* a test can be easily encompassed by the domain-sampling model. As has been illustrated, this actually includes many types of error other than the sampling of items per se. Consequently, for any test the sampling of items from a domain can be thought of in terms of not only the physical collection of items, but also the sampling of the many situational factors (e.g., guessing) that will influence responses to those items. In essence this broadens the assumption of the domain-sampling model to include the sampling of situational factors which influence reliability as well as items only. Thus not only would each person be administered a random sample of items from the domain, but also each item would be accompanied by a random set of situational factors. Then whether or not a person passes any item drawn at random from the domain is a function of which item is selected and the situational factors that accompany the item. All such sources of error will tend to lower the average correlation among items within the test, but the average correlation is all that is needed to estimate the reliability.

**Structured samples** As was mentioned in the previous chapter, rather than think of the random sampling of items from a domain, one can think of a structured sample in terms of a factorial design for systematically dividing items into "cells." An example was given of multiple raters, ratees, rating scales, and test items. An overall domain-sampling model based on such structured samples is presented by Cronbach et al. (1971). One can think in terms of sampling items corresponding to the different cells and correlating sums of these to obtain many different measures of reliability relating to different possible sources of error variance. More generally, one can apply procedures related to analysis of variance and obtain correlation ratios corresponding to the different facets of the factorial design for content in the domain. Such complex approaches to designating components of reliability and investigating related components of measurement error are interesting from the standpoint of basic research in psychometrics and important for use by specialists in studying issues relating to reliability. However, some more direct, simpler approaches to assessing reliability are sufficient for both applied work and basic research in the behavioral sciences. Some of the sources of measurement error that must be considered in those circumstances will now be discussed.

**Variation between tests** The study of measurement error relating to variation between tests most typically is performed with *alternative forms,* which are intended to approximate randomly parallel tests. It will be remembered from Chap. 6 that randomly parallel tests are all random samples from the same domain of content and thus tend to have the same scores for any group of people. However, in many cases no actual sampling is done; rather, an individual constructs two tests which are intended to be similar in content. Since there is no guarantee that all the characteristics of randomly parallel tests are present, these are called *alternative forms* rather than randomly parallel forms. An example would be constructing two vocabulary tests, each of which would be an alternative form for the other. The availability of two such tests would be useful for many applied purposes as well as for measuring reliability relating to alternative forms administered on the same or different occasions. (Incidentally, one way to construct such alternative forms would be to take the set of combined items and randomly shuffle them into two equal groups.)

If alternative forms of a test are administered two weeks apart, the two sets of scores will almost never correlate perfectly. The domain-sampling model provides a prediction of the correlation; and, as was shown in the previous section, the prediction takes account not only of the sampling of content, but also of many sources of error within each testing session. There are, however, three major sources of error intervening between administrations of different tests that are not precisely estimated from the average correlation of items within each test. (For an extensive list of sources of measurement error see Stanley 1971.) The first is due to systematic differences in content of the two tests. The model envisions an actual sampling of items from a hypothetical domain, but in practice items are composed rather than drawn from a hat. For example, two spelling tests independently composed by two persons might emphasize different kinds of words. Then the correlation between the two tests might be less than would be predicted from the average correlation among the items within each test. Similarly, alternative forms of a measure of attitudes toward the United Nations might be systematically different in content, and consequently the correlation between the two forms would be less than that predicted by the domain-sampling model.

A second factor causing variation in scores on some tests from one occasion to another is due to subjectivity of scoring. For example, on an essay examination or a projective test, the same examiner might give somewhat different scores to the same persons; and even larger differences would be expected between the scores given by two examiners. Previously it was said that some of the error because of the subjectivity of scoring by one person could be estimated from the correlation among items within one test if items are scored independently; but this might tap only part of the error. The scorer might change standards somewhat from one occasion to another. For example, between the two testings, the projective tester might come to regard a particular type of response as more pathological than he or she previously had regarded it. Earlier it was said that if different parts of a test are independently scored by different examiners, the correlation between the parts would be indicative of the error entailed in using different examiners; but since two examiners rarely collaborate in that way, there is an unassessed amount of error because of the examiner who "happens" to score responses for a particular person. Then the average correlation among items on a test scored by one person would tend to overestimate the correlation between alternative forms scored by different persons.

Another source of variation in test performance from one occasion to another is because people actually change with regard to the attribute being measured. A person might feel much better on one occasion than on another, might study in the domain of content, or might change attitudes toward the United Nations. It is reasonable to think there is some fluctuation in abilities from day to day, depending on a host of physiological and environmental factors. Even more expected are variations in moods, self-esteem, and attitudes toward people and issues. Such changes in people would tend to make correlations between alternative forms less than what would be predicted from the average correlation among items on each test.

Systematic differences in content of tests and variations in people from one occasion to another cannot be adequately handled by a model which is based on the random sampling of items. For adequately handling these factors, the model must be extended to consider the random sampling of *whole tests*, in which case the tests are thought of as being randomly sampled for particular occasions and correlations among tests are permitted to be somewhat lower than would be predicted from the correlations among items within tests. In that case the average correlation among a number of alternative forms administered on different occasions, or the correlation between only two such forms, would be a better estimate of reliability than that provided by coefficient alpha or KR-20 for one test administered on one occasion only.

## ESTIMATION OF RELIABILITY

Because reliability is an important issue in the use of any measurement method, investigations of reliability should be made when new measures are developed. Following are some recommendations regarding how such investigations should be undertaken.

**Internal consistency** Estimates of reliability based on the average correlation among items within a test are said to concern the "internal consistency." This is partly a misnomer, because the size of the reliability coefficient is based on both the average correlation among items (the internal consistency) and the number of items. Coefficient alpha is the basic formula for determining the reliability based on internal consistency. It, or the special version applicable to dichotomous items (KR-20), should be applied to all new measurement methods. Even if other estimates of reliability should be made for particular instruments, coefficient alpha should be obtained first.

Coefficient alpha sets an upper limit to the reliability of tests constructed in terms of the domain-sampling model. If it proves to be very low, either the test is too short or the items have very little in common. In that case there is no need to make other estimates of reliability (e.g., correlation of alternative forms), because they will prove to be even lower. If, for example, coefficient alpha is only .30 for a 40-item test, the experimenter should reconsider the measurement problem.

Even though potentially there are important sources of measurement error that are not considered by coefficient alpha, it is surprising what little difference these sources of measurement error usually make. This is particularly so if the test instructions are easily understood and there is little subjectivity of scoring. If coefficient alpha for a particular test is compared with the correlation between alternative forms and at least 300 persons are studied, the two coefficients typically are very close. If, say, the former is .85, it might be found that the latter is .80, but it is rare to find the latter as low as .60. There are exceptions, which will be discussed in the next section, but reliability estimated from internal consistency usually is very close to the reliability estimated from correlations between alternative forms.

Coefficient alpha provides a good estimate of reliability in most situations, since *the major source of measurement error is because of the sampling of content.* Also, previously it was shown that reliability estimates based on internal consistency actually consider sources of error that are based not, strictly speaking, on the sampling of items per se, but on the "sampling" of situational factors accompanying the administration of items.

**Alternative forms** In addition to computing coefficient alpha, with most measures it also is informative to correlate alternative forms. Ideally, the alternative forms would be strictly parallel tests; but as mentioned previously, often they are not constructed in such a way as to ensure that this is the case. Usually the forms would be administered about two weeks apart. This would provide time for variations in ability and attitude to occur. If the correlation between alternative forms is markedly lower than coefficient alpha, say by as much as 20 points, it indicates that considerable measurement error is present because of some combination of the three sources of error mentioned previously: systematic differences in content, subjectivity of scoring, or large variations in people over short periods of time. Investigations can be made to determine which of these factors is causing the reduction in reliability.

To investigate variation in scores over short periods of time (two weeks), the correlation obtained on one group of subjects with a two-week interval between testings can be compared with the correlation between forms when both are administered on the same day. If the correlation between forms administered on the same day is much higher than that between forms administered two weeks apart, it indicates that the trait being measured tends to fluctuate somewhat over short periods of time. In one sense this is not measurement error, since such changes need not be random. For example a measure of moods would be expected to change somewhat from one occasion to another, because we all have ups and downs in that regard. Usually, however, the effort is to measure some relatively enduring characteristic, one that at least stays largely stable over a period of two weeks. Consequently, for most purposes, such variations in traits over short periods of time *act* like measurement error in that they tend to attenuate correlations with other variables.

If the correlation between alternative forms administered two weeks apart is low and the correlation between those administered on the same day is equally low, the indication is not that people are changing over time, but that the two forms have largely different types of content. If the average correlation among the items on one form is higher than that among items on the other form, then one form is more reliable than the other. This would suggest that something went wrong in the construction of one of the forms. The decision might be to construct a new form and then correlate that with the existing reliable form.

If the average correlation within the two test forms is substantial, but the average cross correlation between items in the two forms is low, it indicates that the two forms reliably measure somewhat different traits. For example, if the average correlation within each of the two sets of items were .20 and the average correlation between items in the two sets were .10, it would indicate systematic differences in content. This should lead the investigator to think more carefully about the intended domain of content. An inspection of the content might make it evident why the forms differ, which could lead either to emphasizing in the future the type of content on one of the forms or to seeking a type of item that bridges the gap between the two types of content. This circumstance will not arise if alternative forms are constructed by the method mentioned previously of randomly dividing a larger collection of items in half to form two randomly parallel tests.

It is somewhat more difficult to determine the measurement error because of subjectivity of scoring. Let it be assumed that differences in content of the two forms and variations over short periods of time have been ruled out as major sources of unreliability by the methods described above. Then a separate set of comparisons would be needed for each scorer. Each would score responses to alternative forms given (1) two weeks apart to one group of subjects and (2) on the same day to another group of subjects. If correlations between scorers are high for both groups, it indicates that there is little unreliability from any source, including that due to subjectivity of scoring. If the correlation for the two-week interval is substantially less than the correlation for tests taken on the same day, it indicates that scoring is reliable but the trait varies over short periods of time. If both correlations are low in a number of studies made of different scorers, it is difficult to tell whether the measurement error is because of subjectivity of scoring or some other factor. Since in essence the scorer is "a part of the item," there is no easy way to pick apart the contribution of scoring to the measurement error. There would be many hints as to the possible unreliability of scoring, such as (1) good reason to believe that the trait actually exists, e.g., intelligence, (2) the existence of reliable objective tests of the trait, and (3) considerable variability in the reliability of raters. If the measurement problem is important and it is felt necessary to continue employing subjective methods of scoring, the rules for scoring should be improved. If this results in an increased reliability, it would indicate that unreliability of scoring contributed to the earlier amount of measurement error.

If raters do tend to agree with themselves when scoring the same subjects on alternative forms, another question which arises is whether or not there is measurement error because of differences in scoring by different scorers. This can be easily determined by correlating scores obtained from different scorers on the same and alternative forms of the measure. It is sometimes found that scorers develop their own idiosyncratic methods of scoring, and although each scorer is consistent in employing his or her method, the scorers do not agree with one another. This works like other sources of measurement error to attenuate relations found between variables in research.

The need to investigate alternative forms of a measure depends very much on the type of measure. Where the domain of content is easily specified, where there is little subjectivity of scoring, and where people tend to vary little over short periods of time, coefficient alpha will provide an excellent estimate of reliability. This is the case, for example, for most tests of aptitude and achievement. It is necessary to investigate alternative forms if the trait is suspected to vary considerably over relatively short periods of time, as would be true for measures of moods and some measures of attitudes. In some cases the experimenter is challenged to compose alternative forms to satisfy others that there is a definable domain of content. This occurs with some projective techniques, such as the Rorschach, where there is some question as to whether or not it is possible to construct an alternative form. If an alternative form cannot be constructed, it is not possible to define the domain of content, and there is no way to accurately communicate what is being measured; furthermore, it is doubtful that anything of importance is being measured.

**Other estimates of reliability** Coefficient alpha and correlations between alternative forms (under the various conditions mentioned previously) are the basic estimates of reliability. There are other ways of estimating reliability which, though not recommended for most measurement problems, are frequently encountered in research reports (see discussions of these works cited in the Suggested Additional Readings). Instead of employing coefficient alpha or KR-20, one may estimate reliability from various subdivisions of a test. The most popular method is the *split-half* approach, in which items within a test are divided in half and scores on the two half-tests are correlated. Usually the items are halved by placing the even-numbered items in one group and the odd-numbered items in the other group. There are many other ways to make the division, e.g., randomly dividing items into two groups or separately scoring the first and second halves of the items. After the correlation is obtained, it must be corrected by Eq. (6-19) to obtain the reliability coefficient for the whole test.

The difficulty with the split-half method is that the correlation between halves will vary somewhat depending on how the items are divided, which raises some questions regarding what *the* reliability is. Actually, it is best to think of the corrected correlation between any two halves of a test as being an estimate of coefficient alpha. Then it is much more sensible to employ coefficient alpha than any split-half method. The only reason for employing a split-half method occurs when the items are scored not dichotomously, but on three or more points. In that case it is not possible to use the KR-20 version of coefficient alpha. With KR-20, it is very easy to obtain the $p$ values for items and thus the variances of items; but if the number of items is large and computer services are not available, it might prove excessively time-consuming to compute variances for multipoint items (which would be required by coefficient alpha). It is much easier to separately score odd and even items, correlate the two sets of scores, and make the necessary correction [Eq. (6-9)]. However, subsequently coefficient alpha should be obtained.

There are many other ways to obtain reliability estimates from subdivisions of items. For example, the items can be randomly divided into four equal parts. The average correlation among the four sets of scores can be placed in Eq. (6-18) to obtain an estimate of the reliability of the whole test. However, there would be nothing to gain by such methods of estimating reliability. The results would serve only to estimate coefficient alpha. If items are scored dichotomously, there is no excuse for not computing KR-20. If items are scored on more than two points, it is wise to compute coefficient alpha. When saving computational time is an important consideration, the corrected correlation between odd and even items will provide a good approximation of coefficient alpha.

One appropriate use of the split-half method is in measuring variability of traits over short periods of time when alternative forms are not available. For example, the odd items can be given as one test on the first occasion, and the even items can be given as an alternative form on the second occasion. The corrected correlation between the two sets of scores will indicate the relative stability of the trait over that period of time.

In place of using the alternative-form method for determining reliability, the *retest method* can be used, in which the same test is given to the same people after a period of time. Except for certain special instances, there are serious defects in employing the retest method. The major defect is that experience in the first testing usually will influence responses in the second testing. To the extent that responses to the first testing are remembered, they will tend to be repeated on the retest. Also, the individual will tend to repeat work habits and make much the same guesses on items where she or he is unsure. This makes the correlation between testings higher than it would be for alternative forms.

Another difficulty with the retest method is that it does not fit very well into the domain-sampling model. In the model, the reliability of any fixed-length test is strictly a function of the average correlation among items. As was mentioned previously, estimates derived from that model, e.g., KR-20, tend to be approximately the same as correlations actually obtained between alternative forms. The reason the retest method does not fit the model is that the retest correlation is only partly dependent on the correlation among items within a test. Thinking back about principles concerning the correlation of sums will show why that is the case. Even if the items within each testing correlated zero on the average with one another, it still would be possible to obtain a positive correlation between scores in the two testings. The numerator of the correlation of sums is the sum of all the cross covariances (correlations, if scores are standardized) between the two sets of items being summed. Even if all the cross correlations between different items were zero, each item might correlate well with itself on the two testings. Such correlations would be expected to be much higher than those usually found between different items, and they could produce a substantial but misleading correlation between retests.

If coefficient alpha is low for a test, a relatively high correlation between retests should not be taken as an indication of high reliability. As has been mentioned in a number of places, a test should "hang together" in the sense that the items should correlate with one another. Otherwise it makes little sense to add scores over items and speak of the total scores as measuring any attribute. The major information supplied by the retest method is "negative": if the retest correlation is low, the alternative form correlation will be even lower. If a test does not even correlate with itself when administered on two occasions, it is hopeless to seek other evidence of reliability and hopeless to employ the test in correlational studies.

It is recommended that the retest method generally not be used to estimate reliability, but there are some exceptions. In some types of measures, the retest probably would not be markedly affected by the first testing. This would tend to be the case, for example, if an individual were required to rate the pleasantness of 200 designs. The sheer number of ratings and the nature of the stimuli would make remembering the ratings of individual designs very difficult, and consequently the retest would be largely independent of the earlier testing. Also, scores would be more nearly independent if there were a relatively long time between testings, say, several months.

**Long-range stability** Previously it was said that alternative forms should be administered about two weeks apart to permit short-range fluctuations in abilities and personality characteristics to be manifested. Another issue concerns the stability of scores over relatively long periods of time—upward of six months.

If, for example, alternative forms given six months apart correlate less than those given two weeks apart, in a sense the difference is not because of "error," but because of systematic changes in people. As was mentioned previously, what is considered error and what is considered systematic change depend on the way measurement tools are used (the types of scientific generalizations that are made). If a measure is intended to represent the *relatively enduring* status of a trait in people, it would need to remain stable over the period in which scores were employed for that purpose. A good example is the IQ, which is considered by most people to be a relatively enduring characteristic of the individual, something that might change gradually over a period of years, but not markedly in a period of only one year (unless a retarded child was placed in an intensive training program). If an earlier measurement is used at a later time either to make practical decisions about people or to make decisions about the outcomes of research, then to the extent that the trait being measured has not remained stable, measurement error will reduce the validity of the decisions. As a practical example, if scores on intelligence tests given in the second year of high school are used to make decisions about college entrance for students two years later, the effectiveness of such decisions will be limited by (among other things) the extent to which the trait of intelligence has remained stable during that time. If the correlation between alternative forms of the test over that period of time were very low, some bad mistakes would be made in advising students about college. If, for example, on the earlier testing the student had an IQ of 130 and no later testing were made, it would be tempting to strongly encourage the student to enter college. But suppose that an alternative form of the test were administered near the end of high school and the student's IQ were only 95; with this new evidence in hand, it would be a bad mistake to strongly recommend college training.

As an example of how long-range instability can attenuate research results, suppose that an experiment is being conducted to measure the effect of anxiety on difficult learning tasks. Also, suppose that the test of anxiety is administered six months prior to the learning tasks. If the retest correlation or correlation with an alternative form over the six-month period were low, the possible results from using the first test would be misleading. Of course, instead of relying on measures administered much earlier, it is far better to make measurements shortly before practical decisions are to be made about people or shortly before they are used in experiments.

Aside from questions of measurement error, long-range stability is an important research issue in its own right, as, for example, in studies of the growth and decline of human abilities. Some have accused measurement specialists of assuming that psychological traits remain largely stable throughout life and, thus, that very little can be done to improve people. Such a philosophy is not at all necessary for the theory of measurement error. The theory would hold as well if people changed markedly in their characteristics from day to day; but if that occurred, it would make chaos out of efforts to formulate practical decisions about people and to find general principles of human behavior. People do change, but in most traits they change slowly enough to allow valid uses of psychological measures in daily life and in research investigations.

## USES OF THE RELIABILITY COEFFICIENT

In the previous section it was shown that it is meaningful to think of a test as having a number of different coefficients of reliability, depending on the major sources of measurement error that are considered. In practice, however, it is useful to speak of *a* reliability coefficient for a test which summarizes the amount of measurement error expected from using the instrument. This striving for simplicity is understandable, but at least two types of reliability coefficients should be computed and reported for any test that will be employed widely. First, coefficient alpha or KR-20 should be reported for at least one form of the test—for all forms if alternative forms are available. Second, correlations should be reported among alternative forms. Alternative forms are not available for many tests employed in basic research in the behavioral sciences, but they are available for many commercially distributed instruments. Previously it was discussed why correlations among alternative forms potentially tap some sources of measurement error not detected in coefficient alpha (but, as was also discussed, the difference tends to be small in most cases). The correlation should be reported between alternative forms administered at least two weeks apart, in order to tap sources of measurement error due to changes in people over relatively short periods of time. If, in separate investigations, it is possible to obtain correlations between alternative forms administered on the same day, this will provide important supplementary information about reliability. Regardless of how elaborately the investigations are undertaken, at least one measure of reliability based on the logic of coefficient alpha and another based on the logic of correlating randomly parallel tests over time should be computed. In addition, if time and resources are available, there are other measures of reliability that provide important information about the types of scientific generalizations that can be made about the effort to measure a particular trait with a particular measurement method.

If there is an element of subjectivity in the scoring, alternative forms should be independently scored by different persons. If, for example, five persons score the first form and five other persons score the second, the average correlation between the two sets of scores (five correlations in this instance) would provide a good reliability coefficient. If alternative forms are not available, the corrected correlation between split-halves given two weeks apart can be used as the reliability coefficient. To the extent that different approaches to obtaining the reliability coefficient produce somewhat different results, the coefficient that should be used in gauging the stability of traits and in making statistical corrections depends upon the way in which the measurement method will be employed. If, for example, raters will be used as part of the measurement method, then the reliability coefficient should be employed for making statistical corrections that take account of measurement error due to raters. When there is any doubt which reliability coefficient to employ in gauging the worth of an instrument, then the *lowest* one obtained by any of the sensible approaches discussed above provides a conservative estimate. In other words, then one can say that the reliability is "so much" at the very least. Fortunately, with most well-standardized tests, the several approaches to estimating the reliability provide results that are so similar that the differences can be ignored in practical work.

The major use of reliability coefficients is in communicating the extent to which the results obtained from a measurement method are repeatable. The reliability coefficient is one index of the effectiveness of an instrument, reliability being a necessary but not sufficient condition for any type of validity. In addition there are other uses that can be made of the reliability coefficient; the major uses are discussed in the following sections.

**Corrections for attenuation** One of the most important uses of the reliability coefficient is in estimating the extent to which obtained correlations between variables are attenuated by measurement error. Previously it was shown that the correction for attenuation is as follows:

$$\bar{r}_{12} = \frac{r_{12}}{\sqrt{r_{11}r_{22}}}$$

In this case, $\bar{r}_{12}$ is the expected correlation if both variables are perfectly reliable. If the correction is to be made for only one of the two variables, the reliability coefficient for only that variable will appear under the radical in the denominator.

There is some controversy about when the correction for attenuation should be applied. One could argue that the correction for attenuation provides a way of fooling oneself into believing that a "better" correlation has been found than that actually evidenced in the available data. Another justifiable criticism of many uses of the correction for attenuation is that the so-called correction sometimes provides a very poor estimate of the correlation actually obtained between variables when they are made highly reliable. This can occur if a poor measure of reliability is made, in terms of principles discussed previously, and/or if the reliability coefficient is based on a relatively small number of persons (less than 300). That poor estimates are often obtained is illustrated by the fact that corrected correlations sometimes are greater than 1.00!

If, however, good estimates of reliability are available, there are some appropriate uses of the correction for attenuation. The most important use is in basic research, where the corrected correlation between two variables is an estimate of how much two traits correlate. In an investigation of the correlation between anxiety and intelligence, for example, the real question is how much the two traits go together. If the two measures have only modest reliability, the actual correlation will suggest that the two traits go together less than they really do.

Another important use of the correction for attenuation is in applied settings where a test is used to forecast a criterion. If, as often happens, the criterion is not highly reliable, correcting for unreliability of the criterion will estimate the real validity of the test. Here, however, it would be wrong to make the double correction for attenuation, since the issue is how well a test actually works rather than how well it would work if it were perfectly reliable. In prediction problems, the reliability of the predictor instrument places a limit on its ability to forecast a criterion, and the correction for attenuation cannot make a test more predictive than it actually is. The only use for this double correction would be in estimating the limit of predictive validity of the test as both test and criterion are made more and more reliable.

Since perfect reliability is only a handy fiction, results from applying the foregoing formula for the correction for attenuation are always hypothetical. It is more important to estimate the increase in the correlation between two variables when the reliability is increased by any particular amount. A formula for doing this is

$$\bar{r}_{12} = \frac{r_{12} \sqrt{r'_{11} r'_{22}}}{\sqrt{r_{11} r_{22}}} \tag{7-1}$$

where $\bar{r}_{12}$ = estimated correlation between two variables if reliabilities are changed
$r'_{11}$ = changed reliability for variable 1
$r'_{22}$ = changed reliability for variable 2

The use of Eq. (7-1) can be illustrated in the situation where two tests correlate .30 and each test has a reliability of .60. If the reliability of each test were increased to .90, the expected correlation between the more reliable tests would be obtained as follows:

$$\bar{r}_{12} = \frac{.3 \sqrt{.9 \times .9}}{\sqrt{.6 \times .6}}$$

$$\bar{r}_{12} = .45$$

For the sake of computations, a handier version of Eq. (7-1) is as follows:

$$\bar{r}_{12} = r_{12} \sqrt{\frac{r'_{11} r'_{22}}{r_{11} r_{22}}} \tag{7-2}$$

Although Eqs. (7-1) and (7-2) were illustrated in the simple case where reliabilities were the same before being increased and after being increased, in practice the formula works equally well if all four of these reliability coefficients are different from one another. The formula also can be used to estimate what the correlation would be if both reliabilities were *lowered*. This is useful when it is necessary to employ shortened versions of longer tests. If the reliabilities are known for both the longer tests and the shortened versions and the correlation is known between the longer tests, the reliabilities of the shortened tests can be placed in Eq. (7-2) as $r'_{11}$ and $r'_{22}$, and the reliabilities of the longer tests as $r_{11}$ and $r_{22}$. Equation (7-2) applies equally well when the reliability of one test is increased and the reliability of the other is decreased. If the reliability of only one of the two variables is to be changed, Eq. (7-2) becomes

$$\bar{r}_{12} = r_{12}\sqrt{\frac{r'_{11}}{r_{11}}} \tag{7-3}$$

This version of the formula is useful in estimating how much the correlation of a predictor test with a criterion will change if the reliability of the test is either increased or decreased by particular amounts.

What should be evident from inspecting the formulas concerning corrections for attenuation is that such corrected correlations seldom are dramatically different from the actual correlations. Thus, in the example above, a dramatic increase in the reliability of each test from .60 to .90 resulted in an increase in correlation from .30 to only .45. Such a difference is important, but it is much less than intuitively might be thought to occur. As another example, if the correction were made for only one variable and the reliability were increased from .60 to .80, a correlation of .30 would be expected to rise only to .35. The author once heard a colleague suggest that some low correlations found in a study probably would have been much higher if test reliabilities had been higher. The average correlation was about .15, and the average reliability was about .60. Even if the average reliability of the tests were increased to .90, the average correlation could be less than .25. The colleague had in mind an increase in average correlation to .40 or .50, which could not possibly occur.

**Confidence zones** Another use of the reliability coefficient is in establishing confidence zones for obtained scores. Previously it was shown that for any variable $x$ the standard error of measurement is

$$\sigma_{\text{meas}} = \sigma_x \sqrt{1 - r_{xx}}$$

The standard error of measurement is the estimated standard deviation of obtained scores if any individual is given a large number of tests from a domain. It then is useful in establishing confidence zones for scores to be expected on many alternative forms of a test. It was pointed out, however, that it is incorrect to establish such confidence zones symmetrically about the score that a person makes on a particular test. If, for example, an individual has an IQ of 130 on a particular test and the $\sigma_{\text{meas}}$ is 5, it is incorrect to say that the 95 percent confidence zone for that person extends from 120 to 140 ($130 - 2\sigma_{\text{meas}}$ to $130 + 2\sigma_{\text{meas}}$). Even though the practice in most applied work with tests has been to center confidence zones about obtained scores, this is incorrect because obtained scores tend to be biased, high scores tending to be biased upward and low scores downward.

[In the literature on psychometric theory, one sees alternative versions of the standard error of measurement depending upon the type of error that is being estimated. For example, an error term can be developed that takes account of possible mean differences between alternative forms of a test, which is not included in $\sigma_{meas}$ as given previously. Another approach is to provide a confidence zone regarding the distribution of estimated true scores in relation to the obtained score continuum. Since the estimated standard deviation of true scores always is smaller than the standard deviation of obtained scores unless the reliability is 1.00, this standard error of measurement tends to be smaller than the one given previously. These and other possible approaches to obtaining statistics relating to the standard error of measurement are discussed in Cronbach et al (1971), Horn (1971), and Stanley (1971). The formula given above for the standard error of measurement, $\sigma_{meas}$, is the classical formula for describing effects of unreliability on test scores. It is employed much more frequently than any comparable statistic both in basic psychometric theory and in the actual use of tests in research. These differences in approach apply only to the standard error of measurement and not to the other statistical formulas discussed in this chapter.]

Before establishing confidence zones, one must obtain estimates of unbiased scores. Unbiased scores are the average scores people would obtain if they were administered all possible tests from a domain, holding constant the number of items randomly drawn for each. These are true scores which are estimated as follows:

$$t' = r_{xx}x \tag{7-4}$$

In the previous example, the individual with an IQ of 130 would have a deviation score $x$ of 30. If the reliability were .90, the estimated true score $t'$ would be 27 in deviation-score units. Adding back the mean IQ of 100 would give an estimated true score of 127 in units of IQ. This approach allows one to establish confidence zones for deviation scores or their raw-score equivalents. Then the correct procedure would be to set the 95 percent confidence zone as extending from two standard errors of measurement below 127 to two standard errors above 127. With a $\sigma_{meas}$ of 5, the zone then would extend from 117 to 137. If a person were administered a large number of alternative forms of the test, 95 percent of the obtained scores would be expected to fall in that zone, and the expected average of the obtained scores would be 127 (not 130).

In most applied work with tests, there is little reason for estimating true scores except for the establishment of confidence zones. Since estimated true scores correlate perfectly with obtained scores and making practical interpretations of estimated true scores is difficult, in most applied work it is better to interpret the individual's obtained score. The estimated true score would be used only to obtain the center for a confidence zone. Thus, in the example above, the individual would be said to have an IQ of 130, with the 95 percent confidence zone extending from 117 to 137. On that same test, a person with an IQ of 70 would have a 95 percent confidence zone extending from 63 to 83. Actually, such asymmetrical confidence zones have a real practical advantage: they continually remind people that scores obtained on any test tend to be biased outward on both sides of the mean. In most test manuals for commercially distributed tests, an extremely poor job is done of reporting estimated true scores and confidence zones for expected obtained scores on alternative forms. Either an incorrect procedure is employed (e.g., most frequently the confidence zone is centered about the actual obtained score), or the matter of confidence zones relating to $\sigma_{meas}$ is not even mentioned.

In contrast to applied work with tests, seldom is there a need in basic research to estimate true scores or establish confidence zones. In basic research the major concerns are with how much the measurement error lowers correlations and how much it contributes to the error components in statistical treatments. It is sometimes necessary in basic research to consider the effect of measurement error on the mean of a group of obtained scores. This would be the case, for example, if extreme groups on a measure were subjected to an experimental treatment and then either a retest were made or an alternative form were applied. The gain or loss scores for individuals, and the average gain and loss scores for the two groups, would be partly determined by regression effects from measurement error. In essence what one must do is estimate average true scores for the two groups on the first test but not the second test, and then see if the average change is different for the two groups. A detailed discussion of measurement error in covariance analysis is given in Huitema (in press).

**Effect of dispersion on reliability** It should be realized that, since the reliability coefficient is a correlation coefficient, the size of the reliability coefficient is directly related to the standard deviation of obtained scores for any sample of subjects. Previously it was shown that the reliability coefficient could be expressed as follows:

$$r_{xx} = 1 - \frac{\sigma^2_{meas}}{\sigma^2_x} \tag{7-5}$$

The variance of the errors of measurement is expected to be at least approximately independent of the standard deviation of obtained scores. In other words, the standard error of measurement is considered to be a fixed characteristic of any measurement tool regardless of the sample of subjects under investigation. This is a relatively safe assumption in most cases unless one is dealing with persons on the extremes of the distribution of scores from a population, e.g., the upper and lower 10 percent of persons in that regard. Then it is apparent that the reliability coefficient will be larger for samples of subjects that vary more with respect to the trait being investigated. An example would be in studying the reliability of scores on a test used to select first-year college students. If the correlation between alternative forms is used as the measure of reliability and the correlation is computed only for persons who actually were accepted for college, the correlation will be less than if persons who were not permitted to enter college had been included in the study.

A look back at Eq. (7-5) will indicate how estimates can be made of how much the reliability would change if the variance of obtained scores were either larger or smaller. If, for one sample, the variance of errors were 2.0 and the variance of obtained scores were 8.0, the reliability would be .75. If a new sample had a variance of 10.0, the variance of errors would be expected to remain at 2.0, and consequently the reliability would be .80. Thus after the standard error of measurement is found for one sample, it is easy to estimate what the reliability would be in another sample with either a larger or smaller standard deviation of scores. The correctness of this estimate depends on the assumption that the standard error of measurement will be the same in the new sample as in the old sample, which is a reasonably safe assumption unless the means of the two samples are extremely different with respect to the trait in question.

Even though it is important to keep in mind that the reliability varies with the dispersion of scores, this does not alter the direct meaning of the reliability coefficient in any particular sample of people. The reliability coefficient is the ratio of true-score variance to obtained-score variance. If that ratio is small, measurement error will attenuate correlations with other variables. If the total group of subjects in a study has a standard deviation of scores which is not much larger than the standard error of measurement, it is hopeless to investigate the variable in correlational studies. Approximately this condition has occurred in some studies. For example, in some studies of creativity, investigations have been made of only those children who had IQs of at least 120. With the children preselected in this way, the standard deviation of IQs in the group being studied would not be much larger than the standard error of measurement for the measure of intelligence. Then if IQs for the preselected groups are correlated with scores on tests of creativity, the correlations obviously will be very low. Paradoxically, in some controlled experiments this can be a welcome condition, because it means that observed variability of scores on the dependent measure is mainly due to measurement error rather than systematic individual differences in response to treatment effects. This could occur if subjects were very homogeneous with respect to the dependent variable before the experiment was conducted. However, in practice, this is a very rare circumstance. Rather, one usually finds substantial, reliable variance in individual differences relating to the dependent variable both before and after the experiment is undertaken.

## MAKING MEASURES RELIABLE

Of course, doing everything feasible to prevent measurement error from occurring is far better than assessing the effects of measurement error after it has occurred. Measurement error is reduced by writing items clearly, making test instructions easily understood, and adhering closely to the prescribed conditions for administering an instrument. Measurement error because of subjectivity of scoring can be reduced by making the rules for scoring as explicit as possible and by training scorers to do their jobs. On the better individual tests of intelligence, even though the scorer is a potential source of measurement error on some items, rules for scoring are so explicit and scorers usually are so well trained that very little measurement error is present. Of course, the ideal always is to completely remove subjectivity in scoring, but for practical reasons sometimes that is difficult to do. For example, in studies of discrimination learning, experimenters have been interested in "observing responses" in the rat—the tendency for the rat at the choice point in a T maze to look back and forth a number of times before making a choice. Conceivably, the number of such observing responses could be objectively recorded with a complex set of instruments, but if different scorers agree reasonably well on the numbers of observing responses made by different rats, the presence of some subjectivity in the scoring may be preferable to the expense and awkwardness of employing objective instruments. Still, though, the ultimate ideal in science is to have measures that are unaffected by errors of human judgment.

**Test length** The primary way to make tests more reliable is to make them longer. (For this and numerous other reasons in psychometrics, the maxim holds that, other things being equal, a long test is a good test.) If the reliability is known for a test with any particular number of items, the following formula can be used to estimate how much the reliability would increase if the number of items were increased by any factor $k$:

$$r_{kk} = \frac{kr_{11}}{1 + (k - 1)r_{11}} \tag{7-6}$$

If, for example, the reliability of a 20-item test is .70 and 40 items from the same domain are added to the test (making the final test three times as long as the original), the estimated reliability of the 60-item test will be

$$r_{kk} = \frac{3(.7)}{1 + (3 - 1).7} = .88$$

The only assumption in employing Eq. (7-6) in this case would be that the average correlation among the 20 items in the shorter test is the same as the average correlation among the 60 items in the augmented test. The assumption would be violated if old items and new items differed systematically in content (if they were from somewhat different domains) or if they differed in reliability (if the average correlation in one set were higher than that in the other set). In spite of these sources of imprecision, it is surprising how accurately the effects of test length on reliability are usually estimated by Eq. (7-6). This is particularly so if the shorter test contains at least 20 items. (As will be remembered, the precision of the reliability estimate is directly related to the number of test items.)

Equation (7-6) also can be used to estimate the effects on reliability of shortening a test. In this case $k$ equals the number of items on the shorter test divided by the number of items in the longer test, $r_{kk}$ is the estimated reliability of the shortened test, and $r_{11}$ is the reliability of the longer test. In the previous example, one could work backward from the reliability of .88 for the 60-item test and estimate the reliability of a 20-item test. Then, by placing .88 as $r_{11}$ in Eq. (7-6) and making $k = \frac{1}{3}$, one recovers the original reliability of .70 for the 20-item test. For either lengthening or shortening a test, the precision of the estimate obtained from Eq. (7-6) depends mainly on the number of items in the *shorter* test. To take an extreme case, one would not expect a very precise estimate if the known reliability of a 5-item test were used to estimate the reliability of a 40-item test, or vice versa.

Since Eq. (7-6) shows the test reliability to be a direct function of the number of test items only, one might wonder how it can give accurate estimates where there are other sources of measurement error in tests, e.g., variation in scores over short periods of time. As was argued previously, many such sources of error are considered by the domain-sampling model. Coefficient alpha is sensitive not only to the sampling of items but also to sources of measurement error that are present within the testing session. The alternative-form measure of reliability can be made sensitive to all sources of error, including subjectivity of scoring and variations in abilities and personality characteristics over short periods of time. If coefficient alpha is placed in Eq. (7-6), the estimated coefficient alpha for a longer or shorter test takes into account the sampling of items and numerous sources of error in the testing situation. If the correlation between alternative forms is placed in Eq. (7-6), the estimate takes account of variations over short periods of time and any factors that have been systematically varied for the two testings, e.g., using different scorers for the two tests. A good estimate would then be obtained of the alternative-form reliability for a longer or shorter test over the same period of time and with the same factors systematically varied.

An inspection of Eq. (7-6) shows that if the average correlation among items in a domain is positive, no matter how small, then as the number of items in a test is made larger and larger, the reliability necessarily approaches 1.00. If the average correlation is positive, the correlation between any two samples of items ($r_{11}$) is expected to be positive. If numerator and denominator of Eq. (7-6) are divided by $k$ and $k$ is allowed to approach infinity, $r_{kk}$ approaches 1.00. At first glance this might seem to be an easy way to obtain highly reliable tests, but often in practice Eq. (7-6) estimates that to reach even a moderately high reliability, a huge number of items would be required. A conversion of Eq. (7-6) can be used to estimate the number of items required to obtain a particular reliability:

$$k = \frac{r_{kk}(1 - r_{11})}{r_{11}(1 - r_{kk})} \tag{7-7}$$

where $r_{kk}$ = desired reliability

$r_{11}$ = reliability of existing test

$k$ = number of times test would have to be lengthened to obtain reliability of $r_{kk}$

In the situation where a 20-item test has a reliability of .50, the estimated lengthening required to obtain a reliability of .80 is found as follows:

$$k = \frac{.8(1 - .5)}{.5(1 - .8)} = \frac{.4}{.1} = 4$$

Thus the estimate is that to reach a reliability of .80 an 80-item test would be required. In many cases it would be feasible to use a test of that length, but let us see what happens when a 40-item test has a reliability of only .20 and a reliability of .80 is desired:

$$k = \frac{.8(1 - .2)}{.2(1 - .8)} = \frac{.64}{.04} = 16$$

It is estimated that 640 items would be required to reach a reliability of .80. Unless the items were of a kind that could be constructed very easily and administered very quickly, such a long test would be impractical in most applied work and in most experiments. Thus one can see that if the average correlation among items in a domain is very low (e.g., only .05), the correlations between samples of items will not be large, and to obtain high correlations would require a prohibitively large number of items in each sample.

**Standards of reliability** What a satisfactory level of reliability is depends on how a measure is being used. In the early stages of research on predictor tests or hypothesized measures of a construct, one saves time and energy by working with instruments that have only modest reliability, for which purpose reliabilities of .70 or higher will suffice. If significant correlations are found, corrections for attenuation will estimate how much the correlations will increase when reliabilities of measures are increased. If those corrected values look promising, it will be worth the time and effort to increase items and reduce measurement error in other ways.

For basic research, it can be argued that increasing reliabilities much beyond .80 is often wasteful of time and funds. At that level correlations are attenuated very little by measurement error. To obtain a higher reliability, say, of .90, strenuous efforts at standardization in addition to increasing the number of items might be required. Thus the more reliable test might be excessively time-consuming to construct, administer, and score.

In contrast to the standards in basic research, in many applied settings a reliability of .80 is not nearly high enough. In basic research, the concern is with the size of correlations and with the differences in means for different experimental treatments, for which purposes a reliability of .80 for the different measures involved is adequate. In many applied problems, a great deal hinges on the exact score made by a person on a test. If, for example, in a particular school system children with IQs below 70 are placed in special classes, it makes a great deal of difference whether the child has an IQ of 65 or 75 on a particular test. (Of course, other standards would be applied in addition to the IQ test.) If a college is able to admit only one-third of the students who apply, whether a student is in the upper third may depend on only a few score points on an aptitude test. In such instances it is frightening to think that any measurement error is permitted. Even with a reliability of .90, the standard error of measurement is almost one-third as large as the standard deviation of test scores. In those applied settings where important decisions are made with respect to specific test scores, a reliability of .90 is the minimum that should be tolerated, and a reliability of .95 should be considered the desirable standard.

## RELIABILITY OF LINEAR COMBINATIONS

So far this discussion of reliability has been concerned with the reliability of particular traits (e.g., spelling ability), as manifested in the average correlation among items. Another issue is that of the reliability of linear combinations of measures of different traits. An example of such a linear combination would be the total score on an achievement test battery for elementary school children, which would be the sum of scores obtained on separate parts of the test for spelling, arithmetic, word usage, and others. This simple linear combination can be depicted as

$$y = x_1 + x_2 + x_3$$

Similar linear combinations are employed very frequently in basic research, such as when $y$ equals a linear combination of different measures of anxiety or accuracy in perception. Then the question is that of estimating the reliability of $y$ from a knowledge of the reliabilities of the $x$ variables and the covariances among them.

At first thought it might seem that the reliability of $y$ could be estimated by coefficient alpha. For this, the sum of the variances of the $x$ variables would be divided by the variance of $y$, the quotient would be subtracted from 1, and the result would be increased by the factor concerning the number of "things" being summed [see Eq. (6-26)]. This could be done, but the result would be quite erroneous unless the $x$ variables were all measures of the same trait, e.g., alternative forms of a test of spelling ability. The reliability of samples of items from the *same* domain depends entirely on the average correlation among the samples, but this does not hold for samples of items from *different* domains. Suppose that, in the example concerning three subtests of an achievement test, each test had a respectable reliability, but the three all correlated zero with one another. In that case coefficient alpha would lead to the conclusion that the sum of the three tests had a reliability of zero, but that would be absurd. The methods which will be developed represent an extension of the domain-sampling model to a consideration of the correlations among items from different domains of content and the reliability of linear combinations of those domains. The formulas which will be developed for the reliability of linear combinations are analogs to those developed from the domain-sampling model, and the formulas really are extensions of those for the one-domain case.

One correct approach to determining the reliability of a linear combination would be to correlate alternative forms of the linear combinations. Thus if there were alternative forms of the test battery, each with tests of spelling, arithmetic, etc., the alternative forms could be administered approximately two weeks apart. The correlation between total scores on the two occasions would be a good measure of reliability for the linear combination.

In cases where alternative forms are not available or administering them is not feasible, an estimate of the alternative-form reliability can be derived as follows. Previously it was shown that the reliability of any variable equals the true-score variance in that variable divided by the variance of that variable. Thus the reliability of the linear combination would be

$$r_{yy} = \frac{\sigma_{t_y}^2}{\sigma_y^2} \tag{7-8}$$

where $\sigma_{t_y}^2$ = variance of true scores for linear combination
$\sigma_y^2$ = variance of obtained scores for linear combination
In the previous example of a simple sum of three variables, the denominator would be the variance of that sum, which equals $\bar{C}_y$, the sum of all elements in the covariance matrix for the three variables. The numerator could be expressed as follows:

$$\sigma_{t_y}^2 = \frac{1}{N} \Sigma (t_1 + t_2 + t_3)^2$$

By definition the variance of true scores on $y$ equals the variance of the sum of true scores ($t_1$, $t_2$, and $t_3$) of the $x$ variables. Previously it was shown how the variance of a linear combination could be obtained by placing the variables in the sum on the sides of a square table, multiplying corresponding elements and dividing each product by the number of persons being studied ($N$). This would result in a covariance matrix of true scores for the three variables. Each off-diagonal element would be the covariance between two sets of true scores. In Chap. 6 it was shown that the covariance of true scores for any two variables is identical to the covariance of obtained scores for those two variables. Thus the off-diagonal elements in the covariance matrix for true scores would be identical to the off-diagonal elements in the covariance matrix for obtained scores. The only difference between the two matrices would be in the diagonal elements. Each diagonal element in the covariance matrix of obtained scores would be a variance of obtained scores. Each diagonal element in the covariance matrix of true scores would equal the sum of squares of true scores for that variable divided by $N$, which would equal the variance of true scores for that variable. Since the reliability of any variable in the linear combination equals the true-score variance divided by the variance of obtained scores, the true-score variance equals the obtained-score variance multiplied by the reliability. Thus the covariance matrix of true scores for the sum of three variables would be as follows:

|       | $t_1$              | $t_2$              | $t_3$              |
|-------|--------------------|--------------------|--------------------|
| $t_1$ | $r_{11}\sigma_1^2$ | $\sigma_{12}$      | $\sigma_{13}$      |
| $t_2$ | $\sigma_{12}$      | $r_{22}\sigma_2^2$ | $\sigma_{23}$      |
| $t_3$ | $\sigma_{13}$      | $\sigma_{23}$      | $r_{33}\sigma_3^2$ |

Since the covariance matrix of true scores in the numerator of the equation differs from the covariance matrix in the denominator only in terms of diagonal elements, the former can be expressed in terms of the latter, as follows. To obtain the sum of the elements in the matrix of true scores, first subtract the sum of variances (the sum of diagonal elements) from the covariance matrix for obtained scores; then add to the remainder the sum of products of reliability coefficients and variances (the sum of diagonal elements in the covariance matrix for true scores). The reliability of the sum of variables will then be as follows:

$$r_{yy} = \frac{\bar{C}_y - \Sigma\sigma_i^2 + \Sigma r_{ii}\sigma_i^2}{\bar{C}_y} \tag{7-9}$$

$$r_{yy} = 1 - \frac{\Sigma\sigma_i^2 - \Sigma r_{ii}\sigma_i^2}{\bar{C}_y} \tag{7-10}$$

Since $\bar{C}_y$ is identical to $\sigma_y^2$, Eq. (7-10) can be rewritten as

$$r_{yy} = 1 - \frac{\Sigma\sigma_i^2 - \Sigma r_{ii}\sigma_i^2}{\sigma_y^2} \tag{7-11}$$

With this version of the formula, one would need to compute only the variance of the linear combination ($y$) and the standard deviation of each variable in the linear combination and to have foreknowledge of the reliability of each variable. A concrete example would be where (1) the variances of three variables are 1, 2, and 3, respectively, (2) the reliabilities are .60, .70, and .80, respectively, and (3) the variance of the sum of the three variables is 12. The reliability of the sum would be obtained as follows:

$$r_{yy} = 1 - \frac{(1 + 2 + 3) - (.6 + 1.4 + 2.4)}{12}$$

$$= 1 - \frac{6 - 4.4}{12}$$

$$r_{yy} = .87$$

If, as is usually the case, variables were placed in the form of standard scores before they were summed, the covariance of the sum of obtained scores would equal the sum of the elements in the correlation matrix for the variables which were summed. The diagonal elements in the matrix would be 1s, and the off-diagonal elements would be correlations between variables in the sum. The covariance matrix for true scores would have off-diagonal elements the same as those in the correlation matrix for obtained scores, but the diagonal elements would be reliability coefficients rather than 1s. Then Eq. (7-11) could be transformed for the case of $k$ variables expressed in standard scores as follows:

$$r_{yy} = \frac{\bar{R}_y - k + \Sigma r_{ii}}{\bar{R}_y} \qquad (7\text{-}12)$$

$$r_{yy} = 1 - \frac{k - \Sigma r_{ii}}{\bar{R}_y} \qquad (7\text{-}13)$$

$$r_{yy} = 1 - \frac{k - \Sigma r_{ii}}{\sigma_y^2} \qquad (7\text{-}14)$$

The standard-score version of the formula for the reliability of a sum can be illustrated in the case where three variables being summed each have reliabilities of .60 and each pair correlates .50. Then $k = 3$, and the sum of reliabilities equals 1.8. The variance of $y$ would equal $k + (6 \times .50)$ (there being six off-diagonal elements in the correlation matrix). The result would be as follows:

$$r_{yy} = 1 - \frac{3 - 1.8}{6} = .8$$

Going back to Eq. (7-14) one can see that in the special case where only two sets of standard scores are summed, the following special formula can be used:

$$r_{yy} = 1 - \frac{2 - r_{11} - r_{22}}{\sigma_y^2} \qquad (7\text{-}15)$$

Where each of the two variables being summed has a reliability of .60 and the correlation between the two is .50, the computations are as follows:

$$r_{yy} = 1 - \frac{2 - 1.2}{3} = .73$$

The variance of $y$ equals the sum of the elements in the correlation matrix for only two variables, which equals 2.0 plus two times the correlation between them. This makes the denominator of the fraction on the right equal 3.0.

**Negative elements** Up to this point it has been assumed that the problem is that of estimating the reliability of positive sums of variables, but the logic applies equally well when some of the variables are subtracted rather than added, as would be the case in the following linear combination:

$$y = x_1 + x_2 - x_3$$

The previously derived formulas for a linear combination apply equally well when some of the variables in the linear combination have negative signs. If the three variables were in standard-score form, Eq. (7-14) could be applied. In the second term on the right-hand side of the equation, the numerator would not be affected by the minus sign for variable 3 in the example above. There would still be $k$ variables (three), and the reliabilities of the three variables would not be affected. What would be affected is the denominator of that ratio, the variance of the linear combination. If variable $x_3$ correlated positively with the other two variables, placing a minus sign before that variable in the linear combination would reverse the signs of the correlations of variable 3 with the other two variables. This would make the variance of $y$ less than it would have been if variable 3 had been added rather than subtracted. But if variable 3 had a negative correlation with the other two variables, the minus sign in the linear combination would serve to make the variance of the linear combination more than it would have been if the variable had been added. Since the larger the variance of the linear combination, the more the reliability, the pattern of positive and negative signs in the linear combination has a direct effect on the reliability of the combination.

**Weighted sums** The method for estimating the reliability of a sum can be extended to the case of weighted sums. A weighted sum of variables expressed as standard scores would be as follows:

$$y = b_1 z_1 + b_2 z_2 + b_3 z_3$$

The variance of $y$ would equal the sum of all elements in the weighted correlation matrix. The diagonal elements would consist of squared weights, and each off-diagonal element would consist of the correlation between two variables multiplied by the products of the weights for the two variables. The sum of elements in this matrix would be divided into the sum of elements in the matrix corresponding to the variance of the sum of true scores. The off-diagonal elements would be the same in the two matrices, but in the latter the diagonal elements would consist of squared weights multiplied by reliability coefficients. Then Eq. (7-14) could be modified to obtain the following formula for the reliability of a weighted sum of variables expressed as standard scores:

$$r_{yy} = 1 - \frac{\Sigma b_i^2 - \Sigma b_i^2 r_{ii}}{\sigma_y^2} \tag{7-16}$$

where $b_i$ = weight for variable $z_i$

$r_{ii}$ = reliability of variable $z_i$

To apply Eq. (7-16), one would first obtain the variance of the sum of weighted standard scores, which would be the denominator of the expression on the far right of the equation. For the numerator, the sum of squared weights would be obtained. The square of each weight would be multiplied by the corresponding reliability, these would be summed, and the sum would be subtracted from the sum of squared weights. Then it would be only a simple problem in arithmetic to obtain the reliability of the linear combination.

When variables are expressed as deviation scores rather than as standard scores, Eq. (7-16) can be modified as follows to obtain the reliability of the weighted sum:

$$r_{yy} = 1 - \frac{\Sigma b_i^2 \sigma_i^2 - \Sigma b_i^2 \sigma_i^2 r_{ii}}{\sigma_y^2} \qquad (7\text{-}17)$$

Equations (7-16) and (7-17) can be applied equally well in the case where some of the weighted variables have minus signs in the linear combination.

**Principles concerning the reliability of linear combinations** Because linear combinations of variables are encountered so frequently in practice, it is important to look at some principles that govern their reliability. The multiple-regression equation is a weighted linear combination of variables, weighted so as to correlate as highly as possible with a criterion variable. Later it will be seen that, in factor analysis, factors consist of linear combinations of variables, and most other methods of multivariate analysis deal with linear combinations of variables. Consequently the reliability of a linear combination of variables is an omnipresent issue in psychological measurement.

Although previously it was said that the reliability of a sum cannot be estimated by coefficient alpha [Eq. (6-26)], a reinspection of the basic formula for the reliability of a linear combination [Eq. (7-11)] will show that the two formulas look very similar. In the former there is a multiplier in which the number of test items is divided by the number of test items minus 1, but otherwise the two equations look much alike. The difference is that, in the formula for the reliability of a linear combination, the sum of reliabilities multiplied by variances is subtracted in the numerator of the ratio from the sum of variances. Thus the reliabilities of the variables tend to increase the reliability of a linear combination over that which would be predicted from coefficient alpha. As mentioned previously, the similarity in appearance of coefficient alpha with formulas for the reliability of linear combinations is no accident—the latter really represents an extension of the domain-sampling model to a multiple domain-sampling model for reliability. This is further evidence of the importance and extreme generality of the domain-sampling model for considering issues relating to measurement error (and for numerous other issues in psychometric theory as well).

When the correlations among items are all zero, coefficient alpha is necessarily zero. A look at the standard-score version of the reliability of a sum of variables [Eq. (7-12)] will show what happens when the correlations between variables are all zero. In that case $\bar{R} = k$, the number of variables. Then Eq. (7-12) can be reduced to the following:

$$r_{yy} = \frac{\Sigma r_{ii}}{k} \qquad (7\text{-}18)$$

Equation (7-18) leads to the important deduction that when the variables in a sum of standard scores correlate zero, the reliability of the sum is the average reliability of the variables. Thus if three variables expressed as standard scores had reliabilities of .60, .70, and .80 and correlations among the three variables were all zero, the reliability of the sum would equal .70. This would hold even if some of the variables had negative signs in the sum. Obviously Eq. (7-18) also applies when the *average* correlation is zero (excluding the diagonal elements in the matrix).

Another look at Eq. (7-14) will show what happens when the average correlation is not zero. It is possible for the average correlation to be negative, which obviously would be the case when two variables correlated positively and one were given a negative sign in the combination. Then there would be only one correlation, which would have to be negative. There is, however, a severe limit to the possible average negative correlation obtainable among the variables of a linear combination. One can readily see what the limit would be. Since the sum of all elements in a correlation matrix (including the diagonal elements) is the variance of the sum of variables expressed as standard scores and since a variance cannot be negative, a negative sum of off-diagonal correlations cannot be greater than the sum of diagonal values, which equals $k$. By expressing the denominator of the ratio in Eq. (7-13) as $k$ plus the sum of off-diagonal correlations, one can see that the reliability approaches zero as the sum of off-diagonal correlations approaches minus the sum of reliabilities.

If, as is usually the case, the average correlation is positive, the higher the average correlation, the higher the reliability of the linear combination. To understand this rule, one must make a very careful distinction between correlations among variables before and after they are placed in linear combinations. The reason this distinction is so important is that the correlation between two variables before they are placed in a linear combination is reversed in sign if they are given *different* signs in the linear combination. In the simplest case, if two variables have a positive correlation and a linear combination is formed by subtracting one from the other, in the linear combination (in the correlation matrix corresponding to the variance of the combination) the correlation will be negative. So far all the discussion of the reliability of linear combinations has concerned correlations *after* linear combinations are formed. To prevent confusion in that regard, all formulas were developed so that sums or averages of correlations did not explicitly appear. Instead, the correlations among variables in the linear combination were "hidden" in the variance of the linear combination. Of course, when actually computing the variance of a linear combination, one would add or subtract variables depending on their signs in the combination. When that is done, the correct value is obtained for the variance of $y$. The remaining terms in the computing formulas are reliabilities for variables expressed as standard scores and both reliabilities and variances for sets of deviation scores. Since these are always positive, regardless of the signs variables are given, there is no way to become confused about the proper use of the formulas.

There is, however, considerable value in looking at correlations among variables *before* they are placed in linear combinations. This will show how much reliability is expected from a particular linear combination. Here is an extreme case. If two variables correlated .60 and each had a reliability of .60, then if one variable were subtracted from the other [Eq. (7-15)], the reliability of the linear combination would be zero. Obviously such a linear combination would be worthless. Less extreme cases occur frequently in practice. In the case where the reliabilities were each .80 and the correlation between the two variables was .60, the reliability of the difference between the two variables would be only .50. In both cases the same reliability would have resulted if before variables were combined, the correlations were negative, and both variables were given a positive sign in the combination.

Since the reliability of a sum increases with the size of the average correlation among variables, any set of signs in a linear combination that maximizes the positive sum of correlations will maximize the reliability. The problem is illustrated in the following correlation matrix for six variables:

|   | *1* | *2* | *3* | *4* | *5* | *6* |
|---|-----|-----|-----|-----|-----|-----|
| *1* | 1.0 | + | + | − | − | − |
| *2* | + | 1.0 | + | − | − | − |
| *3* | + | + | 1.0 | − | − | − |
| *4* | − | − | − | 1.0 | + | + |
| *5* | − | − | − | + | 1.0 | + |
| *6* | − | − | − | + | + | 1.0 |

The matrix is meant to illustrate correlations among variables *before* they are placed in a linear combination. Variables 1, 2, and 3 form a set whose members all correlate positively, and the same is true for variables 4, 5, and 6. All correlations between members of the two sets are negative. If a linear combination were formed in which all six variables had positive signs, the sum of the elements in the above matrix would be the variance of the linear combination. The size of the reliability of the linear combination is positively related to the size of the variance of the linear combination, and thus it is positively related to the sum of correlations among variables. If, in the example above, all variables were given positive signs, there would be more negative correlations than positive correlations, and consequently the sum of correlations might be either near zero or even negative. In this example, one could obtain the maximum reliability for any possible linear combination by giving negative signs to all three variables in *either* set (but not both). If one chose to give negative signs to variables 4, 5, and 6, all correlations among the three would remain positive and would not change in size. They would remain positive because all three variables would still have the *same* sign. The important difference would be that the signs of all correlations between the two sets of variables would change from negative to positive. Then all correlations in the matrix would be positive, the variance of the linear combination would be at a maximum, and reliability of the linear combination would be at a maximum.

The problem is seldom as neat as in the example discussed above; however, an inspection of correlations among variables *before* they are placed in a linear combination will often indicate that a planned linear combination of variables would not be very reliable and that a different linear combination would be much more reliable. Of course, maximization of reliability is seldom the most important goal either in basic research or in applied work. For example, in the former, if a hypothesis concerns how much *better* people do on the sum of three measures than they do on the sum of three other measures, in the linear combination there is no choice but to give positive signs to the first three variables and negative signs to the other three variables. An inspection of correlations among the variables might show, however, that such a linear combination would have a very low reliability, in which case the study might be doomed before it started.

## ALTERNATIVE MODELS FOR RELIABILITY ASSESSMENT

In Chap. 6 it was mentioned that alternative models are available to the domain-sampling model for reliability and that these models supply useful supplementary information. For example, the binomial model teaches us that the distribution of obtained scores relating to the standard error of measurement is likely to be somewhat skewed for extremely high or extremely low scores. Also, that model provides a forewarning about the assumption of homoscedasticity required in corrections of reliability for range of subjects in an investigation.

The concept of a factorial design for the domain of items proves very useful in thinking about the various sources of measurement error that occur in different applied situations. In the chapter it was mentioned that various reliability coefficients could be employed depending upon the sources of error that are encountered, e.g., unreliability because of differences among test examiners or test forms. Although one can actually make statistical analyses of complete factorial designs regarding relevant dimensions along which measurement error is likely to occur, this is very seldom done in practice. However, concepts relating to factorial designs for domains of content are useful in thinking about measurement error and useful to psychometric specialists in both the development of theory and the conduct of basic research on behavioral measurements.

The most important alternative class of models with respect to measurement error concerns item-characteristic curves (ICC theory). The use of models concerning item-characteristic curves of particular mathematical forms (e.g., normal ogives or logistic curves) has been mentioned previously at a number of places in this book and will be discussed more fully at relevant points later. In some cases, ICC theory leads to the scoring of tests in a manner that cannot be directly compared with the usual method of scoring based on the simple summing of item responses. As will be discussed in Chap. 9, for example, in the use of "tailored tests" different subjects are scored over somewhat different collections of items, e.g., for spelling ability. In such highly specialized cases, the traditional formulas for reliability discussed throughout this chapter would not apply. Instead, some special techniques for assessing measurement error are required. However, testing by methods based on ICC theory rather than the traditional approach still are in a highly experimental phase, are controversial, and are not likely to entirely replace traditional psychometric concepts based on the linear or summative model for some time to come, if ever. The reader who has a special interest in ICC theory should consult Lord (1974), Lord and Novick (1968), and Weiss (1976).

## SUGGESTED ADDITIONAL READINGS

Cronbach, L. J. Coefficient alpha and the internal structure of tests. *Psychometrika,* 1951, *16,* 297—334.

Cronbach, L. J., Gleser, G. C., Nanda, H., and Rajaratnam, N. *The dependability of behavioral measurements.* New York: Wiley, 1971.

Guilford, J. P. *Psychometric methods.* New York: McGraw-Hill, 1954, chaps. 13 and 14.

Guilliksen, H. *Theory of mental tests.* New York: Wiley, 1950, chaps. 1 to 8.

Horn, J. L. Integration of concepts of reliability and standard error of measurement. *Educational and Psychological Measurement,* 1971, *31,* 57—74.

Horst, P. *Psychological measurement and prediction.* Belmont, Calif.: Wadsworth, 1966, chaps. 16 to 19.

Lord, F. M. Individualized testing and item characteristic curve theory. In D. H. Krantz, R. C. Atkinson, R. D. Luce, and P. Suppes (eds.), *Contemporary developments in mathematical psychology.* (Vol. 2) *Measurement, psychophysics, and neural information processing.* San Francisco: W. H. Freeman, 1974.

Lord, F. M., and Novick, M. R. *Statistical theories of mental tests.* Reading, Mass.: Addison-Wesley, 1968, chaps. 5 to 11.

Stanley, J. C. Reliability. In R. L. Thorndike (ed.), *Educational measurement* (2d ed.). Washington, D.C.: American Council on Education, 1971.

Weiss, D. J. *Final report: Computerized ability testing, 1972—1975* (Office of Naval Research Sponsored Project Report). Minneapolis: Department of Psychology, University of Minnesota, April 1976.

# EIGHT

## CONSTRUCTION OF CONVENTIONAL TESTS

If a student who was uninformed about such matters asked a professor "What are the best methods for constructing tests?" the professor could answer "It depends on many things." In so responding, the professor would be both uninformative and incorrect, because there are straightforward, understandable, acceptable, general methods for handling 75 percent (to guess a figure) of the needs for constructing tests. For probably another 15 percent, special methods of test construction are available which will be discussed in Chap. 9. For the remaining 10 percent (another guesstimate), mixtures of various approaches are required, or experts disagree about alternative approaches. Tests relating to this final 10 percent of the cases also will be discussed in Chap. 9.

Before we discuss particular methods of test construction, a number of general principles should be mentioned. First, it should be remembered that tests serve three major types of functions and thus are judged by three standards of validity—predictive validity, content validity, or construct validity. As will be seen as the chapter progresses, the methods used for construction of measures intended to have predictive validity and those intended to have construct validity usually are very much the same. However, instruments that are required to have content validity (e.g., achievement tests of all kinds) are constructed in terms of a different logic. Some principles concerning the construction of measures intended to have content validity will be summarized, and then the remainder of the chapter will be devoted to principles concerning the construction of measures intended to serve the other two functions.

Second, this chapter will consider *general-purpose* instruments rather than tests that are constructed for any highly specialized purpose. By general-purpose instruments is meant ones that are intended to be employed very widely with diverse samples of subjects in numerous studies relating to applied problems or in basic research. With such general-purpose instruments, it is assumed that the investigator is interested primarily in studying *individual differences* among subjects and that tests are constructed in such a way as to measure such individual differences. It also is assumed that it is important to make reliable discriminations at all levels of the trait, such as in distinguishing among people who have IQs well above average. In Chap. 9 will be discussed some methods of test construction for highly specialized instruments which do not meet the assumptions of general-purpose tests as described above. For example, the development of measures to be used in basic research will be discussed in which large, reliable individual differences in scores not only are unnecessary but could constitute a statistical nuisance. Also, in Chap. 9 will be discussed the construction of highly specialized achievement tests for measuring mastery of learning at each major step in a program of school instruction.

Third, the methods of test construction discussed in this chapter are based on the summative or linear model. The model stipulates that test scores are to be obtained by summing scores over items. The items can be either weighted or unweighted, and either they can all have positive signs in the combination or some can have negative signs. All these possibilities are subsumed under the concept of a linear combination of test items. Although there are competing models for special problems of measurement, there is no general competitor to the linear model. Alternative models that either supply supplementary information for the linear model or should be employed instead in highly special situations will be discussed in Chap. 9.

Fourth, the methods of test construction discussed in this chapter are for instruments that are *not* highly *speeded*. Although many of the tests which are developed with methods that will be discussed in this chapter have a time limit mainly to expedite test administration, it is assumed that the time limit is sufficiently generous that speed per se has very little influence on the variance of test scores. Methods of constructing highly speeded tests are discussed in Chap. 9; the psychological processes involved in highly speeded tasks are discussed in Chap. 16. In Chap. 16, it will be shown that, unless time limits are highly restrictive, modest limitations on total test-taking time usually have very little effect on results.

Fifth, whereas it will be convenient to speak of "test construction," the principles discussed in this chapter and the following chapter apply to all forms of psychological measurement, e.g., to physiological measures of anxiety, to measures of activity in the rat, and to measures of learning rate in paired-associate word learning. The principles apply to any measure that is obtained from a linear combination of individual responses, items on mental tests constituting only a special case. The principles apply to measures of ability, personality, and attitudes; and they apply both to dichotomous items and to items scorable on more than two points.

## CONSTRUCTION OF ACHIEVEMENT TESTS

As was mentioned in Chap. 3, the achievement test is the most obvious example of a measure that requires content validity. The term *achievement test* will be used in a general sense to refer to (1) examinations in individual courses of instruction in schools of all kinds and at all levels, (2) measures of achievement (course examinations) used routinely by all the instructors in particular units of instruction, and (3) commercially distributed tests of achievement used throughout the country. Such measures of achievement are employed very frequently at all levels of education up through graduate school and professional training, in civil service examinations, and in special training programs in military establishments and in industry. As will be discussed more fully in Chap. 9, specially constructed achievement tests are also used very often in basic research in the behavioral sciences, e.g., in educational experiments to determine the effectiveness of different approaches to instruction in mathematics.

In terms of sheer numbers of tests administered, achievement tests outrank all other tests by far. For three reasons, however, only a summary will be given here of procedures for the construction of achievement tests. First, the basic principles for contructing achievement tests are simple and can be stated rather quickly. Second, although there are hundreds of special techniques for constructing achievement tests of particular kinds for particular purposes, e.g., achievement tests for grammatical skills and mechanical drawing, these special techniques are of interest mainly to professional educators and specialists in measurement. Since this book is aimed at future behavioral scientists in general rather than any special group, a lengthy discussion of such special techniques would be out of place. Third, there are comprehensive books devoted either wholly or in large part to the construction of achievement tests. These are listed in the Suggested Additional Readings—see in particular the very comprehensive volume edited by Thorndike (1971).

**The test plan** As was mentioned in Chap. 3, ensuring the content validity of an achievement test by an explicit plan for constructing the test is more appropriate than determining the content validity after the test is constructed. If representative persons who are to use the test agree in advance on the appropriateness of the plan, arriving at an acceptable instrument is mainly a matter of technical skill and applied research.

The major part of the test plan is an outline of content for the instrument which is to be constructed. Since content validity depends on a rational appeal to an adequate coverage of important content, an explicit outline of content provides a basis for discussing content validity. For example, an outline of content for a comprehensive achievement test for the fourth grade would need to indicate whether or not a section on "study skills" was to be included. If such a section were to be included, it would also be necessary to list the aspects of study skills that would be covered, e.g., use of the dictionary and locating topics in reference books.

In addition to the outline of content, the plan should describe the types of items to be employed, state the approximate number of items to be employed in each section and each subsection of the test, and give examples of the types of items to be used. The plan also should state how long the test will take to administer, how it will be administered, how it will be scored, and the types of norms that will be obtained.

When the plan is completed, it is reviewed by numerous persons, including teachers, subject-matter experts, administrative officials (in public schools, industry, the military, and other organizations), and specialists in educational and psychological measurement. Many suggestions might be made for changes, and the revised plan would be resubmitted to reviewers. Hopefully, the eventual plan is one that receives general approval from reviewers. Of course, such an elaborate plan would be undertaken only for achievement tests that were to be used quite widely, such as for commercially distributed tests of overall achievement for elementary school and achievement tests used in large training programs in military establishments.

**Test items** Of course, a test can be no better than the items of which it is composed. A good plan represents an *intention* to construct a good test, but unless items are skillfully written, the plan never materializes. Although there are some rules for writing good items (see Nunnally 1972, chap. 6, and Wesman 1971), writing test items is an art that few people seem to master. Most frequently, items are marred by two shortcomings. First, they are ambiguous, because they fail to adequately "aim" subjects toward the type of response required. A classic example is, "What happened to art during the fifteenth century?" The question is so vague that the respondent could take many different directions on an essay examination and could legitimately select several different alternatives on a multiple-choice item. A second major fault is that items often concern trivial aspects of the subject matter. To write items that are unambiguous and to write them as quickly as possible, it is tempting to populate tests with items concerning dates, names, and simple facts. Most instructors will agree that the memory for simple details is not the important thing to be measured; what is important is to measure various aspects of reasoning with the subject matter. But regardless of the type of item employed, it takes considerable skill to write items that adequately measure a true understanding of principles.

There is a choice as to which type of item will be employed, including short-answer essay questions, longer essay questions, and numerous types of objective items. Among objective items, the multiple-choice item is considered the best for most purposes. For three reasons, commercially distributed achievement tests rely almost solely on multiple-choice items. First, they are very easy to administer and score. Second, expert item writers who are highly skilled at composing such items are available. Third, when multiple-choice items are skillfully composed, they can accurately measure almost anything. Time and again it has been shown that a test composed of good multiple-choice items correlates with an essay test of the same topic almost as highly as the reliability of the latter will permit. Since the multiple-choice test typically is much more reliable than the essay test, the conclusion is inescapable that the objective test is more valid. This relationship tends to hold even with material where intuitively it would not seem possible, e.g., in comparison of a multiple-choice test for the pronunciation of a foreign language with scores given on oral exercises.

Although in some instances it logically would be very difficult to employ multiple-choice items to measure achievement (e.g., English composition), most of the major commercially distributed achievement tests have no essay questions. In practice, though, this is not always a major disadvantage. When essay questions are used in achievement tests, they usually correlate so highly with other sections of the test that they can be omitted. Thus, for example, when essay questions are tried as measures of English composition, they tend to add little new variance to what can be explained by multiple-choice tests of vocabulary, reading comprehension, and grammar. This is partly because of a much higher reliability for the objective sections of the test and partly because of a high degree of overlap between abilities required in the objective items and ability in English composition.

In addition to higher reliability and ease of scoring, another advantage of multiple-choice items is that they usually sample the topic much more broadly than would be possible on essay examinations. For example, a 50-minute classroom examination could easily employ 50 multiple-choice items without excessively "speeding" students, but it would be difficult to employ more than 5 one-page essay questions in the same amount of time. How well students performed on the essay questions would depend to some extent on their "luck" regarding which questions were asked, but such luck (measurement error because of the sampling of content) would tend to average out over 50 multiple-choice items. Since there is measurement error because of the sampling of content and an equally large amount of measurement error because of the subjectivity of scoring, the multiple-choice examination is usually much more reliable than the essay examination. A typical finding would be an alternative-form reliability between .60 and .70 for the essay examination and a reliability between .75 and .90 for the multiple-choice examination.

Although the skillful item writer can measure almost anything with multiple-choice items, this is not true for many instructors, particularly those not familiar with principles of measurement and without considerable practice in constructing objective tests. In classes with a large number of students (100 or more), there usually is no choice but to employ an objective examination. To do a careful job of grading that many essay examinations would be a monstrous chore. When there are no more than 15 students in a class, it actually saves time to construct and score an essay examination rather than a multiple-choice examination. Even if the multiple-choice examination is very easy to score, a good one is time-consuming to construct. When there are as many as 30 students, the practical advantage is on the side of the multiple-choice examination. When the class contains between 15 and 30 students, there is no strong practical advantage for either type of test, and consequently the decision between them should be made on other grounds. If instructors feel more comfortable in constructing one type of test than the other, they should probably follow their own intuitions in that regard.

The labors of constructing a multiple-choice test are greatly diminished if the instructor has a pool of items that has been accumulated from previous classes. Once such a pool of items is developed, usually most of the items for a new test can be drawn from that pool, with some new items being written to take into account changing emphases in the unit of instruction. When such a pool of items is available, constructing and scoring a multiple-choice test nearly always take less time than constructing and scoring an essay test for the same subject matter.

If essay questions are used, generally it is best to employ short-answer questions which can be answered in no more than half a page. Short-answer questions have a number of advantages over long-answer questions. Since more questions can be included, the short-answer examination makes it possible to provide a broader coverage of the content. In short-answer questions, it is easier to "aim" the student toward the intended types of responses. Then there will be fewer instances in which a student writes brilliantly on something different from what the instructor intended. Also, short-answer questions are much easier for the instructor to grade. Not only do students get lost while responding to long-answer questions, but instructors get lost in trying to grade them. With short-answer questions, it is much easier for the instructor to formulate a concrete basis for grading and to keep the standards in mind while looking at responses. (See Nunnally 1972, chaps. 5 to 7, for a detailed discussion of the development and use of essay questions in teacher-made tests.)

Although there is a definite place for essay questions in some types of teacher-made tests and in some aspects of basic research in the behavioral sciences, nearly all large-scale achievement tests for both applied problems and basic research rely almost exclusively on multiple-choice items. Consequently, only methods of test construction concerning such multiple-choice items will be discussed in the remainder of this chapter.

After test items are constructed, they should be critically reviewed. Of course, for a classroom examination, the instructors probably would do their own reviewing, but for important achievement tests, a careful review is done by a number of persons. First, the items would be reviewed by experts in test construction. They would consider each item for its appropriateness, apparent difficulty, and clarity. The items that survived that review would then be reviewed by teachers and other potential users of the test.

**Item analysis** Although content validity mainly rests on rational rather than empirical grounds, results from applying an instrument do provide some important types of information. Large-scale investigations are undertaken for important achievement tests. In contrast, the individual instructor may not seek such information at all or may obtain it only incidentally. The first step in obtaining such information is to administer a large collection of items to a large sample of persons who are representative of the individuals with whom the final test will be employed. To have ample room to discard items that work poorly, there should be at least from one-and-a-half to twice as many items as will appear on the final test. All items should be administered to at least 300 persons, preferably to 1,000 or more. Because there are so many opportunities for taking advantage of chance in item analysis, unless there are at least five times as many persons as items, the results may be highly misleading. For this reason, few instructors obtain enough data for their items to warrant an item analysis.

If computational resources are available for the purpose, there are some important types of statistical information that are helpful in evaluating items. First, the percentages of response to each alternative should be determined. Usually there are either four or five alternatives for each answer on most tests, and consequently the percentages of responses are divided among these. Such percentages of responses to alternatives would be inspected from a number of standpoints. One would be quite suspicious of any item in which the percent of persons marking the designated correct response was less than that for one of the alternatives designated as incorrect. In that case, the most probable explanations are that either the instruction was misleading or the item itself is misleading in terms of wording. Another type of information that one obtains from inspecting such percentages of responses to the alternatives concerns the credibility of the incorrect alternatives. If a sizable percent of subjects do not mark the correct answer but almost none of them marks one of the "distracters," then that alternative probably is transparently incorrect. Either such incorrect alternatives should be replaced or the item itself should be replaced.

Another type of information that comes from the inspection of percentages of persons marking each alternative concerns the percent who mark the correct alternative, which is symbolized as the $p$ value of the item (probability of any person at random selecting the correct response). For general-purpose tests (e.g., commercially distributed tests of overall achievement in elementary grades), one should be suspicious of items that have extreme $p$ values—those in which nearly everyone gets the item correct or in which the percentage of correct responses is no greater than could be obtained by chance (e.g., if there are four alternative responses, a $p$ value of .25 would be obtained if everyone guessed at the correct answer). Items which are very close in $p$ value to either end of the difficulty continuum will not discriminate among subjects and thus will add no reliable variance to individual differences. In Chap. 9 will be discussed the concept of "mastery learning," where, at least in terms of theory, most students should respond correctly to most items. In that case and for other purposes, one can argue for having some very easy items on achievement tests; but, as was said, they do not produce reliable, individual differences which are required in most general-purpose achievement tests. The author cannot think of any situation in which it is desirable to have items with $p$ values that are near the chance level. Other than for weeding out items that are extreme in terms of $p$ values, it is far better to rely on other considerations in the construction of achievement tests and for general-purpose measures that are intended to have predictive validity or construct validity.

The second type of statistical information that can be obtained if high-speed computational resources are available is the correlation of each item with the total test score, e.g., total scores on an arithmetic test. If the test has different parts for different topics (e.g., reading and science), each item should be correlated with the subscore for its section rather than with scores on the test as a whole. The proper coefficient is point-biserial, which, as was said previously, is the PM formula applied to the relationship between a dichotomous item and a multipoint distribution of scores.

Any item that correlates near zero with test scores should be carefully inspected. In an achievement test, it is possible for an item to correlate near zero with total scores and still be a valid item, but that rarely is the case. It is more likely that the item is excessively difficult or easy, is ambiguous, or actually has little to do with the topic. Unless there are strong grounds for deciding otherwise, such items generally should be discarded. Among the remaining items, the items that correlate higher with total scores generally are the better items. They probably are less ambiguous, they cannot be very extreme in difficulty in either direction, and they will tend to make individual differences on the final test highly reliable.

The next step in item analysis depends on the number of items that have relatively high correlations with total scores. For example, where 100 multiple-choice items are being investigated for a subtest of a large achievement test, most correlations with subtest scores are expected to range from 0 to about .40. In tests of ability, such correlations are seldom negative, and when they are, it usually is due to sampling error. Correlations above .30 are usually considered good. (An artifact in such correlations will be discussed later.) If there are more than enough items at that level, one can proceed to the next step. If there are barely enough items at that level for the eventual test, there is no choice but to employ those items, and consequently there is no room for further pruning of items. If the number of items at that level is far less than required for the eventual test, the only recourse is to start over with a larger collection of items.

When there are plenty of items that correlate well with total scores, the next step is to investigate the reliability for successive collections of the items. First, the items would be ranked in accordance with their correlations with total scores. Successive sets would be selected, and coefficient alpha, or KR-20, would be computed for each set. Since usually at least 30 items are required to have a high reliability, coefficient alpha would be applied to the 30 items having the highest correlations with total scores. If the reliability were as high as desired, one would stop adding items. If not, one would add the 5 or 10 items next in terms of correlations with total scores, and coefficient alpha would be computed for the collection of items. One would keep adding sets of items 5 or 10 at a time until the reliability was as high as desired.

After a set of items which has a high reliability has been obtained, the next step is to plot the frequency distribution for total scores on the items. If the distribution is "satisfactory," the selection of items is complete. For most commercially distributed achievement tests, usually it is helpful to have a symmetrical, approximately normal distribution of scores. The distribution of scores can be compared with that expected from a normal distribution with the same mean and standard deviation. If the distribution of scores is highly skewed in either direction, corrective measures can be taken. If the distribution is skewed toward the higher end, this means that the test is too difficult. If there are some relatively easy items which correlate satisfactorily with total scores and which were not included in the final collection of items, these can be used to replace some of the more difficult items in the final collection. This will tend to make the distribution of total scores more closely resemble the normal distribution. If the distribution is skewed toward the lower end, some more difficult items can be used to replace some of the easier items. Some cut-and-try methods in this regard will make the distribution symmetrical.

Again it should be emphasized that item analysis of achievement tests is secondary to content validity. Contrary to what is done with predictor tests and measures of constructs, with achievement tests considerable pains are taken to ensure that all items have content validity *before* they are submitted to item analysis. Thus all items submitted for analysis are assumed to be good, and the analysis provides additional information only. But more important than the information obtained from item analysis is the initial decision to use a particular item in a tryout form of the test. Also, regardless of what is found in item analysis, the final decision to include or reject an item is based primarily on human judgment. For example, in each section of most achievement tests, the first several items are very easy. These are included to prevent some students from becoming discouraged and to give all students some practice with the particular type of item. Because nearly everyone correctly answers these items, purely on the basis of an item analysis these items might appear nearly worthless.

**Norms** In standardizing achievement tests, one of the most important steps is the establishment of norms. In the broadest sense of the word, *norms* are any scores that provide a frame of reference for interpreting the scores of particular persons. With achievement tests for measuring progress in elementary school, usually the set of norms would be based on scores made by a representative cross section of students across the country. In addition it is useful to have local norms, such as norms based on samples of students in a particular locality and in a particular school. Then the score of a particular student can be compared with scores of students across the country, students in the same locality, and students in the same school.

In the construction of important achievement tests, the construction of norms is almost as much work as the construction of tests. (For some of the particulars, see Angoff 1971.) Great care must be taken to ensure that the sample of students is representative of the country as a whole, and for this purpose, thousands of students must be tested. Then statistical analyses must be undertaken to obtain the final norms. Also, usually it is necessary to obtain separate norms for different parts of the test.

Norms usually are expressed both in the form of transformed standard scores and as percentiles. For the former, a widely used method is to convert raw scores to a distribution having a mean of 500 and a standard deviation of

100. Essentially, a percentile indicates the percentage of persons in the normative sample that is *below* a particular score. Thus if 80 percent of the students score less than 122, a person with a score of 122 is at the 80th percentile. Such percentiles would be completely interpretable, however, only if no two students made the same score. Consequently, in practice, percentiles are computed by dividing the total number of students tested into the number of students below a particular score plus half the students who make that score.

A strong case can be made that percentiles are easier to interpret than are transformed standard scores. The only way to accurately interpret transformed standard scores is to do some mental arithmetic to figure how many standard deviations a person is above or below the mean and how many persons would be above and below that point. Obviously, then, working with percentiles directly is easier than going through such mental gyrations.

Good norms, although crucial for important tests of achievement, mainly supply supplementary information for predictor tests and measures of constructs. For the former, one could effectively employ a predictor test in a particular setting even if one had no idea how people in general would score on the instrument. For measures of constructs, the major effort is to obtain reliable variance for the groups being investigated regardless of any information that might be supplied by norms. With predictor tests and measures of constructs, norms mainly are useful in indicating whether research results might have been somewhat different with different types of people, e.g., effects on correlations because of restriction in range of scores. Although general norms supply useful supplementary information, they are not absolutely essential for achievement tests used in experiments (e.g., on educational practices).

## THE CRITERION-ORIENTED APPROACH TO TEST CONSTRUCTION FOR PREDICTORS AND CONSTRUCT MEASURES

There are two *incorrect* ways to construct tests that are intended to have either predictive validity or construct validity: one is to select items according to their correlations with a criterion and the other is to select items according to their difficulty. Even if both methods are thought to be incorrect, they have been advocated and used so much in the past that it will be necessary to explain them in some detail. In this section will be discussed the criterion-oriented approach. By *criteria* are meant scores relating to some type of performance in daily life, such as school grades, amount of sales by insurance agents, and ratings of the skill of airplane pilots.

The criterion-oriented approach evolved from the following faulty line of reasoning. First, you ask yourself, "Why construct a test?" Then you answer, "To predict a criterion." If that were so, what would be the best items for the test? Obviously, items that individually correlate well with the criterion. The more each item correlates with the criterion, the more the total test score will correlate with the criterion. According to this line of reasoning, the obvious thing to do is (1) compose a large group of items, (2) administer them to a large sample of individuals in the situation where the test will be used, (3) correlate each item with the criterion, e.g., grades in some course of training, and (4) fashion a test out of those items that correlate most highly with the criterion.

Following this line of reasoning further, there is a way to improve on the foregoing method for the selection of test items. Assuming that one has found a large number of items that correlate well with the criterion, one can further select items in terms of their correlations with one another. Should the items in the final test correlate highly with one another? According to the criterion-oriented approach, the answer is *no*. This conclusion follows from the logic of multiple correlation. It will be remembered that, if a number of variables each correlate positively with a criterion, the multiple correlation is higher when the predictors correlate as little as possible with one another. The maximum multiple correlation would be obtained when the predictors had zero correlations with one another. The same logic would hold for a linear combination of items. When items have low correlations with one another and each correlates positively with the criterion, each item adds information to that provided by the other items; and when scores are summed over items, a relatively high correlation with the criterion will be found.

It will be remembered that the average correlation of an item with the other items on a test is highly related to the correlation of that item with total scores on the test. Then, according to this logic, one would select items that correlated highly with the criterion and had low correlations with total test scores. After these two sets of correlations are obtained, they can be plotted as in Fig. 8-1.

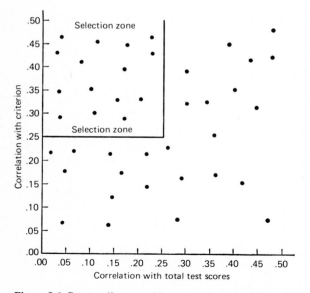

**Figure 8-1** Scatter diagram of item correlations with a criterion and with total test scores.

One then selects items from the indicated region of the figure. If there are enough items in that region, they are used to form the final test.

**What is wrong with the criterion-oriented approach** By this point it must be apparent that something is badly wrong with the criterion-oriented approach. By this method one would select a polyglot group of items with low internal consistency. Coefficient alpha would be low, and consequently there would be no strong common core (factor) in the items. Since the items would tend to measure different things, there would be no rational basis for the construction of an alternative form. The problem could be approached empirically by selecting another set of items that correlated well with the criterion and for which the internal consistency was low, but according to principles concerning the correlation of sums, the "alternative forms" would not correlate highly.

The major error in the criterion-oriented approach is in the original premise that the purpose of constructing a test is to predict a *particular* criterion. This is seldom the guiding principle in constructing a test. Obviously it is not the reason for constructing measures that require content validity and construct validity. In either case, if one had a criterion (whatever that would be), there would be no need to construct tests. As has been argued previously, with measures that require content validity there logically is no empirical criterion. Although construct validity partly depends on correlations among different proposed measures of a construct, no one of them can be considered *the* criterion. Since most measures used in basic research require construct validity, the criterion-oriented approach clearly does not apply. Since in applied work there are many more uses of achievement tests (measures that require content validity) than of predictor tests, the logic obviously does not hold in most applied work.

The only sphere in which the criterion-oriented approach is not obviously inappropriate is in applied work with predictor tests. It will be shown, however, that the logic does not apply there either. It is almost always poor strategy to *construct* a test to measure a particular criterion; it is better to *select* tests of known factorial composition as potential predictors of a criterion. Instead of forming hypotheses about types of *items* that might be predictive of a criterion, it is better to form hypotheses about types of *whole tests* that might be predictive of a criterion.

Other than for measures that require content validity, the purpose of constructing tests should be to investigate factors of human ability and personality. Each test should follow from a hypothesis about relations between a particular type of item and other types of items. Each test should be homogeneous in content, and consequently the items on each test should correlate substantially with one another. Correlations among different tests should be studied by factor analysis. The resulting factors constitute a standard set of yardsticks regarding abilities and personality traits. Gradually, as evidence accrues from factor analysis, the major dimensions of human attributes are determined. In the long run this will result in a catalog of measures for the important dimensions. Then, when one wants to measure a particular factor, the proper measure, or combination of measures, can be taken from a drawer or off a shelf. This logic applies both to measures of psychological constructs and to predictors of particular criteria. The "shelves and drawers" already contain measures of many important factors, and one can select among them for the prediction of particular criteria.

There is no intention to imply here that it is wrong to construct new tests with respect to applied problems of prediction, but when they are so constructed, they should not be constructed according to the criterion-oriented approach. Each such test should be homogeneous in content. Of course, one would want to find the correlation of scores with the criterion, and if that were reasonably high, one would want to learn the factor composition of the measure by correlating it with measures of existing factors. Gradually, in this way, tests constructed for prediction problems add to what is known about factors in general.

As some will argue, the criterion usually is factorially complex and consequently can be predicted best by a factorially complex predictor test. Instead of building the factorial complexity into a particular test, it is far better to meet the factorial complexity by combining tests in a battery by multiple regression, in which case tests would be selected to measure the different factors that are thought to be important. If items are selected by the criterion-oriented approach, one really does not know *what* factors are being measured. Also, the importance of each factor in the test would be determined by the number of items that happened to be present for the factor, and thus would not be rationally related to the importance of the factor in the criterion. The ideal way to combine factors is by multiple regression, and this can be done only by having relatively homogeneous tests relating to each factor. With the criterion-oriented approach, one knows neither what factors are involved in the omnibus test nor what weights are being given to different factors. The fallacy is in assuming that the criterion is to be predicted with *one* test, which to be effective must be heterogeneous in content. It is far better to predict a criterion with a battery of tests, each of which is homogeneous in content.

Even if one accepted the logic of the criterion-oriented approach, it would work poorly in practice. It is very difficult to find items that correlate well with a criterion and have low correlations with one another. Usually the two types of correlations tend to go together, and consequently very few items that met the standards would be found. When the method appears to work, it usually is because only a small sample of subjects are being used, and consequently there is considerable room to take advantage of chance. Subsequent studies would show that the test was not nearly as predictive of the criterion as was suggested by the item analysis. Usually one has a choice of using items that have (1) low correlations *both* with one another and with the criterion or (2) relatively high correlations with one another and with the criterion. Obviously, then, the homogeneous test would predict the criterion as well or better than the heterogeneous test.

Even if one selects items purely in terms of correlations with a criterion and ignores correlations among items, the criterion-oriented approach is not good. Such a test usually would be factorially complex and would run into the difficulties mentioned previously. Also, such a test would contribute very little to one's understanding of either the applied situation or basic issues concerning human attributes. For the former, since one would not fully understand what factors were involved in the test, no information would be supplied about the factors that make for success in a school or on a job. If the factors that lead to success are known, opportunities are provided for training students or employees. For example, if it is known that reading speed is important for success on a particular job, employees can be trained in that respect. If, in a school situation, it is found that successful performance correlates more with memory factors than with other factors, this might suggest changes in the curriculum.

If an omnibus test were constructed for each prediction problem as it arose, we would never come to understand human attributes. Rather than have the "drawers and shelves" filled with measures of a limited number of factors, we would have warehouses filled with thousands of unclassifiable measures.

Even if the weight of argument given so far against the criterion-oriented approach were ignored, one would find that the method works poorly in practice. Obviously, it is very wasteful of time and money to construct tests for each new prediction problem. It is much easier to investigate existing measures with known factor compositions. An omnibus test constructed for a particular criterion often is predictive only of that criterion. For example, in an industrial situation, a psychologist involved in the selection of employees for 20 different jobs might need to construct 20 different criterion-oriented tests. In the same situation, a battery of three to seven tests (with different weights for different jobs) might be predictive of all jobs, and usually the battery would be more predictive of success on any particular job than would the test constructed specifically for that purpose.

The criterion-oriented test that is predictive of a job in one setting often is not very predictive of an apparently similar job in another setting. Thus a test that successfully selects insurance agents might be very poor at selecting real estate sales agents. Also, for any particular job in any particular setting, criteria have a way of changing over time. What people do in particular jobs and the abilities and personality attributes required for successful performance frequently evolve with changes in the organization and developments in technology. Thus the criterion-oriented test that works well now might not work well in five years. One could meet these problems with a battery of tests of known factor composition by investigating different weights required for different jobs and for the same job at different points in time. Also, the evidence might indicate that one or more tests would need to be replaced by more predictive tests.

Because of the obvious bad features of the criterion-oriented approach, it is surprising to find some authors of recent books on psychological measurement flirting with that approach. Related methods of item analysis clearly are not applicable to measures that require content validity or construct validity. Conceivably they would be appropriate for particular problems in prediction, but it is hoped that sufficient arguments have been made against the use of the criterion-oriented approach there also. In prediction problems, a far better approach is to form a battery of tests from homogeneous measures of known factor composition. How to construct such homogeneous measures will be discussed in a later section.

Before concluding this section it should be made clear that the foregoing criticisms are leveled at methods of test construction based on the correlations of items with *criteria of success in daily life*, such as grades in college, amounts of sales by insurance sales agents, and ratings of effectiveness of airplane pilots. Criticisms in this section are not leveled at *all* attempts to construct tests entirely or in part by the investigation of correlations of items with some variable external to the items. An example in point is that of selecting items in terms of their correlations with a known factor of human ability or personality or selecting additional items for an existing good test. These provide useful adjuncts to the methods for constructing homogeneous tests, which will be discussed in a later section.

## CONSTRUCTING TESTS IN TERMS OF ITEM DIFFICULTIES

For developing measures of constructs and measures to be used as predictors, a second *incorrect* approach concerns the selection of items in terms of their difficulties. Although the difficulty levels of items do provide important information, this information is secondary to information obtained from correlations among the items. (How to use the latter type of information will be discussed subsequently.)

It will be remembered that the difficulty of any dichotomous item ($p$ value) is the fraction of persons tested who receive a score of 1 rather than a score of 0. On tests of ability, a score of 1 means that the individual passes the item; on nonability tests (e.g., a measure of suggestibility), a score of 1 is indicative of a high rather than a low score on the attribute. On a spelling test, a $p$ value of .9 would mean that 90 percent of the persons tested passed the item—correctly spelled the spoken word or marked the correct alternative on a printed test.

In test construction, $p$ values are important for two interrelated reasons. First, they influence the characteristics of score distributions. The $p$ values directly determine the mean score, the mean being the sum of the $p$ values. The mean is only of incidental importance, however, in the construction of tests. More important, the $p$ values influence the shape and dispersion of test scores. (These are also influenced by the number of items and the correlations among items.) If the average $p$ value is far removed from .5 in either direction, the distribution will tend to be skewed (particularly when the number of items is small, e.g., less than 20), and the standard deviation will tend to be small. Consequently, since it usually is desired to have an approximately symmetrical distribution and to disperse people as much as possible, an argument can be made for having an average $p$ value of .5. In addition, even if the average $p$ value is .5, the standard deviation of test scores is larger when all the $p$ values are near .5 rather than scattered widely above and below that point. Then, to disperse people as much as possible (to discriminate among them), one could argue that it is desirable for all test items to have $p$ values close to .5. (Of course, on multiple-choice tests, an upward adjustment of this $p$ value to take account of possible guessing would be required, which is a matter that will be discussed subsequently.) A test composed of items of that kind is referred to as a *peaked test*.

The other reason why $p$ values are important is that they relate to the reliability. According to coefficient alpha and KR-20, the higher the items correlate with one another, the higher the reliability. From Chap. 4 it will be remembered that the restriction on the size of the phi coefficient does *not* depend on the $p$ values of either item; rather, it depends on the *difference* in $p$ values of the two items. Thus a correlation of 1.00 can be obtained between two items with $p$ values of .9 as well as between two items with $p$ values of .5. An important point not mentioned previously, however, is that a particular difference in $p$ values has a very different effect on the ceiling of the phi coefficient when it is a difference between items having $p$ values near .5 rather than a difference between items having $p$ values far removed from .5 in either direction. For example, a difference in $p$ value of .4 to .5 would place very little restriction on the phi coefficient, but a difference in $p$ value from .89 to .99 would greatly restrict the maximum size of the phi coefficient. For this reason items with an average $p$ values than for tests with average $p$ values near the middle of the correlations with one another on the average. For the same reason, coefficient alpha and KR-20 tend to be lower for tests composed of items with extreme average $p$ values than for tests with average $p$ values near the middle of the range. Since coefficient alpha and KR-20 usually are good estimates of the alternative-form reliability, a similar lowering of the reliability is expected when alternative forms of a test are correlated if the forms are composed of items whose average $p$ values are extreme in either direction.

From the standpoint of both the desirable properties of score distributions and test reliability, one arrives at the conclusion that a peaked test is best. Although no one would take this argument to the extreme of insisting that all items be at the .5 level, it could be argued that the items should be selected in the range from .4 to .6. This is what one would do to construct a test solely in terms of difficulty levels. (As was mentioned previously, an upward adjustment of this ideal $p$ value would be required to take account of guessing on multiple-choice tests.)

**What is wrong with this approach** The faults in selecting items in terms of $p$ values are not nearly so blatant as those in selecting items in terms of the criterion-oriented approach. Also, the point is not that selecting items in terms of $p$ values is incorrect, but rather that there is a much better way to select them. Purely by selecting items so as to obtain a peaked test, one might end up with a very good instrument. If, after the items were selected, they proved to have a high reliability, it might be found subsequently that the new measure related importantly with other supposed measures of a construct and/or proved effective in predicting particular criteria. If these things happened, after the fact it could be argued that the method of test construction worked well in that instance. The important point, however, is that, a priori, there are reasons why such pleasant results might not be obtained.

For reasons which were discussed previously, "good" items are ones that correlate well with one another. Since the correlations of items with total scores on a test are directly related to their sums of correlations with one another, it thus can be said that "good" items are ones that correlate highly with total test scores. This doctrine will be explained more fully in the next section, but first it will be useful to see what implications this doctrine has for the selection of items in terms of $p$ values.

The $p$ values only place *upper limits* on correlations of items with total scores. A $p$ value near .5 does not *guarantee* a high correlation with total scores. In a particular analysis, it is possible to find that all the items with $p$ values near .5 have correlations near zero with total scores and that items with $p$ values well removed from .5 have respectable correlations with total scores. Actually, in addition to the possible advantages of having $p$ values near .5, in some instances there are reasons to be suspicious of such items. For example, on a personality inventory composed of agree-disagree items, any item that is highly ambiguous will tend to have a $p$ value near .5. Since subjects are unable to understand the item, they mentally "flip coins" in giving an answer.

An item on a peaked test *may* be a good item, the crucial standard being whether or not it actually correlates well with total scores on the test. It is equally possible, however, that the item might not have a high correlation with total scores. This could be either because the item is very unreliable or because it reliably measures something different from the majority of items in the test. Since the crucial consideration is how much the item actually correlates with total scores, why not select items mainly in terms of those correlations? That is what will be advocated in the next section. Before that method is discussed, however, some additional comments should be made about selecting items in terms of $p$ values.

Even if one were to admit that $p$ values are all-important in constructing tests, the logic of so doing is clear only for *free-response* items that are *scored dichotomously*. An example of such an item would be if students were provided a space to answer the question, "When did Columbus discover America?" For two reasons such items are rare. First, most tests employ multiple-choice items rather than free-response items of any kind. Second, even in those tests that employ free-response items, the items usually are scored on a multipoint basis rather than dichotomously. The former would be the case, for example, in scoring each question in an essay examination on a six-point scale.

When multipoint items are employed, there no longer is a "$p$ value." On dichotomous items the $p$ value is the mean, and it is directly related to the variance ($pq$). On multipoint items the mean and variance tend to be related, but they are far from perfectly correlated. For example, on seven-point scales used in measures of attitudes, the nearer the mean score is to the middle of the scale, the larger the variance tends to be. In that case, however, should one select items in terms of the mean score or the variance? One could argue that both should be considered, but there are no obvious principles concerning how these two kinds of information should be combined. It is far better to construct tests concerning multipoint items by methods to be described in the next section.

In considering dichotomously scored multiple-choice items, the selection of items in terms of $p$ values is greatly complicated by the effect of *guessing*. (The effects of guessing will be discussed in detail in Chap. 16.) The $p$ value is determined by both the intrinsic difficulty of the item and the effect of guessing. Guessing tends to make $p$ values higher, the amount of "elevation" being inversely related to the number of alternative responses for each item. Where there are only two alternative responses (a true-false test), obviously it would be inappropriate to peak a test at .5. Less obviously, it also would be inappropriate when there are four or five alternative responses, as typically found on multiple-choice tests. A correction of $p$ values for guessing will be presented later in this chapter.

One might think that the ideal difficulty for test items could be obtained with a proper correction for the expected effects of guessing, but this would solve only part of the problem. Guessing not only tends to raise $p$ values, but also introduces measurement error. Since the less guessing there is, the less measurement error there is, easy items tend to have less measurement error than more difficult items. Consequently the most discriminating item would tend to be somewhere between a corrected $p$ value of .5 and 1.0. There is, however, no certainty as to what the exact value should be. All one can do is generate a model to predict the ideal level and then test how well the model works in practice. Employing one such model, Lord (1952b) deduced that the most discriminating two-choice item would have an *uncorrected $p$* value of .85, a three-choice item .77, a four-choice item .74, and a five-choice item .69. There has not been enough research, however, to determine whether those deductions, or deductions from other models, hold in the general case.

Even if mountains of research were done to find the "ideal" $p$ values for multiple-choice tests with different numbers of alternatives, the previously described shortcomings of selecting items purely in terms of $p$ values still would be present. At best the $p$ values can only indicate the types of items that are not highly restricted in their possible correlations with total scores. It is far more sensible to construct tests primarily in terms of the actual correlations of items with total scores.

## CONSTRUCTION OF HOMOGENEOUS TESTS

Much of what has been said so far in this book argues for the construction of homogeneous tests. Only some of the most important arguments will be reiterated. The first page of Chap. 1 emphasized that measurement always concerns an *attribute*. An attribute is some isolatable characteristic of organisms, some dimension of structure or function along which organisms can be ordered. Items within a measure are useful only to the extent that they share a common core—the attribute which is to be measured. The linear model was accepted as providing a reasonable approach to the construction of most measures in psychology, particularly for the construction of measures concerning individual differences among subjects. Most frequently, the model leads to a simple summation of item scores to obtain total scores. In summing scores, it is assumed that each item adds something to the others, and unless the items shared an attribute, it would not be meaningful to sum scores over items.

The major theory of reliability is based on the domain-sampling model, which assumes that each test is a random sample of items from a domain. Although the model holds when the domain contains items from different factors, it makes more sense, and estimates from it are more precise, when items from the domain share only one major factor. Eventually it will be possible to understand the cardinal dimensions of human attributes only when relatively complete factor structures are known for different types of abilities and personality characteristics. The best measures of each factor will be those that correlate highly with one factor and have low correlations with other factors.

Implicit in the above considerations is the premise that tests should be homogeneous in content. The homogeneity of content in a test is manifested in the average correlation among items and in the pattern of those correlations. If the average correlation among items is very low (and thus the average correlation of items with total scores is low), the items as a group are not homogeneous. This may be because all the correlations are low or because a number of different factors are present in the items. In the latter case there would be a number of item clusters, each cluster being relatively homogeneous, but the clusters would have either correlations near zero with one another or negative correlations. The ideal is to obtain a collection of items which has a high average correlation with total scores and is dominated by one factor only.

**Factor analysis of items** Considering the last statement regarding the ideal statistical properties of a good test, it might be thought that the ideal approach to test construction would be through factor analysis. It will be argued, however, that *constructing* tests on the basis of factor analysis usually is not as wise as investigating the factorial composition of tests after they are constructed. This is a controversial point of view, and it is recognized that those who advocate the construction of tests through factor analysis have some good points on their side.

One important reason for not beginning test construction with factor analysis is that such analyses are seldom highly successful. As will be made evident in Chap. 10, the results from factor analysis usually are clearest when the correlations among whole tests or individual items vary considerably. For example, if some of the correlations among tests are zero and other correlations are as high as .70, this suggests that the tests tend to divide up into clearly defined clusters, or factors. If two tests relate strongly to a factor, they are expected to correlate substantially and to have low correlations with tests that relate strongly to other factors. Then it becomes apparent that for a group of variables (either whole tests or test items) to clearly define a number of factors, there must be a wide range of correlations in the matrix. This occurs very seldom in matrices of correlations among items. On most tests the average correlation among items is less than .20, and the variance of correlations among items is small. A typical finding would be that two-thirds of the correlations were between .10 and .30. To the extent to which the variance of correlations is larger than that, it typically indicates that there is considerable sampling error due to the relatively small number of subjects being investigated. Because of the small variance in correlations among items, it usually is not possible to clearly document a number of factors by the analysis of such correlations. This is particularly so when the items are scored dichotomously. With multipoint items (e.g., rating scales), the correlations among items usually are higher than they are with dichotomous items, and correspondingly the variance in correlations among items is greater with multipoint items. Consequently factor analyses of multipoint items have a higher probability of success.

Another reason for not beginning the construction of tests with factor analysis is that such analysis of test items is extremely laborious. Imagine that one is constructing tests of "dominance" and it is thought that there are a number of different factors concerning different forms of dominance. Many items supposedly concerning different aspects of dominance are collected from the literature or constructed for the particular study. Each item requires agree-disagree responses. Because it is very difficult to tell which items should go with different forms of dominance, the investigator tries to settle the issue with factor analysis. Not only is there a low probability of getting neat factors from this approach; but also the analysis, if properly done, will be extremely tedious. Some rules of thumb will indicate why this is the case. Since about 30 dichotomous items are usually required for respectable reliability, constructing three tests relative to three factors of dominance will require 90 items. Since many of the items either will be very unreliable or will not relate to any of the three factors, a good guess is that it will take a total collection of at least 180 items to obtain the three tests. To prevent taking advantage of chance, a minimum standard (not an ideal) in a factor analysis is that there be at least ten times as many subjects as variables. This means that at least 1,800 subjects are required before a factor analysis can be undertaken. Even with the best of high-speed computers, the actual factor analysis will be expensive. After the analysis is completed, many more hours will be required to study the results, try out different combinations of items for different tests, and investigate reliabilities of the tests and relations among them. Properly done, from start to finish it may take over three years to complete the job, and it will be an expensive operation.

Factor analyses of items seldom are undertaken with the thoroughness described above. Typically, considerably fewer than 100 items are included in the study. Consequently, even if the analysis suggests that there are a number of prominent factors present, there are not enough items to measure the factors. Then another analysis must be done with some of the items from the first collection and with new items that are thought to be related to the factors found in the first analysis. One may need to repeat this process a number of times in order to understand the factor structure and obtain reliable measures of each factor.

Frequently factor analyses of items are undertaken with many fewer subjects than the minimum recommended (10 subjects per item). There are some horrible examples in the literature where the number of subjects was approximately the same as the number of items. Unless the number of subjects is at least ten times as large as the number of items, factor analysis can take great advantage of chance. Then what appear to be factors are only artifacts because of sampling error. For example, if each of 100 subjects flipped coins to decide whether to agree or disagree with 100 questions, a factor analysis probably would indicate a number of apparently strong factors. This is because factor analysis essentially provides a method of searching for clusters of variables that correlate with one another and correlate less with members of other clusters. When the number of subjects is not much larger than the number of items, such clusters of correlations will occur purely by chance. Of course, such "factors" do not hold up in subsequent studies.

For the reasons mentioned above, most efforts to construct tests through factor analysis have not met with notable success. The literature is filled with unclear results from factoring items, disputes about how many and what kinds of factors are present in a particular collection of items, and supposed measures of factors that have very low reliability. This is not to deny that the *logic* of test construction is closely related to factor analysis—it definitely is. The question concerns when factor analysis should be applied. It is argued that factor analysis usually should not be applied to items before tests are constructed, but should be applied to whole tests *after* they are constructed. Although ideally it would be good to know the factor composition of items before they are placed in a test, for the reasons discussed above this is not easy to learn. A wiser strategy is to construct the most homogeneous test possible based on hypotheses regarding the existence and nature of a trait of human ability or personality. Then, in later factor analyses of whole tests, it is possible to learn how successful one has been in developing a relatively pure measure of an important factor. Also, by methods which will be discussed later, at that point it is possible to rid a test of items that prevent it from being a relatively pure measure of a factor.

In addition to the statistical considerations discussed above, there is another important reason for not initiating test construction with a factor analysis of items. This approach tends to encourage an unhealthy form of "shotgun empiricism," which, however, is not a necessary accompaniment of the approach. Although none will admit it, some still work as though factor analyses, and other methods of analysis, automatically grind out the "true nature of things" even if there is no theory at all regarding the construction of items and regardless of the character of the items themselves. One can almost hear such persons saying to themselves, "What I need is a large collection of items to factor-analyze so that I can find the nature of human attributes." The reader surely has heard the evils of shotgun empiricism on numerous other occasions. Progress in science must be guided by theories rather than by a random effort to relate things to one another. Theories serve to greatly reduce the amount of trial-and-error effort, and it is the people who explore theories who tend to stand at the vanguard of each field of science. Some measurement specialists have been rightly criticized for being far more concerned with methods of analysis than with theories regarding the attributes which are intended to be measured. This criticism applies with great force when a polyglot collection of items is factor-analyzed in the hope of obtaining important measures of human attributes.

**The hypothesis** A new measure should spring from a hypothesis regarding the existence and nature of an attribute. In some cases a formal hypothesis is deduced from a theory regarding a construct. An example would be deducing hypotheses from theories concerning the physiological components of arousal (or activation) in human subjects. It has been hypothesized that such activation relates to a variety of neural, glandular, and muscular responses. One such hypothesis is that sudden arousal results in dilation of the pupil of the eye. Based on this hypothesis, one could construct photographic slides to be projected on a screen, some of which were intended to be emotion-provoking, and thus induce arousal. Each such slide could be considered to be a potential test item, and total test scores could be obtained by summing pupillary responses over the items. Although in many cases there are no formal hypotheses regarding the existence of attributes, at least the investigator should have an informal hypothesis that can be communicated to others. For example, it might be hypothesized that reliable individual differences exist in the tendency to have common rather than uncommon associations. Although the hypothesis would not be deduced from a formal theory, such individual differences, if they exist, might be important for cognitive and affective processes. The hypothesis suggests a number of types of items that might be used to measure the attribute in question. In one type of item, the subject would be given a stimulus word and two possible response words. One of the response words would be a highly common associate of the stimulus word and the other would be a less common associate of the stimulus word. On each item, the subject would be required to mark the most appropriate associate. Whether the hypothesis follows from a theory or is only a "good idea," it guides the construction of items. Subsequent investigations of the items provide a test of the hypothesis.

**Construction of items** One cannot know for sure how many items should be constructed for a new measure until *after* they are constructed and submitted to item analysis. If the standard is to obtain a test with a coefficient alpha of .80, item analysis might show that the desired reliability can be obtained with as few as 20 items or that as many as 80 items are required. There are some rules of thumb that can be used to determine the number of items to be constructed. Usually 30 dichotomous items are required to obtain an internal-consistency reliability of .80. Also, usually fewer multipoint items than dichotomous items are required to obtain a particular reliability. For example, it is not unusual to find a coefficient alpha of .80 for 10 agree-disagree attitude statements rated on a seven-point scale. How many more items should be constructed than the minimum required depends on what is known from previous studies about the type of item. If it were known that items of a particular type tended to have high internal consistency (e.g., items on vocabulary tests), at most no more than twice as many items would be constructed as had been found in previous studies to be required for a reliable test. To obtain a reliability of .80 in that case, 30 items probably would suffice for the final test. To provide room for the item analysis to eliminate unsatisfactory items, 60 items would be constructed initially. If very little is known about the homogeneity of items of a particular kind, it is wise to err on the conservative side and construct more items than would be the case in the previous example. For example, with the previously mentioned measure of the tendency to give common word associations, if it were desired to obtain a test with a reliability of .80, it would be wise to construct 100 items.

A somewhat different strategy in deciding how many items to construct starts by purposefully constructing a smaller number of items than is thought to be adequate, e.g., constructing only 30 items when it is suspected that 30 items will be required to obtain a coefficient alpha of .80. These items are then applied to a relatively small sample of subjects (say, 100), and the results are submitted to item analysis. If either the total collection of items (30) or the most homogeneous subset (say, of 15 items) has a coefficient alpha of at least .60, this indicates that it is worth the effort to construct more items, gather responses from a much larger group of subjects, and perform a more complete item analysis. The eventual labor is greater for constructing the test in stages rather than in one large step, but if the results from the first stage of the former method are very discouraging, the project can be abandoned without further loss of time and effort.

**Sample of subjects** After items are constructed and before they are submitted to item analysis, they must, of course, be administered to a sample of people.

So that the required types of analyses may be performed, all the items should be administered to all the people. Of course, the sample of people used in this phase of test construction should be reasonably representative of the types of people that will be studied with the eventual test. To take a very bad example, if a test is intended to be used primarily with children from 8 to 10 years of age, it should not be constructed on the basis of data obtained from college students. Except for such extremes, however, the subjects used in test construction need not be exactly representative of those with whom the final test will be used. The need for a precisely representative sample is much greater in measures that require content validity than in measures that require predictive validity or construct validity. Also, often a test is used with many different types of subjects (e.g., some attitude scales), and in such cases it is very difficult to ensure that the group of subjects used in test construction is highly representative of all the different groups with which the test eventually will be used.

As is true of all methods of analysis, it is not possible to say in advance exactly how many subjects should be used to obtain data for item analysis. A good rule of thumb, however, is that there should be at least ten times as many subjects as items. In some cases this rule is impractical if there are more than about 70 items. For example, if there are 100 items, it might not be possible to obtain 1,000 subjects. In any case, though, five subjects per item should be considered the minimum that can be tolerated.

In gathering data for item analysis, one should administer items under conditions that closely resemble those under which the eventual test will be used. If subjects in the tryout sample are given all the time that they want to complete the items and one intends to place a severe time limit on the eventual test, an item analysis probably will provide very misleading information. If items for a personality inventory are being administered in an atmosphere that encourages frankness and the eventual test is to be administered in an atmosphere where subjects will be reluctant to say bad things about themselves, the item analysis will tell a faulty story.

**Item-total correlations** The remainder of this section will consider methods of item analysis when most of the correlations among items (say, at least 90 percent) are positive. This is almost always the case in measures concerning abilities, i.e., where there is a "correct" response for each item. Some of the correlations may be very close to zero, but if the sample size is large, very few are negative. A later section will consider methods of item analysis when some of the items tend to correlate negatively with the others, as occurs on many personality inventories.

When items predominately correlate positively with one another, those with the highest average correlations are the best items. Since the average correlations of items with one another are highly related to the correlations of items with total scores, the items that correlate most highly with total scores are the best items for a general-purpose test (later this rule will be modified for some special types of tests). Compared to items with relatively low correlations with total scores, those that have higher correlations with total scores have more variance relating to the common factor among the items, and they add more to the test reliability.

The first step in item analysis, then, is to correlate each item with total scores. Thus if there are 60 items, scores are summed over items, and 60 correlations are obtained. If multipoint items are employed, the regular PM coefficient is the correct measure. If dichotomous items are employed, the correct measure is point-biserial, which, it will be remembered, is only a differently appearing version of the PM formula. (If, as usually is the case, these statistics are obtained from high-speed computers, the computer will "not know the difference" and will use the regular PM coefficient anyway.) The obtained coefficients are then ranked from highest to lowest. If numerous correlations are relatively high (with respect to standards that will be discussed shortly), one is "in business," and a few simple steps can be taken to obtain a final test that has (1) a desired level of reliability and (2) a desired distribution form, this usually being a symmetrical distribution.

There are numerous measures of item-total relationship other than point-biserial. An argument can be made for employing the item-total covariance rather than the correlation, because the former takes account of the $p$ values of items as well as the correlation with total scores. The covariance tends to give added weight to items that have $p$ values near .5. Correlational methods other than point-biserial have been employed for item analysis. Biserial can be used; and if the continuous total scores are divided at the mean or median, either phi or tetrachoric can be applied.

In addition to the different measures of correlation that can be used in item analysis, numerous other measures of item-total relationship are available. One of the most popular measures is obtained as follows. First, the top and bottom 25 percent of persons in total test scores is found. Second, for each item, the percentages of persons in top and bottom groups that pass the item are determined. Third, the percentage in the bottom group is subtracted from the percentage in the top group. Items that have a large difference in this regard tend to discriminate persons with high total test scores from persons with low total test scores.

Although many different measures of item-total relationship can be employed in item analysis, there is a wealth of data to demonstrate that they all provide much the same information. In a typical study, four different measures of item-total relationship are applied to the same items, and then items are ranked on the different measures. Typically it is found that correlations between the different sets of ranks are .90 or higher, demonstrating that essentially the same set of items would have been selected by any of the methods.

It is recommended that the PM correlation be used in item analysis, which with dichotomous items is point-biserial. Not only does the PM correlation give very much the same information any other measure of item-total relationship would provide, but to the extent that item selection would be slightly different by different measures, the PM correlation is logically better than the other measures. Also, the use of the PM coefficient at this stage allows one to tie-in with many methods of multivariate analysis that might be useful subsequently.

When the PM correlation is used for item analysis, account must be taken of an artifact in such correlations. In correlating an item with total test scores, one must remember that the item is a part of the total test. This makes the correlation of an item with total scores higher than if the item were correlated with scores on all other items. In the extreme case, if there were no more than five items, even if all correlations among items were zero, each item would correlate substantially with total scores; but if each item were correlated with the sum of scores on the other four items, the correlations would be zero. This spurious source of item-total correlation can be removed with the following formula:

$$r_{1(y-1)} = \frac{r_{y1}\sigma_y - \sigma_1}{\sqrt{\sigma_1^2 + \sigma_y^2 - 2\sigma_1\sigma_y r_{y1}}} \tag{8-1}$$

where $r_{y1}$ = correlation of item 1 with total scores $y$

$\sigma_y$ = standard deviation of total scores

$\sigma_1$ = standard deviation of item 1

$r_{1(y-1)}$ = correlation of item 1 with sum of scores on all items exclusive of item 1

Although the artifact can be large when the number of items is small, with the numbers of items that are involved in most analyses, the artifact is quite small. The effect can be illustrated in the case of 80 items where (1) the item-total correlation is .24, (2) the $p$ value of the item is .5, and (3) the variance of total scores is 191. In this case the corrected correlation would be .22, which is only slightly lower than the item-total correlation. If it is not already available at a particular computing center, the correction given in Eq. (8-1) is easily built into any general computer program for item analysis.

Equation (8-1) is of potential importance mainly in establishing the level of statistical significance in an item analysis. Logically, one should stop adding items to a test when the item-total correlations are well below accepted standards of statistical significance, say, below the .05 level of statistical significance. The significance level should be determined *after* correlations are corrected by Eq. (8-1). In practice, however, it usually is not necessary to bother with the slight artifact that is present. Frequently there are as many as 80 items in the analysis, and thus, as was illustrated above, the bias is slight. If 625 persons were used for the analysis, the standard error of the correlation would be approximately the reciprocal of 25. Then corrected correlations of .08 would be significant beyond the .05 level, which means that uncorrected correlations around .09 or .10 would be significant at that level. Where one has at least 80 items for the analysis, there usually are more items with uncorrected item-total correlations above .10 than are required for the eventual test. Consequently, in most item analysis, one can work directly with the item-total correlations without applying Eq. (8-1). If, however, the number of items is considerably less than 80 and the number of subjects is relatively small, Eq. (8-1) should be employed.

Although it is useful to compute the standard error of the correlation coefficient and let it serve as a guide to the minimum level of item-total correlation that will be used in the selection of items, usually there is no need to be highly concerned about the statistical significance of item-total correlations. Worries in this regard are greatly lessened by dealing with a large sample of persons, e.g., a very minimum of five persons per item. More important, if all or nearly all the item-total correlations are positive, as is frequently the case, the only sensible hypothesis is that *all* the items actually would correlate positively with total test scores in the population of persons being sampled. When over 90 percent of the item-total correlations are positive, as is often the case, one is being conservative to reject items whose correlations with total scores do not reach the .05 level of statistical significance.

**Step-by-step procedures** If there are numerous uncorrected item-total correlations above .25, the remaining steps in item analysis are simple. Since about 30 dichotomous items usually are required to reach a reliability of .80, KR-20 would be computed for the 30 items having the highest correlations with total scores. If the reliability is as high as desired, the item analysis is complete. If it is not, one increases the number of items, adding those items that have the next highest correlations with total scores. How many items are added depends on their correlations with total scores and on the reliability of the first set of 30 items. When the correlations with total scores are very low (e.g., .05), little can be gained by adding more items. When there are numerous additional items with correlations above .20, how many of them are added depends on how much the reliability needs to be increased. If the reliability of the original group of items is .65 and a reliability of .80 is desired, a good strategy is to add 10 items. Then KR-20 is computed for the 40 items. If the desired reliability is obtained, the item analysis is complete; if not, more items are added. If, for example, the 40-item test had a reliability of .75 rather than .80, a good strategy would be to add the next 5 items in terms of their correlations with total scores. If this did not achieve the desired reliability, one could add several more items. If at any point the reliability either fails to increase or decreases, there is no use in trying out larger numbers of items.

When one wants to undertake the labors involved, a highly systematic approach to test construction is to compute KR-20 for cumulative sets of items, starting with the five items having the highest correlations with total scores and adding items in sets of five. Then one can plot a curve showing the size of KR-20 for tests of different lengths. A typical curve is shown in Fig. 8-2. Also shown is the expected increase in reliability from lengthening a five-item test when the five items have a reliability of .40. As can be seen, the empirically obtained reliabilities are lower than the results predicted from Eq. (7-6). This is to be expected, because Eq. (7-6) assumes that the items which are added at each step have the same correlations with total scores as did the original five items. By the method of item analysis recommended here, the first five items would correlate highest with total scores, and later items would correlate less with

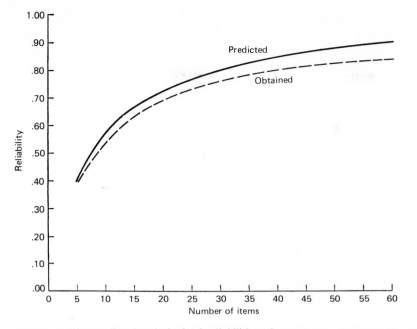

**Figure 8-2** The predicted and obtained reliabilities of tests varying in length from 5 to 60 items when the reliability of the first 5 items is .40.

total scores. Consequently the curve of obtained reliabilities is lower than that predicted from Eq. (7-6). Employing this approach, one would select the number of items that reached a desired level of reliability. Because this method of selecting items takes some advantage of chance, it would be well to continue adding items until KR-20 is comfortably above the reliability needed for the final test. For example, if a reliability of .80 were needed in the final test, it would be wise to select enough items to achieve a KR-20 of .85 or higher. If there were no set standard for the size of the reliability, one would quit adding items when the curve began to level off, as it does in Fig. 8-2 for more than 50 items.

The more complete procedure illustrated in Fig. 8-2 is not necessary in most item analyses. A quicker approach with dichotomous items is to compute KR-20 for the 30 items having the highest correlations with total scores. If the desired reliability is not obtained, adding a few more items usually will suffice. If the analysis is of multipoint items, it is wise to compute coefficient alpha for the 10 items having the highest correlations with total scores, and if the reliability is not high enough, to add several items at a time until the desired reliability is obtained.

What should one do if this approach to test construction fails? It will probably fail if the reliability of the first 30 dichotomous items is no more than .40. Since by this point one could have already used the "cream" of the items, there may not be enough good items left to reach a reliability of .80. There are three reasons why the method may fail to produce a homogeneous test. The first possibility is that the items are from a domain where correlations among items are uniformly low. In that case the reliability would grow slowly as the number of items was increased, but the curve would not flatten out altogether. One could then achieve a reliable test, but it would take a very large number of items.

The second possibility is that the collection of items is factorially complex, in which case clusters of items will tend to have relatively high correlations with one another but very low correlations with members of other clusters. It usually would be very difficult to distinguish this circumstance from the first circumstance discussed. In both cases correlations with total scores would be low; KR-20 would tend to rise as more items were added, but the curve would go up very slowly.

The third possibility is that some of the items have relatively high correlations with one another but the other items have correlations near zero with all items. In that case one would have some good items to form the nucleus of a test, but the reliability could not be increased by adding items. This condition could be detected by a sudden drop-off in the size of item-total correlations as one inspected the correlations ranked from highest to lowest. This would be evidenced, for example, if the 35th item in the list had a correlation with total scores of .21 and the 36th item had a correlation of only .09.

How can one recognize which of the three circumstances prevail and what should be done after the circumstance is recognized? As was mentioned above, it is relatively easy to distinguish the third circumstance from the other two by the marked falloff in item-total correlations at some point in the list of items. If that occurs, one should study the good items and try to determine the nature of their content. Then one should try to construct more items of the same kind, administer them along with the original good items to a new group of subjects, and submit all items to the type of analysis which has been described.

If the average item-total correlation is low, it is very difficult to tell whether this is because of the first or second circumstance. If it is caused by factorial complexity (the second circumstance), it cannot be because of the presence of only two or three strong factors. If that were the case, correlations with total scores would not be very low. Indeed, the major criticism that can be made of selecting items in terms of correlations with total scores is that the method apparently works as well as when several groups of items relate strongly to different factors as when all items relate only moderately to the same factor. From previous discussions of the correlations of sums, one can well see why this would be the case. Where there are 60 items, half of which relate strongly to one factor and the other half to another factor, typically the items belonging to each factor have average correlations with one another of around .20 and with items belonging to the other factor of less than .10. In this case, regardless of the presence of two factors, all items have respectable correlations with total scores. The method of item analysis which has been discussed will select items from both factors. Thus if there are several prominent factors in the items, the problem is not so much that the item analysis will fail, but rather that it will work deceivingly well.

There is another reason why the item analysis probably would not fail because of the presence of several strong factors in the items. The investigator probably would have guessed the presence of the factors and would have constructed different tests to measure the different factors. Consequently it is unlikely that the investigator would construct an item pool containing items relating to several strong factors.

If the reliability of the first 30 dichotomous items is not above .50 and the difficulty cannot be traced to the third circumstance (marked falloff in item-total correlations at some point in the list of items), it can be argued that factor analysis should be applied. For reasons which were discussed previously, this would be very laborious, and the results probably would not be very clear. If the average item-total correlation is low and the variance of correlations is small, the better part of valor in this circumstance might be to abandon the type of item being employed. The investigator would conclude that the attribute either did not exist or needed to be measured by a different type of item. If the investigator were doggedly determined to continue investigating the particular type of item, the only choices would be (1) not to factor-analyze, but to construct a very long test in the hope that later it will be found to primarily measure one factor or (2) to factor-analyze the collection of items in the hope of eventually learning how to measure one, or some, of the factors involved.

**Successive approximations** A possibility not mentioned in the previous section is that the selection of items in terms of item-total correlations can be improved by successively correlating items with subpools of the items. This can be illustrated where an analysis is being made of 100 items and only 50 of them have nonzero average correlations with the others. In this case if it were known in advance that there were only 50 items from which to select the final group of items, the other 50 items would be removed from the analysis. If all items were correlated with total scores on the 100 items, the 50 bad items would tend to "water down" the correlations of the 50 good items with total scores. If one has the time and patience and the problem is sufficiently important, a refinement of the basic approach can be made as follows. In the first go-around, all items are correlated with total scores on all items. All items are removed that have item-total correlations which are either statistically insignificant or below some minimum value, e.g., .15. For example, say that 40 items are removed from a total collection of 100. Total scores are then obtained on the remaining 60 items, and each of the 60 items is correlated with those total scores. Then KR-20 is computed for the items that stand highest in those correlations, and if the desired level of reliability is not reached, successive sets of items are added.

One could go through the above steps a number of times, each step leading to a more and more homogeneous group of items. However, it is seldom necessary to work with anything other than the original correlations of items with total scores. Usually the rank-order of item-total correlations in successive sets of items refined in that way is much the same as it is for the initial item-total correlations. Where such successive refinements are sometimes required is with pools of items where many of the correlations among items are negative, as is sometimes the case with items on personality inventories. This problem will be discussed in a later section.

**The distribution form**   One of the supposed advantages of selecting items in terms of $p$ values is that it permits control of the distribution form for total test scores. How can the same control be exercised when one selects items in terms of item-total correlations rather than $p$ values? As described previously, basing item analysis on correlations of items with total scores will tend to select items that have $p$ values near the middle of the possible range rather than extreme in either direction. Consequently, the frequency distribution will tend to have the desirable characteristics of being symmetrical, being approximately normal, and having a relatively large standard deviation. Also, there is a way to control the distribution form *after* good items have been selected in terms of item correlations. The method will be illustrated in the situation where the first 30 items in terms of item-total correlations produce the desired level of reliability but there still are more items that correlate reasonably well with total scores—say, 20 more such items. The first step would be to plot a frequency distribution for total scores on the first 30 items. If the distribution were symmetrical, the item analysis would be complete. If not, it would be necessary to study the $p$ values of both the 30 items and the remaining 20 good items.

If the distribution is skewed toward the higher end of the continuum, it means that the test is too difficult. To make the distribution more symmetrical, some of the items in the 30-item test having low $p$ values should be replaced by items from the remaining 20 that have $p$ values above .5. If 5 items having $p$ values between .2 and .3 are replaced by 5 items having $p$ values between .5 and .7, this will tend to make the distribution symmetrical. The distribution of the new group of 30 items is then plotted, and if it is symmetrical, the item analysis is complete. If the distribution still is slightly nonsymmetrical, replacement of a few more items will solve the problem. In replacing items in this way, one must recheck the reliability at each step to make sure it is not falling below the desired standard. If it does fall slightly, then at each step in the replacement of items, several more items should be added than are removed. Thus, for example, to achieve both the desired reliability and the desired distribution form, one might end up with a 38-item test rather than a 30-item test.

Actually, though, it is quite unlikely that the distribution of scores will be markedly nonsymmetrical if items are selected purely in terms of correlations with total scores. This method tends to select items in the middle range of $p$ values rather than those at the extremes. Since the restriction on the size of point-biserial is rather severe for items with $p$ values below .2 or above .8, it is unlikely that items with such extreme $p$ values will be high enough in the rank-order of item-total correlations to be included in a test. Since the least restriction in point-biserial is for items having $p$ values at .5, items with $p$ values near .5 have a greater likelihood of having high correlations with total scores, and consequently such items tend to stand high in the rank-order of item-total correlations. (It is important to remember, however, that picking items in terms of item-total correlations favors only those items with $p$ values near .5 that actually correlate well with total scores.) Because choosing items in terms of item-total correlations tends to select items that are "average" in $p$ value, this method of item analysis almost always produces a symmetrical distribution of scores, and consequently no further refinements are necessary. Also, one seldom seeks anything other than a symmetrical distribution.

## SPECIAL PROBLEMS IN TEST CONSTRUCTION

In the remainder of this chapter it will be assumed that the best way to construct most general-purpose tests is in terms of item-total correlations, as described in the previous section. (In Chap. 9 some alternative and supplementary approaches will be discussed.) This section will consider some special problems that arise in employing that method.

**Bipolar domains of items** The discussion in the previous section assumed that most correlations among items are positive, which usually is the case for any items concerning abilities, but is not necessarily the case for measures of personality, attitudes, interests, etc. For example, if an attitude scale regarding the United Nations were being constructed, one approach would be to start by writing 60 statements, half of which were thought to be favorable toward the United Nations and half unfavorable. Each item would require dichotomous, agree-disagree responses. If all agreements were scored 1 and all disagreements scored 0, the negative statements would tend to correlate negatively with the positive statements. Then the average correlation of each item with the others would be close to zero, and thus all the items would have item-total correlations close to zero. Obviously, then, it would not be possible to select items in terms of item-total correlations, and the analyses would provide no hints as to what should be done to improve the situation.

If items are selected purely in terms of item-total correlations, the success of this method depends on the investigator's ability to devise a scoring key initially that will make the majority of correlations among items positive. In most cases this is easily done. In the previous example of constructing a measure of attitudes toward the United Nations, the investigator would score agreements with the positive statements as 1 and *disagreements* with the *negative* statements as 1. Then most of the correlations among items probably would be positive, and there would be no difficulty in selecting items in terms of item-total correlations. Of course, the investigator might misjudge some of the items, and consequently some items would have negative correlations with total scores. For selecting items in terms of item-total correlations, however, it is not necessary that all the correlations among items be positive, only most of them. The method usually will work if a scoring key is devised such that 70 percent of the correlations among items are positive. In this case the majority of item-total correlations are positive, and some probably are sufficiently high to encourage further item analysis.

After the first attempt to devise a scoring key that will make most correlations among items positive, the next step is to rank the items in terms of item-total correlations. If at least 70 percent of the correlations are positive and numerous correlations are above .20, one can proceed to the next step, which is to reverse the scoring for all items having statistically significant negative item-total correlations. Thus if an item that correlated −.15 with total scores previously had been scored 1 for "agree," in the new scoring key it would be scored 1 for "disagree," and vice versa for an item with that same negative correlation which previously had been scored 1 for "disagree." The scoring would not be changed for all items having positive correlations with total scores or nonsignificant negative correlations. Next, a new set of total scores would be obtained with the new scoring key, and each item would be correlated with the new total scores. This time the number of positive, item-total correlations would probably increase markedly, and the average size of the correlations would increase. If there still are numerous items having negative item-total correlations, the process can be repeated.

In most bipolar item domains, it is not necessary to go through the iterative procedure described above. Usually the investigator can intuit a scoring scheme that will make most correlations among items positive. This usually is easy to do with attitude scales, interest inventories, and most personality inventories. It might be necessary to go through one rekeying of the items, but seldom would it be necessary to repeat the process a number of times. But, as was said previously, even if the scoring key produces only 70 percent positive item-total correlations among items, the iterative approach will usually produce the needed positive item-total correlations. After these correlations are obtained, rather than make only one rank-order in terms of item-total correlations, it is better to make a different order for items scored "agree" (or *yes*) than for items scored "disagree" (or *no*). Then one would select an equal number of items from each list to form the first trial test. For example, one would select the top 15 items from both lists and form a 30-item test. If KR-20 is not as high as desired, additional items would be added from both lists. A balanced scoring key of this kind tends to eliminate response styles such as the tendency to agree regardless of the item content. (Response styles will be discussed in Chap. 16.)

**Discrimination at a point** Although it rarely occurs in practice, a potential problem in test construction is to devise a test that will most effectively discriminate persons from one another at a particular point in the distribution of persons, e.g., a test that will most effectively discriminate the lower 30 percent of persons from the upper 70 percent. The problem might occur in a training program in the Armed Forces where only the top 70 percent of the persons at one stage of training are allowed to enter the next stage of training. Another situation in which discrimination at a point would be important is in the selection of students for scholarships. If only 10 percent of the students can be given scholarships, it is important to reliably distinguish the top 10 percent from the bottom 90 percent. The matter of selecting items that discriminate effectively at one point on the continuum also arises in the measurement of educational programs concerned with "mastery learning," which is a matter that will be discussed more fully in Chap. 9.

It has been suggested that the most effective way to discriminate at a point is by controlling the $p$ values of items (Lord 1952a and b). Models used for this purpose lead to the conclusion that one would *not* choose items with $p$ values as extreme as the "cut" desired in the distribution of persons. Thus, to discriminate the upper 70 percent, one would not choose items with $p$ values near .7; instead, one would select items closer to .5. Interesting as such developments are, they are beside the point.

In the linear model, the most discriminating item for any division of distribution is the one that correlates highest with that division. Thus, to discriminate at a point, one would select items as follows. First, one would construct a very long test in terms of item-total correlations, by methods which were described in previous sections. In this case it would be wise to have at least twice as many items in the first test as are thought to be needed for the eventual test. In terms of total scores, subjects would be split into the divisions required, e.g., bottom 30 percent and top 70 percent. Persons in the top group would receive a score of 1, and those in the bottom group would receive a score of 0. A phi coefficient would be computed between each dichotomous item and each dichotomous score on the total test. Items would be ranked from highest to lowest. The items with the highest phi coefficients would be the most discriminating items at the particular point.

One would obtain the final test by selecting enough items high in the rank-order of phi coefficient to obtain the desired level of reliability. Subsequently, of course, one would employ continuous scores on the total test rather than dichotomous scores. One can improve this method of test construction by going through an iterative process as follows. After the first selection of items in terms of phi coefficients and the formation of a test, subjects would again be split into the desired proportions on this new test. Phi coefficients would again be computed between dichotomous items and dichotomized total scores. Items near the top of the list in terms of those correlations would be used to form a new test, and, if required, the procedure could be repeated again. However, such an iterative approach would seldom be necessary. Usually, the items that were high in the first listing of phi coefficients would be high in subsequent listings of phi coefficients.

Even though it is true that, individually, the items that have the highest coefficients with any split in terms of total scores are the most discriminating items, there is no guarantee that the sum of scores on such items will be more discriminating than the sum of scores on some other set of items. The most discriminating *set* of $k$ items will be that set which has the highest multiple correlation with dichotomized total scores. It would, however, be impractical to undertake the analyses that would be involved or to use the differential weights for items required by multiple regression. Also, that approach would take great advantage of chance even if large numbers of subjects were used. The method described above usually will provide better discrimination at a point than any other method that is feasible.

The method described above for discriminating at a point will tend to select items that have $p$ values that are removed in either direction from .5 toward the cutting point. Thus, in using the method to discriminate the upper 70 percent of people and employing free-response items, one would tend to select more items with $p$ values between, say, .5 and .8 than between .5 and .2. The crucial consideration, though, is the phi coefficient between dichotomous scores on the item and dichotomized total scores. In some instances one finds that items with $p$ values near the upper proportion being discriminated have low phi coefficients, and similarly, one frequently finds that items with $p$ values 30 points or more removed from the split have relatively high phi coefficients. What this method does, essentially, is concentrate the test reliability near a particular point in the score continuum; more will be said about this in the next section.

Even though it is recommended that tests constructed to discriminate at a point be developed from item-split correlations rather than $p$ values, the item difficulties do provide important auxiliary information. Before such $p$ values on multiple-choice items are studied, they should be corrected for guessing. The correction for guessing is as follows:

$$p_c = p - \frac{q}{h - 1} \tag{8-2}$$

where $p_c = p$ value corrected for guessing
$\quad\quad p$ = uncorrected proportion of correct responses to items
$\quad\quad q = 1 - p$
$\quad\quad h$ = number of alternative answers for each item

The above formula assumes that all subjects attempt all items. More about this and other matters concerning effects of guessing on test scores will be discussed in Chap. 16. However, because of problems relating to guessing and the difficulties in general of finding the most appropriate $p$ value for making discriminations, one can see that it would be troublesome to construct tests on that basis. As was said above, however, major reliance for construction of such tests should be based on correlations between items and the percentage split rather than on the $p$ values.

Although some exceptions will be mentioned in Chap. 9, usually it is unwise to construct tests on the basis of their ability to discriminate at a particular point on the score continuum. An obvious reason is that such a test will be useful either for only one purpose or for only a narrow range of purposes. In different situations, different points of discrimination are important. The test which has been constructed specifically to discriminate the top 80 percent of the persons in one situation obviously will do a poor job in another situation of discriminating the top 20 percent. Also, the score that would correspond to a particular percentage in one situation might correspond to a very different percentage in another situation. For example, if 70 percent of the persons in one situation had a raw score of 65 or higher, in another situation it might be found that only 30 percent of the persons had a score of 65 or higher. In most cases, one wants to construct a *general-purpose test*, one that is discriminating at all levels of the attribute and hence can be used for many different purposes in many different situations. One can do this by selecting items in terms of item-total correlations as described previously rather than in terms of phi coefficients between items and total scores dichotomized at a point. Also, possibly one would want to employ the refinement described in the next section to ensure approximately equal reliability at different points in the continuum of scores on the eventual test.

**An equidiscriminating test** As was mentioned previously, when items are selected so as to most effectively discriminate at a particular point in the distribution, this tends to concentrate the test reliability at that point. In previous chapters, we were concerned with the *overall* reliability of a test, which is the consistency with which people at all levels of the attribute are differentiated from one another on alternative measures. Thus the overall reliability (coefficient alpha or the correlation between alternative forms) can be thought of as an "average" of the reliabilities at different levels of the attribute. Instead of examining the overall reliability, one could make investigations of reliability at different levels of the attribute, e.g., for people who score between the 20th and 40th percentiles on a particular form of a test. If a test were constructed to maximally discriminate at the 30th percentile by methods described previously, this would provide good reliability (discrimination) in the range from the 20th to the 40th percentile, but would, for example, provide poorer discrimination in the range from the 60th to 80th percentile. On an alternative form constructed by the same standards, the rank-order of persons in the lower range would tend to change less than the rank-order of persons in the higher range. There is a way to partially ensure equal discrimination at different levels of the attribute, this leading to an *equidiscriminating test*.

An equidiscriminating test would be useful in any situation where (1) important practical decisions are made about people with regard to their particular test scores and (2) it is necessary to make highly reliable distinctions at all levels of the attribute. These circumstances occur in some instances with measures of constructs, and they occur very frequently in the use of predictor tests and achievement tests.

For two related reasons, a homogeneous, general-purpose test constructed by the method discussed previously will tend to make more reliable discriminations in the middle of the score range than at either extreme. Because items are selected in terms of their correlations with total scores, this procedure tends to favor items with $p$ values that are near .5 rather than near either extreme.

This is because of the restriction on the point-biserial correlation coefficient as the $p$ value moves in either direction from .5. The second (and statistically related) reason why the method of test construction discussed previously will tend to be more discriminating in the middle of the score continuum than at the extremes is that there simply are many more people in the middle of the distribution, e.g., in an approximately normal distribution. Correlation coefficients are obtained by summing squared differences of standard scores on two tests and dividing by the number of persons involved. Since there would be many more persons in the middle of the score continuum than at the extremes, the sizes of all correlations are determined more by people in the middle of the score continuum than by those at the extremes. This would be the case for all the correlations involved in selecting items discussed previously.

Since KR-20 and coefficient alpha are estimates of the correlation of an existing test with a hypothetical alternative form, it is instructive to look at the problem in terms of the actual correlation of alternative forms. In that case, the reliability coefficient is determined by one correlation. Because there are many more persons in the middle of the score continuum than at either extreme, the middle section of the continuum has much more weight than do the extremes in determining the size of the correlation. Consequently, any method of test construction which tends to maximize overall reliability will capitalize on the fact that the majority of the people are in the middle of the score continuum and ensure reliability in that zone rather than on the extremes. Since the method discussed previously for constructing homogeneous tests does tend to maximize the alternative-form reliability, perforce it concentrates more on stability of scores in the middle of the continuum.

For both of the foregoing reasons, the method which has been described for developing general-purpose tests as predictors and measures of constructs tends to produce instruments that are less reliable on the extremes than in the middle of the score continuum. This same conclusion is reached through use of the models based on item-characteristic curves, which have been mentioned previously and will be discussed more fully in Chap. 9. If one has the resources and can afford to use a relatively long test, a modification of the previously discussed method of developing general-purpose tests leads to the construction of an equidiscriminating test, one that has approximately the same high reliability at all levels of the score continuum.

There are a number of approaches to constructing an equidiscriminating test; the procedure which is recommended is as follows. In essence what one does in constructing an equidiscriminating test is to select items at multiple cutoff levels rather than at only one level. For example, one could select one-third of the items such that they differentiate the top 25 percent of the people from the bottom 75 percent, another third such that they differentiate the top 50 percent of the people from the lower 50 percent of the people, and a final third of the items in such a way that they discriminate the bottom 25 percent of the people from the top 75 percent. Each such subgroup of items would be obtained by the method discussed previously for constructing a test that maximizes discrimination at a particular point. However, with the equidiscriminating test, one selects a number of subsets of items in terms of their ability to discriminate at different levels of the score continuum. Where the divisions are made depends on the points at which it is most important to make discriminations. The number of divisions that are made depends on the resources available for constructing and employing the test. In an equidiscriminating test, it is assumed that there are at least three and perhaps as many as six percentile divisions of the score continuum for which separate sets of highly discriminating items would be selected. By its nature, an equidiscriminating test is usually a long test, because it must discriminate well at all levels of the attribute. Since more room will be required to pick and choose among the items than is required when items are selected purely in terms of item-total correlations, it is necessary to start with a larger ratio of initial-to-final items in constructing an equidiscriminating test. Also, it is wise to construct items that vary greatly in difficulty.

After all items were administered to a sample of subjects, the total sample would be split at a particular percentile level, and phi coefficients would be computed between all items and dichotomized total scores. A good way to start would be to divide the total distribution of persons at the 20th percentile, giving everyone above that point a score of 1 and everyone below a score of 0. Each item would be correlated with that dichotomy. Items would then be ranked in terms of their phi coefficients. Next, the original total-score distribution would be divided at the 40th percentile, persons above that point receiving a score of 1 and persons below a score of 0. Phi coefficients would then be computed for all items with this second set of dichotomized total scores. This would provide a rank-ordering of phi coefficients for the 40–60 split. Subsequently, splits would be made at the 60th percentiles and at the 80th percentiles, which would lead to two more rank-orderings of phi coefficients.

After the four lists of item-dichotomy correlations were obtained, the next step would be to select an approximately equal number of items at each dichotomy to obtain the same average phi coefficient at each level. For example, by this approach one might end up with 20 items at each of the four percentile levels, the average phi coefficients at the respective levels being .19, .21, .23, and .18. Of course, cut-and-try methods would be required to obtain such a result. The average correlations of items at one level (e.g., the 60–40 split) are likely to be higher, in general, than the correlations with respect to another split. Also, an item that correlates well with one split is likely to correlate well with another split, and some of the items are likely to have very low correlations with all splits. One can, however, by a considerable amount of shifting of items from dichotomy to dichotomy achieve approximately the desired properties.

There usually would be little worry about the equidiscriminating test having a high overall reliability. One would not construct such a test unless one already knew that the overall reliability of the type of item was reasonably high. Also, the number of items required for an equidiscriminating test would tend to ensure a high overall reliability. Of course, an investigation would be made of the overall reliability after the test had been constructed through the steps described above.

Issues relating to an equidiscriminating (EQD) test are illustrated in Fig. 8-3. The curves shown there are hypothetical because the exact shapes would depend completely on the intercorrelations of items and the difficulties of items. However, general principles relating to an EQD test are borne out in the figure. Curve A shows what typically would be found for a 40-item test constructed in terms of principles of homogeneity discussed in this chapter, that is, essentially selecting items in terms of their correlations with total scores only. Illustrated in the figure is the fact that the reliability at any particular percentile level declines as one goes in either direction from the 50th percentile. In particular, discrimination at a point tends to be rather low when one gets below the 20th percentile or above the 80th percentile. The highest reliability is at the 50th percentile.

Curve B shows approximately what one would expect for an EQD test also containing a total of 40 items, but with eight items being selected specifically for their relatively high correlations with the 10th, 30th, 50th, 70th, and 90th percentile cutoff points respectively. Thus, one would expect a flatter curve of reliability over various percentile levels. An EQD test with the same number of items as a homogeneous test would have a lower overall reliability, which is illustrated in Fig. 8-3 by the fact that the total area under curve B is less than the area under curve A. However, an EQD test would be more reliable below the 20th percentile and above the 80th percentile.

Curve C represents an estimate of what would be obtained from a very long test (say, with 100 items) constructed by the same method used to develop

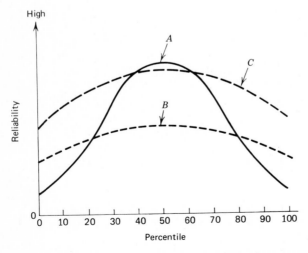

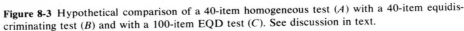

**Figure 8-3** Hypothetical comparison of a 40-item homogeneous test (A) with a 40-item equidiscriminating test (B) and with a 100-item EQD test (C). See discussion in text.

EQD test *B*. The difference would be that 20 items rather than eight items would be selected to represent each of the five percentile cutoff levels. A long test such as illustrated in *C* would be expected to have a much higher overall reliability than *B*, substantially more reliability than *A*, and better discrimination than *A* at every point except the very center of the percentile score range. As illustrated in Fig. 8-3, even with the best of efforts to construct an equidiscriminating test, the reliability would tend to be somewhat higher near the 50th percentile than at either extreme. However, in terms of the general logic for constructing an EQD test, sufficiently long tests can provide excellent discrimination at the higher and lower levels of the percentile distribution.

Numerous refinements of the basic approach described above are possible for the construction of an equidiscriminating test. Dichotomies could be formed at 8 or 10 levels rather than the 4 or 5 mentioned above; however, that probably would do little to improve the final test. After items were selected on the first go-around, one could iteratively improve the results at each stage by forming new distributions of total scores and recomputing phi coefficients with dichotomized scores on the new distributions. Also, new items could be constructed and then correlated with dichotomized scores at different levels of the existing test. A final refinement could be made with respect to adjusting the average phi coefficient at each level. Previously it was said that one should strive for an equal number of items at each level and for equal average phi coefficients in item groups for their respective splits. However, this is only an approximate solution to the ideal, which is to obtain a final collection of items where the average phi coefficient over the *total* collection of items is the same at the different splits. Thus if there are 100 items in the final test and 20 items are selected to represent each of five levels, the ideal is for the 100 phi coefficients with each level to be approximately the same, on the average, as the 100 phi coefficients with other levels. Usually one approximates this ideal by attending to the average correlations of the 20 items selected specifically for each level. Since the correlations of all 100 items at each level would have been obtained for the analysis, the approximation to the ideal can be determined. If there are appreciable differences in the average correlations of the 100 items at the different levels, additional items (if there are any good items left at this point) can be added to increase the average correlation at particular levels.

When the concept of an equidiscriminating test was discussed in the first edition of this book (Nunnally 1967), it was mentioned in passing largely as a hypothetical ideal rather than as a practicable solution to having approximately equal reliability at all levels of the score continuum. However, since the first edition was written, the need for instruments that have the properties of an equidiscriminating test has been spurred on by advances in theory (some of which will be mentioned in Chap. 9), the growing realization that many of the available instruments which have high overall reliability are not highly reliable on the extremes, and the availability of computer hardware and programs that can perform the types of elaborate statistical analyses required. Although one can think of elaborations of the general method discussed here, and there is room for research on many of the technical details, the overall logic for con-

structing an equidiscriminating test is clear. What one does is to employ correlational analysis in such a way as to select subsets of items that are maximally
discriminating at various points along the score continuum and then to combine
these items into one overall test.

In basic research, seldom is it worth the trouble to strive for an
equidiscriminating test. The major requirement in basic research is to have high
*overall* reliability of a size that will support high correlations among different
sources of individual differences. Where sufficient resources are available, at
least an approximation of an equidiscriminating test should be constructed
where (1) people vary considerably with respect to the trait in question, (2) it is
important to make reliable distinctions at all points on the score continuum, and
(3) test results will be influential in making important decisions about people's
lives.

**Weighting of items** The methods of item analysis discussed in this chapter assume that all items are to be weighted equally in the eventual test, and no mention has been made of the possibility of obtaining differential weights for items.
Rather than simply adding the number of correct responses on a test of ability,
one could count correct responses on some items 3, correct responses on some
other items 2, and correct responses on the remaining items 1. This possibility
has not been discussed because it is almost always a waste of time to seek differential weights for items.

A number of different standards could be used for obtaining differential
weights for items. If items were being selected in terms of their correlations
with an external criterion, they could be weighted by a method that would tend
to maximize the correlation of total test scores with the criterion. An approximate method for doing this would be to weight the score on each item by the
item-criterion correlation. Since it was strongly recommended that tests not be
constructed in terms of item-criterion correlations, it also is strongly recommended that items not be weighted by any function of the item-criterion correlations. Also, as was said before, in most test-construction problems there is
no criterion, and consequently there is no possibility of using that method.

A more sensible approach is to obtain differential weights for items by a
method that will tend to maximize the reliability of total test scores. Such a
method would fit well with the procedures described previously for selecting
items in terms of item-total correlations. An approximate method for obtaining
such differential weights is to weight each item by its item-total correlation. To
take an overly simplified example, if 10 items all had item-total correlations of
.15 and 10 more items had item-total correlations of .3, a higher reliability for
the 20 items would be obtained if the former items were weighted 1 and the
latter were weighted 2 than if all items were weighted 1. (Actually, determining
the best weights would be a much more complex matter than this procedure,
but that is beside the point.)

The crucial question in seeking differential weights for items is how much
difference it makes to use differential weights. It would make a difference if the

weighted and unweighted scores on whole tests did not correlate highly and if the reliability of the weighted test were considerably higher than that of the unweighted test. However, there is overwhelming evidence that the use of differential weights seldom makes an important difference. Regardless of how differential weights are determined, typically it is found that on tests containing at least 20 items, the weighted test correlates in the high 90s with the unweighted test. Also, the slight increase in reliability or predictive validity obtained by weighting items can be matched in nearly all instances by adding several items to the unweighted test. Since it is much easier to add several items to a test than to go through the labors of determining and using differential weights for items, seeking differential weights is almost never worth the trouble. (Research on the weighting of items is summarized by Stanley and Wang 1970.)

Differential weights tend to make a difference when (1) the number of items is relatively small (less than 20) and (2) item-total correlations vary markedly. Seldom do both these conditions occur with dichotomous items, since most such tests contain more than 20 items and the item-total correlations are concentrated in a narrow zone. Some measures composed of multipoint items do have considerably less than 20 items, and the item-total correlations vary more than they typically do on tests composed of dichotomous items. This would be the case in a measure of attitudes which contained 10 seven-point rating scales. In this case an increase in reliability of from 5 to 10 points might be achieved by the differential weighting of items. Even there, however, the same increase in reliability probably could be obtained by adding two or three new items.

For the reasons discussed above, in nearly all cases it is recommended that total scores be obtained by an unweighted summation of item scores. If the reliability is not as high as desired, by far the best approach is to increase the number of items.

**Removal of an unwanted factor** Sometimes it is known in advance that items which are being analyzed to measure one attribute will tend to correlate with an unwanted attribute. This is the case, for example, in tests constructed to measure different factors of human ability, where experience has shown that many types of items concerning human ability tend to correlate with the factor of verbal comprehension. Since, no matter what factor is being measured, the items will require some understanding of words and sentences, obtaining relatively independent measures of factors other than verbal comprehension is rather difficult.

Another example is in the construction of a measure of anxiety, where previous studies have indicated that the type of item being used is likely to produce a test which will correlate substantially with measures of intelligence. This will make it somewhat difficult to perform studies on anxiety, since any results obtained will be confounded with intelligence.

An extension can be made of the method of selecting items in terms of item-total correlations to lessen the effect of an unwanted factor. One would need a larger collection of items initially than is usually required in selecting items in terms of item-total correlations. For example, if the best guess is that a 30-item test will be required to achieve the desired level of reliability, it will be well to start with over 100 items. Each item is then correlated with total scores and with scores on the unwanted factor. To facilitate the selection of items, a scatter diagram should be made of correlations of items with both variables. The desired items are those that have relatively high correlations with total scores and relatively low correlations with the unwanted factor.

After a set of items is selected from the scatter diagram, the next steps are to compute KR-20 for the collection of items and correlate the total scores on those items with scores on the unwanted factor. If the former is high and the latter is low, the item analysis is complete. If that is not the case, new items need to be added, and some compromise between the two considerations might have to be reached. If the overlap between measures of the two attributes is a particularly bothersome problem in research, it will be wise to have the reliability of the new test somewhat lower than desired to prevent the new test from correlating substantially with the unwanted factor.

**Taking advantage of chance** All forms of item analysis tend to capitalize on sampling errors relating to the selection of persons, which makes the results appear better than they will in subsequent studies. One tends to take advantage of chance in any situation where something is optimized from the data at hand. This occurs in multiple correlation, in selecting items in terms of item-total correlations, in selecting items for an equidiscriminating test, in seeking differential weights for items, and in purifying a test of an unwanted factor. Since the opportunities to take advantage of chance are related positively to the number of variables and negatively to the number of persons, it was recommended that a bare minimum in item analysis is 5 persons for each item and that a safer number is 10 persons per item.

When there are at least 10 persons per item, the methods of item analysis will take very little advantage of chance. A collection of items found to have a reliability of .84 might in subsequent studies prove to have a reliability of .80, but the drop in reliability is seldom more than a few points. If the exact level of reliability is a crucial issue when items are being selected, a safe procedure is to strive for a reliability at least five points above the crucial level.

The considerable amount of "playing around" with data sometimes required in constructing tests from bipolar domains of items provides more of an opportunity to take advantage of chance than is provided when items are selected in terms of the initial item-total correlations. For this reason, when dealing with such domains of items, one should strive to obtain even more than 10 persons per item if that is feasible. Because of the large number of statistics and the amount of cut-and-try required, it should go without saying that a large sample of subjects is needed for the construction of an equidiscriminating test.

To investigate the extent to which item analyses (and other forms of analysis that strive to optimize some function of the data) take advantage of chance, it has been recommended that a "holdout" group of subjects be employed. For example, if only 600 subjects are available for testing, one approach would be to base the item analysis on half the subjects. Then KR-20 (or whatever else was being optimized) would be computed for the first group and for the holdout group. That certainly would provide evidence about the extent to which the analysis had capitalized on sampling errors, but it would be as imprudent an approach as it would be to permit fire prevention to fall to a dangerously low level in order to invest heavily in firefighting equipment. If the number of subjects is limited, as it usually is, the far wiser strategy is to use every last subject in the item analysis. This way one tends to ensure in advance that the reliability (or any other function being optimized) will not fall off markedly in subsequent studies.

## SUGGESTED ADDITIONAL READINGS

Gerberich, J. R. *Specimen objective test items: A guide to achievement test construction*. New York: Longmans, 1956.

Horst, P. *Psychological measurement and prediction*. Belmont, Calif.: Wadsworth, 1966, chaps. 10 to 15.

Lord, F . M. Individualized testing and item characteristic curve theory. In D. H. Krantz, R. C. Atkinson, R. D. Luce, and P. Suppes (eds.), *Contemporary developments in mathematical psychology*. Vol. 2: *Measurement, psychophysics, and neural information processing*. San Francisco: W. H. Freeman, 1974.

Lord, F. M., and Novick, M. R. *Statistical theories of mental tests*. Reading, Mass.: Addison-Wesley, 1968, chaps. 1, 3, 12 to 15.

Nunnally, J. C. *Educational measurement and evaluation* (2d ed.). New York: McGraw-Hill, 1972, chaps. 5 to 10.

Thorndike, R. L. (ed.). *Educational measurement* (2d ed.). Washington, D.C.: American Council on Education, 1971, chaps. 2 to 5, 17, 19.

# NINE

## CONSTRUCTION OF TESTS
## FOR SPECIAL PURPOSES

In Chap. 8 we discussed principles for constructing general-purpose tests that are intended to have content validity, predictive validity, or construct validity. Although many auxiliary techniques are involved, essentially instruments intended to have content validity are constructed in terms of a rational appeal to the appropriateness of the item coverage, and instruments intended to have both predictive validity and construct validity are constructed in terms of principles of homogeneity. Such general-purpose tests are typically employed quite widely with a variety of subject samples and frequently for numerous purposes. An example would be a comprehensive battery of achievement tests for students in the fourth grade to be used in schools across the country that would supply information relevant to many different kinds of decisions about students and educational programs. A second example of a general-purpose test would be a measure of anxiety which would depend primarily on construct validity but also might be used in some specific prediction problems. The measure would be constructed in terms of principles of homogeneity and would be used with diverse samples of subjects in correlational studies of college students, comparisons of normal mature persons with mental hospital patients, and in experiments on programs of behavior modification intended to reduce certain types of anxiety. As is typical in these cases and typical of all general-purpose tests, it is expected to find large, reliable, individual differences both for broad samples of subjects and for special groups in which they are employed.

Although general-purpose tests as discussed in Chap. 8 are the mainstay of research and applied work in the behavioral sciences, there are some special-purpose tests which require additional considerations. Either they require an entirely different logic of test construction, or the appropriate methods of test construction constitute some modification of the procedures discussed in Chap. 8. Such special-purpose tests will be discussed in this chapter. Test construction methods will be discussed for (1) speed tests, (2) mastery learning, (3) dependent variables for experiments, (4) item-characteristic curves, and (5) tailored tests.

# SPEED TESTS

In Chap. 8 it was assumed that test construction concerns *power tests*, i.e., tests on which subjects are given about as much time as they want. With some types of tests, however, subjects are not given as much time as they want; instead, a highly restrictive time limit is imposed. Issues regarding speed and power tests will be discussed in detail in Chap. 16, but here it is necessary to discuss some of the special principles that apply to the construction of speed tests.

In their purest form, speed tests consist of items of *trivial difficulty*. That is, the difficulties would be trivial if subjects were given as much time as they wanted in making responses. By "trivial difficulty" is meant a $p$ value of .90 or higher when items are administered under power conditions. One type of item that fulfills this requirement is the simple problem in addition or subtraction. If problems of this type were employed in testing normal adults, all persons would answer almost all the problems correctly if they were given as much time as they wanted. The only way, then, to obtain a reliable dispersion of scores is to employ a highly restrictive time limit, in which, for example, the average person has time to answer only about half the questions. Another example of items of trivial difficulty is letter groups used in measures of perceptual speed. Each item consists of two pairs of letter groupings, each group containing about eight letters of the alphabet mixed with numbers and punctuation marks. In each pair of letter groups, either the groups are identical or one letter in one group is different from the corresponding letter in the other group. The subject is asked to indicate whether each pair of letter groupings is identical or not. Obviously, if subjects were given all the time they wanted, all the items would be of trivial difficulty. The only way, then, to obtain a reliable distribution of scores is to employ highly restrictive time limits, e.g., to allow only 10 minutes for responding to 100 items.

Although psychological principles concerning speed tests will be discussed more fully in Chap. 16, a number of points should be summarized here. First, the fact that a time limit is employed for a test does not mean that speed per se is an important ingredient in the variance of test scores obtained from the instrument. In many cases, a relatively generous time limit is set as a practical consideration for expediting a testing session. For example, if a number of tests must be given in a limited amount of time, then some time limits must be employed in order to ensure that the whole group moves along from one test to the next. Otherwise, a few stragglers would greatly hold up the whole group. As will be shown in Chap. 16, however, unless such time limits are severely restrictive, they seldom influence the underlying traits measured by the tests. Second, unless the underlying trait obviously concerns speed, it is generally ill-advised to employ highly speeded tests where power tests logically could be employed instead. Much practical experience and a considerable amount of experimentation as well (e.g., see the investigation by Miller and Weiss 1976) indicate that the introduction of restrictive time limits tends to add unwanted sources of variance into test scores concerning incidental testing-taking habits that are unrelated to the underlying trait. There are some abilities, however, that are intimately related to speed, such as computation of simple arithmetic problems, perceptual speed in detecting details in visual configurations, and such practical abilities as are involved in typing, shorthand, and a variety of other job-related skills.

The rules that apply to the construction of power tests do *not* apply to the construction of speed tests. Rather, a special set of principles applies to the construction of speed tests. These principles will be outlined in this section and further amplified in Chap. 16.

**Internal structure of speed tests**  Previously in this chapter it was shown that the construction of power tests depends very much on the sizes and patterns of correlations among items. Also, in Chaps. 6 and 7 it was shown that the theory of reliability relates directly to the size and patterns of correlations among items. Here it will be shown that with speed tests the size and patterns of correlations among items are artifacts of time limits and of the ordering of items within a test. Consequently test construction cannot be based on the correlations of items with one another, and the reliability of speed tests cannot be based on internal consistency.

In a speed test, the average correlation among items is directly related to the amount of time allotted for taking the test. If subjects are given all the time they want, the $p$ values of all items will be either 1.0 or close to that, and consequently the correlations among items will be either zero or close to zero. At the other extreme, if subjects are given practically no time for taking the test, the $p$ values will all be zero or close to zero, and consequently the correlations among items will be near zero on the average. Between these two extremes of time limits, the average $p$ values of items range from 0 to 1.0. One could, for example, experiment with time limits to obtain an average $p$ value near .5, in which case the average correlation among items might be substantial.

In addition to the average correlation among items being related to the time limit, the patterns of correlations among items are determined by the time limit. Let us look at the case where a time limit is employed such that (1) the average $p$ value of items is near the middle of the possible range and (2), by methods to be discussed later, the distribution of total scores is found to be highly reliable. Suppose that one employed the methods discussed previously for constructing a power test. Essentially this consists of selecting those items that correlate highly with total scores, but on speed tests this depends directly on the ordering of items within the test. Items near the beginning of the test probably would have such high $p$ values that they would tend to correlate very little with the other items, and consequently they would correlate very little with total scores. Items near the end of the test would have such low $p$ values that they also would correlate very little with the other items and with total scores. In contrast, items near the middle of the test would tend to have substantial correlations with one another and with total test scores. Since, in a speed test, the ordering of items is arbitrary, the correlations of items with total scores are arbitrary, and it makes no sense to select items on the basis of item-total correlations. The construction of speed tests, then, must be based on principles other than those that apply to construction of power tests. These principles will be discussed throughout the remainder of this section.

**The item pool**  As is true in the construction of all tests, the first step in the construction of a speed test is to develop an item pool. Usually this is done rather easily, because the items on speed tests usually are so simple that it is easy to compose them by the dozens. Whereas previously it was possible to give some rules of thumb regarding the numbers of items required for the item pool for a power test, this is very difficult to do with speed tests. This is because the reliability of speed tests is not as highly related to the number of items as is the case with power tests. For example, a speed test with 50 arithmetic items might be more reliable than a speed test containing 200 pairs of letter groupings. The reliability of different types of speed tests tends to be related not to the number of items, but to the *testing time* required to obtain the most reliable distribution of scores. Thus if the ideal testing times for two different types of speed tests are both 15 minutes, the tests will tend to have roughly the same reliability regardless of the number of items in each. When one constructs the item pool, the number of items should depend on intuitive judgments about how rapidly the items can be answered by the average person. If later it is found that the original item pool was too small, usually it is easy to construct new items.

**Time limits**  Constructing a speed test consists largely of finding the *time limit* that will produce the *most reliable distribution of total scores*. The amount of experimentation required to find the ideal time limit depends on previous experience with employing time limits with the particular type of item. Say, for example, that the items consist of simple problems in subtraction and addition, and the test is to be used with unselected adults. Previous experience indicates that the average adult can correctly solve such problems at the rate of two per minute. The purpose of test construction is to develop a highly reliable test of numerical computation. The experimenter, thinking that a test of about 80 such items will produce a highly reliable distribution of scores, constructs 80 such items and performs experiments to determine the ideal time limit. Previous experience suggests that the ideal time limit would be somewhere near 40 minutes, but it is safest to perform experiments to make sure. Consequently, the experimenter administers the items with five different time limits to five different groups, the groups consisting of random selections from a larger sample of subjects. The experimenter elects to try time limits of 30, 35, 40, 45, and 50 minutes, respectively.

In the experiment above, the ideal time limit is the one that produces the most reliable distribution of scores, the reliability being determined by methods to be discussed later. Rather than perform studies of reliability at this stage, however, one can use a simpler approach which will usually produce much the

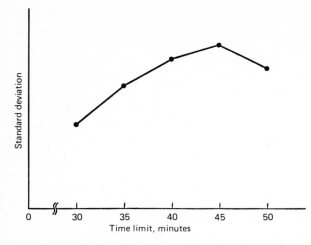

**Figure 9-1** Standard deviation of scores on a speed test as a function of different time limits.

same results. In a speed test the reliabilities produced by different time limits are highly related to the standard deviations of scores produced by those time limits. Consequently one selects the time limit that produces the largest standard deviation of scores. Hypothetical results from the experiment discussed above are shown in Fig. 9-1. As is typically the case, the standard deviation (and thus the reliability) is highest at some point in between the extreme time limits being investigated and tapers off on either side of that point. In this case, however, the ideal time limit is 45 minutes rather than the 40 minutes originally guessed by the experimenter.

**Measurement of reliability** It is not correct to measure the reliability of a speed test in terms of internal consistency, as is the case with coefficient alpha and KR-20. The most appropriate measure of reliability is made by correlating alternative forms. Thus, in the previous example, rather than construct only one 80-item test of numerical computation, one would construct two 80-item tests. The correlation between scores on the two tests would be the best estimate of the reliability. A time-saving approximation to the alternative-form reliability can be obtained by correlating separately timed halves of only one test, which will save the labors of constructing an alternative form. In that case, even-numbered items on the test would constitute one form, and odd-numbered items the other form. The first half of the items would be administered with a time limit equal to half that employed with the test as a whole. Immediately after time is called, the second half of the items would be administered with a time limit equal to half that employed with the whole test. In order to test for stability over short periods of time, another approach is to administer the two half-tests about two weeks apart. The correlation between the separately timed halves would then be corrected by Eq. (6-19) to provide an estimate of the alternative-form reliability of the whole test. The estimate usually is rather precise if (1) the trait does not change markedly over the time used for applying alternative forms and (2) performance within a testing session is not markedly influenced by fatigue.

Why the reliability of speed tests cannot be determined from formulas relating to internal consistency is not as simple as it may seem on first thought. This does not necessarily follow from the fact that the average correlation among items is an artifact of the time limit. It was said that the reliability is closely related to the size of the standard deviation of total scores, and the standard deviation of total scores is highly related to the average correlation among items within the test. There is a subtle reason why formulas concerning internal consistency (for example, KR-20) cannot be legitimately employed with speed tests. Such formulas are predictive of the alternative-form reliability only if it can be assumed that the average correlation (or covariance) among items *within* a test is the same as the average correlation (or covariance) *between* items on alternative forms. On speed tests the average correlation between items on alternative forms tends to be *smaller* than the average correlation between items within each test. For this reason, reliability estimates concerning internal consistency tend to *overestimate* the alternative-form reliability of speed tests.

**Factor composition** As was mentioned previously, the patterns of correlations among items in a speed test are determined almost entirely by the time limit and the ordering of items within the test. Items near the middle of the test tend to correlate more highly with other items than do items near either end of the test. Consequently, in a factor analysis, items near the middle of the test would tend to have the highest loadings on a general factor, purely because of the way items are ordered on the test. In addition, items tend to correlate more highly with items near their ordinal position on the test than they do with items further removed in the ordering. For example, the 14th item would probably correlate more highly with the 13th and 15th items than it would with the 10th and 20th items. Consequently items tend to break up into different factors because of the proximity of items to one another in the test. The factor structure of speed tests is interesting from the standpoint of psychometric theory, but it tells one nothing about factors of ability or personality. The proper way to learn about the factors measured by speed tests is to factor-analyze whole tests *after* they have been constructed by methods discussed previously in this section.

## ACHIEVEMENT TESTS FOR MASTERY LEARNING

The concept of *mastery learning* is a relatively new philosophy concerning education which has grown out of psychological learning theory, changing principles in pedagogy, and social movements regarding equal educational opportunities for all people. Although the concept of mastery learning has been studied most extensively with respect to simple topics in the elementary school grades, such as reading and mathematics, in principle it applies to all types of training programs, such as habituation of the mentally retarded and behavior modification of personality problems.

**Nature of mastery learning**  In essence, mastery learning concerns the effort to train *all*, or at least nearly all, people to an acceptable level of performance in whatever type of training program is being undertaken. Thus, if some individuals are unable to reach a satisfactory level of performance, then they are given more practice with the learning materials until they do reach the specified level of mastery learning. The term *mastery learning* is somewhat of a misnomer in that usually what is sought is a satisfactory level of performance rather than true mastery, in the sense that all persons would be expected to reach outstanding levels.

There are numerous controversies about the concept of mastery learning—what it means, how it should be applied, which subject matters are suitable, if any, practicability of the goals, and problems of measuring results. These controversies are discussed in Nunnally (1976), where references also are given to some of the other major writings on the topic. The purpose here, however, is not to discuss mastery learning in broad detail, but rather to discuss the test construction problems that are posed.

Measurement issues relating to mastery learning can be illustrated with simple skills in arithmetic and language usage. In the former, the goals at a particular grade level could be for the child to understand the processes involved in long division, including "carrying," use of decimals, and backward multiplication to check division. These would constitute the subgoals in an overall mastery of arithmetic at that level. The teacher would intend for all students to demonstrate these skills, and students would continue to receive practice until they all clearly showed a mastery of the concepts. A similar form of mastery learning could be evidenced in goals of instruction for punctuation in language usage. Some of the goals at a particular level of elementary school training would be for the children to understand rules regarding use of commas, capitalization, etc. The children are given continued practice and tested repeatedly to ensure that they develop the required skills, e.g., to always place a comma before *and* in a compound sentence. In both these instances, tests could be developed easily for the simple skills involved, and also it would be a straightforward matter to develop a number of alternative forms that could be administered for whatever number of retestings were required to ensure mastery learning.

**Test construction**  In all cases, measurement of successful performance with respect to mastery learning is done with achievement tests, and these depend on content validity exactly as was specified in Chap. 8. That is, the test is constructed in terms of a rational appeal to the appropriateness of the content rather than in terms of any experimentation or statistical results as would be required for predictive validity or construct validity. What has puzzled some people, however, is that in the ideal situation where all people master the learning tasks (as in the simple examples above), there is little or no variance of test scores. In that case, the internal-consistency reliability would be zero, and the measure could not even correlate with an alternative form. There is no reason to be puzzled about the circumstance arising, if indeed it ever does. Because achievement tests are constructed in terms of content validity, it is not absolutely essential that there be any variance of scores which would support internal-consistency reliability or correlations with other variables. However, this situation almost never occurs, because (1) the concept of mastery learning is limited to only certain types of subject matters; (2) unless an artificial ceiling is placed on test performance, the brighter students will perform much better than average and below-average students even after mastery learning, and thus the variance will remain large; and (3) as will be shown subsequently, mastery learning frequently has to be defined partly in a normative sense rather than purely in terms of the goals of instruction with respect to particular skills. For these reasons, even with the best of efforts to achieve mastery learning, one usually finds large, reliable individual differences on tests intended to measure performance in situations where mastery learning supposedly is at work. There is nothing wrong with attempting mastery learning in any situation, and the appropriateness of the instruments is not directly dependent on any type of empirical evidence or statistical results. However, there is also nothing wrong with examining the variance actually obtained from achievement tests for that purpose and studying internal-consistency reliability, as an incidental form of information about the measuring instruments.

As was mentioned, with many topics there is no direct way to set the level of mastery learning purely in terms of requisite skills, but rather this must be done partly normatively. For example, how would one determine mastery learning in such high school topics as ancient history, political science, or speech training? Normative information must be employed to at least some extent when one evaluates performance in any type of speeded ability. For example, what would constitute mastery learning in terms of reading speed, typing speed, or speed of solving very simple arithmetic problems? Usually in these and most topics where an effort is made to obtain mastery learning, the level of mastery is determined partly by the judgment of the instructor or group of instructors responsible for the training program and partly by norms concerning how well previous groups have performed on general-purpose tests of achievement relating to the topic.

The author was told by a colleague that he employed a form of mastery learning in his college courses in introductory psychology. He gave tests four times during the semester, with the fourth test constituting a final examination. In terms of his own impressions of what students should be able to achieve, he established the mastery level as constituting 80 percent correct responses on multiple-choice items with four alternatives for each item. From previous experience with this type of test in the course, he had learned that the average student could answer approximately 80 percent of the items correctly.

Consequently, henceforth he declared this the mastery level, and any student who reached this level would obtain at least a C grade in the course. Higher grade levels were given B's and A's depending upon the judgment of the instructor regarding the proper cutoff levels. If on a particular test students scored less than 80 percent correct, they were given an opportunity for additional study and administered an alternative form of the test. They could repeat this cycle of studying and being reexamined until they had exhausted five available forms for each of the four tests. The instructor reported that most students improved over taking several alternative forms to where they would reach the mastery level of 80 percent correct. Thus, nearly all students received at least a C in the course. This situation is typical of many of those in which so-called mastery learning is at work—the standards depend partly on the judgment of the instructor regarding acceptable levels of performance and partly on normative data from previous uses of general-purpose tests.

Whereas it is not intended here to assert either approval or disapproval of the above educational practices, some suggestions will be given regarding appropriate methods of test construction where measurement of mastery learning depends partly on normative standards. The original normative information comes from general-purpose achievement tests, either well-standardized tests developed by experts or less formal tests constructed by the individual instructor. In either case the instruments should have content validity and should meet all the standards discussed in Chap. 8 for that purpose. As was mentioned there, some auxiliary forms of empirical information are very helpful regarding percentages of responses to each alternative on each item and correlations of items with total scores. In other words, the original tests from which normative information was gleaned for setting an appropriate mastery level (for example, 80 percent correct responses) should have been good achievement tests in terms of standards for content validity. Although usually it would be satisfactory to continue to employ alternative forms of such general-purpose achievement tests with respect to this approach to mastery learning (partly judgmental by the instructor and partly normative in terms of performance of previous groups of students), some refinements can be made specifically for this purpose. This would entail pruning the items in terms of discrimination at a point, as was discussed in Chap. 8 with respect to the development of homogeneous tests. The same principles of item analysis would apply in selecting items particularly appropriate to discriminating at a point in terms of setting a cutoff standard for mastery learning. If the more complex forms of analysis regarding item-total correlations are not feasible in the situation, at least the test can be slanted toward the difficulty level that would be more discriminating with respect to the cutoff point. In Chap. 8 some rules were mentioned for selecting items purely in terms of difficulty levels if no information is available about item-total correlations.

**Practical problems** Whereas the logic for measuring performance in relation to mastery learning as stated above is reasonably clear, definite practical problems are encountered in carrying out that logic. This is because, by its nature, mastery learning usually requires much more assessment of performance than the more conventional testing of achievement in particular units of instruction. Obviously this was the case in the example mentioned above in which the instructor allowed students to take as many as five alternative forms of each of the four tests. In that case, it was necessary for the instructor to compose a total of 20 tests, which would entail a great deal of effort. Because textbooks and other aspects of instruction change over time, it would be necessary to continually update the tests. The sheer difficulties of scheduling, grading, and communicating test results to students would require considerable effort on the part of the instructor.

In testing for mastery learning with respect to simple skills in the elementary school grades, it would be necessary to continually assess levels of performance in order to properly monitor instruction. This might require many rather brief tests to ensure that nearly all students had mastered each subgoal of the overall unit of instruction. For the foregoing reasons, it is obvious that careful assessment as part of educational programs geared to mastery learning will require (1) considerable effort on the part of the instructor to adequately measure progress, (2) the use of "canned" testing materials that are ready-made for use by teachers, or (3) computerized approaches, which will be discussed subsequently.

The measurement of mastery learning has been tied in with some automated approaches to instruction, where computerized procedures are employed not only for developing skills, as in arithmetic, but also for simultaneously measuring level of performance as the instruction progresses. Thus, the computer would be programmed to continually "feed" the child problems at a level of difficulty that would ensure growth in skill to a point where either a ceiling was reached with respect to the type of instruction or instruction time ran out. Measurement with such automated instruction and testing procedures is tied in rather closely with the advent of *tailored tests*, which will be discussed in a subsequent section.

**Summary** This section on measurement problems with respect to mastery learning should end with a few summary statements. First, the concept of mastery learning is a good idea whether or not it is practicable in many circumstances. Second, the practicability and explicit procedures for carrying out mastery learning are still very much in dispute. Third, where mastery learning can be largely fulfilled, there are no necessary logical problems of measurement. Measurement is made with achievement tests, which should be constructed in such a way as to have content validity. Although some auxiliary forms of empirical information and statistical analysis are helpful, and some new ones were mentioned here specifically related to the measurement of mastery learning, validity depends mainly on a rational appeal to the content and the way it is presented in the form of a test. Fourth, however, unless ready-made testing materials or computerized aids are available, the actual measurement of performance in the learning process can pose extreme practical problems. Fifth, in those few situations (and there are not many) where mastery

learning results in near-zero individual differences in eventual level of performance, no one need be worried that this means almost zero variance, zero reliability, and zero correlations with any other possible measure. These results do
not detract at all from the worth of the test in terms of content validity; and, at
least in principle, there is nothing strange about this circumstance occurring.

## CONSTRUCTION OF MEASURES FOR EXPERIMENTS

One frequently hears a gross distinction made between correlational studies
and experiments. In correlational studies, as the name implies, one computes
correlations between sets of individual differences on tests or other measures.
Also, as the name implies, in experiments one purposely attempts to influence
some attribute of people and observe effects in one or more treatment groups.
An example of the former would be observing the correlations among five tests
of reasoning ability, and an example of the latter would be comparing the effectiveness of three approaches to instruction in reading comprehension. Most
correlational investigations are undertaken with general-purpose tests, which
should be constructed in terms of principles of homogeneity discussed in Chap.
8. This method of test construction leads to large, reliable individual differences among subjects with respect to the attribute being studied. Persons
who work primarily with experiments rather than in studies of individual differences can rightly claim that different standards should be employed in judging the usefulness of measures for experiments, and they are correct.

**Experiments and individual differences** As many people have pointed out, the
dependent measures employed in experiments need not be accompanied by
large, reliable individual differences in responses. An extreme example will
show why that is the case. Imagine that an experiment is being undertaken to
elevate the IQ. Some 300 subjects are selected who have a mean IQ of 100 and
a standard deviation of scores that is the same as the standard error of
measurement. In other words, the differences among people before the experiment is undertaken are totally unreliable. The total group is randomly divided
into three groups of 100 subjects each. Nothing is done with one group, which
constitutes the control group. The other two groups are submitted to six
months of different kinds of training relating to changing the IQ. At the end of
six months, it is found that the mean IQ of the control group is 100, the mean
IQ of one treatment group is 110, and the mean of the second treatment group
is 115. The standard deviations of all three groups are almost equal to the
standard error of measurement, and thus individual differences about each
mean are totally unreliable. An analysis of variance shows that differences
among means are highly significant statistically. The experiment is a whopping
success, and although this is an "Alice in Wonderland" example, there would
be nothing wrong psychometrically if it happened. There is no reason why the
dependent measures employed for experiments necessarily must have large, re-

liable individual differences in pretests before experiments are undertaken or in posttests after the experiments are completed.

**Content validity for dependent measures** Measures constructed specifically for experiments should be constructed in terms of content validity, embodying all the principles discussed in Chap. 8. Most experimenters in the behavioral sciences actually have been doing this all along without ever labeling their procedures as constituting content validity. Examples are legion. A very simple example is in paired-associate learning of words that vary in terms of frequency of usage in the language. The subject is shown a list of 18 words, each of which is paired with one of the numbers from 1 through 18. The number-word pairs are shown in a random order on each trial. The subject is first shown the number, required to verbalize the associated word, and then shown the correct number-word pair. This is continued for a set number of trials or until a specified level of learning is attained for all subjects in the study. In the lists are words of three levels in terms of frequency of usage: very common words, moderately common words, and infrequently used words, such as house, moose, and dredge. (It would be necessary to equate the six words in the three word groups on the average with respect to numbers of letters and other possible confounding characteristics.) Whatever the experimenter finds in the study, the measurement method (the "test") for the dependent measure is, and should be, constructed to have content validity. That is, the words are designated, chosen, and administered in ways that are widely acceptable regarding the scientific generalizations which the experimenter hopes to make about the results. Not only is there no need, but it actually would be quite incorrect, to specifically select the words in such a way as to manifest large individual differences by methods for constructing homogeneous tests.

Content validity also is at issue in most other experiments. Another example would be studying the length of time that people elect to look at geometrical forms that vary in complexity from 3-sided figures to 200-sided figures. The experimenter has constructed eight figures at six different levels of complexity in this range. The method of construction is designed to ensure that the figures are truly random in shape. The randomness and numbers of sides are easily communicated to others, which helps ensure content validity. Each subject is allowed to look at the figures one at a time for as long as desired. The slides are placed in a different random order for each subject. The dependent measure consists of the average amount of time in seconds spent looking at forms at each level of complexity. A regular, monotonically increasing relationship is found between degree of complexity and amount of looking time. The experimental measure is constructed in terms of content validity; i.e., the items are constructed on a rational basis and presented in an acceptable manner in the perception task. Other experimenters can judge to what extent any generalizations from the experiment hold in other possible experimental situations. To the extent to which other experimenters think that alternative procedures should be employed for obtaining the geometrical forms or presenting them in the perception task, this serves only as food for hypotheses to be investigated in subsequent experiments. Actually, the possibility that other experimenters will contest the generality of results obtained from an experiment because of a particular feature of the methodology (a challenge to the content validity) exemplifies a healthy aspect of scientific progress.

Another example would be comparing two computerized approaches to teaching introductory psychology with the usual lecture series and attendant instructional activities. The two computerized approaches differ in terms of the statistical strategy for presenting material, testing for knowledge at each stage, and selecting new material to be presented subsequently. The dependent variable should be an achievement test specially constructed to fit the subject matter being taught, and an achievement test requires content validity.

There has been so much confusion about this point that it needs to be reiterated: measures developed specifically for experiments should be constructed to have content validity. Although there are some experimental approaches and statistical results that provide helpful auxiliary information which were discussed in Chap. 8, these are entirely secondary to the major standards concerning content validity. Measures constructed for experiments should not be item-analyzed in such a way as to produce large, reliable individual differences.

**Incidental individual differences** Even when measures are not constructed specifically for that purpose, however, usually it is found that there are large, reliable individual differences on the measures employed in experiments. Actually, it is quite a rarity to find good measures for experiments (good in the sense that they effectively differentiate treatment groups) that do not also have large, reliable individual differences *within treatment groups*. In many cases, experimenters wish that they could rid themselves of these omnipresent, large, reliable individual differences because they serve to inflate the error variance when a between-groups rather than a within-subjects experimental design is employed.

On the other side of the coin, there is no harm in investigating individual differences that arise as by-products of measures constructed specifically for experiments. For example, although in rat learning, mazes are not constructed specifically to produce individual differences in learning rates, rats do differ reliably in that regard, and some interesting correlations have been found among these sources of individual differences in various types of mazes. Factor analysis studies of such correlations have been undertaken.

What has been said about the construction of measures of dependent variables for experiments is particularly relevant to evaluation research in relation to various programs of social betterment, such as programs of early educational intervention for culturally deprived children and various efforts at school integration of minority group members. The measures employed to assess the results of such programs of social betterment necessarily are constructed to have content validity by the methods discussed in Chap. 8. A special caution in such investigations, however, is that sometimes it is hazardous to employ existing general-purpose achievement tests and other available instruments for measuring the effects of such programs. It is entirely possible that such programs as a whole, and individual segments of them, have their own particular goals that may not be adequately assessed by existing general-purpose instruments. For example, an educational program aimed at young children might have as one of its major goals to increase the awareness of children of differences in sights and sounds in the environment and encourage their categorizing behavior in that regard. Probably it would be necessary to construct tests specifically to measure such behaviors, because they probably would not be adequately measured on any available, widely used instruments. Although the logic is clear that such instruments should be constructed to have content validity, some of the particular goals of programs of social betterment are difficult to measure adequately. This is particularly the case with respect to goals concerning noncognitive functions involving attitudes, interests, and various forms of social behavior.

## ITEM-CHARACTERISTIC CURVES

As has been mentioned at a number of places so far in this book, special psychometric theories exist regarding the specific mathematical form of the relationship between hypothetical attributes and the probability of responding in one way (manner alpha) rather than another (manner beta) to dichotomously scored items. (See summary articles by Lord 1974; Weiss 1976; and relevant sections of other listings in the Suggested Additional Readings.) Hypothetical curves for three such items are illustrated in Fig. 9-2. It should be understood

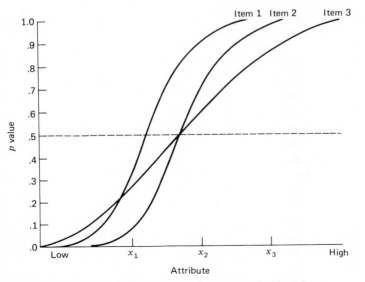

**Figure 9-2** Hypothetical item-characteristic curves for three items.

that the attribute is entirely hypothetical and can be only inferred from the items and never known directly. The attribute sometimes is spoken of as a *latent trait*. With respect to the issues illustrated in Fig. 9-2, it might be useful to think of the attribute as constituting word knowledge (vocabulary) and the $p$ value as representing the probability of people at any level of the attribute responding correctly to a particular item. It is useful to think of a very large number of persons being located at each point on the hypothetical attribute. For all persons located at point $x_1$, there would be a probability of less than .5 of passing any one of the three items. For persons at points $x_2$ and $x_3$, the probability of passing the items would be higher than for persons at $x_1$.

In Chap. 2 it was said that the model which is used most frequently in the actual development of tests, the linear model, makes no assumption about the specific mathematical form of the item trace line, but rather only assumes that the items are monotonically increasing. (On nonability tests, such as measures of attitudes, this would be the case after negatively worded items were reversed in terms of scoring.) In the linear, or summative, model a total score consists of number of responses indicative of high rather than low score with respect to a noncognitive attribute, such as positiveness of attitude toward abortion. Psychometric theories relating to item-characteristic curves (ICC theory) do make explicit assumptions about the mathematical form of item trace lines. The most common assumption has been that the curves are normal ogive in form. The normal ogive is simply another word for the cumulative normal distribution. In Chap. 2 it was said that it makes sense to hypothesize this form of curve for a trace line because so many types of judgments in psychophysics tend to obey this function. One could see why curves like those shown in Fig. 9-2 would make sense with vocabulary items. An example would be asking persons the meaning of the word *severe*. For people at a very low level in this attribute, there would be a near zero probability of correctly defining the word. In contrast, for people at a high level of ability in vocabulary, there would be a very high probability of defining the word correctly. One would expect the curve to be rather steep near the point on the attribute continuum where people had a 50-50 chance of correctly defining the word. At least slightly S-shaped curves would be expected with many types of items on ability tests and personality tests. In considering the shapes of item-characteristic curves, an important point is that every item in a long test need not have exactly the prescribed mathematical form, whether the form is hypothesized to be a normal-ogive or a similar form, but rather each item tends to have the hypothesized shape. Because it is more convenient to work with mathematically, it frequently is assumed that items form a logistic curve rather than a normal-ogive curve. The two curves are almost identical in appearance (see discussion in Lord and Novick 1968).

**Properties of item curves** Even if all the items tend to form normal-ogive relationships or some other type of curve, as can be seen in Fig. 9-2, the items differ in a number of important ways. First, the items differ in terms of *difficulty* (*d*), which concerns how far to the left or right the whole curve for an item is displaced on the attribute. *Difficulty* usually is defined as the point on the attribute where the curve crosses the .5 *p* value line shown in Fig. 9-2. Thus, the difficulty levels are higher for items 2 and 3 than for item 1, and the difficulty levels for items 2 and 3 are identical. In ICC theory, difficulty level is analogous to the *p* value of items in the summative model. With the curves shown in Fig. 9-2, however, *p* value refers to the probability that all persons at a particular point on the latent attribute will respond in manner alpha (e.g., will pass) to an item rather than the probability that *all* persons in the study will respond in manner alpha. Thinking about this, the reader will see that the two statistics are analogous.

The second feature of item-characteristic curves as illustrated in Fig. 9-2 is the steepness or *discriminability* (*r*) of the item. Thus, in Fig. 9-2, items 1 and 2 are equally steep even though they vary in difficulty, but item 3 is noticeably flatter than items 1 and 2. The higher the value of *r*, the more sharply the item discriminates among people on the latent attribute who are in a zone corresponding to a .5 *p* value. If it can be assumed that the latent attribute is normally distributed, then there is a direct relationship between the steepness of the curve (discriminability) and the biserial correlation of the item with the latent trait, which is why the symbol *r* is used for discriminability. Note that with items of the normal-ogive form, curves are always steepest at a point corresponding to a *p* value of .5, which is a matter that will be discussed subsequently.

A third property of item-characteristic curves (not shown in Fig. 9-2) is that of the probability of getting a correct response by chance—guessing on a multiple-choice test. For example, if there were five alternative answers for each of the items illustrated in Fig. 9-2, all three of the curves would flatten out at a *p* value of .20 regardless of their other characteristics. This property will be denoted *g*, for guessing. The chance probability *g* has posed a severe problem for ICC theory, one which has proved to be very difficult to handle in the numerous mathematical models. One of the difficulties in understanding material written on ICC theory is that authors differ in symbols that they employ for the various characteristics of curves, and usually the system of symbols bears no helpful relationship to the characteristics being symbolized. Worse, many authors almost exhaust the Greek alphabet to further confuse readers in this regard. Here has been adopted a simple set of alphabetical letters that are meaningfully related to the things being symbolized.

**Uses of ICC theory**   Whereas ICC theory provides a useful way of thinking about relationships between items and hypothetical traits, and the indices of *d*, *r*, and *g* are informative, it would not be worthwhile to consider the theory in detail if that was all that was provided. ICC theory is useful because it leads to numerous mathematical models for actually estimating latent attributes. Thus, if any score on the attribute is *a*, then various mathematical models allow one to estimate the score *a'* statistically by combining information from the hypothetical curves. If one can assume that the individual item-characteristic curves are normal ogives (and that other assumptions hold which will be discussed subsequently), then one can mathematically combine these ogives to best estimate $a$ by $a'$. This requires a statistical approach, and a variety of competing approaches are available. In addition, numerous auxiliary statistics can be obtained from these mathematical models. One of the most useful is the precision of discriminating at any point on the attribute, which is analogous to the reliability at any point on a test scored in terms of number of correct responses. Numerous other important psychometric deductions can be obtained from ICC theory that would not be possible to obtain from conventional test theory based on the summative model, at least not without the help of some auxiliary models.

A detailed discussion of ICC theory would be too specialized for this book. Also, an understanding of ICC theory in detail requires more mathematical background than is assumed for the average reader. However, because of the useful ideas that have been produced and the possibilities of developing tests for some special purposes which will be discussed later, the reader should be informed about the basic nature of ICC theory, the properties of the psychometric models, and the limitations for actual measurement of human attributes.

**Deductions from ICC theory** If for no other reason, ICC theory is useful because it has led to many mathematical deductions that can be tested with actual data obtained from the linear model or from other statistical methods rather than dealing with "ghostly," hypothetical latent traits. One such set of deductions was mentioned previously—that regarding the precision of measurement at any point on the latent-trait continuum. Because of the analogy between the latent trait and ability as manifested in number of correct responses on conventional tests, investigations can be made of conventional tests in terms of the principles derived from ICC theory. As a particular example, ICC theory leads to the deduction that, on a free-response test, the most discriminating item at any point on the attribute continuum is one with a $p$ value of .5. Thus, numerous other things being equal, the most reliable discrimination at a point would be with items with $p$ values close to .5 for people in a narrow zone on the attribute continuum corresponding to that $p$ value. Rather than resorting to mathematical deductions from ICC theory only, one can test this hypothesis directly with conventional measurement methods and actual data. There are many other interesting deductions from ICC theory that can be tested with actual data, and for this reason ICC theory has proved to be a valuable theoretical adjunct to psychometric theory in general.

**Construction of tests from ICC theory** It is in the actual construction of tests with ICC theory that matters become quite controversial and issues relating to practicability become very important. Some enthusiasts for ICC theory talk as though *all,* or at least most, important tests some day will be constructed on the basis of ICC theory rather than in terms of the linear model or other conventional approaches to test construction. Perhaps that is so, but, for reasons which will be described, that time certainly is not at hand.

Proponents of constructing tests in terms of ICC theory point to two cardinal limitations of conventional tests, as constructed in terms of the summative model. First, the method for selecting test items is dependent to some extent on the particular sample of subjects used for test construction. Because the method for constructing homogeneous tests described in Chap. 8 depends heavily on the correlation of individual items with total scores, that criticism is correct. If a sample of subjects is studied that is more or less diverse than the one employed in a particular item analysis, the item-total correlations will change. Thus, the particular statistics used for test construction are not *sample-free*, which has been used by enthusiasts for ICC theory as a criticism of conventional tests. However, on careful thought this is not really a severe criticism. Even though the item-total correlations would change in absolute size with different samples of subjects, the rank-order of item-total correlations would tend to remain the same. Thus what would appear to be a good item in terms of one sample would tend to give the appearance of being a good item in terms of another sample, even if these samples were somewhat different with respect to the attribute in question. However, such item-total correlations might be quite different if they were derived from subjects on one end of the trait continuum rather than a group of subjects at the other extreme.

Whereas the criticism that statistics employed in test construction are not sample-free usually is not a serious problem, a more telling criticism of conventional tests by proponents of ICC theory is that scores of people are not sample-free. Usually any interpretations of scores on conventional tests are made *normatively* with respect to the mean and standard deviation of the sample of subjects on which the test was standardized or with respect to the particular group of subjects in an experiment. Usually this is done with percentiles, standard scores, or a linear transformation of standard scores. This scoring of tests on a normative basis offers no problem if all new groups of subjects are tested with the *same* items that are employed in previous groups. In the use of conventional tests, it is assumed that the set of test items is fixed and that henceforth all subjects will be administered the same items, at least as regards use of that particular test to measure that particular attribute. For some special problems in testing, however, there are advantages in administering to different groups of subjects only some of the same items or even nonoverlapping sets of items in an effort to measure exactly the same attribute. This matter will be discussed more fully in the following section concerning tailored tests, but the possibility is mentioned here.

From ICC theory it is possible to estimate scores that people would make on items to which they do not respond from scores that they make on items to which they do respond. This is illustrated in Fig. 9-2. Suppose that a person is administered items 1 and 2 but not item 3. If one actually knew the three item-characteristic curves, obviously one could estimate the probability of passing item 3 from one's position on the attribute. For all persons at $x_2$, for example, it can be seen that the probability is .6 of passing item 3. For persons at point $x_3$, the probability of correctly responding to item 3 is approximately .86. Thus, if sufficient information can be obtained from a subset of a total collection of items, one can estimate scores on the underlying attribute. Then these scores, in turn, permit one to estimate scores on the attribute that would be obtained from the total collection of items. Theoretically, this can be done even with extreme groups on the attribute. As long as at least some of the subjects in the group pass the item and some of the subjects fail the item, theoretically there is a possibility of estimating the item-characteristic curves and in turn estimating abilities of subjects. (Keep in mind that the reasonableness of doing this depends on sets of assumptions that differ from model to model, and that to actually do this in practice might be highly unfeasible.) However, the need to administer the same items to all subjects, as is done in conventional testing, very seldom constitutes a serious practical problem. Rather, it constitutes a major problem only in employing tailored tests, which will be discussed subsequently.

**Problems with ICC theory** Whereas ICC theory has proved important for psychometric theory, it remains to be seen how important it will prove to be for psychometric practice. If there were no serious technical and practical problems involved, one wonders why ICC theory was not adopted long ago for the actual construction and scoring of tests. Lord (1952b) described numerous deductions from the normal-ogive model many years ago, and actually the basic ideas of ICC theory existed a long time before that. In spite of the intense activity among a relatively small group of superspecialists on the topic, one still finds almost no actual employment of ICC theory in developing practicable tests. Partly this may be because ICC theory is highly mathematical and thus difficult for many persons to understand. Partly, though, the paucity of "hardware" arising from ICC theory is inherent in the difficulties of the theory itself.

A potential fault of ICC theory in the eyes of some is that it is based on the ghostly concept of a latent attribute rather than on statistical analyses of actual data. To some extent the same criticism can be made of conventional test theory, which usually is accompanied by the theoretical notion of true scores underlying fallible scores. However, the logic of constructing conventional tests is much closer to the actual data than is the case with ICC theory. ICC theory leads to important psychometric deductions only if one is willing to make a variety of assumptions about the data and their relationship to the underlying trait. These assumptions tend to differ from model to model, and in many cases there is no way to know whether the assumptions are correct other than in terms of the reasonableness of the final products. Some of the assumptions made in some of the models are blatantly incorrect, such as assumptions that (1) all the items have the same discriminatory power, (2) only one factor is involved in the items, and (3) guessing has no influence on scores. What has been remarkable is that in some cases deductions from the models have fit actual data well in spite of the unreasonableness of the assumptions involved in the version of ICC theory; but in other cases, the fit has been poor (see discussion in Weiss 1976).

One of the reasons why various forms of ICC theory are still of unknown general merit is that they have been tried out only on several very simple types of abilities, mainly those represented by vocabulary items and mathematical items of the type encountered on college entrance examinations. Almost nothing has been done with a wider range of abilities (e.g., items relating to reasoning) or with respect to noncognitive functions concerning personality, attitudes, values, interests, etc. Whereas the assumption in ICC theory that collections of items mainly concern one factor is relatively safe with the simple tests of vocabulary and mathematics that have been investigated extensively to date, this assumption is not at all safe with many other collections of items that might be studied.

Even if there were no theoretical problems with employing ICC theory to actually construct tests, most investigators would be discouraged by the practical problems involved for what usually proves to be very little gain in terms of the quality of the eventual test. If, as is usually the case, the same set of test items is administered to all examinees, scores obtained from a test constructed and scored by ICC theory usually correlate very highly with those obtained from the much simpler approaches to constructing homogeneous tests discussed in Chap. 8. Frequently these correlations are in the high .90s. In some instances the two types of scorings of the items have proved to be slightly nonlinear, particularly at the extremes. Any difference between the two types of scoring, however, frequently comes at the very heavy expense of the assumptions, complexities, and practical disadvantages of working with a test developed by ICC theory.

For the foregoing reasons, conventional tests, as discussed in Chap. 8, have continued to dominate the scene even though ICC theory provides some very important perspectives on psychometric theory concerning human traits and their measurement. Perhaps eventually ICC theory will lead to many practical applications, but that time is not yet in sight. In addition to the important theoretical advantages that ICC theory offers to specialists in psychometrics, the theory mainly has practical implications for tailored tests which will be discussed subsequently.

A final point of criticism concerns not so much ICC theory itself as the overall conceptual framework in which it has been developed. In spite of the large literature on the topic, there is almost no mention of the *purpose* for which tests would be constructed in general or in particular instances. When validity is discussed, typically no mention is made of either content validity or construct validity; and although the authors do not make it clear, from discussions of validity the impression is given that only predictive validity is important. This is suggested also by the types of items which have been investigated most extensively in ICC theory—vocabulary and mathematical items that either came from predictor tests for college aptitude or were of a kind usually employed for that purpose. Pains have been taken in numerous places in this book to argue that the most important thing to consider about any test is the purpose, namely, the type of validity that is necessary. This also was evidenced in Chap. 8 and in the early sections of this chapter, which have discussed broad categories of validity and validity for particular purposes, e.g., for measuring effects of experimental treatments. The author maintains that issues regarding validity should be settled first; then test construction methods for particular circumstances should follow as a logical consequence.

## TAILORED TESTS

Mention was made previously of giving individuals "a test" in which not all subjects would be administered all the same items. Of course, this does not occur with conventional tests. For example, if the test consists of 80 multiple-choice items concerning vocabulary items, all subjects are administered all items. For reasons which will be discussed in detail in Chap. 16, it is recommended that all subjects *attempt* all items even if they feel that they are only guessing in some instances.

For practical reasons one could argue that time and effort could be saved by a flexible procedure in which subjects would not all be administered the same items but rather would be administered a subset of the total available items that was particularly tailored to their level of ability or other type of latent trait involved. An introduction to the topic and literature related to tailored testing can be obtained from Lord (1974) and Weiss (1976). The topic is discussed also in some of the other citations in the Suggested Additional Readings. An example will show the underlying logic for tailored testing. Suppose that, by one method or another, it is known in advance that one person has relatively low ability and another person relatively high ability in vocabulary. Then one could argue that it is a waste of time to give a whole general-purpose test to these two individuals. Rather, one should give rather easy items to the first person and rather difficult items to the second person. As mentioned previously, from ICC theory and from other theoretical points of view, the most discriminating free-response items would be ones that had $p$ values of .5 for all persons at the particular trait level. Required to take the whole test, the person with low ability in vocabulary simply would be presented with many items that he or she would not get correct; and if the person with high ability were administered all items, he or she would be presented with many items that were trivially easy. One could further argue that not only does this represent a waste of time and effort, but employing the whole test would not serve to concentrate the reliability at the point at which it was most needed for each of the individuals. For the sake of economy, of time and effort on the part of the subject, and for ensuring precision of measurement, a case can be made for tailoring tests with respect either to prior information that is available about subjects or, more importantly, to information that is obtained early in the sequence in which items are presented to the subject.

**Methods for constructing tailored tests** The development of approaches to tailored testing has become a "hot" item among psychometric specialists during recent years. There has been a flood of experimentation and literature on the topic (for example, the extensive series of investigations summarized by Weiss 1976).

The development of tailored tests has been closely wedded to ICC theory, because that theory is needed to suggest effective methods of item presentation and to provide individuals with scores that estimate their position on the latent trait. Regarding the latter consideration, obviously one cannot score tailored tests in terms of number of correct responses because subjects are responding to different items. In the example given previously of two persons being given items at two levels of difficulty in a vocabulary test, they might get exactly the same number of items correct—one person 20 easy items, and the other person 20 difficult items. Regarding the former consideration, where does one start in "probing" to adjust the difficulty level of the tailored test in such a way as to be most appropriate for each examinee?

One approach to tailored testing is really a rather old idea. It consists of testing in stages. First the individual is given a relatively brief general-purpose test. On the basis of obtained scores, subjects are divided into a high group, a low group, and an in-between group; the majority of the subjects fall into an in-between group. Then the three groups are given three different types of tests in the second stage. The majority of the students who fell in the middle of the distribution are given a general-purpose test constructed by the methods discussed in Chap. 8 for the development of homogeneous tests. It will be remembered, however, that this approach tends to slight subjects on both extremes of the distribution in terms of reliability of measurement. A two-stage testing approach could help counteract this problem. The two groups who were extreme on the first-stage test could be given tests of appropriate difficulty for their indicated general levels of ability. Assuming that one could devise a sensible scoring procedure whereby all subjects could be compared with one another, this would tend to accomplish one of the goals of tailored testing, namely, maintaining precision of discrimination at different levels of estimating the trait. This would approximate what would be obtained from the type of equidiscriminating test discussed in Chap. 8. However, such a two-stage approach to testing might result in the subjects spending more rather than less total time in testing, and more rather than fewer items might be administered than on a relatively long general-purpose test administered initially.

Most approaches to tailored testing do not employ fixed tests, either one-stage or two-stage tests. Rather they have available a rather large item pool, from which items are presented serially to each subject by a strategy that moves as rapidly as possible toward items that are particularly suited to the subject's estimated position on the latent attribute. To do this requires a strategy for presenting the items (and there are numerous competing ones) and rather elaborate computer facilities. The computer facilities are needed for the very complex decision processes required to determine the particular order of presenting items to each subject. Typically, the items are presented on the equivalent of a television screen, and the subject pushes buttons to indicate responses. Depending upon the response to each item, the computer program (designed to implement a particular strategy) selects the next item, and so on, until some optimum state of affairs exists with respect to estimating the subject's score on the latent trait.

Although only moderate-sized item pools (e.g., about 80) are necessary for some of the experimental work with tailored tests, actual applied work with tailored tests would require that hundreds of items would be stored in the computer, which would require a rather mammoth job of item writing. It goes without saying that the items should range very broadly in terms of difficulty, $p$ value—the ideal being a rectangular distribution of $p$ values for a representative sample of subjects with whom the tailored test eventually will be used. Obviously, accurate information about this and other aspects of the item pool would be dependable only if large numbers of subjects were tested prior to the development of tailored testing strategies.

Numerous strategies and combinations of strategies have been developed for tailored testing. Findings with respect to the most promising of these are summarized by Weiss (1976). One of the simplest strategies will be discussed to give the reader a concrete idea of how one might proceed. The method is referred to as the "up-and-down" procedure or the staircase procedure. When the subjects sit facing the viewing screen of a computer console, they are automatically presented an item with a $p$ value of .5. If they answer the first item correctly, the computer selects a slightly more difficult item and displays it on the screen. If they answer the first question incorrectly, the computer selects a slightly easier item and displays it on the screen. If the people who were given a more difficult item on the second trial get that item correct, then on the third trial they are given a slightly more difficult item; but if they fail the second item, they are given an item that has a $p$ value between that of the first item and that of the second item administered. A similar strategy is employed in selecting a third item for the people who fail the first item. By continuing up and down in this way, the automated routine obtains a level of item difficulty where the subjects are responding correctly very close to 50 percent of the time. The same is done for all subjects.

This up-and-down strategy typifies all the more elaborate strategies that have been developed. Thus, rather than continue the up-and-down process on later trials, one can use the results obtained from earlier trials to estimate the latent-trait level of the subject and thus skip ahead to a level that probably is particularly relevant to the individual. For example, if from the earlier items it is estimated that the individual has a very high ability, the up-and-down strategy could be augmented by jumping ahead to a rather grossly different level of difficulty. There are many refinements and combinations of strategies, all of which consist of a hunt-and-search probing technique to find an appropriate level of difficulty for precisely documenting the position of the individual on the hypothetical latent trait.

**Perspectives on tailored tests** It is obvious that the art of tailored testing is in a highly experimental phase, and it may be quite some time before sufficient theoretical and empirical work is completed that will indicate which, if any, of the approaches actually leads to viable methods of psychological measurement. Because the development of tailored tests depends so heavily on ICC theory, all the problems inherent in employing that theory are encountered also with tailored tests; and tailored tests have some special problems of their own. The major advantage that can be claimed for tailored tests is that *potentially* such tests could produce highly reliable discriminations all along the test continuum with fewer items than general-purpose homogeneous tests or equidiscriminating tests (described in Chap. 8). However, the specific methods obviously have not been developed. The different strategies for selecting items sometimes lead to rather different results, and in numerous cases the results are demonstrably erroneous. Even such a crucial issue as how to score the test is still very much in doubt (see the discussion in Weiss 1976). Even if the potential advantages are obtained, they will come at quite a price. Operational tests probably would have to employ at least several hundred test items to be stored in a computer. The test would need to be constructed and calibrated by specialists in tailored testing. The test would have to be administered, scored, and analyzed by computers. There are not likely to be many situations in which such expertise and computer hardware will be available for routine testing. Although one can think of some special circumstances in which testing time is so precious that it is extremely important to wring the last possible ounce of reliable discrimination out of the smallest possible number of items, such circumstances are uncommon. For these reasons, it will be interesting to see in the years ahead to what extent practicable tailored tests are actually developed and employed widely.

## SUGGESTED ADDITIONAL READINGS

Glaser, R., and Nitko, A. J. Measurement in learning and instruction. In R. L. Thorndike (ed.), *Educational measurement* (2d ed.). Washington, D.C.: American Council on Education, 1971.

Henryssen, S. Gathering, analyzing, and using data on test items. In R. L. Thorndike (ed.), *Educational measurement* (2d ed.). Washington, D.C.: American Council on Education, 1971.

Lord, F. M. Individualized testing and item characteristic curve theory. In D. H. Krantz, R. C. Atkinson, R. D. Luce, and P. Suppes (eds.), *Contemporary developments in mathematical psychology.* Vol. 2: *Measurement, psychophysics, and neural information processing.* San Francisco: W. H. Freeman, 1974.

Nunnally, J. C. Vanishing individual differences—Just stick your head in the sand, and they will go away. *Journal of Instructional Psychology,* 1976, *3*, 28–40.

Weiss, D. J. (ed.). *Computerized adaptive trait measurement: Problems and prospects.* Minneapolis: Department of Psychology, University of Minnesota, November 1975.

Weiss, D. J. *Final report: Computerized ability testing, 1972–1975.* Minneapolis: Department of Psychology, University of Minnesota, April 1976.

Wright, B. D., and Douglas, G. A. Best test design and self-tailored testing. *Research Memo No. 19.* Chicago: Statistical Laboratory, Department of Education, University of Chicago, 1975.

## MULTIVARIATE ANALYSIS

# FUNDAMENTALS OF FACTOR ANALYSIS

Factor analysis is not *one*, simple, statistical method that can quickly be described as a whole and exemplified with one or several equations, with the matter then settled. Rather, the term *factor analysis* stands for a broad category of approaches to conceptualizing groupings (or clusterings) of variables and an even broader collection of mathematical procedures for determining which variables belong to which groups. As an example, a theory of personality leads an investigator to the conclusion that there are two major types of individual differences in anxiety—anxiety concerning physical harm and anxiety concerning social embarrassment. The investigator either finds in the literature or constructs for this purpose two sets of four tests to measure different aspects of these two types of anxiety. The tests in each group would not be duplicates of one another in the sense that they would be alternative forms for the same test, but rather they would be meant to share a common core and concern different-appearing item content. In essence, the investigator has conceptualized the problem in terms of factor analysis. Subsequently, mathematical and statistical procedures can be employed to test the adequacy of the hypothesis. The hypothesis would receive substantial support if (1) the four tests supposedly concerning bodily harm correlated substantially with one another, (2) the four tests supposedly concerning social embarrassment correlated substantially with one another, and (3) the average correlation *between* tests in the two groups was low. Essentially, then, the investigator has hypothesized two factors in relation to anxiety, and the hypothesis would be borne out by the mathematical procedures of factor analysis.

Another example of conceiving the problem of grouping variables as one in factor analysis would be studying factors of human reasoning abilities. In this case let us say that the investigator does not have strong hypotheses about the numbers and kinds of major factors that underlie tests of reasoning ability; the investigator rather has only hunches in this regard. Consequently, rather than explicitly test hypotheses, as in the example of anxiety factors, the investigator conceptualizes the problem as one of discovering factors by mathematical procedures of factor analysis. Subsequently, many tests are collected from the literature that supposedly concern various types of reasoning; then the investigator constructs numerous other tests, all this being guided by the hunches regarding tests that might be important with respect to underlying groups (clusters or factors) concerning human reasoning. Then methods of factor analysis are applied which essentially speak for themselves in helping the investigator to explore statistically the number and kinds of factors underlying the particular tests. Whether the stage of conceptualization concerns explicit hypotheses, half-formed hypotheses, good hunches, or simply a broad search, factor analysis involves conceptualizing variables as relating to underlying factors and performing analyses that will test for or discover such factors.

Factor analysis is a very broad topic in terms of both the number of particular mathematical methods that are available and the amount of existing literature. Hundreds of articles are written in professional journals on one aspect or another of factor analysis. Since its inception, the journal *Psychometrika* has devoted more pages to factor analysis than to any other quantitative topic in the behavioral sciences. Articles on various aspects of factor analysis consume sizable amounts of space in numerous journals in education, psychology, and other behavioral sciences. One or more chapters on factor analysis appear in numerous books broadly concerned with quantitative methods in the behavioral sciences. The four most recent comprehensive texts on factor analysis are given in the Suggested Additional Readings. The reader who wants to follow up methods that are mentioned but not described in detail in this and the following chapter will find them adequately discussed either in those readings or in specific references that will be given to proper sources. In particular the individual who wants to learn more about factor analysis in general should read the comprehensive text by Gorsuch (1974).

Although they are usually wedded in practice, it is important to maintain the distinction between factor analysis as a set of concepts and factor analysis as a set of mathematical procedures. In some cases, theories of human ability and personality characteristics are related to concepts of factor analysis without explicitly employing the related mathematical techniques. For example, some batteries of aptitude tests are constructed to measure a number of underlying factors, but the tests are not actually developed mathematically from factor analysis. On the other hand, sometimes the mathematical techniques are applied willy-nilly without actually considering the conceptual model for performing such analyses. This is the case, for example, when an individual takes a miscellaneous collection of tests that concern theoretically unrelated variables and forces them through an arbitrary, meat-grinder, computerized approach to finding factors. In the better factor analysis investigations, the conceptual models and the mathematical models are both carefully thought out and interwoven. How this is done will be discussed at numerous points in this chapter and in Chap. 11.

Factor analysis is a natural outgrowth of all topics that have been discussed so far in this book. As examples, previous chapters have concerned the basic logic of measuring individual variables, statistical characteristics of individual variables, reliability and validity of individual variables, and statistical relations among variables in the correlation of sums, in multiple correlation, and in other multivariate measures of relationship. The two previous chapters have discussed methods for constructing individual tests. Of course, from the standpoint of both common sense and the many things that have been said so far in this book, ultimately psychometrics is concerned not only with such individual variables, but with the way that they relate to one another. As a simple example, in multiple correlation, the interest usually is in the extent to which a group of predictor variables is related to a criterion variable. As was illustrated above, factor analysis also is intimately concerned with the relationships among variables.

A very important way in which factor analysis concerns relationships among variables is in the explication of constructs. As was said in Chap. 3, one of the major aspects of the explication of constructs is in determining to what extent hypothesized measures of a construct measure the same thing or break up into clusters of variables that measure different things. In Chap. 3 it was also said that the explication of constructs requires studying the statistical structure not only among variables that measure a construct but between sets of variables that measure different constructs. Obviously, then, the conceptual problem concerns possible different groupings of variables intended to measure each construct and possible correlations between such groupings relating to different constructs. There are other aspects of construct validity which were mentioned in Chap. 3, such as performing experiments to determine whether supposed measures of a construct fit predictions from a well-accepted theory. But the clustering of variables as done in factor analysis constitutes a very important aspect of construct validation. This is particularly true if the construct concerns measures of individual differences (e.g., intelligence, reasoning ability, anxiety, or attitudes toward abortion) rather than measures of the results of experiments (e.g., learning rate, perceptual accuracy, or amount of activity in rats). As was said in Chap. 9, it is not necessary to find large, reliable individual differences in the measures employed as dependent variables for experiments. Consequently, factor analyses of individual differences in that regard might not be very important for explicating a construct relating to such dependent variables. However, as also was mentioned in Chap. 9, one usually does find large, reliable individual differences in measures employed in experiments; and if that is the case, factor analysis of different supposed measures of a construct would provide important information about construct validity.

In applied work with tests, usually one is also interested in underlying groupings of variables rather than individual variables. As one example, in the use of achievement tests for the elementary school grades, the subtests of a battery are given names such as reading comprehension, mathematical skills, language usage, and others. The use of such names implies a generality of individual differences beyond the specific tests employed in the particular battery. Thus, if an individual rightfully can employ the name *reading comprehension*, then the test in his or her battery should correlate substantially with tests given the same or similar names in other batteries. In other words, various tests purported to measure the same thing should constitute a factor and be evidenced in actual factor analysis investigations. Another example is in applied programs of personnel selection and classification. There is, for example, a well-documented factor of *perceptual speed* which tends to be present in any task requiring the rapid recognition of similarities and differences in visual patterns. Tests relating to this factor are useful in programs of personnel selection, e.g., for the selection of filing clerks. Different tests purported to measure this ability frequently have different-appearing items, but they all correlate substantially with one another. Consequently, research results obtained with one of these measures tend to be general to the other measures. Thus, the various purported measures of perceptual speed tend to form a factor of human ability, which has been found in numerous factor analysis investigations to date.

It should be obvious that factor analysis concepts and methods of analysis are intimately related to *scientific generalization.* Hypotheses about factors concern statements regarding the extent to which one can generalize results across variables (e.g., typical mental tests) that are given the same name. Such hypotheses require confirmation from factor analysis. When no definite hypotheses are available at the start of the experiment and the analyses are mainly exploratory, the results suggest groups of variables across which one can generalize and which can be given the same name. In either case, obviously factor analysis is intimately related to issues concerning scientific generalization.

Properly considered, factor analysis is only a prelude to more extensive investigations of constructs. Factor analysis is useful only to the extent that it aids in the development of principles of human behavior, and the best methods of analysis are those that aid most in the search. Because of the opportunities for developing elegant, highly complex methods related to factor analysis, there has been a tendency to overdo the mathematical requirements of factor analysis and underdo the requirements of factor analysis for empirical research. This is a bad case of the "tail wagging the dog." In judging the usefulness of a particular method of analysis, the experimenter should ask, "How much will this help in my program of research?" Looking at it in this way, one will see that many of the mathematical issues in the literature on factor analysis concern inconsequential problems for empirical research and that some of the most important problems for empirical research frequently are subverted by unnecessarily complex mathematical developments. In some cases very complex mathematical methods actually are required for the scientific problem at hand. But in many other cases much simpler approaches are not only more practicable but also more commensurate with the strategies of empirical research. As will be seen in the pages ahead, the basic ideas and principles underlying factor analysis are easy to understand. When particular problems are encountered that require specialized mathematical methods, the reader will have to do what even most specialists in psychometrics have to do—go to the detailed accounts in the Suggested Additional Readings or other referenced sources.

## SOME IMPORTANT DISTINCTIONS

In learning about and employing factor analysis, it is very important to recall the meanings of some key terms and watch carefully how such terms are used in the literature. A slight change in terminology may make a very large difference in what the author is discussing. Also, there are many inconsistencies in the literature regarding the use of these terms. In particular, in the journals in the behavioral sciences often editors permit authors either to employ terms loosely or not to employ terms that correctly specify the procedures of factor analysis. Some of the most important distinctions are as follows.

**Exploratory and confirmatory analysis** As illustrated previously, the conceptual basis for a factor analysis may be a set of hypotheses held by the investigator, such as those illustrated for two factors of anxiety. In this case, it is said that one performs hypothesis-testing, or *confirmatory*, factor analysis (this latter term is employed more frequently). In contrast, the method of analysis might be guided by hunches or simply an open question about the number and kinds of factors which might be derivable from a collection of variables. This was illustrated in the study of factors underlying a broad collection of tests concerning reasoning. In this case, it is said that the problem concerns *exploratory* factor analysis. Of course, as one would expect, most investigations constitute a mixture of these two antipodes. Seldom does an investigator perform a factor analysis of a nearly random collection of tests. Usually, at least the investigator has some strong hunches about some of, if not all, the underlying factors. At the other extreme, seldom does the investigator have such firm initial hypotheses that surprises fail to come from the analysis. However, it is important to keep in mind the extremes of this continuum of confirmatory versus exploratory analysis. First, highly exploratory analyses should be undertaken with caution, which is a matter that will be discussed subsequently. Second, even though many methods of analysis can be employed in the same or a modified version in both exploratory and confirmatory analysis, some methods are distinctly different for the two approaches.

**Component factors and common factors** We will find it necessary to make a distinction between common factors and component factors even though (1) the terms are not precisely defined in the literature, (2) they hide an important distinction that we will need to make later, and (3) they are given somewhat different meanings by different authors. Some writers simply speak of one term as constituting *components* and the other as constituting *factors*, but the author thinks that this is a misleading, partisan effort to demean component factors as though they were not legitimate factors. As the terms are commonly employed, in essence component factors are *real* factors, in the sense that they can be directly derived from the data in a particular study. In contrast, as the term *common factors* is employed (and it is employed with various meanings by different authors), basically it pertains to *hypothetical factors*, in the sense that the factors can be only *estimated* from the actual data at hand. These matters will be discussed in detail throughout this and the subsequent chapter; however, as a prelude to that discussion, a number of points should be kept in mind. Components analysis is conceptually simple and straightforward mathematically. There are only several highly desirable mathematical solutions, and these solutions are very practicable. In contrast, there is a multitude of hypothesized solutions for common factors, journals are filled with controversies about the most appropriate approaches, no one is even sure how to define common factors, some of the mathematical approaches are extremely difficult to understand and compute, and there are other unpleasant prospects in wandering into the domain of common factors.

From what was said previously, one could conclude that everything is in favor of component-factor analysis and everything is against common-factor analysis (which is not a bad argument). However, component-factor analysis has a cardinal fault in some types of factor analysis studies (which will be specified in detail later). In spite of all the annoying problems and perplexities involved, there is a conceptual elegance behind the notion of common factors which tends to lure psychometricians. If the concept of common factors had never been developed or the reader of this book had never heard about it, probably the reader could work successfully in all the research with components analysis and never suffer any adverse consequences—*if* the reader looked carefully at several places where components analysis can produce misleading results. As will be discussed in detail, the results from applying components analysis and common-factor analysis usually lead one to approximately the same conclusions about the number and kinds of underlying groups of variables in a problem.

As will be seen in Chap. 11, the supposed distinction between component factors and common factors is further complicated by the fact that there is a middle ground of methods that partakes of both approaches. That is, there are methods of obtaining common factors which are *real* factors, in the sense that they can be actually derived from the data at hand rather than only estimated. These approaches are usually referred to as *image analysis*.

It should be made very clear to the reader that the remainder of this chapter will be concerned with components analysis (with one exception, which will be noted later) and that methods concerning hypothetical common factors and real common factors will be discussed in Chap. 11. In studying the material in this chapter, however, the reader should understand that the principles which will be discussed are general to all forms of factor analysis and that common hypothetical factors represent only modifications of the basic ideas and mathematical models for component factors.

**Other important distinctions** As will be discussed subsequently, it is necessary to keep a careful eye out for other differences among terms used in discussing factor analysis. For example, whether a table is labeled "factor structure" or "factor pattern" is very important. And it makes a great deal of difference when, in speaking of a "factor," a person is referring to the scores of people on the factor or the correlations of tests with the factor. Efforts will be made to sharply distinguish among these and other important terms in factor analysis. It is hoped that succeeding generations of behavioral scientists do a much better job than present professionals in discussing the theory and results of factor analysis.

## MATHEMATICAL BASIS

Component-factor analysis concerns a rectangular matrix (table) of data such as that illustrated in Table 10-1. A data matrix (or *score matrix,* as it frequently is named) will be symbolized as $S$. The matrix contains the scores of $N$ persons on $k$ measures. Thus $a_1$ is the score of person 1 on measure $a$, $a_2$ is the score of person 2 on measure $a$, and $k_N$ is the score of person $N$ on measure $k$. It is assumed that scores on each measure are standardized. Then the sum of scores in any column of the table is zero, and the variance of scores in any column is 1.0.

The term *measures* is used in a very general sense to refer to any set of attributes that can be quantified. The measures might be printed tests, scores in different types of learning tasks, physiological variables, or items of personal history. The term *persons* is used in an even more general sense to refer to any class of objects on which measurements are made. The problem is the same whether the measurements are made on people, insects, vegetables, countries, rocks, or rivers. For example, the objects could concern the 50 states, and the measures could be such as area, average rainfall, population, average annual income, and numerous other variables which potentially are important in distin-

**Table 10-1  Data matrix**

|  | | *a* | *b* | *c* | $\cdots$ | *k* |
|---|---|---|---|---|---|---|
| | | | *Measures* | | | |
| | | | *(Variables)* | | | |
| | *1* | $a_1$ | $b_1$ | $c_1$ | $\cdots$ | $k_1$ |
| | *2* | $a_2$ | $b_2$ | $c_2$ | $\cdots$ | $k_2$ |
| | *3* | $a_3$ | $b_3$ | $c_3$ | $\cdots$ | $k_3$ |
| | *4* | $a_4$ | $b_4$ | $c_4$ | $\cdots$ | $k_4$ |
| *Persons* | . | . | . | . | $\cdots$ | . |
| *(Objects)* | . | . | . | . | $\cdots$ | . |
| | . | | | | $\cdots$ | |
| | *N* | $a_N$ | $b_N$ | $c_N$ | $\cdots$ | $k_N$ |

guishing among the states. Actually, this would represent a very interesting problem in factor analysis, in which one would investigate, say, the factors among measures of 20 variables relating to the 50 states (objects, as depicted in Table 10-1). The only essential is that there be a score for each object on each measure. In practice, the data matrix is much taller than it is wide, because to keep from taking advantage of chance in the factor analysis of measures, it is necessary to have many more persons (or objects) than measures.

**Factors** Any linear combination of the variables in a data matrix is said to be a *factor* of that matrix. That is all there is to it. Any linear combination $A$ would be as follows:

$$A = w_a a + w_b b + w_c c + \cdots + w_k k \tag{10-1}$$

If, for example, the weight for variable $a$ ($w_a$) is .8, the score for each person on measure $a$ is multiplied by .8. The weights can be either all the same or different. Some can be positive, and some can be negative. Different methods for deriving component factors are defined in terms of the *ways that weights are used for obtaining linear combinations*. Any consistent method, whether it makes sense or nonsense, for determining such weights is the basis for a particular type of component factor analysis. For example, as will be made clearer in a later section, the centroid method requires that all weights be either $+1$ or $-1$.

It must be kept in mind that any component factor is a real, observable set of scores; i.e., each person has a score on the factor. Thus one obtains the score for person 1 on factor $A$ by combining that person's scores on measures $a$ through $k$. The same weights are used for all persons; but since people will tend to have different scores on the various measures, they also will tend to have different scores on the factor. It is useful to express factor scores in standard form. This is done either in the course of the analysis itself or after the weights are applied.

Although conceivably factor analysis could employ nonlinear combinations of variables, nearly all existing methods are based on linear combinations. A nonlinear combination would be involved if, for example, one of the terms in the combination were $w_{ab}ab$, which would be the weighted product of variables $a$ and $b$. When the basic data of psychology merit such complex methods of analysis, nonlinear methods of factor analysis may be employed more frequently. It is possible to develop such nonlinear methods of factor analysis as extensions of presently available linear methods, but for the time being the linear methods are sufficient for nearly all problems that are encountered in research.

**Factor correlations** After a factor is obtained, scores on the component factor can be correlated (PM formula) with scores on each of the individual variables in the data matrix. Since the factor is a column of numbers, that column of numbers can be directly correlated with any column of numbers in the data matrix. Such correlations usually are spoken of as *factor loadings*. In this book factor loadings will always refer to factor-variable correlations. (The reader should keep in mind that, in this discussion and throughout the chapter, we are talking about component factors and not hypothetical common factors.) Depending on the nature of the variables and the method of factor analysis employed, some of the correlations might be high and others low, and some might be positive and others negative. It is important to make a very clear distinction between factor scores and factor loadings. The former are the actual scores of people obtained from a linear combination of variables; the latter are the correlations of the variables with factor scores.

**Successive factoring** In most problems, it is important to go beyond one factor and see what, if any, other factors are involved in the data matrix. The number of factors to be obtained is suggested by the first set of factor loadings. If these are very high, it suggests that only one factor is needed. If they are near zero, it suggests that there are no common factors. If they are moderately high (e.g., around .60), more factors may be needed.

Basic to obtaining factors after the first one is the concept of partialing, as it has been examined in detail in previous chapters. The way to obtain a second factor $B$ is as follows. Partial factor $A$ from each of the variables. For partialing factor $A$ from variable $a$, the loading of $a$ on $A(r_{aA})$ is multiplied by each standard score on $A$. This is subtracted from each score on $a$. When $A$ is partialed from $b$, $r_{bA}$ is used to perform the operation. It would then require $k$ different formulas to transform the original variables to partialed variables. The partialed matrix of data will be symbolized as $S_1$ to indicate that one factor has been removed. All variables in $S_1$ are converted to standard scores to facilitate subsequent analyses.

By definition, $A$ correlates precisely zero with each variable in $S_1$. What is not immediately apparent is that it necessarily follows that $A$ will correlate precisely zero with any linear combination of the variables in $S_1$. Then, no matter what linear combination of the variables in $S_1$ is used to obtain a second factor $B$, $r_{AB}$ must be precisely zero. This fact provides the basis for obtaining a set of uncorrelated (orthogonal) factors.

Factor $B$ can be obtained by any linear combination of the variables (partialed variables) in $S_1$. (This is not to imply that some types of linear combinations are not better than others, a matter which will be discussed in detail later in the chapter.) For convenience, $B$ would be placed in standard form. How, then, would one obtain loadings on factor $B$? Here it is easy to make a mistake by assuming that the loadings would be obtained by correlating the partialed variables in $S_1$ with $B$. What is done instead is to correlate the original variables (in $S$) with $B$. This is done because the effort is to "take apart" the original variables in terms of a number of uncorrelated linear combinations or factors. The matrix $S_1$ is important only as a way of obtaining $B$.

After obtaining factors $A$ and $B$, one can then go on to obtain additional factors by the same iterative approach. With second-order partial correlations, $A$ and $B$ could be simultaneously partialed from $S$. An easier way to arrive at the same result is to partial $B$ from $S_1$. This results in $S_2$, and any linear combination of the twice-partialed variables in $S_2$ would produce another factor; that factor necessarily would be uncorrelated with the first two factors. Mathematically, the only general limit on the number of factors obtained in that way is the number of variables. If, for example, there are 20 measures, all scores in $S_{20}$ will be zero. If some smaller number $k$ of factors will explain all the original variance, then all the scores in $S_k$ will be zero. The hope is to find a relatively small number of linear combinations of factors that will explain the relationships among variables. For example, it would be desirable to find that about four factors did a good job of explaining relationships among 20 tests. In exploratory factor analysis, this results in scientific parsimony, because it is much easier to deal conceptually and mathematically with four factors than with 20 individual tests.

**The matrix of factor loadings** A matrix of factor loadings is shown in Table 10-2. Variables $a$, $b$, and $c$ tend to have substantial loadings only on factor $A$; $d$, $e$, and $f$ have substantial loadings only on factor $B$; and $g$, $h$, and $i$ have substantial loadings only on factor $C$. There are some principles concerning the properties of matrices of factor loadings which form the basis for interpreting results. The square of any factor loading tells the proportion of variance explained in a particular variable by a factor. The correlation of a variable with a factor has the same interpretation that any correlation coefficient does. Thus since variable $a$ has a loading of .60 on factor $A$, it can be said that factor $A$ explains 36 percent of the variance of $a$ and vice versa. The sum of squares in any column of the factor matrix indicates the total amount of variance explained by that factor for the variables as a group. More important, the average squared loadings in a column is the proportion (without the decimal, a percentage) of variance of the variables as a group explained by that factor. Thus factor $A$ explains 19 percent of the total variance in the original data matrix $S$. The sum of average

**Table 10-2 Matrix of component-factor loadings**

|  |  | Factors | | | |
|---|---|---|---|---|---|
|  |  | $A$ | $B$ | $C$ | $h^2$ |
|  | $a$ | .60 | −.06 | .02 | .36 |
|  | $b$ | .81 | .12 | −.03 | .67 |
|  | $c$ | .77 | .03 | .08 | .60 |
| Variables | $d$ | .01 | .65 | −.04 | .42 |
|  | $e$ | .03 | .80 | .07 | .65 |
|  | $f$ | .12 | .67 | −.05 | .47 |
|  | $g$ | .19 | −.02 | .68 | .50 |
|  | $h$ | .08 | −.10 | .53 | .30 |
|  | $i$ | .26 | −.13 | .47 | .31 |
| Sum of squared loadings |  | 1.76 | 1.56 | .98 | |
| Var. |  | .19 | .17 | .11 | (total) = .47 |

squared loadings (.47) for the several factors indicates the percentage of variance explained by the factors, which provides an indication of the extent to which a set of factors does a good job of explaining the original variables. Note that the sum of squared loadings over the three columns equals the sum of $h^2$, and the sum of variance proportions (denoted "Var") over the three factors equals the average $h^2$.

The sum of squared loadings in any row of factor loadings $h^2$ tells the proportion (or percentage) of variance of the variable which is explained by the factors. The more a variable tends to share common factors with the other variables, the larger $h^2$ will be. In this context it would be useful to think of how one would estimate one of the original variables from the factors. If as many factors are extracted as there are variables, then any variable can be perfectly "estimated" from those factors. But usually the number of factors is small relative to the number of variables, and thus it is not probable that a perfect estimate can be obtained. In terms of the principle of least squares, the best estimate of any variable would be obtained from the multiple regression of the variable on those factors. Thus one would obtain an estimation of variable $a$ from three factors as follows:

$$a' = \beta_a A + \beta_b B + \beta_c C \tag{10-2}$$

where $a'$ = least-squares estimate of $a$ from multiple regression
$A, B, C$ = standard scores on three factors
$\beta_a, \beta_b, \beta_c$ = multiple-regression weights

The above approach to estimating any variable from a set of factors leads to some useful deductions. It will be remembered from Chap. 5 that when the predictor variables are uncorrelated, the squared multiple correlation equals the sum of squared predictor-criterion correlations. Since in this discussion the factors are assumed to be uncorrelated, the sum of squared loadings in any row of the matrix of factor loadings is the squared multiple correlation of the factors with the particular variable. Consequently the column in Table 10-2 labeled $h^2$ shows the squared multiple correlations of the three factors with the nine variables. This is why $h^2$ can be interpreted as a percentage of variance explained.

Another deduction from Eq. (10-2) is that the factor loadings in any row are the beta weights ($\beta_i$) required for multiple regression:

$$a' = r_{aA}A + r_{aB}B + r_{aC}C \tag{10-3}$$

Equation (10-3) holds in any instance where (1) all variables are in the form of standard scores and (2) all predictor variables (factors, here) are uncorrelated. This holds regardless of how the linear combinations (factors) are determined. One might choose a method of obtaining linear combinations that would lead to a very poor estimate of the original variables; but regardless of how good or poor the estimate, the multiple-regression weights would equal the factor loadings. Also, the reader should not confuse the present issue concerning the estimation of variables from factors with the issue of going the other way around—estimating factor scores from variables. The latter issue will be discussed in Chap. 11.

Another important principle follows from the discussion above. If all the variables are reproduced perfectly by the factors, the correlation between any two variables equals the sum of products of the loadings of the variables on the factors:

$$r_{ab} = r_{aA}r_{bA} + r_{aB}r_{bB} + \cdots + r_{aK}r_{bK} \tag{10-4}$$

This principle can be derived from the discussion in Chap. 5 regarding the correlation of sums. If any variable can be reproduced perfectly from a set of factors, that variable can be expressed as a linear combination of those factors. The correlation between any two such variables can be expressed in terms of the correlation of sums, in the usual way. As will be remembered, the correlation of sums equals the sum of elements in the cross-covariance matrix divided by the square root of the product of the sums of elements in both covariance matrices. If the factors are uncorrelated, all the terms in each covariance matrix vanish except those on the diagonal. The diagonal terms are the squares of the loadings of the variables on the factors. Since the sum of these is 1.0 in each of the two covariance matrices whenever the variables are perfectly reproduced, the denominator of the formula for the correlation of sums "falls out." The correlation then equals the sum of elements in the cross-covariance matrix. Since factors are uncorrelated, only terms involving the same factor are different from zero, for example, $r_{aA}r_{bA}$. Thus the correlation between any two variables equals the sum of cross products of their factor loadings.

Of course, seldom will the number of factors actually used in a study exactly reproduce the original variables. It would be a waste of time to employ as many factors as there are variables, and when that is not done, the factors being used frequently do not account for as much as 80 percent of the total variance. Even when only part of the variance is explained by the factors, however, the cross products of factor loadings provide a partial explanation of the correlations among variables. Thus if only three factors are used, a partial explanation of the correlation between variables $a$ and $b$ is as follows:

$$r'_{ab} = r_{aA}r_{bA} + r_{aB}r_{bB} + r_{aC}r_{bC} \tag{10-5}$$

That is why it is said that factors serve to *explain correlations* among variables or explain the common variance among variables. For any set of factors, one can attempt to reconstitute the original correlation matrix by forming all possible pairs of cross-product terms, as was illustrated above for variables $a$ and $b$. This can be subtracted, element by corresponding element, from the matrix of correlations among the original variables. These are then *residual coefficients*. If they are small (by standards that will be discussed later), the set of factors does a good job of explaining the common variance; but if they are large, it indicates that prominent factors are still to be obtained from the data.

**The correlation matrix** Frequently it is said that one "factors a correlation matrix." In previous sections it was stated that it is more appropriate to think of factoring the data matrix. For two reasons, however, correlations among the variables play important parts in factor analysis. Preparatory to any factor analysis, the first step is to compute the full matrix of correlations among variables. The first important part played by the correlation matrix is in determining the signs and sizes of coefficients in the linear combinations that produce factors. For example, if all the correlations are positive, which tends to indicate that all the variables have something in common, one might decide to give all variables positive weights in the first linear combination. If, on the other hand, some of the variables tend to correlate negatively with the others, one might decide to give negative weights to those. If, instead of assigning weights on some a priori basis, one derives weights mathematically in a way that optimizes some property of the factors, then the correlation matrix indicates how that optimization is to be done. Thus the correlation matrix is very useful in determining the signs and sizes of coefficients in linear combinations. Without the information provided by the correlation matrix, it would be very difficult to form useful linear combinations.

A second importance of the correlation matrix is that it greatly facilitates the correlation of variables with factors. Since each component factor is a linear combination of the variables, the correlation of any variable with a factor can be obtained from the correlation of sums by the usual formulas (Chap. 5). A simple example will illustrate how this is done; in a later section the methods will be discussed in detail. In this example, imagine that there are only five variables; say that they are supposed measures of anxiety. A hypothetical correlation matrix for the variables is shown in Table 10-3.

In Table 10-3, all the variables correlate positively with one another, but some tend to have higher correlations than others. Since the variables all correlate positively, a decision is made to give all the variables positive weights in the first linear combination. Also, it is decided to give them all equal weights. Since all the weights are equal, it is easier to give all variables a weight of 1 than to employ any other weight. In other words, one obtains the first linear combination (factor) by simply adding scores on the five variables. One would obtain the factor score for person 1 by simply adding that person's scores on the five tests, and so on for the other persons. For convenience, factor scores would then be standardized. Finally, each of the variables would be correlated with the factor to obtain factor loadings.

**Table 10-3 Correlation matrix for five measures of anxiety**

|   | *1* | *2* | *3* | *4* | *5* | *A* |
|---|------|------|------|------|------|------|
| *1* | 1.00 | .43 | .18 | .08 | .48 | .60 |
| *2* | .43 | 1.00 | .51 | .49 | .63 | .84 |
| *3* | .18 | .51 | 1.00 | .27 | .55 | .69 |
| *4* | .08 | .49 | .27 | 1.00 | .44 | .63 |
| *5* | .48 | .63 | .55 | .44 | 1.00 | .91 |

If the correlation matrix is available, there is an easier way to obtain factor loadings. Since in the example above the factor is a simple sum of the variables, the correlation of variables with the factor can be obtained from the correlation of sums. When all variables are in the form of standard scores, it was shown in Chap. 5 that the correlation of one variable with the sum of other variables is as follows:

$$r_{1y} = \frac{\Sigma r_{1i}}{\sqrt{\bar{R}}} \tag{10-6}$$

where $y$ = linear combination

$1$ = variable being correlated with $y$

$\Sigma r_{1i}$ = sum of correlations between variable 1 and each variable in $y$

$\bar{R}$ = sum of all elements in correlation matrix for $y$ variables

To put it in words, the numerator equals the sum of correlations between variable 1 and each of the variables in the linear combination. Under the radical in the denominator is the sum of all elements in the matrix of correlations among the $y$ variables. This includes the diagonal 1s.

The formula for the correlation of sums was developed in Chap. 5 for the situation where one variable is correlated with the sum of a number of *other* variables, but the formula applies equally well when the variable itself is a member of the linear combination. Thus the formula can be applied in the above situation where, for example, variable 1 in Table 10-3 is to be correlated with the sum of all variables in the matrix. In this case, variable 1 is to be correlated with the sum of variables 1 through 5. In the numerator of Eq. (10-6), there are five correlations. One of these is the correlation of variable 1 with itself, which by definition is 1.0. The other four correlations are between variable 1 and the other four variables. The sum $T$ of all elements in the correlation matrix is 13.12. The square root of $T$ is 3.6221, which is the denominator of Eq. (10-6). The correlation of variable 1 with the sum of variables 1 through 5 would then be obtained as follows:

Sum of variable 1's correlations = 2.17

$$\frac{2.17}{3.6221} = .60$$

In the same way, the loadings of all five variables on the factor would be computed. These are shown in column $A$ of Table 10-3.

In the example above, a very simple linear combination was used to illustrate how factor loadings can be computed from the correlation matrix rather than from the data matrix itself. The logic applies, however, to *any* type of linear combination. All such possibilities are covered by formulas for the correlation of individual variables with the weighted combination of a set of variables (see Chap. 5). For example, in the method of principal components (to be described later), the first factor is determined so as to maximize the "variance explained"—maximize the sum of squared loadings on the first factor. To do this requires a set of weights determined by a particular method of analysis. The weights could be applied to the data matrix; then the factor loadings could be obtained by correlating each variable with the weighted combination of variables. It is easier to use the same weights in the correlation of weighted sums, which can be done directly on the correlation matrix. Actually, in most of the factoring methods, this resort to the correlation of weighted sums is hidden in the overall computations, but the methods basically are founded on correlations of weighted sums.

To obtain a succession of uncorrelated (orthogonal) factors, a method was described previously for partialing each factor in turn from the original matrix of data. One can accomplish the same thing, and much more easily, by partialing the factor loadings from the correlation matrix. For example, previously it was shown how a second factor could be obtained as a linear combination of the partialed matrix of data, the influence of the first factor having been removed. Factor loadings on the second factor were obtained by correlating each of the original variables with a linear combination of the partialed variables. The same can be obtained from the correlation matrix as follows. First, by formulas for the correlation of sums, loadings on the first factor are determined. These correlations are partialed from the original correlations by the usual methods of partial correlation. This can be illustrated for variables 1 and 2. Each variable has a loading on (correlation with) factor $A$. It is an easy matter to partial factor $A$ from the correlation between variables 1 and 2. All that is needed are three correlations: $r_{12}$, $r_{1A}$, and $r_{2A}$. In the same way, correlations with factor $A$ can be partialed from all correlations in the original matrix. Loadings on the second factor can then be determined from the matrix of partial correlations rather than from the matrix of partialed scores. It is the same either way, but working from the matrix of correlations is much more convenient than working from the data matrix.

The original correlation matrix supplies all the information required for determining factor loadings on any kind, and any number, of factors. However, this fact should not be allowed to obscure the basic nature of factors. Even if loadings of variables on factors can be computed from the correlation matrix, the component factors themselves are linear combinations of the actual variables. Also, after factor loadings are obtained, to obtain scores of people on factors one must return to the data matrix and apply methods that will be described in Chap. 11.

**Geometric interpretations** There are some very useful analogies between factor analysis and geometry. The correlation between any two variables can be pictured as the angle between two vectors (straight lines). Specifically, the correlation is pictured as the cosine of the angle between two vectors. Both vectors have the same origin, and both are of length 1.0 (unit length). Each vector can be thought of as a "correlation yardstick" with the numbers .00, .01, .02, . . . , .99, 1.00 along it. One obtains the correlation between any two variables by extending a perpendicular line from either one of the vectors to the tip of the

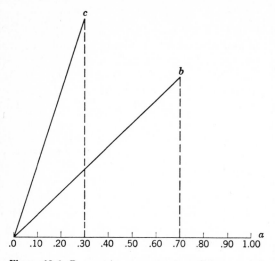

**Figure 10-1** Geometric representation of the correlations among three variables.

other. This is illustrated in Fig. 10-1 for the correlations of variables $b$ and $c$ with variable $a$. Variable $b$ correlates .70 with variable $a$, and variable $c$ correlates .30 with $a$. One would find the same correlations by lowering perpendiculars from $b$ to $a$ and from $c$ to $a$. Also, the cosine of the angle between $b$ and $c$ specifies their correlation, this being .91. Two vectors at right angles have a cosine of .00 and a correlation of .00; two vectors that lie atop one another have a cosine of 1.00 and a correlation of 1.00. For two vectors having a 45° angle of separation, the cosine and correlation are .71. In between these points are represented all possible sizes of correlations.

Negative correlations are represented by angles greater than 90°, as is illustrated in Fig. 10-2 for a negative correlation of .50. Each vector can be thought of as extending in both directions from the origin, as is illustrated by the dashed line extending past the origin at the end of variable $a$. Usually only one end of the vector is shown in illustrations, but it is understood that vectors go to length 1.00 on both sides of the origin. This permits the depiction of all possible correlations, positive and negative, by the cosines of angles. Angles between 90° and 180° have negative cosines. For example, an angle of 180° has a cosine of −1.00, and an angle of 135° (45° beyond a right angle) has a cosine of −.71. Of course, cosines related to any angle can be sought directly in books on trigonometry and related topics.

Any matrix of correlations can be thought of as a matrix showing all possible cosines among a set of vectors, each vector representing one of the variables. Thus the correlation matrix in Table 10-4 can be thought of as a matrix of cosines. The geometric configuration for the variables is shown in Fig. 10-3. Such configurations have an arbitrary frame of reference. That is, as long as the cosines among angles are left the same, the whole configuration can be rotated about the origin without changing the problem. Whereas in Fig. 10-1 variable $a$

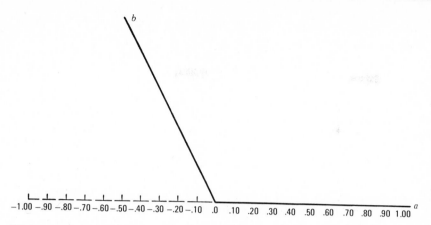

Figure 10-2 Geometric representation of a negative correlation between two variables.

## Table 10-4 Correlation matrix for four variables

|   | *a* | *b* | *c* | *d* |
|---|-----|-----|-----|-----|
| *a* | 1.00 | .73 | −.04 | −.67 |
| *b* | .73 | 1.00 | .66 | .05 |
| *c* | −.04 | .66 | 1.00 | .78 |
| *d* | −.67 | .05 | .78 | 1.00 |

is shown as coming out horizontally to the right of the origin, one could represent the same set of cosines among vectors equally well by having variable *c* come out horizontally to the right of the origin. In that case all variables would be rotated to the right through equal angles. Then, for example, the vector for variable *b* would slope downward to the right of the origin. All that is important is that the configuration correctly show the cosines of angles corresponding to the correlations among variables.

The matrix of correlations in Table 10-4 is an idealization of what is found in practice. It is unusual in that all the cosines (correlations) can be represented in two dimensions (a two-space). Usually the correlations cannot be repre-

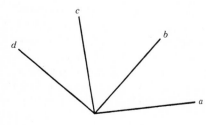

Figure 10-3 Geometric representation of the correlations in Table 10-4.

sented even in three dimensions. Then it is necessary to think of the correlations as being represented in a *hyperspace*, or a space of more than three dimensions. Of course, there is no physical representation of spaces of more than three dimensions, but this does not hinder the use of geometric conceptions.

The use of unit-length vectors in physical space to portray matrices of correlations in terms of corresponding matrices of cosines is part of a more general geometric analogy in which the relationship between any two variables is expressed as the cosine of the angle between their vectors multiplied by the lengths of the vectors. In the example given in Table 10-4 and displayed in Fig. 10-3, all the variables are of the same length, namely 1.00. In the more general model, different possible lengths of the variables can be taken into account. The length is $h$, which is the square root of the diagonal element shown in a matrix of relationships. In components analysis, since unities are placed in the diagonal spaces of the matrix, these need not be shown in the more general expression, which for two variables would be $h_1\cos_{12}h_2$. In the more general model, $h$ represents the standard deviation of a variable, which of course is 1.00 in a real correlation matrix, as depicted in Table 10-4. In the discussion of common factors in Chap. 11, as opposed to component factors which are discussed in this chapter, the diagonal elements will usually be less than 1.00, which means that all the variance of standard scores from the score matrix will not be included in the factor analysis. In this case, the diagonal elements can vary anywhere from 0 to 1.00. The diagonal element is symbolized as $h^2$ and referred to as the "squared length" of the corresponding vector for the variable in the geometric representation of relationships among the variables. Then, $h_1$ is the length of vector 1, $h_2$ is the length of vector 2, and so on for the vectors corresponding to other measures in the score matrix. When the original diagonal elements of the correlation matrix are less than 1.00, then the geometric representation of correlations is obtained by multiplying the cosine by the product of the lengths for any two variables, that is, $h_i\cos_{ij}h_j$. For example, if $h_1$ is .8 and $h_2$ is .9, then a correlation of .5 would correspond to a cosine of .69. In this way all the correlations in a matrix can be depicted in terms of vectors in space regardless of the diagonal elements placed in the original matrix of correlations. More broadly speaking, in the discussion of multidimensional scaling in Chap. 12 and in other places, it will be important to know that *any* system of vectors such as that depicted in Fig. 10-3 can be subjected to factor analysis regardless of variations in lengths of the vectors and whether the relationship $h_i\cos_{ij}h_j$ concerns correlation coefficients or other measures of relationship among variables or objects. The geometric model is perfectly general to all such possibilities and the depiction of a correlational matrix with unities in the diagonal simply in terms of the cosines among unit-length vectors is a highly useful special case.

Often factors are spoken of as dimensions, and factoring is spoken of as dimensionalizing a space of variables. Imagine, for example, that the vectors for 20 variables all lie in a three-dimensional space. Factor analysis can be thought of as inserting a framework of three new vectors (factors) to explain the correlations (cosines) among the variables. If all 20 vectors lie in a three-space, the variables are "redundant" of one another. They all can be "explained" by three factors. Following are some useful principles regarding relations between factoring and hyperspace geometry.

If a set of variables is represented in an $r$-dimensional space, any linear combination of the variables is also represented in that $r$-dimensional space. This would apply in the example above where 20 variables are represented in a three-dimensional space. *Any* linear combination of those variables would also be a vector in that space. This applies no matter what the coefficients are for the linear combination; e.g., some of the coefficients can be zero, and some can be negative. In other words, a factor (a linear combination of variables) is another vector in the same space as that of the variables themselves. Thus factoring can be thought of as putting new variables in a space of variables. The important point is that the vector representing any factor cannot "get out of" the space formed by the variables themselves.

If any set of variables lies in an $r$-dimensional space, any $r$ number of nondependent linear combinations of those variables is said to constitute a *basis* for the space. The term *nondependent* means that none of the linear combinations can be expressed as a linear combination of the other linear combinations; e.g., none of five factors can be totally explained from the others by multiple regression. The principle is easier to visualize when all factors are uncorrelated with one another, in which case the vectors for the factors are all at right angles to one another. If the vectors representing variables lie, say, in three dimensions, any three uncorrelated (orthogonal) factors will explain all the correlations among the variables.

The loading of a variable with a factor is represented by the cosine of the angle between the vector for the variable and the vector for the factor. If the variables lie in an $r$-dimensional space, any $r$ orthogonal factors will explain the vectors for all variables. In that case the sum of the squared loadings in each row of the matrix of factor loadings will equal 1.00, and the sum of cross products of loadings in any two rows of that matrix will equal the correlation between the two variables. Thus a row of factor loadings can be thought of as a row of cosines between a variable and a number of factors.

Usually the number of factors employed will not explain correlations perfectly. In other words, the space of variables has more dimensions than factors. In that case the factors are said to form a *semibasis* for the space of variables. Suppose, for example, that the variables cannot be represented in less than 10 dimensions, but only five factors are used. Some of the variables might lie almost entirely in the space of factors, and others might lie mainly outside that space. The sum of squared loadings for any variable is a direct measure of the extent to which that variable lies in the space defined by the factors. Then $h^2$ is the squared length of a vector explainable by a space of factors. If, for example, $h^2$ for a variable on five factors is .64, then .8 is the explained length.

The number of dimensions required to represent a matrix of correlations is said to be the *rank* of that matrix. Consequently factor analysis is often said to involve finding the rank of a matrix of correlations.

As useful as these geometric interpretations are, it is possible to carry them too far. First, there is nothing necessarily geometric about factoring. It can all be developed and used without ever talking about cosines of angles, dimensions, and the like. Geometric interpretation is a useful isomorphism which sometimes helps one to think about problems of factoring, but it should be invoked only when it is useful. Second, the talk about rank and the basis for a space can easily mislead one into assuming that these are frequently obtained. In nearly all problems in component factoring, the rank is as large as the number of variables. This is mainly because each variable has its own unique source of variance which cannot be explained by other variables. Even in the ideal situation where variables could be entirely explained by a relatively small number of common factors, for example, 20 variables and five factors, the sampling error of correlations would usually prevent a perfect "fit." Also, in most problems, no one is interested in completely explaining the correlations among variables. Usually one is interested in the prominent factors, the ones that have at least moderate-sized loadings. Typically, the factors with very small loadings (e.g., none higher than .30) are not interpreted.

In terms of hyperspace geometry, it is most useful to think of factoring as establishing a semibasis for a space of variables. Then, from a statistical point of view, a good factoring method is one that constitutes a semibasis which explains as much as possible of the variance $h^2$ of the variables. From the standpoint of empirical research, a good semibasis is one that (1) is easily interpreted and/or (2) relates most clearly to psychological theories.

**Components of variance** In the general factor analysis model, the total variance of any variable (1.00 when in standard score form) can be partitioned into three uncorrelated components respectively concerning (1) common variance, (2) specific variance, and (3) error variance. Look at the three in reverse order: the error variance is nothing other than the standard error of measurement squared ($\sigma^2_{meas}$) from reliability theory, which equals $1 - r_{aa}$ for variable $a$. Thus, if the reliability of variable $a$ is .80, then the variance attributable to error is .20 and the variance not attributable to error is .80. In addition to measurement error, each variable is thought of as having a specific factor or source of variance that cannot be explained by its relationship with other variables. For example, a particular test of anxiety would have some variance due to unreliability, some variance that could be explained by other tests of anxiety, and a source of variance that was specific to itself. In the general factor analysis model, the specific variance is thought of as being uncorrelated with either error variance or common variance. Theoretically common variance is that proportion of the total variance of a measure that can be explained by common factors (although there are uncertainties and disputes as to exactly how this should be done). Then the total variance of any variable can be sectioned into the following three uncorrelated components:

$$\sigma_a^2 = \text{variance explainable by common factors}$$
$$+ \text{variance because of specific factor}$$
$$+ \text{variance because of errors of measurement} \qquad (10\text{-}7)$$

In most actual analyses, no effort is made to separate specific variance from error variance, and consequently these are lumped together and called *unique variance* $u^2$. Then Eq. (10-7) reduces to

$$\sigma_a^2 = h^2 + u^2 \qquad (10\text{-}8)$$

It is apparent, then, that the unique variance equals the sum of squared loadings on common factors subtracted from 1.0 (which is $1 - h^2$).

Although usually no effort is made to take apart $u^2$ in terms of specific variance and error variance, one could make a good argument for doing so. In factor analysis this can be done by placing reliability coefficients in the diagonal spaces of the correlation matrix rather than unities, if excellent measures of reliability are available. There is nothing wrong with directly factoring such a matrix by any of the procedures which will be discussed subsequently. Although the resulting factors will not separate the common components from the specific components, factoring with reliability coefficients in the diagonal spaces offers one sensible approach which, however, is seldom actually used.

Frequently it is said that factor analysis serves to partition variables into sources of common and unique variance. In component analysis, one attempts to explain common variance with linear combinations of the variables, and the unique variance is the part not explainable by the obtained factors. As was mentioned previously, though, this is only approximately done in most studies. There still is common variance left in most studies after the investigator stops factoring. The portion of variance left over is due partly to unique variance and partly to nonanalyzed common variance. Also, for reasons which will be made clear later, there is no foolproof way to distinguish common variance from unique variance. In component-factor analysis, this is because in forming linear combinations, the unique variance of each variable becomes part of the factors, which tends to confound the two sources of variance. An attempt to separate common variance from unique variance is done with the methods of common-factor analysis which will be discussed in Chap. 11, but an entirely acceptable method for doing this has not been found. Since we lack exact methods for partitioning variance into these components, it is best to think of Eqs. (10-7) and (10-8) as idealizations of what actually is done in factor analysis. However, it is useful to think of the variance of any variable as being partitionable into three uncorrelated components—common variance, specific variance, and error variance (the latter two summing to equal the unique variance).

**Confirmatory and exploratory analysis** In confirmatory factor analysis, typically one employs a *direct* solution. For example, if the hypothesis was that six measures of introversion are dominated by only one common factor, one would obtain a direct solution to test that hypothesis, e.g., by correlating each test with the simple sum of the six tests. As another example, it might be hypothesized that six tests concerning introversion evolve into two common factors, with three of the tests belonging to one factor and the other three belonging to another factor. One could then obtain a direct solution to test this hypothesis, e.g., by making the first linear combination (factor) a simple sum of the first three variables and the second factor a simple sum of the second three variables. One might hypothesize as many as half a dozen or more factors and then form linear combinations accordingly. The essence of any direct solution is that (1) it is performed so as to test hypotheses about the existence of factors and (2) the nature of linear combinations is stated in advance of obtaining the correlation matrix.

Although for obvious reasons it is better to begin an analysis with hypotheses, this has not been done in most factor analyses to date. Investigators are unwilling to formulate hypotheses, do not trust the hypotheses they have, or have so many variables to analyze that the end result is difficult to estimate. In these cases one starts with a large collection of "interesting" measures (for example, 30 tests concerning different aspects of memory) and leaves it to the statistical methods to say what factors are present. Many attempts have been made in this way to explore "interesting" domains of variables, e.g., motor skills, perceptual abilities, interests, and personality characteristics.

In exploratory factor analysis typically one employs a *stepwise* analysis rather than a direct analysis. The first step is to *condense* the variables into a relatively small number of factors. In this case the standard of statistical parsimony is given paramount consideration. It does not matter in the first step how interpretable the factors are; the only concern is with the extent to which they serve to condense the data. The degree to which condensation is obtained is reflected in the average percentage of variance explained (average $h^2$) by a number of factors. If a method of condensation is used in which each factor takes out more variance than the succeeding one, the rate at which variance is extracted indicates the degree of condensation. Imagine that in the analysis of 20 tests, the first five factors explain 50 percent of the variance and the succeeding five factors explain another 10 percent of the variance. This means that the first five factors do a good job of condensing the correlations among the 20 variables. Another way of looking at it is that, after the first five factors are partialed from the correlation matrix, the partial correlations among variables are near zero, and thus there is little common variance left to analyze. In other words, five factors provide a good semibasis for the space of variables.

After one has used one of the methods for condensing a space of variables, the next step usually is to *rotate* factors. This is done because usually it is very difficult to interpret the original factors. They are good from a statistical point of view; but when the loadings of variables on factors are inspected, it is hard to find clear-cut patterns of loadings. A rotated factor is simply a linear combination of the original factors. Thus a rotated factor is simply a linear combination of the other linear combinations. If one has five factors which condense the variables reasonably well, one can rotate those factors by making five linear combinations of the original factors. Means are available for ensuring that the rotated factors are orthogonal if that is desired. The important point is that any set of rotated factors explains exactly the same variance as the original factors. Variables will have different patterns of loadings on the rotated factors than they have on the original factors, but the $h^2$ for each variable will remain exactly the same (assuming that the rotated factors are uncorrelated). The rotated factors explain the same amount of variance as the original factors, but they "slice it up" in a way that is more interpretable. In the remainder of the chapter, methods of condensation for exploratory factor analysis, methods of rotation, and methods of confirmatory factor analysis for testing hypotheses will be discussed.

## CENTROID METHOD OF CONDENSATION

Until about 1950, the centroid method of condensation was employed more frequently than any other method. Whereas here it is referred to as a method of condensation, generally it is referred to simply as the centroid method of factoring. Actually it is not quite as efficient at condensing variables as a method to be discussed in a later section—the method of principal components. The effectiveness of the centroid method, however, usually is rather close to that of principal components. Also, the centroid method is far simpler to compute and understand. Understanding the centroid method will give readers a good grasp of the mechanics involved in all methods concerned with condensation.

**Geometric configuration** A geometric interpretation of the centroid method starts with the space of variables as shown in Figs. 10-3 and 10-4. In Fig. 10-4 only the end points of vectors are shown for four measures. This is an idealized example, because all the vectors go to unit length in a two-space, which means that two factors can perfectly explain all variables. If more than two factors were required, the vectors would not go to unit length in the figure, because part of the length would be evidenced in other dimensions.

As was mentioned previously, a factor can be thought of as a new vector which is obtained from a linear combination of the variables. The first centroid factor produces a vector which is the *average* of the vectors for the variables. That is, it is the *mean,* or *centroid,* of the other variables, and thus the vectors for the variables balance in all directions about the centroid. In Fig. 10-4, the first centroid factor ($A$) is inserted. As can be seen, it is precisely in the middle of the vectors for the variables, with only the end points of these vectors being shown. Just as the vectors for the variables can be thought of as extending in both directions from the origin, this is also true of factor vectors.

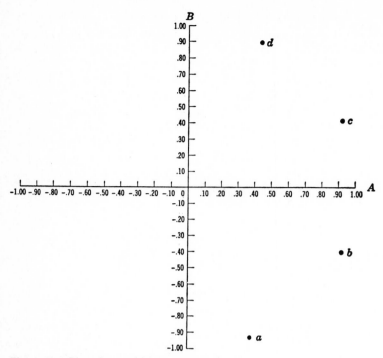

**Figure 10-4** Plot of centroid factor loadings.

The correlation (loading) of each variable with the first centroid can be read from the factor axis, as noted previously. The factor axis is sectioned in tenths to show how this is done.

The second centroid factor is made orthogonal (uncorrelated, or at a right angle) with the first. Since the variable can be represented perfectly in a two-space, there is only one place for the second centroid to go. It is shown in Fig. 10-4 as vector $B$. Loadings on $B$ can also be read directly. Loadings on the two centroid factors are shown in Table 10-5. In each case $h^2$ is 1.00, and the loadings are exceptionally high, which would be true only in an idealized example like the one here.

**Table 10-5 Centroid loadings for factors shown in Fig. 10-4**

|  |  | Factor | |
|---|---|---|---|
|  |  | A | B |
|  | a | .38 | −.93 |
| Variable | b | .92 | −.40 |
|  | c | .91 | .42 |
|  | d | .44 | .90 |

**Table 10-6 Correlation matrix for six variables and computation of loadings on first centroid factor**

|  | 1 | 2 | 3 | 4 | 5 | 6 |
|---|---|---|---|---|---|---|
| 1 | 1.00 | .55 | .43 | .32 | .28 | .36 |
| 2 | .55 | 1.00 | .50 | .25 | .31 | .32 |
| 3 | .43 | .50 | 1.00 | .39 | .25 | .33 |
| 4 | .32 | .25 | .39 | 1.00 | .43 | .49 |
| 5 | .28 | .31 | .25 | .43 | 1.00 | .44 |
| 6 | .36 | .32 | .33 | .49 | .44 | 1.00 |
| Column sums | 2.94 | 2.93 | 2.90 | 2.88 | 2.71 | 2.94 |

$$T = 17.30 \qquad \sqrt{T} = 4.1593 \qquad M = .2404$$

|  | 1 | 2 | 3 | 4 | 5 | 6 |
|---|---|---|---|---|---|---|
| A | .71 | .70 | .70 | .69 | .65 | .71 |

**Correlation matrix** Like other forms of factor analysis, a centroid analysis starts with the computation of a matrix of correlations. A matrix for six variables is shown in Table 10-6. The PM formula should always be employed, which results in point-biserial and phi for special cases where one or both variables are dichotomous. Non-PM estimates of PM coefficients such as biserial and tetrachoric cannot be used legitimately in factor analysis. This is because the correlation of a variable with a linear combination of variables requires the use of PM coefficients in the correlation of sums. This cannot be done legitimately with biserial or tetrachoric. Numerous analyses have been undertaken with these formulas, and perhaps the results have been approximately correct. There is, however, no mathematical basis for employing such coefficients in component factor analysis.

The correlation matrix in Table 10-6 has been arranged to indicate that the six variables tend to break up into two clusters, one formed by variables 1, 2, and 3 and the other formed by the remaining three variables. A person who is experienced with factor analysis could see at a glance that the common variance among the variables can be condensed to a high degree by two factors. For the factor analysis, *unities* are placed in the diagonal spaces of the matrix. (So-called *communality estimates* are frequently placed in the diagonal spaces, a matter which will be discussed in the next chapter.)

**First centroid factor** As was mentioned previously, factoring methods are defined in terms of the way they form linear combinations of variables. The centroid method is defined by linear combinations in which all weights are either $+1.0$ or $-1.0$. In other words, the variables are simply summed, with the possibility that some of them might be given negative weights (subtracted rather than added).

To simplify the discussion, let it be assumed that the sum of correlations in each column (and thus each row), disregarding the diagonal unities, is positive. This would mean that, disregarding the diagonal elements, each variable has a larger sum of positive correlations than of negative correlations. This usually holds for the original correlation matrix. When this condition holds, the matrix is said to be of *positive manifold*. For the following discussion, it is not necessary that all correlations be positive, only that the sum of nondiagonal entries in each column be positive. What to do if the sum of one or more columns is negative will be discussed later.

If the correlation matrix is of positive manifold, the centroid method requires that the weights for all variables be $+1.0$. In other words, the variables are not weighted; they are simply summed. After the sum of variables is standardized, it is a unit-length vector at the centroid of the other vectors, as was illustrated in Fig. 10-4. It is then the mean vector—the one that balances the others in all directions.

In Table 10-6 are shown the steps required to obtain factor loadings on a first centroid factor. The correlation of each variable with the sum of all six variables (the first centroid factor) is determined as follows. First, the sum of coefficients in each column of the matrix is computed. This includes every element from the top to the bottom of each column, *including* the diagonal unity. The sum of the column sums $T$ is obtained, which, of course, is the sum of all elements in the correlation matrix including diagonal elements. To compute each centroid loading, the sum of elements in each column is the numerator in the correlation of sums, and the square root of $T$ is the denominator. It is easier to multiply the former by the reciprocal of the latter $(M)$. Thus when each column sum is multiplied by $M$, a loading on the first centroid factor is obtained. The full set of loadings on the first centroid is shown in row $A$.

**Matrix of residual coefficient** After the first factor is obtained, by the centroid method or by any other method, and as a prelude to seeking a second factor, one must obtain a matrix of residual coefficients. The residual coefficient corresponding to any element in the original correlation matrix is obtained as follows. First, the loadings for the two variables on the first centroid factor are multiplied. For variables 1 and 2, this product is .50. This is done for all possible pairs of variables. One simplifies the computations by placing the loadings at the proper points on the top and side of an empty matrix and then multiplying corresponding pairs of elements. This is shown in Table 10-7. In each diagonal space is the square of the particular factor loading. The resulting matrix is labeled $Q_1$, to stand for the first matrix of factor cross products. Then $Q_1$ is subtracted element by element from the original matrix of correlations $R$, resulting in the first matrix of residual coefficients $R_1$, shown in Table 10-8.

**Table 10-7 First matrix of factor cross products ($Q_1$)**

|      | .71  | .70  | .70  | .69  | .65  | .71  |
|------|------|------|------|------|------|------|
| .71  | .50  | .50  | .50  | .49  | .46  | .50  |
| .70  | .50  | .49  | .49  | .49  | .46  | .50  |
| .70  | .50  | .49  | .49  | .48  | .45  | .49  |
| .69  | .49  | .49  | .48  | .48  | .45  | .49  |
| .65  | .46  | .46  | .45  | .45  | .42  | .46  |
| .71  | .50  | .50  | .49  | .49  | .46  | .50  |

## Table 10-8  First matrix of residual coefficients ($R_1$)

|   | 1 | 2 | 3 | 4 | 5 | 6 |
|---|------|------|------|------|------|------|
| 1 | .50 | .05 | −.07 | −.17 | −.18 | −.14 |
| 2 | .05 | .51 | .01 | −.24 | −.15 | −.18 |
| 3 | −.07 | .01 | .51 | −.09 | −.20 | −.16 |
| 4 | −.17 | −.24 | −.09 | .52 | −.02 | .00 |
| 5 | −.18 | −.15 | −.20 | −.02 | .58 | −.02 |
| 6 | −.14 | −.18 | −.16 | .00 | −.02 | .50 |

It is important to understand the nature of the elements in the residual matrix. They are sometimes mistakenly spoken of as "residual correlations." Each diagonal element is a partial variance, the variance remaining after the influence of the first factor is partialed. Each off-diagonal element is a partial covariance, the covariance between two variables after the influence of the first factor is removed. One can see why this is so by looking at the partial correlation between variables 1 and 2 when factor $A$ is held constant:

$$r_{12.A} = \frac{r_{12} - r_{1A}r_{2A}}{\sqrt{1 - r_{1A}^2}\;\sqrt{1 - r_{2A}^2}} \tag{10-9}$$

In the partial correlation formula, the numerator is the partial covariance for the two variables being partialed, and the denominator is the product of the square roots of the partial variances for the two variables. The numerator is exactly what is found in $R_1$ corresponding to the entry for variables 1 and 2. In the denominator, the square of the term on the left (the partial variance for variable 1) is exactly what is found in the diagonal element for variable 1 in $R_1$. Likewise, the partial variance for 2 is found in the diagonal space for that variable in the residual matrix.

Since in $R_1$ the diagonal terms are partial variances and the off-diagonal terms are partial covariances, it is easy to convert the entire table to a matrix of partial correlations. One can accomplish this by dividing the elements in each row by the square root of the diagonal element for that row and then dividing the elements in each column by the square root of the diagonal element for that column. To obtain a second factor (by the centroid method or by any other method), it is not necessary to convert residual coefficients to partial correlations. The computations can be performed more easily on the partial variances and partial covariances. It will be remembered that formulas for the correlation of sums apply as easily to covariance matrices as they do to correlation matrices.

**Reflection**  One obtains a second factor by applying formulas for the correlation of sums to $R_1$. In $R_1$, however, it is not a good strategy to make the second factor the sum of partialed scores because this matrix has an even balance of negative and positive coefficients. Consequently, the sum of elements in each column of $R_1$ differs from zero by only rounding errors. Since the first centroid is the mean vector, when its influence is partialed, the residual coefficients in the whole table sum to zero. Obviously, then, it is not possible to compute factor loadings for the second factor by the same method of weighting used for the first factor.

What is done to remedy this situation is to *reflect* some of the variables in $R_1$. All this means is that some of the variables are given negative signs in the sum. For any variable which is so reflected, the signs of all coefficients in that column and row of the residual matrix are changed. Thus, rather than actually changing the signs of scores in the matrix of partialed scores (making positive standard scores negative and negative standard scores positive), one can obtain the same final result by changing the signs of rows and columns of $R_1$. There is nothing "wrong" with performing such reflections; it is simply a step required in correlating each of the variables with a particular linear combination of the partialed variables. All that is required is that, after the loadings are obtained from the reflected variables, the variables which were reflected be given negative signs for their loadings.

The aim of reflecting variables is to obtain a reflected matrix (symbolized as $R_1'$) which will have the highest possible sum of coefficients ($T$). This is because the sum of factor loadings increases with $T$. Since, in any method of condensation, the object is to make each factor account for as much variance as possible, one should reflect in a way that makes $T$ as large as possible (which is routinely done these days on computer programs for the centroid method). The ideal is when reflections can be made so that all coefficients in $R_1'$ are positive, in which case it is obvious that $T$ is a maximum. Frequently it is not possible to make all coefficients positive, so some cut-and-try methods are necessary for finding the largest sum of coefficients. Detailed methods for doing this are described by Thurstone (1947).

When only a few variables are involved in the analysis (which is rarely the case these days), the best method of reflection can be determined by inspection. In Table 10-8, it can be seen that the two groups of variables have all negative coefficients between them. Then one can make most of the coefficients in the table positive by giving negative signs to variables 4, 5, and 6. (The same could have been accomplished by giving negative signs to variables 1, 2, and 3.) The resulting matrix of reflected residuals ($R_1'$) is shown in Table 10-9.

Loadings on the second centroid factor are obtained from $R_1'$ (not from $R_1$). The same procedures are employed as were employed with the original matrix of correlations. First, one finds the sum of coefficients in each column, including the diagonal term. One then finds the sum of the column sums ($T$), the square root of that, and the reciprocal of that, which is $M$. Each column sum is multiplied by $M$. Then the proper signs must be given to these values before they become loadings. All variables which were reflected receive minus signs, and all nonreflected variables receive positive signs. When the proper sign changes are made, the second centroid factor $B$ is obtained.

Although one can easily get lost in the mechanics of reflection to obtain linear combinations and the subsequent reflections to obtain the proper signs for loadings, actually it is only a computational routine for doing something

**Table 10-9 Reflected residual matrix ($R_1'$) and extraction of second centroid factor**

|  | 1 | 2 | 3 | 4* | 5* | 6* |
|---|---|---|---|---|---|---|
| 1 | .50 | .05 | −.07 | .17 | .18 | .14 |
| 2 | .05 | .51 | .01 | .24 | .15 | .18 |
| 3 | −.07 | .01 | .51 | .09 | .20 | .18 |
| 4* | .17 | .24 | .09 | .52 | −.02 | .00 |
| 5* | .18 | .15 | .20 | −.02 | .58 | −.02 |
| 6* | .14 | .18 | .16 | .00 | −.02 | .50 |
| Column sums | .97 | 1.14 | .91 | 1.00 | 1.07 | .96 |
|  | $T = 6.05$ | | $\sqrt{T} = 2.46$ | | $M = .406$ | |
| B | .40 | .46 | .37 | −.41 | −.43 | −.39 |

*These variables were reflected.

very simple. Since after the influence of the first centroid factor is removed from the variables there is a balance of negative and positive correlations among the partialed variables, the partialed variables do not add up to anything. Each variable would correlate zero with the simple sum of partialed variables. To obtain a linear combination that correlates highly with each of the variables, one must give some of the partialed variables negative signs. The ideal system of signs makes all correlations among partialed variables positive or, if that is not obtainable, makes the sum of correlations as large as possible. Instead of determining signs for reflection from the matrix of partialed scores, it is much easier to see how this should be done from an inspection of the matrix of residual coefficients.

Once the sign changes are made, the correlation of each variable with the second centroid factor can be determined directly from the correlation of weighted sums, in which some weights will be +1.0 and others will be −1.0. A computational shortcut is to change the signs of coefficients in the appropriate rows and columns of $R_1$ producing $R_1'$, compute the loadings from the latter matrix, and then reverse signs for variables that were reflected.

In obtaining loadings on the first centroid factor, it was assumed that a positive manifold exists. If that is not the case, reflections must be made before the first centroid factor is obtained. One does this by exactly the same procedures described above for the more usual case where reflection is required only after the first factor is extracted.

**Additional factors** There is little more to explain about the centroid method of factoring. Most methods of condensing variables are repetitive procedures. Once one knows how to obtain loadings and residual matrices and make reflections, one simply repeats the same process over and over for subsequent factors. After the second centroid factor is obtained, cross products are computed, forming matrix $Q_2$. This is then subtracted from $R_1$ (the unreflected residual

**Table 10-10 Second residual matrix ($R_2$)**

|   | 1 | 2 | 3 | 4 | 5 | 6 |
|---|------|------|------|------|------|------|
| 1 | .34 | −.13 | −.21 | −.01 | −.01 | .02 |
| 2 | −.13 | .29 | −.16 | −.05 | .05 | .00 |
| 3 | −.21 | −.16 | .37 | .06 | −.04 | −.02 |
| 4 | −.01 | −.05 | .06 | .36 | −.20 | −.16 |
| 5 | −.01 | .05 | −.04 | −.20 | .39 | −.19 |
| 6 | .02 | .00 | −.02 | −.16 | −.19 | .35 |

matrix), not from $R_1'$ (the reflected residual matrix). This produces $R_2$, which for the six-variable problem is shown in Table 10-10.

To obtain a third factor, one would operate on $R_2$ in the same way as on $R_1$. First, some of the variables would have to be reflected to maximize the sum of loadings, which would produce $R_2'$. Loadings would be computed from $R_2'$ as they were from $R_1'$. Again it would be necessary to give negative signs to the loadings of variables which were reflected, which would result in factor $C$.

Two factors are sufficient to explain much of the common variance in our illustrative problem; but if the problem warrants it, the methods which have been described can be applied repeatedly until any number of factors (up to the number of variables) is obtained.

**Characteristics of the centroid method** The ideal standard for any method of condensation is that it extract as much variance as possible with each factor. This is done by the method of principal components and it is approximated by the centroid method. In the centroid method, if reflection at each stage is done so as to maximize $T$, the centroid method has definable statistical characteristics. In that instance the sum of absolute loadings (disregarding signs) for each factor is a maximum. If one looks back at the way unreflected loadings were obtained from the reflected residual matrix, one can easily see that the sum of such loadings necessarily equals the square root of $T$. Thus before loadings are reflected, their sum increases with $T$. After loadings are reflected, the sum of absolute loadings also increases with $T$.

It will be remembered that the variance explained by any factor equals the sum of *squared* loadings in a column of the matrix of factor loadings. Thus a method which maximizes that sum (which the method of principal components does) extracts more variance than any other method. Instead of maximizing the sum of squared loadings, the centroid method tends to maximize the sum of loadings, disregarding signs. It is said that the centroid method "tends" to do this, because in practice this will be the case only if reflections are made so as to maximize $T$. An example will serve to illustrate why this does not always occur. Suppose that one is reflecting elements in the first residual matrix and sufficient reflections have been made to produce positive sums for each column of the matrix. One could then go on to obtain loadings on a second factor. It is possible, however, that a better system of sign changes could have been employed, which would have made $T$ larger and thus would have produced a larger sum of absolute loadings. When computer routines are employed which guarantee that $T$ is maximized before each factor is extracted, the centroid method is strictly defined: It is the method which extracts the largest sum of absolute loadings for each factor in turn.

The centroid method, it should be pointed out, is a "good" method of condensation. It is a very simple method to understand, and consequently one does not have to be an expert to grasp the mathematical essentials of the method. Also, compared to some other methods, it requires relatively simple computations. For this reason, before the advent of large-capacity, high-speed computers, the centroid method was by far the most favored method of condensation. Now it is being edged out by the method of principal components. From the standpoint of the degree of condensation, however, the advantage of the principal-components method is not great. The centroid method still is very useful for special problems in factor analysis and as a general method of condensation for small matrices when computer services are not readily available.

## PRINCIPAL-COMPONENTS METHOD OF CONDENSATION

There are three major mathematical approaches to obtaining effective methods of factor condensation. The first is a rational approach, in which one purposefully selects a weighting method for extracting factors irrespective of the nature of the data. This approach is exemplified by the centroid method of condensation, which was discussed previously. The second approach is through statistically optimizing some aspect of the data at hand which are actually obtained from a sample of subjects. The preferred method in this case is principal-components (PC) factor analysis, which will be discussed in this section. The third approach is to employ the results obtained from a sample of subjects to optimally predict the characteristics of a population at large. The approach which is usually employed in that case is referred to as *maximum-likelihood* factor analysis, which will be discussed in a later section.

In many ways, the principal-components method represents an optimum approach to condensation prior to rotation. Whereas the centroid method extracts factors in a way that maximizes the sum absolute of loadings on each factor in turn, the method of principal components maximizes the sum of squared loadings of each factor extracted in turn. This means that each principal-component factor explains more variance than would the loadings obtained from any other method of factoring.

A solution for the weights which can be employed to obtain each principal-components factor involves a classic problem in matrix algebra which is referred to as the *characteristic equation* of a matrix, a matrix of correlations being a prime example. The problem is one of best estimating (in the sense of least squares) a "target matrix," in this case the correlation matrix with unities in the diagonals. To do this requires two sets of values. The first set of values is spoken of as the *characteristic vectors* of the matrix, which will be symbolized as $V_i$. They also are called *latent vectors* and *eigenvectors*. The second set of values are referred to as *characteristic roots*, and they also are referred to as *latent roots* and *eigenvalues*. These will be symbolized as $l_i$. Although the mathematical solution is complex, the basic idea is rather straightforward. When the method of principal components is applied to a correlation matrix, what is meant by a characteristic vector $V_i$ is simply a column (or row) of weights, with each weight pertaining to one of the variables represented in the matrix. Thus, if there are 10 tests being studied, then there would be 10 weights in the first characteristic vector, corresponding to the first factor. Columns in the resulting matrix of factor loadings for factors $A$, $B$, $C$, etc., will be symbolized as $F_a$, $F_b$, $F_c$, etc. Corresponding to each column of factor loadings will be a characteristic vector, appropriately labeled $V_a$, $V_b$, $V_c$, etc. It will be shown that each characteristic vector is proportional to its corresponding column of factor loadings, and the coefficient of proportionality is the square root of the numerical value of the characteristic root for that factor. For example, $F_a$ would be obtained from multiplying each element of $V_a$ by the square root of $l_a$. The same would be done for all factors.

For simplicity in conceptualizing the problem and performing mathematical operations, each characteristic vector is derived so that it has *unit length;* that is, the sum of squares of the weights equals 1.00. In the computations, this can be done easily by dividing each element in a set of weights obtained at any step by the square root of the sum of the squares of the raw weights. This is referred to as *normalizing* a vector. Thus, when one speaks of a characteristic vector (latent vector or eigenvector) $V_i$, it is known that the sum of squares of the weights corresponding to the variables equals 1.00. In practice, one obtains as many characteristic vectors $(V_a, V_b, \ldots, V_r)$ as one wants to obtain factors, i.e., factors that prove to be statistically significant or that explain most of the common variance represented in the correlations of $R$. If one knew these characteristic vectors in advance, then only one more step would be required to obtain the PC factors. What is lacking is a set of *characteristic roots* $l_i$ (latent roots or eigenvalues) for converting corresponding characteristic vectors into PC factors.

Although the sum of squares of each characteristic vector is 1.00, the sum of squares of the factor loadings of any column of the factor matrix will not be 1.00, but rather will represent the total amount of its variance explained by the factor. This total amount of variance explained by each factor is the characteristic root $l_i$ for the factor. The factor with the largest root explains the most variance of the original variables and of the correlation matrix, the characteristic vector with the second largest characteristic root explains the most remaining variance, and so on for as many factors as one wishes to extract.

The mathematical rationale for the PC method and various computational approaches are discussed in the Suggested Additional Readings. Also see Harris (1975) and Tatsuoka (1971) for a mathematical treatment of the topic. Although the concepts underlying the PC method had been around for some time previously, it was left to Hotelling (1933) to specify both the rationale and a practicable computational approach. Rather than derive characteristic vectors and roots directly from the correlation matrix, an iterative solution is employed. Thus, as in any iterative solution, one first takes a trial vector (e.g., a provisional set of 10 weights for 10 variables) and performs a test to determine how close this is to a statistical criterion value. To the extent to which the trial vector is different from the criterion value, the iterative procedure stipulates an approach for modifying the first trial vector to obtain a second trial vector, which logically should be closer to the criterion vector. One continues this iterative process until the solution "converges," that is, until additional iterations produce almost identical results. The final set of values is so close to the actual solution of the equation that any differences are entirely inconsequential.

The method that will be described for iteratively obtaining characteristic roots, characteristic vectors, and PC factors is the outgrowth of a set of mathematical proofs by Hotelling (1933). A method will be described which readers should find highly understandable and which will provide insights about the nature of PC analysis. The method can be cast in computationally more convenient forms, but in forms which would be rather meaningless to the reader. Also, whereas the method which will be described is the same in principle as that developed by Hotelling (and still is a perfectly legitimate procedure), much more efficient computational routines have been developed that are particularly suited to use on computers.

In the iterative approach, characteristic vectors are derived one at a time, and the corresponding characteristic root is obtained as a by-product of the computations. Thus, the first set of calculations would concern a derivation of $V_a$ and $l_a$. To obtain the final characteristic vector $V_a$, form a sequence of trial vectors $V_{a1}, V_{a2}, V_{a3}, \ldots, V_{an}$, where $n$ represents the number of trial vectors required to reach a "goodness of fit" criterion. The criterion concerns the fact that, in the method which will be described, the trial vectors become more and more alike to the point where they are nearly identical up to several decimal points in their calculations. It is said, then, that the iterative solution has *converged*, and Hotelling (1933) proved that convergence must occur with this method. When convergence occurs, one may accept the final vector as being so close to the actual characteristic vector as to be identical for all practical purposes. When this occurs (e.g., at $V_{a9}$ or $V_{a26}$), then the converged vector is designated simply as $V_a$. A method is then available for finding $l_a$ as part of these computations. Then one goes on to search for a second characteristic vector $V_b$ and corresponding characteristic root $l_b$ by the same iterative approach.

The iterative approach shares some computational procedures with the centroid method, and for that reason the reader might want to glance back at earlier sections of this chapter while the method is being discussed. The derivation of $V_a$ starts with the original matrix of correlation $R$. If $R$ has a mixture of negative and positive correlations, then appropriate reflections should be made as described previously for the centroid method. Such reflections usually are not necessary with the original correlation matrix; but if they are, reflections should be performed so as to maximize the sum of coefficients in the matrix as a whole. To simplify the discussion, let us assume that correlations in the original matrix are overwhelmingly positive and the sums of coefficients in all columns (and thus all corresponding rows) are positive. The first step is to obtain the sum of coefficients in each column, including the diagonal element. Thus if $R$ is a 10-by-10 matrix, there would be a diagonal unity and nine actual correlation coefficients to be summed in each column. The 10 column sums could be said to constitute a vector of such sums, and it will be remembered that this vector of column sums could be converted to a vector of loadings on the first centroid factor by dividing each column sum by the square root of the sum of the elements in $R$. Because of the close similarity between centroid factor loadings and PC factor loadings, particularly for the first several factors, one would expect the column sums of $R$ to be closely proportional to the elements in $V_a$. However, in deriving $V_a$ one operates directly off the column sums rather than off the centroid loadings. The vector of column sums is referred to as $U_{a1}$. When $U_{a1}$ is normalized, it becomes $V_{a1}$. This is done by squaring and summing the column sums in $U_{a1}$ and then dividing each element in $U_{a1}$ by the square root of the sum of squares. Thus, $V_{a1}$ is nothing more than a normalized vector of column sums $U_{a1}$ of $R$.

The second trial vector $V_{a2}$ used to estimate $V_a$ is obtained as follows. Elements in $V_{a1}$ are accumulatively multiplied by the first row of $R$ to obtain the first element in a new vector $U_{a2}$. For example, in multiplying $V_{a1}$ by the first row of $R$, the first element in $V_{a1}$ would be multiplied by the diagonal 1; this would be added to the product of the second element in $V_{a1}$ multiplied by $r_{12}$, which would be added to the third element in $V_{a1}$ multiplied by $r_{13}$, and so on for all corresponding elements in $V_{a1}$ and the first row of $R$. Next, the same $V_{a1}$ would be accumulatively multiplied into the elements of the second row of $R$ to obtain the second element of $U_{a2}$. This process would be repeated for each row in turn, which would result in the vector $U_{a2}$. If $R$ is a 10-by-10 matrix, there would be 10 elements in each row of $R$ and 10 elements in $V_{a1}$, and the process of accumulative multiplication would result in a new vector $U_{a2}$ that contains 10 elements. Next, $U_{a2}$ would be normalized by dividing each element by the square root of the sum of the squared elements, which would result in $V_{a2}$. One would then compare $V_{a1}$ and $V_{a2}$. If they were nearly identical, then convergence would have occurred. This actually might happen for the first PC factor because it is derived by a method that is very similar to the first centroid factor, but usually numerous trial vectors are required before convergence occurs.

The next step in estimating the first characteristic vector $V_a$ is to employ $V_{a2}$ in the same way that one employed $V_{a1}$ and accumulatively multiply the elements in each row of $R$, which would result in $U_{a3}$. After $U_{a3}$ is normalized, it becomes $V_{a3}$. Thus one keeps operating off the same correlation matrix but successively trying out altered vectors $V_{ai}$ as accumulative multipliers of the matrix.

The iterative process of deriving trial vectors for factor A would continue. For example, if by this method $V_{a8}$ and $V_{a9}$ were nearly identical, the solution would have converged. In that case, $V_{a8}$ would be declared $V_a$. This would be the first characteristic vector. When $V_a$ is accumulatively multiplied into $U_{a9}$, the result is the first characteristic root $l_a$. Factor loadings for the first factor $F_a$ are obtained by multiplying each element in $V_a$ by the square root of $l_a$. Then $V_a$ can be used as a set of weights for combining the original variables (tests) in a linear combination in such a way PC to produce the actual factor $A$. The loadings of $F_a$ are the correlations of the variables with the linear combination. Thus, in one final move the three desired values are obtained—the characteristic vector, the characteristic root, and the factor loadings for the first PC factor.

Like most methods of condensation, the iterative approach for finding PC factors is repetitive. To obtain factor $B$, one seeks solutions for $V_b$, $l_b$, and the actual factor loadings $F_b$. The same procedures are used as for finding the first factor, except that one operates off the first residual matrix $R_1$ rather than the original correlation matrix $R$. In this case it definitely would be necessary to reflect rows and corresponding columns in $R_1$ to maximize the sum of correlations in the table. With the centroid method, such a reflected matrix was referred to as $R'_1$, off of which one would operate to obtain the necessary ingredients for the second PC factor. First, one would obtain the column sums in $R'_1$, which would constitute $U_{b1}$. This would be normalized to obtain $V_{b1}$. $V_{b1}$ would then be accumulatively multiplied row by row into $R'_1$ to produce $U_{b2}$, which in turn would be normalized to produce $V_{b2}$. The accumulative multiplication is applied to the reflected first residual matrix by the same procedures described previously with respect to obtaining the first PC factor from the original correlation matrix. The procedure would be applied over and over to $R'_1$ until the trial characteristic vectors converged. In this instance, let us say that $V_{b13}$ and $V_{b14}$ prove to be identical. Then: (1) $V_{b13}$ would be declared $V_b$, (2) this would be accumulatively multiplied into $V_{b14}$ to obtain $l_b$, and (3) each element of $V_b$ would be multiplied by the square root of $l_b$ to obtain $F_b$. Proper signs for the factor loadings in $F_b$ would be obtained by giving negative signs to variables that has been reflected in transforming $R_1$ to $R'_1$. Usually this will result in about half of the variables having negative loadings on the second PC factor.

The procedure described above is repeated over and over to obtain each successive PC factor. To obtain the ingredients for the third factor, one would compute a residual matrix by multiplying the loadings in $F_b$ (after negative signs were given to variables that had been reflected), and these would be subtracted element by element from $R_1$—*not* from $R'_1$. This would lead to a second matrix of residual coefficients $R_2$, which also would need to have signs properly reflected so as to maximize the sum of coefficients, resulting in $R'_2$. The iterative procedure described above would be employed to obtain a third characteristic vector, characteristic root, and set of PC factor loadings.

One would continue to obtain PC factors successively until (1) the investigator arbitrarily decided to stop, (2) the elements in a residual matrix proved to be close to zero, (3) a residual matrix proved to be statistically insignificant, or (4) a criterion of goodness of fit was reached. These approaches will be discussed subsequently. In this way one ends up with loadings for all variables on all factors, as well as characteristic roots and vectors corresponding to the factors.

Although the method described above is correct and is probably the most understandable that could be used to introduce someone to the topic, much more rapid approaches have been developed for obtaining PC factors, particularly methods for use on computers. For example, convergence occurs much more rapidly if the iterative process is applied to a *higher power* of the correlation matrix than to the correlation matrix itself, typically the fourth or eighth power. By raising a matrix to a power, however, the reader who is not familiar with matrix algebra should not assume that this means raising the individual elements in the correlation matrix to that power, e.g., squaring $r_{12}$, $r_{13}$, etc. Rather, when one "squares a matrix," one must accumulatively multiply rows in such a way as to obtain a second matrix, which is referred to as the square of the first matrix. The same process can then be applied to the squared matrix to obtain a matrix which is said to be to the fourth power, and so on to higher powers. There are numerous other iterative approaches which have been developed mathematically and used in various computer programs. These approaches are discussed in the Suggested Additional Readings and in various books on multivariate analysis such as Harris (1975) and Tatsuoka (1971). However, all the approaches boil down to essentially the same logic as embodied in the simple, straightforward approach described above. They all produce the same characteristic roots, vectors, and PC factor loadings.

**Mathematical properties of principal components** In many ways, the method of principal components is ideal for selecting a method of condensation prior to rotation that optimizes some function of the actual data. Tables 10-6 through 10-10 showed the derivation of two centroid factors from a 6-by-6 matrix of correlations. Table 10-11 shows those same centroid factors compared with PC factors obtained from the same $R$ matrix. In this case the results are very close; however, in large problems where the factors are not nearly as clear as in this case, the results of the two approaches can be noticeably different. The

**Table 10-11 A comparison of factors obtained by the centroid method with factors obtained by the method of principal components**

| | Centroid Factors | | | | Principal Components | | |
|---|---|---|---|---|---|---|---|
| | $A$ | $B$ | $h^2$ | | $A$ | $B$ | $h^2$ |
| *1* | .71 | .40 | .66 | | .71 | .39 | .66 |
| *2* | .70 | .46 | .70 | | .71 | .48 | .73 |
| *3* | .70 | .37 | .63 | | .70 | .32 | .59 |
| *4* | .69 | −.41 | .64 | | .69 | −.42 | .65 |
| *5* | .65 | −.43 | .61 | | .64 | −.45 | .61 |
| *6* | .71 | −.39 | .66 | | .71 | −.38 | .65 |
| Var | .48 | .17 | (total = .65) | Var | .48 | .17 | (total = .65) |

**Table 10-12 Principal-components factor loadings for 24-ability tests**

| Tests | Factors | | | |
|---|---|---|---|---|
| | A | B | C | D |
| 1. Visual perception | .61 | −.02 | .43 | −.21 |
| 2. Cubes | .40 | −.06 | .41 | −.22 |
| 3. General information | .69 | −.33 | −.33 | −.06 |
| 4. Paragraph comprehension | .69 | −.41 | −.26 | .08 |
| 5. Sentence completion | .69 | −.41 | −.35 | −.06 |
| 6. Word classification | .69 | −.24 | −.16 | −.12 |
| 7. Word meaning | .69 | −.45 | −.30 | .07 |
| 8. Add | .47 | .54 | −.45 | −.19 |
| 9. Code | .57 | .42 | −.21 | .02 |
| 10. Counting groups of dots | .49 | .54 | −.12 | −.35 |
| 11. Straight and curved capitals | .62 | .28 | .03 | −.38 |
| 12. Word recognition | .44 | .10 | −.03 | .57 |
| 13. Number recognition | .40 | .16 | .10 | .52 |
| 14. Figure recognition | .54 | .10 | .40 | .29 |
| 15. Object-Number | .50 | .27 | −.06 | .48 |
| 16. Number-Figure | .55 | .38 | .19 | .14 |
| 17. Figure-Word | .48 | .13 | .10 | .21 |
| 18. Deduction | .65 | −.19 | .14 | .08 |
| 19. Numerical puzzles | .62 | .24 | .10 | −.19 |
| 20. Problem reasoning | .65 | −.15 | .11 | .07 |
| 21. Series completion | .71 | −.11 | .15 | −.09 |
| 22. Woody-McCall test | .67 | .20 | −.23 | −.05 |
| 23. Paper form board | .44 | −.20 | .47 | −.10 |
| 24. Flags | .51 | −.18 | .33 | −.21 |
| Sum Sq. = $l_i$ = | 8.16 | 2.06 | 1.70 | 1.48 |

*Source*: Adapted from R. L. Gorsuch, *Factor Analysis* (Philadelphia: W. B. Saunders Co., 1974). By permission of the author and W. B. Saunders Co.

results of applying the PC method to an actual investigation of human abilities are given in Table 10-12. The original data came from an old study by Holzinger and Swineford (1939), and the analysis shown in Table 10-12 was performed by Gorsuch (1974) and adapted from that source.

Some interesting and useful mathematical properties of PC factoring are as follows:

1. Each factor in turn maximizes the variance explained from the correlation matrix. This has several important implications. First, the sum of squared loadings is as large as possible for any PC factor. Second, the sum of squared loadings in the residual matrix including the diagonal elements is as small as possible for any factor that could be extracted. In other words, the sum of squared partial correlations that could be obtained from the first residual matrix is as small as possible. Third, the first principal component, as a linear combination of variables, explains more of the actual standard score variance in the data matrix $S$ than would any other linear combination of the variables in that matrix. These represent several ways of saying

that each PC factor explains the most variance possible of the data obtained from a sample of subjects (but not necessarily from a hypothetical population from which the sample may have been drawn, which is a matter which will be discussed subsequently).

2. Any $h$ principal-component factors ($h$ being equal to or less than the number of variables $k$) will explain as much or more total variance than any $h$ component factors obtained by any other method. This is a fortunate circumstance which does not necessarily follow from the first statement above, because it is entirely possible that a method could derive the most variance possible from the original correlation matrix and from each residual matrix but not be the best in that regard for any set number of factors. It turns out that the PC method does maximize the variance explained for any number of factors.

3. The amount of variance explained (sum of squared loadings) by each PC factor is equal to the corresponding characteristic root. The roots for factors $A$ and $B$ in Table 10-11 are 2.89 and 1.01 respectively. When these are divided by the number of variables, they show the characteristic roots as proportions (spoken of as percentages) of total variance explained. Thus, the first factor explains 48 percent of the total variance, and the second factor explains 17 percent of the total variance.

4. In a "legitimate" PC analysis of a correlation matrix, all the characteristic roots are either zero or positive—never negative. The reason that the term *legitimate* is employed is that one actually can obtain negative characteristic roots by using measures of relationship other than product-moment correlation coefficients. For example, instances have been found of negative characteristic roots obtained from applying PC analysis to tetrachoric correlation coefficients. The fact that characteristic roots must be either zero or positive offers an after-the-fact test for the legitimacy of the analysis—the measures of relationship employed and any departures from using the standard PC approach. Although tiny negative characteristic roots frequently are obtained in computer outputs, these usually are due to rounding errors in the multitudes of computations required. If large negative latent roots are obtained, however, this is a sure indication that something illegitimate was performed in the analysis.

5. The number of positive (nonzero) latent roots represents the number of PC factors needed to explain all the variance in a correlation matrix. For example, if only five characteristic roots are greater than zero in a matrix of correlations among 20 tests, then (1) five factors would provide a complete basis for the analogous representation of correlations in terms of hyperspace geometry, (2) all the coefficients including the diagonal elements would be precisely zero in the residual matrix after the fifth factor was extracted, and (3) all the scores in the original $S$ matrix would be precisely zero after the five factors were partialed. In component analysis, it is usually the case that *all* characteristic roots are positive; consequently it is necessary to extract as many factors as there are variables to totally reduce

the correlation matrix to zero and thus totally explain the original variance of scores and correlations in $R$. However, as will be discussed more fully subsequently, the roots frequently become so small after a number of factors are extracted that subsequent roots can be ignored. The factoring can be considered complete at that point. Thus one would achieve a solution that did a good job of approximately explaining all the variance with a relatively small number of factors.

6. The sum of characteristic roots equals the sum of diagonal elements in the original correlation matrix. When PC analysis is performed with unities in the diagonal spaces, this means that the sum of characteristic roots equals the number of variables. Thus, in the solution depicted in Table 10-11, there are six variables; consequently, the sum of all characteristic roots would be 6.00. In that solution the first characteristic root is 2.89, and the second characteristic root is 1.01, for a total of 3.90, which when divided by 6 gives the total 65 percent variance shown in the table. When PC analyses are performed on measures of relationship other than correlation coefficients (e.g., covariances and other measures to be discussed later), the sum of characteristic roots still equals the sum of diagonal elements. In any case this sum is referred to as the *trace* of the matrix.

7. Earlier in the chapter it was said that a component factor is a linear combination of the actual scores in $S$. The linear combinations that underlie PC analysis are mutually orthogonal, or uncorrelated with one another. Even though the mathematical operations might be employed directly on the correlation matrix to obtain the matrices of factor loadings, such as illustrated in Tables 10-11 and 10-12, these loadings can be used in conjunction with the correlation matrix to actually obtain the linear combinations that constitute the factors (by methods which will be discussed in Chap. 11). Such scores of people on the factors can be only estimated when one employs a method of common-factor analysis rather than a method of component-factor analysis.

8. In addition to the other aspects of PC factoring mentioned above, the results and by-products of solutions of the characteristic equation provide many incidental advantages which are not provided by other methods. To illustrate the point, several of these will be mentioned. First, not only are the actual linear combinations of scores underlying the factors orthogonal, but the characteristic vectors, and thus the columns in the original matrix of factor loadings, are uncorrelated (orthogonal) to one another. Even some professionals who should know better get confused on this point. The orthogonality of the factors, as linear combinations of the variables, does not guarantee that the columns in the matrix of factor loadings are uncorrelated with one another. Indeed, this is necessarily true only for the unrotated PC solution and not even for the PC solution after the factors are rotated by methods to be discussed subsequently. Thus, whereas the factors, as linear combinations of the variables, can remain uncorrelated, the columns of correlations of variables with those factors (as shown in

Tables 10-11 and 10-12) after rotation may correlate substantially either positively or negatively. The orthogonality of the original PC factor loadings greatly simplifies some mathematical operations that might be performed on them. A second mathematical advantage is that the product of all characteristic roots of a matrix is equal to the *determinant* of the matrix. The reader will remember that the determinant of a matrix of coefficients in simultaneous equations is very useful in solving for the unknown values. In this case, a knowledge that the product of characteristic roots is equal to the determinant of $R$ greatly simplifies the solution of mathematical equations that involve the whole original correlation matrix. Previously it was said that the number of factors required to explain a matrix of correlations (the rank of the matrix) is equal to the number of positive characteristic roots. Obviously, then, if the number of factors is less than the number of variables, some of the roots will be zero, the product will be zero, and the determinant will be zero. Again, from a mathematical point of view, this offers some very interesting perspectives and permits numerous mathematical derivations. A third incidental mathematical advantage of working with characteristic roots, characteristic vectors, and the other by-products of the PC method is that all the related developments lend themselves quite nicely to the employment of inferential statistics (e.g., in determining the statistical significance of individual factors), which will be discussed in Chap. 11.

**Examples of principal components** Some features of matrices of factor loadings before they are rotated are evident in Tables 10-11 and 10-12. Typically the first factor explains the lion's share of the variance, and the percentage or proportion of variance falls off rapidly (the sizes of the characteristic roots decline). All 24 characteristic roots for the problem concerning 24 tests shown in Table 10-12 are as follows: 8.16, 2.06, 1.70, 1.48, 1.01, .92, .89, .83, .78, .73, .64, .54, .54, .51, .47, .42, .39, .36, .33, .32, .31, .25, .20, and .17. Only the four factors corresponding to the first four largest roots are shown in Table 10-12. As can be seen, the first factor explains almost four times as much variance as the second, and the sizes of the roots tend to level off rapidly after that.

In Table 10-11 it can be easily shown that the two columns of factor loadings are orthogonal, in that the sums of products in the two columns are zero, within rounding error. As can be seen in both Table 10-11 and Table 10-12, if the correlation matrix has predominantly positive correlations, then typically one finds large, positive loadings for nearly all variables on the first PC factor. A factor of this kind frequently is spoken of as a *general factor* because nearly all the tests have strong positive loadings, and the factor does not serve to distinguish among the tests very well. As is shown in both tables, there is a balance of positive and negative loadings on all factors subsequent to the first. As can be seen by inspecting the two tables, it is rather difficult to give meaningful interpretations to the raw PC factors. For the 24 tests whose loadings are shown in Table 10-12, one could call the first factor "general ability," but it would be quite difficult to give meaningful interpretations to the other factors. Partly this is due to the complex configuration of loadings, which makes it difficult to untangle the groupings or clusterings of tests from one another. Partly this is due to the negative loadings that necessarily occur on raw PC factors. This is particularly confusing when one is analyzing tests of ability rather than tests of personality or other noncognitive functions. The difficulty in directly interpreting the raw PC solution is the reason that rotation usually is employed as a second step in exploratory factor analysis.

## MAXIMUM-LIKELIHOOD METHOD OF CONDENSATION

As mentioned previously, there are three major mathematical approaches to determining the weights required for linear combinations of variables in factor analysis. These are (1) a rational approach in which one simply asserts the way in which weights will be applied, (2) a statistical approach in which one optimizes some aspect of data from a sample of subjects, and (3) a statistical approach in which one maximizes some relationship between the sample of data and the population from which the sample was drawn. The first approach is epitomized by the centroid method; the second approach is epitomized by the principal-components method; and the third approach is epitomized by the maximum-likelihood (ML) method of factoring.

The maximum-likelihood method differs from the PC method in that the ML method obtains sets of factor loadings successively in such a way that each in turn explains as much as possible of the *population* correlation matrix as estimated from the sample correlation matrix. For convenience in this discussion, special symbols will be used: $R_s$ stands for the correlation matrix actually obtained from the data in a sample (e.g., of test scores), and $R_p$ stands for the correlation matrix that would be obtained if the whole population were tested. Of course, $R_s$ is only an estimate of $R_p$, the goodness of the estimate depending on the adequacy of the sampling techniques and on the number of subjects. The PC method maximizes the variance explained in $R_s$. Whereas the PC method is statistical in the sense of optimally describing some aspects of the data obtained from a sample, namely as much as possible of the correlations in $R_s$, the ML method is statistical in a more general sense of inferential statistics in that it seeks to extrapolate what is known from $R_s$ in the best possible way to estimate $R_p$.

**Usefulness of ML factoring** For a number of reasons, the ML method will be described here only in general terms rather than spelled out in more detail. First, whereas the ML method is an approach to condensation which can be used in exploratory factor analysis as a prelude to rotations, it is even more useful as part of a general approach to confirmatory factor analysis, which will be discussed later. Second, it was said that this chapter would be confined to *component analysis*, in the sense that the factors are real, linear combinations of variables rather than hypothetical common factors. Although one can employ the ML method with reliability coefficients or other prespecified indices of variance, most frequently the method is used to search for hypothetical common factors. One obtains almost identical results from the PC method and the ML method when (1) communalities are very high, (2) high reliabilities are employed in the diagonal spaces, or (3) one intentionally puts values in the diagonal spaces that are .90 or higher. Since the PC method is far easier to compute and understand than the ML method, the ML method seldom has any advantage purely as an approach to condensation when all or nearly all the total variance is being explained. In exploratory factor analysis, those who favor the ML method do so because (1) they consider it an excellent approach to deriving common factors, as distinct from components, and (2) it is accompanied by a significance test for the extraction of each successive factor that is superior to that which is employed with any other type of common-factor analysis.

**Properties of maximum-likelihood estimators** Because mention is made of maximum-likelihood statistical methods with respect to various psychometric procedures in addition to ML factor analysis, such as the use of ML methods in multidimensional scaling, it would be useful to look briefly at some of the characteristics of ML statistical methods in general. The ML methods constitute one approach to obtaining statistical estimators, in which one uses the information obtained from a sample to estimate some characteristic or parameter of a population from which the sample was drawn. Thus, the formulas used to obtain the mean and standard deviation (with $N$ rather than $N - 1$ in the equation) happen to be ML estimators of the population mean and standard deviation. In an analogous fashion, one can obtain ML estimators of the population correlation matrix, covariance matrix, and complex mathematical functions of those. Because many different choices of statistical estimators can be employed, it is useful to look for important characteristics in selecting among them:

1. *Consistency.* An estimator is *consistent* if in a probabilistic sense it converges on the population parameter as the sample size increases without limit.
2. *Efficiency.* An estimator is *efficient* if it has the smallest error variance over different samples.
3. *Sufficiency.* An estimator is said to be *sufficient* if it utilizes all the relevant information from the sample in estimating the parameter.
4. *Bias.* An estimator is unbiased if the expected value is the same as the population parameter, i.e., if the probability is 50-50 that a particular estimate is above or below the population value.

Not all parameters have sufficient estimators, but if one exists, the maximum-likelihood statistic is a sufficient estimator. In that case, there is a maximum-likelihood estimator that satisfies the first three of the above criteria for selecting statistical estimators. Regarding the fourth criterion, sometimes the ML estimator is slightly biased (e.g., as illustrated above with respect to the estimator of the population standard deviation); but this slight bias, if present, usually is offset by the many advantages of ML estimators. In addition to the advantages of ML estimators with respect to the characteristics mentioned above, ML estimators prove to be applicable to an extremely wide variety of problems. Even though they prove to be complex for individuals who are not familiar with the mathematics involved, persons who do understand the mathematics can derive maximum-likelihood estimators for almost anything, or at least so it seems. Also, such ML estimators tie in very neatly with a wide variety of related statistical procedures and auxiliary methods of mathematics. For these reasons, ML estimators have proved to be very attractive in factor analysis and a wide variety of other problems in multivariate analysis and psychometric theory generally.

**Computation of ML factors** From a number of standpoints, the actual arithmetic underlying the ML method is quite difficult. First, the mathematical derivations are much more complex than even those with the PC method. The underlying mathematics would be understandable only to the individual who had a solid grounding in calculus, higher algebra, and matrix algebra in particular. The basic mathematical derivations are well explained in Mulaik (1972). Second, as with the PC method, in the ML method an iterative approach is employed to find each factor. However, whereas highly acceptable iterative procedures have been worked out for the PC method, this has proved much more difficult to do with the ML method. Third, although some breakthroughs have been made in recent years in developing iterative computer programs for the ML method [discussed in Gorsuch (1974) and Mulaik (1972)], these are still more complex to employ and require considerably more computer capacity and computer time than the PC method.

**Products of the ML method** On the surface, the products of the ML method are essentially the same in appearance as those of the PC method. Actually, when both methods are applied to the same data, the results frequently are highly similar—so much so that one would reach essentially the same conclusions regardless of which of the two types of analyses one had in hand. The ML method is quite flexible in that one can simultaneously extract a specified number of factors initially; but for exploratory factor analysis, this is usually done one factor at a time successively. The loadings obtained on the first factor are employed in the usual way to obtain a matrix of residual coefficients. A significance test is applied to the matrix of residuals, in order to indicate whether it would be reasonable to extract a second factor. Then a second factor is obtained iteratively, a second matrix of residual coefficients is obtained, and again one employs a significance test to determine if additional factors should be extracted. One stops factoring after the significance test fails to reject the null hypothesis for the residual matrix (e.g., not significant beyond the .01 level), or the experimenter stops at some earlier point in the extraction of factors for a different reason. The final product is a matrix of factor loadings. Since such matrices of factor loading for all intents and purposes look like they do with those obtained from the centroid method and PC methods, there is no need to provide a special illustration. In exploratory factor analysis, one would rotate the ML factor loadings. For this purpose one could employ any method of rotations, including those that typically are employed with the centroid method, the PC method, and other methods of condensation.

## OTHER METHODS OF CONDENSATION

In addition to the three major methods of condensation that have been discussed, numerous other methods are available. Now many are largely of historical importance, and they have been succeeded by better approaches; others are useful for only highly specialized purposes, such as making mathematical transformations in the process of rotating factors. Such other approaches to condensation are discussed throughout the Suggested Additional Readings. Gorsuch (1974) provides easily understood descriptions of many different factoring methods. For descriptions of methods which are now mainly of historical value, see Thurstone (1947). As was mentioned earlier in this chapter, *any* rule for weighting the variables in a data matrix constitutes a legitimate approach to factor analysis, and consequently there are as many different possible approaches to factor analysis as there are ways to specify methods for obtaining weights. It was said that the major approaches to condensation rely on three general approaches, namely those concerning rational specifications of weights, specifications of weights in such a way as to maximally explain the variance in the sample correlation matrix $R_s$, and methods to maximally estimate the variance in the population correlation matrix $R_p$ from mathematical derivations relating to the sample correlation matrix $R_s$. By far the best methods available for these purposes are the centroid method, the PC method, and the ML method respectively. Nearly all other modern methods of factor analysis really are only special cases of these, even though other methods go by a variety of names.

## ROTATION OF FACTORS

The second step in a stepwise analysis is to rotate factors. Although some factorists try to interpret factors obtained in the first step (e.g., factors obtained from the PC method), by far the majority of factorists prefer to rotate factors. This is done to obtain a more interpretable set of factor loadings and to facilitate estimations of the scores of people on the factors.

**Geometric analogy** It is in the rotation of factors that the analogy between factoring and hyperspace geometry proves most useful. In Fig. 10-4 the placements of two centroid vectors in a two-space of four variables were shown. There is nothing to prevent one from rotating those two factor vectors. The problem of rotation is the same regardless of the method of condensation employed, e.g., centroid, PC, ML, or any other. If one wants to maintain un-correlated (orthogonal) factors, the rotation must be done so as to keep the ro-tated factor vectors at right angles to one another. Rotation can be illustrated by imagining that the factor vectors are movable like the hands on a clock. One of the factor vectors then could be moved to any position desired. The other would be moved to a position where it formed a right angle with the rotated first factor vector.

The geometry of rotation is illustrated in Fig. 10-5, which is a graphic plot of loadings on two centroid factors for the six-variable problem shown in Table 10-6. $A$ and $B$ are the centroid factor vectors, and $A_1$ and $B_1$ are the ro-tated vectors. Loadings for the six variables can now be read off the rotated fac-tors in the same way that they were from the unrotated factors. Rotated factors $A_1$ and $B_1$ can be transformed into "yardsticks" by spacing deciles along them ranging from 0 to 1.00 in the same way as was done for the original factors. Then a perpendicular line is raised from the point on each rotated factor to the point corresponding to the variable. Where the perpendicular line touches the rotated factor axis is the loading of the variable on the rotated factor.

Loadings on the rotated factors are shown in Table 10-13. If rotated factors are orthogonal, two important properties of the unrotated matrix of factor load-ings carry over to the rotated matrix of factor loadings. First, the sum of squared loadings in any row ($h^2$) remains the same. That is, the rotated factors explain the same amount of variance as the unrotated factors did. Second, the sum of products of loadings in any two rows of the rotated factor matrix is the same as that in the unrotated matrix. Thus the same common variance is explained in both the rotated and unrotated matrices. In other words, from a statistical point of view, the rotated factors are "just as good" as the unrotated factors. Thus if rotated factors are more easily interpreted than unrotated fac-tors, the investigator has every right to rotate. The first step in a stepwise analy-sis (e.g., use of the PC method) can then be thought of as determining the start-ing points for rotation. The first step serves its purpose in condensing the com-mon variance, and the second step (rotation) serves its purpose in "slicing up" that common variance in a manner that is more easily interpreted.

**Table 10-13 Loadings on orthogonally rotated centroid factors**

|   | $A_1$ | $B_1$ | $h^2$ |
|---|---|---|---|
| 1 | .23 | .78 | .66 |
| 2 | .18 | .82 | .70 |
| 3 | .25 | .75 | .62 |
| 4 | .78 | .18 | .64 |
| 5 | .77 | .14 | .61 |
| 6 | .78 | .21 | .65 |
| Var | .33 | .32 | (total = .65) |

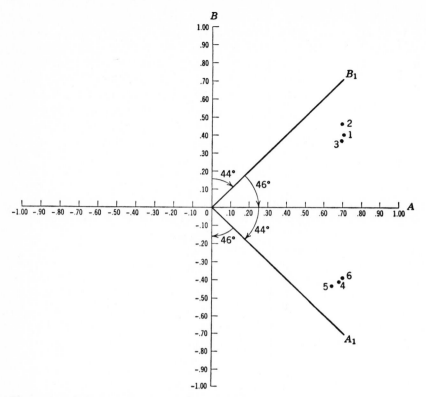

**Figure 10-5** Orthogonal rotation of centroid factors.

**Mechanics of rotation** One way to rotate is illustrated in Fig. 10-5. First, one plots loadings on factors with graph paper. The rotated loadings can be read directly from the rotated factors. One way to do this is to develop a transparent grid that can be placed over the graph. The zero point on the grid is placed over the zero point on the graph. The abscissa of the grid is placed along the vector for $A_1$, which makes the ordinate of the grid fall along the vector of $B_1$. Loadings on $A_1$ and $B_1$ are read from the grid in the same way that they were read from the graph for unrotated factors $A$ and $B$. What rotation does is to construct a new coordinate system.

Although it is seldom done these days in large analyses, one can perform all rotations by the graphical method described above. This method requires that only two factors be rotated at a time. Thus one might start off by rotating $A$ and $B$ to $A_1$ and $B_1$. Then $A_1$ would be rotated with factor $C$, which would lead to $A_2$ and $C_1$. $B_1$ and $C_1$ could then be rotated to obtain $B_2$ and $C_2$, and so on. If there are numerous factors, there are even more numerous possibilities for rotating factors two at a time.

One can rotate factors two at a time and still maintain the essential properties of the original matrix of loadings. If orthogonal rotations are made in each binary comparison, no matter what pairs are formed for rotation and no matter how many such rotations are done, $h^2$ for each variable will remain the same. Also, the sum of cross products in any two rows of factor loadings will remain the same, and all factors will remain orthogonal.

If more than three or four factors are submitted to rotation, the graphical method of rotation may take considerable time. This is because there are so many possible comparisons of the factors two at a time. Suppose, for example, that in the first round of rotations, five factors are compared two at a time in all possible pairs. This would require 10 graphical comparisons, rotations, and the computation of rotated loadings. Usually the full matrix of rotated factors would not produce the desired structure of loadings (according to standards which will be discussed later). Then it would be necessary to start in again and rerotate the once-rotated factors. From 10 to 20 such rounds of rotation might be required to reach the desired solution, which would be very time-consuming. For this reason, numerous efforts have been made to develop *analytic methods of rotation*, ones that "do the job for you" on computers. These will be discussed later.

**Mathematics of rotation** It will be recalled that a component factor is a linear combination of variables. A rotated factor is simply a linear combination of a set of factors. In other words, a rotated factor is a linear combination of a set of linear combinations. For example, the rotation of factor $A$ in Fig. 10-5 can be done with the following linear equation:

$$r_{iA_1} = a_1 r_{iA} + b_1 r_{iB} \tag{10-10}$$

where $r_{iA_1}$ = rotated loadings on $A_1$

$r_{iA}$ = unrotated loadings on $A$

$r_{iB}$ = unrotated loadings on $B$

$a_1, b_1$ = weights for rotation

In the rotation shown in Fig. 10-5, $a_1$ is .72, and $b_1$ is $-.69$. The weights are the cosines of the angles of rotation of $A_1$ with $A$ and $B$, respectively. Rather than rotate visually with the use of a grid as was discussed previously, one can use the graph of factor loadings to obtain the proper weights and then perform the rotations on a desk calculator. This is not necessarily faster than using a grid, but it is somewhat more accurate.

Rather than form a rotated factor as the linear combination of only two factors, as is illustrated in Eq. (10-10), one can form a factor as a linear combination of a larger number of factors. Thus a set of rotated factor loadings $A_1$ could be obtained from a linear combination of four factors as follows:

$$r_{iA_1} = a_1 r_{iA} + b_1 r_{iB} + c_1 r_{iC} + d_1 r_{iD} \tag{10-11}$$

When a rotated factor is formed as a linear combination of more than two factors, it is difficult to obtain the weights from graphical comparisons. This is because one is rotating simultaneously in more than two dimensions, and consequently the weights cannot be determined by the movement of factor vectors on the flat surface of a piece of graph paper.

Equations (10-10) and (10-11) illustrate an important principle concerning rotation. If the original factors are orthogonal (which has been assumed in all discussions so far), the sum of squared weights for rotation must equal 1.0. This is true both for the rotation in Eq. (10-10) and for that in Eq. (10-11). This is necessary for the rotated factor to remain at unit length.

Another important principle about rotation can be illustrated by the linear combination that would produce $B_1$ in Fig. (10-5). In general terms the formula would be as follows:

$$r_{iB_1} = a_2 r_{iA} + b_2 r_{iB} \tag{10-12}$$

The weights for obtaining loadings on $B_1$ are $a_2$ and $b_2$. For the rotation in Fig. 10-5, $a_2$ is .69 and $b_2$ is .72. Note that the sum of the squares of these two coefficients equals 1.0, as it must. The principle to be illustrated is this: If the original factors are orthogonal and the rotated factors are orthogonal, the sum of products of the two sets of factor weights must equal zero. Thus in this instance $a_1 a_2 + b_1 b_2$ does, and must, equal zero. This is true regardless of how many terms there are in the linear combination used to obtain rotated factors. Thus if factors $A_1$ and $B_1$ are orthogonal rotations of factors $A$, $B$, $C$, and $D$, it necessarily follows that

$$a_1 a_2 + b_1 b_2 + c_1 c_2 + d_1 d_2 = 0 \tag{10-13}$$

If that condition does not hold, $A_1$ and $B_2$ are not orthogonal; i.e., the correlation between the two factors is different from zero. If all rotated factors are orthogonal, the sum of cross products of weights for rotation for any pair of rotated factors equals zero.

**Oblique rotations** Up to this point it has been assumed that, in rotation, the original factors are orthogonal and the rotated factors also are orthogonal. There is, however, no mathematical necessity for maintaining right angles among rotated factors. Nonorthogonal (correlated) factors are referred to as *oblique*, because the angles among them differ from 90°. It is tempting to employ oblique factors to place rotated factor vectors through clusters of variables, which tends to maximize the loadings on a factor for the members of a cluster. An oblique rotation for the data from Fig. 10-5 is shown in Fig. 10-6, and the corresponding loadings on oblique factors are shown in Table 10-14. The cosine of the angle between $A_1$ and $B_1$ is .48, which is the correlation between the two factors. One can determine loadings on oblique factors by raising a perpendicular line from the rotated factor vector to the tip of the vector for a variable. This also can be done with a transparent grid in a manner similar to that described previously for orthogonal rotations. First, one obtains loadings on $A_1$ by placing the abscissa of the grid along $A_1$. Then, to obtain loadings on $B_1$, it is necessary to rotate the grid to a point where the ordinate of the grid lies on $B_1$. Loadings on $B_1$ can then be read from the ordinate of the grid.

Rather than compute loadings on obliquely rotated factors with a grid, one can form linear combinations of the unrotated factors. Contrary to what is true of orthogonal rotations, the sums of cross products of weights for rotation of two rotated factors would not equal zero. Also, if obliquely rotated factors

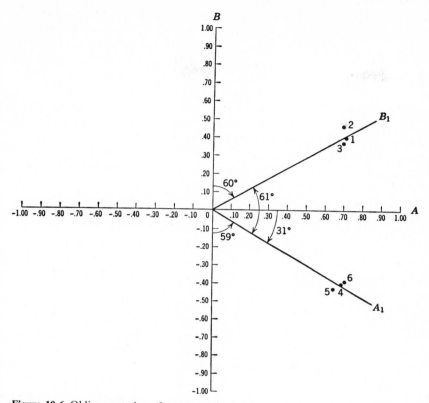

**Figure 10-6** Oblique rotation of two centroid factors.

subsequently are rerotated, the sum of squared weights for rotation would equal 1.00 only by chance.

Oblique rotations change some of the essential characteristics of the original matrix of factor loadings. The sum of squared loadings in any row would equal $h^2$ only by chance, and the sum of average squared loadings in the columns of the matrix would equal the total variance explained only by chance.

**Table 10-14 Loadings on obliquely rotated factors**

|   | $A_1$ | $B_1$ |
|---|---|---|
| 1 | .40 | .81 |
| 2 | .36 | .84 |
| 3 | .41 | .79 |
| 4 | .80 | .39 |
| 5 | .78 | .35 |
| 6 | .81 | .42 |

Also, the sum of cross products in any two rows of the matrix of rotated loadings would be unlikely to equal the same quantity computed from the unrotated loadings. In this case, the sum of cross products could be greater than $+1.00$ or less than $-1.00$ which, to say the least, would make it evident that sums of cross products of oblique factor loadings do not serve to explain the original correlations.

There are numerous other "statistical losses" in employing oblique rather than orthogonal rotations. For example, in an orthogonal rotation, the sum of squared loadings in any row of the matrix of factor loadings equals the squared multiple correlation of the factors with the particular variable; in oblique rotations, this would not be the case. Also, in numerous auxiliary methods of analysis that cannot be discussed here, working with orthogonal factors is far simpler than working with oblique factors.

The supposed advantages of oblique rotations are mainly conceptual rather than mathematical. As we mentioned previously, when one looks at plots of factor loadings, it is intuitively appealing to place factor vectors through dominant clusters of variables, which usually leads to oblique rotations. Also, it is easy to think of many variables that are conceptually independent but are correlated in real life. For example, it is meaningful to discuss heights and weights of people as separate dimensions of size, but the two are correlated. Also, it is meaningful to discuss verbal ability and mathematical ability as constituting different factors of intellect, but these two factors have a substantial positive correlation. From this and other examples, it can be argued that it is meaningful to work with correlated factors in factor analysis.

Because there are good things to say about both orthogonal rotations and oblique rotations and because both are mathematically legitimate, which is used boils down to a matter of taste. In the early years of factor analysis, most rotations were orthogonal. Then, from about 1940 until recent years, there was a swing toward the use of oblique rotations, but now one gets the impression that orthogonal rotations are predominating. Also, since most rotations are performed today by analytic methods on high-speed computers, the type of rotation is determined by the particular analytic method. The method which is used most frequently (the Varimax method) results in orthogonal rotations.

The author has a mild preference for orthogonal rotations, because (1) they are so much simpler mathematically than oblique rotations, (2) there have been numerous demonstrations that the two approaches lead to essentially the same conclusions about the number and kinds of factors inherent in a particular matrix of correlations, and (3) as will be discussed more fully subsequently, there are numerous ways to fool oneself and other people by some types of oblique rotations. This preference is "mild," because as will be discussed more fully later, in the act of estimating the scores of people on orthogonal factors, one frequently does the equivalent of additional rotations. After estimates of factor scores are obtained, usually it is found that the estimates are correlated even if the factors themselves are orthogonal. Also, in the multiple-group method and other approaches to confirmatory analysis that will be discussed subsequently, frequently it is logical to derive correlated factors. For these reasons, the author can understand why some persons prefer the use of oblique rotations to place factor axes through dominant clusters of variables. There are some systems of oblique rotation, however, which definitely are not recommended; these will be discussed subsequently.

**Criteria for rotation** What is a *good* set of rotations? As was mentioned previously, the unrotated factors are as good in a statistical sense as any rotation of them. The major reason for rotating factors is to obtain a more interpretable solution. The ideal case of an easily interpreted solution is illustrated in Table 10-15, where an $X$ stands for a substantial positive loading. There are at least three "pure" variables for each factor. Factor $A$ can be interpreted in terms of whatever variables 1, 2, and 3 have in common. Since the variables that define one factor have zero loadings on the other two factors, this aids the interpretation of factors. In addition to simplifying the interpretation of factors, an ideal rotation like that in Table 10-15 would make it very easy to estimate scores of people on factors. One could estimate scores on factor $A$ by simply summing (and then standardizing) scores on variables 1, 2, and 3. Similarly, one could obtain factor scores for the other two factors by averaging scores on the related clusters of variables.

If it were reasonable to expect factor results like those in Table 10-15, it would be easy to get almost everyone to agree on the criterion for rotation: *Rotation should be performed so that each variable loads on one and only one factor.* The rule need not require that there be the same number of pure variables for all factors, only that there be some pure variables for each factor. Attempts to approximate this ideal led to Thurstone's (1947) concept of *simple structure.* The concept is embodied in a set of rules regarding the form of the rotated matrix of factor loadings; e.g., each row of the factor matrix should have at least one zero.

Although most factorists today talk about "rotating to simple structure," no one can say for sure what constitutes simple structure. The rules given by Thurstone and others are not nearly sufficient. The condition is definable in the

**Table 10-15 Ideal set of rotated factor loadings**

|  | *Factor* | | |
|---|---|---|---|
|  | *A* | *B* | *C* |
| *1* | *X* | 0 | 0 |
| *2* | *X* | 0 | 0 |
| *3* | *X* | 0 | 0 |
| *4* | 0 | *X* | 0 |
| *Variable* *5* | 0 | *X* | 0 |
| *6* | 0 | *X* | 0 |
| *7* | 0 | 0 | *X* |
| *8* | 0 | 0 | *X* |
| *9* | 0 | 0 | *X* |

ideal case, as in Table 10-15, but when one departs from the ideal case, no one can completely specify the best approximation of simple structure. It is like trying to specify the essential physical ingredients that combine to form a beautiful woman. In both cases, by looking at the product, one can form an impression of how well the criterion is met, but the processes of judgment are illusive. Also, even to the extent to which one can specify the characteristics of simple structure, there is no reason why nature must be displayed in this precise form, particularly when one is performing exploratory analyses of polyglot collections of tests.

Rather than talk about simple structure, perhaps it would be better to talk about *simpler structures*. Thus a rotated factor matrix usually is simpler to interpret than the unrotated matrix, and some rotations are simpler to interpret than others. Generally what one seeks is a rotation where there are *some relatively pure variables for each factor*. The orthogonal rotation in Table 10-13 meets this standard. Variables 1 through 3 have much higher loadings on $B_1$ than on $A_1$, and vice versa for variables 4 through 6. Such simpler rotations can be sought either with graphic comparisons of factors two at a time or with one of the analytic methods used on computers.

Efforts can be made to find a simpler structure either with orthogonal factors or with oblique factors. The example in Table 10-13 shows how this can be done with orthogonal rotations. In searching for methods to define simple structure, Thurstone (1947) and his colleagues developed a special system of oblique rotation, one that is *not* recommended by the author of this book. Although the method is mathematically and psychometrically elegant, frequently the results are very misleading, particularly for individuals who are not experienced in the use of factor analysis. The usual difficulty in approaching the ideal of simple structure is that the clusters of variables (when the variables tend to cluster) are not at right angles. Typically, if factors are rotated into clusters, the factors will correlate positively. This is particularly likely to occur in studies of human abilities, because all abilities tend to correlate positively with one another. Thus if one rotates in this way rather than using orthogonal rotations, the rotated factors will look less "simple." One can see this by comparing the orthogonal solution in Table 10-13 with the oblique solution in Table 10-14.

Instead of placing oblique vectors through clusters of variables, the method employed by Thurstone essentially backs off each oblique vector 90° from one of the clusters. This method of oblique rotation is illustrated in Fig. 10-7 for the six-variable problem used in the preceding figures. In the figure are shown (1) factor axes for the original centroid factors $A$ and $B$, (2) the positively correlated rotated factors that go through the two clusters $A_1$ and $B_1$, and (3) $A_1'$ and $B_1'$, which are the vectors rotated at right angles to $B_1$ and $A_1$. The axes for $A_1$ and $B_1$ are the same as those shown in Fig. 10-6 and Table 10-14. When factor vectors are backed off from a cluster, the members of that cluster are made to have near-zero loadings on the factor. Thus, in Fig. 10-7, variables 4, 5, and 6 are made to have near-zero loadings on $B_1'$, and variables 1, 2, and 3 are made to have near-zero loadings on $A_1'$. The resulting oblique rotation is shown in Table 10-16.

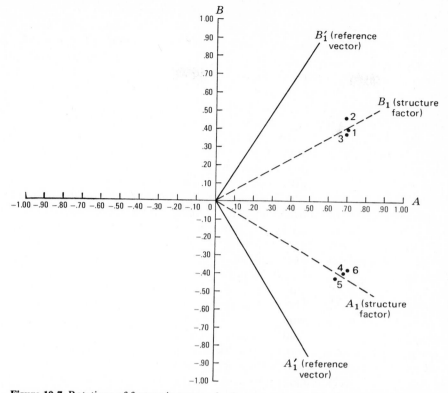

**Figure 10-7** Rotations of factors in terms of reference vectors $A_1'$ and $B_1'$ and structure factors $A_1$ and $B_1$.

When the effort is made to place factor vectors (frequently called axes) through clusters of variables, as was illustrated in Fig. 10-6, the resulting projections of variables on the rotated factor loadings are said to constitute a factor structure. These are the actual correlations, or loadings, of the original variables on the obliquely rotated factors. As was mentioned, although it is geo-

**Table 10-16  Loadings on oblique reference vectors depicted in Fig. 10-7**

|   | $A_1'$ | $B_1'$ |
|---|---|---|
| 1 | .01 | .71 |
| 2 | −.05 | .76 |
| 3 | .02 | .69 |
| 4 | .70 | .02 |
| 5 | .70 | −.02 |
| 6 | .69 | .04 |

metrically tempting to place the axes through such clusters, this does not necessarily result in simpler-appearing tables of factor loadings, which was illustrated in Table 10-14. That is, variables that do not "belong" to the cluster have at least moderate-sized loadings on factors that pertain to other clusters. Note in Table 10-14 that although factor $A_1$ is defined mainly by variables 4, 5, and 6, variables 1, 2, and 3 also have appreciable loadings. The reverse is the case for factor $B_1$. In an effort to find an approximation of simple structure through statistical manipulations, Thurstone conceived of the statistical method in which one would back off vectors 90° from the cluster, thus guaranteeing near-zero correlations (loadings) of members of the cluster on this new vector. The vectors that are backed off this way are called *reference vectors*. The loadings on reference vectors can be calculated in the same way as for vectors going through the clusters, which usually are referred to as constituting a *factor structure* for the variables in contrast to a *reference vector structure*. However, for a number of reasons, these are rather peculiar correlations or loadings, which frequently are misleading or difficult to interpret. Note that whereas the structure factors (the ones that go through clusters) correlate positively ($r = .48$), the reference vectors correlate negatively ($r = -.48$).

Although the use of oblique reference vectors like those shown in Fig. 10-7 can lead to a simple-appearing matrix of factor loadings, it comes at quite a price in terms of the confusion that is wrought. In books, journal articles, and other places, authors frequently label tables simply as "factor matrix" without saying whether the matrix concerns loadings on reference vectors, vectors placed through clusters, or, worse yet, some statistical products of the factor analysis that are not even correlations or loadings (which will be discussed subsequently). In the reporting of numerous other results relating to a factor analysis study, such as equations for estimating scores of people on the factors, frequently the reader is not given enough information to determine whether the equations concern reference vectors or structure factors. This author strongly feels that one should not display loadings on such reference vectors in the literature as representing the actual factor structure of the variables.

A second criticism of the Thurstone approach to oblique rotation is that it can, and often does, fool the investigator into thinking the data are simpler than they actually are. In most problems, even an approximation to simple structure by this method forces negative correlations among the factor axes (the reference vectors). Whereas thinking in terms of positively correlated factors is difficult enough, it is even more difficult to think in terms of negatively correlated factors. Thus the simple-appearing table of loadings comes at the expense of confusion in interpreting the overall results. Such confusion can be illustrated with the following example. This method of rotation can be used to show that an arithmetic test has a substantial loading on factor $A$ and a zero loading on factor $B$, and vice versa for a vocabulary test. But since the two variables would be positively correlated, the only way to obtain the rotation would be by making the factors correlate negatively. If one does not look at the negative correlation between the two factors, one might be misled into thinking that the two variables are independent. There are, in the literature, many examples of confusion resulting from efforts to interpret oblique rotations made in this way.

A third criticism of reference vectors, as illustrated in Fig. 10-7 and Table 10-16, is that much of the clarity of the original geometric model for depicting the factoring problem is lost. It is easy and helpful to think of the original correlation matrix as portrayed by a system of vectors, whose angles and lengths specify the correlations. It is easy to think of inserting new vectors in that space, factor vectors which help to summarize the whole system of vectors in some parsimonious way. After factor vectors are used to condense the space, it is also useful to think of rotating those vectors to positions that help one interpret the results. It is also easy to think of oblique factors being placed through the clusters, but the geometric analogy breaks down badly when one switches to employing a system of reference vectors. When there are three rather than two factors, one does not simply back off a factor vector 90° from a cluster—one backs off a *plane* 90° from a cluster. If, as is very frequently the case, there are more than three factors, then one must back off a hyperplane 90° from a cluster. It is questionable whether many people find it helpful to think of rotated factors in terms of spatial positioning of variables with respect to such hyperplanes. Some superspecialists on the topic of factor analysis apparently find this geometric analogy appealing, but the author has more than enough experience to know that it confuses even most professional people in the behavioral sciences who either conduct factor analyses of their own data or try to understand those reported in such geometric terms in the literature.

It is recommended that only one system of rotated factors be shown or discussed in research reports, the rotated factors being referred to simply as factors. Their geometric counterparts can be referred to as factor vectors or factor axes. If it is decided to rotate these factors obliquely rather than orthogonally, it is recommended that the oblique factors not be backed off 90° from clusters. Rather, it is recommended that factors be placed through clusters. This seldom will lead to a simple-appearing matrix of factor loadings, but it will clearly represent the actual relations among variables.

**Pattern matrix** If sufficient confusion has not been wrought over several decades by the introduction of matrices of reference vector loadings in research reports, that confusion has been compounded even more by presenting in such research reports a *pattern matrix*. A pattern matrix frequently looks very much like a factor matrix (usually very much like one obtained from reference vectors), but it is really not a matrix of factor loadings at all. Rather it is a matrix of weights, which will be labeled $P$. To clarify this issue, some old symbolism will be reiterated, and some new symbols will be developed. The reader already is familiar with the symbol $S$ which refers to the score matrix showing the scores of all people in a sample of $N$ subjects on $k$ tests or other variables. The reader also has been acquainted with the use of $R$ to stand for the original correlation matrix with unities in the diagonal spaces and $R_1$, $R_2$, etc., to refer to various residual matrices of coefficients when factors are successively extracted. In general, a matrix of factor loadings will be symbolized as $F$, and where necessary, subscripts will be used to denote any particular characteristic of the factor matrix. $F$ means the correlations of variables with the linear combinations of variables which constitute the factors. Either these are real, linear combinations of variables, as component analysis has been discussed throughout this chapter, or they are hypothetical, linear components of the variables, as will be discussed in Chap. 11 in terms of common-factor analysis. In factor analyses there are as many rows of factor loadings as there are variables in $R$, but the number of columns of factor loadings usually is far less than the number of variables—otherwise, there would not have been much purpose to performing the analysis. The symbol $F_r$ will be used specifically to designate a factor matrix obtained from reference vectors as illustrated in Fig. 10-7 and discussed previously. The symbol $F$ will be used with respect to a factor matrix showing loadings of variables on orthogonally rotated factors or rotated in such a way as to go through whatever clusters of variables are present. (Of course, in a particular analysis, there may be no neat clusters or statistical manipulations with reference vectors that will produce a simple-appearing factor matrix.) If factors are orthogonal, either before or after rotation, then $F_r$ and $F$ are identical. In that case, one could simply refer to $F$ without employing a subscript to distinguish between reference vectors and factor structure.

Another important matrix in factor analysis is $S_f$, which is used to denote the scores of people on the factors. Thus, if four factors are shown in the factor matrix, as in Table 10-12, then correspondingly there is an $S_f$ matrix of four rows showing the actual scores of people on those factors. The factor matrix, then, is nothing other than a table of correlations of the original variables from $S$ with the factor scores of people from $S_f$. When factors are orthogonal, either before or after rotation, there is a simple relationship between $F$, $R$, and $S_f$. If the factors are orthogonal, by definition the rows of scores in $S_f$ mutually correlate zero with one another—they are orthogonal. For example, if there are five factors in $F$, then there are five rows of factor scores in $S_f$, all of which are uncorrelated with one another. Then $F$ shows loadings on uncorrelated factors, regardless of whether they have been rotated previously. One can either obtain $S_f$ directly when component analysis is employed or estimate $S_f$ when common-factor analysis is employed. In either case, there are simply relationships between the three matrices. However, when oblique rotations are performed, those simple relationships no longer exist. Then, rather than use $F$ in conjunction with $S_f$ to determine or estimate original scores, one must employ a special matrix of weights, called the *pattern matrix* and symbolized as $P$. The pattern matrix $P$ is *not* a matrix of factor loadings, in the sense of showing correlations with the original variables or anything else. Rather it is a special set of weights that has the same number of columns and rows as an $F$ matrix and frequently has entries that deceptively appear to be factor loadings or correlations. Basically the pattern matrix $P$ is useful only in determining scores in $S$ from the factor score matrix $S_f$, which is of theoretical interest but almost no practical use. However, many specialists in factor analysis derive methods of rotation which operate on the $P$ matrix rather than on the $F$ matrix, which does offer a potentially useful mathematical approach. What is misleading, however, is that the so-called factor matrices shown in many publications actually are pattern matrices rather than factor matrices—$P$ rather than $F$.

Mathematically it turns out that each column of a $P$ matrix is proportional to a corresponding column of reference vector loadings $F_r$. That is, the first column in one will correlate perfectly with the first column in the other, but they will differ by a constant proportion. For example, in one instance the proportion might be 1.2 in going from the reference vector loadings to the pattern coefficients; thus reference vector loadings of .00, .10, and .50 would become .00, .12, and .60 respectively. The coefficients of proportionality linking reference vector loadings to weights in the pattern matrix differ from factor to factor depending upon the correlations among rotated reference vectors. For these reasons, if the reference vector matrix of loadings $F_r$ looks "simple," the corresponding pattern matrix $P$ will also look simple. This is why many factorists find it appealing to work with the pattern matrix. That the $P$ matrix is not a matrix of correlations and can lead to confusion is illustrated by the fact that elements frequently are greater than $+1.00$ or less than $-1.00$.

Whereas the pattern matrix $P$ is useful mathematically in various aspects of factor analysis, particularly in computer programs, the author strongly feels that such $P$ matrices ordinarily should not be given in research reports. If they are, they should be carefully labeled and explained to the reader, because even the expert might be fooled. The difficulties in interpreting the reference vector loadings are made even worse in any attempt to interpret coefficients in the pattern matrix. Unfortunately, in many research reports, even in very reputable publication outlets, frequently one finds tables labeled only as "factors." Only by playing around with some of the calculations or actually writing the author can one find out whether the rotation is orthogonal or oblique, whether the table shows a pattern matrix or a matrix of factor loadings, and, if it is a matrix of factor loadings, whether the loadings are shown on reference vectors or rotated through clusters. For all the foregoing reasons, in most uses of factor analysis, it is strongly recommended that either rotations be kept orthogonal or if they are allowed to be oblique, only one system of factor vectors be used, and these be placed through the dominant clusters.

## ANALYTIC METHODS OF ROTATION

Since the advent of methods of factor rotation, there have been numerous attempts to formulate analytic criteria. An analytic criterion is one that is stated in precise mathematical terms rather than as verbal description. The many different approaches to analytic rotation usually are prefixed or suffixed by "max" or "min," because they are intended to either maximize something good with respect to the rotation or minimize something bad. Nearly all these methods of analytic rotation are based on Thurstone's general conception of simple structure, although, as was stated previously, it is difficult to give precise formulations of the concept. Generally, the various analytic procedures are to obtain "simpler structures," in the sense in which it was discussed previously.

Because all the analytic methods of rotation require extremely complex computations, they necessarily are performed on computers. Consequently, selecting among the various methods to apply in a particular factor analysis problem consists of selecting among the various computer programs available for that purpose. Analytic methods of rotation are discussed in the Suggested Additional Readings. Gorsuch (1974) gives a good overview of the major existing methods. A more mathematical overview is presented by Kaiser (1970) and Kaiser and Rice (1974). There are far too many methods, variations on methods, and combinations of methods (all with strange-sounding min and max names) to discuss even the majority of analytic approaches. Analytic methods are available for both orthogonal rotations and oblique rotations, although generally solutions to the orthogonal case are better.

Early attempts to develop an orthogonal, analytic method of rotation resulted in the *Quartimax method*. Although at least a half-dozen other persons were working on essentially the same approach, credit is usually given to Neuhaus and Wrigley (1954) for producing the first major method. The Quartimax method is based on one of the salient requirements of simple structure—that the variance of loadings in each row of the factor matrix is as large as possible. When a variable has substantial loadings on a number of factors, it is not a pure measure of any of them, and the variance of loadings is then relatively small. If the factors can be rotated so that a variable loads mainly on one factor, then that variable is a relatively pure measure of that factor and the variance of loadings is relatively large. Thus, by maximizing the sum of variances in rows of the factor matrix, one approaches one of the goals of simple structure. However, since the actual variance in any row would be affected by both the sizes of loadings and their signs, the criterion is applied to the squared loadings rather than to the loadings themselves. A number of different investigators independently arrived at this criterion. The particular method used to maximize the sum of variances of rows in the factor matrix is called Quartimax. Wrigley and his associates developed numerous variants of the method and provided workable computer programs.

The Quartimax method, although still used in some studies, has not proved very successful in producing simpler structures. The difficulty is that it tends to produce a general factor in the rotations. One can see why this would be so, because the criterion would be perfectly satisfied if all variables had a loading on only one factor. Regardless of one's concept of a "simpler structure," inevitably it involves dealing with clusters of variables; and any method that tends to create a large general factor (e.g., as on the first PC factor) is not in line with the goals of rotation. Consequently, the Quartimax method is now mainly of historical significance.

Kaiser (1958) approached the problem in a somewhat different way. Rather than maximize the sum of variances of squared loadings in rows in the factor matrix, his *Varimax* method maximizes the sum of variances of squared loadings in the columns of the factor matrix. In each column of the matrix, this tends to produce some high loadings and some loadings near zero, which is one aspect of simple structure. The Varimax method is applied to the squared loadings rather than to the loadings themselves. This makes all entries in the column positive, which offsets the artificial effect on the variance of column entries because of the possible presence of some large, negative loadings. Such large, negative loadings could occur purely in terms of the way some tests are scored, e.g., scoring number of errors rather than number of correct responses. Also, before the variance of squared loadings in each column is computed, the squared loadings in each row of the factor matrix are divided by the sum of squares. This serves the purpose of making all variables equally important in determining the rotated solution.

The Varimax method has proved very successful as an analytic approach to obtaining an orthogonal rotation of factors. Even in those cases where the results do not meet the investigator's concept of a simple structure, the solution usually is close enough to greatly reduce the labor of finding a satisfactory rotation. During a period of more than 20 years, Kaiser and various associates have continually improved the Varimax method, developed readily available computer programs, and performed a great deal of research on results obtained from applying the method to a wide variety of factor analysis problems.

Kaiser and his associates have amply documented what has been found by numerous other investigators, namely that the various approaches to analytic, orthogonal rotation all tend to produce the same final result. Although individual loadings may differ somewhat, if there is a definite factor structure that would be found by any one of the methods, the same structure would be found by the other methods as well. To the extent to which one of these methods of orthogonal, analytic rotation has a slight advantage over others, it is generally accepted that Varimax is the best.

In addition to the analytic method of rotation itself, Kaiser and his associates have embedded the Varimax method of rotation in a whole package of related methods of factoring and assessing the results. The most recent version of this package containing Varimax and related statistics is referred to as Little Jiffy Mark IV (Kaiser and Rice 1974). Either this most recent statistical package or an earlier version of it can be found in almost any large computer facility in a university setting. Although it is desirable to have available the most recent set of computer programs for the purpose, the programs that were available for Varimax 20 years ago will do essentially the same job of rotation but without some of the useful auxiliary statistics. Although the Varimax method can be applied to any orthogonal factors obtained by any method, it is applied by far most frequently to either principal components or the common factor counterpart. When a person has a large-scale problem (at least 20 variables) in exploratory factor analysis, the usual advice is "Get the computer center to run the principal components plus Varimax program." This combination of methods has worked so well for exploratory factor analysis that it has become hard to improve upon. When an investigator is dissatisfied with the PC plus Varimax solution, usually it is because no simple, clear factor solution could be obtained by any method—which frequently occurs when a polyglot collection of poorly constructed tests is thrown together without any sensible psychological theory and/or the sample of subjects is far too small to produce clear results.

## Table 10-17 Varimax solution for the box components

| Variables | Factors | | |
|---|---|---|---|
| | A | B | C |
| 1. Length squared | .92 | .23 | .22 |
| 2. Height squared | .35 | .40 | .82 |
| 3. Width squared | .35 | .81 | .38 |
| 4. Length plus width | .77 | .52 | .31 |
| 5. Length plus height | .75 | .30 | .56 |
| 6. Width plus height | .48 | .60 | .63 |
| 7. Longest inner diagonal | .79 | .37 | .39 |
| 8. Shortest inner diagonal | .62 | .39 | .58 |
| 9. Space inner diagonal | .79 | .37 | .47 |
| 10. Thickness of edge | .28 | .87 | .23 |

*Source*: Adapted from R. L. Gorsuch, *Factor Analysis* (Philadelphia: W. B. Saunders Company, 1974). By permission of the author and W. B. Saunders Co.

An example of a Varimax solution is shown in Table 10-17. As an example to be used in testing various methods of factor analysis, Gorsuch (1974) collected 100 miscellaneous boxes from the homes of friends. On each box he performed the 10 measurements indicated in the table. Because boxes usually are described in terms of the dimensions of length, width, and height, one would expect a good method of factor analysis to produce these dimensions. In Table 10-17 one can see that such factors tend to be borne out. Variables related to factor A tend to concern length, those related to factor B tend to concern width, and those related to factor C tend to concern height. However, one can see that this is by no means a simple structure in the Thurstonian ideal sense, because variables other than key variables have substantial loadings on each of the

## Table 10-18 Promax rotation of box components

| Variables | Reference vector correlations | | | Factor pattern | | |
|---|---|---|---|---|---|---|
| | Length | Width | Height | Length | Width | Height |
| 1. Length squared | .71 | −.06 | −.11 | 1.18 | −.09 | −.20 |
| 2. Height squared | −.06 | .01 | .58 | −.11 | .02 | 1.05 |
| 3. Width squared | .00 | .53 | .10 | .00 | .83 | .17 |
| 4. Length plus width | .48 | .22 | −.05 | .80 | .34 | −.09 |
| 5. Length plus height | .41 | −.07 | .24 | .69 | −.10 | .43 |
| 6. Width plus height | .08 | .23 | .32 | .13 | .36 | .58 |
| 7. Longest inner diagonal | .50 | .05 | .05 | .83 | .07 | .09 |
| 8. Shortest inner diagonal | .27 | .03 | .27 | .45 | .05 | .50 |
| 9. Space inner diagonal | .45 | .01 | .12 | .79 | .02 | .22 |
| 10. Thickness of edge | −.02 | .66 | −.05 | −.03 | 1.02 | −.08 |

*Source:* Adapted from R. L. Gorsuch, *Factor Analysis* (Philadelphia: W. B. Saunders Co., 1974). By permission of the author and W. B. Saunders Co.

three factors. Actually, this particular example is loaded against the Varimax method of factor rotation, because in this collection of 100 boxes and in the real world at large, length, width, and height tend to be highly correlated in boxes. This particular example was chosen so that comparisons could be made with oblique, analytic methods of rotation, which will be discussed subsequently.

There are numerous oblique, analytic methods of rotation having prefixes or suffixes with the terms *max* or *min* in them, e.g., Oblimax, Biquartimin, Binormamin, etc. The problem of achieving an acceptable oblique, analytic solution has proved to be far more difficult than that of achieving an acceptable orthogonal solution. Many different methods have been proposed, and none of them clearly dominates the field in terms of acceptability (see discussion in Harman 1976). The problems with oblique, analytic methods are partly conceptual and partly statistical. The conceptual problem concerns the difficulties in making sense out of reference vectors, factor patterns, factor structures, and correlations among factors. The statistical problems arise from the much greater complexity that occurs in seeking an oblique solution. There simply are many more possibilities and many more degrees of freedom for producing oddball results in order to achieve anything approaching Thurstone's ideal concept of simple structure. Frequently it is necessary to interpret the reference vectors or the factor pattern rather than the actual factor structure (the correlations of variables with the factors). Also, in order to achieve even a simple-appearing set of loadings on reference vectors or a simple-appearing factor pattern, it is necessary to have unacceptably high correlations among the factors relating to the factor structure. All these problems are evidenced in the Promax rotational solution shown in Table 10-18 corresponding to the Varimax solution shown in Table 10-17. The table shows the correlations or loadings of the variables on the reference vectors. One notes that there is the nice appearance of simple structure which is the Holy Grail of so many specialists in factor analysis. This same neat appearance of simple structure is shown in the col-

**Table 10-18** (*Continued*)

| Factor structure | | | Correlations among factors 1, 2, and 3 | | |
|---|---|---|---|---|---|
| Length | Width | Height | Length | Width | Height |
| .96 | .58 | .66 | (1) 1.00 | | |
| .73 | .72 | .98 | (2) .69 | 1.00 | |
| .71 | .96 | .79 | (3) .78 | .74 | 1.00 |
| .96 | .82 | .78 | | | |
| .95 | .69 | .89 | | | |
| .83 | .88 | .95 | | | |
| .95 | .71 | .79 | | | |
| .87 | .73 | .88 | | | |
| .98 | .73 | .86 | | | |
| .62 | .94 | .66 | | | |

umn titled Factor Pattern, which contains the factor pattern. As discussed previously, this is the set of weights required for estimating the original variables from the scores of people on the factors. As noted previously, these are not correlation coefficients, which is amply indicated by the fact that three of the elements are greater than 1.00. Each column in the factor pattern differs from its corresponding column in the matrix of reference vector loadings by only a constant of proportionality.

In looking at the column of factor structure, one finds that in order to achieve the neat-appearing simple structure in the reference vectors and the factor pattern, one makes a mess out of the actual factor structure, which is the set of correlations of the original variables with the actual underlying linear combinations. Nearly all variables load highly on all factors. The reason for this rather confusing situation is shown in the rightmost column of the table, where it can be seen that the three factors have correlations on the average of over .70. These are the correlations among the factors underlying the factor structure. It will be noted that not only are these very high correlations necessary to give a simple-appearing picture with respect to the reference vectors and the weight pattern, but they also force the very high loadings in the factor structure shown in the column Factor Structure. Note there that not only is the structure not "simple," but it is quite confusing in that many of the loadings are extremely high. Because of the high positive correlations among the factors, the sums of squared loadings on some rows are well above 2.00, when of course the maximum for orthogonal factors would be 1.00. Admittedly, Table 10-18 shows the results of an oblique, analytic rotational method like Promax at its worst—in the sense that in order to fool oneself into believing that a simple structure exists in the reference vectors and in the proportional sets of factor pattern weights, one sometimes must force very high correlations among the factors underlying the actual factor structure loadings and obtain as a result a very peculiar, difficult-to-interpret, actual set of loadings, as in the column Factor Structure.

Among the various analytic procedures for oblique rotation, apparently Promax is being employed as widely as any other [see the discussion in Gorsuch (1974) and in Harman (1976)]. In contrast to some of the other methods, Promax can be programmed for computers rather easily, and such programs are already available at numerous computer centers. The results provided by Promax and comparable methods usually are not as misleading as those depicted in Table 10-18. Gorsuch (1974) provides a number of illustrations of the application of Promax in which readily interpretable solutions are obtained, including a Promax solution for the 24-variable problem depicted previously in Table 10-12.

## CONFIRMATORY FACTOR ANALYSIS

The methods of factor analysis discussed so far concern stepwise exploratory solutions. These methods are dominated by statistical criteria concerning the formation of linear combinations in the first step of the analysis and the rotation of factors in the second step. The methods are used primarily to *discover* factors rather than to test theories regarding the existence of factors. Because these methods are sometimes used in the absence of explicit theory, some investigators feel that factor analysis, in all its forms, is an unhealthy type of "shotgun empiricism." In this section it will be shown that some forms of factor analysis are very useful for testing theories regarding the existence of factors. These methods are usually referred to as *confirmatory* factor analysis, as distinct from *exploratory* factor analysis.

As is true of all methods for testing hypotheses, methods of factor analysis used for that purpose hypothesize the existence of particular patterns of relationship in the data. In factor analysis, the patterns of relationship concern properties of the correlation matrix. For example, if one hypothesizes that a single general factor accounts for the correlations among a set of variables, this is the same as hypothesizing that the correlation matrix will possess certain mathematical properties. By testing to see if the mathematical properties are present, one makes a test of the tenability of the hypothesis. If, instead of hypothesizing one factor, it is hypothesized that particular collections of variables will evolve into a number of factors, this also can be tested by an analysis of particular characteristics of the correlation matrix.

Although, in the best scientific tradition, the hypotheses should be available before data are collected, in testing hypotheses with factor analysis the hypotheses frequently are formulated only after an inspection of the correlation matrix. This can be thought of as halfway between pure efforts at discovery and pure efforts at the testing of hypotheses. Also, frequently hypotheses arise not so much from explicit psychological theories as from past experience in performing exploratory factor analyses. This is the case with the 24-variable problem depicted in Table 10-12. The tests that were employed for the study had been investigated in numerous previous studies, and the experimenters specifically included tests that they thought would form particular factors, i.e., factors relating to verbal comprehension, numerical skills, spatial visualization, and perceptual detection. That particular matrix has been analyzed by so many different methods and so frequently to demonstrate that four major factors are present, that one could rightly employ confirmatory factor analysis rather than exploratory factor analysis, as was illustrated previously. It is a healthy scientific trend when earlier exploratory factor analyses gradually produce enough evidence that confirmatory methods of factor analysis can be employed to neatly test hypotheses about groupings of variables.

In most methods of factor analysis used for the testing of hypotheses, one goes directly to the desired solution, and rotations are not required. If the hypotheses are supported poorly by the obtained factors, one might start over and employ one of the stepwise methods. In other words, if the theory does not lead to a good explanation of the matrix of correlations, an effort can be made to discover factors by the stepwise approaches.

First we will discuss a method which mainly is of historical interest—Spearman's general-factor solution and some extensions. Then we shall discuss the confirmatory methods which are used most frequently today for test-ing hypotheses.

## SPEARMAN'S GENERAL-FACTOR SOLUTION

Charles Spearman was the originator of factor analysis, (1904), and more recent theorists have been strongly influenced by his ideas. Although he modified his ideas later (Spearman 1927), his early theory was that all mental abilities are underlaid by one general factor $G$. The general factor was thought of as a type of mental yardstick of intelligence, and only one yardstick was thought neces-sary to explain the common ground among all forms of individual differences in abilities. Thus measures as diverse as tests of arithmetic, spelling, and the judg-ment of illusions were thought to share in $G$. In addition, it was theorized that each source of individual differences (test) possessed a unique factor. Since by definition the unique factors in different tests are uncorrelated, all correlations among tests could be accounted for by one general factor. The theory is some-times called Spearman's *two-factor theory,* because it hypothesized that each test could be explained by a general factor and a unique factor.

Spearman developed a test for his general factor according to the following lines of reasoning. If correlations among tests can be accounted for by one common factor $G$, this means that the correlations among the tests can be ac-counted for by the correlations of the tests with (loadings on) $G$. If the loadings of tests on $G$ were known, these could be used to predict the correlation be-tween any two tests. To use a concrete example, say that there are five tests numbered 1 through 5. Their correlations would be $r_{12}$, $r_{13}$, etc., and the load-ings of these on $G$ would be $r_{1G}$, $r_{2G}$, etc. According to the logic of PM cor-relational analysis, if one variable can explain the correlation between two other variables, the partial correlation between the latter two variables (par-tialing the first variable) is zero. Consequently, if $G$ explained the common variance among the five variables, the partial correlations among those five variables (holding $G$ constant) would all be zero. In that case it would necessar-ily follow that the correlation between any two variables would equal the prod-uct of their loadings on $G$. Why this is so can be seen from the following formula for partialing $G$ from the correlation between variables 1 and 2:

$$r_{12.G} = \frac{r_{12} - r_{1G}r_{2G}}{\sqrt{1 - r_{1G}^2}\ \sqrt{1 - r_{2G}^2}} \tag{10-14}$$

The only way for the expression on the right to be zero is for the numerator to be zero, and the only way for the numerator to be zero is for the correlation be-tween the two tests to equal the product of their loadings on $G$. Thus the corre-lations in any matrix explainable by a general factor would be the products of loadings on the general factor.

To simplify the following discussion, let the loadings of the five tests on $G$ be symbolized as $a$, $b$, $c$, $d$, and $e$, rather than as $r_{1G}$, $r_{2G}$, etc. Then, if the corre-

**Table 10-19 Correlations among five tests expressed in terms of loadings on a general factor**

| | | | Test | | |
|---|---|---|---|---|---|
| | | *1* | *2* | *3* | *4* | *5* |
| | *1* | | *ab* | *ac* | *ad* | *ae* |
| | *2* | *ab* | | *bc* | *bd* | *be* |
| *Test* | *3* | *ac* | *bc* | | *cd* | *ce* |
| | *4* | *ad* | *bd* | *cd* | | *de* |
| | *5* | *ae* | *be* | *ce* | *de* | |

lations can be explained by a general factor, $r_{12} = ab$, $r_{13} = ac$, $r_{23} = bc$, etc. The full matrix of correlations would equal the products of loadings on $G$, as shown in Table 10-19. (For the time being, it will be assumed that there is no concern with the diagonal elements, and consequently they are left blank in Table 10-19. In Chap. 11, when the concept of *communality* is discussed, we shall consider questions regarding the diagonal elements.)

Matrices that can be explained by a general factor have some interesting characteristics. One characteristic of Table 10-19 is that, exclusive of diagonal elements, the elements in each column are proportional to those in other columns. For example, taking elements from columns 1 and 2 gives the following:

$$\frac{r_{13}}{r_{23}} = \frac{r_{14}}{r_{24}} = \frac{r_{15}}{r_{25}} \qquad (10\text{-}15)$$

One can prove this by substituting for the correlations their counterparts in terms of products of loadings on $G$:

$$\frac{r_{13}}{r_{23}} = \frac{ac}{bc} = \frac{a}{b}$$

$$\frac{r_{14}}{r_{24}} = \frac{ad}{bd} = \frac{a}{b} \qquad (10\text{-}16)$$

$$\frac{r_{15}}{r_{25}} = \frac{ae}{be} = \frac{a}{b}$$

Thus the elements in any two columns (ignoring those pairs of elements where either is a diagonal element) are proportional to the loadings of the two variables on $G$. Obviously, this holds for any two rows of the matrix as well as for any two columns.

Before methods were developed for calculating loadings on $G$, the test for a general factor essentially concerned a test for the proportionality of columns in the matrix of correlations. This was done by examining *tetrads,* each of which consisted of two elements from any column and the corresponding two elements from any other column. The pairs of elements from the two columns should be proportional, and it is a simple matter of arithmetic to determine how far off from proportionality they are. There are many different such tetrads in a matrix, and it proves quite laborious to compute the extent to which these are discrepant from zero. [See Harman (1976) for a discussion of how such tetrads were investigated for the general-factor case and how Spearman's model was later augmented to include the possibility of factors in addition to $G$.]

In the ideal case where columns of the correlation matrix are exactly proportional, the loading of any variable on $G$ can be directly computed from equations formed among the correlations. One equation for determining the squared loading $a^2$ of variable 1 on $G$ is as follows:

$$\frac{r_{12}r_{13}}{r_{23}} = \frac{(ab)(ac)}{bc} = \frac{a^2\,bc}{bc} = a^2 = r_{1G}^2 \tag{10-17}$$

The same result can be obtained from different equations:

$$\frac{r_{14}r_{15}}{r_{45}} = \frac{(ad)(ae)}{de} = \frac{a^2\,de}{de} = a^2 = r_{1G}^2 \tag{10-18}$$

In a matrix of five variables, there are six equations for computing the loading on $G$ for any one of the variables. If the proportionality requirements were met exactly, all the equations would give the same result. Since this is not likely to occur, the different equations provide somewhat different estimates of loadings on $G$. One can combine all equations to obtain an overall estimate of the loading. In our illustrative problem, one does this by adding the numerators of all six equations and adding the denominators of all six equations:

$$a^2 = \frac{r_{12}r_{13} + r_{12}r_{14} + r_{12}r_{15} + r_{13}r_{14} + r_{13}r_{15} + r_{14}r_{15}}{r_{23} + r_{24} + r_{25} + r_{34} + r_{35} + r_{45}} \tag{10-19}$$

The denominator contains the sum of all correlations exclusive of those of variable 1 with the other variables. The numerator contains the sum of paired products of correlations of variable 1 with the other variables. When the proportionality criterion is not met exactly, as it almost never will be, Eq. (10-19) provides an estimate of the loading of variable 1 on $G$. Similar expressions could be generated for determining the loadings of the other variables.

Rather than go through the arithmetical operations required to estimate loadings by the method illustrated in Eq. (10-19), one can use the available computational routines. The same results are obtainable from the following formula:

$$r_{iG}^2 = \frac{L^2 - Q}{2(M - L)} \tag{10-20}$$

where $r_{iG}^2$ = squared loading of any variable on $G$
$\quad L$ = sum of correlations in column $i$ excluding diagonal element
$\quad Q$ = sum of squared correlations in column $i$
$\quad M$ = sum of all correlations below diagonal of matrix
The computations are illustrated in Table 10-20.

After the estimated loadings on $G$ are obtained, a matrix of cross products of the loadings would be obtained in the usual way. The matrix of cross products would be subtracted from the matrix of correlations, which would produce a matrix of residual coefficients. An examination of the size and patterning of

## Table 10-20 Computational procedures for determining loadings on a general factor

*Correlations*

|  | 1 | 2 | 3 | 4 | 5 |
|---|---|---|---|---|---|
| 1 |  | .48 | .40 | .40 | .30 |
| 2 | .48 |  | .40 | .40 | .25 |
| 3 | .40 | .40 |  | .34 | .28 |
| 4 | .40 | .40 | .34 |  | .20 |
| 5 | .30 | .25 | .28 | .20 |  |
| Column sums ($L$) | 1.58 | 1.53 | 1.42 | 1.34 | 1.03 |
| Sum of squares ($Q$) | .6404 | .6129 | .5140 | .4756 | .2709 |
| $M = 3.45$ |  |  |  |  |  |
| $r_{iG}^2$ | .50 | .45 | .37 | .31 | .16 |
| $r_{iG}$ | .71 | .67 | .61 | .56 | .40 |

*Residual coefficients*

|  | 1 | 2 | -3 | 4 | 5 |
|---|---|---|---|---|---|
| 1 |  | .00 | -.03 | .00 | .02 |
| 2 | .00 |  | -.01 | .02 | -.02 |
| 3 | -.03 | -.01 |  | .00 | .04 |
| 4 | .00 | .02 | .00 |  | -.02 |
| 5 | .02 | -.02 | .04 | -.02 |  |

residual coefficients would lead to either the acceptance or the rejection of the general-factor hypothesis.

Although Spearman laid the foundation for all factor analysis studies since that time, his hypothesized omnipresence of a *G* factor rapidly became untenable in the light of numerous departures from the ideal. Thus, when larger matrices of tests were investigated and diverse measures were included concerning verbal skills, spatial skills, perceptual skills, numerical skills, and numerous others, it became quite obvious that a single factor would not explain the correlation matrices. The residual coefficients as shown in Table 10-20 usually were quite large. By inspecting residual coefficients among different tests, it became obvious that additional factors were needed. This required both an augmentation of theory and the development of mathematical procedures of factor analysis that would go beyond testing for a general factor only.

Various efforts were made to extend the logic of Spearman's factoring method to the multifactor case. Most of these consisted, in essence, of applying the formula for *G* to clusters of partial correlations in the residual matrix after the influence of *G* was removed. One such method that was used widely is Holzinger's (1941) bifactor method. In essence what was done was to first extract a *G* factor and then search for group factors in the residual matrix corresponding to observed clusters of tests. However, two things went very wrong in this effort to patch up Spearman's original theory and extend it to the multifactor case. First, without anyone actually saying so, the factoring methodology gradually switched from that of confirmatory analysis to exploratory analysis.

This is because the groupings of tests after the influence of a general factor was removed were determined largely with regard to the observed sizes and interrelationships or variables in the first, second, and successive residual matrices. Thus the groups or clusters of variables were not specified in advance of the analysis, but were determined in large measure by the observed patterns of relationships in the correlation matrix and subsequent residual matrices. This eventuates in exploratory analysis rather than confirmatory analysis. Second, the mathematical procedures for obtaining loadings on $G$ did not provide an adequate basis for developing a powerful mathematical logic for exploratory factor analysis in general. The efforts to extend the methods for deriving $G$ to obtaining additional factors consisted largely of cut-and-try techniques in which numerous assumptions had to be made about relationships among patterns of correlations in the matrix. These methods have no solid mathematical basis such as the centroid, PC, or the ML methods have.

For the above two reasons, beginning in the early 1930s, the emphasis gradually shifted from confirmatory to exploratory analysis. Such forms of exploratory analysis (for example, PC plus Varimax) have been greatly refined and applied to an immense number of problems. During the last 10 years or so, however, both psychological theories and evidence accumulated from numerous past studies have brought us to the point where more definite hypotheses can be formulated about the number and kinds of existing factors of human ability and personality. Consequently, hypothesis testing with factor analysis has come back into vogue, and there is much renewed interest in confirmatory methods of analysis. In that connection, Spearman's old, elegant model for $G$ still is a perfectly good procedure for testing the hypothesis that a particular collection of variables is dominated by one common factor only.

## MULTIPLE-GROUP METHOD OF CONFIRMATORY ANALYSIS

The multiple-group method offers the most generally useful approach to testing hypotheses about the existence of factors. In the limiting case, it can be used to test for the presence of a general factor, much as is done with the general-factor solution. At the other extreme, it can test for the presence of any number of hypothesized factors.

The multiple-group method will be illustrated with the six-variable problem used to illustrate methods of condensation. For example, suppose that the problem concerns hypotheses about two factors of anxiety. One factor is hypothesized to concern bodily harm, and the other is hypothesized to concern anxiety in social situations. Tests 1 through 3 are hypothesized to concern the first factor, and tests 4 through 6 are hypothesized to concern the second factor. It is also hypothesized that, in an oblique solution, there will be a moderate correlation between the two factors.

The mathematics of the multiple-group method are very simple. They are obtained directly from formulas for the correlation of sums, about which much has already been said in this book. The multiple-group method might better be called the "group-centroid method," because it is only a variation of the centroid method which was discussed previously. Although one can place a centroid among *all* the variables, it is equally easy to place a centroid among only some of them. In the example above, the first centroid factor is placed among variables 1, 2, and 3 only. (It could be placed equally well among the other three variables only.) Then the correlations of *all* variables with this centroid are obtained, which are the loadings on the first factor. Next, a second centroid is placed among variables 4, 5, and 6 only. The correlations of all six variables with the second centroid will be the loadings on the second factor.

Going back to the basic concept of factor analysis as concerning the linear combination of variables in a matrix of data, we find that a group centroid equals the sum of scores over a specified set of variables. One obtains loadings on the factor by correlating all the variables (including ones not included in the sum) with the factor scores. It is easier to perform these calculations on the matrix of correlations than on the data matrix, which can be done with formulas for the correlation of sums. It will be remembered that the general formula for the correlation of sums of standard scores is as follows:

$$r_{xy} = \frac{\bar{R}_{xy}}{\sqrt{\bar{R}_x} \sqrt{\bar{R}_y}} \tag{10-21}$$

The numerator is the sum of all elements in the cross-correlation matrix for the two sums $x$ and $y$. Under each radical in the denominator is the sum of elements in the correlation matrix for the variables in a sum. If either $x$ or $y$ is not a sum of other variables but an individual variable instead, one term of the denominator equals 1.0, and the numerator equals the sum of correlations between the individual variable and the members of the sum of variables. Various uses of Eq. (10-21) constitute the major computational steps in the multiple-group method.

A worked-out example of the multiple-group method is shown in Table 10-21. The first factor consists of the sum of variables 1, 2, and 3. The loading of any variable on this group-centroid factor is obtained from Eq. (10-21), as follows. Since a loading will equal the correlation of an individual variable with the sum of variables 1 through 3, only one term appears in the denominator. The square of the denominator equals the sum of all the elements in the submatrix of correlations for variables 1 through 3. This part is blocked off in Table 10-21. The sum $T_1$ includes the correlations above and below the diagonal of the submatrix for the three variables, and it also includes the three diagonal unities. The square root of this sum is the denominator in the equation for computing each loading, but again it is easier to multiply by $m$, the reciprocal of the square root of $T_1$. The numerator of the equation equals the sum of correlations of each variable with variables 1 through 3. Each variable has three correlations with these three variables. Since variables 1 through 3 are members of the group which defines the factor, one of their three correlations is 1.0. Thus the sum of correlations for variable 1 equals $1.0 + r_{12} + r_{13}$. For any variable not included in the group defining the centroid, there are three empirical correla-

## Table 10-21 Computational procedures for obtaining multiple-group factors

### Correlation Matrix

|   | 1 | 2 | 3 | 4 | 5 | 6 |
|---|---|---|---|---|---|---|
| 1 | 1.00 | .55 | .43 | .32 | .28 | .36 |
| 2 | .55 | 1.00 | .50 | .25 | .31 | .32 |
| 3 | .43 | .50 | 1.00 | .39 | .25 | .33 |
| 4 | .32 | .25 | .39 | 1.00 | .43 | .49 |
| 5 | .28 | .31 | .25 | .43 | 1.00 | .43 |
| 6 | .36 | .32 | .33 | .49 | .43 | 1.00 |

$T_1$  (sum 1, 2, 3) = 5.96  $\sqrt{T_1} = 2.4413$  $m_1 = .4096$
$T_2$  (sum 3, 4, 5) = 5.70  $\sqrt{T_2} = 2.3875$  $m_2 = .4188$

|  |  | Sums of Correlations with Groups | | Factor Loadings | |
|---|---|---|---|---|---|
|  |  | First group | Second group | A | B |
|  | 1 | 1.98 | .96 | .81 | .40 |
|  | 2 | 2.05 | .88 | .84 | .37 |
| Variable | 3 | 1.93 | .97 | .79 | .41 |
|  | 4 | .96 | 1.92 | .39 | .80 |
|  | 5 | .84 | 1.86 | .34 | .78 |
|  | 6 | 1.01 | 1.92 | .41 | .80 |

tions, and the diagonal entry would not enter the computations. Thus for variable 4, the numerator equals $r_{14} + r_{24} + r_{34}$. In this way, loadings of the six variables on the first group-centroid factor are obtained.

How loadings are obtained on the second group factor depends on whether one decides to use oblique factors or orthogonal factors. The former case will be considered first. In this case loadings on the second centroid factor can be obtained directly from the original matrix of correlations as illustrated in Table 10-21. In Eq. (10-21), the denominator is the square root of the sum $T_2$ of all elements in the submatrix of correlations for variables 4, 5, and 6. This submatrix is blocked off in Table 10-21. The numerator of the equation for each variable equals the sum of correlations of that variable with variables 4, 5, and 6. In this instance the numerator for each of the variables in that group contains two empirical correlations and a diagonal unity. For variables 1, 2, and 3, the numerator will equal the sum of three empirical correlations with the other three variables. Thus the numerator for variable 1 equals $r_{14} + r_{15} + r_{16}$. In this way all loadings on the second group factor are obtained.

After the two factors are obtained, it is easy to compute the correlation between them from Eq. (10-22). The matrix of correlations can be sectioned as follows:

| $R_A$ | $R_{AB}$ |
|---|---|
| $R_{AB}$ | $R_B$ |

According to formulas for the correlation of sums, the correlation between the two factors $A$ and $B$ is obtained as follows:

$$r_{AB} = \frac{\bar{R}_{AB}}{\sqrt{\bar{R}_A} \; \sqrt{\bar{R}_B}}$$

$$r_{AB} = .48 \tag{10-22}$$

Since the two terms in the denominator have been obtained for previous computations, all that is needed is to compute the sum of elements in the cross-correlation matrix $R_{AB}$ and use this as the numerator.

It will be noted that the loadings on the two oblique group-centroid factors in Table 10-21 are almost identical to the loadings shown in Table 10-14 for an oblique rotation of two centroid factors, except that what was designated factor $A$ there is designated factor $B$ here, and vice versa. In both cases, the final factors go through clusters of variables. There is, however, a very important difference in how the two sets of results are obtained. In rotating the centroid solution, it is necessary to search for factors. In the group-centroid solution, the factors are hypothesized in advance of the analysis, and a direct solution for the factors is made. In general, there is no assurance that the two approaches will lead to the same results, particularly when the number of variables is large (more than 20) and numerous factors are extracted.

Note that the factor matrix in Table 10-21 does not look very "simple." The variables that define factor $A$ have appreciable loadings on factor $B$, and vice versa. Typically this occurs when centroids are placed through the dominant clusters. However, the loadings of the three salient variables on each factor are so much higher than the other three variables in each case that there would be no doubt as to the nature of each of the two factors.

If orthogonal factors are desired when hypotheses are tested with the multiple-group method, the procedures are slightly different from those discussed for the oblique case. Factor $A$ would be obtained from the correlation matrix as was shown in Table 10-21, but factor $B$ would not be obtained from the correlation matrix. A matrix of residuals would be obtained in which the influence of factor $A$ is removed. This would be done in the usual way. Products of loadings would be obtained for factor $A$, and these would be subtracted from the correlation matrix. Then the computations for $B$ would be performed on the residual matrix. The same procedures would be applied that were illustrated in Table 10-21.

Although one can obtain loadings on orthogonal group-centroid factors by operating on successive residual matrices as described above, there is an easier way to perform the computations. First, oblique factors are obtained from the correlation matrix. Then a mathematical transformation is made which orthogonalizes the oblique axes. (The computations are discussed in the Suggested Additional Readings and in many other sources where factor analysis is discussed extensively.)

The multiple-group method can be used to test for any number of hypothesized factors. If a group of variables is hypothesized to be explainable by only one common factor (a general factor), the first "group" centroid will go among all the variables. In other words, the first factor will be the first factor obtained from applying the regular centroid method of condensation, discussed previously.

The multiple-group method can be easily applied to more than two groups of variables. Oblique factors can be determined directly from the correlation matrix. One does this by sectioning off the variables that constitute the different groups. From these sections, one obtains the proper quantities for formulas concerning the correlation of sums. After all factors are extracted from the correlation matrix, they can be mutually orthogonalized by the transformations mentioned above. These loadings can be used to obtain a final matrix of residuals. If, for example, four factors have been obtained, one can compute the fourth residual matrix without going through the steps of computing the earlier residual matrices (discussed in Suggested Additional Readings).

When the multiple-group method is employed, it is not necessary for all variables to be assigned to one of the groups. In some analyses, there are firm hypotheses about the factorial composition of some of the variables, but other variables are included in the analyses purely in the hope that interesting relations will be discovered. In the analysis in Table 10-21, six additional variables could have been included but assigned to neither of the two groups. It should be obvious how their loadings would be computed via the correlation of sums. The loadings for the original six variables would not change, but loadings would be obtained for the six additional variables.

In previous years the multiple-group method frequently was used as a method of condensation in a stepwise analysis rather than as a method for testing hypotheses. When clusters are judiciously chosen in terms of the correlations, a number of group-centroid factors will explain considerable common variance. Then some of or all the factors obtained in this way can be rotated. The multiple-group method is not as efficient in condensing common variance as either the full centroid method or the PC method. Since the availability of computers makes it practicable to employ the latter two methods in stepwise analyses, there is no longer any need to employ the multiple-group method for this purpose. This fact has probably led to the unfortunate conclusion by some persons that the multiple-group method is "not as good" as the full centroid method or the PC method. It is not as good for condensing common variance in a stepwise analysis, but it is far better for testing hypotheses.

In using the multiple-group method, it is appropriate to ask whether it is possible to find *disconfirming* results regarding the existence of factors. There are a number of ways for this to happen. First, a variable assigned to a group might not correlate highly with the centroid for that group, which would mean that the variable does not strongly share a common factor with the other variables. This is not as likely to happen when the groups contain only a small number of variables, because each variable is then prominently represented in the centroid. In actual research, however, frequently there are half a dozen or more variables assigned to each group, and thus it is possible to obtain rather low correlations of variables in a group with the centroid for that group. Even when there are a half-dozen or more tests in each of the groups, however, the factor loadings tend to look "too large" when component analysis is being used—when unities are placed in the diagonal spaces. This matter will be discussed much more fully in Chap. 11, but several relevant comments should be made here with respect to the multiple-group method of confirmatory analysis.

In addition to reporting all factor loadings on the multiple-group factors, it is also wise to report the average off-diagonal correlation within each group of variables used to define each factor. For example, in Table 10-21 the average correlation is .49 for the variables that define factor *A* and .42 for the variables that define factor *B*, both of which are lower than one might guess when looking at the loadings in the .80s in the factor matrix. Because factors represent something central about a group of variables, it is to be expected that the loadings will be higher than the individual correlations among variables. However, the factor loadings give a misleading impression of the sizes of average correlations within groups when unities are placed in the diagonal spaces and only a small number of variables belong to each group. These mathematical procedures are absolutely legitimate, but they can be misconstrued by unwary individuals. If the average correlations within groups are reported, then readers can judge for themselves how well the various hypothesized groupings of variables "hang together." Another possible way to handle the potentially misleading picture of having large factor loadings when correlations among variables really are not high is to place something other than unities in the diagonal space of the correlation matrix before the group centroids are extracted. Various approaches to doing this will be discussed in Chap. 11; but readers will be on safe ground if they apply the multiple-group method of confirmatory analysis exactly as it was illustrated in Table 10-21 and simply take the precaution of reporting average correlations within groups.

A second type of disconfirming information is obtained when variables assigned to one cluster correlate substantially with the centroid for another cluster. For example, it might be found that a test intended to measure anxiety regarding bodily harm actually correlates more with the centroid for tests intended to measure anxiety in social situations than with the centroid for tests of the former kind.

A third type of disconfirming information is obtained from an inspection of the final residual matrix after all the hypothesized factors have been extracted. The average absolute value of those residuals should be low. If that quantity is large in proportion to the average absolute correlation in the original matrix, it means that the hypothesized factors do a poor job of explaining the common variance.

Obviously the author is "sold" on the general usefulness of the multiple-group method for performing confirmatory factor analysis. The essence of any form of confirmatory analysis is that at least some of the groupings of the variables be designated in advance of the analysis. There also is ample room for including variables that do not obviously belong to any of the a priori groups and ample room for extending the confirmatory analysis to an exploratory analysis of the final residual matrix, after the hypothesized factors have been extracted. Although the centroid method is by far the simplest to understand and apply to multiple-group solutions, and for most purposes works as well as any other, one can employ a very wide variety of methods to determine the factors for multiple-group solutions. For example, it is perfectly permissible to place principal-component factors or maximum-likelihood factors within the groups rather than centroids, and there are numerous other possibilities. The use of the multiple-group approach to confirmatory analysis epitomizes something that was said in the early pages of this chapter, namely that many of the methods of factor analysis that do exactly the right job from the standpoint of a practicing behavioral scientist are simple to understand, employ, and communicate.

## PROCRUSTES METHODS OF CONFIRMATORY ANALYSIS

Another approach to confirmatory factor analysis is through *forced rotation* in such a way as to approximate a hypothesized factor structure for a set of variables. These are referred to as *Procrustes* solutions from the story in Greek mythology about the innkeeper who had a bed that would fit anyone. If the visitor was too short for the bed, Procrustes stretched the visitor on a rack. If a visitor was too tall to fit the bed, Procrustes trimmed the length of the visitor's legs to fit the bed. In essence, what is done with this family of methods is to best estimate a "target" factor matrix from a sample correlation matrix. The hypotheses to be confirmed are stipulated by the nature of the target matrix. For example, if one hypothesizes three factors to exist among 12 tests with 4 tests representing each factor, one would simply compose a target matrix that would show three columns of a factor matrix of that kind. If, from previous studies or from a theory, estimates can be made of the loadings of the variables on those three factors, these are placed in the target matrix. If the hypotheses are not so precise as that, one can place 1.00 in each column of the factor matrix for tests that are thought to belong to the factor. Instead, one could place reliability coefficients, or some type of communality estimate, based on either some characteristic of the sample correlation matrix or statistics obtained from previous studies employing the test. Some of the entries in the target matrix could be negative as well as positive, some could be zero, and some could be high and others low. The various Procrustes methods available are quite flexible with respect to the formulation of the target matrix. The target matrix can be stipulated as concerning orthogonal factors only, or oblique factors can be permitted. If oblique factors are used, in some methods the experimenter can stipulate the sizes of correlations among factors, or this can be determined by the computerized method of forced rotation. If oblique-factor rotations are performed, most frequently the transformations are made on the pattern matrix, which of course can then be mathematically converted to the factor structure showing the actual correlations of variables with the factors. The methods are discussed in the Suggested Additional Readings, where references can be found to more detailed descriptions and computerized computational procedures. A person who develops a serious interest in Procrustes methods of rotation should see the article by Cramer (1974), which discusses mathematical developments for the major methods and clarifies numerous issues.

The major classes of forced Procrustes methods of confirmatory analysis are based on the principle of least squares, and therein they bear a close kinship with PC factoring. In essence, one factors and rotates a sample matrix of correlations in such a way as to fit the target matrix as closely as possible, in the sense of minimizing the squared errors of estimation. As has been mentioned at numerous places so far in this book, such a minimization of squared errors of estimation is only the other side of the coin from maximizing the variance explained, which is done by the use of the characteristic roots and vectors underlying the PC method of factoring. In essence, one employs the *characteristic equation* in conjunction with auxiliary mathematical devices in such a way as to maximize the fit (minimize the misfit) of a sample correlation matrix to a hypothesized target matrix. Various computer programs are available for accomplishing this, but they are not as generally available as more widely used methods, such as the Varimax method of rotation. Frequently one has to study the research reports of individuals who originate the different methods and sometimes contact them directly in order to learn about available computer programs. These can be tracked down from the references in the Suggested Additional Readings and from the previously mentioned article by Cramer (1974).

The Procrustes methods of confirmatory analysis suffer from two major faults, the first a matter of strategy and the second a matter of statistics. In terms of strategy, if clear hypotheses are available regarding factors, the multiple-group method, as described previously, is much simpler, more direct, and more understandable than the Procrustes methods. In terms of strategy, the only clear advantage of the Procrustes methods would be in employing as the "hypothesis" a target matrix which consisted of the actual factor matrix obtained from studying some other sample than the one under consideration. For example, the Procrustes methods could be employed to determine whether a factor solution found in studying abilities in male college students could be borne out in a subsequent study employing female college students. However, this is only hypothesis testing in a rather limited meaning of the term.

The second major fault of Procrustes methods, the statistical one, is that the methods are "too flexible," to the point where very frequently one can fit a target matrix literally by statistically cutting and stretching until the appearance of a reasonable fit occurs. Saying it another way, the Procrustes methods are excellent for taking advantage of chance. One allows so many parameters to "float free," such as the correlations among factors, that unless the computer burns itself out in the process, frequently it will come up with something resembling the target matrix. Horn and his associates (e.g., Horn and Knapp 1973) have provided numerous demonstrations of the extent to which unreasonable results could be obtained from Procrustes methods simply because of the many opportunities to take advantage of sampling error in the correlation matrix. One such form of evidence came from studies of *random* correlation matrices which were obtained quite simply by forming sets of test scores from tables of random numbers, intercorrelating these, and applying Procrustes methods. They report instances in which the Procrustes methods produced good "simple structures," which of course was purely because of the computerized, statistical playing around with chance variance.

Because of the two major faults mentioned above, the Procrustes methods are not employed widely for confirmatory factor analysis. Although the concepts are interesting to psychometric theorists, and there are some special statistical problems to which they apply, the Procrustes methods definitely are not recommended for general use. The methods are still in an experimental phase, and they should be left in the hands of psychometric specialists until more satisfactory solutions are developed.

## MAXIMUM-LIKELIHOOD CONFIRMATORY ANALYSIS

Previously the ML method was discussed in relation to methods of condensation, where it was mentioned that in relation to confirmatory factor analysis the method is as useful, or more useful, than in exploratory factor analysis. The ML method of confirmatory analysis bears kinship to both the multiple-group method and the Procrustes methods. It is similar to the former in that one applies a direct solution to the correlation matrix, rather than going through the steps of condensation and subsequent forced rotation (which most of the Procrustes methods do). In this and other ways, confirmatory ML analysis takes less advantage of chance than Procrustes methods, although it still has problems in that regard. To be on the safe side in employing the ML method for confirmatory analysis, one should surely have a large sample of subjects, with 10 subjects per variable being an absolute minimum and 20 being a much more comfortable number. An advantage of the ML method over the Procrustes methods for confirmatory analysis is that there are some easily applied inferential statistics that can be used to test for the statistical significance of factors and establish confidence zones for the interpretation of loadings.

The ML method of confirmatory analysis employs a target matrix, as is done with the Procrustes method, but one need fill in only some of the hypothesized loadings of the matrix or some of the correlations among factors if an oblique solution is sought. For example, one need specify only a number of the variables for which zero loadings are hypothesized for each of the factors; and the ML method of analysis will do the rest in obtaining an overall factor matrix which will, if statistically possible, meet that criterion and produce loadings for all variables on all factors.

The ML method of factor analysis is part of a highly flexible, highly general mathematical model developed by Jöreskog (1974) that incorporates ML condensation, rotation, confirmatory analysis, and numerous other multivariate statistical methods, all in one computerized mathematical package. A simplified discussion of the overall model is given in Gorsuch (1974) and in the other references in the Suggested Additional Readings. The overall model is very complex and difficult for nonspecialists to understand. However, it has caught on among psychometric specialists, who find it extremely useful for handling a wide variety of problems, including confirmatory factor analysis. The computer program developed by Jöreskog and his associates (see Jöreskog 1974 and Gorsuch 1974) is gradually being adopted at major university computer centers across the country. Some uses of the overall computer program would tax the capacity of anything other than large-scale computers, and the average professional person in the behavioral sciences who employed the method might need some help in interpreting the results from a person with specialized knowledge of the method. However, other than for those inherent problems, the ML method of confirmatory analysis has much to recommend it; but it would be foolish to employ such a complex approach if hypotheses are sufficiently clear that they can be tested more simply and directly by the multiple-group method, as discussed previously.

## COMPUTERIZED APPROACHES

In closing this chapter, it should be reiterated that nearly all major problems in multivariate analysis are performed these days with computers. This includes all aspects of factor analysis, large-scale problems in multiple and partial correlational analysis, and the numerous other methods of multivariate analysis that will be discussed in the following two chapters. Anyone who works extensively with such statistical methods relating to multivariate analysis should become familiar with the computer programs that are available at local computer centers and with those that can be obtained elsewhere. Gorsuch (1974) gives an excellent overall discussion of the methods and problems in developing an extensive library of programs for factor analysis, and programs for specific purposes are mentioned at various points in the other references cited in Suggested Additional Readings. A number of manuals are available for specifying the actual procedures required to develop programs for a wide variety of problems in multivariate analysis for the behavioral sciences (see, in particular, the handbook by Nie et al. 1975). Most major computer centers have an up-to-date manual which describes available programs that can be used to solve many types of mathematical problems including those required for multivariate analysis in the behavioral sciences. Typically, the manual describes the available methods (e.g., most of them will list PC plus Varimax) and a variety of alternative approaches. Usually they describe all the procedures required for submitting data in a suitable form (which programs are necessary) and the kinds of "output" results. To the extent that a program is not available at a local computer center, it can be sought from one of the handbooks mentioned previously or, if it is a rather specialized program, by contacting the originator of the program. If one works extensively with factor analysis and other complex forms of multivariate analysis, there is no better advice than "get to know your local computer center."

## SUGGESTED ADDITIONAL READINGS

Comrey, A. L. *A first course in factor analysis*. New York: Academic, 1973.
Gorsuch, R. L. *Factor analysis*. Philadelphia: Saunders, 1974.
Harman, H. H. *Modern factor analysis* (3d ed.). Chicago: University of Chicago Press, 1976.
Mulaik, S. A. *The foundations of factor analysis*. New York: McGraw-Hill, 1972.
Thurstone, L. L. *Multiple-factor analysis*. Chicago: University of Chicago Press, 1947.

# CHAPTER ELEVEN

## SPECIAL ISSUES IN FACTOR ANALYSIS

Although the fundamentals of factor analysis were covered in the previous chapter, still special issues need to be discussed. These include the estimation of factor scores, comparisons of factors in different analyses, statistical decisions in factor analysis, and other relevant issues. One of the major topics which has not been discussed in detail up to this point concerns the *common-factor model*.

## THE COMMON-FACTOR MODEL

In the previous chapter it was assumed that unities are placed in the diagonal spaces of correlation matrices before factor analysis is undertaken. This was done for two reasons. First, the actual correlation of any variable with itself is 1.0, and consequently the diagonal elements of any real correlation matrix are unities. Second, if a factor loading is defined as the correlation of a standardized variable with a standardized linear combination of a set of variables, then to compute that loading from the correlation of sums, the formulas require that unities be placed in the diagonals of the correlation matrix. If anything other than unities are placed in the diagonal spaces, one is not correlating an *actual variable* with a *linear combination of actual variables*.

Ideally the factorial model concerns three independent sources of variance—common variance, specific variance, and variance because of errors of measurement. In most models for factor analysis, specific variance and measurement error variance are lumped together to form the unique variance, and the problem is stated as one of separating common-factor variance from unique variance. When unities are placed in diagonal spaces of the correlation matrix, this goal is only approximately accomplished. The two sources of variance become somewhat mixed, because the variables themselves, including their uniqueness, determine the factors. It can be further understood why common and unique variance become mixed when one considers factors as linear combinations of scores, in which case one mixes the unique characteristic of each variable (or test) with aspects that the variables have in common.

Perhaps it would be best to speak of the approach developed in the previous chapter as concerning *actual factors*, since the factors are actual combinations of the variables and loadings are actual correlations with those factors. The other approach is concerned with *hypothetical factors*—hypothetical because they can only be estimated from the actual variables. The second approach is to seek mathematical solutions that specify factors entirely in terms of the common variance among variables. Such approaches usually involve *communalities*—numbers in the diagonal spaces of the correlation matrix which generally are less than 1.0. For example, one approach to common-factor analysis is to employ communality estimates in the diagonal spaces of the correlation matrix and then submit it to a principal-factor analysis (which is identical to a principal-components analysis except that communality estimates rather than unities are used in the diagonal spaces). Also, there are some special methods of factor analysis which are specifically intended to derive common factors, methods that are not used for components analysis.

**The case for common-factor analysis** The search for hypothetical common factors is appealing for a number of reasons. First, because if there were some way to cleanly disentangle common variance and unique variance, it would accomplish one of the major purposes of factor analysis. From the standpoint of parsimony, relationships among variables would be simplified if the unique components could be neatly distinguished, because in many cases these unique components represent "garbage" that is of no general scientific interest. The approach is appealing also because it would help explain the influence of hypothetical factors on correlation matrices, which presents a more theoretical approach to understanding the underlying traits. One can see why this is so by returning to the general-factor solution.

A general factor $G$ is thought of as a hypothetical factor. It accounts for the correlations among variables, but it is not completely defined by the actual variables. In other words, even if the proportionality criterion is met, the multiple correlation of the variables with $G$ could be much less than 1.0.

If a hypothetical general factor accounts for all the correlations in a matrix, the products of loadings on $G$ equal the correlations. When that notion was introduced earlier, no mention was made of the diagonal spaces of the correlation matrix. In the matrix of products of $G$ loadings, in each diagonal space would be the squared loading for the variable. Thus the diagonal terms would be $a^2$, $b^2$, etc., as illustrated in Table 11-1. These terms would equal 1.0 only if each variable correlated perfectly with $G$, in which case all the correlations would be 1.0.

If a matrix of correlations like that in Table 11-1 meets the requirements for a general factor and unities are placed in the diagonal spaces of that matrix, no existing method of condensation will arrive at only one factor. If, for ex-

**Table 11-1 Correlation matrix computed from loadings of four variables on a general factor**

|   | 1 | 2 | 3 | 4 |
|---|---|---|---|---|
| 1 | $a^2$ | $ab$ | $ac$ | $ad$ |
| 2 | $ab$ | $b^2$ | $bc$ | $bd$ |
| 3 | $ac$ | $bc$ | $c^2$ | $cd$ |
| 4 | $ad$ | $bd$ | $cd$ | $d^2$ |

ample, the centroid method is applied, probably there will be as many factors as there are variables. There will be a general factor, and the remaining factors will tend to explain rather small percentages of variance; but certainly not all elements in the first residual matrix will be zero. There is, however, a way to accomplish this feat if the squared loadings on $G$ are placed in the diagonal spaces, which is illustrated in Table 11-1.

The foregoing result can be accomplished by applying the usual method of centroid condensation to the matrix in Table 11-1, in which communalities are inserted in the diagonal spaces. The sum of coefficients in the first column equals $a(a + b + c + d)$. The sum of coefficients in any column equals the loading of the particular variable times the sum of loadings for all variables. Then the sum of column sums $T$ equals the squared sum of all loadings, which shows that the square root of $T$ equals the sum of loadings. By the usual method of centroid analysis, one finds the loading of any variable by dividing the column sum for that variable by the square root of $T$. Then the centroid loadings would be $a$, $b$, $c$, and $d$—the hypothetical loadings on G. The products of these loadings would equal the coefficients in Table 11-1, including the communality values. All elements in the first residual matrix would be precisely zero. (Exactly the same result would have been obtained from applying the PC method.) Such a beautiful result as this appeals to the imagination and makes one wonder if all factor analysis could not be founded on the search for hypothetical factors. Before the difficulties in this line of reasoning are discussed, the issue of communalities in the general case will be examined.

Artificial examples like that for the general factor case illustrated in Table 11-1 can be extended to *any* number of contrived common factors. One can make up such matrices of factor loadings at will, with only some rather lenient statistical limits. The artificial matrix is illegitimate if (1) any $h^2$ is greater than 1.00, (2) the sum of products of any two rows is greater than 1.00 or less than −1.00, or (3) if any multiple or partial correlations among variables are spuriously greater than 1.00 or less than −1.00. Actually, it is very easy to avoid these pitfalls, which rarely occur if sums of squared loadings on rows ($h^2$) are not above about .80. (The reader may remember from the last chapter that in PC analysis all characteristic roots are either positive or zero if a legitimate factor analysis is performed, which provides a test for any correlation matrix that is composed from an artificial factor matrix. The cautions mentioned above are summarized by saying that the artificial matrix is legitimate if none of the characteristic roots are negative.)

One can make up an artificial matrix as discussed above for any number of factors. For example, a simple case would be to make up an example for 10 hypothetical variables showing loadings on two hypothetical factors. One could put any 20 numbers ranging between −1.00 and 1.00 in the 20 vacant spaces in the matrix as long as they did not violate the three stipulations given above. For testing the effectiveness of a particular method of common-factor analysis, usually one puts in artificial loadings which depict some type of neat pattern of results, such as a perfect simple structure. The rows of the matrix can be multiplied in pairs to form a corresponding artificial matrix of correlations. In this case, rather than place unities in the diagonal spaces, one would place $h^2$ for each variable in the appropriate diagonal space. Then one can take this artificial matrix and apply any one of many different methods of condensation (e.g., principal-factor analysis) and find exactly two factors. Residual coefficients in the second residual matrix will be zero, including the diagonal spaces. One can then rotate the obtained factors so as to obtain the original set of artificial factors composed for the problem. The fact that such clear-cut results can be obtained from common-factor analysis when factors are artificially composed motivates specialists in psychometrics to search for such common factors in correlation matrices obtained from real data. However, this line of reasoning can lead one into conceptual pitfalls and numerous statistical dead ends. These points will be made clearer after various approaches for tackling the problem of common-factor analysis have been discussed.

**Matrix rank** It was Thurstone who first conceptualized the problem of factor analysis in terms of the *rank* of a matrix (see the discussion of these early developments in Thurstone 1947). He saw that the solution to Spearman's $G$ constituted a hypothesis of a rank of 1 for the correlation matrix. The concept of rank was discussed in Chap. 10 where it was said that the rank of a correlation matrix consists of the number of factors required to explain all the correlations exactly. In terms of the picturization of correlations as cosines among vectors, it was said that the number of linear combinations required to serve as a basis for the space constituted the rank of the space. Because matrices of correlations obtained in practice could not be explained by one factor only, Thurstone posed the problem of common-factor analysis as one of finding the rank of a matrix. Thus if five common factors could entirely explain the correlations in a matrix (coefficients in the fifth residual matrix were all exactly zero), then one could say that the rank of the original correlation matrix with communalities in the diagonal spaces was 5.

Although the concept of rank is mathematically important and provides a useful way of thinking about common-factor analysis, there are numerous difficulties in putting the concept to use in the actual study of correlation matrices.

First, even if a relatively small number of underlying traits were involved in the tests employed in a particular analysis, the actual correlations would be "thrown off" in unpredictable ways purely because of the sampling error involved; and, of course, such random distortions would be inversely related to the number of subjects in the sample. Consequently, sampling error alone would prevent any small number of factors from exactly explaining all the correlations in relatively large matrices. Second, even if one attempts to mathematically force entries into the diagonal spaces (communalities) other than unities, the solution of the necessary equations would require an inordinately large number of factors (see the discussion in Harman 1976). Even when one places various restrictions on the nature of the correlation matrix, the rank required to find exact diagonal elements frequently is more than half the number of variables. Thus, to find a unique set of communality estimates to fit a derived rank, one might have to use more than 10 factors to explain a matrix of correlations among only 20 variables.

Because of both sampling error and the very large number of factors that would be required for an exact fit to any rank, it becomes obvious that determining the number of factors required in a particular problem consists of finding a "good fit" to the correlations rather than explaining them exactly. When unities are placed in the diagonal spaces of the correlation matrix and some method of condensation is applied (PC analysis), it is almost always found that the rank is as large as the number of variables, even though many of the factors might be quite small. Even when one attempts to estimate communalities for the diagonal spaces and subsequently employs a method of condensation, usually the rank is as large as the number of variables if one speaks in terms of residual coefficients at any point all being precisely zero. Frequently, however, residual coefficients become very small after only a small number of common factors are extracted. In summary, the concept of rank is theoretically useful mainly in pointing out the need for efficient methods of estimating the number of common factors required in particular problems.

**Communality estimation** It was Thurstone who most fully explored the derivation of hypothetical common factors through the use of communality estimates. When the rank of the matrix actually is less than the number of variables (hopefully much less), if one could somehow guess the correct communalities, one of the methods of condensation, such as the centroid method, could be used to obtain the proper loadings. If, for example, the "true" rank is 4, all coefficients in the fourth residual matrix will be zero, and the sum of squared loadings for any variable ($h^2$) will equal the communality for that variable. This then turns into a bootstrap operation, in which, by some means, the communality must be known before the analysis is undertaken. If one can ascertain the correct values for the communalities and place these in the correlation matrix, any method of condensation applied to that matrix will reveal the "true" rank and will determine loadings on the factors. Many models have been developed for determining hypothetical factors, and many particular methods have been proposed for estimating communalities (see the discussions in works cited in the Suggested Additional Readings).

The method of estimating communalities proposed by Thurstone, which is still used frequently, is an iterative approach. First, by some means, estimates are made of communalities, and these are placed in the diagonal spaces. One of the methods of condensation is applied, typically principal factors or the centroid method, to the point where the matrix of residual coefficients contains only very small values. The number of factors required to do that is considered the rank of the matrix. To obtain proper loadings, the following steps are then required. First, $h^2$ is computed for each variable and compared with the estimated communality used in the analysis. Unless the differences are very small (e.g., an average absolute difference over all variables of only .02), the analysis must be performed again. This time, instead of the original estimates of the communalities, the $h^2$ found for each variable in the first analysis is used. These new communality estimates are placed in the diagonal spaces of the correlational matrix, and the same number of factors is extracted as was obtained in the first analysis. The new set of $h^2$ values is then compared to the ones used in the second round of factoring. If the differences are not small, the obtained communalities in the second analysis are used as estimated communalities for a third analysis. One can keep going in this way until differences between estimated communalities and derived communalities are very small. The loadings obtained in the final analysis are taken as the correct loadings.

There are major difficulties with the iterative method discussed above for determining the number and nature of common factors. The solution is not unique, because at one stage of the analysis, an assumption must be made about the rank (about the number of hypothetical factors). Then one can iteratively find a set of communalities that will fit that rank, but there is no assurance that the rank is correct. No complete solution is known in the case where both the number of factors and communality estimates are allowed to vary simultaneously. Also, even if one accepts particular ways of estimating the rank, iterative approaches have their problems. Different initial estimates of communalities result in convergence to somewhat different iterative solutions for communalities and factor loadings. Also, the iterative approach sometimes leads to the conclusion that the communalities for some variables are greater than 1.0, which certainly casts suspicion on all attempts to obtain communalities through iterative approaches.

In addition to the iterative approach, another approach to estimating communalities is with multiple correlation. The squared multiple correlation (SMC) for estimating each variable from the remaining variables is obtained. Thus, for variable 1 in a group of 20 variables, this would be the SMC for variables 2 through 20 with variable 1. Guttman (1956) proved that the SMC is a *lower bound* for the communality. If the rank of a matrix is less than the number of variables, $h^2$ for any variable will be at least as large as the SMC for that variable. There are three major difficulties with the use of SMCs as estimates of communalities. First, they obviously determine one type of common variance—the variance that a particular variable has in common with the other variables in a matrix. However, this is not the intuitive concept of common variance that many people have in mind. To many people, common variance concerns how much a particular variable has in common with a set of hypothetical factors, not just how much it has in common with the variables in a particular study. A second problem is that SMCs do not reproduce the expected results in artificial problems where stated sets of factor loadings are used to generate tables of correlations. In those cases SMCs seldom reproduce the initial loadings used to obtain the artificial matrices, and thus SMCs do not entirely match the intuitive concept of common factors. In other words, when by the use of an artificial matrix of factor loadings the rank is known, that rank will not be reproduced in general with the use of SMCs in the diagonal spaces.

Third, there are some purely statistical problems in employing SMCs as communality estimates. SMCs tend to grow larger as the number of variables grow larger. This is because each new variable added has some possibility of explaining another portion of each variable already present; also, the more variables there are, the more opportunity there is to take advantage of chance. Regarding the first consideration, although people who deal with the concept of common factors realize that communalities would not necessarily be the same in different collections of variables, it is disturbing to find that they systematically increase when variables are added, as would be the case with SMCs. Of course, the amount of increase would be more noticeable when the original set of variables was small rather than large. The tendency for the SMC to be spuriously large because of taking advantage of chance can be largely offset by having a large sample of subjects—no less than 10 subjects per variable as recommended previously.

Although the use of SMCs for communality estimates has the problems mentioned above, if one insists upon employing a form of communality estimation rather than actual component analysis, then use of SMCs is a sensible approach. This also can be done when ones uses SMCs as the starting point in an iterative approach to obtaining final communality estimates, as mentioned previously. The SMCs have the advantages of being (1) unique, (2) directly obtainable on computers, and (3) definitive of at least one type of common variance.

**Statistical criteria of rank** Rather than employ one of the various procedures of estimating communalities in order to determine rank by an iterative approach or some other procedure of estimation (such as with SMCs), another approach is to consider the rank to be the number of *statistically significant* factors. Tests of statistical significance are available for both the principal-components method (with unities in the diagonal spaces) and the maximum-likelihood method of condensation (with communality estimates in the diagonal spaces). (See the discussion in works cited in Suggested Additional Readings.) With either method, first the test is applied to decide whether the original correlation matrix is due entirely to sampling error. If the null hypothesis is rejected (e.g., significant beyond the .01 level), one can extract a first factor. The same test is applied to the first residual matrix, and to each subsequent residual matrix, until one reaches the number of factors for which the residual matrix is statistically not significant. The number of factors up to that point is declared the rank of the matrix, and the obtained factors are considered an appropriate solution. The statistical tests in both cases are entirely appropriate, but they utterly fail in what the factorist wants to do, namely describe a collection of variables with a relatively small number of factors. There have been numerous demonstrations that the statistical tests are correct but far too lenient in accepting large numbers of factors. Even in problems where considerable previous experience and factor analysis work indicate that no more than four or five factors are required with respect to a particular collection of tests (e.g., those shown in Table 10-12), typically the significance tests accept a rank that is twice as large. In many cases these "statistically significant" factors are utterly insignificant in terms of the amount of variance which they explain. Although the inferential statistical tests themselves are elegant, they are not a solution to the psychometric problem of obtaining a parsimonious solution to common factors. On the other hand, one certainly would not place any faith in a factor that was not statistically significant by this extremely lenient standard.

**Minimum-residual analysis** Because of the difficulties in the methods which require some type of communality estimates, for over 70 years the dream of psychometric specialists has been to find a method of common-factor analysis that works entirely on the off-diagonal correlations and ignores the diagonal elements altogether. (See proposed solutions in the works cited in Suggested Additional Readings.) If the factors could be derived entirely from the off-diagonal elements, then subsequently $h^2$ could be obtained for each row, which would, after the fact, give the proper communalities. Although there would be no reason to do so, except to demonstrate the generality of the solution, one could then take the reproduced matrix with the deduced communalities and refind the factors by any of the standard methods of condensation (e.g., the centroid method).

The most promising approach to factoring the off-diagonal elements in the correlation matrix has been with *minimum-residual factor analysis*. Surprisingly similar methods were developed independently by Comrey (1973) and by Harman (1976). The major difference in approach is that Comrey's method derives one factor at a time until a satisfactory solution is achieved, and Harman's method simultaneously extracts a specified number of factors before the residual matrix is examined. The criterion for determining each set of loadings is the obverse of the principal-components criterion. With principal components, each factor is extracted so as to explain as much as possible of the variance; with minimum-residual analysis, factors are extracted in such a way as to minimize the sum of squared off-diagonal residuals after factors are extracted. The methods developed by Comrey and his associates and by Harman and his associates are based on computer algorithms that consider only the off-diagonal elements. A sufficient number of factors are extracted to reduce the next remaining residual matrix of coefficients either to near zero or to elements that are considered tolerably small. Various statistical and psychometric criteria are used to determine the number of factors required to obtain a sufficiently good estimate.

The method developed by Comrey seems to be a very flexible approach. He has developed extensive computer programs which tie in the method with analytic methods of rotation and auxiliary statistics. Mathematically, his method is very similar to the iterative procedures required for PC analysis, except adjustments are made to prevent the diagonal elements from being involved in the computations. As with the PC method, the same iterative procedure is applied to each successful residual matrix in turn.

The Minres method, developed by Harman and his associates, minimizes residual coefficients for a specified number of factors rather than, as in Comrey's method, for each successive factor. In a sense this is a more elegant approach, and theoretically it should lead to a better fit for the specified number of factors than the approach given by Comrey. However, as Harman freely admits (Harman 1976, chap. 9), his Minres solution suffers from a number of mathematical and practical problems. In terms of practical problems, even the most recent computer algorithms require immense amounts of calculation. There are several mathematical problems that occur with the method. The major one is that, by some form of prior knowledge, one must know the proper number of factors for which to obtain a fit with the Minres approach. Of course, if the fit is not good with a particular specified number of factors, one either increases or decreases the number of factors which are sought until a good fit is obtained. However, this may require a great deal of time for the investigator and the computer. Also, there are some mathematical anomalies that can arise in the use of Harman's Minres method; for example, occasionally one finds a communality that is spuriously larger than 1.00 (for which Harman supplies a correction procedure) or a misleading solution in the iterative process. However, these problems mentioned with respect to the Minres solution by both Comrey and Harman tend to occur infrequently, and in general very reasonable solutions are obtained by both methods.

Minimum-residual methods of factor analysis apparently have not been employed very widely, in spite of the fact that a workable method was developed long ago (Comrey 1962). Probably the methods would have been used more if they were widely known among researchers other than specialists in psychometric methods. Much more theoretical and empirical research should be done with methods based on minimum residuals because at least theoretically they represent an ideal approach to estimating common factors without becoming embroiled in the very knotty issues surrounding communality estimation. Actually, the Minres approaches boil down to very useful ways of estimating the communalities for a regular principal-factor procedure. After communalities are deduced by the Minres approaches, these communalities in turn can be placed back in the original correlation matrix, the regular principal-factors approach can be employed, and the results are the same as those obtained from a Minres analysis.

**Image analysis** Strangely enough, one of the most appealing solutions to the search for common factors is through an interesting adaptation of components analysis, which is referred to as Guttman's *image analysis* (discussed in detail in Suggested Additional Readings). Previously mentioned was Guttman's suggestion for employing the SMC as a communality estimate to be placed in correlation matrices prior to factor analysis. This use of the SMC, however, is only an incidental aspect of a broader methodology for getting at the extent to which variables in factor analysis share common cores of meaning rather than measure different things. In image analysis, the "common" part of a variable in the data matrix is that part which can be predicted by multiple regression from the remaining variables in the matrix. For example, if there are 20 tests represented in the data matrix, one can consider the first test as a criterion variable and predict it with multiple regression from the other 19 variables. Then one would take the second variable, use it as the criterion variable, and predict it from the other 19 variables (including the original scores on the first variable). One would end up with an image score matrix consisting of scores that were predictable from one another in the original score matrix. It should be kept firmly in mind that one ends up with actual scores in the image score matrix, and that these are in no way only hypothetical. One can then perform components analysis on the image score matrix. However, to do this one does *not* correlate the image scores; rather one forms a matrix of *covariances* among them. One would not study the correlation matrix among the image scores, because to do so would automatically standardize all scores, equating all their variances to 1.00. Variables in the image matrix have variances corresponding to their respective SMCs, which of course would differ from variable to variable in terms of the overall pattern of correlations among their original scores. According to this logic of factoring, the geometric analogy for the variables should depict them as having different lengths $h_i$ in the vector space, with $h^2$ equaling the SMC for any variable.

After the image score matrix is obtained, the corresponding covariance matrix with SMCs in the diagonal spaces can be factored by any of the methods of condensation or confirmatory analysis discussed so far in this book. For example, one could employ either principal components or the centroid method to the image covariance matrix. Whereas it has not been necessary to mention this matter so far, the same methods of factor analysis that apply to correlation matrices also apply to covariance matrices. Actually, even if one mistakenly interpreted factor loadings from an image analysis as representing correlations with factors rather than covariances, probably one would not mistakenly interpret the overall results. This is because the image factor loadings look very much like the usual factor loadings based on correlation coefficients, except that they tend to be smaller—how much smaller depending on the sizes of the SMCs.

Of course, a correlation matrix is nothing other than a covariance matrix in which all scores are standardized before the covariances are obtained. In the actual factor analyses, it is not necessary to go the long way round of computing the image score matrix; rather appropriate mathematical manipulations can be made of the correlation matrix to transform it to the necessary image covariance matrix.

Image analysis has a number of attractive advantages. First, it provides a sensible, unique solution to the study of one type of common variance, namely the part which each variable holds in common with other variables in the particular investigation. Second, the solution for the covariance matrix is unique and simple to obtain in any case. It is known that SMCs go in the diagonal spaces—there is no argument about it and no need to make estimates of communalities. Third, image analysis is on very firm mathematical footing, because factors are actual linear combinations of scores (in the image score matrix but not in the original score matrix). Consequently, image analysis has all the advantages of components analysis, such as allowing one to obtain scores of people on the image factors directly rather than to just estimate them as must be done when communalities are employed in common-factor analysis.

In spite of its numerous attractive advantages, image analysis poses some practical and theoretical problems. The major practical problem is that most nonexperts are not used to interpreting the results of covariance analyses, which restricts the general usefulness of the procedures. The obtained loadings are legitimate loadings. However, they are not correlations of variables with the factors, but rather covariances of the image variables with linear combinations of the image variables. This is all perfectly legitimate mathematically, but it tends to be somewhat confusing to many people who must read and understand research reports on factor analysis.

The second disadvantage is conceptual rather than practical: image analysis does not fit what many theorists "have in their heads" when they talk about common factor analysis. Image analysis serves to explain the variance that is common in a particular set of variables; but although many of the proponents of common-factor theory are rather fuzzy about the matter, they apparently have in mind a much broader concept of common variance which extends far beyond the actual data at hand. A third problem with image analysis is that it does not reproduce artificial factors and resulting artificial correlation matrices put together by methods discussed previously. Thus, if one makes up a two-factor problem, image analysis is likely to produce considerably more than two factors; and even after rotation, usually one could only approximate the clean appearance of the factors built into the artificial matrix of correlations. This is not a disadvantage for an individual who favors the image conception of common variance, but it is disturbing to those people mentioned previously who hold a broader meaning for the term.

Image analysis has been around for a long time (see Guttman 1953). Although frequently it has proved useful in mathematical derivations by psychometric specialists, it is not used often in actual substantive studies employing factor analysis. This may be unfortunate, because image analysis does represent an elegant halfway house between full components analysis and common-factor analysis (e.g., minimum-residual analysis). To paraphrase comments that have been made recently by a number of psychometric theorists, image analysis is and is not factor analysis. It is factor analysis in the sense that it derives factors only from the common core of statistically overlapping variance within a data matrix, but it is components analysis in the sense that the factors are actual linear combinations of the image scores. Growing dissatisfactions with the general ambiguities in the common-factor model (e.g., with estimated communalities) have renewed interest in image analysis, which may play a more important part in future factor analysis studies.

**The conceptual dilemma** The major problem with common-factor analysis (as distinct from component analysis) is neither mathematical nor statistical but rather conceptual—no one can say unambiguously what is meant by either common or unique variance. Whereas the various experts have tended to be quite elegant with their mathematical and statistical developments, most have been vague in discussing the question of "common to what?" If one defines common variance as that explained by a number of component factors which are actual linear combinations of variables in the score matrix, then that problem is solved by any of the methods of condensation, for instance, PC analysis. If common variance is defined as the part that each variable has in common with other variables in a particular matrix, then that problem is solved by image analysis. If one defines common variance as all the *reliable* variance of each variable in a data matrix, then that problem is solved too. One needs only to put reliability coefficients in the diagonal spaces and factor-analyze by any of the available methods of condensation (e.g., the centroid method). Beyond those three ways of defining common variance, all other ways are either loosely defined or really not defined at all. Frequently the common variance is rather loosely defined as that portion of the variance that a variable would have in common with a *domain* of variables, but there is no simple way to define such a domain. In discussing reliability theory, it was convenient to postulate a domain-sampling model (e.g., of spelling words). Although that required some stretch of the imagination, it is stretching the imagination much too far to consider a domain of all the possible *variables*, particularly when it is not even stated what kinds of variables would be included. For example, in studying domains of abilities, would one include pole vaulting, speed of counting backward from 100 by $2\frac{1}{2}$, and numbers of Presidents of the United States that one can recall? Obviously, such domains really are not defined, but are casually mentioned on the way to some rather abstruse mathematical and statistical approaches to estimating what has not been defined originally.

There are numerous other possible models for deriving hypothetical factors, but none of these has led to acceptable solutions. All estimates of communality tend to increase (for example, SMCs) as the number of variables in the study is increased. If, by common-factor variance, one has in mind the SMC that a variable would have with an infinitely large, random sample of variables, then if there were any sampling error at all, the SMC would approach unity (because of the tendency for the multiple correlation to take advantage of chance). If there were no sampling error, the SMC would equal the reliability of the variable in question. This is because in an infinite sampling of variables, one would obtain alternative forms of all measures.

There simply is no way to cleanly define common-factor variance when the common factors are not completely specified by the variables at hand. As these words are being written, the author has on his desk stacks of personal communications and prepublication copies of manuscripts which lament the conceptual muddle surrounding the general model for common-factor analysis.

**Perspectives on common-factor analysis** The reader has been led through some of the major issues with respect to common-factor analysis because there are lively controversies in the literature regarding the matter and because these controversies lead to different factor analysis practices. In this section we will try to stand back, take a clear look at the problem, and make some straightforward recommendations regarding the use of factor analysis in research. There is a great deal of evidence now to show that nearly all factoring methods provide much the same results if there really are any clear groupings of variables in the correlation matrix. If a clear solution is found by one approach, almost always it will be found by any other widely used approach. For example, in the 24-variable problem shown in Table 10-12, almost everyone finds the same four factors regardless of the method used. Some people find several small, inconsequential, additional factors; but the four main ones keep popping up by widely different methods of factor condensation, rotation, etc.

If a clear factor structure were found by any one method of factor analysis, almost always it would be found by another method. All the methods of component analysis discussed in the last chapter tend to lead to the same conclusions about the numbers and kinds of factors in major analyses. The different methods of orthogonal rotation tend to produce similar results, and usually the orthogonal results would lead one to essentially the same major conclusions as the oblique methods of rotation. Most important for the discussion here, in *most* analyses one obtains almost identical results from component factors as from different approaches to common factoring, and one finds essentially the same results from different approaches to common factoring. These results are amply documented in the books listed in the Suggested Additional Readings and in the numerous references they cite to particular studies. The author personally has had a great deal of experience in comparing factor analyses by different approaches and uniformly finds that if a clear factor structure is obtained by one approach, it will be apparent by another approach.

The reason that the word *most* was emphasized above is that there are a few exceptions to the rule that all roads in factor analysis lead to essentially the same conclusions, if there are any conclusions to be reached by any one of the methods. Different results from different approaches to analysis can be obtained in two circumstances. The first is when there is a very "weak" factor structure, as opposed to a "strong" structure, found by one of the methods. By a strong structure is meant one in which there are obvious groupings of the variables, as evidenced in substantial correlations among members of the groups and much lower correlations between members of different groups. In terms of factor analysis products, this means that each factor has some variables that load mainly on it alone, and there are at least four tests with loadings above .50. Unless a factor is at least that strong, it would be best to ignore it. Factor analyses of correlation matrices that possess no clear-cut groupings are subject to change by different approaches to factor analysis. In such cases it makes a difference whether one employs component analysis or common-factor analysis, and it makes a difference in terms of how one rotates. However, if the correlation matrix is of a kind that such different approaches would lead one to very different conclusions about the overall results, it might be best to relegate the results to the wastebasket.

Although there are numerous special approaches to common factoring, most of these boil down to what will be placed in the diagonal spaces of the matrix—unities, reliability coefficients, SMCs, or some type of communality estimate. It is very safe to say that if there are as many as 20 variables in the analysis, as there are in nearly all exploratory factor analyses, then it does not matter what one puts in the diagonal spaces. For example, when communality estimates are placed in the diagonal spaces, typically these estimates range between .50 and .80. If there are at least as many as 20 variables, one can randomly shuffle them initially, perform a number of different factor analyses, and find the resulting loadings on factors almost identical to one another.

For the above reasons, when there are at least 20 variables to be employed in exploratory factor analysis, it is strongly recommended that unities be placed in the diagonal spaces and that component analysis be undertaken. Further, it is recommended to use PC plus Varimax, particularly in the overall computer package which Kaiser calls "Little Jiffy Mark IV" (Kaiser and Rice 1974).

Although 20 variables is not a magic number in following the rules stated above, one is surely safe by that point in pursuing the recommended course. To look at the other extreme, *exploratory* factor analysis does constitute a problem when only a small number of variables are being studied, say less than 10. In that case, if one employs component analysis with unities in the diagonal spaces, then these unities can have a substantial influence on the resulting factor structure. This is illustrated in Table 11-2. Except for the last row, the table shows the average centroid loading that would be obtained for different numbers of variables and different average sizes of correlations among them. As an interesting base of comparison, the last row marked $20_z$ shows the average centroid loadings that would be obtained if zeros were placed in the diagonal spaces and the regular centroid method were applied. First it is instructive to look down the column corresponding to an average zero off-diagonal

**Table 11-2 Average loadings on the first centroid factor with unities in the diagonal spaces when number of variables ranges from 5 to 25 and average off-diagonal correlations range from 0 to .60\***

|  | Average Correlations among Variables | | | |
|---|---|---|---|---|
|  | .00 | .20 | .40 | .60 |
| 5 | .45 | .60 | .72 | .82 |
| 10 | .32 | .53 | .68 | .80 |
| 15 | .26 | .50 | .66 | .79 |
| 20 | .22 | .49 | .66 | .79 |
| 25 | .20 | .48 | .65 | .78 |
| $20_z$ | .00 | .40 | .62 | .76 |

*Number of Variables*

*The last row marked $20_z$ shows the results for 20 variables with zeros placed in the diagonal spaces.

correlation among variables. Note that because of the diagonal unities, the loadings on the first centroid are not zero, but the size of such spurious loadings declines rapidly as the number of variables increases. Naturally, if zeros are put in the diagonal spaces, then the average centroid loading would be zero, as indicated in the last row of the table. Whereas no one would be likely to factor-analyze a matrix with zero off-diagonal correlations, it is not unheard of to factor-analyze correlation matrices with an average correlation of .20. In that case, one could see that the diagonal unities would contribute importantly to the first factor if there were only five variables; but this effect tends to dwindle rapidly as one goes to 10 and 15 variables.

When the average correlation in the matrix is as high as .40, then the diagonal unities play less of a part even when the number of variables is small. The most important point to note is that by the time one reaches 20 variables, the influence of the diagonal unities has come to be very insignificant. It is instructive to look at the last row, which shows the average centroid loadings for different numbers of variables when zeros are placed in the diagonal spaces. Note that these are not very different from what is obtained with 20 variables when the unities are placed in the diagonal spaces and the average correlation is at least .20. This serves to demonstrate that it really does not matter *what* you put in the diagonal spaces if you have as many as 20 variables. Many other examples could be composed, and the results from many actual studies could be cited to show that the only problems in employing unities in the diagonal spaces come when the correlations in the matrix are small and particularly when the number of variables is small. However, even with as few as 10 variables, typically one finds the same factor solution regardless of what is put in the diagonal spaces. In most problems where some type of communality estimate is employed, typically the average correlations range between .50 and .80—not between 0 and 1.00. Therefore the range of choice is not as broad as one might think. Just for the fun of it, the author once compared the results of a carefully done centroid factor analysis of a 10-variable problem in which communalities were estimated with the same problem performed when those communality estimates were randomly shuffled from one variable to another. The three factors found in the two studies were almost identical.

If an exploratory factor analysis is being undertaken, there are less than 20 variables, and the groupings of variables in the correlation matrix are not clear, there are several sensible choices for the experimenter: (1) place SMCs in the diagonal spaces before the analysis, (2) employ minimum-residual analysis, or (3) use image analysis. If there is anything worth finding in the matrix, the investigator probably will find essentially the same thing with any one of these approaches. Although the second two alternatives are more elegant mathematically, the use of SMCs probably is easier for most people to understand. One of these three approaches, rather than component analysis with unities in the diagonals, is strongly recommended for any exploratory study that has no more than, say, 12 variables. However, when one is speaking of exploratory studies, these problems almost never arise. Nearly all exploratory factor analyses have more than a dozen variables, and many have well over 50.

Having given these recommendations for exploratory factor analysis, let us consider what should be done in *confirmatory* factor analysis. The multiple-group centroid method is highly recommended if clear-cut hypotheses are available. As was mentioned in Chap. 10 and evidenced in Table 11-2, the diagonal unities can make the loadings seem spuriously high for small clusters of variables containing no more than a half-dozen tests. In a sense, there is nothing wrong with this, because it is the correct mathematical solution. Also, the loadings obtained from such an analysis are exactly the ones required for computing factor scores and other statistics that will be needed subsequently. The illusory appearance of large loadings could be reduced by following one of the three procedures mentioned above for small exploratory factor analyses—use of SMCs as communalities, minimum-residual analysis, or image analysis. However, this is not really necessary if the reader will faithfully observe the sizes of correlations that determine each of the group factors and report those average correlations along with other statistics relating to the study. The other method that was recommended for confirmatory factor analysis, the ML method, has a built-in procedure for deriving communality estimates as part of its overall strategy for estimating the population correlation matrix from the sample correlation matrix. Therefore the problem takes care of itself even when each group or cluster involved in confirmatory factor analysis has a half-dozen members or less.

## STATISTICAL DECISIONS

Factor analysis in psychology, as the name implies, has been considered mainly as a mathematical method of analysis rather than as a statistical tool, in the sense of inferential statistics. That is the way the author thinks it should remain. There are, however, some points in factor analysis where decisions must be made regarding the statistical confidence to be placed in results. Chief among these is a question of when to stop factoring. The answer is different both in terms of component and common-factor analysis and in terms of whether confirmatory or exploratory analysis is being undertaken.

Regardless of which of the two types of analyses is being performed, one should make questions of sampling error trivial by employing a large sample of persons. Since there are so many opportunities to take advantage of chance in factor analysis, particularly in employing one of the methods of condensation prior to rotation, a good rule is to have at least 10 times as many subjects as variables. Then there will be little sampling error, and as experience has shown (e.g., Gorsuch 1974), probably there will be more "significant" factors than the investigator will care to interpret. First we will consider inferential statistics relating to confirmatory analysis. Then we will consider such inferential statistics relating to exploratory factor analysis.

With methods for testing hypotheses, the chief method being with the use of group centroids, as many factors should be extracted as were hypothesized initially. The question then concerns whether the average loading on each factor is significantly high to lend confidence that the factor exists beyond the confines of the particular group of subjects. A highly conservative rule of thumb will usually suffice for that purpose. First, one computes the average correlation among the variables hypothesized to form a particular factor. If some of the variables were hypothesized to have negative loadings, signs of their correlations would be reversed in the proper columns and rows of the correlation matrix. The average value would be over all nondiagonal elements. This average value would then be compared with the usual standard error of a correlation coefficient. An example will help illustrate this rule of thumb. It is hypothesized that six variables form a factor. All correlations among the variables are positive, and the average correlation is .30. There are 300 subjects, and consequently the standard error for a correlation coefficient (*not* for the average correlation among variables) is approximately the reciprocal of the square root of 300. Then a correlation as low as .15 would be significant beyond the .01 level. Thus one could have a great deal of confidence in a factor based on an average correlation of .30. If the factor does not possess a high degree of confidence by this very conservative standard, either the number of persons is too small to provide meaningful results or the variables are related so weakly that substantial factor loadings probably cannot be obtained.

If the ML method is used rather than the multiple-group method for confirmatory analysis, the ML method has a built-in significance test. The test will usually produce many more "significant" factors than one would care to interpret. However, one certainly would not want to make any effort to interpret a factor in confirmatory analysis that was not significant by this very generous standard.

In confirmatory factor analysis, an acceptable test of significance is available for the principal-component solution, that is, when unities are placed in the diagonal spaces rather than some type of communality estimate (see works cited in Suggested Additional Readings). Essentially what one does is to test the original correlation matrix for statistical significance before even the first factor is extracted. The same test is applied to each successive residual matrix. One would discontinue factoring when a residual matrix proved to be insignificant. It would be wise to accept a very stringent level of significance in this regard, i.e., the .001 level of significance. Even so, if there are at least 10 persons per variable, the significance test is likely to lead one to accept factors as significant whose largest loadings are less than .20. Consequently, it is better to use rules of thumb which will be discussed subsequently for terminating the factoring rather than to rely solely on such tests of significance.

The available computer programs for the ML method have "built-in" procedures for communality estimation and significance tests corresponding to the correlation matrix and each subsequent residual matrix. As mentioned previously, however, this test proves to be very generous when ample subjects are included in the analysis, and consequently it would be better to rely on the rules that will be given subsequently regarding decisions about numbers of factors to employ. It should be emphasized that, in both PC analysis and ML analysis, the available significance tests apply to the number of factors *before* they are rotated. The equivalent inferential statistics for rotated factors are theoretically much more complex [see the discussion in works cited in the Suggested Additional Readings and in Archer and Jennrich (1973); Jennrich (1973); and Jennrich and Thayer (1973)].

Although available tests of statistical significance should be considered with respect to the results of exploratory factor analysis, it is more important to heed the following rules of thumb for accepting unrotated and subsequently rotated factors. On theoretical grounds and from a great deal of experience in factor analysis, Kaiser has shown that a suggestion made earlier by Guttman serves very well to determine the number of PC factors that should be accepted prior to rotation. The solution is to use all unrotated factors that have characteristic roots (latent roots or eigenvalues) that are greater than 1.00 for subsequent rotation. This criterion is employed frequently in the computerized statistical package related to the Varimax criterion of rotation. The logic, use, and history of this criterion are discussed in Kaiser and Rice (1974). This rule of thumb sometimes has been applied when communalities are used rather than unities, but this is not correct.

There are several other useful rules of thumb for exploratory analysis, all of which will probably lead to essentially the same rotated factor solution, if there are any substantial factors to be found in the matrix. An old rule is to delete any factors for which there are no loadings greater than .30. This is not a bad principle since no variable would have a loading with more than 9% of its variance explained by the factor. Another rule of thumb is to extract approximately one-third as many factors as there are variables, somewhat more for small matrices and somewhat less for large matrices. Thus in exploratory factor analysis with 12 variables, one might extract as many as five factors prior to rotation; with 100 variables, one might extract as many as 25 factors prior to rotation. Whereas this rule of thumb to extract approximately as many as one-third of the number of variables may seem overly liberal (and so may other rules of thumb in that regard), there is a great deal of practical experience to show that it is sensible to "overfactor" in exploratory analysis (whether in components analysis or in common-factor analysis) prior to rotation. There are good, logical grounds for believing that rotation usually will serve to separate the wheat from the chaff in the sense of building up the "real" factors and rotating spurious factors to the vanishing point. Although one can find exceptions to this rule, in general the factors that prove to be real, in the sense that they appear in subsequent analyses, do tend to make their appearance known after factors are rotated in which purposeful overfactoring is done of the original correlation matrix.

In exploratory analysis, after factors are rotated, the next step is to note the number of variables that have loadings of .30 or higher. It is doubtful that loadings of any smaller size should be taken seriously, because they represent less than 10 percent of the variance. Imagine in a particular study that on factor 5 there are six variables with loadings of .30 or higher. Since these variables must be used to interpret the factor, it is proper to ask how well the factor is defined by these variables. This is determined by the multiple correlation of the six variables with the factor, about which more will be said in a later section. After that multiple correlation is computed, a conservative rule of thumb for accepting the factor as real is obtained as follows. First, to partially take account of the extent to which advantage is taken of chance, the obtained multiple correlation should be "shrunk" with the use of Eq. (5-23). In Eq. (5-23), rather than use the number of variables employed to compute the multiple correlation, one should use the total number of variables in the study. Then the shrunken multiple correlation is compared with the standard error for a multiple correlation. So that one can have any real confidence in the factor, the shrunken multiple correlation should be considerably larger than the multiple correlation, which would be significant at the .01 level. Thus if a multiple correlation of .30 would be significant at the .01 level, one would hope to have a shrunken multiple correlation of at least .50.

The results of any factor analysis should be "more significant" than would be required by any exact statistical test. If the variables used to interpret a factor do not have a multiple correlation with the factor of at least .50, the estimates of factor scores will be highly inexact. Since there are very few instances in which an investigator would attempt to interpret a factor which failed to meet that criterion, the question is one of how much confidence can be placed in a multiple correlation of .50. If there are at least 10 times as many people as variables, such a multiple correlation will be highly significant in most instances.

Worrying about exact tests of statistical significance or employing the conservative rules of thumb discussed above, however, is of far less importance than considering the "reality" of factors as a problem of replication. No factor analysis should be an end in itself. If the results are interesting, some of the same variables will be included in other investigations. Then it will be found to what extent the variables used to define a factor actually "hang together" and measure something different from variables used to define other factors. This can be illustrated in the problem where two factors are thought sufficient to explain most of the common variance among 20 supposed measures of anxiety. Suppose it is found that three variables have a high multiple correlation with one factor and three other variables have a high multiple correlation with the second factor. Scores on these variables are then used to estimate the two factors, and these estimates of factor scores are used as dependent measures in subsequent investigations. In addition to examining the treatment effects (whatever the purpose of the study), the experimenter should also inter-correlate the six measures used to define the two factors. These correlations would show in a direct way whether the two groups of variables "hung together" and tended to measure two factors.

## ESTIMATION OF FACTOR SCORES

If factors are linear combinations of actual variables, factor scores for people can be perfectly "estimated." An exact determination of factor scores can be made in components analysis regardless of how many factors are extracted relative to the number of variables. This is true in PC analysis and in the use of the centroid method with unities placed in the diagonals. Factor scores also can be exactly determined in image analysis. With information provided by the matrix of factor loadings, equations can be established for determining factor scores from the data matrix. (These equations are discussed in the works cited in the Suggested Additional Readings.) Essentially these equations concern a multiple-regression analysis in which the factor is the variable to be predicted and all the variables are the predictors. Each loading is a correlation with the factor, and correlations among the predictor variables are obtained from the original matrix of correlations. A different prediction equation would be required for each factor. When unities are placed in the diagonal spaces of the correlation matrix preparatory to the analysis, the multiple correlations of variables with the factors are precisely 1.0. So in this instance one uses the equivalent of multiple regression in the trivial cases where all multiple correlations are known in advance to be 1.0.

With any of the methods concerned with hypothetical factors, scores of people on the factors can only be estimated, not directly measured. This is true in Spearman's general-factor solution and in any method of condensation where values other than unities are placed in the diagonal spaces. The preferred procedure in these cases is to estimate factor scores with multiple-regression analysis. This can be done either with all the variables in the analysis or with a subset of the variables. In either case, however, the multiple correlation will almost always be less than 1.0, and in most cases it will be considerably less. Alternative methods of estimating factor scores are described in the works cited in Suggested Additional Readings, but none of these are as widely accepted as multiple-regression analysis.

The estimation of factor scores is a crucial step in the continuing explication of constructs. For example, suppose it is found that two factors do a good job of accounting for the correlations among 20 supposed measures of anxiety. The next step would be to use the two factors in controlled experiments and in investigations concerning correlations among sources of individual differences. Unless there are continuing investigations of this kind, a factor analysis does little to advance the science. A very important point, however, is that in such continuing investigations of the factors, it is quite unlikely that all 20 tests will be employed. The hope in factor analysis is to reduce a larger collection of variables to a smaller set of "potent explainers." In the example above, it might be found that three tests relate strongly to one factor of anxiety and another three tests relate strongly to the second factor of anxiety. These tests can then be used to estimate factor scores in subsequent studies. In this instance, however, factor scores could be only estimated, and not perfectly so. This is true regardless of whether unities or communality estimates are placed in diagonal spaces of the correlation matrix. If unities were employed, even if each factor has a perfect multiple correlation with *all* the variables, a perfect multiple correlation with only some of them is not likely.

For the above reasons, in nearly all empirical studies it is better to think of *estimating* factor scores rather than of measuring them directly. Of course, if unities are employed, one can directly measure factor scores for the particular people used for the factor analysis, but this is the trivial case. Exact determinations of factor scores sometimes are useful as part of overall mathematical analyses, but they are of very little use in continuing actual research with factors beyond the original situation in which the factors are found. If a factor is of any importance, it will be used in many investigations, and employing all the tests used to define the factor initially is not feasible.

That factor scores usually must be estimated by multiple regression is a fact which provides some perspectives on other issues in factor analysis. Frequently only one variable is used to estimate factor scores in subsequent investigations; e.g., only one test is used to measure a factor of anxiety in a controlled experiment on the effects of anxiety on the rate of solving particular types of problems. For two interrelated reasons, usually this is bad practice. First, a variable seldom loads so heavily on a factor that it provides precise estimates of factor scores. In this instance the "multiple correlation" with the factor is simply the loading of the variable on the factor. Then, even if the variable has a loading as high as .70, only about 50 percent of the variance of the factor can be accounted for by the variable. Second, estimates of factor scores in this instance would be heavily weighted by the unique variance of the particular variable. Almost always, at least two variables are needed to estimate a factor. The multiple correlation between the two variables is likely to be considerably higher than the loading of either, and combining the two variables in multiple regression averages out some of the unique variance in each variable.

At the other extreme, in continuing studies of a factor, it is seldom feasible to use more than three or four variables to estimate factor scores. This has two important implications. The first is that one should look carefully at the multiple correlation of the variables with the factor. Regardless of how "statistically significant" the factor may be in other ways, if the multiple correlation is not high, the factor is not ready for continuing investigations. If the multiple correlation is less than .70, one is in trouble. In that instance the error variance in estimating the factor would be approximately the same as the valid variance. At a very minimum, one should be quite suspicious of factor estimates obtained with a multiple correlation of less than .50, because in that case less than 25 percent of the variance of factor scores can be predicted from the variables. Then one could not trust the variables as actually representing the factor, and it would be of dubious value to perform further studies supposedly concerning the factor. For these reasons, decisions about the acceptance or rejection of a factor as real should be based on the size of the multiple correlation with the factor for those variables which will be used to estimate the factor in subsequent studies. Thus mere statistical significance of a factor is not nearly as important as having a factor that can be estimated well from a relatively small subset of the variables. When the latter standard is employed, frequently factors are rejected that would appear "highly significant" by the former standard (assuming that there are at least 10 subjects per variable). Of course, even if a factor fails to meet the requirement of having a high multiple correlation, it might be investigated with new variables in a new factor analysis. But the factor should be "released" to other scientists only when good estimates of factor scores are possible.

A second implication of the fact that only a relatively small subset of variables can be used in continuing investigations of a factor concerns the rotation of factors in stepwise analyses. As was mentioned previously, the estimation of factors usually results in an additional rotation, one beyond that performed in the rotational process per se. If, for example, three variables are used to define a factor, in essence one is placing a factor axis among those variables. If the factor is estimated by a simple sum of scores on three variables, it is rotated to the centroid of those three variables. Then even if factors are kept orthogonal in the rotations, the estimates of factor scores are likely to be correlated.

## FACTOR ANALYSIS DESIGNS

The problem of factor analysis was posed with respect to a data matrix, which was illustrated in Table 10-1. The columns of the table were different variables, and the rows showed the scores of persons on those variables. The problem was posed in terms of the correlations between column variables. This type of analysis is referred to as $R$ techniques, which is to be distinguished from numerous other possibilities for factor analysis designs. These possibilities have been discussed in detail by Cattell (1952) and Gorsuch (1974). A variant of *R* technique is to have the *same* person on each row of the data matrix, showing changes in scores at different points in time and/or under different circumstances. An example would be in the study of physiological processes in one person from day to day. Measurements on the same variables are made each day for a period of several months. These measures are intercorrelated and factor-analyzed. A factor would concern a group of physiological variables that tend to go up and down together from day to day. This variant of *R* technique is called *P* technique, the *P* standing for observations at different points in time. It is similar to *R* technique in that it concerns the factor analysis of correlations among variables. *P* technique also can be employed when each row of the data matrix shows the average scores of a group of subjects on different occasions. This might be useful in the study of longitudinal trends in physiological processes or personality characteristics for people in general.

In contrast to *R* and *P* techniques, there are designs concerning correlations among the rows of the data matrix rather than among the columns. These methods are frequently referred to as *transposed* analyses. The parent name for these different possibilities is *Q* technique.

A study performed by Fiedler (1950) will serve to illustrate *Q* technique. (A more detailed description of *Q* technique will be given in Chap. 15.) The study was of 60 psychotherapists who represented three different approaches to treatment. Each therapist rated his or her agreement with a list of statements concerning different ways of conducting therapy sessions. The columns of the data matrix related to the statements and the rows showed the ratings of each therapist. Scores were standardized *over statements* for each therapist separately, *not* over therapists for each statement, as would be the case in *R* technique. Correlations were computed between therapists, showing the relative amount of agreement between therapists. Factor analyses were then performed to describe the different schools of thought.

A variant of *Q* technique, which some call *O* technique, is to have the same person on all rows of the data matrix, showing different scores on the same variables for the same individual on different occasions. This is the same type of data matrix employed in *P* technique. With *O* technique, however, one correlates rows of the data matrix with one another rather than columns. An example of this variant of *Q* technique is a study by the author (Nunnally 1955), in which an individual was required to make ratings of her self-concept from 16 different points of view, e.g., "the way you really are," and "the way your parents view you." These were intercorrelated, resulting in a 16-by-16 matrix of correlations. A factor analysis found "three selves," and changes in these were investigated over the course of psychotherapy.

In both *R* and *Q* techniques, one must be careful how scores are standardized before correlations are computed. In the typical *R*-technique study, common sense indicates how this should be done. Scores should be standardized over people separately for each variable. Essentially the same should be done in *P* technique, in which case scores are standardized over occasions for one person (or group of persons) on each variable separately.

In the $Q$-technique family of designs, more thought is required to determine the proper approach to standardization. An example would be where the columns represented different tests of ability and rows showed the scores of different subjects. It would be misleading to standardize over tests for each person and then intercorrelate persons. Since the tests probably would have different means over persons, the correlations between persons would be strongly influenced by these mean differences. In that case, the proper approach would be to first standardize over persons on each variable and then restandardize over variables for each person. This would remove spurious effects because of differences in means and standard deviations of variables. In some types of studies, this can be accomplished by the method of collecting data. This cannot be done with tests of ability, but it can be done with ratings concerning preferences and agreement. One does this by forcing all subjects to have the same mean rating and the same standard deviation of ratings. The method for doing this is called the $Q$ *sort*, which will be discussed in detail in Chap. 15.

There are some obvious differences between $R$-technique and $Q$-technique families of designs. In the former, the variables have factor loadings, and the persons have factor scores, and vice versa in $Q$ technique. Another obvious difference between the two approaches concerns the number of persons and variables required for meaningful analyses. In $R$ technique, the number of persons should be much larger than the number of variables, and vice versa in $Q$ technique. Whereas in the former it is meaningful to apply inferential statistics to correlations, this poses some problems in the latter. In $Q$ technique, the sample size consists of the number of variables, and to employ that as $N$ in the usual formulas (e.g., significance of difference from zero correlation) forces one to consider random samples of variables in a specifiable domain, which stretches the logic of applying many inferential statistics. This matter will be discussed more fully in Chap. 15.

There have been numerous attempts to show that nothing can be obtained from $Q$-technique designs that could not be obtained from $R$-technique designs. For several reasons, this is not correct. In certain hypothetical cases there are some equations that will permit a transformation of the results obtainable in $Q$ technique to results obtainable in $R$ technique, and vice versa (Burt 1941). The circumstances in which that can be done, however, are not likely to prevail in actual studies. Second, even if there were precise mathematical relations in all cases, the rotational choice in one method of analysis probably would not lead to the most desirable solution in the other method of analysis. Third, and most important, the different approaches have very different implications for psychological theory. If one has theories concerning factors among variables, one should use $R$ technique. If one has theories concerning factors among persons, one should employ $Q$ technique. Even if it were true that transforming one type of analysis to the other usually would be possible, this would be beside the point. To think otherwise would be analogous to thinking that because the same machine could be used to measure heart rate and brain waves, it would make no difference which was measured.

The difference between the two basic approaches to factor analysis is in terms of the ease with which they can be fitted into psychological theories. The constructs in most theories concern clusters of related variables (e.g., anxiety, intelligence), and $R$ technique is the proper approach. In contrast, $Q$ technique concerns clusters of persons, and each factor is a hypothetical "person." The hypothetical person is defined in terms of "his" or "her" complete set of responses to the variables involved. Factors must be thought of as idealized "types" of persons, and the loadings of actual people specify to what extent they are mixtures of the various types. Such constructs simply are more difficult for most psychologists to "think with" than are the constructs of concern in $R$ technique. For this reason, the $R$-technique family of possible analyses is used much more frequently than the $Q$-technique family. There are, however, some types of studies where $Q$ technique is sensible and where interesting results have been obtained in studies to date (some of these are mentioned in Chap. 15). $Q$ technique also is closely related to profile analysis, which will be discussed in the next chapter.

## CLUSTER ANALYSIS

The purpose of cluster analysis is very similar to that of factor analysis (see Tryon and Baily 1970 for an extensive discussion of cluster analysis). As the name implies, *cluster analysis* consists of methods of classifying variables into groups, or clusters. A *cluster* consists of variables that correlate highly with one another and have comparatively low correlations with variables in other clusters. This is essentially what a factor is in factor analysis. Instead of formal methods of factor analysis, however, there are some ways of searching for clusters in the correlation matrix. An approximate approach is as follows. First, if some variables have a negative sum of correlations in the correlation matrix, one reflects variables so as to obtain a maximum sum of positive correlations for the matrix as a whole. Next, the highest correlation in the matrix is found. The two variables involved form the nucleus of the first cluster. Then one looks for variables that correlate highly with these and includes them in the cluster.

One obtains the nucleus for the second cluster by finding two variables that correlate highly but have low correlations with members of the first cluster. Variables that correlate highly with the two variables serving as the nucleus of the second cluster are included in the cluster. Then one proceeds in this way to search for a third cluster, and so on.

If clusters were quite clear, as is seldom the case, it would be better to use cluster analysis than to go the long way round through formal procedures of factor analysis. For a number of reasons, however, frequently this is not the best strategy. When the number of variables is small, often one can see the patterns of relationship simply by inspecting the correlation matrix, which was the case for the six-variable problem in Table 10-6. When there are many variables in the study (e.g., more than 20), it is easy to get lost in the maze of correlations and become entirely confused about which variables should be placed in clusters. Also, since successive matrices of residual coefficients in factor analysis can be converted directly to partial-correlation coefficients, frequently clusters which make themselves apparent after a number of factors have been extracted from a matrix would not be discernible in the original correlation matrix. Consequently, some more formal methods of analysis are necessary in addition to simply grouping variables in terms of their original correlations. For problems concerning large numbers of variables, numerous cut-and-try methods have been proposed for locating clusters. McQuitty developed a number of rather elaborate computational routines for that purpose (e.g., McQuitty and Koch 1976). There are two major problems with these methods. First, they are mathematically "messy." Numerous, semiarbitrary decisions must be made about the number of clusters and the composition of clusters. Second, these methods require as much computational time as a formal factor analysis.

If one likes to think of all factor analysis as being forms of cluster analysis (a point of view which has considerable merit), the multiple-group approach to factor analysis is recommended. If clusters are hypothesized in advance, the multiple-group method can test for how well the clusters actually hang together. If clusters are not defined a priori with regard to hypotheses about constructs, one can search for clusters with the multiple-group method. A first group centroid can be placed among those variables that have the highest correlations with one another. The residual matrix is obtained, and a second factor is placed among those variables that have high residual coefficients with one another, and so on for additional factors.

Whether one uses the cut-and-try methods of cluster analysis or formal methods of factor analysis, in the end all factors can be thought of as clusters. As was mentioned previously regarding the estimation of factor scores, almost always no more than three or four variables are used to measure a factor in studies subsequent to the factor analysis. Then, for all intents and purposes, those several variables define the factor, and in practice a factor is a linear combination of the scores on a cluster of variables.

## AD-LIB FACTORING

In obtaining successive factors from a particular matrix of correlations, it is not necessary to employ only one method of factoring. It is entirely legitimate to extract the first factor by the PC method, the second factor by the centroid method, the third factor by a method based on minimum residuals, and the fourth factor by still another method. Factor analysis can be applied to the successive matrices of residual coefficients without regard to the methods used to obtain the factors. When there are hypotheses to guide the analysis, an ad-lib approach to factoring offers a flexible method for "taking apart" the common variance among variables. An example of how this is done comes from a study by Nunnally and Hodges (1965) in which the variables were measures of individual differences in word association. Each variable concerned the tendency to give a particular type of associate. Prior to the analysis, three scales had been studied extensively, and these were included as variables in the factor analysis. The other variables were new scales intended to measure five new factors. The first step was to employ the square root method (the method is discussed in Harman 1976). The three old scales were used successively as pivots. This tested for the relative independence of the old scales and removed their variance from that of the new scales. The group-centroid method was then applied to the residual matrix. Five group centroids were placed among the five hypothesized groups of variables. The complete-centroid method was then applied to the resulting residual matrix, in an effort to discover factors that had not been hypothesized originally. Rotations were made of the complete-centroid factors by the Varimax method, but the three factors derived by the square-root method and the five factors obtained by the group-centroid method were not included in the rotations. A flexible approach to factor analysis of this kind allows one to directly test the explanatory power of hypotheses regarding the nature of psychological constructs and to explore new groupings of variables as well. It is easy to let good ideas about a domain of variables get lost in the brutish mechanics of a ready-made, rigid approach to factoring.

## HIGHER-ORDER FACTORS

If correlated factors are obtained, it is possible to factor the correlations so as to obtain higher-order factors. The original factors are called *first-order factors*. Say, for example, that 10 first-order factors are obtained and the correlations among those factors are known. Then the 10-by-10 matrix of correlations among factors can be submitted to any desired method of factor analysis, and the obtained factors can be rotated. In this example, say that four factors are obtained. These would be called *second-order factors*. The correlations among the second-order factors also could be analyzed to obtain third-order factors. A first-order factor is a linear combination of the variables, a second-order factor is a linear combination of the first-order factors, and so on for higher-order factors. Since there is a direct link between the original variables and higher-order factors, there are methods for computing the loadings of all variables on higher-order factors (Gorsuch 1974).

For two reasons, the author has somewhat ambivalent feelings about the usefulness of higher-order factors. First, they tend to confuse nonspecialists. The average psychologist has difficulty in understanding first-order factors, and this difficulty is increased with higher-order factors. This is not such a problem if loadings are interpreted only with respect to the highest order of factors investigated—e.g., if the loadings of all variables are shown and discussed only for the second-order factors. If, however, the average psychologist must interpret loadings on first- and second-order factors, she or he is likely to make some misinterpretations. Also, if factor analysis is partly founded on the principle of parsimony, it is reasonable to question the parsimony of having different orders of factors. For the sake of parsimony, the fewer the factors, the better; but the use of higher-order factors adds more and more factors. In this way one could end up with more factors than variables.

A second reason for the author's ambivalent feelings about the use of higher-order factors is that, in some cases, approximately the same information can be obtained in a simpler way. This is particularly true with second-order factors. Loadings on a second-order general factor mainly reflect the tendency of variables to correlate positively or negatively with the other variables. Much the same information is obtained from the loadings of variables on a first-order factor obtained by either the centroid method or the method of principal axes. There is nothing wrong with interpreting such loadings on a general factor even if that factor subsequently is rotated in conjunction with other factors.

In a number of investigations, second-order factor analysis has proved helpful in summarizing the results of large analyses that produced many factors. For example, although many tests that we think of as being related to intelligence can be broken down into 10 or more oblique factors, a second-order factoring produces strong loadings on a general factor. This shows that, in addition to talking about separable factors of intellect, it is also meaningful to talk about general ability or, as it is popularly known, intelligence. Some second-order analyses have also proved helpful in making sense out of the many factors found in personality inventories. A final observation about the employment of higher-order factors: if first-order factors are kept orthogonal, of course there is no possibility of obtaining higher-order factors.

## COMPARISONS OF FACTORS IN DIFFERENT ANALYSES

An important problem in research is to determine the similarity of factors in different analyses. For example, in the literature, frequently one finds discussions of whether two factors from two different analyses actually are the same. In deriving methods for settling such issues, it is important to remember that factors are linear combinations of the variables—actual linear combinations in component analysis and hypothetical linear combinations which are estimated in common-factor analysis. These are to be distinguished from factor loadings, which are the correlations of variables with the factors. It is a mistake to argue about the comparability of factors in terms of the tables of loadings in two analyses. One proposal, for example, has been to correlate the loadings on factors in different analyses to measure their comparability. Various other indices have been proposed for comparing two matrices of factor loadings (see the discussion in Gorsuch 1974). These, however, all miss the point, because the loadings are not the factors. It is easy to rig an example where the loadings on two orthogonal factors in the *same* analysis correlate highly. One can do this by drawing two orthogonal axes and then putting in points for variables so that a high correlation is obtained.

The proper method of comparing factors in different analyses is to compare *factor scores* in the different analyses. This can be done straightforwardly only if the same persons are involved in the different analyses. If such is the case, it does not matter whether all the variables are the same in the different analyses, only some of the variables are the same, or all the variables are different. The first step is to obtain factor scores on all factors. For this, it is better to use all the variables in the analysis to obtain factor scores than to estimate them from subsets of the variables. The next step is to correlate the factor scores in the different analyses. The comparability of factors is judged by the sizes of the correlations. If only some of the persons participate in two studies, one can obtain an approximate notion of the comparability of factors by correlating factor scores for those persons.

If different persons are involved in the different analyses, it is arguable what method should be used to compare factors. If in that case the variables also are different in the different analyses, there is no conceivable way of comparing factors. If the variables are the same, one method of comparing factors is as follows. To obtain factor scores in one analysis, a set of weights must be applied to the variables. The set of weights required in one analysis can be applied to the scores of the different people in a different analysis. In each analysis, this would then provide two sets of factor scores—the weights for one obtained from the analysis of a different group of subjects. The correlations between these two sets of factor scores could be used to judge the comparability of factors in the analysis of the same variables in different groups of subjects. If only some of the same variables are involved in the two analyses, an approximate test of comparability can be made as follows. Factor scores are estimated from only those variables that appear in both analyses, if that is possible, and correlations of the type described above are computed between the sets of factor scores.

In most cases where comparisons are made between factor scores in different analyses, it is not necessary to actually obtain the scores unless they are wanted for some other purpose. Instead, the correlations between factor scores can be calculated from the weights required to obtain the scores. This is done by the correlation of weighted linear combinations discussed in Chap. 5. Special formulas for this purpose are found in the works cited in the Suggested Additional Readings.

## HOW TO FOOL YOURSELF WITH FACTOR ANALYSIS

It would be appropriate at this point to mention some cautions regarding the use of factor analysis. One way to fool yourself with factor analysis is to ignore the correlations that are used to define a factor. In some cases the variables used to define a factor have correlations near zero with one another. This can happen because of the successive partialing that goes on in the derivation of factors. An example will indicate how this occurs. Suppose that two variables each have loadings of .50 on one of two factors; on the second factor, one variable has a loading of .50, and the other has a loading of −.50. If one were not careful, one might use the two variables to define the first factor, but the set of loadings on the two factors could stem from a correlation of zero between the two variables. Mathematically there is nothing wrong with this eventuality, but it might lead to some misinterpretations. It is mathematically possible for variables that have very low correlations to have substantial loadings on a factor, but if those variables are used to define a factor in studies subsequent to the factor analysis, people will tend to expect substantial correlations among the variables.

A second way to fool yourself with factor analysis relates to the first way. It is easy to overinterpret the meaning of small factor loadings, e.g., those below .40. It must be remembered that in some methods of factor analysis, such as the PC method, factor vectors are placed so as to make loadings on successive factors as large as possible. Even if the average correlation in the matrix (disregarding signs) is rather low, the factor loadings may look substantial. This is particularly true when unities are placed in the diagonal spaces of the correlation matrix. As an extreme example, suppose that there are only four variables and all correlations are precisely zero. Each variable will then have a loading of .50 on the first centroid factor. When unities are placed in the diagonal spaces and the number of variables is small, one should be cautious in interpreting small loadings. As was advised previously, the safe procedure is to inspect the original matrix of correlations to ensure that variables used to define a factor actually have substantial correlations.

A third way to fool yourself with factor analysis is to misinterpret the meaning of orthogonal factors. Although the factors themselves are uncorrelated, this does not mean that estimated factor scores are uncorrelated. If unities are placed in the diagonal spaces and all variables in the study are used to obtain (not estimate) factor scores, the factor scores will be uncorrelated; but this is seldom the way factor scores are obtained. Usually, they are only estimated, not obtained directly. This is true in all cases where anything other than unity is placed in each diagonal space of the correlation matrix prior to factoring. Even if unities are placed in the diagonal spaces, usually, for practical purposes, factors are estimated by no more than four variables. In these cases the estimated factor scores are likely to correlate substantially even if the factors themselves are orthogonal. Consequently, one should be careful in using the word orthogonal to discuss a particular set of factors, and the actual correlations among estimates of factor scores should be reported.

A fourth way to fool yourself with factor analysis is to employ variables that are experimentally dependent, which can occur in a number of ways. One way is in employing variables that have overlapping items. This happens most frequently in personality inventories, where it is common practice to derive a number of different scales from the same items. An outstanding example is in the Minnesota Multiphasic Personality Inventory (MMPI), where numerous scales are based on the same items. The overlapping items force correlations among the scales, which produce "factors." A study by Shure and Miles (1965) showed that when overlapping items are removed from the scales, the factor structure of the MMPI is different from what was thought. Another way to obtain experimental dependence is by including in the analysis various combinations of the separate variables. This would be the case, for example, if one variable equaled the difference between two other variables. The difference scores necessarily would correlate with the two variables used to obtain the differences, which would tend to confuse the results of a factor analysis. Generally it is best to avoid any form of experimental dependence among variables employed in factor analysis. The intention is to investigate "natural" correlations among variables, not the correlations that are forced through experimental dependence.

A fifth way to fool yourself with factor analysis concerns the selection of subjects. If subjects are relatively heterogeneous with respect to age, sex, and education, factors sometimes are produced by differences in those regards. Whether one should permit samples of persons to be heterogeneous with respect to such variables depends on the population over which the results of factor analysis are to be generalized. For example, if the factors are to be interpreted with respect to individual differences in children *within* particular age levels, the sample of children investigated in the factor analysis should be relatively homogeneous with respect to age. On the other hand, if one is interested in factors relating to developmental trends in children, the sample of children should vary over the age range under consideration.

If both sexes are included in an analysis, it is wise to standardize scores separately for the two before correlations are computed. If that is not done, sex should be included as another variable in the analysis. Either group can be given a score of 1, and the other group can be given a score of 0. The correlation of sex with the other variables can be observed. The influence of sex can then be removed by the square root method, and factor analysis can be done on the matrix of residual coefficients. Unless one is interested specifically in factors relating to age and education, it is wise to employ groups that are rather homogeneous in those regards. Otherwise, one often finds large general factors that disappear when more homogeneous groups are studied. Rather than seek homogeneous groups, another approach is to include age and years of education as additional variables in the analysis and to remove their influence by the square root method [see the discussion in Gorsuch (1974) and Harman (1976)].

A sixth way to fool yourself with factor analysis is to take great advantage of chance and thus be able to spuriously demonstrate almost anything. This can be done with any of the factoring methods when the sample of subjects is small. The author has seen some horrible examples in which the number of subjects was no more than the number of variables, in which case one is bound to find what appear to be handsome factors, purely because of taking advantage of chance. As mentioned throughout this and the previous chapter, there are many other places in which one can take advantage of chance and thus spuriously demonstrate in one analysis factor results that definitely will not hold up in subsequent investigations. It was mentioned that this is easy to do with some of the Procrustes methods of rotation, where even if the number of subjects is moderately large (for example, 10 subjects per variable), the methods are so ideally equipped to take advantage of chance that quite spurious results frequently are obtained.

A seventh way to fool yourself and/or other people with factor analysis is to employ a method of rotation that does more to obscure the actual groupings of variables than to adequately depict them. This was mentioned with respect to methods of oblique rotation, where in order to have a simple-looking set of results, the pattern matrix rather than the actual matrix of factor loadings (usually called the factor structure) is frequently interpreted. Also, in such rotations, high correlations among the oblique axes frequently can lead one to quite erroneous conclusions about the overall results of a factor analysis.

## AN OUTLOOK ON FACTOR ANALYSIS

More important than an understanding of the technical details of factor analysis is a proper outlook on the methods. Factor analysis is neither a royal road to truth, as some apparently feel, nor necessarily an adjunct to shotgun empiricism, as others claim. Since usually it is necessary to combine scores on a number of variables to obtain valid measures of constructs, some method is required for determining the legitimacy of forming particular combinations. Important in determining this legitimacy are the patterns of correlations among variables. Also, in order to make valid scientific generalizations over sets of variables that are given the same name (e.g., verbal comprehension or numerical skill), it is important to determine whether members of each group of variables correlate substantially with one another and correlate less with members of other groups. Factor analysis is nothing more than a set of mathematical aids to the examination of patterns of correlations, and for that purpose it is indispensable.

## SUGGESTED ADDITIONAL READINGS

Comrey, A. L. *A first course in factor analysis.* New York: Academic, 1973.
Gorsuch, R. L. *Factor analysis.* Philadelphia: Saunders, 1974.
Harman, H. H. *Modern factor analysis* (3d ed.). Chicago: University of Chicago Press, 1976.
Mulaik, S. A. *The foundations of factor analysis.* New York: McGraw-Hill, 1972.
Thurstone, L. L. *Multiple-factor analysis.* Chicago: University of Chicago Press, 1947.

# PROFILE ANALYSIS, DISCRIMINATORY ANALYSIS, AND MULTIDIMENSIONAL SCALING

Although factor analysis of measures (e.g., typical tests of ability and personality) is used more frequently than any other form of analysis, it is only one of a number of types of multivariate analysis that are useful in psychometric research. The three classes of multivariate analysis to be discussed in this chapter by no means exhaust the multivariate methods that are available, but they are the ones employed most frequently in addition to factor analysis. Like factor analysis, profile analysis and discriminatory analysis usually are concerned with the scaling of people, although they can be applied to the scaling of stimulus objects as well. Multidimensional scaling usually is concerned with the scaling of stimuli, but also has some special uses in the scaling of people. It is employed when data fail to "fit" the models for unidimensional scaling of stimuli discussed in Chap. 2. First will be discussed profile analysis and discriminatory analysis, and then the final section of the chapter will be devoted to multidimensional scaling.

Like factor analysis, profile analysis and discriminatory analysis are concerned with a rectangular data matrix, with variables appearing on the columns of the matrix and persons appearing on the rows. The major purpose of factor analysis is to examine relations between the columns to test for, or discover, clusters of variables. Each such cluster consists of variables that tend to measure the same thing and to measure something different from what is measured by other clusters. Instead of being concerned with relations among the columns (variables), profile analysis and discriminatory analysis are concerned with relations among the rows (persons). Just as factor analysis is concerned mainly with clusters of variables, profile analysis and discriminatory analysis are concerned mainly with clusters, or groups, of persons. It will be seen that the mathematical procedures which underlie conventional factor analysis underlie profile analysis and discriminatory analysis as well.

## PROBLEMS IN PROFILE ANALYSIS

*Profile analysis* is a generic term for *all* methods concerning groupings of persons. What is spoken of here as profile analysis frequently is called *cluster analysis*. However, there is some danger of confusing the clustering of persons in profile analysis with the clustering of variables usually undertaken in conventional factor analysis. One class of problems in profile analysis is that in which the groups are known in advance of the analysis, and the purpose is to distinguish the groups from one another on the basis of scores in the data matrix. For example, the problem would start with groups of normals, neurotics, and psychotics; and the purpose of the analysis would be to distinguish these three groups in terms of scores on a dozen tests. This type of problem relates to *discriminatory analysis,* which is concerned with a priori groupings of people and is one class of analysis in the more general family of profile analyses. Thus, in discriminatory analysis, one simultaneously tests hypotheses regarding the differentiation of a priori groups with a set of measures and forms linear combinations of those measures that will most effectively differentiate in that regard.

The other major class of problems in profile analysis occurs when groupings of people are not stated in advance of the analysis, in which case the purpose of the analysis is to "cluster" persons in terms of their profiles of scores. Thus discriminatory analysis is concerned with testing hypotheses about the extent to which a priori groups "hang together" in the data matrix, and the clustering of profiles is concerned with discovering groups of persons that "hang together." It is usually suspected that only some of the people will be members of relatively pure clusters and that most people will prove to be mixtures of the traits which define the clusters.

**Characteristics of score profiles** The term *profile* comes from the practice in applied work with tests of plotting scores on a battery of tests in terms of a graph or profile. Examples of profiles for two persons on six variables are shown in Figure 12-1. The variables can be thought of as six tests of ability, six measures of physiological responses to stress, or six measures of different traits relating to mental illness. For convenience, the variables are expressed as standard scores (standardized separately over all persons in the study), but this relates to an issue which will be discussed later.

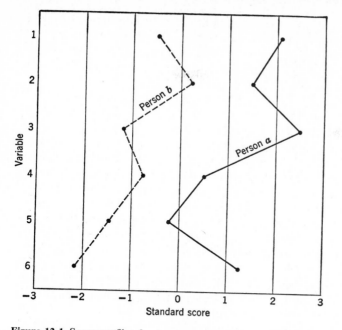

**Figure 12-1** Score profiles for two persons on six variables.

There are three major types of information in the profile of scores for any person: level, dispersion, and shape. The *level* is defined by the mean score of the person over the variables in the profile. In Fig. 12-1, for person *a*, one would obtain this by adding scores on the six variables and dividing that by 6, and one would do the same for person *b*. It can be seen that the level for *a* is higher than that for *b*. Without the application of other forms of analysis, the level is directly interpretable only if all variables are "pointed" in the same direction and only if they concern the same domain of behavior. This would be the case if all variables concerned different tests of reasoning and the profile was plotted so as to show high scores on the right and low scores on the left. The level is not directly interpretable if the variables are from very different domains of behavior, as would be the case if they consisted of two personality tests concerning mental illness, two reasoning tests, and measures of height and weight. Although it is conceivable that such a polyglot collection of variables would relate to the same construct, it is doubtful that a sensible interpretation could be made of the mean score (level) on those measures. Even if the variables all relate to the same domain of behavior, the level is difficult to interpret if variables are "pointed" in different directions. This would be the case with six tests concerning aspects of mental illness if on half the tests a high score indicated "sickness" and on the other tests a high score indicated adjustment.

As the word implies, the *dispersion* relates to how widely scores in a profile diverge from the average (level). Some speak of this as the *scatter* rather than the dispersion. A measure of the dispersion is the standard deviation of scores for each person. In Fig. 12-1, one would determine this for person $a$ by subtracting his or her level from the scores on each of the six variables, squaring these six deviates, and obtaining the square root of their average. The same would be done to obtain the dispersion for person $b$.

Whereas under the conditions stated previously it is possible to make a direct interpretation of level, this is difficult to do for the profile dispersion. It is difficult because the profile dispersions for people in general depend upon the correlations among variables in the profile. If high positive correlations exist among the variables, people in general will tend to have small dispersions. If the correlations among variables are low, the dispersions will tend to be relatively large. If some of the correlations are positive and others are negative, the dispersions will be even larger. The most sensible way to interpret the dispersion of scores for a particular person is to compare it with the dispersions of scores for other persons. For example, if person $a$ has a much larger dispersion than person $b$ on six physiological measures, it can rightly be concluded that person $a$ is much more variable than person $b$. Also, although it is seldom done, the interpretation of profile dispersions is facilitated by obtaining a distribution of dispersions over people. The distribution could then be converted to percentiles, which could be used as a basis for interpreting the profile dispersions for particular persons.

The last remaining information in the profile, the *shape,* concerns the "ups and downs" in the profile. Even though two persons have the same level and dispersion, the high and low points for the two might be quite different. The shape is defined by the rank-order of scores for each person. Thus in Fig. 12-1, person $a$ is highest in variable 3, next in variable 1, and so on to the lowest score, which is on variable 5. As can be seen, the order (the shape) is quite different for person $b$. In studies of human abilities, the shape indicates the particular talents of the person. If one is interested only in similarities of profile shapes, then a sensible measure is the PM correlation between any two profiles.

It should be obvious that level, shape, and dispersion are not entirely independent in samples of persons. If the level is either very high or very low, the dispersion must be relatively low. Thus one would expect to find at least a moderate curvilinear correlation over people between level and dispersion. Although shape is not directly related to level, in a sense it is related to the dispersion. If the dispersion is small, the ordering of variables for a person (the shape) may represent only tiny differences in performance. Also, if this is the case, the observed differences may be due to measurement error. (This point was discussed in Chap. 7 in terms of the reliability of linear combinations of variables.) Consequently, unless the dispersion is relatively large, it may be hazardous to interpret the shape of a particular profile.

It should be obvious that the physical appearance of a particular profile depends on the way variables are listed. Since it is arbitrary which variable is listed in which position, the physical appearance of the profile can be arbitrarily changed without affecting level, dispersion, or shape.

The profiles shown in Fig. 12-1 could have depicted the average scores for two groups of individuals rather than the scores for two persons. The term *profile analysis* frequently is used in referring to statistical tests of overall significance of differences between two such profiles of means. Similarly, one could have shown numerous profiles of mean scores of groups and performed statistical analyses to test for significance of differences among groups on all variables considered simultaneously (by methods discussed extensively in those books in the Suggested Additional Readings concerned with multivariate analysis). However, the problem of testing for significance of difference between groups on a number of variables considered simultaneously should not be confused with the major problem of profile analysis being considered here, namely that of the clustering of profiles and discriminatory analysis.

## CLUSTERING OF PROFILES

In spite of the considerable controversy over proper methods for clustering profiles, there are some straightforward methods for handling the problem. The problem starts with the measurement of $N$ persons on $k$ variables. The variables can be anything, but to place the problem in focus, imagine that each variable concerns a physiological response to stress. (Readers with different turns of mind can imagine that the variables are MMPI scales or tests of abilities.) The experimenter is curious regarding possible individual differences in patterns of responses and so plots profiles for some of the subjects. The experimenter sees not only marked differences in levels, but also what appear to be marked differences in shapes. The experimenter would like to perform some type of analysis to determine whether people fall into different clusters regarding their measurements. This is the problem of clustering profiles.

Over the last quarter-century, many methods for clustering profiles have been proposed. Most of these are cut-and-try methods which lack any solid mathematical foundation. A careful logical analysis of issues in the clustering of profiles was given by Cronbach and Gleser (1953). Nunnally (1962) placed the problem of clustering profiles in perspective with multivariate analysis generally and demonstrated that all major problems in the clustering of profiles could be handled by the same powerful methods of factor analysis that more traditionally are employed to study correlations among variables. [See Tryon and Bailey (1970) for a wide variety of proposed methods for cluster analysis.]

**Measures of profile similarity** Before it is possible to develop methods for clustering profiles, one must define measures of profile similarity. In the clustering of variables with factor analysis, the measure of relationship is the PM correlation coefficient. In some instances the PM coefficient has also been used to measure the similarity of profiles. This is what is done in $Q$ technique, as it was described in the previous chapter. In our illustrative problem, the physiological measurements for each person would be standardized. The level would be subtracted from scores on each of the variables, and each deviation score would then be divided by the profile dispersion for that person. In the same way, the profiles for all persons would be standardized. (Keep in mind that this is very different from standardizing scores over persons on each variable. The probability is near zero that the two approaches to standardization would produce the same scores.) The PM correlation between two standardized profiles would be computed in the usual way, and the correlation would constitute one measure of the degree of relationship between two profiles.

If, however, it is important to consider profile level and profile dispersion, the PM correlation is not a proper measure of the degree of similarity of two profiles. The mechanics of computing the PM formula equate all profiles for level and dispersion. The level of all profiles is 0, and the standard deviation of all profiles is 1.0. Thus it is apparent that the PM coefficient is sensitive only to similarities in shape and not to similarities in level and dispersion. Two examples will indicate how this could produce misleading results. If a moron and a genius had exactly the same shapes of profiles on tests of abilities, the PM coefficient would be 1.00, but this would hide the fact that they differed markedly in level. If two persons had the same shape on profile variables and had the same level, the PM correlation would be 1.00, but this could hide the fact that they differed greatly in dispersion.

There are two primary standards in choosing any measure of relationship: first, it should include all the information important in making comparisons; second, it should lend itself to powerful methods of mathematical analysis. The first is largely a matter of taste and judgment, but once the measure is selected, it may place severe limits on the methods of analysis that can legitimately be employed. If it is thought wise to cluster profiles with consideration of level, dispersion, and shape, obviously the measure of relationship should consider all three types of information. (Later it will be argued that in some instances it is better to use measures of relationship that ignore one or more of the three sources of information.) Numerous measures have been proposed for this purpose (Cronbach and Gleser 1953; Helmstadter 1957; Muldoon and Ray 1958; Tryon and Bailey 1970).

An example will serve to illustrate one possible measure that considers level, dispersion, and shape. One obtains this measure by summing the absolute differences in scores for any two profiles. This would be zero for two identical profiles and would tend to grow larger as profiles differed in level, dispersion, or shape. Although this measure makes sense as a descriptive index, it suffers from the same fault as do most of the other proposed measures of profile similarity: it does not lend itself to powerful methods of analysis.

**Distance measure** The most appealing measure of profile similarity is the distance measure $D$ which was proposed by Osgood and Suci (1952) and by Cronbach and Gleser (1953). $D$ is simply the generalized Pythagorean theorem for the distance between two points in euclidean space. In the case of two persons and two variables, this is the length of the hypotenuse of a right triangle, as illustrated in Fig. 12-2. The distance between the points for persons $a$ and $b$ is obtained as follows:

$$D_{ab}^2 = (X_{a1} - X_{b1})^2 + (X_{a2} - X_{b2})^2 \qquad (12\text{-}1)$$

The square root of the above expression is the distance between points $a$ and $b$. For any number of variables $k$, the squared distance is as follows:

$$
\begin{aligned}
D_{ab}^2 &= (X_{a1} - X_{b1})^2 + (X_{a2} - X_{b2})^2 + \cdots + (X_{ak} - X_{bk})^2 \\
&= \Sigma(X_{aj} - X_{bj})^2
\end{aligned}
\qquad (12\text{-}2)
$$

The distance $D$ between the two points corresponding to the profiles for two persons equals the square root of the sum of squared differences on the profile variables.

All the scores for one person on $k$ variables serve to define one point in a $k$-space of variables, each variable being plotted as orthogonal to the others. The point for the person then summarizes all the information in the profile. Although there is no physical representation for such points when more than three variables (dimensions) are involved, the logic of measuring distance with $D$ still holds.

$D$ is intuitively appealing because it considers profile level, dispersion, and shape. Also, it does lend itself to powerful methods of analysis. For these reasons, the author recommends, as others have, that problems of profile analysis be discussed in terms of the $D$ measure. For reasons which will be discussed

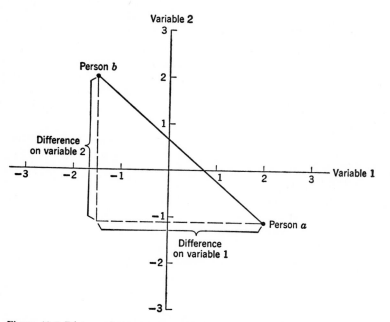

**Figure 12-2** Distance between two persons on two variables.

later, however, in deriving methods for the clustering of profiles, it is better to use a conversion of $D$ rather than $D$ itself.

To return to the illustrative problem concerning profiles of physiological variables, the experimenter could use the $D$ measure to search for clusters of people. First, $D$ would be computed between all possible pairs of persons, forming an $N$-by-$N$ symmetric matrix of distances. Persons with small $D$'s have similar profiles, and persons with relatively large $D$'s have dissimilar profiles. Numerous methods of cluster analysis have been employed for determining the numbers of clusters and the membership of each cluster. [For some proposed solutions, see Osgood, Suci, and Tannenbaum (1957); Sawrey, Keller, and Conger (1960); Tryon and Bailey (1970).]

## RAW-SCORE FACTOR ANALYSIS

Most of the methods of cluster analysis that have been proposed for the analysis of matrices of distance measures suffer from the same faults as all such cut-and-try methods: they lack any general algebra, they are indeterminate, and they are computationally messy. Powerful methods for this purpose are available, which will be discussed in this section. The answer is to factor-analyze the raw-score cross products of pairs of profiles.

To set the issues in focus, imagine that a problem concerns the profiles of six persons on 10 physiological variables (or on 15 measures of abilities). The distances $D$ between all pairs of persons are obtained, and these are shown in Table 12-1 and plotted in Fig. 12-3. In this hypothetical example, the distances were formed so that they could be exactly portrayed in a two-space, which would almost never be the case in actual research. In Fig. 12-3 there is nothing sacred about the way points are positioned on the page. They could be moved to the right or left or rotated in circles as long as the final positions maintained the same distances among the six points. Also, as will be discussed more fully later, the geometric configuration will maintain the same appearance if all distances are multiplied by the same constant. For example, if one multiplied all the distances in Fig. 12-3 by 2.5, the same geometric configuration would be apparent, only spread out more on the page. However, a rule that will become

**Table 12-1 Matrix of $D$'s for points shown in Fig. 12-3**

| | | *Person* | | | | | |
|---|---|---|---|---|---|---|---|
| | | *a* | *b* | *c* | *d* | *e* | *f* |
| | *a* | .0 | 1.0 | 1.4 | 7.8 | 7.1 | 6.4 |
| | *b* | 1.0 | .0 | 1.0 | 7.2 | 6.4 | 5.8 |
| *Person* | *c* | 1.4 | 1.0 | .0 | 6.4 | 5.7 | 5.0 |
| | *d* | 7.8 | 7.2 | 6.4 | .0 | 1.0 | 1.4 |
| | *e* | 7.1 | 6.4 | 5.7 | 1.0 | .0 | 1.0 |
| | *f* | 6.4 | 5.8 | 5.0 | 1.4 | 1.0 | .0 |

**Figure 12-3** Interpoint distances for six persons.

more important later is that one cannot *add* any arbitrary constant to all the distances without throwing off the appearance of the configuration of points; indeed, one might even increase the number of dimensions required to contain the points.

In looking at Fig. 12-3 and Table 12-1, one can see that there are two clusters, defined, respectively, by persons *a, b,* and *c,* and persons *d, e,* and *f.* If, in actual research, there were so few cases involved and such definite clusters were present, no refined method of analysis would be needed; but this is almost never the case. A method of analysis will be described which can recover those clusters and can be used equally well with any number of persons and regardless of the relative "visibility" of clusters.

It apparently is not widely known that matrices of $D$'s such as that in Table 12-1 can be factored. The method was derived by G. J. Suci [Osgood, Suci, and Tannenbaum (1957)]. Suci and this author cooperatively explored his method of factoring $D$ and found it to be a special case of raw-score factor analysis. This is where a major misconception arises: some persons are evidently unaware that raw-score cross products can be factored in the same way that correlation coefficients are factored. The failure to realize that factor analysis is not restricted to correlation coefficients is either directly evident or implied in many papers concerning methods of clustering profiles.

**An example of raw-score factor analysis** Because of the unfamiliarity of factoring raw-score cross products, a worked-out example will be given. The first step is to obtain the sum of raw cross products over the profile variables. An example follows for the profiles of persons *a* and *b* on four variables:

|  | Person *a* | Person *b* | Cross products |
| --- | --- | --- | --- |
| Variable 1 | 1.5 | 1.0 | 1.5 |
| Variable 2 | .5 | 2.0 | 1.0 |
| Variable 3 | −2.0 | −1.0 | 2.0 |
| Variable 4 | 1.2 | −.5 | −.6 |
| Sum |  |  | 3.9 |

The sum of cross products for persons $a$ and $b$ is 3.9. In the same way, the sum of cross products is obtained for all pairs of persons, resulting in a symmetric matrix of terms. It is said that these are sums of *raw* cross products because the mathematical procedures to be described place no limits on the scoring units employed for each variable. Later will be discussed the question of employing a common system of units for all variables, e.g., expressing all variables as standard scores, as was done in Fig. 12-1.

A hypothetical matrix of cross products for physiological variables is shown in Table 12-2. The matrix was constructed so as to be compatible with the $D$'s shown in Table 12-1 and the plot of those distances shown in Fig. 12-3. Actually, the matrix of cross products was constructed by working backward from the distances in Fig. 12-3, but one could obtain them equally well by actually summing cross products on 10 physiological variables (or 15 tests of abilities). Each diagonal space contains the sum of cross products of a person with herself or himself, which is simply the sum of squared scores over the profile variables. (This is analogous to placing unities in the diagonal spaces of a correlation matrix preparatory to factoring correlation coefficients.) It will be noted that large sums of cross products in Table 12-2 correspond to small $D$'s in Table 12-1, and vice versa. One could perform various types of cluster analysis

**Table 12-2 Raw-score cross products and factor solution for points shown in Fig. 12-3**

|  | | $a$ | $b$ | $c$ | $d$ | $e$ | $f$ |
|---|---|---|---|---|---|---|---|
|  | | | | *Cross Products Person* | | | |
|  | $a$ | 36 | 30 | 30 | 6 | 6 | 12 |
|  | $b$ | 30 | 25 | 25 | 5 | 5 | 10 |
|  | $c$ | 30 | 25 | 26 | 11 | 10 | 15 |
| Person | $d$ | 6 | 5 | 11 | 37 | 31 | 32 |
|  | $e$ | 6 | 5 | 10 | 31 | 26 | 27 |
|  | $f$ | 12 | 10 | 15 | 32 | 27 | 29 |
| Column sums | | 120 | 100 | 117 | 122 | 105 | 125 |
| First factor | | 4.58 | 3.81 | 4.46 | 4.65 | 4.00 | 4.77 |

| | | $a$ | $b$ | $c$ | $d$ | $e$ | $f$ |
|---|---|---|---|---|---|---|---|
|  | | | | *First Residuals* | | | |
|  | $a$ | 15.02 | 12.55 | 9.57 | −15.30 | −12.32 | −9.85 |
|  | $b$ | 12.55 | 10.48 | 8.01 | −12.72 | −10.24 | −8.17 |
|  | $c$ | 9.57 | 8.01 | 6.11 | −9.74 | −7.84 | −6.27 |
| Person | $d$ | −15.30 | −12.72 | −9.74 | 15.38 | 12.40 | 9.82 |
|  | $e$ | −12.32 | −10.24 | −7.84 | 12.40 | 10.00 | 7.92 |
|  | $f$ | −9.85 | −8.17 | −6.27 | 9.82 | 7.92 | 6.25 |
| Column sums after reflection | | 74.61 | 62.17 | 47.54 | 75.36 | 60.72 | 48.28 |
| Second factor | | −3.89 | −3.24 | −2.48 | 3.92 | 3.16 | 2.51 |

## Table 12-2 Raw-score cross products and factor solution for points shown in Fig. 12-3 (*Continued*)

*Second Residuals*

|          |     | a     | b     | c     | d     | e     | f     |
|----------|-----|-------|-------|-------|-------|-------|-------|
|          | a   | −.11  | −.05  | −.08  | −.05  | −.03  | −.09  |
|          | b   | −.05  | −.02  | −.03  | −.02  | .00   | −.05  |
|          | c   | −.08  | −.03  | −.04  | −.02  | .00   | −.05  |
| Person   | d   | −.05  | −.02  | −.02  | −.07  | .01   | −.02  |
|          | e   | −.03  | .00   | .00   | .01   | .01   | −.01  |
|          | f   | −.09  | −.05  | −.05  | −.02  | −.01  | −.05  |

*Centroid Factors*

|          |     | A    | B     | $h^2$ |
|----------|-----|------|-------|-------|
|          | a   | 4.58 | −3.89 | 36    |
|          | b   | 3.81 | −3.24 | 25    |
|          | c   | 4.46 | −2.48 | 26    |
| Person   | d   | 4.65 | 3.92  | 37    |
|          | e   | 4.00 | 3.16  | 26    |
|          | f   | 4.77 | 2.51  | 29    |

*Transformation Matrix*

|     | $A_1$  | $B_1$ |
|-----|--------|-------|
| A   | .763   | .647  |
| B   | −.647  | .763  |

*Rotated Factors*

|          |     | $A_1$ | $B_1$ |
|----------|-----|-------|-------|
|          | a   | 6.01  | .00   |
|          | b   | 5.00  | −.01  |
|          | c   | 5.01  | 1.00  |
| Person   | d   | 1.01  | 6.00  |
|          | e   | 1.01  | 5.00  |
|          | f   | 2.02  | 5.00  |

on the matrix of cross products as well as on the matrix of distances, but there are much better ways to go at it.

How should one analyze the sums of cross products to obtain clusters? The answer is to factor-analyze, and *all* the methods used with correlation coefficients can be applied: multiple group, centroid, principal components, maximum likelihood, minimum residual, or whatever. In doing this, one applies the customary formulas in the customary ways. Let us see what a centroid analysis provides.

For the first centroid factor, one sums the elements in each column, finds the square root of the sum of the column sums, and divides this into each of the column sums. These are loadings on the first centroid factor in the raw-score space. One uses the first factor loadings to obtain a first set of residuals, reflects, extracts a second set of factor loadings, and continues in this manner until residuals are small (relative to the sizes of the original sums of cross products) or until enough factors have been obtained to satisfy one's curiosity.

By choosing a set of points in a two-space, one needs only two factors to explain the cross products, and consequently the second residuals differ from zero only by rounding errors in the computations. Also, as would necessarily be the case, the sums of squares of loadings in rows of the factor matrix are identical to the original diagonal elements in the matrix of cross products.

After raw-score factors are obtained, there is nothing to prevent rotating them in the same way that one rotates factors obtained from correlation matrices. (Also, there is nothing to prevent employing analytic methods of rotation such as those discussed in Chap. 10.) In Table 12-2, an orthogonal transformation of centroid factors $A$ and $B$ is made to obtain rotated factors $A_1$ and $B_1$. The clusters shown in Fig. 12-3 and Table 12-1 are clearly evidenced in the rotated factor loadings, and the factor loadings tell how strongly each person relates to each factor. In Fig. 12-4, the rotated factor loadings are plotted, and it can be seen that the obtained set of interpoint distances is identical to that shown in Fig. 12-3.

**How raw-score factor analysis works** Variables in profiles (e.g., physiological measures or tests of abilities) can be considered as mutually orthogonal axes in euclidean space. Each profile can be plotted as a point in the space, and $D$ measures the distance of such points from one another. Raw-score factor analysis provides a basis (or semibasis) for the profile space; i.e., the factors provide a geometric frame of reference where no frame of reference existed originally. Because any sufficient basis preserves distances between points, the factor loadings preserve the original $D$'s. In the example shown in Table 12-2, this can be tested by obtaining $D$'s from the rotated factor loadings. This shows, for example, that the $D$ between persons $a$ and $b$ is almost exactly 1.0,

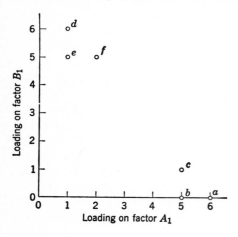

Figure 12-4 Loadings on rotated factors.

which is what was given in Table 12-1. Similarly, all the $D$'s can be calculated from the matrix of centroid loadings or from the matrix of rotated loadings. If factoring is not complete, the factor matrix will serve to explain the bulk of the distances. Thus any information regarding clusters that could be obtained from a matrix of $D$'s also can be obtained from a matrix of cross products; and whereas it is difficult to directly factor matrices of $D$'s, this is very easy with matrices of cross products. Consequently, although it is useful to think of profiles as represented by points in euclidean space, it is better to analyze those points with the sums of cross products than with $D$.

Since it has been shown that working with sums of cross products is more useful than working with $D$, it is instructive to examine the relationship between the two measures:

$$
\begin{aligned}
D_{ab}^2 &= \Sigma(X_{aj} - X_{bj})^2 \\
&= \Sigma(X_{aj}^2 + X_{bj}^2 - 2X_{aj}X_{bj}) \\
&= \Sigma X_{aj}^2 + \Sigma X_{bj}^2 - 2\Sigma X_{aj}X_{bj}
\end{aligned}
\tag{12-3}
$$

$$
\Sigma X_{aj}X_{bj} = \frac{\Sigma X_{aj}^2 + \Sigma X_{bj}^2 - D_{ab}^2}{2}
$$

If both profiles are standardized over the $k$ profile variables and both sides of Eq. (12-3) are divided by $k$, the following is obtained:

$$
r_{ab} = 1 - \frac{D_{ab}^2}{2K}
\tag{12-4}
$$

Thus it can be seen that when the two profiles are in the form of standard scores (standardized over profile variables, not over people), the PM correlation between the two profiles is a monotonically decreasing function of $D^2$, and thus of $D$.

The solution to the problem of clustering profiles through raw-score factor analysis illustrates a very general principle regarding factor analysis. Whereas cross-products analysis can be applied to raw-score profiles as well as in correlational analysis, both approaches to factor analysis are part of an even more general model concerning the factor analysis of vector products. It was said in Chap. 10 that a general geometric model for depicting elements in a correlation matrix consists of translating any correlation into $h_i \cos_{ij} h_j$, where $h_i$ and $h_j$ equal the lengths (square roots of diagonal elements) and $\cos_{ij}$ equals the cosine of the angle between the two vectors depicting the two variables. The geometric analogy of $h_i \cos_{ij} h_j$ was used to depict the elements in correlation matrices, but it can be used to depict the elements in raw-score factor analysis. In that case, for example, $h_1$ would equal the square root of the sum of squared elements in the profile for person 1, $h_2$ would equal the square root of the sum of squared elements in the profile for person 2, and $\cos_{12}$ would equal the cosine between their two vectors. Of course, the lengths would not be 1.00 as in the component factoring of correlation matrices, but would be determined by the actual sums of squared scores in profiles. Raw-score factor analysis is part of an even more general method which permits one to factor-analyze *any* matrix of elements $h_i \cos_{ij} h_j$ that can be legitimately construed to lie in a euclidean space. Thus, later in the chapter we will consider problems of factoring in multidimensional scaling where there are no variables over which cross-product terms could be summed. Rather, only a symmetric matrix of measures of relationship is obtained from people's judgments of similarities among stimuli. If either their raw judgments or some modifications of them can be construed as vector products $h_i \cos_{ij} h_j$, then they can be factored directly by all the methods of factor analysis discussed up to this point. Thus, we see that factor analysis is an extremely general tool for handling many problems in multivariate analysis.

**Transformations of variables** Much of the controversy about the clustering of profiles has concerned what transformations, if any, should be made of the raw data prior to the analysis. There are two kinds of transformations that can be made: transformations of distributions of individual differences on the separate variables and transformations of intraindividual profile scores. The former will be discussed in this section, and the latter will be discussed in the next section.

One reason why it is important to consider possible transformations of the variables prior to the search for clusters is that the variables may have very different standard deviations (over people). For example, a number of physiological variables are likely to be expressed in very different units. Then, purely as an artifact, the standard deviation of one variable might be 1.2, and that of another, 522.8. Less extreme differences might be expected on different tests of abilities or different scales of adjustment. If such differences are allowed to remain, some variables will more strongly influence the clustering of profiles than others. If the variables differ markedly in standard deviations, usually it is wise to equate variables in that regard prior to the analysis of cross products. One way to do this is to convert all variables to standard scores.

Another possible type of transformation of variables must be considered because of the correlations among variables (over people). In most problems where one might consider the clustering of profiles, it would be expected to find nonzero correlations among the variables; and in some cases such correlations might be substantial. For example, one would expect at least moderate-sized positive correlations among different tests of abilities. Also, one might find a pattern of moderate-sized negative and positive correlations among 10 physiological variables.

Some have argued that if the variables are correlated, it makes no sense to employ $D$ or to perform analyses of cross products. There are two classes of arguments involved in this matter—one mathematical and one theoretical. Let us consider the mathematical issue first: the use of $D$ and cross-products analysis are not restricted to the case where variables correlate precisely zero with one another. In mathematical analyses, it is quite common to depict variables with orthogonal axes even if they are substantially correlated with one another, with the purpose of such depiction often being the determination of the degree of correlation. For example, in performing the correlation of any two variables, it is customary to form a scatter diagram in terms of orthogonal or uncorrelated coordinates for the variables. A more general example will help to show why it is sensible to depict variables as orthogonal in performing mathematical analyses even if they are correlated with one another. Equation (12-4) shows that the correlation coefficient can be expressed as a monotonically decreasing function of $D$. When the correlation is between two variables rather than between two profiles, $D$ is the distance between two variables (not two persons) in a space of persons. In that instance, each person can be represented by an axis which is orthogonal to that for all other persons. The correlation between any two variables can be obtained either as a function of $D$ or, more customarily, as the average product of standard scores. Would anyone seriously question the customary use of correlational analysis simply because it can be depicted in a space of orthogonal persons? Of course, since profiles will tend to correlate with one another, people will not be orthogonal in that sense. But does that prevent the use of the correlation coefficient? It is doubtful that anyone would answer *yes,* but for some reason, there are people who think it is not correct to use $D$ or the sum of cross products unless the variables are orthogonal. For the above reasons, there is no strong mathematical argument for insisting upon variables being uncorrelated in order to compute the $D$ statistic or perform cross-products analysis.

Although there is no obvious mathematical necessity for having uncorrelated variables, the presence of substantial correlations among the variables may cause a theoretical problem regarding interpretation of the results. On the one hand, it is not likely that a well-thought-out problem would concern the clustering of profiles in situations where variables correlated near zero with one another. If the variables are part of an overall theoretical system, it is more probable that at least moderate-sized correlations will appear among them. The sizes of such correlations determine the extent to which the variables are redundant with one another and thus the extent to which they differentially influence $D$ and any cross-products factors used to explain the distance space. For example, in a study of reasoning tests, if there are two tests that correlate very highly, they will make approximately the same contribution to $D$ and have essentially the same influence on raw-score cross products. Then, if two persons had similar scores on those two tests, this would tend to make them appear similar over the profile as a whole, even though they may differ substantially on other variables in the profile. The potential problems caused by substantial correlations among the profile variables relate to the generalizability of results that can be obtained from profile clustering. Ideally, the variables included in a cluster analysis should be *representative* of some specified domain of variables, e.g., physiological variables relating to stress or tests representative of different factors of reasoning. The $D$ statistic is an index of similarity (more strictly speaking, dissimilarity), which raises the knotty question of "similarity with respect to what?" That question can be answered only if investigators can say what the domain of variables represents and thus declare the kinds of traits over which results can be generalized. There are two approaches to helping ensure generalizability in this regard. The first is to "sample" the variables thought to be important in a specified domain, e.g., reasoning abilities or physiological indicators of stress. In that case one includes a little bit of everything that is thought to be important, includes the broadest coverage that is feasible, and generally ends up with a relatively large number of measures for the analysis of profile clusters. A complementary approach to selecting variables can be used if a more definite theory is available regarding the domain of variables. For example, if there are thought to be six major types of reasoning ability or six major factors relating to physiological indicators of stress, tests for these specific traits can be used in the profiles.

If generality can be ensured either by a sampling approach or by a structured selection of variables, as mentioned above, then the $D$ statistic and the results of cross-products analysis can be interpreted directly even if there are some substantial correlations among the variables. That is, it makes sense to say that two individuals are similar over a sufficient mapping of the variables from a domain, even if some of the correlations are substantial among the variables.

After variables are either sampled or purposely selected to represent the tests in profiles, if high correlations exist among the variables, then one could factor-analyze the variables before performing cross-products analysis. For example, if the investigation started with a dozen variables, the variables could be first intercorrelated and factor-analyzed by all the procedures discussed in Chaps. 10 and 11. It might be found, for example, that four factors were sufficient to explain most of the common variance. Factor scores could be obtained on the four factors, the $D$ statistic could be computed among these scores for descriptive purposes, and cross products over the four profile points could be submitted to factor analysis. In resorting to factor analysis in this way, however, one usually raises more problems than are solved. First, often one ends up with so few variables (e.g., only four in the illustrative problem above) that there is not much room to perform cross-products factor analysis. Second, if the number of factors is no more than about one-third the number of variables, then much of the unique variance of each variable might not be included in the $D$ measure or in any cross-products analysis. If the individual variables are important, then one may be throwing away the very important unique contribution of each variable in the clustering of profiles. One could make a case for employing components analysis and extracting as many factors as there are variables. Then the total variance of all variables would be represented, $D$ would be computed in an orthogonal space, and cross-products analysis could be performed on the results. Then all would be mathematically proper, but it might make the results difficult to interpret. However, usually this is the wisest approach to transforming profiles prior to studies of profile clustering if (1) the investigator finds it difficult to clearly define the domain of variables, and/or (2) the correlations of the variables indicate that a number of strong factors could be derived.

**Transformations of profiles** Regardless of what transformations, if any, are made of distributions of individual differences on separate variables, it is also necessary to consider possible transformations of intraindividual distributions of profile scores. If it is meaningful to consider level, dispersion, and shape in clustering profiles, these should be permitted to vary when cross products are analyzed. If, however, one or more of these aspects are considered irrelevant, then it, or they, should be equated before the analysis is undertaken.

If level is considered unimportant in a particular analysis, the means of all profiles should be equated, preferably to zero. Then cross products would be formed among profiles expressed as deviation scores (deviates about the level for each person). It facilitates working with such sums of cross products to divide them by the number of variables. In that case relations among profiles would be expressed as *covariances*. These can be factored by cross-products analysis in the same way as shown previously for the analysis of cross products of raw scores. This is called *covariance analysis*, but it is only a special case of cross-products analysis (which in turn is only one form of vector-products analysis).

## DISCRIMINATORY ANALYSIS

Discriminatory analysis is employed when groups of persons are defined a priori and the purpose of the analysis is to distinguish the groups from one another on the basis of their score profiles. Examples of groups are different types of mental patients, different vocational groups, and college seniors majoring in different fields. From a mathematical point of view, there is no limit to the types of variables that can be employed. Questions regarding the interpretability of results with different types of variables will be discussed later.

There are three related problems in discriminatory analysis: (1) determining whether differences in score profiles for two or more groups are statistically significant, (2) maximizing the discrimination among groups by combining the variables in some manner, and (3) establishing rules for the placement of new individuals into one of the groups. The first of these is the least important for most research in psychology; however, appropriate statistical tests are available. Hotelling's $T$ test can be used to test the statistical significance of the differences between the average profiles of two groups. It could be used, for example, in testing the significance of differences in profiles of physiological variables for males and females. If the null hypothesis is rejected in this case, it is inferred that the total profiles for the sexes are different. Analogous methods are available for testing the significance of differences among more than two average profiles. These are discussed in the books on multivariate analysis included in the Suggested Additional Readings. Such significance tests also are by-products of the discriminant function, which will be discussed later.

For two reasons, it was said that statistical tests like those described above are not highly important in most research problems. First, the results of such tests frequently are difficult to interpret. It is possible for two groups to have nonsignificant differences on each of the variables but for the overall difference between profiles to be significant. Such tests combine all the information from the different variables in one overall test of significance. Unless there are significant differences on some of the variables, preferably on a majority of them, it is difficult to interpret the significance of difference in overall profiles. At best such tests provide rather meager information about significance of differences. Second, and more important, merely finding that the average profiles for two or more groups are significantly different does not solve the major problems, which are problems 2 and 3 as stated above.

The major problem in discriminatory analysis is problem 2, that of maximizing the discrimination among groups. A discussion of issues related to that problem will occupy most of this section. Later in the section, the problem of the placement of new individuals (problem 3) will be discussed.

**Geometric interpretation of discriminatory analysis** The geometric interpretations given previously for profile analysis will help one understand some of the issues in discriminatory analysis. If there are $N$ persons and $k$ variables, the profile for any person can be represented by a point in a $k$-dimensional space. Each axis of the space consists of one of the variables, and the variables are depicted as orthogonal to one another. In discriminatory analysis, it is useful to think of the region of that space occupied by a particular group. If discriminatory analysis is to provide useful information, it is necessary for the members of each group not to be scattered randomly over the space, but it is necessary for the members of the different groups to occupy somewhat different parts of the space of variables. To the extent that individuals in each group are tightly clustered in a particular region of the $k$-space, and to the extent that there is little overlap between the regions occupied by different groups, discriminatory analysis can provide useful information.

A simplified example of a space for two groups on two variables is shown in Fig. 12-5. The groups are males and females, and $X_1$ and $X_2$ are raw scores on two physiological indices of reaction to stress. The profile point for each male is represented by an $M$, and likewise the point for each female is represented by an $F$. It can be seen that the two groups tend to occupy different regions of the space. Males tend to be high on $X_1$ and low on $X_2$, and vice versa for females; however, there is a moderate amount of overlap between the two groups on both variables.

In Fig. 12-5, $C_m$ and $C_f$ represent the centroids for males and females, respectively. A centroid is simply the point representing the average profile of a group. The average score for the group is obtained for each variable, and the resulting means are plotted as though they were scores for an individual. The centroid is the point about which the points for individuals in a group balance in all directions. It is analogous to a centroid vector as it was discussed with regard to centroid factor analysis. If groups are well discriminated, centroids are far apart, and the members of each group hover near their centroid.

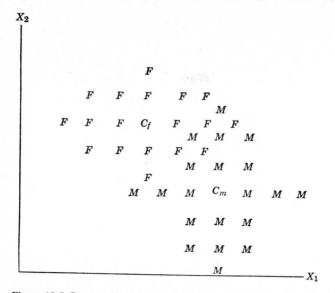

**Figure 12-5** Scores of males $M$ and females $F$ on two measures of physiological reaction to stress.

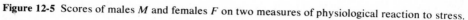

Instead of depicting a point for each person in each group, it is more convenient to depict only regions of scatter for the groups. This is done in Fig. 12-6 for the profile points depicted in Fig. 12-5. The amount of overlap between the contours of scatter indicates the extent to which the two groups are not discriminated by the two variables.

**Figure 12-6** Areas of scatter for males and females on two measures of physiological reaction to stress.

**Linear discriminant function** What would be helpful in the problem depicted in Figs. 12-5 and 12-6 would be some means of combining the information from the two variables so as to discriminate the members of the two groups as well as possible. Potentially this could be done with a number of types of functions of the variables, but a simple linear function has been used most often. Such a function is referred to as a *linear discriminant function:*

$$Y = a_1 X_1 + a_2 X_2$$

where $Y$ = scores on discriminant function

$X_1$, $X_2$ = raw scores on variables

$a_1$, $a_2$ = weights for variables

Weights $a_1$ and $a_2$ are applied to raw scores on variables $X_1$ and $X_2$. The same set of weights is applied to the scores of each person in each group. This results in a new score for each person, $Y$, which combines the information from $X_1$ and $X_2$ regarding discrimination of the groups.

Before we discuss how the weights are obtained for the discriminant function, the example in Fig. 12-6 illustrates how such a linear function can serve to discriminate two groups. After the weights are applied, a new line can be drawn in the space $Y$, and the scores of all persons can be projected on that line. This is done in Fig. 12-7. Whereas there is considerable overlap between the two groups on each of the variables $X_1$ and $X_2$, there is less overlap on $Y$. The scores for persons on $Y$ can be "taken out" of the space for the variables and depicted separately as a frequency distribution, which is shown in Fig. 12-8. There it can be seen that the means for the two groups are far apart and there is little overlap between the two distributions. Then $Y$ serves to condense the discriminatory information in the two variables.

As is true in all situations where optimum weights are sought, the method for obtaining the weights depends on a rule for optimization. For example, it will be recalled that the weights in multiple regression are obtained according to the principle of least squares: the sum of squared errors of prediction is minimized. In the linear discriminant function, the weights are obtained so as to maximize the following ratio:

$$\frac{\text{Variance between means on } Y}{\text{Variance within groups on } Y}$$

After any set of weights is employed, the discriminant function $Y$ is obtained, and each person has a score on $Y$. Then one can find the quantities required for the numerator and denominator of the above ratio. This is similar to what is done when one calculates the ratio of the "between" to "within" variance in a one-classification analysis of variance. Thus it is seen that the rule of optimization with the linear discriminant function is to obtain weights so as to maximize the $F$ ratio of between-means variances to within-groups variances. This rule was proposed by Fisher (1936) and has been the basis of most work in discriminatory analysis since that time.

After a rule for optimization is proposed, then one resorts to calculus to see if a mathematical solution is obtainable. It turns out that there is a solution,

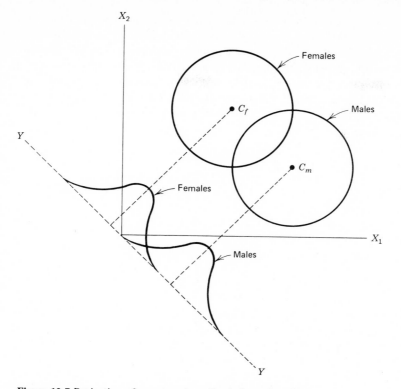

**Figure 12-7** Projection of scores onto a discriminant function $Y$.

which results in a set of computational procedures for deriving the weights for linear discriminant functions. With only two groups and any number of variables, this proves to be very simple. In this case a solution is obtainable through a special use of multiple-regression analysis. The variable to be predicted consists of "group scores." The members of one of the two groups receive a score of 1, and the members of the other group receive a score of 0. It does not matter which group is given which score. Also, since correlational analysis is concerned only with standard scores, any other two numbers do as well. The variables are then used in multiple regression to estimate the group scores.

**Multiple linear discriminant function** In most research problems, there are more than two groups. Then it is possible, and usually desirable, to derive more

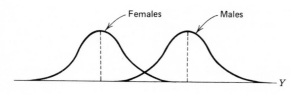

**Figure 12-8** Distribution of scores on a discriminant function.

than one linear discriminant function, and for this we employ the *multiple discriminant function* (MDF). The first discriminant function derived is that linear combination of the variables which maximizes the ratio of the between-means variance to the within-groups variance. Next, a second discriminant function is derived which serves as the second-best explainer of variance. In any problem, it is possible to obtain as many discriminant functions as variables, or one less than the number of groups, whichever is less. This leads to a family of linear discriminant functions, as follows:

$$Y_1 = a_1 X_1 + a_2 X_2 + \cdots + a_k X_k$$
$$Y_2 = b_1 X_1 + b_2 X_2 + \cdots + b_k X_k$$
$$Y_3 = c_1 X_1 + c_2 X_2 + \cdots + c_k X_k$$

.

.

.

$$Y_h = h_1 X_1 + h_2 X_2 + \cdots + h_k X_k$$

After the weights are obtained, each person receives a score on each discriminant function. The discriminant functions are computed so that the scores on all functions are uncorrelated with one another (orthogonal). For example, the correlation between $Y_1$ and $Y_2$ over all persons in all groups combined would be zero. (This, however, does not necessarily hold for the correlation between two sets of discriminant scores *within* a particular group.)

The computational procedures underlying the MDF are discussed in detail in those works cited in the Suggested Additional Readings concerned with multivariate analysis, e.g., Tatsuoka (1971). The mathematical procedures of MDF embody a special use of PC analysis, including the derivation of characteristic roots and vectors. However, rather than apply PC analysis to a correlation matrix, in the MDF analysis the same PC method is applied to a special matrix, which we will designate $A$. The problem can be posed as that of differentiating among six groups of people (such as occupational groups or people with different types of chronic diseases). The same measures must be applied to all subjects, and in this case say there are 10 measures. The numbers of individuals in each group can vary, but it is wise to have at least 30 subjects in each group for each measure. Whereas in the data matrix $S$ depicted in Table 10-1 subjects were not classified into a priori groups, they would be for discriminatory analysis, as indicated in Table 12-3. The groups can contain persons or material objects, and the variables can consist of anything that can be objectively measured. $G_1, G_2, \ldots, G_h$ stand for the various groups. In the table only the general element is shown for each group on each measure, for example, $z_{ij}$. Conceptually it is helpful to think of the matrix being in the form of standard scores—standardized separately for each variable over the members of all groups combined. Then, for example, whereas the sum of standard scores for measure 3 would be zero over all groups, the groups could have very different

**Table 12-3 Data matrix partitioned for discriminatory analysis**

| Person (objects) | Measures (variables) | | | | |
|---|---|---|---|---|---|
| | $z_1$ | $z_2$ | $z_3$ | $\cdots$ | $z_k$ |
| Group 1 | | | $z_{1j}$ | | |
| Group 2 | | | $z_{2j}$ | | |
| Group 3 | | | $z_{3j}$ | | |
| . . . | | | | | |
| Group $h$ | | | $z_{hj}$ | | |

average standard scores. Also, whereas the variance over all groups combined for one measure would equal 1.00, one would expect the variance to be less within each of the groups. The solution to finding a first discriminant function (DF) consists of obtaining a set of $k$ weights by which scores on the variables can be multiplied to maximize the criterion of variance explained. The set of weights with $k$ elements can be referred to as a *vector of weights*, and the first such vector $V_a$ is mathematically equivalent to the first characteristic vector derived in PC analysis. A first vector of weights $V_a$ is sought in such a way that the ratio of the sums of squares between group means divided by the sums of squares within groups is as large as possible. Both of these sums of squares can be cast in the form of matrices symbolized as $B$ and $W$ respectively. Then one seeks $V_a$ such that it fulfills the following requirements:

$$\frac{BV_a}{WV_a} = \text{a maximum}$$

Thus, as in employing trial vectors to accumulatively multiply into correlation matrices as illustrated in Chap. 10 for deriving PC factors, one can perform the same operations on any matrix with vectors of weights. Whereas it is customary to think of sums of squares as being computed directly from lists of scores, as in analysis-of-variance tables, it has been shown at numerous places in this book that the variances of sums and weighted sums can be depicted by covariance matrices. In this case the covariance matrix $B$ can be used to display the sums of squares between the six groups, and the covariance $W$ can be used to display the sums of squares within the six groups. A set of weights $V_a$ is obtained such that when it is applied to $B$ and $W$, the ratio of the weighted sums of elements in the two matrices is as large as possible. The above expression can be simplified by an analogy with what usually is done in multiplying the numerator of a ratio by the inverse of the denominator. In this case one multiplies $B$ by the inverse of $W$, which is symbolized in matrix algebra terminology as $W^{-1}$. However, the reader who is unfamiliar with matrix algebra should not assume that the inverse of a matrix bears a simple relationship to the matrix, such as might be obtained by taking the reciprocal of each element in the original matrix. Rather, the inverse is a matrix which is specially computed so that when it is multiplied by the original matrix, there results a symmetric matrix with unities on the diagonals and zeros in the off-diagonal spaces. Thus, the inverse of a matrix is the analog of the inverse of any variable in ordinary algebra. Once the inverse is obtained for $W$, then the problem of finding the normalized vector of weights for the first DF can be stated as follows:

$$W^{-1}BV_a = \text{a maximum}$$
$$AV_a = \text{a maximum}$$

The product of $W^{-1}$ and $B$ can be referred to as the matrix $A$. This then puts the problem in exactly the same form as that for PC analysis. One can derive $V_a$ by applying the same computational routine to matrix $A$ as was done in the iterative procedure applied to the correlation matrix $R$ in PC factoring. After the iteration converges, the procedure will produce the first vector of discriminant weights $V_a$ and a corresponding characteristic root $l_a$. The characteristic root equals the amount of total variance explained by the first DF.

In obtaining $Y_1$, there are as many weights in $V_a$ as there are variables, although some of them may be near zero. If, for example, there are 15 variables involved in the different groups depicted in Table 12-3, then $V_a$ would contain 15 weights. When these weights are accumulatively multiplied by the standardized variables, this produces scores for all people on the first DF, $Y_1$. As by-products of these computations, one can obtain mean scores on the discriminant for each group, standard deviations of scores of subjects within each group, and a test of statistical significance regarding mean differences of the groups on the DF.

After the first DF is obtained and the related statistics are computed, one can seek a second DF, $Y_2$, by obtaining a second normalized vector of weights $V_b$. This is done by operating off of a residual matrix $A_1$ in an analogous way to that which is done in deriving the second factor in PC analysis. After trial vectors converge, then $V_b$ can be used to calculate the second DF, $Y_2$, and the attendant descriptive and inferential statistics. In this way, one can continue to derive DFs until (1) a significance test fails to lend support to a function, (2) successive discriminants explain only tiny portions of the original variance (as evidenced in their characteristic roots), or (3) the experimenter discontinues the derivation of discriminants because additional ones would be of neither theoretical nor practical importance.

**Examples of multiple discriminants** A large-scale example of the use of the multiple discriminant function is from a study by Tiedeman, Bryan, and Rulon (1952). The groups were eight technical specialties in the Air Force. The persons in each group had received satisfactory scores on achievement tests in their specialties. The number of persons in a group varied from 99 to 2,084. The variables consisted of 17 tests, mainly concerning intellectual functions such as word knowledge and knowledge of mechanical principles. After the first two DFs were obtained, subsequent discriminants explained very little variance.

After DFs are obtained, all persons can be depicted in the discriminant space rather than in the space of variables. One does this by plotting scores on

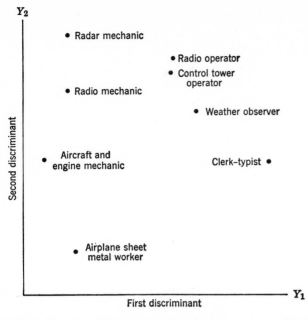

**Figure 12-9** Centroids of occupational groups on two discriminant functions. (*Adapted from Tiedeman, Bryan, and Rulon 1952.*)

the discriminants, as is done in Fig. 12-9. In the figure are shown only the centroids for the groups. If the scores were shown for each person, one would see that there is considerable overlap among groups. The authors interpreted the first discriminant as a mechanical dimension, since the groups clearly are lined up in that way. Low scores on $Y_1$ correspond to specialties with high mechanical achievement, and vice versa for high scores on $Y_1$. Less definitely, the second discriminant was interpreted as an intellectual dimension, because specialties high on it tend to require more intellectual aptitude than those that are low. These interpretations were also supported by the sizes of the weights involved in the two DFs.

Another example of the MDF regards the interests of college students who elect different majors in college. The measures consisted of six tests from an interest inventory developed by the American College Testing Program concerning (1) social service, (2) business contact, (3) business detail, (4) technical work, (5) science, and (6) creative arts. The groups consisted of students in the major programs shown in Fig. 12-10. Over 12,000 college seniors in 24 major fields of study were tested in a national cross section of 32 institutions (Hanson 1974). It was found that the six interest tests combined into two DFs which served well to describe the overall interests of students selecting different majors. Of course, there was considerable overlap among the different groups, and only the group centroids are shown here. As is usually the case, the interpretation of the discriminants (referred to here as *coordinates*) is made both

# MAP OF COLLEGE MAJORS

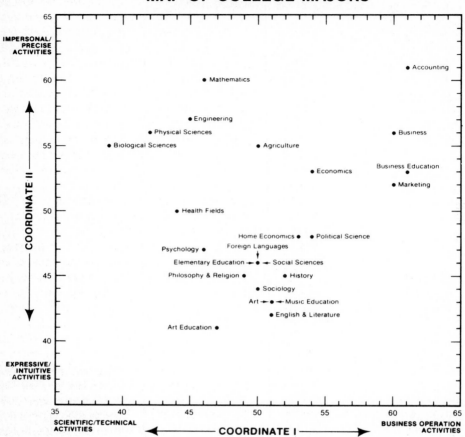

**Figure 12-10** Centroids of students in 24 college major programs on two discriminant functions for ACT interest inventory scales. (*Used with permission of the American College Testing Program.*)

by inspecting the distributions of centroids and by considering the weights that the variables have on the two DFs. The descriptions on the figure apparently provide good interpretations of the two DFs. The results of an analysis such as this are helpful in both understanding differences among existing groups of individuals and helping place new individuals in groups (e.g., in this case advising a new student about a possible major program).

**Placement** Placement concerns the assignment of new individuals to a group when their membership is unknown. With respect to the examples above, this would be the case for a new member of the Air Force who is to be assigned to a technical specialty or, with respect to the second example, a student who has not yet selected a major program. To undertake such placement, one must compare the profile of scores for a person with the profiles of scores for persons who are known to belong to a group. Herein lies a potential difficulty of the placement problem, because first one must know the group membership of at least some persons to make valid decisions about the group membership of other persons. Also, if the average profiles of the groups are not different, placement is hopeless. In that case, flipping coins would do as well. Whereas the MDF is very useful in many aspects of basic research as well as in applied work, the placement problem mainly is important in psychological applications. Examples will be given later of uses of the MDF in controlled experiments where no subsequent problem of placement arises.

Placement can be performed either in the space of variables or in the discriminant space. (For all the pros and cons of these approaches and for an excellent overall discussion of logic and methods for placement, see Cooley 1971).

Assume that the MDF has been applied. Then in our illustrative problem the scores of all persons in the various groups are known for the discriminants, and the centroid for each group is computed. It is necessary to assume that scores on each discriminant are normally distributed within each group. Then it is possible to compute contours of equal density about the centroid for each group. Since these contours are about the centroid for a group, they are referred to as *centours*. (How to obtain such centours is discussed in Cooley 1971.) It is easiest to visualize such centours in the two-space of only two discriminants, but the logic applies as well with any number of discriminants. In a two-space, the scatter of a group about its centroid can be pictured by a series of ellipses, as in Fig. 12-11. As was mentioned previously, even though DFs correlate zero with one another over all persons in all groups, this does not necessarily hold within any particular group. If the correlation is high (which is

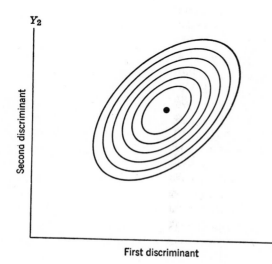

**Figure 12-11**  Centour ellipses around the centroid for one group on two discriminant functions.

very rarely the case), the centours will be highly elliptical; if the correlation is zero, the centours will be circles. Regardless of which is the case, the centours indicate the percentages of persons "farther in" and "farther out" about the centroid.

In the use of centours, placement is performed by the assignment of the individual to the group where his or her centour score is highest. The centour score for an individual estimates the percentage of persons in a group that are further from the centroid. For example, if an individual has a centour score of 75 percent, this means that 75 percent of the members of the group are farther from the centroid (irrespective of direction) than the centour on which the profile point for the subject lies. If an individual had centour scores of 75, 25, and 10 percent, respectively, for three groups, the individual would be assigned to the first group. Such centour scores usually do not add up to 100 percent. Depending on the discrimination among groups, one person could have a high centour score on a number of groups, and another person could have a very low centour score on all groups.

The extent to which centour scores are successful in placing people is directly related to the variability of such scores for each person. If such scores are much the same for a person, placement is performed about as well by flipping coins. If that is the case for most subjects in a study, placement had better be based on variables other than those employed in the study. The reader who develops a special interest in solutions to the placement problem should consult the comprehensive paper on the topic by Cooley (1971).

**Evaluation of discriminatory analysis** In spite of the differences in purpose of factor analysis and discriminatory analysis, mathematically they are closely related. The MDF is based on a linear combination of variables. So in that sense, a linear DF is a factor. Also, as was mentioned previously, linear DFs are obtained by an application of PC factoring to a special matrix concerning indices of discrimination among and within groups. DFs, then, are special types of factors—ones that serve to discriminate among a priori groups of subjects. It would be mere accident if scores on any such DF corresponded perfectly to scores on any factor obtained from analyzing correlations among variables.

Both conceptually and mathematically the MDF constitutes a powerful tool which has not been employed nearly as much as it should have been in the behavioral sciences. The MDF was introduced to psychology in relation to applied programs of testing involving personnel selection and placement. The results of one of the first major analyses appearing in the literature are shown in Fig. 12-9. The early examples tended to be with tests of ability rather than noncognitive functions such as personality traits, interests, and values. The aim of these early applications was to develop an effective strategy for assigning people to jobs or training programs. It turned out that these early applications were not highly successful, and also the close association of the methods with rather specialized problems of personnel selection tended to hide the methodology from the broader field of psychology. Now the MDF is being employed much more widely, both with a wide variety of problems in applied psychology and with respect to numerous problems in basic research.

Potentially, discriminatory analysis is useful in applied problems concerning the assignment of persons to jobs, students to courses of training, and patients to diagnostic groups. However, there are some logical difficulties in employing discriminatory analysis in that way. One logical difficulty is in deciding how to designate the members of groups prior to performing discriminatory analysis. In some cases this is rather obvious, such as in comparing males versus females or members of different professions with one another, but this is by no means simple in other cases. As one example, if the MDF is applied to different classifications of mental patients, such classifications are not reliable enough to produce clear results. Another problem is illustrated in Fig. 12-9 concerning ability test scores of Air Force personnel. In each group, should one include all persons who are presently in each training program, persons who meet at least a minimum level of satisfactory performance, or only outstanding individuals?

Another problem that arises in employing the DF with ability tests is that it works well only if there are curvilinear relationships between test scores and desirability (however defined) of the individual being placed in a particular group. This can be clearly seen by looking at the centour method of placement. If the individual is far removed from the centroid in any direction, then the individual is declared not fit for that group. This strategy would lead one to reject an individual for a particular job because his or her scores were too high in mathematics, vocabulary, etc. Such an approach makes some sense in the context of an even more elaborate strategy for the overall best utilization of talent and job satisfaction considered simultaneously, but this is a complex strategy that goes far beyond the use of the MDF and related procedures currently available for placement.

Discriminatory analysis might be much more fruitful with respect to noncognitive attributes such as the MDF related to interests shown in Fig. 12-10 or with personality characteristics, attitudes, and values. With such noncognitive attributes, the assumption of a "just right" amount of an attribute for determining group compatibility makes much more sense than with most tests of ability.

Another logical difficulty in employing the MDF and related procedures of placement in problems of personnel selection is that it is easy to accept the hidden premise that people who currently are members of definable groups (e.g., different training programs or college majors) *should* be in those groups. Actually, there are reasons to believe that frequently people become members of occupational and training groups partly because of prior procedures of selection which are based on ill-formed research or poor intuition in assigning individuals to groups.

There are several principles regarding the use of discriminatory analysis in applied problems. First, the overall strategy probably will work better with noncognitive attributes such as interests and personality characteristics than with cognitive attributes such as scores on aptitude and achievement tests. Second, discriminatory analysis will be more fruitful where there are obvious, qualitatively different groups rather than groups that are formed partly on the basis of chance or formed in such a way that membership is arguable. Such groups are: (1) men versus women; (2) normal, blind, and deaf people; (3) people with different, definite diseases; and (4) categories concerning family constellations for a child relating to presence or absence of father and mother, siblings, and other aspects of the family structure. When such definite a priori groupings of these kinds can be formed and have some relevance for questions in the behavioral sciences, then the MDF might serve a very useful purpose.

In most studies to date, the MDF has proved more helpful in *understanding* differences among central tendency (the centroids) of various groups than it has in clearly pinpointing group membership or placing new individuals in groups. This is because the scatter about the group centroids tends to be large in comparison to distances among centroids. Another way of saying it is that the DFs frequently do not explain a large amount of variance. For example, the differences shown in Figs. 12-9 and 12-10 do help one to understand the "types" of persons on the average who are in the various designated groups, but the amount of scatter about those points would be so large as to greatly lower the effectiveness of the DFs in a placement problem.

There are many possible uses for the MDF in basic research, and apparently this is not widely realized. In any experiment where there are multiple dependent measures, potentially the MDF would be useful in summarizing the results. A simple example would be in determining the effects of a new drug on five strains of rats which are known to differ in terms of temperamental characteristics. On each of the eight days, 20 rats from each strain are given the drug; after an appropriate amount of time, a dependent measure is taken. A different measure is taken on each day (and measures on different days are given in some type of counterbalanced order). The measures would concern different types of activity, conditionability, discrimination learning, and memory. The results would consist of the scores of all five groups of rats on all eight measures. Of course, one would analyze each measure separately to determine the amount of variance explained. Also, it would be useful to employ the MDF as a way of best combining the eight measures to maximally discriminate among the groups and to summarize the overall results. (Of course, such designs could be made more elaborate by employing appropriate control groups and groups given different dosage levels.)

Another example of where the MDF would be useful in basic research is in a comparison of four methods of instruction in elementary school mathematics for male and female students. An equal number of boys and girls is included, which constitutes one facet of an a priori grouping. Both sexes are broken down into four randomly constituted groups. The first is a control group, which is taught in the usual way. The other three groups are taught in different experimental approaches employing computerized routines. After three months a long test is administered with subtests concerning various mathematical processes, e.g., understanding long division and solution of simultaneous equations. There are 15 subtests in the battery. In addition to examining the main effects of the experimental design by analysis of variance, it also would be instructive to perform an MDF analysis of the eight groups on the 15 measures. A DF analysis of this kind is particularly useful when numerous "interactions," in the statistical sense, occur in the results. For example, since girls and boys are known to differ in spatial relations ability, any method of instructing mathematics that relied heavily on spatial examples might help boys much more than girls. The MDF would help to summarize the overall results and provide a basis for maximally discriminating among the groups. There are many other possible uses of the MDF in basic research. The concepts, mathematical methods of analysis, and attendant statistics have not been employed nearly as much as they should have been.

## PATTERN ANALYSIS

What is spoken of in this chapter as profile analysis is called *pattern analysis* by some persons. Here it will be useful to make a distinction between the two in terms of the types of scores employed in each. The term *profile analysis* will be used for those situations in which variables are relatively continuous, e.g., when all variables consist of total scores on tests or when they consist of ratings obtained from seven-step scales. The term *pattern analysis* will be used for those situations in which the variables are dichotomous rather than relatively continuous. Most typically, pattern analysis is employed with the dichotomous items within a test. In addition to test items, there are many other dichotomous scores that occur in the behavioral sciences, such as the presence or absence of symptoms related to brain damage, correctly remembering or forgetting each word in a list, or a rat making the correct versus an incorrect choice at each point in a maze. Another possibility would be to dichotomize scores on continuous variables (e.g., dichotomize scores at the median), but that would be throwing away much valuable information.

Even though two persons obtain the same total score on a test, it is unlikely that they have the same scores on all items. On a personality inventory concerning adjustment, two persons could obtain the same adjustment score but have different "patterns" of responses to the items. A *pattern* is simply any complete set of responses to a collection of items. A pattern would be the actual responses of a particular individual, the most popular responses in a group of persons, or even a hypothetical set of responses. It has been suggested that an analysis of such patterns might offer improvements over measures obtained from the linear model.

**Clustering of patterns** Numerous cut-and-try techniques have been proposed for the clustering of persons in terms of patterns of responses (see discussions of many of these in Tryon and Bailey 1970). The proper approach, however, is to employ cross-products analysis, similar to the way that it is employed with relatively continuous measures. The first step in such an analysis is to compute an index of response agreement over items for each pair of individuals. If two individuals give the same response to an item, regardless of what that response is, that is counted as an agreement. In tests of ability, one type of response would consist of passing the item, and the other type of response would consist of failing the item. In nonability tests, one type of response would consist of agreeing with a statement, and the other would consist of disagreeing with the statement. An index of agreement in responses over dichotomous items is the mean cross product of scores when one of two dichotomous responses is scored 1 and the other is scored −1. Thus if two persons either pass or fail an item, the cross product is 1; but if one person passes the item and the other fails the item, the cross product is −1. Similarly for nonability tests, if two persons give the same response to an item, the cross product is 1; but if they give different responses, the cross product is −1. Sums of such cross products over items are then divided by the number of items. These can be factor-analyzed by all the methods employed with other types of sums of cross products.

In spite of the ease with which cross-products analysis can be applied to the problem of clustering patterns, the author knows of no instance in which this has been done. The theoretical possibilities are interesting. The loadings of each person on each factor could be considered as a score, each such score indicating how strongly each person related to each pattern (factor). Rather than having only one score on the collection of items, as would result from applying the linear model, each person would have a score on each factor. Such scores could be employed in subsequent investigations, either as variables in basic research or as predictor variables in applied problems.

**Discriminatory analysis of patterns** Analogous to methods of discriminatory analysis applied to sets of relatively continuous scores (profiles), there are methods of discriminatory analysis that can be applied to sets of dichotomous scores (patterns). For example, the MDF can be applied. Discriminatory analysis with score patterns is discussed by Maxwell (1961). An illustrative problem would be that of discriminating different types of mental patients on the basis of patterns of symptoms, in which each symptom would be scored 1 when present and 0 when absent.

**Evaluation of pattern analysis** In spite of the interesting possibilities for clustering persons in terms of patterns and for applying discriminatory analysis to patterns, pattern analysis has produced very little in the way of important research findings. When pattern analysis is applied to typical items on mental tests, it suffers from a crippling flaw: it takes individual items too seriously. As has been noted previously, the individual item usually is heavily loaded with uniqueness, part of which is pure measurement error and the rest reliable variance specific to the item. Remember that items within a test usually have low correlations with one another, with correlations above .30 being the exception. In other words, most of the variance in each item is trivial, and pattern analysis seeks to find important information in that trivia. It has not worked. Studies in which pattern analysis has been employed either failed to obtain clear results or, when they apparently did, the results did not hold up in subsequent samples. Regarding the latter point, pattern analysis applied to test items is the "ideal" method for taking advantage of chance. This is because (1) there is a large component of measurement error in each item, (2) such studies usually employ a relatively large number of items, which gives more room for taking advantage of chance, and (3) the methods of analysis, such as the MDF, are ones that capitalize on chance variance. Much more interesting results might have been obtained from applying pattern analysis to sets of dichotomous variables other than test items, such as presence or absence of symptoms relating to various types of brain damage or various items concerning biographical information. There is still hope for the future, but so far pattern analysis has not added substantially to the linear model in the scoring of responses to collections of items.

## MULTIDIMENSIONAL SCALING

Although MDS is based on the same mathematical models as factor analysis and discriminatory analysis, it is used for a different purpose. As the term will be used in this book, *multidimensional scaling* usually is concerned with the scaling of stimuli rather than the scaling of people. Some of the methods actually can be used to study individual differences among people, but (1) studies of individual differences are adequately handled by the multivariate procedures discussed previously in this book, and (2) the procedures which will be discussed are mainly important for the scaling of stimuli. MDS is an extension of the methods of unidimensional scaling of stimuli which were discussed in Chap. 2.

From Chap. 2 it will be remembered that methods of unidimensional scaling are applied only in those cases where there is good reason to believe that one dimension is sufficient. This would be the case, for example, in developing an interval scale for judgments of weight. In unidimensional scaling, the experimenter tries to control extraneous differences among the stimuli to prevent them from influencing judgments or preferences. For example, in a study of lifted weights, the experimenter would ensure that the weights are all the same shape and color. More important than these efforts to control extraneous differences among stimuli is the control obtained from instructions to subjects. In unidimensional scaling, the investigator knows in advance of the study the dimension on which responses are to be made. Each subject is carefully instructed to make judgments or preferences with regard to the dimension of interest and is warned about letting other variables influence the responses.

In MDS subjects usually are not instructed to make responses with respect to a particular dimension; rather, they are asked to respond only in terms of similarities and differences among the stimuli, e.g., judging whether stimulus *a* is more similar to stimulus *b* or to stimulus *c*. MDS is used in two related types of studies. In one type, the investigator does not know what dimensions people typically use in responding to a class of stimuli, and the purpose of such investigations is to learn the dimensions. This would be the case in studying responses of college students to 20 well-known members of the United States Senate. Similarity judgments about the senators might be explainable by only one dimension of good-bad, or other dimensions might be evidenced in the judgments, such as liberal-conservative, North-South regional affiliation, and so on. The purpose of the study would be to learn something about the dimensions that people employ in judging senators. In this and other instances, MDS allows the investigator to learn something about the "natural" dimensions that subjects employ in judgments and sentiments about a class of objects.

In the second type of study in which MDS is employed, the investigator is concerned with judgments rather than sentiments. Although the investigator knows what the major physical dimensions are that differentiate the stimuli, it is not clear how such dimensions are actually involved in psychological processes underlying judgments. An example would be in obtaining similarity judgments regarding colored chips. All chips would be of the same hue, but they would be systematically varied in terms of brightness and saturation. An analysis of the responses might indicate that subjects actually employ only one dimension rather than two; e.g., both saturation and brightness are combined into one overall dimension of "vividness." Equally possible would be to find that more than two dimensions are required to represent the responses. A third possibility would be that subjects employ only two dimensions in making responses, but one is much more influential than the other.

MDS has become a very popular topic among specialists in psychometrics during the last 20 years. This is probably because (1) many behavioral scientists are becoming sufficiently sophisticated in mathematics and statistics to derive and understand the complex methods involved, (2) high-speed computers are available for the immense computations that often are required, and (3) the products actually are proving useful in various areas of the behavioral sciences. The most comprehensive recent sources on the topic are listed in the Suggested Additional Readings. An excellent overall discussion from a mathematical point of view is given in Shepard (1974) [he also provides a less technical, general overview of purposes and methods in Shepard, Romney, and Nerlove (1972)].

**Spatial conceptions of MDS** It is with MDS that spatial models play an extremely important part, more so even than in factor analysis and profile analysis. Even the terms that are used to refer to the experiments and methods of analysis are spatial in nature, e.g., dimension, proximity, origin, rotation, and numerous others. Indeed, as one of the most prominent developers of MDS has said (R. N. Shepard in Shepard, Romney, and Nerlove 1972), one of the attractive features of these scaling methods for many people is that they allow one to summarize complex relations among numerous stimuli in terms of simple pictures in two dimensions or two-dimensional graphs showing each pair of relations for three or four dimensions. In gathering data for MDS, in essence one requires the subject to make some type of response which is susceptible to a spatial representation, either directly in terms of the form in which the response is made or in terms of a mathematical model by which the experimenter converts responses into a spatial representation.

By far the most frequently employed "spatial" geometric model for MDS has been the euclidean space. Since this is the space that is actually observed in the world around us, it is referred to geometrically as *real* space. Thus, while sitting in a room, one is literally in a euclidean three-space. All the geometric properties of the room could be computed from familiar theorems of geometry, such as the area of one wall and the length of a diagonal extending from a ceiling corner to an opposing floor corner. It is very useful to conceptualize MDS and other forms of multivariate analysis in terms of euclidean spatial models because very powerful systems of mathematics can be adopted, e.g., those in factor analysis and discriminant analysis. Actually, there are alternative spatial representations that have been mentioned as possibilities for MDS—see discussions of these in Coombs, Dawes, and Tversky (1970), Shepard, Romney, and Nerlove (1972), and Torgerson (1958). For example, one proposal is the "city block" spatial model, in which distance literally is measured in terms of the way in which one would get from the point on one corner of a city block to the opposing point two blocks away. Thus one would have to walk down to the corner, turn left, and walk another block. This would be the shortest distance between the two points in terms of the city-block model. Of course, if one could walk straight through the buildings from one corner to the opposing corner, this would be the shortest distance in euclidean space.

Another spatial model that has been proposed, and for which methods of MDS have been developed, is the purely nonmetric space, in which no distances at all are known; rather only rank-orders are known for stimuli on the various dimensions. For discussions of these various possibilities, see Coombs in Coombs, Dawes, and Tversky (1970), Shepard in Shepard, Romney, and Nerlove (1972), and Torgerson (1958). However, none of the noneuclidean models have led to any powerful methods of MDS, and mainly they are important theoretically as reference points for theorizing about euclidean models.

Once points are located in (mapped into) a euclidean space, then powerful methods of analysis are available for dimensionalizing the space, placing it in a coordinate system, and locating each stimulus with respect to the resulting coordinate axes. The logic of how this is done was discussed previously with respect to the $D$ measure and raw-score factor analysis. All the necessary mathematical methods are available for handling the problem once a euclidean space of points is formed. The logic grew out of a historic paper on the matter by Young and Householder (1938) and has been manifested subsequently in numerous mathematical methods for handling problems of multivariate analysis such as is evidenced in factor analysis, clustering of profiles, and the multiple discriminant function. From the standpoint of psychological experimentation, the primary problem is that of obtaining responses to stimuli from subjects in a way that is susceptible to mapping into a euclidean space. The subsequent problem for mathematical models is to transform the raw responses of subjects into an altered form which results in a mapping of stimuli in a euclidean space.

**Responses in terms of similarity** Nearly all methods of MDS are based on responses of subjects in terms of similarities and differences of stimuli rather than in terms of specified attributes. Examples of collections of stimuli that might be studied in that regard are names of United States Senators, colored chips that vary on different dimensions concerning color, names of countries, adjectives, and almost any other stimuli to which subjects can respond in terms of similarities and differences. Such responses are said to concern *proximities.*

There is a hierarchy in terms of the amount of information that one tries to obtain from subjects with respect to the underlying scales being developed. At one extreme, one can make the assumption that subjects are capable of supplying complete metric information about the stimuli, and thus that subjects can produce ratio scales or interval scales of proximity directly, e.g., as with the methods of ratio estimation. At the other extreme, either subjects are not required to give responses that directly produce higher-order measurement scales concerning proximities (e.g., they are only asked to rank-order stimuli in terms of proximity) or, regardless of the types of responses subjects are required to make, the experimenter takes seriously only the rank-ordering or even categorical information that is supplied. Another way of saying it is that one can order psychophysical scaling methods for MDS from those that are very "strong" to those that are very "weak" in terms of what they require subjects to do in the scaling task and how seriously one takes subjects' responses.

Thus, within the extremes that usually are interesting in MDS, the strongest set of assumptions involves subjects directly producing a vector space showing $h_i \cos_{ij} h_j$ among all pairs of stimuli. That is, under the strongest set of assumptions, one asks subjects to produce distances among stimuli and distances of each stimulus from a common origin. Methods will be described by which this can be done.

At the other extreme, subjects can be asked only to rank-order stimuli in terms of how similar or dissimilar they are to one another. For example, in a set of 10 stimuli, one stimulus could be chosen and the subject could be asked to rank-order the other nine stimuli in terms of how similar or different they are with respect to the chosen stimulus. Then one could apply a model which made rather weak assumptions about the information that could be obtained from such data and be limited to methods of MDS that resulted in rank-order spaces only.

Thus, one can think of a continuum in terms of what the subject is required to do in the psychophysical scaling task ranging from very strong to very weak assumptions, and one can think of attendant methods of MDS that also vary in terms of the strength of the assumptions regarding efforts to map responses into spatial configurations. However, in practice the two sets of assumptions tend to be closely parallel. When subjects are required to give a great deal of information about the spatial properties in relation to one another (e.g., to directly produce distances among stimuli by one or another scaling technique), then usually one employs a method of MDS that also is based on strong mathematical assumptions about permissible methods of analysis. If initially one requires subjects to produce a rather high order of information about the mapping of points into a euclidean space, one tends to throw away information by using a subsequent method of MDS that does not utilize all the potential information.

Of course, there are advantages and disadvantages to employing "strong" psychophysical scaling methods and "strong" methods of MDS. The more assumptions that are made, the more places in which one can be incorrect and thus the more spurious results that can be produced (fortunately there are ways of testing the validity of many of these assumptions). On the other hand, to the extent to which one employs a psychophysical method that obtains only "weak" information about the mapping of stimuli into a euclidean space, and/or employs a method of MDS which provides only meager information (e.g., only rank-order), there is little danger from faulty assumptions. To put it simply, one can obtain a great deal of information rather easily if one is willing to make a variety of assumptions about the data-gathering process and methods of analysis, but one runs the risk of producing spurious results because the assumptions are not entirely correct. At the other extreme in terms of caution, the experimenter can require subjects to supply only weak information in the psychophysical method (e.g., rank-order information) and apply only those methods of MDS that make few assumptions about the spatial representation of the stimuli; but in so doing, the experimenter is doomed at the outset to obtain only meager information from the overall results.

**Vector-product MDS** By far the most powerful method of MDS in terms of what is required of subjects and what can be done subsequently with the data is based directly on the concept of vector-product geometric models, where the relationship between any two variables is represented by $h_i \cos_{ij} h_j$. In terms of psychophysical scaling methods, the most direct approach is to ask the subject to judge the percent to which pairs of stimuli are similar rather than different on a percentage continuum running from 100 percent similar through 0 to 100 percent different. (In some cases it is logical to go only from 100 percent "similar" to 0 percent, as in the example which will be shown subsequently.)

An example of applying the vector-product model comes from some unpublished research by the author which concerns the scaling of adjectives relating to emotions. The overall purpose is to derive a set of factored rating scales for a wide variety of emotions. The illustrative study here represents some pilot work which was done to test the feasibility of the rating task and attendant methods of MDS. In this study, nine adjectives related to emotion were investigated, with three adjectives hypothesized to be related to three underlying factors. The adjectives in group A are happy, contented, and pleasant; B are vigorous, healthy, and strong; and C are loving, romantic, and warm. There are 36 possible pairs of relations among the adjectives. For each pair, subjects were asked to mark on a percentage continuum from 0 to 100 the extent to which the words were similar in meaning. It was explainable that this percentage indicated the proportion of stimulus contexts in which one word could be substituted for the other and the meaning of a sentence would not be substantially altered. Since all nine of the adjectives are positive in connotation, rather than employ a bipolar scale, only the range from 0 to 100 percent similarity was used.

For the pilot study, responses were obtained from 34 college students. This resulted in a matrix of percentages analogous to a correlation matrix. The highest percentage was 80 percent between the adjectives *happy* and *contented*, and the lowest percentage was 30 percent between *pleasant* and *strong*.

Responses in terms of similarity on a percentage scale such as this can be converted directly to vector products. Each percentage should be considered a proportion; for example, 74 percent is expressed as .74 and 8 percent is expressed as .08. The square root of each proportion (for example, .86 and .28 in the examples above) equals the vector product, which leads to what will be called *PS* (proportion square root) *analysis*. The square roots of such proportions meet all the requirements for a vector-product space and thus can be factor-analyzed directly. Basically one conceives of the vectors as being of unit length, and thus 1.00 is placed in each of the diagonal spaces. (However, concepts of common factoring can be employed in which communality estimates are placed in the diagonal spaces also.) The average of percentages (expressed as proportions) obtained from a group of individuals can be thought of as the percentages that represent the group as a whole or, alternatively, as the percentages that would be produced by a *modal* individual. Then one would take the square root of each average proportion and form a symmetric table of PS coefficients.

It is perfectly logical to apply conventional methods of factor analysis to such vector-product matrices. The "loadings" obtained from the analysis represent projections on underlying factors. The square of each loading indicates the percent (proportion) to which the stimulus is related to the attribute associated with the factor (which is similar to a squared loading in the factor analysis of correlation coefficients equaling a "percent of variance explained"). In this case, the first step was to employ confirmatory, multiple-group analysis, with proportions of 1.00 in the diagonal spaces. Simultaneously, three group centroids were placed in groups A, B, and C, each containing the three adjectives mentioned previously. Whereas generally the results tended to confirm the hypotheses, as usual there were some departures from an ideal solution. The words in group A tended to overlap rather highly with the words in group C, and some of the words did not "behave" exactly as expected. Regarding this last consideration, the words *pleasant* and *warm* did not load as highly with their hypothesized factors as had been anticipated, and they shared enough meaning to form a fourth factor of their own. Subsequently, the matrix of PS coefficients was submitted to a PC analysis with unities in the diagonal spaces, and four factors were extracted. What was said above was also borne out in the four Varimax rotated PC factors shown in Table 12-4. Boxes have been drawn around the loadings of the three variables that were intended to represent each of the three factors. It can be seen that the hypotheses are largely confirmed, but there were the unexpected results mentioned previously. This pilot work suggested that the original hypotheses were generally along the right lines, indicated improvements in the groupings of words, and provided a starting point for much more extensive investigations of emotion-related words. More important for the discussion here, the study provides a clear case of vector-product, multidimensional scaling—in this instance with PS analysis. Whenever one can obtain such vector products directly from the responses of subjects, then powerful methods of factor analysis can be applied.

PS analysis can be applied when the rating scale ranges between 100 percent agreement through 0 to 100 percent disagreement. In that case, percentage disagreements would be converted to proportions, square roots would be taken, and negative signs would be attached prior to factor analysis. For example, percentage disagreements of 25 and 64 would be converted to PS coefficients of $-.50$ and $-.80$ prior to factor analysis.

Vector-product MDS can be applied to a wide variety of classes of stimuli, particularly anywhere it is sensible to have subjects give responses in terms of the similarity of stimuli two at a time. In the example given above, the method applies equally well when bipolar percentage scales rather than unipolar scales are used. Of course, in employing vector-products MDS in this way, one runs the risk of requiring subjects to do more than they are capable of doing, namely, directly producing the vector space for the experimenter. The wisdom of this

**Table 12-4 Varimax rotated vector-product PC factors for emotion-related words**

| Words | Factors | | | |
|---|---|---|---|---|
| | A | B | C | D |
| 1. Happy | .66 | .39 | .45 | .42 |
| 2. Contented | .70 | .34 | .49 | .26 |
| 3. Pleasant | .53 | .26 | .35 | .69 |
| 4. Vigorous | .15 | .84 | .24 | .36 |
| 5. Healthy | .55 | .74 | .20 | .15 |
| 6. Strong | .22 | .87 | .33 | .10 |
| 7. Loving | .45 | .29 | .75 | .31 |
| 8. Romantic | .28 | .31 | .85 | .21 |
| 9. Warm | .19 | .32 | .64 | .62 |

approach depends on the criteria, which will be discussed later, that should be applied to all methods of MDS. One obvious criterion in any case where stimuli are mapped into a euclidean space is to ensure that a euclidean space is actually appropriate. In vector-products MDS, this assumption would be violated if any of the characteristic roots obtained from applying the PC method or the principal-factors counterpart produced any negative characteristic roots. In the example shown in Table 12-4, none of the nine possible characteristic roots were negative. Vector-product psychophysical methods and related MDS can be applied to such collections of stimuli as geometric forms, political viewpoints of United States Senators, styles of various authors, and anything else than can be sensibly rated in terms of percentages of similarity. It is an extremely powerful method that should be used very frequently in the future.

**MDS with known euclidean distances** Some approaches to psychophysical scaling lead to estimations of distances among stimuli. In the simplest case, one asks the subjects to provide such distances in a rather direct manner. As a very simple example, consider MDS with the names of six well-known senators. The subject is required to make ratio estimates among the distances of senators from one another when they are compared in triads. The subject would be asked first which two of the three senators are most similar and then which two are most different. This provides one with a rank-ordering of the distances between the three senators in a hypothetical space. After the three distances were placed in rank-order, the subjects could then be asked to make ratio judgments among these distances, e.g., how much larger the distance between senators A and B is than between senators B and C. In this way, one could obtain ratio estimates of distances among all the stimuli in the set. These could be averaged over subjects to obtain a matrix of ratios among distances for a group as a whole. If one will assume that subjects can sensibly make such responses, then the obtained ratios among distances can be analyzed directly as distances in a euclidean space. In the use of the euclidean model, it is important to realize that only ratios among distances are important, because the dimensionality and configuration are not influenced when all distances are multiplied by the same constant (but this is not the case when one *adds* a constant to all distances). Thus, if one knows the distances up to a criterion of proportionality, the distances can be analyzed appropriately. What is not known in this case, however, is the distance of each stimulus point from an origin. If this were known, the distances could be converted directly to vector products; and then all methods of factor analysis could be applied to the resulting matrix. Later will be discussed some methods for estimating distances with data in which subjects are not required to directly produce the distances. By whatever methods the distances among stimuli are obtained, let us assume here that these distances are known, and the issue is one of MDS for the distances. An illustration of how this situation is handled follows.

In Fig. 12-12 are shown hypothetical results for distances among six senators, the senators being labeled *a, b, c*, etc. It is a simplified example, because (1) most studies would employ considerably more than six stimuli (senators in

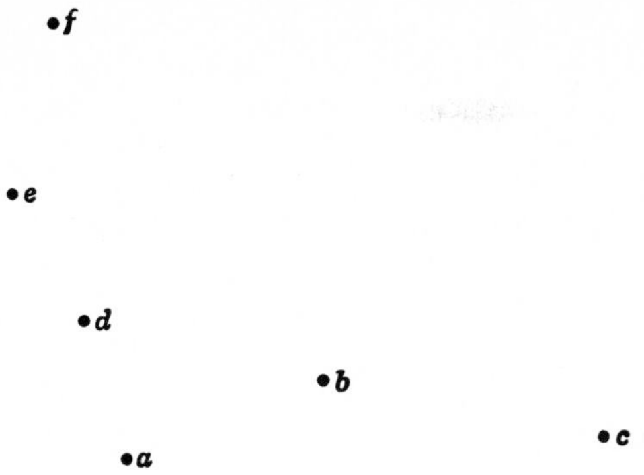

•*f*

•*e*

•*d*

•*b*

•*c*

•*a*

**Figure 12-12** Space of distances of six senators.

this case) and (2) probably more than two dimensions would be required to portray the distances exactly.

In Fig. 12-12, lines could have been drawn between all pairs of stimuli to represent distances, but to simplify the illustration, that was not done. After distances among stimuli have been obtained, how are these to be dimensionalized? If the points fit as neatly in a two-space as those shown in Fig. 12-12, there would be no problem. One could simply pencil in two dimensions with a ruler. In that case the number of dimensions must be neither more nor less than 2; but the exact placement is a matter of choice, as it is in the rotation of factors in factor analysis. One could employ an arbitrary scale for each dimension; for example, $\frac{1}{4}$ inch equals a score of 1, $\frac{1}{2}$ inch equals a score of 2, $\frac{3}{4}$ inch equals a score of 3, and so on. Then interpretations could be made of the dimensions in terms of the scores of senators, and the dimensions could be investigated in subsequent studies. However, since stimuli can seldom be represented in a two-space, it is necessary to develop methods of analysis that can handle all cases.

The set of distances provides no hint about an origin, as is evidenced by the lack of an origin in the space of distances portrayed in Fig. 12-12. There are a number of ways to put an origin in a space of distances. One way is to make one of the points the origin. Then all the other points could be represented by vectors extending from the point designated as the origin. It would not be satisfactory to define the origin as the point of a particular stimulus, because (1) there is some error in establishing the point and (2) even if that were not the case, the results of subsequent analyses would depend very much on the point which was chosen. A solution which tends to circumvent these problems is to place the origin at the centroid of the space of points. In a two-space of points, this could be easily done by (1) putting any pair of orthogonal coordinates in the space and (2) computing the average scores of all points on the coordinates. Remember that the centroid of points (for persons or stimuli) is represented by the average score of those points on any orthogonal basis for the space. In Fig. 12-13 are shown the points from Fig. 12-12 represented by vectors extending from the centroid of the space.

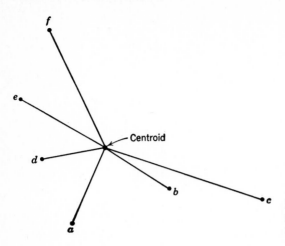

**Figure 12-13** Space of points for six senators with an origin at the centroid.

When all points cannot be exactly represented in a two-space, as they almost never will, there are straightforward ways of calculating the distance of each point from the centroid of the space. Thus, all that is required is a matrix of distances of stimuli from one another, and then simple formulas are available for calculating the distance of each stimulus from the centroid of these differences, without any additional information being required. (These methods are discussed by Torgerson 1958, Chap. 11.) After these distances are obtained, the matrix of distances among stimuli can be converted to a matrix of vector products. These can be factored by any method of factor analysis. Also, there is nothing to prevent rotation of factors to positions that are more interpretable.

In Fig. 12-14 are shown the results of a centroid factor analysis of the vectors shown in Fig. 12-13 (centroid factors are not to be confused with the centroid point of a space of points). These are rotated, and loadings for stimuli on the rotated factors are shown in Table 12-5. (The units in which loadings are expressed are the same as those used to express the distances of points from one another and from the centroid of the space.) If we consider the patterns of loadings for the senators, it might be suggested that factor $A_1$ concerns liberalism versus conservatism and factor $B_1$ concerns attitudes regarding foreign affairs.

**MDS with estimated distances** In the previous section it was assumed that distances among stimuli are known, in which case it is an easy task to convert these to vector products and factor-analyze. One of the major controversies in MDS, however, concerns how those distances are obtained initially. Before particular methods for estimating those distances are discussed, it would be worthwhile to examine the requirements for the obtained distances.

In multidimensional scaling, the distances must be established on a ratio scale of measurement; that is, it must be possible to say, for example, that the distance between points $a$ and $b$ is twice the distance between points $b$ and $c$.

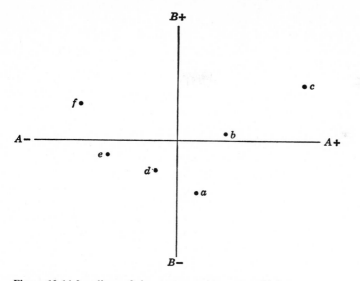

**Figure 12-14** Loadings of six senators on two centroid factors.

Also, since a ratio scale must have a rational origin, it must be possible for the distance between two stimuli to be zero. In Chap. 1 it was said that a ratio scale is invariant only over transformations of the type $aX$. Any ratio scale $X$ can be multiplied or divided by an arbitrary constant $a$, and the resulting scale $X'$ will also be a ratio scale. Then the distances used for multidimensional scaling must be determined only up to a criterion of proportionality.

Even if a ratio scale of distances (or anything else) is invariant under transformations of the form $aX$, it is *not* invariant under transformations of the form $aX + b$, where $b$ is different from zero in either the positive or negative direction. Thus one cannot add an arbitrary constant to a set of distances and maintain the same configuration of points. Then, for example, adding an arbitrary constant might change the shape of the triangle connecting three points or

**Table 12-5 Loadings of six senators on two rotated factors**

|  |  | Factor | |
| --- | --- | --- | --- |
|  |  | $A_1$ | $B_1$ |
| Senator | a | .02 | −.31 |
|  | b | .26 | −.05 |
|  | c | .74 | .07 |
|  | d | −.16 | −.13 |
|  | e | −.37 | .03 |
|  | f | −.42 | .35 |

might change the number of dimensions required to represent half a dozen points. Another possibility is that the space would become noneuclidean; i.e., the points could not be represented in any physical space or any extension of the properties thereof to hyperspaces.

The lesson to be learned from the above discussion is that before one can dimensionalize distances among stimuli, those distances must be obtained on a ratio scale of distances. Then either some method of ratio estimation must be employed in gathering data from subjects or, if methods are employed that lead to an interval scale, some rationale must be developed for transforming the interval scale of distances to a ratio scale of distances. Regardless of which of these two approaches is used, the distances are only estimated, and there must be an examination of the extent to which the distances actually are euclidean. Although there are a number of ways one can do this, the easiest is to examine the results of a PC factor analysis of the space of distances after the distances have been transformed to vector products. If the space is noneuclidean, results of the analysis will violate some rules regarding possible outcomes. Primarily, at least one characteristic root of the matrix of vector products will be negative. No root can be negative if the space is euclidean. Thus, if the PC method is used to dimensionalize the space of vector products, there is a built-in check on the legitimacy of analyzing the space as though it were euclidean. Very small negative characteristic roots might be accepted as inconsequential departures from the requirements for a euclidean space, but large negative characteristic roots (e.g., less than $-1.0$) would seriously challenge the assumptions of the model. Extensive research needs to be performed on the consequences of obtaining negative characteristic roots of various sizes.

**Ratio estimates of distances** As was mentioned previously, a careful distinction must be made between obtaining ratio estimates of distances, as they will be discussed here, and obtaining ratio estimates of scale values, as they were discussed in Chap. 2. In the latter, for example, the subject would be required to estimate the ratio of brightness of one light to another. In the ratio estimation of distances, the analogous task would be to judge the ratio of *differences* in brightness of lights $a$ and $b$ to that of $b$ and $c$. In MDS, the scaling tasks concern judgments about the relative size of differences among the stimuli rather than about the amount of an attribute possessed by the stimuli.

Some investigators are reluctant to employ methods of ratio estimation to obtain distances among stimuli because they feel that such methods require too much of subjects. Instead they feel that it would be better to require much simpler responses from subjects and then estimate a ratio scale of distance with mathematical models. The author is not one of those who is skeptical about making the strong assumptions required to employ methods of ratio estimation of distances (as in PS analysis), but this is a matter that remains to be settled by continued research on MDS.

**Interval estimates of distances** Instead of employing methods of ratio estimation with differences among stimuli, one could employ methods of interval estimation. For example, the experimenter shows the subject two pairs of stimuli, one pair consisting of stimuli $a$ and $b$ and the other pair consisting of stimuli $c$ and $d$. The subject is asked to pick a pair of stimuli from a set so that the distance between them is midway between the distances of $a$-$b$ and $c$-$d$. Such methods of interval estimation of distances, however, would confuse the experimenter, and the subject would be even more perplexed. Even if this were an understandable task for subjects, it would lead only to an interval scale for the distances. Since methods of ratio estimation are more understandable to subjects and are intended to produce ratio scales for distances, those methods are preferable to methods of interval estimation. (This is so in multidimensional scaling, but it is not necessarily so in unidimensional scaling, as it was described in Chap. 2.) The alternative is to start with methods of ordinal estimation, which is discussed in the following section.

**Ordinal estimates of distances** Much of the work on multidimensional scaling so far has been based on ordinal estimates of distances. The method of *triads* is used frequently for this purpose. Subjects are shown three stimuli from a larger set. First, they are asked to indicate which two of the three stimuli are most similar; next, they are asked to indicate which two are most different. This produces a rank-ordering of the three differences possible among three stimuli. Judgments can then be made of the ordering of distances in all possible triads in a set. (Under the stronger assumptions required for the vector-products approach to MDS, subsequently subjects are required to make ratio estimates of distances within the triad.)

Another method of ordinal estimation employed with distances among stimuli is the method of *multidimensional rank-order*. An example would be as follows. The subject is given stimulus $a$ and asked to rank the remaining stimuli in a set in terms of their similarity to $a$. Next, the subject is given stimulus $b$ and asked to rank all other stimuli in terms of their similarity to $b$. As many rank-orderings are made as there are stimuli.

Either of the above methods of ordinal estimation can be used to generate an interval scale of distances. This is an instance in which the requirements placed on the subject in making responses are weaker than the requirements placed on the subsequently employed model for generating an interval scale of distances. Thus, whereas subjects merely rank-order distances, a scaling model is then applied which attempts to convert these to an interval scale of distances. The basic data obtained from subjects are the proportions of times that one stimulus is judged more similar to a second stimulus than to a third stimulus. For stimuli $a$, $b$, and $c$, this would be symbolized $_aP_{bc}$, which indicates the proportion of subjects that say $a$ is more similar to $b$ than to $c$. Since such proportions provide only ordinal information about distances, some type of mathematical model must be used to convert the proportions to intervals. This is most frequently done with models relating to Thurstone's law of comparative judgment, which was discussed in Chap. 2. There are, however, two very important differences between the way those scaling methods are applied in unidimensional scaling and in multidimensional scaling. In the former, the methods are applied to proportions of persons who say that one stimulus is greater than another with respect to a stated attribute; in multidimensional scaling, the methods are applied to the proportions of people who say, in effect, that the distance between two stimuli is greater than that between two other stimuli. In the former case, the methods result in an interval scale of the stimuli with respect to an attribute; in the latter case, the result is an interval scale of *distances* among stimuli, with the attribute(s) involved in the distances not being known at that stage of the analysis. An illustrative interval scale of distances among three pairs of stimuli is as follows:

| Smaller | $ab$ | $bc$ | | $cd$ | Larger |
|---------|------|------|--|------|--------|
| distances | | | | | distances |

The interval of distance between pairs $ab$ and $bc$ is much smaller than that between pairs $bc$ and $cd$. Since it is an interval scale rather than a ratio scale, no zero point is shown, and the ends of the line are anchored only by "smaller" and "larger." However, one can take seriously the ratios of the three intervals depicted. For example, one can see that the interval $bc$-$cd$ is several times larger than the interval $ab$-$bc$. The purpose of applying Thurstone's law of comparative judgment would be to obtain an interval scaling of all possible distances among stimuli in a set. Then, by methods to be discussed later, the interval scale would be transformed to a ratio scale, and the resulting distances would be factor-analyzed by the methods discussed previously.

**The additive constant** If the methods discussed in the previous section are employed to obtain an interval scale of distances, still there is the problem of converting to a ratio scale of distances. As was mentioned previously, to factor-analyze the distances among stimuli, one must measure distances on a ratio scale. After an interval scale is obtained for the distances, one can convert it to a ratio scale by adding or subtracting the proper quantity. This can be illustrated where one knows in advance the distances among stimuli on a ratio scale. Suppose that the distances $a$-$b$, $b$-$c$, and $c$-$d$ were known to be 6, 5, and 2, respectively. If one were to subtract 2 from each of the distances, they would be 4, 3, and 0, respectively. The converted distances would be on an interval scale of measurement but not on a ratio scale. Obviously, one could add 2 to all the converted distances and reachieve the ratio scale of distances. Thus in this case the proper additive constant would be 2.

Of course, with an interval scaling of distances, there is no direct way to determine the additive constant that will produce a ratio scale. Rather, one must make some assumptions about the nature of the additive constant and then derive the constant on the basis of those assumptions. Most frequently, it is assumed that the additive constant should be selected so that (1) it results in euclidean distances and (2) the dimensionality of the space of distances is as small as possible. (Methods for doing this are discussed by Torgerson 1958.)

The above objectives are achieved iteratively. In doing this, it is important for one to know that the space of distances can be made euclidean by making the additive constant large enough. As the additive constant is made larger and larger, the dimensionality of the space approaches the number of stimuli minus 1. When that limit is reached, any set of distances must necessarily fit the requirements of euclidean space. Then it would not be possible to find illogical relations among distances like those illustrated previously. Also, nothing would "go wrong" in applying PC factoring methods to the distances, as it would if the space of points were noneuclidean. In principle, then, the problem of finding the correct additive constant boils down to finding the smallest number of dimensions that will preserve the euclidean properties of the space.

The additive constant usually is estimated in the following steps. First, a trial value is chosen, with the average of all distances among stimuli on the interval scale being a good choice for this. Second, all distances on the interval scale are converted to distances on an approximate ratio scale. Third, the distance of each point is determined from the centroid of the points by methods discussed previously. Fourth, distances are converted to vector products by methods which also were discussed previously. Fifth, the matrix of vector products is factored by the PC method, and the results provide a check on the euclidean properties of the space. Sixth, if the space is noneuclidean, as usually will be the case, a larger additive constant must be selected, and the analysis must be redone from the beginning. This iterative approach is employed until the space is approximately euclidean. Since there is some error in the data, an exact fit to euclidean requirements is not expected; consequently the iteration is stopped when the fit is close. If, in the fifth step above, the space is euclidean, a smaller additive constant is employed, and the resulting matrix of vector products is analyzed by the PC method. Successive iterations in this way will lead to the smallest additive constant that approximately meets the requirements of a euclidean space. The results on one iteration suggest how much larger or smaller the next trial value should be. (The particulars of these steps are discussed by Torgerson 1958 and Messick 1956.) In studies to date, only several iterations have been required to achieve a good fit.

When the proper additive constant is determined, simultaneously a multidimensional scaling is achieved for the stimuli. The number of factors in the last iteration is taken as the dimensionality of the space, and the loadings of stimuli on those factors indicate the amount of each attribute (dimension) possessed by each stimulus.

**An example of MDS with ordinal estimation** The examples shown previously concerned MDS when distances were known before MDS per se was applied. As discussed previously, in obtaining ordinal estimates of distance, it is necessary to use a mathematical model to estimate the actual distances. Among other things, this requires seeking the proper additive constant. An excellent example of this approach was presented by Torgerson (1958). The problem concerned judgments about the similarity of colored chips. There were nine chips, all the same red hue but varying in terms of saturation and brightness. The physical

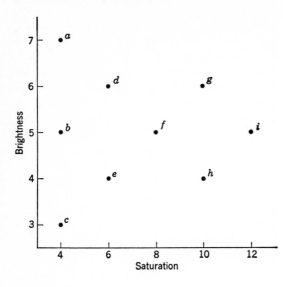

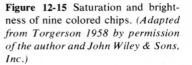

**Figure 12-15** Saturation and brightness of nine colored chips. *(Adapted from Torgerson 1958 by permission of the author and John Wiley & Sons, Inc.)*

characteristics (not necessarily the psychological characteristics) of the nine chips with respect to saturation and brightness are shown in Fig. 12-15. The problem was to determine the dimensions that subjects employ in making similarity judgments about the colored chips.

The method of triads was employed with 38 subjects. The responses were then converted to the form $_iP_{jk}$, showing the proportion of times that stimulus $i$ was judged more similar to stimulus $j$ than to stimulus $k$. Those proportions were then scaled by a method (Torgerson 1958) which provides a least-squares fit to interval scales based on Thurstone's law of comparative judgment. An additive constant was then sought to convert the interval scale of distances to a ratio scale of distances, the latter being shown in Table 12-6. Next, the distance of each stimulus from the centroid of the space of distances was determined, and these distances were used to transform distances to vector products by the

**Table 12-6  Distances among nine colored chips**

|   | a | b | c | d | e | f | g | h | i |
|---|---|---|---|---|---|---|---|---|---|
| a |      | 2.98 | 5.83 | 1.23 | 4.69 | 3.83 | 3.48 | 5.62 | 5.16 |
| b | 2.98 |      | 2.88 | 1.67 | 1.85 | 2.82 | 4.30 | 3.88 | 4.85 |
| c | 5.83 | 2.88 |      | 4.38 | 2.30 | 4.09 | 6.22 | 4.02 | 5.48 |
| d | 1.23 | 1.67 | 4.38 |      | 3.13 | 2.70 | 2.59 | 4.65 | 4.40 |
| e | 4.69 | 1.85 | 2.30 | 3.13 |      | 2.37 | 4.67 | 2.42 | 4.17 |
| f | 3.83 | 2.82 | 4.09 | 2.70 | 2.37 |      | 2.28 | 1.95 | 2.58 |
| g | 3.48 | 4.30 | 6.22 | 2.59 | 4.67 | 2.28 |      | 4.30 | 2.93 |
| h | 5.62 | 3.88 | 4.02 | 4.65 | 2.42 | 1.95 | 4.30 |      | 2.93 |
| i | 5.16 | 4.85 | 5.48 | 4.40 | 4.17 | 2.58 | 2.93 | 2.93 |      |

*Source:* Adapted from Torgerson (1958) by permission of the author and publisher.

**Table 12-7 Vector products among nine colored chips**

|   | a | b | c | d | e | f | g | h | i |
|---|---|---|---|---|---|---|---|---|---|
| a | 10.35 | 2.41 | −5.70 | 6.09 | −3.99 | −1.62 | 3.11 | −7.12 | −3.55 |
| b | 2.41 | 3.36 | 3.65 | 1.95 | 1.80 | −1.76 | −3.57 | −2.35 | −5.50 |
| c | −5.70 | 3.65 | 12.24 | −1.80 | 5.31 | −1.70 | −9.23 | 1.54 | −4.31 |
| d | 6.09 | 1.95 | −1.80 | 3.34 | −1.40 | −1.43 | 2.31 | −5.64 | −3.42 |
| e | −3.99 | 1.80 | 5.31 | −1.40 | 3.66 | −.44 | −5.08 | 2.40 | −2.28 |
| f | −1.62 | −1.76 | −1.70 | −1.43 | −.44 | 1.08 | 1.93 | 2.14 | 1.80 |
| g | 3.11 | −3.57 | −9.23 | 2.31 | −5.08 | 1.93 | 7.99 | −1.75 | 4.29 |
| h | −7.12 | −2.35 | 1.54 | −5.64 | 2.40 | 2.14 | −1.75 | 7.00 | 3.79 |
| i | −3.55 | −5.50 | −4.31 | −3.42 | −2.28 | 1.80 | 4.29 | 3.79 | 9.17 |

*Source:* Adapted from Torgerson (1958) by permission of the author and publisher.

method discussed previously. The vector products shown in Table 12-7 were factor-analyzed, for which purpose Torgerson employed the centroid method. The first two centroid factors, and rotations of them, are shown in Table 12-8, and a plot of the rotated factors is given in Fig. 12-16. Except for the placement of the origin at the centroid of the space, the configuration of points in Fig. 12-16 is rather similar to the physical configuration of points (Fig. 12-15) with which the problem began. Of course, in multidimensional scaling, one should not expect an exact correspondence between physical dimensions of stimuli and psychological dimensions of stimuli. In the case where stimuli can be described by physical dimensions, the problem is to determine the similarities and differences between the two types of spaces. Because this example was intended to test and demonstrate the effectiveness of MDS, rather simple stimuli were employed that were known to differ initially on two physical dimensions. Of course, with this and other approaches to MDS, the real value

**Table 12-8 A factor analysis of the vector products among nine colored chips**

|   | Centroid Factors | | Rotated Factors | |
|---|---|---|---|---|
|   | A | B | $A_1$ | $B_1$ |
| a | −3.12 | .18 | 2.71 | −1.55 |
| b | −.59 | 1.78 | −.27 | −1.85 |
| c | 1.86 | 2.84 | −2.92 | −1.69 |
| d | −1.94 | .49 | 1.52 | −1.31 |
| e | 1.23 | 1.30 | −1.68 | −.62 |
| f | .41 | −.90 | .04 | .99 |
| g | −1.40 | −2.44 | 2.34 | 1.56 |
| h | 2.39 | −.77 | −1.80 | 1.76 |
| i | 1.16 | −2.45 | .06 | 2.71 |

*Source:* Adapted from Torgerson (1958) by permission of the author and publisher.

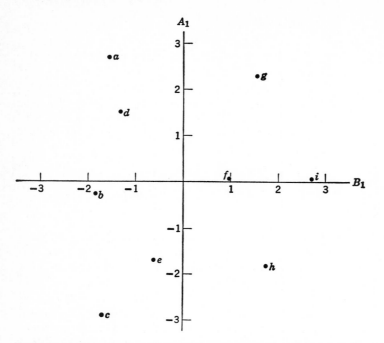

**Figure 12-16** Plot of rotated factor loadings for nine colored chips (*Adapted from Torgerson 1958 by permission of the author and John Wiley & Sons, Inc.*)

will come eventually in applying the methods to many classes of stimuli in which the underlying dimensions are very much in doubt.

**MDS with monotonicity analysis** A third approach to MDS has some points in common with vector-products MDS and MDS conducted on derived distances, but there are also a number of important differences. Whereas the methods discussed up to this point assumed that distances in a euclidean space could be either determined directly or derived by some scaling method (e.g., by using the law of comparative judgment and then seeking an additive constant), the method to be described makes rather weak assumptions about the nature of the distances *before* the process of seeking underlying dimensions is undertaken. The scaling method can operate off almost any measure of similarity or difference among stimuli, for which reason frequently it is spoken of as *proximity analysis*. At the beginning of the analysis of underlying dimensions, the various methods are extremely flexible with respect to the kinds of measures of similarity and/or difference (proximities). For example, measures of similarity among various countries could be obtained by having people rate pairs of countries in terms of a list of traits (e.g., economically developed, overpopulated, democratic, etc.) and simply requiring them to rate the pair on each trait as similar or different. The percentage of "similar" marks could be used as an indication of closeness or proximity in space. Conversely, the percentages of "different" marks could be taken as an index of distance of two countries in a spatial model. As another example, countries could be rated in pairs simply in terms of how similar they were as measured by a verbally anchored, eight-step rating scale ranging from extremely similar on one end of the continuum to extremely different on the other end. As still another example, MDS with monotonicity analysis could start with the raw scales of distances derived from either ratio estimates or rank-order estimates obtained from comparing the stimuli in triads, as discussed previously. In the latter case, one could convert rank-order estimates of distances into interval scales of distances with the law of comparative judgment and then seek an additive constant, which in turn converted the original responses into presumed distances in euclidean space. Rather than go through the steps of deriving an interval scale and seeking an additive constant, one could use MDS with monotonicity analysis to operate directly off the average ranks of subjects regarding perceived sizes of distances among stimuli.

If subjects are under instructions to rate similarity (by whatever method), then the first step in MDS with monotonicity analysis is to convert such measures of closeness to measures of distance. In either case, one is working with a symmetric matrix of proximities. If these are expressed as similarities, one simple way to convert them to measures of difference is to subtract each element in the matrix either from the highest index of similarity that could be obtained with the psychophysical method or from the largest element in the matrix. Whether such measures of difference are obtained directly from ratings of subjects or by a conversion of some type of rating of similarity, the resulting matrix concerns *quasidistances*. They are not to be considered in any rational sense as distances in a euclidean space, as one would assume with the first two approaches to MDS which were discussed. Rather these are considered only an approximation up to at least a rank-order of the distances to be derived from applying MDS. Thus, in a symmetric matrix of difference measures, one could rank-order them in size cell by cell. The only firmly held assumption in subsequently applying MDS by monotonicity analysis is that the rank-order of proximity measures is the true rank-order. Because this is the hard-core assumption upon which remaining aspects of monotonicity analysis are based, frequently it is said that such methods of MDS are "nonmetric." However, that is a misnomer for two reasons. First, a rank-order metric is assumed for the quasidistances represented in the difference matrix. Second, whereas the method of MDS can operate off proximities that are little more than rank-orderings of distance, frequently the data can reasonably be construed to be at least approximately close to actual distances in a euclidean space.

The tendency to refer to MDS with monotonicity analysis as being nonmetric is due to the extreme "robustness" that the methods have shown regarding the almost casual way in which one can obtain proximity judgments from people, apply the computerized techniques of MDS, and end up with very sensible distances and factors in a supposed euclidean space. Thus, whereas only very weak assumptions are made regarding the metric on which subjects operate in making their judgments, strong assumptions are made regarding the eventual metric for distances and dimensions used to explain those distances.

Actually, except for the proved robustness of MDS based on monotonicity analysis, most people would not have taken it very seriously because, on the face of it, the methods seem to be based on an overly simplified concept of how one can transform only rough estimates of distance into coordinate points of stimuli in a neat euclidean space. However, there have been numerous demonstrations of the surprising generality of results obtained from different approaches to establishing the proximity matrix prior to the application of monotonicity analysis. In one example, Kruskal (1964) used these methods to recover the actual distances among physical stimuli. The analysis started with a set of dots on a piece of graph paper, where it is known that (1) the distances are the real distances in a euclidean two-space and (2) the axes of the graph can serve as two factors for describing the space. First, these actual distances were distorted by a monotonic transformation, and then random numbers were added to the resulting values. These were only roughly approximate to the actual distances. The quasidistances were submitted to monotonicity analysis. The obtained configuration of points was amazingly similar to the actual configuration of points. Other demonstrations are quite convincing regarding the ability of these methods to produce results similar to those produced by different methods of multidimensional scaling.

There has been almost an explosion of interest in MDS with monotonicity analysis since the appearance of landmark papers by Shepard (1962a, 1962b), in which he spelled out the basic ideas and presented a workable, computerized method of analysis. Since then literally hundreds of journal articles have been written on monotonicity analysis. There are many supposedly competing approaches available which, as it turns out, tend to produce very similar results. The person who develops a serious interest in MDS with monotonicity analysis should read the two volumes of *Multidimensional Scaling* [by Shepard, Romney, and Nerlove (1972) and by Romney, Shepard, and Nerlove (1972)]. More recent important papers on the topic are Girard and Cliff (1976), Kruskal and Shepard (1974), Lingoes and Roskam (1973), McClelland and Coombs (1975), and Shepard (1974). Anyone who wants to carefully study MDS with monotonicity analysis will find the relevant information either in the above-mentioned sources or in the detailed references to other works in those sources.

There are three stages to MDS with monotonicity analysis. First, by one method or another of obtaining and aggregating human responses, a matrix of quasidistances is constructed. Second, one performs monotonic transformations of the quasidistances so as to obtain the best (by some standards) set of actual distances, which is a matter that will require some additional explanation and illustration. Third, once those actual distances are known, they are dimensionalized by methods that should be very familiar by this point in the book. For example, after such distances are known, one could employ the centroid of the space as the origin, convert all distances to vector products, and factor-analyze by any method selected. Actually, with most methods of MDS based on monotonicity analysis, steps 2 and 3 are combined so that the overall computational approach makes monotonic transformations and simultaneously derives coordinates for the resulting space of points. Both stages 1 and 3 are rather noncontroversial and simple to do. However, stage 2 is quite complex both conceptually and mathematically, and there have been many proposals for the most effective solution (although it is becoming increasingly apparent that the major methods bear strong kinship and produce very similar results).

Only monotonic transformations of the original matrix of quasidistances are allowed because a nonmonotonic transformation would violate the only strong assumption about the proximity matrix, namely, that the rank-order of proximity measures is the same as the rank-order of actual distances, however one obtains such actual distances. In other words, if after applying complex methods of MDS one obtains a matrix of supposed actual distances, one should be able to rank-order the distances in that matrix and obtain exactly the same ranks as those from the original matrix of quasidistances. Within this one limitation, however, the kinds of monotonic transformations that one can make are left entirely free. The simplest of all possible monotonic transformations was that shown previously with respect to seeking an additive constant for distances known on an interval scale—namely, adding the same number to all the quasidistances. A linear transformation of the quasidistances also would be a monotonic transformation, and there are many other possibilities.

There are two standards for determining the *best* monotonic transformation of quasidistances $D'_{ij}$ to obtain the derived distances $D_{ij}$. The first is that all $D_{ij}$ fit into euclidean space. Most versions of MDS with monotonicity analysis are euclidean models, and consequently the derived distances must fulfill the fundamental axioms of the representation of points in euclidean space. There are a number of ways to test whether or not the derived distances $D_{ij}$ violate principles of euclidean space. A primary indicator would be that some large negative characteristic roots were found in the application of principal components analysis to vector products derived with respect to the obtained distances.

The second requirement for the *best* monotonic transformation is that the space of $D_{ij}$ have the smallest number of dimensions possible, but with an allowance for some error with respect to the "best fit." Mathematically one must seek the monotonic transformation that provides a small number of dimensions but simultaneously maintains the euclidean properties of the space, and this requires a great deal of checking back and forth with computerized methods. The various methods of doing this are called *computer algorithms*. The term *algorithm* is a fancy word for a method of solving a problem. The theoretical arguments concern the reasonableness of jamming and packing spatial representations of psychological reactions to relations among stimuli into the smallest number of dimensions possible. This technique certainly has parsimony on its side, but one could debate whether such a purely statistical standard has the best interest of psychological theory at heart.

An extremely simple example will illustrate the issues associated with MDS with monotonicity analysis. Figure 12-17 shows an approximate space of

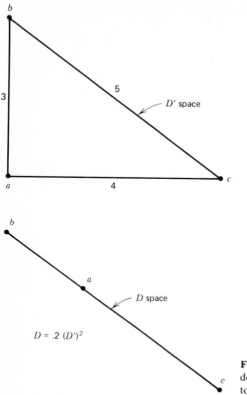

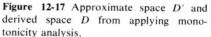

$D' \text{ space}$

$D = .2 \ (D')^2$

**Figure 12-17** Approximate space $D'$ and derived space $D$ from applying monotonicity analysis.

points labeled $D'$ and a space of points derived by a monotonicity analysis labeled $D$. This is a "rigged" example which produces a very simple solution, but it illustrates some important principles about monotonicity analysis. In the $D'$ space, points $a$ and $c$ are 4 units apart, points $a$ and $b$ are 3 units apart, and points $b$ and $c$ are 5 units apart—with the "units" simply being the spacings on the graph paper which the author used in drawing the example. The $D'$ space is constructed in such a way as to form a right triangle; then the sum of the squares on the sides equals the square of the hypoteneuse. Thus, by squaring the distances one can force all three points to lie on a straight line.

To place the resulting configuration in perspective with the original space, squared distances were divided by 5, which makes the length of the line segment $bc$ the same as it was previously. This is the same as squaring each $D'$ value and multiplying the result by 0.2. This is then a very simple monotonic transformation of $D'$. This example shows how one can monotonically transform a space of larger dimension, in this case two, into one of smaller dimension and still maintain the euclidean properties of the space.

The monotonic transformation required to convert the original approximate distances $D'$ into the derived distances $D$ is shown in Fig. 12-18. Note

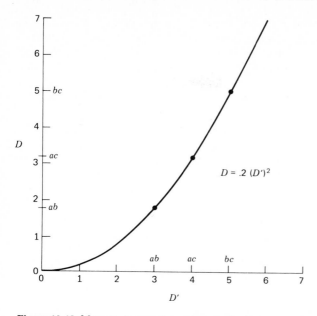

**Figure 12-18** Monotonic transformation required to convert a two-dimensional space of approximate distance $D$. to a resulting one-dimensional space $D$.

that the scales for both $D$ and $D'$ are in terms of distances, not in terms of the metric for any particular measure. The distance from $a$ to $b$ is 1.8 and the distance from $a$ to $c$ is 3.2; these add up to a distance of 5 from $c$ to $b$. O course, this is the condition for three points to lie on a straight line.

One could make the example more realistic by including more points in Fig. 12-17, so that they would not fit exactly on a straight line but would vary about it by relatively small amounts. Then, with the transformation shown of $D'$ to $D$, the additional distances would not lie exactly on the line of transformation but would tend to scatter about it. In practice, usually one seeks a transformation where the sum of squared deviates about the line of transformation is as small as possible; in other words, the principal of least squares is used as the criterion of fit. Of course, use of the least-squares criterion for minimizing error opens up many statistical procedures, in particular those which are related to characteristic roots and vectors of a matrix of relationships.

An example of the results from an MDS with monotonicity analysis is shown in Fig. 12-19, reported in a chapter by Wish, Deutsch, and Biener in Romney, Shepard, and Nerlove (1972). Their studies were concerned mainly with differences in MDS solutions obtained from different types of people. Figure 12-19 shows results obtained from male "doves," male students who at the time of the investigation were opposed to United States participation in the Vietnam war. This aspect of the study is unimportant for the example shown here. Figure 12-19 both shows an interesting application of MDS with monotonicity analysis and illustrates some principles. In this case the analysis was based on ratings of similarity on a nine-point scale, which in the analysis were converted to approximate distances. In turn these were subjected to monotonicity analysis according to principles discussed above. The results for the two most salient dimensions are shown in Fig. 12-19. As is illustrated, after the "raw" dimensions are obtained, it is perfectly permissible to translate the origin and rotate the dimensions. This results in an easily visualized, meaningful depiction of dimensions underlying perceived similarities among nations.

Initially, MDS with monotonicity analysis was intended to make only very weak assumptions about the relationship between the proximity indices obtained from subjects and the eventually derived euclidean distances. For this reason frequently it was referred to as nonmetric MDS. However, for two reasons MDS with monotonicity analysis has grown much closer in psychometric theory and in results to MDS based on strong assumptions regarding the nature of distances, such as in vector-product analysis and in distances derived from the law of comparative judgment plus a best-fitting additive constant.

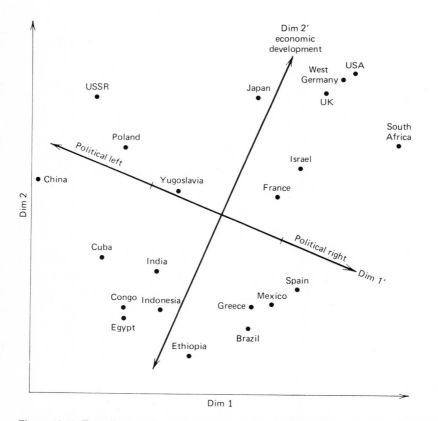

**Figure 12-19** Two dimensions obtained from applying MDS with monotonicity analysis to perceived similarities among nations. (*Adapted from Wish, Deutsch, and Biener in Romney, Shepard, and Nerlove 1972 by permission of the authors and Seminar Press.*)

More recent algorithms for seeking an MDS solution with monotonicity analysis actually begin with a matrix of distances derived from one of the two procedures of MDS described previously, such as in the example from Torgerson that is depicted in Fig. 12-16. Not only does MDS with monotonicity analysis tend, in many cases, to produce results very similar to MDS based on stronger assumptions about the original distances, but there is a growing realization that there are some formal mathematical connections among the methods (see the discussion in MacCallum 1974).

**MDS to rank-order** In addition to the powerful methods of MDS discussed previously that by one approach or another lead to projections of stimuli on coordinate axes in euclidean space, there have been numerous proposals regarding much weaker structures in terms of both what is assumed about the responses of subjects and what is considered permissible in forms of analysis. At root these models are based on representations of proximity relationships in terms of set theory concepts concerning inclusion, exclusion, greater than, less than, union, intersection, ordering, and other primitive logical relations. Such primitive logical systems have vast generality indeed, in that they can be shown to underlie all forms of measurement and all forms of unidimensional and multidimensional scaling (for a comprehensive discussion of this matter, see Chaps. 1 through 4 in Coombs, Dawes, and Tversky 1970). Coombs has been the leader in a careful classification and axiomization of various approaches to measurement and scale development. [See Coombs (1964) for a summarization of theory and research up to 1964; see the article by McClelland and Coombs (1975) for more recent developments and some advanced computer algorithms for nonmetric scaling.]

As will be seen in the previously mentioned references, methods of nonmetric MDS vary in terms of the strength of assumptions and methods of analysis, ranging on the one extreme to MDS which produce coordinates among a number of underlying dimensions expressed as rank-order, but also partaking of some characteristics of euclidean space too. At the other extreme, MDS produces "dimensions" in which only some of the stimuli can be shown in rank-order and the rest are simply tossed together into an undifferentiated group.

Perhaps the nature of nonmetric scaling can best be shown by two illustrations. First, in terms of the underlying logic, the most easily understood would be the case where the proximity matrix could be broken down into two or more (in practice seldom more than two) Guttman scales. Guttman scales for unidimensional scaling were discussed in Chap. 2. What was not mentioned at that point is that it is possible for a collection of responses of subjects to stimuli to be subsumed by more than one underlying Guttman scale. Whereas Guttman scales were discussed in the context of scaling people, the logic and method apply equally well in scaling stimuli. An example would be having each of 30 countries rated on a list of statements ranging from neutral to strongly positive. The subject would simply agree or disagree with each of the statements. Whereas it might be found that the total matrix of data failed to produce a clear Guttman scale, a considerable amount of cut-and-try might break down the statements into two groups, each of which formed a clear Guttman scale. One can imagine that one such scale would concern political attitudes and the other would concern economic attitudes. Then, if two clear Guttman scales were found (and the odds against this are low), it would be meaningful to speak of two nonmetric, rank-order scales being found. The countries simply would be ranked 1, 2, 3, etc., on each of the two scales. There would be no indication of how far apart the countries were on each scale; and since no assumptions are being made about euclidean properties, it would not be possible to state how relatively independent the scales were (without some appended model being supplied). Rather than cut and try in this way, complex computer algorithms have been developed that uncover such rank-order scales, both Guttman scales and rank-ordering based on other principles. These algorithms are discussed throughout the references given earlier in this section on nonmetric MDS, e.g., McClelland and Coombs (1975). Although the results of such nonmetric MDS frequently are not very informative about relations among stimuli, some of the attendant mathematics and computer algorithms are complex indeed.

The second illustration with respect to MDS with rank-order concerns the example given in Table 12-4, which showed the application of vector-products, psychophysical scaling and analysis to dimensions underlying emotion-related words. There, very strong assumptions were made about the nature of human judgments of similarity and about the resulting spatial configuration in the proximity matrix. What is lost in going from a "very" metric model to one based entirely on rank-order can be visualized if one will simply write the rank-orders for the four columns corresponding to the factors in Table 12-4. Actually, in this case we are being kind to the concept of MDS with rank-order, because after the fact we are rank-ordering the projections of stimuli on a coordinate system obtained from a euclidean space with a rational origin. Be that as it may, one can see that the conversion of the loadings in each column into ranks would only throw away much valuable information. Since no euclidean model would be employed, one would not know that the factors were orthogonal nor even legitimately discuss possible relations among factors in such terms. Second, even though the defining three adjectives for each of the three major factors would be in the top three in each case, much information would still be lost. It would not be seen that the three defining adjectives in each case have high loadings in an absolute sense. It would not be seen that on each of the three factors ($A$, $B$, and $C$) the loadings drop off markedly for adjectives not hypothesized to belong to the factor. The tendency for factors $A$ and $C$ to share substantial loadings with one another would not be apparent, and conversely the tendency of factor $B$ to be more independent in that regard would not be apparent. On factor $D$ it would not be apparent in the rank-order that after "pleasant" were ranked 1 and "warm" were ranked 2, the remaining ranks would be for entirely inconsequential loadings. Whereas in considering individual measurement scales one throws away a great deal of information when going from either a ratio scale or interval scale to a rank-order scale, even more information is lost when one sacrifices all metric information other than rank-order in employing MDS. MDS with rank-order mainly is useful for basic theory in psychometrics and as a benchmark for the development of more powerful methods of MDS. It provides very little in the way of usable scaling techniques for empirical researchers in the behavioral sciences.

**Evaluation of multidimensional scaling** Among psychometric specialists, MDS has become a very attractive topic during the last 20 years. Partly this is because potentially the methods are scientifically useful, and partly this is because some behavioral scientists have become rather sophisticated mathematically in developing complex multivariate methods such as MDS. The interest in MDS certainly has been encouraged by the advent and wide availability of high-speed computers. Many of the methods of MDS (e.g., monotonicity analysis) would be totally unusable without excellent computer services.

A now classic book by Torgerson (1958) introduced a wide spectrum of behavioral scientists to some developments in MDS that had been going on among specialists for the prior decade. In a significant pair of papers Shepard (1962a, 1962b) discussed the first successful MDS method based on monotonicity analysis and described the computerized computational approaches. This opened a flood of psychometric research on monotonicity analysis and MDS generally. Coombs and his associates have been the major proponents of nonmetric MDS (see the discussion in Coombs, Dawes, and Tversky 1970) and have made outstanding contributions to the development of MDS for the general case (see discussion in McClelland and Coombs 1975). The literature on MDS is expanding so rapidly that new approaches or modifications of approaches are seen frequently in journals in psychology and education.

If one chose to do so, one certainly could find numerous points on which to criticize MDS as a class of psychometric tools. First, many of the methods are extremely laborious in terms of both the collection of data and the subsequent analyses. With respect to the collection of data, usually one must compare stimuli two or more at a time, as in vector-product analysis of the scaling of emotion-related words and in the use of triads with respect to the interval scaling of distances prior to employing MDS. Whereas in many types of investigations it is only necessary for subjects to rate each stimulus separately, in MDS they must be rated in pairs or triads; thus the number of responses that each subject must make is increased immensely. The time and effort required have limited most demonstrations to less than 20 stimuli, which would not be sufficient for mapping the dimensions underlying the class of stimuli.

A second potential criticism of MDS concerns the types of psychophysical responses required of subjects. Whether people are capable of making some of the kinds of discriminations required in the data-gathering processes might be rightly questioned. For example, whereas the author is enthusiastic about the possibility of employing PS analysis, he is alert to the possibility that the underlying responses of percentage similarity among stimuli may be elusive in general and simply not understandable to subjects with some classes of stimuli. However, the results have been quite encouraging. Even though on a rational basis one might question the ability of subjects to perform some of the complex types of responses requested of them, one tends to find highly reasonable results in many cases, such as was illustrated in Table 12-4.

Third, as with any mathematical model, one can rightly question the assumptions employed in the different models for MDS. For example, one can question the logic of employing Thurstone's law of comparative judgment to obtain interval scales of distances, as illustrated previously. An important counterargument is that various models all tend to produce very much the same results when they are pitted against one another (this is particularly true when the problem is posed with respect to distances in euclidean space).

A fourth criticism is double-barreled, namely that MDS is largely a "play toy" for psychometric specialists which will not be adopted for general use in day-to-day research in the behavioral sciences. To some extent, both aspects of this criticism are valid. Some of the methods of MDS which have been developed do have a Rube Goldberg look about them and seem unnecessarily complex for the actual problems of collecting and analyzing data in empirical science. Also, frequently it is found that supposedly different methods really are quite closely related, if not formally connected mathematically. As for the other aspect of the criticism, it is certainly true that MDS has not been used very widely in the behavioral sciences. For example, one sees some, but not much, use of MDS in substantive articles in social psychology, perception, learning, physiology, and other areas. But the author thinks that this trend is more a "cultural lag" than an indictment of MDS as a class of useful psychometric tools. One sees many instances of research reports in which relatively straightforward methods of MDS would have helped clarify a research issue, but no such method was employed by the author.

In the long run, the worth of MDS will be determined by the extent to which it advances the behavioral sciences. If anything, more methods are available than would be required to handle the substantive problems to which they might be applied. Also, there have been hundreds of convincing demonstrations of sensible results obtained from illustrative problems, such as those given in this chapter. What is needed now is to actually apply MDS quite generally as a tool for deciphering the underlying dimensions for the stimuli which are employed in research. If such dimensions actually are important psychological dimensions, they should, for example, predict (1) amounts of facilitation and inhibition in various types of learning, (2) generalization gradients in studies of classical conditioning, and (3) kinds and amounts of attitude change in social psychology.

## SUGGESTED ADDITIONAL READINGS

Cronbach, L. J., and Gleser, G. C. Assessing similarity between profiles. *Psychological Bulletin,* 1953, *50,* 456–473.

Harris, R. J. *A primer of multivariate statistics.* New York: Academic Press, 1975.

Shepard, R. N. Representation of structure in similarity data: Problems and prospects. *Psychometrika,* 1974, *39,* 373–421.

Shepard, R. N., Romney, A. K., and Nerlove, S. B. (eds.), *Multidimensional scaling:* Vol. 1. *Theory.* New York: Seminar Press, 1972.

Tatsuoka, M. M. *Multivariate analysis.* New York: Wiley, 1971.

Timm, N. H. *Multivariate analysis.* Monterey, Calif.: Brooks/Cole, 1975.

Torgerson, W. S. *Theory and methods of scaling.* New York: Wiley, 1958.

Tryon, R. C., and Bailey, D. E. *Cluster analysis.* New York: McGraw-Hill, 1970.

Van de Geer, J. P. *Introduction to multivariate analysis for the social sciences.* San Francisco: Freeman, 1971.

## FOUR

## THE CONTENT AREAS

# THIRTEEN

## MEASUREMENT OF ABILITIES

Before we discuss human abilities, a definition is in order: *Abilities* concern individual differences in how well people perform different tasks when they try. The definition says that abilities concern "individual differences," but perhaps it would be better to say that psychologists mainly are interested in individual differences in abilities rather than in relatively constant characteristics of people. For example, abilities certainly are required, and important ones, to lift objects from a table, but since individual differences in this regard are not very important, there would be little there to interest psychologists. In the definition, the words *how well* signify that abilities concern performance with respect to specified criteria of success. Examples are correct answers to factual questions, correct solutions of mathematical problems, accuracy of reproducing a geometric figure from memory, and speed of response in a study of reaction time. Before a particular type of ability can be studied, the "how well" of performance must be objectively defined. The definition speaks of performance when people "try," which indicates that abilities can be measured only in those situations where all subjects are motivated to do their best.

Because this book is mainly concerned with measurement theory and methodology rather than with surveying empirical findings, this chapter will be principally concerned with theory and methodology also. To satisfy that concern, however, it will be necessary to summarize some trends in studies of human abilities. Descriptions of particular measurement techniques and detailed accounts of research on human abilities can be found in the Suggested Additional Readings at the end of the chapter.

There is no end to the ways in which people differ from one another in abilities, but only some of these have proved worthy of attention. Most thoroughly investigated have been the so-called intellectual abilities, which are distinguished from the "special" abilities. There is no way to clearly make the distinction, but *intellectual abilities* are usually thought of as those forms of ability that are important for scholarly accomplishment and scientific work. In contrast, *special abilities* are those that are thought to be important for mechanical skills, artistic pursuits, and physical adroitness. Although the evidence to be summarized in this chapter will primarily concern the intellectual abilities, the theories and methods which will be discussed are general to all forms of ability.

## HISTORICAL PERSPECTIVE

It is surprising that systematic studies of human abilities were not undertaken until the second half of the last century. This cannot be explained in any large measure by physical problems of instrumentation, because even today most measures of human ability are paper-and-pencil instruments, and writing equipment has been available for thousands of years. Also, one can find examples of elaborate written examinations being required in schools and for civil service positions in China hundreds of years before the birth of Christ. Partly, the failure to perform systematic studies of individual differences may have been due to the lack of adequate methods of statistical analysis — correlational analysis, factor analysis, and related methods of multivariate analysis. Although many forms of mathematics had reached a high level of development by 1800, it was not until over 100 years later that statistical methods were developed that would be required to construct psychometrically sound tests of ability and to investigate their inner relationships.

Partly, the slowness with which measures of human ability were developed seems to have paralleled the slowness with which people came to consider themselves a proper object of scientific investigation. The attitudes that led to those imbalances in scientific approach may have resulted from religious compunctions about investigating people, or from people taking one another so much for granted that they saw nothing to study in human beings. But whatever the causes, systematic studies of human abilities were late in coming, and they still have a long way to go.

**Darwin** The work of Charles Darwin had an immense influence on all studies of living organisms, including studies in psychology. If there is a "survival of the fittest" among plants and lower animals, there may also be a "survival of the fittest" among people. If it is meaningful to think of plants and lower animals as adjusting to, or coping with, the environment, it may be meaningful to think of much of human activity as serving the same purpose. If individual differences among fish in a species relate to differences in survival rate, individual differences in humans may be similarly important. If differences in survival rate result in slow changes in species of fish over many generations, individual differences in humans may slowly lead to changes in the average characteristics of the species as a whole. If physical characteristics of fish tend to be passed on from generation to generation, some individual differences in people may be influenced by heredity. The theory of evolution caused humans to look more carefully at themselves and helped open up the study of individual differences in human abilities as an important object of scientific inquiry.

**Galton** Particularly important in the history of studies of individual differences was the influence that Darwin had on Francis Galton. Through this influence, Galton became interested in the heritability of human traits. He became convinced that most human traits are inherited, not only such physical characteristics as height and eye color, but also abilities and personality characteristics. Galton founded the *eugenics* movement, whose avowed purpose is the betterment of the human race through selective mating. (The movement is still active today in England.) Being a scientist, he saw that before a program of eugenics was possible, it would be necessary to understand the principles whereby traits are passed from father to son, and before that could be done, it would be necessary to measure human traits.

Galton coined the term *mental test* and made efforts to measure many human attributes. He recognized the need for standardization in testing—that all subjects should be presented the same problems under uniform conditions and instructions. Galton's tests bore little resemblance to those used most widely today. He and his immediate followers in England made much of the philosopher Locke's dictum that all knowledge comes through the senses. Their reasoning was that the person with the most acute "senses" would be the most gifted and knowledgeable. Most of Galton's tests were measures of simple sensory discrimination: the ability to discriminate tones from one another, the acuteness of vision, the ability to differentiate colors, and many other sensory functions.

Galton began the first large-scale testing program at his Anthropometric Laboratory in the South Kensington Museum in 1884. Each visitor was charged threepence for having measurements taken on a variety of physical and sensory tests, including height, weight, breathing power, strength of pull, hearing, sight, and color sense. To analyze the obtained data, Galton made use of statistical methods, and with these he determined averages and measures of dispersion. He particularly needed a measure of association, or correlation, to determine the amount of resemblance between the characteristics of fathers and their sons. For this purpose, he made the first steps in the development of correlational analysis.

Galton's work came at a very important time, because during the last quarter of the nineteenth century, the newly founded field of psychology was concerned almost exclusively with the mental makeup of the typical person, and there was very little interest in individual differences. Galton's work made it obvious that the new field of psychology could not ignore individual differences. The study of individual differences has been an important activity in psychology since that time, particularly in the United States.

**Pearson** Galton supported a younger colleague, Karl Pearson, in the development of statistical methods for the study of individual differences. Pearson was the genius in mathematical statistics that Galton was in studies of individual differences. He derived the PM correlation coefficient, multiple correlation, and partial correlation, and he laid the groundwork for factor analysis and other methods of multivariate analysis. Once Galton pointed to a need for mathematical methods to deal with the measurement of human abilities, it did not take Pearson long to develop them.

**Binet** During the last quarter of the nineteenth century, along with his many other interests in psychology, Alfred Binet became interested in individual differences in human ability. This interest may have been fostered by his work with hypnotism, in which there had been much speculation about individual differences in hypnotizability. Also, his interest probably was fostered by the developing field of psychiatry in France at the time, with which he had been associated. By their nature, psychiatry and clinical psychology are concerned with individual differences, and it is only to be expected that persons in those fields would foster studies of human abilities and personality attributes.

Binet's early work on human abilities resembled the work of Galton in that he worked mainly with simple variables of sensory discrimination and physical attributes. He even studied palmistry as a possible source of measures of abilities. Binet's work on abilities took a practical turn in the opening years of the twentieth century, when he was commissioned by the French government to study mental deficiency in French schools. The French government had become alarmed by the number of children who were apparently unable to perform normal schoolwork, and some means was needed for distinguishing those children who could profit from remedial instruction from those who lacked the capacity to advance in school. Faced with this practical problem, Binet did what most other psychologists would have done in the circumstances: he turned from investigating the "elements" of human ability to investigating the use of a global measure of overall intellectual ability, or intelligence.

Binet, working in collaboration with Théodore Simon, completed his first test in 1905. It consisted of a list of 30 problems concerning the child's ability to understand and reason with the objects in the cultural environment. The problems ranged in difficulty from those that could be solved by very young children to those that would be difficult for the average adult. Five of the problems were as follows:

1. Touch head, nose, ear, cap, key, and string.
2. Judge which of two lines is longer.
3. Repeat immediately three digits read by the examiner.
4. Define house, horse, fork, and mamma.
5. Repeat a sentence of 15 words after a single hearing.

The list of problems was tried on about 50 children, and provisional norms were established. Obviously the test was only a rough beginning to the measurement of intelligence, but it constituted a very important first step. A revision of the test was made in 1908, in which items were arranged in terms of age levels, with a group of items representing average intelligence for each age. The highest age level at which a child could perform adequately was called *mental age*. Later, William Stern suggested that this be divided by chronological age for each child, which (when multiplied by 100) is the IQ as it has come to be known.

It is hard to overstate Binet's influence on later investigations of human abilities. The measurement of intelligence was then, and still is, of immense practical importance. The thought that intelligence could be measured, even if only approximately, stirred many investigators to develop measures of intelligence and to use such measures in research. The scene soon shifted to America, where there were numerous translations and modifications of the Binet tests. The important point, however, is that all subsequent work on the measurement of intelligence has been modeled after Binet's work, to the extent that many of the items on modern tests of intelligence are very similar to ones that Binet used.

The strong influence that Binet's tests had on subsequent efforts to measure intelligence was, in one sense, very good, but in another sense it might have worked a harm. Binet's tests concerned the end products of intelligence —the mastery of language, reasoning, and the assimilation of facts. This is where one naturally would look for evidence of differences in overall intellectual ability. By weaving a measuring instrument from the global end products of intellectual functioning, one has a high probability of obtaining a valid measure. The type of test developed by Binet obviously has a rather high level of construct validity for the construct of intelligence. The influence of his tests in this regard was very good, because it rapidly led to the development of measures of intelligence with real practical importance.

Binet's influence may have worked a harm in that subsequent studies along the same lines as his work have not taught us much about the *nature* of human intellect. It is one thing to be able to measure an attribute and quite another to understand it. In turning away from the elements of intellect to work with global end products, Binet certainly was on the right course for the development of valid measures of intelligence. If one is interested only in measurement, rather than in understanding, one should always turn to global end products rather than try to pick apart an attribute in terms of simple functions. For example, if one wanted to measure the quality of different wines, the safest approach would be to have judgments made by professional wine tasters. Such judgments probably would be valid in the sense that they would predict what wines people would like and what they would purchase, but they would tell us nothing about how grapes should be grown or how wine should be made.

**Applied psychology** The work of Binet had a strong influence on applied psychology, particularly in the United States. Tests of the type developed by Binet have been exceedingly useful in schools, psychological clinics, the armed forces, and industry. There is hardly anyone today who has not taken an intelligence test of some kind, and the lives of many people have been strongly influenced by decisions based in large part on the results of such tests, e.g., a child who is placed in a special school for retardates and a man who is allowed to undertake officer training in the armed forces.

Because tests of the Binet type have worked so well in applied settings, in turn applied psychology has had a very strong influence on concepts of human abilities and on the research into human abilities. This has been particularly true during the two great wars of this century, in which many psychologists were called to develop large-scale testing programs for many purposes in the selection of men, the measurement of progress in programs of training, and the assignment of men to sundry duties.

It would be silly to suggest that it is wrong for measures of human ability to have practical importance or that applied concerns should not influence the directions of research on human abilities. This applied influence, however, has probably had some adverse effects on the study of human abilities. There has been too much concern with predictive validity, whereas, as was mentioned previously, the major concern in most basic research in psychology is the explication of constructs. For example, in the use of multiple regression to predict a criterion, the applied psychologist usually loses interest in those measures that fail to add to predictive validity, but such measures might be of great importance in basic research on the nature of human abilities. Also, partly because of the applied influence, there has been too little theory about human abilities and too much "shotgun empiricism." Even worse, many studies of human abilities have been largely divorced from experimental psychology, where we probably should go to seek interesting new measures of differences in abilities and to investigate the importance of different factors of intellect. Of course, the applied psychologists cannot wait while the basic researcher wanders through the crannies of natural phenomena; on the other hand, the basic researcher should not be limited by the scope of present practical concerns or dominated by the concepts and procedures relating to applied efforts.

One of the important influences of applied psychology on the study of human abilities has been in terms of money. Much of the research support for studies of human abilities has come from government agencies, industry, and commercial distributors of tests. Apparently there still are not a lot of grant funds from government agencies and philanthropic organizations being given for basic research on human abilities, and this being so, it is only natural for researchers in this area to seek funds from applied enterprises. In consequence, research on human abilities, particularly in this country, has been strongly influenced by the needs and outlooks of applied psychology. For the sake of applied psychology, that is good, but for the sake of promoting the science of psychology, one would hope to see more basic research on human abilities and a closer tie with psychological theories and with experimental psychology.

**The British factorists** After having followed the threads of the Binet influence up through modern applied psychology, we will return to Galton's followers in England. There was a remarkable parallel during the first several years of this century between the work of Binet in France and the work of Charles Spearman in England. (The work of Spearman is summarized in his book *The Abilities of Man,* 1927.) Like Binet, Spearman was concerned with the nature of human abilities, but his was a much more scholarly approach based on psychological theories concerning the nature of abilities and buttressed by mathematical models for studying human abilities. Implicit in Binet's efforts to measure intelligence was the assumption that either there is only one factor of intelligence or intelligence is dominated by one factor. Spearman asserted the presence of a general factor as a hypothesis to be tested. He developed the mathematical criteria for the presence of a general factor in a matrix of correlations among tests (discussed in Chap. 10) and gathered data to test the hypothesis of a general factor.

In his early work, Spearman concluded that individual differences in all tests of ability can be accounted for by two factors: a general factor $G$ and a specific factor for each test. Later Spearman had to recognize that $G$ was not sufficient to explain the correlations among all tests of ability. It became obvious that more than one factor would be required to explain correlations among tests of ability. Now that we have "splintered" human abilities into numerous factors, we have come to realize that much, but far from all, of the common variance among tests of abilities can be explained by a general factor.

Although, in a sense, the theories and findings of Spearman tended to support the type of test developed by Binet, Spearman proposed a more refined method for measuring $G$. First, it would be necessary to determine those tasks which, rather than being dominated by specific factors, actually measure $G$; second, to measure $G$ would require a proper weighing of each intellectual task. Spearman was critical of Binet's practice of assembling a hodgepodge of problems without first testing for the presence of a general factor or without properly weighing the problems in terms of their loadings on the general factor. Since, however, Spearman was concerned more with basic research on human abilities than with the development of practical measures, he developed no tests with the wide appeal of the Binet measures of intelligence.

Spearman's work continues to be important for two major reasons. First, while developing mathematical models for studying $G$, he laid the foundation for factor analysis. He could see that in the end, questions regarding the generality of intelligence rested on the nature of correlations among tests of ability. Once he showed how such correlations could be studied with respect to a general factor, it encouraged others to extend the logic to methods for investigating any number of factors among tests.

The second major importance of Spearman's work is that, in contrast to the tradition of applied work that followed from Binet's tests, it established a scholarly tradition in the investigation of human abilities. Spearman was concerned much more with *understanding* human abilities than with just measuring them. Spearman had many interesting theories about $G$, its biological basis, the influence of culture, the interaction of $G$ with manifestations of abilities in daily life, and the relations of $G$ to speed, fatigue, and other variables.

From 1930 until recent years, there was a tendency, particularly in this country, to dismiss Spearman as having been "wrong" and to forget the achievements of the man and the potency of his ideas. The statistical evidence is that he really was not entirely wrong about the importance, if not omnipotence, of a general factor. Also, Spearman's theories about human abilities still are stimulating, and they should provide a lesson to some of those modern factorists who are less concerned with a real psychology of human abilities than with obtaining more and more factors.

Spearman's influence is still strong among British psychologists. They no longer cling to Spearman's $G$ as the sole factor of intellect, but they recognize the presence of a general factor in addition to a number of group factors. Perhaps because of Spearman's influence, they are reluctant to accept all the factors found by American psychologists as being important dimensions of intellect. Also, in Spearman's tradition, British psychologists have tried to make sense of the structure of human abilities by proposing "factor hierarchies," a matter which will be discussed later in this chapter. Although picking names tends to slight the numerous unmentioned British psychologists that have made major contributions to the study of human abilities, the names that stand out are Godfrey Thomson, Cyril Burt, and Phillip Vernon.

## PIONEERING RESEARCH BY THE THURSTONES

Just as Binet's ideas about the testing of intelligence were rapidly imported to the United States, Spearman's ideas were also; but psychologists in this country were concerned not so much with Spearman's theories of human abilities as with his methods of factor analysis. During the 1920s and 1930s, American psychologists pushed mathematical methods of factor analysis far ahead of those developed by Spearman. Prominent in this work were T. L. Kelley and K. J. Holzinger. Subsequently, L. L. Thurstone did so much to develop mathematical methods of factor analysis and to explore human abilities with them that it is fair to say that he is the father of the American school of factorists.

The American school of factorists has, at least until recent years, been typified by a rough-and-ready bedrock empiricism. There has not been nearly enough theory, but there has been a great deal of technical elegance in the measurement of human abilities and in the mathematical analysis of correlations among them. Later it will be shown how this technical elegance has produced factors to the point of confusion, but before that stage in the history of the study of human abilities is discussed, let us see what the scene was like in the early 1940s when psychologists were learning about Thurstone's investigations of the "primary mental abilities."

Thurstone was an engineer before he was a psychologist, and as an engineer he worked for a time with Thomas Edison. Perhaps genius is infectious, because Thurstone became an Edison in the field of psychology. Although he is best known for studies of human abilities, particularly for his contributions to factor analysis, his inventive mind ranged over studies of learning, perception, personality, and other topics. For many years his Psychometric Laboratory at the University of Chicago was the world center for studies of human abilities, and many of the persons who are prominent today in psychometric work studied there with him. Thurstone made not only outstanding contributions to the theory and methodology of individual differences, but also made the first large-scale onslaughts on the empirical problems.

Up until about 1930, the major argument in studies of human ability concerned whether or not Spearman was correct about the omnipresence of $G$. Thurstone, as he often stated it, turned the question around and asked *how many* and *what kinds* of factors are needed to account for the observed correlations among tests of ability. To answer these questions, Thurstone made major improvements in existing methods of factor analysis and gathered data on a scale that was unheard of in that day.

Before Thurstone's studies of human ability, most studies had been based on 6 to 20 tests, and frequently the number of subjects was too small to obtain stable results. In one major analysis, Thurstone employed 60 tests, most of which had to be developed for the purpose. Only those who have participated in such studies can appreciate the labor that is involved in constructing instruments, administering them to subjects, and analyzing the data. Inherent in such studies is the great difficulty of administering all tests to all subjects. If a subject takes 59 tests but, for some reason, is unavailable to take the 60th test, none of the subject's scores can be used in a factor analysis. Over 1,100 school children were given all tests in one of the major studies by Thurstone and his wife. When Thurstone performed his major studies of human abilities, only the most rudimentary of computational equipment was available. Consequently it was an immense and highly time-consuming job to compute all possible correlations among tests, employ methods of condensation (the centroid method being used most frequently for that purpose), and rotate the factors. Some of the Thurstones' major findings (reported in Thurstone 1941) are summarized in the following quote:

> Several of the primary factors are not yet sufficiently clear as regards psychological interpretation to justify an attempt to appraise them generally among school children. The primary fac-

tors that do seem to be clear enough for such purposes are the following: Verbal Comprehension $V$, Fluency $W$, Number $N$, Space $S$, Rote Memory $M$, and Induction or Reasoning $R$. The factors which in several studies are not yet sufficiently clear for general application are the Perceptual factor $P$ and the Deductive factor $D$.

## SOME OF THE MAJOR FACTORS

Most of the factors that were found in the sequence of analyses by the Thurstones have proved to be important both in basic research on human abilities and in many types of applied work with tests. Even numerous factors that were only suggested by their findings have been well documented in subsequent investigations. Below will be described some of the most important factors of human ability—important in ways that will be discussed subsequently. Most of them either were found directly in the work of the Thurstones or were suggested by their research.

**Verbal factors** Some of the most important factors concern abilities relating to the understanding and use of written and spoken language. As is true of the factors in most subdomains of human abilities, verbal factors can be broken down into four or more separable factors. Two of these have proved to be more important by far than any others. They are *verbal comprehension* and *verbal fluency*, which will be discussed in turn.

The most important verbal factor concerns the ability to understand written and spoken language. The factor extends to what we call reading skill in elementary schools and more generally to the ability to deal with written material. Although the factor extends far beyond sheer vocabulary, a vocabulary test provides one good measure of verbal comprehension.

*Typical items:*

1. Which one of the following words means most nearly the same as salutation?
   a. Offering
   b. Greeting
   c. Discussion
   d. Appeasement

2. Which one of the following words is most nearly the opposite of languid?
   a. Unemotional
   b. Sad
   c. Energetic
   d. Healthy

In contrast to verbal comprehension, verbal fluency concerns the ability to produce words and sentences rapidly. It can be thought of as the rate-of-production aspect of verbal ability in contrast to verbal comprehension, which concerns the depth of understanding of verbal material.

*Typical items:*

1. Write as many names of foods as you can in the next 2 minutes.

 

_____     _____     _____

_____     _____     _____

_____     _____     _____

2. In each of the following rows write three words that mean almost the same as the given word:

Small     _____     _____     _____

Helpful     _____     _____     _____

Kind     _____     _____     _____

Verbal comprehension comes into play when rather complex words, sentences, and paragraphs are being dealt with. Verbal fluency comes into play when the verbal material is relatively simple and when fluidity of expression is at issue. The two types of abilities are somewhat correlated. Correlations of about .40 or .50 are typically found between the tests used to measure verbal comprehension and verbal fluency. On the other hand, the two types of abilities are far from perfectly correlated. Children can understand what they read very well but have great difficulty in explaining it because of a lack of verbal fluency. On the other hand, talkative children who produce a torrent of words in ordinary conversation do not always have the depth of comprehension to match. People are sometimes fooled by children who are quite facile in expression but who do rather poorly when they are required to read and understand material or to analyze poetry or essays.

**Numerical facility** One very clear factor of numerical facility has been found in many different studies. It concerns the speed and accuracy of solving arithmetic problems of all kinds—addition, subtraction, multiplication, division, finding square roots, and others.

*Typical items:*

$$\begin{array}{r} 246 \\ +943 \\ \hline \end{array} \qquad \begin{array}{r} 8,754 \\ -381 \\ \hline \end{array} \qquad 16 \times 22 = \underline{\hspace{1cm}} \qquad 284/4 = \underline{\hspace{1cm}}$$

In addition to items that obviously concern arithmetic computations, the factor also extends to almost any type of task in which quantitative operations are involved, such as the following items:

1. Which one of the following numbers is closest to 8.2?
   - *a.* 8.1
   - *b.* 8.3
   - *c.* 8.18
   - *d.* 8.23
2. Which one of the following numbers is most nearly the same as the square root of 15?
   - *a.* 225
   - *b.* 4
   - *c.* 5
   - *d.* 1.5
3. Which one of the following would be the largest *positive* amount?
   - *a.* $-10 \times -10$
   - *b.* $-5 \times -5$
   - *c.* $10 \times -10$
   - *a.* $9 \times 9$

It should be clearly understood that not all problems containing numbers measure numerical facility. Numbers also appear in many of the reasoning tests, which will be discussed in the next section, but mainly such problems do not concern numerical facility. The numerical facility factor comes into play when some complex (for the age group) numerical solutions must be obtained. If the numbers involved are very simple and are included only as a way of providing a useful method of expressing the solution to a problem, numerical facility as such may be very unimportant. This distinction will be made clearer in the discussion of reasoning factors.

Tests of numerical facility usually show moderate correlations (about .40) with measures of verbal ability. As was mentioned previously, all measures of human ability tend to correlate positively with one another, but numerical facility has a far from perfect relationship with other factors of ability. Numerical facility is not the same as mathematical reasoning, which is involved in simple algebraic problems. Although algebraic problems require some numerical computations, usually these are relatively simple. Instead, algebraic problems relate more prominently to the reasoning factors, which will be discussed below. The fact that children are very good in number skills in the elementary grades does not mean that they are likely to be good later in mathematical subject matter, such as algebra, geometry, and trigonometry.

**Reasoning factors** Reasoning is a complex domain in which the abilities involved tend to blend in different ways in different tests, making it hard to separate the reasoning factors from one another and to find good measures of any of them. The most clearly determined factors are discussed below.

The *general reasoning factor* is found most frequently in different studies of the factors underlying reasoning tests. It concerns the ability to invent solutions to many different types of problems. Arithmetical reasoning problems are most characteristic of the factor.

*Typical items:*

1. If a machine produces bolts at the rate of two each 15 minutes, how many bolts does the machine produce in 3 hours?
2. How would you get exactly 7 quarts of water from a stream if you had one 5-quart container and one 3-quart container?

As was mentioned previously, even though such simple algebraic problems involve numbers, the main ability being measured is not that of numerical computation. In order to solve the problems, the student must invent a solution and grasp some principle by which each can be solved.

The general reasoning factor also appears in items concerning series completion, in which the subject is required to supply the next entry in a patterned series of letters or digits. Two examples are as follows:

zzxxyyw _____

2132435465 _____

There is an element of discovery in all the tests that measure the factor of general reasoning—the discovery of some principle whereby a correct solution is obtained.

**Deduction** The *deductive reasoning factor* is concerned with the drawing of conclusions. In this type of reasoning there is nothing in particular to be discovered or invented; the ability concerns evaluating the implications of an argument.

*Typical items:*

1. John is younger than Fred. Bill is older than Fred. Therefore,

   Bill is _____ than John.

2. A student has 10 marbles. No one else in the class has 10 marbles. This means that:
   *a.* No one else in the class has marbles.

*b.* All the other students have fewer than 10 marbles.
*c.* Some of the students have fewer than 10 marbles.
*d.* Some of the students have more than 10 marbles.
*e.* Only one student has exactly 10 marbles.

Whereas the factor of general reasoning is represented by a very wide variety of items concerning the solution of problems, the deductive factor is more narrowly concerned with only those items pertaining to logical syllogisms.

**Seeing relationships** A third factor of reasoning involves the ability to see the relationship between two things or ideas and to use the relationship to find other things or ideas. This factor is best represented by verbal analogies and design analogies.

*Typical item:*

1. *Ship* is to *sail* as *automobile* is to
   *a.* Ship
   *b.* Seat
   *c.* Motor
   *d.* Wind
   *e.* Driver

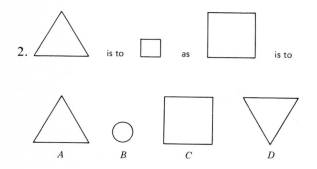

Some items concerning reasoning abilities represent a blend of the factor of seeing relationships and the factor of general reasoning. This is the case, for example, with the series-completion items illustrated previously.

**Memory factors** As is true of the other areas of human ability that we have discussed, there is more than one type of memory. Some of the better established factors of memory are discussed as follows. *Rote memory* is the best established factor of memory. It concerns the ability to remember simple associations where meaning is of little or no importance.

*Typical item:*

The person is given a list of names, each of which is paired with a number. A minute or so is given to memorize which number goes with which name. Then the person is told to turn the page. The next page contains the list of names without the numbers. The person is instructed to write the proper numbers next to the names. Other items which concern rote memory are of the same general kind, involving, for example, pairing colors with words, initials with last names, and letters with geometric forms.

There is substantial evidence to indicate the existence of a *meaningful-memory factor.* The factor of meaningful memory appears when the individual is requested to memorize sentences, meaningfully related words, and lines of poetry.

*Typical items:*

1. The individual is asked to read and to try to remember a list of sentences like the following:

   John repaired the wagon by welding the broken axle.

   The list of sentences is taken away, and then the student is given the same sentences with one or more of the words deleted from each, like the following:

   John repaired the wagon by welding the broken _____ .

2. The student is shown a list of meaningfully related pairs of words such as the following:

   dog–bark
   shoe–leather
   hard–candy
   small–box

   The list is taken away, and the student is presented with only one member of each pair as follows:

   dog–_____        hard–_____

   shoe–_____        small–_____

There is evidence for several other memory factors. A number of investigators have reported a memory span factor concerning the ability to recall perfectly for immediate reproduction a series of unrelated items. A typical item would be to read a series of 5 to 12 digits and ask the student to give the digits back in their exact order. There is some evidence for a visual memory factor in which the ability to grasp the relationships within a picture or pattern is important. A typical item would consist of showing an individual a landscape picture and asking the person to remember the details. Then the picture would be taken away, and the student would be asked questions like "How many sheep were in the picture?" "What was the boy handing to the man?" and "Where was the swing located?" The visual memory factor might be related to the ability to remember faces and witnessed events.

**Spatial factors** Most frequently encountered in factor-analysis investigations is the *spatial orientation* factor. This factor concerns the ability to detect accurately the spatial arrangement of objects with respect to one's own body. The factor would be necessary in deciphering pictures taken from a maneuvering airplane. If the plane is simultaneously turning and climbing, the landscape looks very different from the normal view. The individual who can accurately detect what maneuver the airplane is going through from looking at only a picture of the landscape from that vantage point has good spatial orientation. The factor appears most prominently when the spatial problems are presented under "speeded" conditions.

*Typical items:*

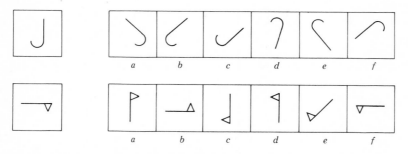

Every alternative that could be obtained by a rotation of the first figure is to be marked.

(From *Primary Mental Abilities*—Ages 11 to 17, Manual. © 1958, Thelma Gwinn Thurstone. Reprinted by permission of the publisher, Science Research Associates, Inc.)

The second most frequently found spatial factor is that of *spatial visualization*. It is present when the individual is required to imagine or *visualize* how an object would look if its spatial position were changed. Although there is good statistical support for both of these factors, it has proved somewhat difficult to interpret the difference in underlying processes. (For this reason, frequently items pertaining to the two factors are combined into one overall test of spatial

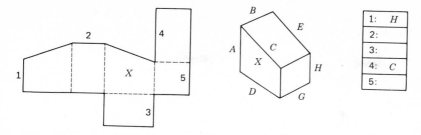

**Figure 13-1** Sample item from the Surface Development Test. The subject's task is to visualize how a piece of paper will be folded to make an object. The subject is asked to indicate which lettered edge of the object on the right corresponds to each numbered edge of the piece of paper at the left. *(From* Surface Development Test. *Copyright © 1962 by Educational Testing Service. Reproduced by permission.)*

relations.) Spatial orientation seems to require either an actual or an imagined adjustment of one's own body. In spatial visualization the individual cannot solve the problem by a bodily adjustment; instead the individual must conceive of how an object would look if its spatial position were markedly changed. In contrast to spatial orientation, spatial visualization is best tested under relatively "unspeeded" conditions.

*Typical item:*

The person is shown a folded piece of paper with a number of holes punched in it. The person is asked to choose from a number of unfolded pieces of paper the one that would be the same as the first.

Another type of item concerning spatial visualization is shown in Fig. 13-1.

**Perceptual factors** A number of factors have been found which concern the ability to detect visual patterns and to see relationships within and between patterns. Some of these factors are apparently of only limited importance, such as the ability to judge certain types of illusions. Several of the more important factors will be described.

The factor that has been found most frequently in the perceptual domain is that of *perceptual speed*. This factor concerns the rapid recognition of perceptual details and particularly the recognition of similarities and differences between visual patterns.

*Typical items:*

1. The person is shown a complex geometric form and is asked to choose from a number of other forms the one that is the same as the first.

2. The person is told to make a check mark by each pair of letter groupings if they are identical and to make no mark beside groups that are different.

x′#·Iq _____ X′#·IQ

a&30(k _____ a&3(oK

—ro–/w _____ —ro–/w

(Fifty to several hundred pairs would be used, depending on the time allowed.)

A second factor that is found frequently is *perceptual closure*. This factor concerns the perception of objects from limited cues. The word *closure* means a sudden awareness of an obscure object or relationship. Perceptual speed requires only the recognition of a perceptual form. Perceptual closure requires the "putting together" of a perceptual form when only part of it is presented.

*Typical items:*

In the items on the left, the individual is required to recognize the incomplete words; in the items on the right, the number or letter that is partially outlined.

There is evidence for a *flexibility-of-closure factor* in problems which require the subject to detect a perceptual pattern that is embedded in a distracting or competing pattern. This factor is found in such items as the hidden-picture games that are printed in newspapers and some children's magazines. For example, a picture that looks like a normal landscape at first glance is found, after careful scrutiny, to contain a number of faces hidden in the trees and rocks. In order to see the faces, it is necessary to resist or "break down" the perception of the object in which the faces are embedded.

## PRESENT OUTLOOKS ON STUDIES OF HUMAN ABILITIES

Since the monumental work by the Thurstones, factor analysis studies of human abilities have pushed far ahead. In the early 1940s, many psychol-

Typical items:

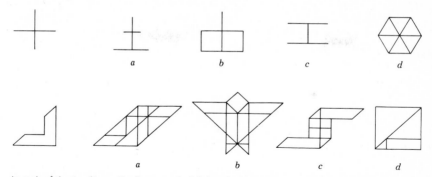

In each of the two items, the figure on the left is embedded in one or more of the four alternative figures on the right.

(These items were reproduced by permission of Science Research Associates, Inc.)

ogists were developing tests for the armed forces. Tests were developed for so many special types of aptitudes and with respect to so many types of training programs that excellent opportunities were provided to extend what was known about factors of human ability. Up through 1950, it could be reported that there were over 40 known factors of ability. [These are described in detail by French (1951).] This was a far cry from the conception of human abilities originally held by Spearman, and it suggested that the Binet type of test was based on very false assumptions about the generality of intellect.

The number of factors of intellect has continued to grow since the survey by French, and now one could argue that there are between 50 and 100 factors, depending on how cautiously one interpreted the evidence. These are discussed in detail in Guilford (1967) and Guilford and Hoepfner (1971). Whereas the purpose of employing factor analysis was to provide an understanding of the nature of human abilities, the results of factor-analysis studies were, in a sense, "too plentiful." Spearman hoped to show that only one factor of intellect was important, and one gathers that the Thurstones hoped to show that no more than about 10 would be required to cover the important ground of human intellect. Probably no one wanted to find over 50 factors, because if so many are found, what is one to do with them? Is human intellect really splintered into so many separate dimensions?

In the search for factors, gradually it became apparent that one can artifactually force factors to occur in a number of ways. One way to do this is to compose several tests that are highly similar in terms of operations and materials. An example is as follows. On the first test, the subject is presented with a page of randomized alphabetical letters and told to circle as many a's as possible in 60 seconds. On the next test, the subject is presented with another page of randomized letters and told to circle b's; then on the third test, the subject is told to circle c's. The three tests will correlate well with one another, and the correlations among them cannot be accounted for by factors relating to other types of tests. Then, from a purely mathematical point of view, it must be admitted that the three tests define a factor; but is a factor that is so narrowly defined likely to be of any importance?

## JUDGING THE IMPORTANCE OF FACTORS OF ABILITY

Aside from the point that many of the supposed factors that have been found would be better classed as *artifactors* (to coin a word), it is becoming increasingly clear that, to prevent chaos in the accumulation of factors, consideration must be given to the *importance* of factors. Since it is now quite obvious that "laboratory" tests can be constructed so as to produce an almost endless array of factors, some means must be devised for separating the wheat from the chaff. How to determine the importance of factors will be the major issue of discussion in the remainder of the chapter.The principles that will be discussed pertain to factors in all domains of individual differences as well as to human intellectual abilities, such as social traits, values, interests, and other types of traits that will be discussed in subsequent chapters.

**Mathematical importance of factors** One way in which a factor can be important is in its relations to mathematical models for human abilities. For example, to the extent that a general factor is found in tests of human ability, that factor is important because it goes a long way in explaining correlations among all tests of ability. Similarly, a factor is mathematically important if it keeps cropping up in very different methods of applying factor analysis. However, the mathematical importance of a factor depends to some extent on the nature of the mathematical model being used. Thus a general factor would be important in a model that concerns a general factor and group factors, but it would not be important, or would be a downright nuisance, in other models. A later section will consider some of the methods that have been proposed for explaining human abilities.

**Content generality of factors** A second way in which a factor can be judged important is with respect to the range of test materials involved. Previously it was described how an "artifactor" could be produced by the development of three almost identical tests (the circling of alphabetical letters). Although there are no concrete standards by which one can gauge the relative breadth of content covered by factors, some of the factors appearing in the literature appear to relate to very narrow domains of content. For example, French (1951) reports a factor of *length estimation*, for which some of the tests with highest loadings concern (1) estimating length with a meter stick, (2) estimating length with a meter stick after practice, (3) selecting the shorter of straight lines radiating from a point, and (4) selecting the shortest crooked line. This may prove to be an important factor, but from the narrowness of its content, one would suspect that it is not. There would be more intuitive support for the factor if it extended to judgments of area and volume and it related to both regular and irregular figures.

At the other extreme of content generality is the *verbal comprehension factor* which relates to almost any type of test that directly or indirectly concerns the understanding of words and connected discourse. That factor relates to so many types of intellectual tasks that sometimes there is a problem in reducing its effects in tests that are intended to measure other factors, e.g., because of the wording of written or oral instructions and because of the verbal material in test items.

There is no way to specify the ideal level of generality for a factor. At the upper extreme, one could argue that a factor is not sufficiently analytic; i.e., it tends to hide subdimensions of abilities in a particular area. This has often been said about the factor of verbal comprehension, and consequently efforts have been made to break down this factor into several correlated factors. As was mentioned previously, the ideal generality of a factor depends in part on the mathematical model which is used to guide research on human abilities. At the lower extreme of content generality, however, it is doubtful that some of the highly specialized factors that have been reported will ever prove to be of general importance. Such is the case with the factor of *length estimation*. That factor might be important only for predicting success on a job concerned purely with the estimation of the length of things, and if there is such a job, it probably is so unimportant in the total enterprise that success in it would not be worth the labors of employing psychological tests. Also, aside from the possible use of tests as predictor instruments, it is doubtful that such a narrowly defined factor would prove to be important in the other ways discussed in this chapter. One gets the impression that this is true of many of the factors which have been reported: they are so narrowly defined in item content that, unless they can be shown to be somewhat more general in that regard, they have little likelihood of becoming important.

In a sense, one can argue that a factor is important partly to the extent that it produces some surprises. If, for example, one tells a colleague that a factor of length estimation has been found among half a dozen tests all obviously related to the same thing, one is likely to be met with a yawn. (Of course, in some instances the yawn is undeserved, because what frequently appear to be "obviously" similar tasks fail to correlate well with one another.) At the other extreme of surprise value are some of the perceptual and spatial factors, where moderate-sized loadings are found for some tests that do not obviously concern either perception or spatial relations. An example is the *gestalt flexibility factor* (French 1951), which primarily concerns the ability to detect simple geometric configurations within complex configurations. The surprise value of the factor comes in the fact that a *motor* test (two-handed coordination) has a high loading. Anyone who is interested in the nature of human abilities would not yawn upon learning that. Such surprises stimulate us to think about the more basic factors of ability that underlie test materials that superficially are so different.

**Importance in prediction** One obvious way in which a factor can be important is in the prediction of significant criterion variables, such as success in pilot training, grades in college, and improvement in psychotherapy. As was mentioned previously, in a sense it is unfortunate that so much of the effort to understand human abilities has hinged on applied concerns. To some extent this has caused us to ignore factors that may be very important for understanding the nature of human abilities but have little predictive validity for the criteria most frequently investigated. However, whether in basic research or in applied settings, it is very comforting to find that a newly found factor of ability or personality predicts *something* of importance.

In spite of the many potential uses for factors of ability in predicting performance in real-life situations, most of the uses have been with respect to either success in school at all levels or success in specific occupations. The most outstanding results have been with respect to the former, where it has been found that success in many different types of school settings is reasonably well predicted by factors of verbal comprehension, reasoning, numerical computation, and some of the perceptual and spatial factors; but beyond those, other factors tend to have little predictive validity. The validity of factors of human ability for predicting success in particular occupations depends considerably on the occupation. Much more success has been had with high-level occupations (e.g., engineers) than with low-level ones (e.g., truck drivers).

Although it is doubtful that studies of predictive validity alone will do all that one requires to gain an understanding of the importance of different factors of human ability, there are ways in which such studies could help. For example, it would be informative to learn more about how factors of ability relate to particular topics in college and to subparts of those topics. It would be instructive to learn more about how factors of verbal ability relate to the mastery of foreign languages, not only to overall grades in learning languages, but also to the rate of mastering various aspects of the language, e.g., grammar as opposed to vocabulary.

**Ecological importance of factors** Eventually, what will be needed for an understanding of the importance of factors in daily life is a correlation of those factors with individual differences manifested in real-life situations. Presently we do not know to what extent our factors of human ability extend beyond the laboratory to the things that people do every day. Are those factors of any importance for making change on a bus, recalling phone numbers, or giving a talk to the PTA? Of course, it is not possible to measure performance in a multitude of real-life situations, but at least it would be possible to conduct informal surveys of what people do in daily life. Persons who are familiar with the known facts of human ability could literally follow people around and watch the things that they do, and any task that possibly concerned one of the known factors could be noted. Also it would be useful to list important tasks that apparently do not relate to any known factors of ability. Gradually, in this way, a classification scheme could be developed for areas in real life that need to be explained by factors of ability, and studies could be made of the correlations between laboratory tests and daily behavior. It may sound rather extreme to talk of such developments now, but issues relating to human abilities are sufficiently important to merit the efforts. In this process, we certainly will find much "chaff" among presently known factors of human abilities, but the remaining "wheat" will stimulate further basic investigations.

**Importance for psychological constructs** More than anything else, factors need to prove their importance for controlled experiments in general psychology. There has always been a great deal of talk about the need to consider measures of individual differences in controlled experiments, but not much has been done about it. One can see numerous parallels between factors of human ability and processes that are investigated in controlled experiments. For example, one would expect to find individual differences in some of the perceptual factors to correlate with individual differences in various aspects of tachistoscopic recognition experiments. As another example, one would expect to find relations between verbal factors, memory factors, and various aspects of studies on verbal learning and verbal behavior. Interesting hypotheses can be generated about relations between various factors of ability and the functions mediated by different parts of the brain. It would be important to investigate the variance explained by factors of ability not only in highly controlled experiments but also in observational studies, such as in data collected regarding social relationships in play activity of children and in many types of investigations of personality and clinical psychology where problems of experimental control and measurement frequently are difficult.

A suggestion by Ferguson (1954) illustrates the many possible links between factors of human ability and basic processes in controlled experiments. He suggested that transfer of training in experiments on learning is governed by factors of human ability. It is well known that practice in one type of learning situation may facilitate learning in new situations, but there has been no way of predicting the amounts and kinds of transfer that would occur. Ferguson's suggestion is that if a person is given training with respect to one type of problem relating to a particular factor of ability, there will be positive transfer to other types of problems relating to the same factor. For example, if an individual is given training with respect to one task concerning a particular factor of reasoning, that might transfer somewhat to different-appearing tasks concerning the same factor. This suggestion offers the possibility of investigating many links between the results of controlled experiments and factors of ability.

Guilford (1961) has pointed out numerous relations between factors of human ability and the processes that are investigated in controlled experiments—concept formation, learning, reinforcement, memory, and others. Fleishman and Hempel (1954) pioneered a type of study which relates factors of ability to control experiments: they investigated correlations between factors of ability and progress in different trials of a learning task. They found that the importance of different factors differed with the stage of learning. In learning a psychomotor task, a factor of spatial relations was important in the early trials, but in later trials it correlated much less with performance. On the early trials, factors concerning speed of movement had relatively small correlations with performance, but by the end of training they were the most important factors. There are many other possibilities for investigating relations between factors of ability and learning processes.

## ARENAS OF RESEARCH ON HUMAN ABILITY

As has been described so far in this chapter, the typical approach to the study of human abilities has been through the development of printed tests and their subsequent investigation as predictor variables either in applied settings or in factor-analysis studies. Although this approach has produced very valuable results and will probably continue to be relied on heavily, there are some allied approaches that potentially are very helpful. These are discussed as follows.

**Developmental psychology** Potentially, many hints about important variables to investigate with respect to human abilities can be derived from typical studies in developmental psychology. The developmental theories of Jean Piaget have been most influential in that regard. They concern a complex series of steps in cognitive development that range from a prelogical stage in infancy up through various stages of sophistication in ability to understand the world. For example, there is a very early stage before "object permanence" develops; e.g., if a hat is placed over a block, then apparently the child thinks that the block has gone away. When the hat is removed, the child thinks that the block comes back. Only later can the child conceive of the block still being there but being covered by the hat. Another stage of development that typically occurs between 5 and 7 years of age is that of size conservation. If the liquid from a short, wide glass is poured into a tall, narrower glass, typically the child will say that there is "more" liquid in the tall glass. Similarly, if a large ball of clay is broken down into a number of smaller balls, the child will state that there is more clay, apparently confusing numbers of balls with total amount of clay. In these and other ways, the child must develop the concept of conservation in terms of various types of physical quantification.

The early logical developments involve "concrete operations," which are closely tied to actually seeing and manipulating material, such as seeing that one can take apart a large ball of clay and then put it back together to form the same overall amount. Later the child develops the ability to handle the same problem symbolically with the use of language without actually physically manipulating the materials. At further stages of intellectual development, the budding adult learns to handle logical problems on an entirely abstract level without talking about particular instances but rather using general logical principles; e.g., the whole equals the sum of the parts regardless of the object involved.

Piaget has interwoven his developmental sequence with numerous concepts concerning the nature of human thinking. For example, much of human thinking takes place either by assimilation or by accommodation. *Assimilation* consists of fitting some new idea into an existing set of conceptions, such as learning how to solve a new type of arithmetic problem with the same set of arithmetic principles that one has known up until that time. *Accommodation* requires a modification of the existing ways of classifying and understanding objects and events to take account of a new percept that simply will not fit into current ways of thinking. An example would be having to learn a new form of mathematics (e.g., solution of simultaneous equations) because new problems being given in school simply could not be solved by previously known mathematical approaches. Frequently in daily life accommodation consists of discovering new principles of reality to fit apparently enigmatic events, as in developing new principles of meteorology to explain previously unpredictable events of weather that are related to changes in solar radiation.

The many concepts that have been developed by Piaget and other theorists regarding developmental psychology provide many hints about interesting and important types of human abilities. For example, Piaget discusses the ability of children to "centrate," or to focus on a relevant aspect of a perceptual problem, such as in a visual illusion or in a concept-formation task where a child must learn to pick up one geometric form rather than another in order to receive prizes. In order to solve these kinds of problems, the subject must concentrate, or perceptually "centrate," on relevant aspects of the problem and ignore potentially distracting stimuli. The ability to do this tends to grow with age; but, as with so many of the variables that are investigated in developmental psychology, individuals differ in their abilities to do this at all age levels. There have been numerous suggestions, for example, that inability to centrate is typical of adult schizophrenics, autistic children, and mental retardates.

Although the theories of Piaget and those of most other developmental psychologists primarily are concerned with an ordering of growing abilities in a developmental sequence, the problem can easily be turned around to investigate individual differences at each age level and at adulthood in the various processes involved. Although one can make very bad mistakes, it is a good hypothesis that almost anything that changes markedly with age is potentially important to investigate as a source of individual differences in adulthood. There are numerous counterexamples, such as the use of foot length to measure intelligence; but such examples aside, the tendency for abilities to develop with age—at least through adolescence—has been documented for many important types of abilities. Indeed, this was one of the major bases on which the early intelligence tests were developed; i.e., items were selected on which children tended to improve with age. It was from scales constructed on this principle that the concept of *mental age* was developed. Although one can push this analogy too far, the theories regarding developmental psychology and findings regarding improvements in abilities over time offer very rich ground for exploring human abilities both developmentally and at adulthood. These days one sees many tie-ins between developmental psychology and studies of individual differences in human abilities, which is a healthy sign. Some efforts to develop standardized tests based on Piaget's theories and those of others are discussed by Anastasi (1976).

**Experimental psychology** Laboratory experimental psychology and applied-oriented studies of mental testing went their own ways for over half of this century, but they have been reuniting in recent years. Unfortunately, there has been a tendency for the two camps to criticize one another in a partisan manner regarding which was more correct in orientation and which was more fruitful. Now that such nonsense is no longer prevalent, the two subfields are making important contributions to one another (e.g., see discussion by Carroll 1974). As illustrated by the work of Carroll, two of the most prominent areas have been reaction time and memory. Various cognitive processes have been proposed to account for the types of tasks that are involved in related laboratory experiments. For example, if the subject is told that alphabetic letters will be flashed on a screen one at a time, the most primitive stage is that of sheer recognition that something has been presented. A second stage requires classifying what is presented, e.g., the letter A. In more complex tasks, the subject can be presented randomly selected strings of alphabetic letters varying in length from 3 to 10. At varying times after the first presentation, the subject can be presented a single alphabetic letter and asked to indicate whether it appeared previously on the screen. The space between presentations can either be left "empty" or be filled with a second cognitive task. As such tasks are made more and more complex, supposedly more and more complex mental processes are involved. For example, when someone is shown a string of letters, after the phase of categorizing objects, supposedly there is a "short-term memory storage" that is hypothesized to dissipate over time unless some type of rehearsal or second presentation of the material occurs. On being shown the single test stimulus, one must make mental comparisons between what is on the screen and memory for letters presented previously, which requires a cognitive comparison process with what is in short-term storage. At each stage in these and more complex tasks, subjects usually are required to respond as rapidly as possible, and both correctness of response and time taken to respond are used as indicators of task difficulty. By varying the parameters of the task (e.g., length of strings of letters or amount of time between first and second presentations), the difficulty of performing a particular cognitive operation should be increased. In all the hypothesized stages that are required to perform such cognitive tasks concerning memory and reaction time, there are important individual differences among subjects, which one would expect to relate in some logical manner to overall ability to solve the types of problems in question. Numerous investigations are now being made of individual differences in performing the subprocesses, and these are being correlated with one another. As a simple example, it is important to learn whether ability to solve a problem depends more on individual differences in coding time (classifying a letter as "A") than on raw reaction time to the presence of anything.

These days one sees many other instances in which part of the concern in traditional laboratory studies of learning, memory, perception, and other processes is attumed to studies of individual differences as well as to the performance of the average person. One can hope not only that experimental psychology will be enriched in this way, but also that many hints will be obtained about the potential importance of both the numerous existing measured and yet unmeasured factors of human ability (for some possibilities, see discussion by Messick 1972).

**Task analyses** Related to the above-mentioned analyses of laboratory tasks in experimental psychology are analyses of more complex, lifelike types of performance found in human engineering and in applied performance situations. Studies of this type have been pioneered by Fleishman (1975). A typical complex task investigated by Fleishman is a mock-up of the controls of an airplane. Over a number of practice sessions, the subject learns how to manipulate the controls to simulate the correct flight of an airplane. In order to understand the importance of various factors of ability at different stages of training, Fleishman and his colleagues administered a wide variety of psychological tests at different points, e.g., tests of spatial relations, verbal comprehension, reaction time, and various measures of motor skills. He found that the amount of variance explained by each of these factors changed markedly as a function of numbers of trials. For example, factors concerning spatial relations were very important in the early trials but of relatively little importance near the end of training. In contrast, discrimination reaction time was not very important in the early trials but became much more important later. Fleishman and others have analyzed a number of types of complex performances in terms of the contribution of underlying factors. This same type of analysis can be applied to numerous types of complex performance in jobs such as learning computer programs and operations, development of athletic skills, driver training, etc. By working directly with important types of performance in real life, one has some assurance that the studies of human abilities are more than illusory products of the psychometric laboratory. Also, in the process of investigating the importance of known factors of human abilities, one obtains many hints about important types of abilities that have not yet been measured.

**Physiological psychology** In spite of the truism that important individual differences manifested on psychological tests and in various ways in daily life must be represented somehow or other in the human brain, it is surprising that physiological psychology has contributed so little about possibly important forms of human abilities that could be turned into practicable tests. Partly this may be because some types of human abilities depend on extremely subtle aspects of brain processes which are unknown at the present time, but partly this is because of the immense technical difficulties encountered in learning about ongoing processes in the human brain. Some technical breakthroughs in learning about ongoing electrical activities of the brain (see the discussion in Goleman 1976) give reason to hope that more can be learned in the future. In the investigation of abilities through brain functions, one logical problem is that abilities as manifested at any particular point (e.g., verbal comprehension and perceptual accuracy) may be represented in the form of "achievements" or, in other words, in terms of previous learning. Such previous learning may have no structural or obvious chemical quality in the brain, but rather may be manifested in immensely complex "traces" of some kind or other, which may prove to be impossible to unravel for the individual. However, there may be some general electrical, chemical, or other physical representations of abilities which can be measured in terms of ongoing brain activity, e.g., some type of electrical activity while the individual is trying to solve problems. However, the study of ongoing brain processes in healthy people in this way is only in an embryonic stage.

Most of what has been learned from physiological psychology with respect to human abilities is negative, in the sense that one can learn which types of conventional measures of ability are affected by various kinds of disease and injury. Foremost in this regard have been studies of various types of brain damage. It is found, for example, that damage to the dominant brain hemisphere (the left hemisphere for a right-handed person) tends to affect various types of verbal and symbolic learning more than learning that is based on spatial abilities and visual configurations, and vice versa for damage to certain areas of the nondominant hemisphere. Many other instances have been noted in which damage to certain areas of the brain influenced scores on typical tests of motor skills, memory, verbal comprehension, etc. However, this has been largely a one-way street, in which the technology of mental testing has been used to indicate something about the nature of brain disorders. Not a great deal has come from such investigations of brain disorders to suggest the importance of various existing tests of human abilities or to provide hints about important, yet unmeasured types of human abilities. Surely in the future one can expect to see a rather close tie-in between studies of human ability and studies in physiological psychology, and studies of human ability should be much enriched in the process. But for the present, conventional psychological testing mainly is an assistant in brain research.

## STRUCTURES OF ABILITY

Previously it was said that (1) many factors of ability have been found so far, (2) some of these may be unimportant with respect to the various standards that were discussed, and (3) some very important types of abilities (e.g., those relating to creativity) probably are yet to be discovered. In order to make sense out of what we know now and to conceptually manage the accumulation of knowledge about human abilities, some type of structure is required—some type of verbal or mathematical scheme for comprehensively but parsimoniously cataloging human abilities. Some of the most promising approaches are treated in the discussion that follows.

**Conceptual models** As is true in all science, one of the basic approaches to classifying phenomena (e.g., classifying insects) is to develop a system of verbal categories in terms of relevant features of the objects or activities being investigated. Numerous verbal classification schemes have been proposed for this purpose. The first grew out of findings from factor analysis as exemplified in the work of the Thurstones, where groups of factors were simply named *verbal, numerical, spatial, perceptual, reasoning,* etc., as they arose. However, such verbal classification schemes came about more as an incidental feature of the investigations than as any systematic way of cataloging.

By far the most influential verbal categorization scheme for factors of human ability is that advocated by Guilford [see Guilford (1967); Guilford and Hoepfner (1971)]. This verbal classification scheme and attendant research have grown over a period of more than 20 years. The scheme has come to be referred to as *Guilford's structure of intellect.* The classification scheme is presented in Fig. 13-2.

In discussing the classification scheme, it is easiest to start with *operations,*

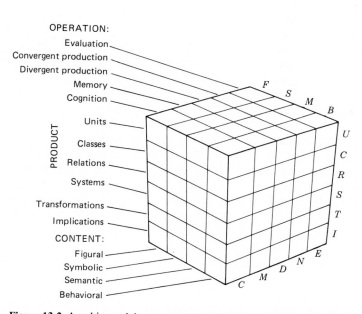

**Figure 13-2** A cubic model representing Guilford's structure of intellect. (*Adapted from* The nature of human intelligence *by J. P. Guilford,* © *1967. Used by permission of the author and McGraw-Hill Book Company.*)

which concern the type of mental activity going on while an ability is being tested. It is in this five-fold breakdown that Guilford has made perhaps his most important contribution in categorizing human abilities. *Cognition* consists of knowing something, such as knowing how to spell a particular word or knowing the author of a particular book. *Memory,* as the word implies, concerns the ability to retain facts, pictorial material, and other types of content. *Divergent production* (frequently called *divergent thinking*) consists of the ability to come up with interesting ideas when no specific solution is sought for a problem. A classic example is a typical test of verbal fluency in which an individual is asked to supply all the names of objects that he or she can think of that begin with the letter S. *Convergent production* consists of thinking when a specified solution is required for a problem. Simple examples are taking a scrambled set of letters and rearranging them to spell a real word or determining the letter that comes next in a series-completion reasoning problem. *Evaluation* consists of judging the soundness of solutions to problems, as it is manifested in nearly all multiple-choice tests. For example, for a test of mechanical aptitude, a number of brief descriptions can be given for approaches to repairing a broken bridge over a river, and the subject is asked to rank-order the solutions in terms of how well they would work.

*Content* concerns the nature of the test materials, which Guilford breaks down into figural, symbolic, semantic, and behavioral. [For a thorough discussion of these and other aspects of the classifications scheme, see Guilford (1967) and Guilford and Hoepfner (1971).] Figural content concerns geometric forms and pictures of other physical objects. As the term is used, symbolic material also can be figural in content or even contain words, but in essence it relates to groupings of things and principles by which they are grouped. An example is showing an individual four groups of letters with four alphabetic letters in each. The subject is asked to pick the one group that does not belong with the other three. In one example, three groups have two A's in them, and the fourth does not. Semantic content, of course, consists of dealing with words and written material generally, such as in a vocabulary test. The "behavioral" type of content was put in more as a possibility than as a viable alternative for many types of testing. An example that Guilford gives is a multiple-choice test of people's facial expressions and postural gestures. Three of these symbolize happiness, and the subject is to pick the one picture from four alternatives that also symbolizes the same thing.

The facet of the classification scheme concerning *products* relates to the end result of the subject's problem-solving activity. These were illustrated by Guilford (1967) with the content and operations listed in Fig. 13-2. One would need to inspect the numerous examples of items relating to products to fully understand this facet, as also is the case for the other two facets of the classification system.

Admittedly the classification scheme by Guilford is quite complex; in dealing with actual test items, it is difficult to discriminate some of the categories, and, as Guilford freely admits, the classification scheme probably will be augmented and improved in the future. One could argue that classification schemes of this kind do more to complicate the overall picture of human abilities than to simplify it, because if one sought a factor for each cell in the design portrayed in Fig. 13-2, it would require 120 factors. However, as Guilford recognizes, many of the possible factors may be implausible to measure or of no theoretical interest. Also, Guilford recognizes the need for superordinate classification schemes regarding the potential importance of all the many different factors that might be derived from a verbal classification scheme of this kind. Guilford and his colleagues have done a great deal of research over several decades trying to document the factors implied by the classification scheme and to improve the scheme in the process. This is an immensely laudatory enterprise, but there are those who challenge the success of the venture so far [see the very strong criticisms by Horn and Knapp (1973)].

Guilford's model has already had one very beneficial effect—it has suggested numerous interesting new measures of human ability. Perhaps most important is the distinction between divergent and convergent thinking. Guilford has helped make researchers realize that most of the effort in the development of tests of human ability has involved items in which the solution of a specific problem was required, one in which only one answer was correct. This is typical of most multiple-choice items, regardless of what is measured. People who study creativity frequently have mentioned that creative thinking to a large extent consists of going off in numerous directions with respect to a general question or issue rather than seeking a specific solution to a problem. In many cases, creativity consists of asking previously unasked questions rather than answering any at all. Such divergent thinking makes everyone aware of many new questions, problems, modes of solving problems, and general approaches to problem solution. Frequently the products of such divergent thinking are more significant than those of more conventional convergent thinking, which has been the most widely tested mental operation in psychometrics. These and other distinctions made by Guilford have led to some interesting individual tests and batteries of tests [see the discussion in Anastasi (1976) and Guilford and Hoepfner (1971)].

In a test of *associational fluency*, the subject writes words that are similar in meaning to a given word. In a *utility test*, the subject lists as many uses as possible for common objects, such as for empty food cans. In the test of *alternative uses*, the subject is required to list uses for objects other than those for which they are primarily intended, e.g., putting Ping-Pong balls inside airplane wings to keep the craft afloat. Another test concerns *ideational fluency*, which consists of naming all the objects or substances in a particular class, such as fluids that will burn. These and many other interesting tests have been suggested by Guilford's structure of intellect.

The work by Guilford and his colleagues on the structure of intellect certainly is an impressive and praiseworthy venture. Whether it stands or falls on logical or empirical grounds, this research by Guilford and his colleagues certainly has been a very important stimulus to others. The classification scheme definitely has stimulated a great deal of research and led to the development of interesting new measurement methods. Any investigators who criticize Guilford's classification scheme should feel challenged to produce a better one.

**Facet models** Although it is not necessarily a fault, what is lacking in Guilford's classification scheme is any attendant mathematical model stating proposed relations among the various "cells" or stipulating any procedures of mathematical analysis that are particularly appropriate for exploring the usefulness of the scheme. Thus, although this was not made highly explicit originally, the apparent implication was that each cell would constitute a possible factor which potentially is measurable by conventional approaches to correlational and factor analysis. Actually, this has been the approach employed by Guilford and his colleagues. Starting off with the most promising parts of the matrix of 120 possible factors, they have accrued evidence over a period of several decades and have attempted to document as many factors as they could. However, this is a slow, tedious process. Purely in terms of possibilities, one could obtain 120 factors from the existing cube depicted in Fig. 13-2; and as Guilford states, there may be other facets that should be considered in an overall classification scheme. What are needed are some more comprehensive mathematical models that help one to analyze results of particular tests and portray their overall patterns of correlation in a parsimonious way. Facet theory is one proposed solution to this problem. In essence, each dimension of the cube presented in Fig. 13-2 can be thought of as a facet, much as each dimension of an analysis of variance design for an experiment can be spoken of as a facet of the design. A facet is nothing other than a system for classifying things, in this case test materials. There are as many "levels" to each facet as there are ways of categorizing things. Thus, there are five "levels" in thinking operations, but the frequent use of the word *levels* should not imply a quantitative ordering of the categories. In most verbal classification schemes and in facet theory as it will be discussed here, each facet consists of a nonordered set of categories. A facet design can have a number of facets; three are depicted in Fig. 13-2. However, resemblances between factor analysis and Guilford's verbal classification scheme diverge in terms of what is done to the facets and the types of mathematical analyses that are performed.

Although the idea of facet analysis really is quite old, ` owe it to Louis Guttman to bring the matter to the attention of psychologists in terms of some intriguing mathematical models. Guttman's contributions along with modern developments in facet analysis are discussed in Foa (1965) and Wiggins (1973).

There are four aspects, or stages, in any facet analysis. First, there must be a classification scheme, such as that for Guilford's structure of intellect. Second, rather than simply look throughout the whole scheme for factors, one *hypothesizes* the presence or absence (potentially to some degree) of variance associated with each level of each facet in a collection of measures. Thus, one has a collection of measures for which one proposes a facet structure, which is a highly specific combination of the total possibilities in the classification scheme. Second, this proposed facet structure leads to a hypothesized matrix of correlations among tests, with the hypothesized pattern depending on the particular theory of facet combinations one has for the domain being investigated (e.g., leadership ability). Third, a statistical test is made to determine the extent to which the hypothesized pattern of correlations actually is manifested in the data. Fourth, if the hypothesized correlations among variables are found, subsequently one would need to arrange test-scoring schemes so as to best measure the underlying factor combinations.

Facet analysis frequently is spoken of as *molar correlational analysis,* because it is concerned with hypothesized structures for whole correlation matrices rather than individual factors. Thus, in this way, one can think of "super" factors or underlying facets which in various combinations can help explain the individual factors obtained from factor analysis. Although there are possible inroads to deriving the underlying facets from correlations among tests, ideally facet analysis starts off with explicit hypotheses about the nature of the underlying facets and the facet combinations in each test.

As the name implies, the simplest of all structural hypotheses in facet analysis is the *simplex,* which is illustrated in Table 13-1. This example can be thought of as concerning five facets, labeled $A$, $B$, $C$, $D$, and $E$, respectively. Each facet represents a potential source of variance, and whether a facet is present in a particular performance variable is represented by an X or a 0. In this simplex each facet has only two levels, usually relating to the presence or absence of a "causal agent." In the example shown in Table 13-1, the performance variables differ only in terms of how many of the facets are involved. Thus only facet $A$ is involved in the first performance variable (or test), two fac-

**Table 13-1 Facet levels and corresponding correlation matrix for a perfect simplex**

|  |  | *Facets* | | | | |
|---|---|---|---|---|---|---|
|  |  | $A$ | $B$ | $C$ | $D$ | $E$ |
|  | *1* | X | 0 | 0 | 0 | 0 |
| *Performance* | *2* | X | X | 0 | 0 | 0 |
| *Variables* | *3* | X | X | X | 0 | 0 |
|  | *4* | X | X | X | X | 0 |
|  | *5* | X | X | X | X | X |

|  |  | *Correlation Matrix of Variables* | | | | |
|---|---|---|---|---|---|---|
|  |  | *1* | *2* | *3* | *4* | *5* |
|  | *1* | 1.00 | .80 | .60 | .40 | .20 |
| *Performance* | *2* |  | 1.00 | .80 | .60 | .40 |
| *Variables* | *3* |  |  | 1.00 | .80 | .60 |
|  | *4* |  |  |  | 1.00 | .80 |
|  | *5* |  |  |  |  | 1.00 |

ets are involved in the second variable, and all five are involved in the fifth variable. This arrangement of facet compositions results in neighboring tests being more similar to one another in terms of their variance components and thus correlating more highly with one another. An ideal correlation matrix in this circumstance is presented in the bottom half of Table 13-1. Note that the correlations adjacent to the diagonal unities are high (.80 in this case), and they trail off in size as one goes away from the diagonal. Thus the lowest correlation is between tests 1 and 5, which is .20 in this case. Any table of correlations that can be arranged in such a way as to display the pattern exemplified in Table 13-1 is said to "fit" a simplex.

Despite what one might think at first, a correlation matrix typical of a simplex is not dominated by one factor only, nor does it display the number of common factors corresponding to the number of underlying facets (which would be five in this case). Rather, a simplex is dominated by two factors; one relates to the common variance which can be explained by the first variable in the list, and the other relates to the common variance that can be explained by the last variable in the list.

Although no one expects to find a correlation matrix that will fit a simplex pattern perfectly, there are numerous cases in which reasonably good approximations are obtained. Theoretically, correlation matrices relating to the simplex should be found in many types of investigations. This is the case in almost any type of repeated measurement over time, such as in developmental psychology or in the correlations among different trials in a learning task. In terms of individual differences, correlations are higher among the earlier testings than among later testings, and vice versa. Thus if one repeatedly applied a broad-range intelligence test over a period of years from ages 6 through 16, one would expect to find a pattern of correlations like that in the simplex. In the studies reported previously by Fleischman relating to changes in the factor composition of tasks concerning airplane flying, the correlations over trials tended to fit the simplex pattern. In those instances the factor composition was simpler near the end of learning trials, resembling the facet composition of variable 1 shown in Table 13-1, and more complex initially, resembling variable 5.

It is sensible to hypothesize a simplex only when some of the performance variables are thought to be rather complex with respect to the underlying sources of variance (or facets), and the variables included in the analysis can be arranged from very simple to very complex. When it is sensible to hypothesize a simplex for a correlation of variables and a good approximation of the predicted correlations is found, this provides a type of scientific parsimony in summarizing overall performance.

A more complex structural hypothesis in molar correlational analysis is referred to as the *circumplex* as illustrated in Table 13-2. In contrast to the simplex, the facet structure cannot be explained by a simple ordering of performance variables from simple to complex; rather they literally go in circles. Each variable is referred to as a *cluster* because each is a mixture of facet components, as in clusters of people found in profile analysis. Starting with variable

**Table 13-2 Facet levels and amount of overlap for a perfect circumplex**

| | | Facets | | | | | | | |
|---|---|---|---|---|---|---|---|---|---|
| | | A | B | C | D | E | F | G | H |
| | 1 | X | X | X | X | 0 | 0 | 0 | 0 |
| | 2 | 0 | X | X | X | X | 0 | 0 | 0 |
| | 3 | 0 | 0 | X | X | X | X | 0 | 0 |
| Clusters of | 4 | 0 | 0 | 0 | X | X | X | X | 0 |
| Variables | 5 | 0 | 0 | 0 | 0 | X | X | X | X |
| | 6 | X | 0 | 0 | 0 | 0 | X | X | X |
| | 7 | X | X | 0 | 0 | 0 | 0 | X | X |
| | 8 | X | X | X | 0 | 0 | 0 | 0 | X |

| | | Number of Facets in Common to Clusters of Variables | | | | | | | |
|---|---|---|---|---|---|---|---|---|---|
| | | 1 | 2 | 3 | 4 | 5 | 6 | 7 | 8 |
| | 1 | — | 6 | 4 | 2 | 0 | 2 | 4 | 6 |
| | 2 | | — | 6 | 4 | 2 | 0 | 2 | 4 |
| | 3 | | | — | 6 | 4 | 2 | 0 | 2 |
| Clusters of | 4 | | | | — | 6 | 4 | 2 | 0 |
| Variables | 5 | | | | | — | 6 | 4 | 2 |
| | 6 | | | | | | — | 6 | 4 |
| | 7 | | | | | | | — | 6 |
| | 8 | | | | | | | | — |

1, each variable has more in common with its neighboring variable (for example, 1 with 2 and 7 with 8); but they go in a circle in the sense that variables in the middle (e.g., variables 4, 5, and 6) have less to do with the extremes than with one another, and variables on the extremes overlap in terms of facet composition. Note, for example, that variables 1 and 8 have six facets in common (considering 0 as one level of each facet and X as the other level). A simple count of the number of facets common to each variable is shown in the lower half of Table 13-2. Note that adjacent variables all have six out of a possible eight facets in common, variables one step removed from one another have four facets in common, and variables four steps removed from one another have no facets in common. What is important to note in the matrix concerning facets in common is that, as one goes away from the diagonal part of the matrix, the numbers of facets in common decline to zero but then pick up in size, indicating the circular nature of the shared variance because of common facets. Whereas the structure underlying a simplex can be described in terms of one hierarchy —an ordering of variables from simple to more complex—a circumplex represents a circular ordering. Such a circular ordering is illustrated in Fig. 13-3. The circumplex shown in the figure fits the hypothetical data depicted in Table 13-2. In this case there are eight social traits (personality variables) which combine into eight clusters or "types" of individuals, such as one might derive from the clustering of profiles. Obviously, if one finds a hypothesis relating to a cir-

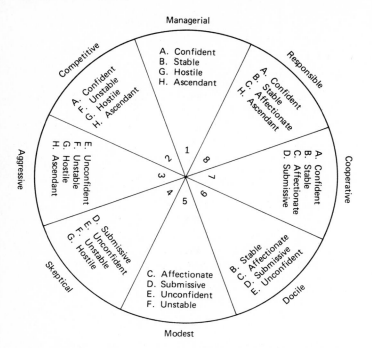

**Figure 13-3** A circumplex corresponding to the facet design shown in Table 13-2. *(Adapted from Wiggins,* Personality and prediction: Principles of personality assessment, *1973, Addison-Wesley.)*

cumplex so neatly manifested in data, then the overall results can be easily pictured literally in the form of a figure such as is illustrated; and the circumplex pattern provides an easy summarization of the overall findings.

Whereas the simplex was illustrated with a correlation matrix, to simplify the problem, the circumplex was illustrated with numbers of facets held in common. However, that part of Table 13-2 showing numbers of facets in common could easily be converted into a hypothetical correlation matrix. Thus, if two variables have six out of eight facets in common, this could be related to percents of variance in common, the square roots of which would lead to correlation coefficients. The whole table of facets in common could be converted to a corresponding matrix of correlations showing the same pattern.

The simplex and the circumplex represent only some of the simpler possibilities in molar correlational analysis. Some of the theoretical possibilities are discussed by Foa (1965); some efforts to develop test batteries on the basis of the simplex, circumplex, and other molar structures are discussed by Wiggins (1973). Before we leave the discussion of facet analysis, a number of points should be kept firmly in mind. First, factor analysis and theories regarding correlational structures generally are praiseworthy in that they intend to summarize complex relations among individual factors of ability and personality.

As was mentioned at a number of points in this chapter, more general summarizing principles certainly are needed.

Second, in a few instances (but not many), actual test data have been found to provide reasonable fits to the simplex, circumplex, and other proposed facet models. However, facet models and molar structural correlational analysis generally are beset by a number of difficult problems. The methods are both theoretically and statistically complex, which is probably the reason that many investigators have shied away from employing them.

Third, those who deal in facet theory and molar structural correlational theory generally are somewhat vague in what they mean by a facet and a variable. Generally, the theory is not nearly as clear as it should be in terms of the hypothesized components and the proposed statistical structures.

Fourth, facet analysis and molar structural correlational analysis in general are mainly *hypothesis-testing* models rather than statistical methods of discovery. Not only are such models aimed at hypothesis testing, but the hypotheses frequently are quite complex indeed, as is the case in hypothesizing the results to be obtained from a whole correlation matrix with the circumplex. Obviously, there are not many situations in which one has sufficient foreknowledge to confidently predict such a pattern of results.

Fifth, there is nothing "illegal" about the use of cut-and-try experimentation and the gradual assembling of a set of variables over successive analyses that fit a facet model. To say it another way, it is not necessary for the facet model to work out beautifully on the first problem to which it is applied. Rather, it might be necessary to build up the essential test variables over numerous analyses to eventually achieve a matrix of correlations that will "prove out" as predicted by the facet model.

Sixth, as they are usually presented, facet designs do not take account of the fact that frequently it would be necessary to use different weights with respect to the *degree* to which facets were present in various tests or other variables. Thus the examples given in Tables 13-1 and 13-2 show facets being present or absent on an all-or-none basis, but this is unrealistic regarding what would be obtained from psychological tests or from scores in relation to any type of real-life performance. The need to introduce such weights into facet design does not make the situation impossible, but it certainly makes it more complex. Additional complexity would be introduced if facets had more than only two levels, as used here to illustrate the simplex and circumplex.

A seventh important point is that facet theory and molar structural correlational analysis more generally have not been supplied with attendant methods for discovering underlying facets, as is the case in exploratory factor analysis. Actually, many possibilities have not been fully explored. For example, the circumplex illustrated in Fig. 13-3 is ready-made for methods concerning the clustering of profiles discussed in detail in Chap. 12. Numerous other adaptations of available mathematical approaches (e.g., second-order factoring) are appropriate to one type or other of theoretical facet design. In the future, one hopes to see more use of facet theory and powerful related methods of analysis to help summarize already discovered and still undiscovered factors of human ability.

**Higher-order factor models** One approach to simplifying the overabundance of factors obtained in the area of human abilities and in other areas of individual differences is to take seriously only higher-order factors obtained from factor analysis. From Chaps. 10 and 11 remember that if one derives correlated factors, then a matrix can be obtained of the correlations among factors. Such correlated factors may come from a direct hypothesis-testing approach, such as with the multiple-group method, or from an exploratory approach in which an analytical method of rotation (e.g., Promax) is employed. There is nothing to prevent factor-analyzing these correlations among the first-order factors. Thus, in employing oblique "hand" rotational methods, the Thurstones obtained a matrix of positive correlations among their factors. Interestingly enough, this matrix was dominated by a general factor, which resembles in structure the type of matrix hypothesized by Spearman for his $G$; indeed, the pattern of loadings supported Spearman's interpretation of the underlying general factor.

Because of the huge matrices of correlations that are investigated these days (frequently more than 60 whole tests or as many as 200 individual test items), often one has more than a dozen correlated factors which can be subjected to higher-order factor analysis. One might obtain as many as four or five factors which, if they are allowed to be correlated, produce a small matrix of correlations among the second-order factors. These in turn can be factor-analyzed to produce one or more third-order factors; indeed, if enough variables and factors are available, there is no end to the levels of factoring that one can use. Also, statistical methods can be easily applied for correlating all the original tests with each of the factors at each level (such procedures are discussed in detail in Gorsuch 1974).

There are some good things and some bad things to say about higher-order factor analysis as a way of condensing the plethora of individual factors being found year by year. To start with the bad things, one major disadvantage is that such higher-order factor analyses are not possible if the first-order factors are uncorrelated. The Varimax analytical method of rotation is used very frequently these days in computer packages for factor analysis, and it results in orthogonal factors. As mentioned in Chaps. 10 and 11, the author has a mild preference for dealing with orthogonal factors, but appreciates the potential value of oblique factors for some purposes, one of which is when higher-order factoring is contemplated. The second bad thing to say about higher-order factoring as a method of achieving parsimony is that the statistical complexities sometimes are overwhelming, are difficult to assimilate, and lend themselves to misinterpretation.

A third problem with higher-order factor analysis is that sometimes the highly important unique variance in a factor gets lost in higher-order factoring. Many examples could be given of how this is a potential problem. This might occur, for example, if several tests of motor coordination were being investigated in a large battery of tests used for selection of men for industrial training programs relating to skilled mechanical work. The tests concerning motor coordination might correlate well with one another and thus form a factor, but the resulting factor might correlate near zero with more intellectual factors like verbal comprehension, numerical skills, spatial relations, etc. Then, although that factor would be very important in its own right and important for many jobs, it would have zero loadings on all higher-order factors. Thus the very important unique variance of the factor simply would not make itself known in any form of higher-order factor analysis. The potential of losing the very important unique variance of a factor in higher-order factor analysis can be realized in many circumstances, and this is the major problem that the author finds in using this as a sensible approach to parsimoniously condensing factors of ability.

One good thing to say about second-order factoring of abilities (and other types of individual differences as well) is that at least it is an attempt to statistically boil down the huge numbers of factors that can be obtained by the endless generation of "laboratory" tests. Examples were given previously of how rather trivial variations on the same theme could be employed to generate a number of tests that would correlate well enough with one another to form a very narrowly defined factor. Second-order factoring tends to combine such "splinter" factors into more meaningful superordinate groupings, which is praiseworthy. Actually, this is more of an advantage with nonability tests of personality and other characteristics, as they will be described in subsequent chapters, where it is difficult to hypothesize whole tests. Consequently many investigators have resorted to deriving dozens and dozens of tiny factors from individual test items. In a statistical sense, second-ordering factoring is helpful in boiling down what would otherwise be a rather messy statistical situation. The second major good thing to say about higher-order factoring is that some of the results obtained so far have been interesting, as mentioned in the previous case of the Thurstones rediscovering general intelligence as a second-order factor.

## HIERARCHICAL MODELS

A conceptual-mathematical approach that is akin to both facet analysis and higher-order factoring is that of hierarchical models. In essence a hierarchical model presupposes that traits of individual differences in any domain can be successively ordered at various levels from the more general to the more specific. A hypothetical example of factors that would fit such a model was given by Humphreys (1962, p. 476):

> I shall assume that there are four discriminable levels of specificity of tests of mechanical information. These are as follows: (a) information about specific tools, e.g., the cross-cut saw or the socket wrench; (b) information about groups of tools having a common function, e.g., saws or wrenches; (c) information about areas of mechanical interest, e.g., carpentry or automotive; (d) general mechanical information, sampling from several areas such as carpentry, automotive, metal work, and plumbing.

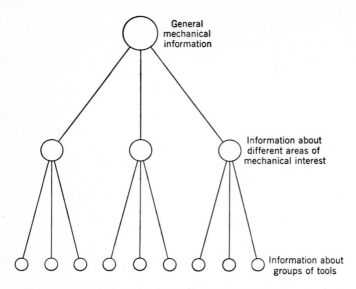

General
mechanical
information

Information about
different areas of
mechanical interest

Information about
groups of tools

**Figure 13-4** Factor hierarchy for mechanical information.

A graphic representation of the above hierarchy is shown in Fig. 13-4. At the top is general mechanical information, immediately below are broad group factors relating to particular areas of mechanical interest, and below that are narrow group factors relating to information about different groups of tools. Further down could have been shown specific factors relating to information about particular tools within each group of tools.

A test of the adequacy of the above hierarchy for mechanical information could be obtained as follows. First, one would construct tests at level *b* above, concerning information about tools having a common function, e.g., saws or wrenches. (Little information probably would be supplied by starting at level *a*, concerning particular tools.) Scores on the tests would be intercorrelated and factor-analyzed to test for the adequacy of the hierarchy shown in Fig. 13-4. One could make a test for the general factor by obtaining the first PC factor or the first complete-centroid factor. The influence of the general factor would be removed from the correlation matrix in the usual way. Next, one could obtain group-centroid factors corresponding to the three hypothesized broad group factors relating to areas of mechanical interest. If the nine tests formed the hypothesized hierarchy, the matrix of factor loadings would appear like that in Table 13-3 (with each *x* representing a substantial positive loading). Not shown in the table are the specific factors (reliable unique variance) for the tests corresponding to the nine hypothesized narrow group factors.

There are other statistical approaches to obtaining hierarchies. To some extent one does this in higher-order factoring, particularly if one keeps track of factors obtained at each level of factoring, including the unique variance in first-order factors and the unique variance in individual tests. Also, it would

**Table 13-3   Matrix of factor loadings corresponding to the factor hierarchy shown in Fig. 13-4**

|  |  | General Factor | Group-Centroid Factors | | |
|---|---|---|---|---|---|
|  |  | A | B | C | D |
|  | 1 | x | x |  |  |
|  | 2 | x | x |  |  |
|  | 3 | x | x |  |  |
|  | 4 | x |  | x |  |
| Tests | 5 | x |  | x |  |
|  | 6 | x |  | x |  |
|  | 7 | x |  |  | x |
|  | 8 | x |  |  | x |
|  | 9 | x |  |  | x |

be simple to posit facet models corresponding to any hypothesized hierarchy and test the resulting correlation matrix for goodness of fit. One might even fly entirely by intuition, compose tests for all levels of a hierarchy, and find that the resulting statistical structure fit the model; but that is improbable without the aid of a series of investigations using factor analysis or other mathematical models.

Another example of a hierarchy was given by Guilford (1959), concerning possible relations among different types of factors in his scheme of factors. The hierarchy is shown in Fig. 13-5. Only the hierarchy for productive thinking is shown in detail. At the top is overall intellectual ability (like Spearman's

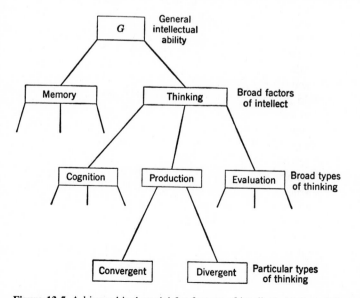

**Figure 13-5** A hierarchical model for factors of intellect. *(Adapted from Guilford 1959.)*

$G$), below which is "thinking" as opposed to "memory." Below "thinking" is "productive thinking," and below that are two types of productive thinking. To make the hierarchy for productive thinking complete, one would need to put in additional lines going down to different types of convergent and divergent thinking.

As one can see from Fig. 13-5, to propose a complete hierarchical structure for human intellect would result in a very complex system, and to find tests to fit the system would be difficult. Also, one can always find tests that will not fit the system, e.g., a test that has substantial loadings on more than one group factor at a particular level.

There are several principles that should be heeded in the search for hierarchical arrangements of factors. First, in the long run probably it will be more fruitful to start from near the bottom and work upward rather than start at the top and work downward. For example, rather than start off at the top with "intellect" and look for hierarchical arrangements of factors below it, probably it would be better to start with, say, "productive thinking" and seek a hierarchy below that. One of the problems in so many studies of human abilities is that they bite off far more than they can chew. Consequently factors are poorly defined, and so many factors are found in each analysis that it is hard to make sense of the results. It would be better to make careful investigations of restricted aspects of intellectual functioning, such as productive thinking. If hierarchies can be found at a lower level, gradually these can be welded into larger hierarchies at higher levels.

A second principle in searching for hierarchies of factors is that such work has little chance of success without credible theories of human abilities. The importance of theory is evidenced in the hypotheses about hierarchical relations among factors that follow from Guilford's theories about the structure of intellect. It is inconceivable that one would find neat hierarchical structures in miscellaneous collections of tests covering a hodgepodge of abilities.

A third principle in searching for hierarchies is that we should abandon the needless assumption that *all* tests in a factor analysis must fit the hierarchy. As was mentioned previously, it would always be easy to produce a test that did not fit a hierarchy (or any other mathematical model concerning relations among factors of human ability). What is important is to find tests that *do* form a hierarchy regardless of how many other tests in an analysis do not conform to the hierarchy. If the tests that do fit the hierarchy explain most of the common variance among all tests in the analysis, then the hierarchy offers a sufficient scheme of explanation. One can then throw away the tests that do not fit the hierarchy and continue to expand the hierarchy upward and downward in new investigations. The purpose of such studies should be to *impose* lawfulness on nature, not to hope vainly that it will be discovered in anything that anyone wants to call a test.

It may be too much to hope that hierarchies of factors can be found which will meet the mathematical requirements. To find such hierarchies will require a great deal of work and more careful thought and investigation than have characterized many previous efforts. If such hierarchies can be found, they will go a long way toward making human abilities understandable. If they cannot be found or if some other conceptual-mathematical model cannot be shown to fit, it will have to be admitted that there are many separate factors of intellect with no logical order among them. Then the only recourse will be to examine the importance of each separate factor with respect to criteria discussed previously. Not only would that take a long, long time, but it would be a rather uninteresting pursuit.

## SUGGESTED ADDITIONAL READINGS

Anastasi, A. *Psychological testing* (4th ed.). New York: Macmillan, 1976, chaps. 9 through 13.

Guilford, J. P. *The nature of human intelligence.* New York: McGraw-Hill, 1967.

Guilford, J. P., and Hoepfner, R. *The analysis of intelligence.* New York: McGraw-Hill, 1971.

Horn, J. L. Human abilities: A review of research and theory in the early 1970's. In M. Rosenzweig and L. Porter (eds.), *Annual review of psychology*, Vol. 27. Palo Alto, Calif.: Annual Reviews, Inc., 1976.

Nunnally, J. C. *Introduction to psychological measurement.* New York: McGraw-Hill, 1970, chaps. 9 to 11.

Tyler, L. E. Human abilities. In P. Mussen and M. Rosenzweig (eds.), *Annual review of psychology*, Vol 23. Palo Alto, Calif.: Annual Reviews, Inc., 1972.

# FOURTEEN

## MEASUREMENT OF PERSONALITY TRAITS

Used in the broadest possible sense, the term *personality* refers to any feature that characterizes individuals and distinguishes them from one another. To many nonpsychologists, the word *personality* refers to social charm and effectiveness, which is, of course, a limited aspect of the matter. Some psychologists have given overly comprehensive and elegantly vague definitions of personality, such as "the total functioning individual interacting with the environment." Whereas such definitions certainly do not lack inclusiveness, they do more to confuse than enlighten the individual who would like to learn about the scientific study of personality. Such broad definitions would include all traits of human ability, which would be a mistake because a meaningful distinction can be made between abilities and personality characteristics. One can make a good argument for including measures of attitudes, values, interests, and other sentiments in a definition of personality; but, at least for the sake of compartmentalizing issues concerning the measurement of human traits, such measures of sentiments will be discussed separately in the next chapter.

The overall study of personality concerns two broad issues: (1) what people are like at any point in time and (2) how they got that way. Personality measurement is concerned mainly with the first issue, the purpose of measurement being to describe individuals in terms of traits relating to adjustment, dominance, extraversion, etc. The second issue relates to heredity and past experience. To explain how an individual developed a particular set of traits, one must resort either to genetic mechanisms or to learning theory. Of course, at the present time we are only beginning to learn about possible genetic mechanisms relating to human traits; although we know considerably more about the kinds of social learning that lead to the development of personality traits, still there is much left undiscovered.

Specialists in the study of personality can, and sometimes do, argue that a discussion of personality measurement is not a total discussion of personality. There is much merit in this argument. Although this chapter will be concerned with personality measurement, it is freely recognized that this is only the first of the two issues discussed above. Also, we might have better measures of personality if all the persons who specialize in personality measurement had closer contacts with studies and theories concerning personality development.

This chapter is concerned with *personality description* as evidenced in standardized measurements of psychological traits. It is assumed that the same general principles underlie the measurement of personality traits as those discussed so far in this book for the measurement of all other forms of individual differences among people. In particular, it is assumed that (1) personality traits exist as consistent sources of individual differences, (2) standardized measurement of such traits is possible, if not always easy in practice, (3) measures of individual traits should be constructed in terms of principles discussed in Chaps. 8 and 9, (4) such measures of individual traits should be investigated and combined in terms of factorial models like those employed with human abilities, and (5) test validity must depend on one of the three standards discussed extensively so far, namely, predictive, content, or construct validity.

It is both an advantage and a disadvantage that many personality traits which might be investigated are necessarily couched in everyday language, such as aggressiveness, adjustment, sociability, and so on. The advantage is that efforts to measure such traits are of immediate interest to most people; the disadvantage is that such terms adopted from everyday parlance are far from precise, which creates considerable difficulties for psychologists in communicating with one another about personality measurement and in transmitting their research results to lay persons. Psychologists frequently disagree with one another about what they mean in referring to a personality trait such as anxiety, and the person in the street may either hold still different meanings or not understand the term very well in any sense. Thus the study of personality is beset by severe semantic problems. If the psychologist uses terms that are familiar to most people, considerable "noise" is introduced into any effort to communicate scientifically. On the other hand, if the psychologist divorces the studies from popular language by referring to traits as only alpha, beta, gamma, etc., then it is impossible to communicate even to colleagues, much less to lay people. The only way out of the semantic problem is to gradually delineate different types of personality traits and gradually refine their meanings in ways that meet the requirements of both scientific accuracy and richness of interpersonal communication. Some overlapping categories of personality traits that are subject to measurement follow.

1. *Social traits:* The characteristic behavior of individuals with respect to other people. Typical social traits are honesty, gregariousness, shyness, dominance, and humor. Also included are aspects of character such as social responsibility, religiosity, charity toward others, and personal integrity. Social traits are often said to constitute the surface layer of personality—the way an individual appears in society.

2. *Motives:* Individual differences in "needs" or "drives," particularly the "nonbiological" drives such as the needs for affiliation, aggression, achievement, and hostility. In contrast to social traits, motives are not "on the surface" but lie within the person. They must be measured either in terms of self-description or indirectly in terms of behavior. Although motives and social traits sometimes go by the same or similar-sounding names, they are quite different: consistent, strong motives may be diversely represented in social traits; e.g., a person who consistently has strong hostile feelings may learn how to suppress these into a form of overt kindness as a social trait.

3. *Personal conceptions:* This difficult-to-define but very important category of personality traits concerns the ways in which the individual judges and understands the social and material environment. Examples of these are whether the person views (1) other people as basically friendly or hostile, (2) getting ahead in life dependent more on luck than on personal striving, (3) being liked by others as depending more on kindness toward them than on mastery of them, and (4) long-range planning of personal goals as more important than day-by-day adjustment. Many other interesting facets of individual differences concerning "world outlooks" can rightly be considered aspects of human personality. These potentially can be measured from either self-report or inferences from overt behavior.

4. *Adjustment versus maladjustment:* The relative freedom from emotional distress and/or socially disruptive behavior. Maladjustment is said to occur when an individual is very extreme with respect to any of the three categories mentioned above (e.g., extremely unhappy or hostile). Also, there are some rather specific forms of maladjustment that are not ordinarily included in any of the above three categories, such as the tendency to have hallucinations, to have paranoid delusions, or to develop "psychological" illnesses.

5. *Personality dynamics:* The so-called personality dynamics consist of organizational principles whereby the above four types of traits are "put together" and articulated in the form of a walking, thinking person. The traits involved in personality dynamics constitute rather high-level constructs such as ego strength, disunified self-concept, amount of repression of motives, identification with various role models, and other such complex

constructs which serve to explain the articulation of traits into a whole person.

Of course, the classification scheme above is not the only way in which personality traits could be categorized. The scheme is not exhaustive, and the traits for different categories will overlap one another. However, the five-fold classification scheme is useful in discussing potentially measurable aspects of personality. Actually, most approaches to measuring personality have contained separate tests or mixtures of items within tests that covered two or more of the above categories. Thus, it is not uncommon to see the results of projective techniques discussed in terms of all the above categories, and this is also the case for many methods of self-report. A classification scheme such as the one above is helpful in two ways. First, it points to different arenas of measurement, where approaches to measurement and special problems may differ from category to category. Second, it helps settle many arguments about the nature of personality traits and the study of personality in general which spring from semantic problems in discussing the issues. For example, whereas two psychologists may disagree about the best approaches to measuring hostility, one psychologist may be thinking mainly in terms of hostility as a social trait, whereas the other may be thinking of hostility as a covert motive.

**Personality traits** The title of this chapter speaks of the measurement of personality traits, the word *trait* being a synonym for *attribute* or *characteristic* as those terms have been used in previous chapters. A trait is simply a measurable dimension of behavior, either one that is measurable only dichotomously or one that is measurable in finer gradations. Traits vary in generality from specific habits, such as smoking rather than not smoking, to very general dimensions of behavior, such as extraversion rather than introversion. To have parsimonious descriptions of personality, it is necessary to find general traits, ones more general than specific habits. In spirit, this chapter is entirely in the camp of those who seek standardized yardsticks for describing individual differences among people, particularly as such measurement is developed in accord with the general factorial model for the investigation of homogeneous tests. This stance is taken not so much as a theory, a point of view, or a matter for debate, but rather as the only sensible approach known to the author for a description of personality characteristics in scientifically useful terms. As will be seen subsequently, however, there are others who view these matters quite differently.

## IDIOGRAPHIC AND NOMOTHETIC THEORIES

For some years now there has been a controversy as to whether general traits of personality exist. The controversy has been between those who espouse a *nomothetic* and those who espouse an *idiographic* point of view, the former referring to "general laws" applicable to all people, and the latter referring to an individualized approach. Essentially, the idiographic point of view is that each person is a law unto herself or himself. In terms of factor-analysis approaches, this means that either there are no general factors among personality characteristics, or those which do exist fail to capture the "essence" of the individual. The idiographic approach is used by novelists who explore in detail the inner workings and behavioral characteristics of one person. This is in contrast to the nomothetic approach, which strives to represent the important personality characteristics of all people in terms of profiles of measurable traits.

The idiographists have an important point: To find general traits (factors) of personality, it is necessary to find correlations among specific traits (habits); but everyday experience suggests that such correlations frequently are either very low or absent altogether. For example, it makes sense to deal with a general trait of dominance only if there are positive correlations among tendencies to be dominant in specific situations. But there are so many examples of persons who are dominant with their spouses but not dominant at work, dominant with men but not with women, dominant in intellectual matters but not in practical matters, and so on.

To be successful, the nomotheticist must hypothesize a general trait of personality and find it evidenced in the correlations among more specific traits; or if there are no hypotheses, such clusters of correlated traits must be found in factor-analysis explorations. If important factors are not found with these approaches (important in terms of criteria discussed in the previous chapter), then the nomotheticist has failed. Enough failures of this kind would eventually lead to the admission that the idiographist is correct: personality traits are "scattered" among people in such a way that the only approach to understanding individuals is by tracing out the life threads of how they came to be the way they are. Then it would have to be admitted that there are no general traits of dominance, extraversion, or others; instead, each individual would need to be considered a unique configuration of specific traits (habits).

The idiographists may be entirely correct, but if they are, it is a sad day for psychology. Idiography is an antiscience point of view: it discourages the search for general laws and instead encourages the description of particular phenomena (people). This would be like the astronomer who gave up on finding any general laws relating to heavenly bodies and instead devoted the rest of his or her life to describing the particular features of the planet Neptune.

Efforts to measure personality traits are based on the hypothesis that the idiographists are not entirely correct—that there are some general traits of human personality. The nomothetic point of view should be tested to the limit; otherwise, to accept an idiographic point of view in advance is to postulate that only chaos prevails in the description of human personalities. The remainder of this chapter concerns efforts to find general traits of personality.

**Approaches to the measurement of personality** In contrast to the measurement of human abilities, there are a number of different basic approaches to the measurement of personality traits. Most measures of human ability, particularly those of the "intellectual" functions, are printed tests. Although apparatus tests are employed in the measurement of some types of ability (e.g., motor coordination), most intellectual functions can be successfully measured by printed tests. Broadly speaking, in each such test the subjects understand that they are required to solve some type of problem. In most tests of human ability, it is obvious how responses should be scored; with measures of personality, these matters are not nearly so clear. Tests of personality traits are not highly concerned with "how well" a person can perform; rather, they are mainly concerned with the typical behavior of people in daily life, e.g., the typical amount of gregariousness or hostility. How such typical behavior is to be measured, if it can be, is a matter of dispute, and consequently various schools of thought have come forward. Also, the logic of measurement depends on the kind of personality trait being studied. Thus the logic of measurement required for the measurement of social traits might be different from that required for the measurement of motives.

The diversity of types of personality traits and the difficulties of measuring them have resulted in a very wide variety of proposed procedures. Although many personality tests consist of printed forms, which on first glance look like printed tests of abilities, a wide variety of procedures has been tried for the measurement of one or more aspects of personality. These consist of such measurements as the products of group discussions, physiological reactions to stress, brain waves in response to specific forms of stimulation, composing stories regarding make-believe situations, and many other such exotic approaches. Numerous books have been written on the plethora of possible approaches to measuring different types of personality traits [e.g., Cattell (1957), Guilford (1959), and Wiggins (1973)].

The major approaches to the measurement of personality traits are with (1) self-inventories, (2) observational methods, (3) projective techniques, (4) physiological variables, (5) perceptual-judgmental variables, and (6) a mixed bag of "other" approaches. In the remainder of the chapter each of these approaches will be discussed in turn (see the works cited in the Suggested Additional Readings for in-depth discussions of measures derived by all these approaches and research results obtained from employing them).

**Current status of personality measurement** Before particular approaches to the measurement of personality characteristics are discussed, it should be admitted that the development of valid measurement methods has proved more difficult in this area than in studies of human abilities and in studies of types of sentiments (e.g., interests) that will be discussed in the following chapter. In speculating why psychologists have met numerous difficulties in the measurement of personality attributes, one must realize that this is not because the problem has been neglected. Galton was interested in the measurement of personality traits, and he made some attempts to develop valid instruments; the same was true of Binet, Spearman, Thurstone, and the other "greats" in psychometric theory. On the present scene are numerous distinguished psychologists who have devoted themselves in large measure to the study of personality traits. At present, it is safe to say that more effort is being expended to develop measures of personality traits than to develop measures of human ability. In spite of all this effort and in spite of the talent that has been associated with some of it, the search has met with only modest success.

The rapid success of early efforts to measure human abilities may have beguiled psychologists into thinking it would be easy to measure personality traits. Also, since printed tests of human abilities proved successful, this probably encouraged the idea that printed tests of personality would be equally successful.

Part of the difficulty in measuring personality traits is that, as the idiographists claim, there may be few important general traits of personality, if any. If, as the idiographists claim, specific traits (or habits) combine idiosyncratically in people, there is no hope of measuring general traits of personality. One cannot measure a trait that does not exist, no matter what approach is followed. Let us hope, however, that the idiographists are not entirely correct and that, when we find the correct approaches, some important general traits of personality will be measurable.

The slow development of adequate personality measurement methods is in strong contrast to the need for such measures. Psychological theories are populated with personality traits such as anxiety, self-esteem, ego strength, dogmatism, empathy, rigidity; and many of these traits must be measured by approaches which are not well tested in research and/or have proved to be largely invalid when the evidence is in. In addition, there are many needs for measures of personality traits in applied settings—in psychological clinics, schools, psychiatric practice, industry, the armed forces, and so on. In spite of these obvious needs, there are very few instances in which supposed measures of personality traits have proved to be consistently valid in applied programs of personnel selection, classification, and management. This point is exemplified by the fact that, whereas vocabulary tests are consistently valid for selecting first-year college students for many different colleges, no personality test (as far as the author knows) has shown itself to be consistently valid for the same purpose.

In spite of the inherent problems in measuring different types of personality traits, the situation is far from hopeless. As will be mentioned, some highly useful "hardware" already is available for basic research and applied usage. Some of the older, simpler methods (e.g., problem checklists) have fewer faults and more virtues than was thought some years ago. Many of the methods in which hindsight shows that psychologists wasted much energy (e.g., intuitively interpreted projective tests and simple physiological functions) have largely fallen by the wayside as viable approaches to a scientific description of personality. Although much of the search for adequate measures of personality traits has been disappointing and frustrating, at least this has served to separate the wheat from the chaff and has provided many suggestions for more effective personality measurement in the future.

Before particular approaches to the measurement of personality characteristics are discussed in detail, let the tone of this discussion be set with a personal comment. I am asked on many occasions how to measure one aspect or another of personality, or one of the forms of sentiment that will be discussed in the following chapter. During the month prior to writing these lines, I was asked how to measure personality traits by a friend concerned about the moodiness of his son, an undergraduate student working on a project in psychology, a graduate student concerned with the self-concepts of overweight persons, physicians concerned with changes of personality of patients suffering kidney failure, psychologists directing habilitation programs for the mentally retarded, and government officials concerned with the impacts of various human services programs on the recipients. In these and in many other cases, in essence what I tell each person who inquires is that in most personality measurement, *ask the individual or ask someone who knows her or him.* In other words, most valid measures of personality available at present grow out of someone's impressions—the individual's impressions of herself or himself or some other person's impressions of the individual. These allied approaches fall under the rubric of *self-report* and *observational methods* respectively. These two major methods will be discussed in turn, and then alternative approaches will be pursued.

## SELF-INVENTORY MEASURES

By far the most frequently employed approach to personality measurement is printed tests in which individuals are required to describe themselves. A typical item, for which the subject is required to answer *yes* or *no*, is, "Do you usually lead the discussion in group situations?" Although such self-inventories have been used for a long time (Galton used one to measure individual differences in imagery), the first systematic effort to develop them is credited to Woodworth (1918). During World War I, the army needed some means for weeding out emotionally unfit men before they were sent overseas. Previously such screening had been done by psychiatric interviewers, but there were not nearly enough interviewers to do the job. Woodworth's solution essentially was to have each man "interview himself." Questions were obtained from a search of the psychiatric literature and from conferences with psychiatrists. The questions were those that psychiatrists frequently used in interviews. Some of them were as follows:

1. Do you often have the feeling of suffocating?
2. Did you ever have convulsions?
3. Can you stand the sight of blood?
4. Did you have a happy childhood?
5. Have you ever had a vision?
6. Did you ever have a strong desire to commit suicide?

A list of 116 such questions constituted a printed form called the Personal Data Sheet. A neurotic-tendency score for each person was obtained by counting the number of problems marked by each man. A small amount of standardization research was performed with the  instrument. Items were eliminated if the "neurotic" response was given by more than 25 percent of normal soldiers. Comparisons were made of responses given by unselected soldiers and by a small group of diagnosed neurotic soldiers.

The Personal Data Sheet was considered not as a test, in the stricter meaning of the term, but as an aid to interviewing. Persons who gave numerous "neurotic" responses were called in for detailed psychiatric interviews. Although little direct evidence of validity was obtained, persons who worked with the Personal Data Sheet during World War I were generally pleased with it. After World War I, an interest developed in the construction of tests of all kinds, personality self-inventories included. Many of the inventories were modeled after the Personal Data Sheet, to the extent of using some of the same items. Now there are literally hundreds of self-inventories employed for one purpose or another.

**Types of inventories** In a discussion of inventories, it is important to make a distinction between self-inventories and other types of inventories, even though the distinction sometimes is not clear. By a *self-inventory* is meant one in which individuals describe their own traits, such as is the case in the Personal Data Sheet. Self-inventories essentially ask the individual: "What are you like as a person? Show us by responding frankly to the following items." Such self-inventories should be distinguished from inventories that do not require subjects to describe themselves. Self-inventories are used very widely with respect to the different types of personality characteristics mentioned previously. Although they are most easily adapted to the study of social traits, they are also quite useful for studying adjustment, motives, personal conceptions, and various characteristics relating to personality dynamics. In all such cases, however, it is important to keep firmly in mind that individuals are trusted to frankly tell what they know about their own personality characteristics. It has been the custom to refer to any objective (as regards scoring) printed test as an *inventory*. An example of an inventory that does not concern self-description is one in which the individual answers multiple-choice questions concerning what the average person would do in certain social situations, e.g., whether the average person would return money which he or she found. As another example of an inventory which does not directly concern self-description, efforts have been made to develop measures of personality attributes from esthetic preferences among different types of geometric forms, e.g., choosing between regular and irregular forms. The reason for the importance of distinguishing self-inventories from other types of printed tests of personality is that self-inventories have their own logic and their own particular problems, ones that do not necessarily hold with other printed tests of personality. This section concerns self-inventories; other printed tests for measuring personality traits will be mentioned at various points in the remainder of the chapter.

**Types of self-inventory items** Numerous types of items can be used in self-inventories. Most typically, the subject is presented with a list of statements and asked to mark yes-no, true-false, or agree-disagree. Various types of rating scales can also be employed with such statements, such as seven-step scales of agreement-disagreement, percentage scales comparing the individual with people in general, and others. Various types of comparative rating methods, in stead of such absolute rating methods, can be employed. These include forced-choice scales, ranking of statements, and $Q$ sorts. Issues regarding the psychometric properties of these different ways of obtaining responses were discussed in Chap. 2. Special issues in the development and use of rating methods in the study of personality and in the study of attitudes will be discussed in the next chapter. Such technical considerations regarding how responses are elicited, however, are secondary to other problems in the measurement of personality traits. If it were not for the other problems discussed in this chapter, any and all of the rating methods probably could be successfully employed in the measurement of personality.

**Factors in self-inventory items** There is an interesting parallel in the growth of knowledge about factors in self-inventories and the growth of knowledge about factors in tests of human abilities. At first only several factors were proposed, e.g., adjustment and introversion-extraversion. Then others were proposed, such as dominance and sociability, and the list grew and grew. In the attempt to make sense out of the increasing list of proposed factors, factor-analysis studies were undertaken. [Guilford (1959) provides a comprehensive discussion of the history of this work, the many factors which have been proposed, and one person's view of the evidence.] Just as it was necessary to make yearly revisions of the number of factors of human ability that existed, it was necessary to make yearly revisions of the number of factors of personality that existed. At the present time, it is difficult to say how many factors have been found in self-inventories, because (1) the statistical evidence for some of the factors is so weak, (2) different investigators include different types of traits under the heading of personality, and (3) it is very difficult to compare factors reported by different investigators. The most conservative estimate, however, is that over 20 factors have been reported in self-inventories. Cattell (1957) reports over 45 factors of personality, and Guilford (1959) apparently thinks in terms of similar numbers (some of these factors are defined mainly by measurement methods other than self-inventories). Subsequent research on the factors inherent in self-inventories is summarized by Edwards (1970) and Wiggins (1973).

By far the most widely used self-inventory is the Minnesota Multiphasic Personality Inventory (MMPI) (Hathaway and McKinley 1967). The inventory is specifically aimed at various forms of maladjustment, particularly at differentiating various types of psychotic states. Although originally the instrument was not developed from factor analysis, the different scales were developed in such a way as to potentially measure separate factors relating to psychoses. Each scale was developed to differentiate patients that had been diagnosed as having a particular type of mental disorder from groups of individuals having different types of mental disorders and from normal control subjects. The scales were refined in terms of principles of homogeneity similar to those discussed in Chap. 8. The most frequently employed version of the MMPI has eight scales relating to different forms of mental illness. In addition, there is a ninth scale intended to measure masculinity versus femininity and a variety of scales concerned with the extent to which the individual was frank in giving responses and understood the questionnaire. Two related items are shown for each type of mental illness. A plus sign means that persons who have the illness are likely to agree with the item; a minus sign means that they are likely to disagree.

**Hypochondriasis (Hs).**   This illness is characterized by overconcern with bodily functions and imagined illness.
> *Related items:*
> I do not tire quickly. (−)
> The top of my head sometimes feels tender. (+)

**Depression (D).**   The term *depression* is used in the conventional sense to imply strong feelings of "blueness," despondency, and worthlessness.
> *Related items:*
> I am easily awakened by noise. (+)
> Everything is turning out just as the prophets of the Bible said it would. (+)

**Hysteria (Hy).**   The development of physical disorders such as blindness, paralysis, and vomiting as an escape from emotional problems is termed *hysteria*.
> *Related items:*
> I am not likely to speak to people until they speak to me. (+)
> I get mad easily and then get over it soon. (+)

**Psychopathic deviate (Pd).**   An individual who lacks "conscience," who has little regard for the feelings of others, and who gets into trouble frequently is called a *psychopathic deviate*.
> *Related items:*
> My family does not like the work I have chosen. (+)
> What others think of me does not bother me. (+)

**Paranoia (Pa).**   Extreme suspiciousness to the point of imagining elaborate plots is *paranoia*.
> *Related items:*
> I am sure I am being talked about. (+)
> Someone has control over my mind. (+)

**Psychasthenia (Pt).**   The term *psychasthenia* indicates strong fears and compulsions.
> *Related items:*
> I become impatient with people easily. (+)
> I wish I could be as happy as others seems to be. (+)

**Schizophrenia (Sc).** Bizarre thoughts and actions out of communication with the world characterize *schizophrenia*.

*Related items:*

I have never been in love with anyone. (+)

I loved my mother. (−)

**Hypomania (Ma).** Overactivity and inability to concentrate on one thing for more than a moment are typical of *hypomania*.

*Related items:*

I don't blame people for trying to grab everything they can get in this world. (+)

When I get bored, I like to stir up some excitement. (+)

Research on the MMPI has gone on for almost 40 years. Many new scales have been derived from the old items, and many new items have been added to measure factors in addition to the eight illustrated above. Numerous factor analyses have been performed on these items, resulting in new groupings into scales. Also, a great deal of empirical research has been undertaken to determine how effectively the instrument works and to assess the influence of various situational factors (e.g., instructions regarding frankness) on the different scale scores. [See discussions of this large mass of research in Edwards (1970), Wiggins (1973), and other works cited in the Suggested Additional Readings.]

Typical of the inventories that are primarily concerned with social traits is the Guilford-Zimmerman Temperament Survey (GZTS) (Guilford 1959). The GZTS grew out of many years of factor-analyzing groups of self-inventory items by Guilford and his colleagues. The inventory contains 300 items concerning social traits. Each of 10 factors is measured by 30 of the items. The factors are as follows:

*General activity* High energy, quickness of action, liking for speed, and efficiency

*Restraint* Deliberate, serious-minded, persistent

*Ascendance* Leadership, initiative, persuasiveness

*Sociability* Having many friends and liking social activities

*Emotional stability* Composure, cheerfulness, evenness of moods

*Objectivity* Freedom from suspiciousness, from hypersensitivity, and from getting into trouble

*Friendliness* Respect for others, acceptance of domination, toleration of hostility

*Thoughtfulness* Reflective, meditative, observing of self and others

*Personal relations* Tolerance of people, faith in social institutions, freedom from faultfinding and from self-pity

*Masculinity* Interest in masculine activities, hard-boiled, not easily disgusted versus (for femininity) romantic and emotionally expressive

The GZTS was constructed much more carefully than many of the multifactor self-inventories. It has been progressively refined over many years, and investigations have been made of both the internal characteristics of the instrument and correlations with numerous other variables (for much of the earlier research results see the discussion in Guilford 1959). The GZTS also is discussed in a number of the works cited in the Suggested Additional Readings.

**Evidence for the factors** In spite of the many reported factors in self-inventories, presently it is unknown how many important factors exist (important in terms of standards discussed in Chap. 13). Because in many cases it has been necessary to factor-analyze collections of items rather than whole tests, many of the factor-analysis results have not been clear. In subsequent uses of the factors, in many cases less than 20 items were used for each factor, reliabilities of factors were rather low, and correlations among tests used to measure different factors had excessively high correlations among them. Whereas extensive, careful research has gone into the development of multifactor tests such as the MMPI and the GZTS, many of the supposed factors that have been found in personality inventories are based on very skimpy evidence. This has tended to create a statistical mess, in which it is difficult to separate the wheat from the chaff. Part of the problem is that the domain of possible factors covered by self-inventories of personality potentially is quite large, but part of the problem is also due to inadequate research.

The whole area of research into the factors that underlie personality inventories badly needs to be cleaned up. A number of approaches would help. First, where possible, it would be better to hypothesize and construct whole tests relating to personality than to rely on factor analyses of individual items, which causes all the difficulties mentioned in Chap. 8. Second, in those areas where it is necessary to factor-analyze items rather than whole tests (if it ever is the case), it would be far better not to take seriously the numerous "splinter" factors obtained in this way. Typically they have low reliabilities and correlate excessively with one another. It would be better to intercorrelate the relatively small groupings of items that supposedly measure such factors and to factor-analyze these. Third, it would be wise to perform second-order factor analyses of the dozens of statistically flimsy factors that have been found so far and take seriously only these more general underlying factors. These and other sound alternatives are available for constructing adequate measures of the different factors. The resulting factors need to be highly reliable, have a substantial amount of independence among them, and prove their importance by criteria discussed in Chap. 13. Until that is done, it will be unknown how many important factors exist in personality inventories.

Because of the statistical mess resulting from a careless overuse of factor analysis with conglomerate collections of inventory items, Peterson (1965) came to the following conclusions:

> Factor analyses of verbal personality measures have typically generated highly complex multidimensional structural systems. Available evidence now suggests that the most dependable

dimensions drawn from conventional factor analyses of ratings and questionnaires are simple, familiar dimensions of broad scope. It also appears that most of the initially obscure, apparently more precise, more narrowly defined factors many investigators claim to have revealed are either trivial, artifactual, capricious, or all three. Verbal descriptions of personality were reduced to two factors, and the two factors were reduced to two ratings, one concerning perceived adjustment and the other related to introversion-extraversion.

Although Peterson is correct that much of the common variance in personality inventories can be explained by global factors of adjustment and introversion-extraversion, there is ample evidence that numerous other important factors can be obtained from self-inventories—if careful research is undertaken.

**Social desirability**  One of the major problems in developing multifactor batteries of personality tests from self-inventories is that such inventories tend to be dominated by a general factor of *social desirability*. Although this was suspected for a long time, it remained for Edwards and his colleagues to thoroughly explore the matter. A great deal of research in this regard is summarized in Edwards (1970). In the first major study (Edwards 1953), 152 subjects rated the social desirability of 140 self-inventory items. Each item was rated on a nine-point scale. The mean rating of each item represented the social desirability of the item as viewed by the subjects as a group. Next, Edwards placed the 140 items in a self-inventory and obtained yes-no responses from a group of subjects. He found a correlation (over items) of .87 between the mean desirability ratings and the proportion of people endorsing each item. This is strong evidence that the average person tends to describe himself or herself in a socially desirable manner on self-inventories.

The above evidence regarding social desirability, however, said nothing directly about individual differences in the tendency to say good things about oneself; rather, it pointed to a bias in that regard for the average person. However, a variety of forms of evidence make it clear that individual differences are very important with respect to self-inventories. When an effort is made to develop a relatively pure measure of the tendency of people to say good rather than bad things about themselves, it is found that such social desirability scales correlate highly with many factors, such as some of those in the MMPI and in other multifactor batteries. The evidence is so strong now that no longer is there any argument about the statistical importance of self-desirability in explaining the variance of self-inventories. Rather, the question is whether a sufficient amount of independent variance remains in self-inventories to produce other strong factors.

Research evidence during the last 10 years shows that careful research can produce numerous strong factors of personality in self-inventories, but only if efforts are made to prevent the tests and individual items from being dominated by social desirability. A major argument now concerns the psychological nature of self-desirability scores. Some speak of such scores as concerning only *response styles*—individual differences in test-taking habits which are unrelated to the purpose of the instruments. (Response styles will be discussed more fully in Chap. 16.) Others have gone so far as to suggest that the variance in self-desirability ratings represents individual differences only in conscious faking, which in turn implies that self-inventories in general tend to measure only individual differences in the tendency to "fake well." At the other extreme, some argue that the correlations between self-desirability scores and scores on self-inventories do not invalidate the latter, but rather show that adjustment and self-desirability (or self-esteem) are much the same thing.

Admittedly the dominant factor in self-inventories (social desirability) is quite complex. Probably it is a pure measure of neither adjustment nor faking, but rather a combination of those and other attributes. The major components of social desirability probably are (1) actual adjustment of individuals, (2) knowledge individuals have about their own traits, and (3) frankness of individuals in stating what they know. Individuals could be maladjusted (by popular standards) and not know it, and thus they might rate themselves as being high in social desirability. In contrast, individuals could be maladjusted and know it but consciously distort their responses so as to appear socially desirable. Another possibility would be individuals who are highly adjusted, know it, and frankly describe themselves as being high in social desirability. Since each of these three component characteristics can be thought of as relatively continuous, the expressed self-desirability of each person can be thought of as some combination of the three.

Social desirability is an interesting variable that should be investigated in detail. There is enough circumstantial evidence to show that it is related to adjustment, but also there is enough circumstantial evidence to show that some part of its variance concerns other traits, such as self-knowledge and frankness.

**Other problems with self-inventories** In addition to the problems that have been discussed so far in the use of self-inventories to measure personality traits, there are other problems that should be mentioned. Such inventories are beset with severe *semantic problems*, which occur in communicating both the meaning of items to subjects and the results of studies to researchers. The former type of problem can be illustrated with the following item: "Do you usually lead the discussion in group situations?" First, the individual must decide what is meant by "group situations." Does this pertain to family settings as well as to groups found outside the home? Does it pertain only to formal groups, such as clubs and business groups, or does it also apply to informal group situations? Second, the subject must decide what is meant by "lead." Does this mean to speak the most, make the best points, or to have the last say? Third, the subject must decide what is meant by "usually." Does that mean nearly all the time, most of the time, or at least half the time? It could be said that these semantic problems constitute a "language barrier" which makes it difficult for individuals to frankly report what they know about their own personality characteristics.

Anyone who works with self-inventories should, on at least one occasion, ask several subjects how they interpret each item on a typical inventory. When that is done, one is rather disturbed by the differences in meanings held by different subjects and by the extent to which all subjects are somewhat confused by some items. For these reasons, frequently subjects give different responses to appreciable percentages of the items when responding to the same self-inventory on two or more occasions. This, of course, relates only to the general confusion about the meanings of items. In contrast, if an individual has a definite but erroneous interpretation of an item, he or she will consistently respond erroneously to the item.

A second semantic problem occurs in communicating the results of studies with self-inventories to other researchers. Factor names and descriptions tend to be less clear than factors of human ability. This is partly because researchers employ terms in common parlance to describe factors, and people do not entirely agree about the meanings of such terms. For example, the factor that Guilford calls thoughtfulness might be misinterpreted by many as relating to considerateness, whereas it relates to contemplativeness. Admitting that it is difficult to find precise terms for communicating about personality traits, some investigators have gone out of their way to employ vague terms, e.g., rhathymia and adventurous cyclothymia.

Another major problem with self-inventories is that scores are somewhat affected by situational factors. (Evidence for this is summarized by Guilford 1959.) For example, if a self-inventory is used in personnel selection, individuals are likely to give somewhat different answers when applying for a job than they will sometime later when they are performing satisfactorily on the job. Numerous studies have shown that responses are somewhat different when the same subjects are required to take the same inventory under different instructions, e.g., under instructions to appear adjusted, appear maladjusted, and to be frank. Although there is not enough evidence to know for sure, self-inventories used in basic research might be affected to some extent by the subject's conceptions of the intents and purposes of the research. For example, if the subject thinks the research concerns emotions, the subject might give somewhat different responses to an inventory than if the research concerned learning.

Another potential problem with self-inventories is that they may be affected by response styles—test-taking habits that are unrelated to the purpose of the instruments. For example, there is some evidence regarding a response style of *acquiescence*, the tendency to say *yes* or to agree regardless of the item content. In most cases the variance attributable to such response styles is logically unrelated to the trait being measured; consequently, such variance should be limited as much as possible in terms of the way that instruments are constructed, administered, and scored. As will be shown in Chap. 16, most of the concerns about self-inventories being dominated by response styles have proved to be largely false alarms.

**Directions for research** In spite of the problems with self-inventories, they play a very important part in research and applied work today, and probably they will continue to do so for a long time to come. Even though considerable negative evidence has been obtained regarding the validity of some self-inventories, and there are reasons to question the validity of others, in most cases such inventories apparently are more valid than the measures provided by any other approaches. For example, even though practically no one in psychology would claim that self-inventories to measure anxiety have more than a modest level of validity, certainly they are more valid than existing projective instruments, physiological indices, and other approaches. The problem is that we have few, if any, highly valid measures of personality traits provided by any approach, and the measures provided by self-inventories currently are the best of the lot.

Since individual differences in social desirability are so strongly represented in most self-inventories, plans for improving such inventories must consider what is to be done about that variable. As was mentioned previously, it is an interesting variable which merits investigation in its own right, but it is serving to cloud the measurement of other personality traits. Numerous suggestions have been made for ways to delete the social desirability factor in self-report inventories, but none of these has proved entirely satisfactory. One suggestion is to measure social desirability separately and then partial such scores from the scores on self-inventories. There are two large problems in doing that. First, even if one were successful, it would markedly reduce the reliable variance in existing self-inventories. Such partialed scores would have reliabilities predictable from equations for the reliabilities of linear combinations (Chap. 7). Since it is known that social desirability correlates substantially with most self-inventories, partialing social desirability would result in rather unreliable "corrected" self-inventory scores. Another way of looking at this matter is in terms of correlations among self-inventories. Since it is known that social desirability can explain a sizable percent of the common variance among self-inventories (in factor analysis), correlations among self-inventories would be rather small if scores on social desirability were partialed. Then it would be very difficult to find statistically strong factors among such partialed scores.

The second major problem with attempting to partial social desirability from self-inventories is that, before this can be done, it is necessary to measure some components of social desirability. The problem with present measures of social desirability is that they lump together several underlying traits, i.e., adjustment, self-knowledge, and frankness. Rather than partialing these in conglomerate form from self-inventories, it would be better to partial only one or two of these, particularly frankness and/or self-knowledge. Before this can be done, it will be necessary to measure the different components of social desirability, but at the present time, there are no appealing suggestions as to how that can be managed.

One possible way to deal with social desirability without encountering the problems mentioned above is to employ items that are neutral with respect to social desirability. Logically this is very difficult, because to varying degrees personality traits are intrinsically related to social desirability. Thus dominance is considered more desirable than submissiveness, sociability is considered more desirable than nonsociability, energeticness is considered more desirable than laziness, and so on for other personality traits. For these reasons, it is very difficult to find neutral items that actually measure personality traits; however, by using items that are not extreme with respect to social desirability, one should be able to reduce the importance of that factor. This represents the best hope of limiting the variance of social desirability in self-inventories so that additional strong factors relating to personality can be documented.

Rather than attempt to employ items that are neutral with respect to social desirability, another approach is to employ forced-choice items that are matched for social desirability. Two examples are:

Do you worry more about
_____ social problems
or _____ health problems

Most of your friends consider you as more
_____ frank
or _____ tenderhearted

Although the use of forced-choice self-inventories has stirred much interest, and considerable work has been done to develop such inventories, the forced-choice item by no means constitutes a panacea for the problems that beset self-inventories. [In a review of the literature on forced-choice inventories, Zavala (1965) paints a much more sanguine picture of the effectiveness of forced-choice inventories than is being painted here. For some other positive outlooks on the use of forced-choice items, see Edwards (1970).]

One major problem is that it is very difficult to equate alternatives for social desirability. Even when the alternatives have almost identical ratings of social desirability when rated separately, they are not rated equal in social desirability when paired. This is probably because relative ratings are more precise in this instance, for reasons that were discussed in Chap. 2. For example, even if frankness and tenderheartedness receive the same mean rating of 6.0 on a seven-step social desirability scale, 60 percent of the people may say that frankness is more desirable than tenderheartedness when they are actually paired. Apparently, in forced-choice inventories, people are able to detect fine differences in social desirability, which partly destroys the purpose of using such instruments. However, in terms of both the logic of the problem and the available evidence, one would expect that the variance because of social desirability could be reduced with the use of forced-choice items; consequently, future research along those lines should be encouraged.

In summary, even though personality inventories have their problems, they represent the best general approach currently available to measuring personality characteristics. Many of the supposed problems are not inherent in self-inventories and can be avoided by proper methods of test construction and use. The people who have poked fun at self-inventories as being unscientific have failed to produce more valid approaches for general use. Perhaps there are some breakthroughs on the horizon that will lead to highly valid measures of personality which are different in kind from self-inventories; but unless and until such things happen, there is no choice but to rely heavily on self-inventories for the measurement of a wide variety of personality traits.

## OBSERVATIONAL METHODS

Related to self-inventories are observational methods for the measurement of personality traits. The difference is that in the latter method individuals are asked to describe someone else rather than themselves. In most observational methods, the interest is in the personality traits of the person being observed, and the intention is for the observer to be an impartial, accurate judge of the traits of the other person.

In most observational methods, the validity of the measurements is completely at the mercy of the observers. They make judgments about the personality traits of other people, and such judgments can be accurate only if the experimenter asks the right questions of the observers and only if the observers know the correct answers. It is proper to say that observational methods of these kinds are "subjective," in that judgments necessarily flow from the silent intuitive processes of the observers. Such subjective judgments surely constitute the oldest approach to the understanding of personality traits. People have always observed other people and tried to describe their characteristics with words relating to personality. What has been done in psychometric research on observational methods is to objectify the recording of impressions (e.g., with rating scales) and the analysis of results.

In contrast to most observational methods, which are based on subjective judgments of personality traits, some observational methods are quite objective, in that all the observer does is record what the subject actually does, e.g., how many questions a child asks in an interview situation. In other instances, observational methods are "almost" objective, in that the observer is required to make ratings that entail only a low level of inference, e.g., that a child is shy in an interview. Typically, the more objective the behavior to be observed, the more molecular the trait involved. It is easy to be objective about traits at the level of simple "habits," e.g., number of questions asked, amount of time spent in different activities, and number of words of different kinds uttered by the person being observed. When observations are being made of more general personality traits, however, judgments usually are highly subjective, e.g., judging personality traits like anxiety, dominance, and achievement motivation. Thus efforts to make observational methods more objective usually result in narrowing the traits under investigation to the level of highly specific modes of response (or habits). Then there is a question of how to combine such highly specific responses into measures of more general personality traits. To do so requires a great deal of construct validation, very little of which has been done at the present time. If one goes to the other extreme and deals directly with general traits of personality, much reliance must be placed on the accuracy of subjective judgments by observers.

Most observational methods employ rating scales to record impressions, e.g., a seven-step scale anchored by the adjectives *anxious* and *calm* to be used in rating psychiatric patients in an interview. Some psychometric properties of rating methods will be discussed in Chap. 15; here will be considered the types of situations in which such rating scales are employed. There is a large literature on observational methods, so large that it is not possible to summarize here all the evidence about the many approaches that have been explored. In this section only some of the outstanding properties of the major observational methods will be mentioned. [See Guilford (1959) and Wiggins (1973) for comprehensive discussions of many types of observational methods and research evidence from employing them.]

**Observations in daily life** Observation in daily life probably is employed more frequently than any other observational method for the measurement of personality traits. Examples are a teacher rating the personality traits of students, parents rating the traits of their children, and students rating the personality traits of one another. Such observations are analogous to having one individual fill out a self-inventory for someone else, and consequently both methods tend to run into the same types of problems. Ratings of persons in daily life tend to be dominated by a general factor, not unlike the factor of social desirability found in self-inventories (Peterson 1965). Such ratings tend to concern rather obviously good- and bad-sounding traits, e.g., anxious rather than calm, friendly rather than hostile. Although only moderate correlations typically are found among different rating scales, this is mainly due to only a moderate level of reliability. Much of the common variance among scales in a typical study can be accounted for by a general factor. This is particularly so in ratings of social traits and motives of normal people. Apparently there is less tendency for a general factor to prevail in studies of symptoms of maladjustment in groups of neurotics and psychotics. An example is the study by Grinker (1961) and his colleagues, which produced 15 factors relating to the symptoms of depressed patients.

The general factor that usually appears in self-inventories concerns self-desirability (or rated self-esteem). The general factor that appears in most ratings of normal people concerns *leniency*—the tendency to say good things or bad things about people in general. This might be thought of as other-desirability rather than self-desirability. Individual differences in the former tendency have been documented on numerous occasions, where it has been found that raters differ in their average ratings of other people.

In addition to making it difficult to document additional factors in ratings, the factor of other-desirability introduces a source of bias into ratings. Since the ratings of a person depend to some extent on the level of other-desirability held by the rater, this is a source of unreliability. Obviously this bias would lead to some faulty decisions about people in applied situations, e.g., in ratings of workers by supervisors and in the rating of psychiatric patients by nurses.

Just as self-desirability in self-inventories is influenced by the frankness of the subject, the rated social desirability of other persons is influenced by personal prejudices. For example, parents are prone to give more favorable ratings to their own children than to other peoples' children, and teachers are influenced in the ratings of students by their personal likes and dislikes.

Just as self-inventories are limited to what individuals know about themselves, ratings in daily life are limited to what the observer knows about the person being rated. Actually, this is more of a problem with observational methods than with self-inventories, because with the former it can at least be assumed that individuals "live with themselves," and whether or not they take advantage of it, they have myriad opportunities to observe themselves in action. Frequently ratings are made by people who barely know the person being rated or who have had opportunities to observe the person only in highly restricted settings. In this connection, the author once performed a study of ratings (unpublished) in a military setting, in which officers were asked to identify by name the photographs of men that they previously had rated. On the average, they could identify less than 50 percent of the men, and interestingly enough, the men identified were predominantly from the "good" and "bad" ends of the rating continuum rather than from the middle.

Even if the observer has had considerable opportunity to observe an individual in one type of situation, there may have been practically no opportunity to observe the individual in situations relevant to the traits being rated. This frequently occurs in university settings, where professors are asked to rate personality characteristics of students in applications for graduate work or for a particular position. The professor may have only the vaguest idea about some of the social traits of the student.

In spite of their problems, observations in daily life tend to be superior to the other types of observational methods. Although such ratings frequently suffer because the observer has not had sufficient opportunities to observe the individual in circumstances relevant to the traits being rated, the situation tends to be much worse with the other observational methods. Typically the latter methods permit the observer to witness only a small sample of the individual's behavior, and frequently that is done in highly artificial situations. If nothing else, observations in daily life provide a much more economical way of obtaining approximate information about personality characteristics than is provided by other observational methods.

**Peer ratings** A particularly useful form of observations in daily life is *peer ratings,* in which all members make ratings of the traits of other members within a closed group of people who have had ample opportunity to become acquainted with one another, such as students in a classroom, members of a fraternity, players on a football team, members in the same platoon in the Army, and other such closely affiliated groups (see the discussion of peer ratings in Wiggins

1973). A typical method of peer ratings requires each member of a group to rate each other member of the group on a list of personality traits. The types of traits in the list would vary in terms of the kinds of acquaintances the subjects had had with one another and the purposes of obtaining the ratings. For example, peer ratings in military settings would tend to emphasize leadership qualities, ability to accept discipline, thoughtfulness of others, problem-solving ability in military situations, job knowledge, social relationships, and personality traits that would be particularly important for effectively working with others in a military role. In contrast, peer ratings obtained among sixth-grade students might be slanted more toward studiousness, athletic ability, cooperation with school officials, likability, possession of particular talents, and other characteristics that are important in the world of the schoolroom and might be important for researchers to investigate.

There is a wealth of research evidence to show that peer ratings usually are highly reliable and valid *if* excellent rating methods are employed and the traits are ones that can be adequately judged from the kinds of acquaintances raters have had with one another. Regarding the former consideration, a poorly constructed measuring instrument can blur even the best of peer ratings. Regarding the latter, valid ratings of traits cannot be obtained unless there is some opportunity for behavior relative to those traits being observed in the social situation from which peer ratings are obtained. For example, whereas members of a platoon in the army might provide very valid peer ratings of the types of traits mentioned previously, they might provide rather invalid rating of personality traits that would be manifested in situations where there has been no opportunity to observe the individual, such as in his relationships with members of the opposite sex, in relation to parents, or in his religious beliefs.

The major problem in employing peer ratings is a practical matter: it simply is difficult in most instances in which one wants to measure personality traits to have available a relevant peer group such as those described previously. Peer ratings constitute very useful measures of personality traits when (1) an individual is a member of such a peer group, (2) the traits in question are ones that would probably manifest themselves in the group situation, and (3) it is feasible to obtain peer ratings.

**Interviews** The interview is simply one type of observational situation. It is seldom used for observing personality traits in general; rather, it usually is restricted to sizing up individuals with respect to particular decisions about them, e.g., as in a job interview or a psychiatric interview. Usually the interviewer either has never previously met the person being interviewed or has known the person only casually. Because of the small amount of time to observe the individual (usually less than one hour), interviews make sense only if it can be assumed that (1) the interviewer is particularly talented at observing some important traits and (2) the interview is limited to obtaining information about only a small number of traits. Because the results of interviews naturally depend on the questions asked by the interviewers, efforts have been made to "structure" such interviews with standard lists of questions and other ways of establishing uniformity.

Even with the best efforts, ratings based on interviews tend to have only a low level of reliability and validity [Guilford (1959) and Ulrich and Trumbo (1965)]. Since interviews usually are employed in making personnel decisions, validity is determined by correlating ratings with specific criteria. When that is done, usually it is found that ratings add little to the predictive validity obtainable from objective tests of ability, personality, and interest. In spite of this fact, interviews probably will continue to be used for some time, because in some instances there is nothing else that can be used, e.g., as is the case with psychiatric interviews. It is surprising, however, that some people who castigate standardized tests place inordinate faith in what can be obtained from a 30-minute interview. Mainly, interviews are useful in obtaining idiosyncratic information about people that would not be obtained from standardized measures or application forms. For example, with respect to job interviews for various positions, it would be useful to learn that (1) a particular person has a speech defect that would make it difficult to use the telephone extensively, (2) a second individual would be required to perform periodic military duty which would interrupt employment, and (3) an individual has had considerable experience as a mechanic which would be incidentally helpful in a job relating to another type of activity. These and other idiosyncratic bits of information can be obtained from interviews, and for this reason such interviews frequently are worth the time and expense. However, it is clear that the interview does not provide a valid general tool for the measurement of personality traits.

**Observations in contrived situations** One approach to observation is to have the individual participate in a contrived situation, which is frequently spoken of as a *situational test*. One of the pioneering efforts of this kind was the screening program developed by the Office of Strategic Services during World War II, which was modeled on earlier screening programs developed first in the German army and subsequently in the British army (these are discussed in detail in Wiggins 1973). The purpose was to select men for military intelligence work, espionage, and other dangerous assignments. In addition to taking standardized tests of personality and ability, each candidate was given a series of situational tests, with each situation involving a type of problem that might be encountered in actual duty. The candidate's performance was rated in terms of ability to think quickly and effectively and in terms of emotional stability and leadership. In one such situation, the candidate was told to imagine that he was caught in a government office going through files marked "secret," that he did not work in the building, and that he carried no identification papers. The candidate was given 12 minutes to construct an alibi for his presence in the suspicious circumstances. Then he was subjected to a harrowing interrogation, in which attempts were made to break his alibi and make his statements appear foolish. The candidate was rated on how convincing his story was and his ability to support it under interrogation.

A large-scale use of situational tests was in a study to develop selection instruments for clinical psychology trainees [Kelly and Fiske (1951)]. In one such test, each candidate was required to express in pantomime the meaning of different emotions. In that study, situational tests added nothing to the prediction of success in clinical activity over what was provided by standardized tests of ability and personality (and the same was true for interviews).

By their nature, observations in contrived situations are not suited to the measurement of personality traits in general; rather, they are restricted to a very limited number of traits relating to the particular contrived situations. Also, since in many cases they are extremely laborious and time-consuming, they should not be employed unless they add something to simpler methods of measurement, and most of the evidence on that score is negative. Perhaps in some situations such observations are no more valid than they are because the situations are so obviously contrived. Some situations amount to "play acting," and it is reasonable to believe that such play acting is not entirely representative of behavior in real life. For example, the individual who shows leadership qualities in daily life might regard situational tests as silly and thus might appear to perform rather poorly. Although there are some exceptions, generally situational tests have proved to be highly laborious, time-consuming, expensive efforts that largely met with failure [see the discussion in Guilford (1959) and Wiggins (1973)].

**Behavioral tests**  In some observational situations, directly observable aspects of the subject's behavior are used as measures of personality characteristics. Because the observations concern observable behavior, the situations in which such observations are made are usually referred to as *behavioral tests*. Like situational tests, behavioral tests also consist of contrived situations. One of the earliest and still the best-known use of behavioral tests was that of Hartshorne and May in the Character Educational Inquiry. They wanted to measure traits in schoolchildren such as honesty, truthfulness, cooperativeness, and self-control. Rather than use conventional tests or ratings to measure those characterics, they chose to observe the actual behavior of children with respect to the traits. The observations were made in the normal routine of school activities—in athletics, recreation, and classroom work.

Observations were made so as to provide objective scores. For example, one of the measures of honesty was made by allowing students to grade their own papers; then a check was made as to the student's honesty in correctly scoring the paper. Since a duplicate copy of each paper had been prepared before it was given to the student, it was a simple matter to check the student's honesty in that situation. Another behavioral test in that study concerned the trait of "charity," in which children were first given an attractive kit of school supplies and were then allowed to donate some of the items to "less fortunate children." The donations appeared to be anonymous, but the experimenters had marked the items so as to be able to count the number of items donated by each child.

Another type of behavioral test is the Minimal Social Behavior Scale

[Farina, Arenberg, and Guskin (1957)], in which mental patients are submitted to a structured interview. In one "item," the interviewer offers the patient a pencil, and the item is scored "correct" if the patient accepts the pencil or acknowledges the offer in some other way. In another item, the interviewer places a cigarette in her or his mouth and fumbles for a match, during which time a book of matches is in plain view of the patient but is not visible to the interviewer. The item is scored "correct" if the patient mentions the matches or offers a match from his or her own pocket.

When behavioral tests can be employed, they have a number of attractive advantages. The use of actual behavioral products frees the measurement methods from the subjectivity of rating scales. If observations can be made in natural settings where the subject is unaware of being tested in any sense, the results are probably more valid. However, there have been so few systematic uses of behavioral tests that it is difficult to judge how useful they will be in the measurement of personality traits. They probably will continue to be used more with children than with adults. This is because it is easier to place children in test situations without having them suspect an ulterior purpose. Also, the relevant behaviors of children are more easily observed than complex adult interactions.

For a number of reasons, it is doubtful that behavioral tests will occupy more than a modest place in the measurement of personality traits. Like all observations in contrived situations, they are expensive and time-consuming. More important, it is very difficult to think of behavioral products that might relate to most personality traits. For example, what behavioral products in adults might relate to dominance or sociability? Behavioral tests will probably continue to be used only for rather special purposes, such as in the basic research of Hartshorne and May on character traits in children or for diagnosing rather specific traits in clinical populations.

**Summary of observational methods**  In spite of the many strenuous efforts to develop highly structured situations for measuring personality with observational methods, it has become clear that observations in daily life not only are far more economical but also are far more valid in general than other approaches. Observations in daily life tend to be particularly effective if, as with peer ratings, the individuals are well acquainted with one another in situations that relate to the traits being rated. It has become a truism in studies of ratings based on observational methods that far more important than any type of professional qualification or special training of the rater is the amount of experience that the rater has in lifelike situations where behaviors related to the traits being rated can be easily observed.

## PROJECTIVE TECHNIQUES

Projective techniques are based on the principle that, when a situation is open to a variety of interpretations, interpretations sometimes differ in accordance with the personalities of people. There is a great deal of everyday experience to support the principle, which is evidenced, for example, in the individual who, while suppressing intense hostility, attributes hostile motives to other people. As another example, the principle is clearly evidenced in the writings of children, where children are given a few lines of a story and told to complete it. The achievement-oriented child writes about prizes and conquests; the highly anxious child writes about explosions and mayhem; and the child with harsh parents populates the story with unkind adults.

Whereas the techniques employed with respect to these phenomena are called *projective*, in a strict sense projection is only one of the mechanisms involved. *Projection* refers to the tendency of people to attribute their own unwanted motives and social traits to other people, as in the case of the hostile person mentioned above. Actually, projective techniques are used to measure numerous types of social traits, motives, and forms of maladjustment. Although it would be better to speak of the methods as concerning interpretation rather than projection, the name *projective techniques* is too well ingrained in psychology to allow the change. In addition to relevant sections in the works cited in the Suggested Additional Readings, research on projective tests is summarized in Klopfer and Taulbee (1976) and in Molish (1972).

Frequently it is said that the essence of projective techniques is that they are *unstructured*, in contrast to self-inventories and rating methods, which are said to be *structured*. If there is an agreed-on public meaning for a stimulus configuration, it is said to be structured; but if there is no agreed-on public meaning, it is said to be unstructured. For example, a structured stimulus would be employed in the situation where an individual is shown an outline drawing of a house and asked to tell what she or he sees. Since there is an agreed-on public meaning for the stimulus configuration, nearly all subjects are likely to say that it is a house. In other words, there is little room for interpretation of a highly structured stimulus, and consequently individual differences in interpretation are not very important. In contrast, an unstructured stimulus would be used if the individual were presented with some random smudges of color on a piece of paper and asked to tell what it is. Another example of an unstructured situation is that in which the individual is shown a drawing of a house and asked to tell what the people are like who live there. In both instances, there are no agreed-on ways of responding. The individual must make an interpretation rather than give an objective description, and it is reasonable to think that the nature of the interpretation will depend on the personality characteristics of the individual. Even if there is much truth in that principle, however, there still is the chore of turning such interpretive responses into valid measures of personality characteristics, which apparently is much easier said than done.

Since self-inventories and projective techniques are used more often than any other methods for the measurement of personality traits, it is important to make some comparisons between them. Whereas the essence of projective techniques is that they are unstructured, self-inventories are intended to be structured. That is, on a self-inventory, regardless of what motivates an individual to respond in one way or another to an item, the person should clearly understand the item. Previously it was mentioned that this goal is only approximately achieved because of the language problems in the development of self-inventories.

Sometimes it is said that projective techniques are subjective methods, whereas self-inventories are objective methods. Actually, both are subjective but in different ways. The objectivity in self-inventories is in the scoring, but the validity of the results depends on the subjective processes of the subjects. In contrast, the projective techniques do not depend on the subjective processes of subjects to describe their personalities, but most of these techniques depend very much on the subjective processes of test examiners to interpret the responses. Rather than speak of objectivity, it would be better to say that self-inventories are much more highly *standardized* than most projective techniques, a matter that will be discussed in more detail later.

The growth of projective techniques has paralleled the growth of self-inventories, but they have been nourished by somewhat different traditions. Projective techniques have been developed mainly in conjunction with psychiatry and clinical psychology, but to a large extent, self-inventories have been developed in conjunction with basic research on personality traits and with personnel selection programs in military and vocational settings. Because of the affiliation of projective techniques with clinical activities, frequently they are spoken of as "diagnostic instruments." In clinical settings, projective techniques are mainly used to specify what is particularly "sick" about an individual who, at the outset, is known to have serious problems.

**Types of projective techniques** The projective techniques do not fall into neat types with common properties, as do observational methods. Rather, the apparent differences among them mainly concern the physical characteristics of the stimulus materials. Some consist of pictures of nonhuman objects, others consist of written material, and still others consist of three-dimensional materials of one type or another. Detailed descriptions of particular techniques are found in the Suggested Additional Readings at the end of this chapter.

The most widely used projective technique is the Rorschach inkblot test, which, as almost everyone knows, consists of 10 inkblots. Individuals are asked to tell what they see on each blot, and for this reason, the Rorschach is frequently called a *perceptual* test. The word *perception* in this context, however, is rather inappropriate, because other than for reasons of poor eyesight, everyone can see the blots, and what is at issue are the individuals' interpretations of what they see. Because of the wide use of the Rorschach, much of the evidence regarding the psychometic properties of projective techniques is based on research with that instrument.

The Thematic Apperception Test (TAT) is next in popularity to the Rorschach. It consists of pictures of people in different types of social situations. Perhaps more than any other instrument, it is directly concerned with motives. For this reason, the pictures that are used lend themselves to interpretations of motives of aggression, affiliation, security, achievement, and others.

Whereas on the Rorschach the subjects are required to tell what they see, on the TAT they are asked to make up a story about each picture.

Probably third in popularity are tests consisting of incomplete sentences such as the following:

1. I most dislike to _____
2. I wish that I had never _____
3. The people I like most _____

In some cases, semiobjective scoring systems have been developed for tests employing incomplete sentences (e.g., Rotter, Rafferty, and Schachtitz 1949).

In addition to the major methods discussed above, many other types of projective techniques have been developed. Various play activities of children have been used for that purpose, such as doll play, finger painting, and molding of clay.

**Validity** Apparently most projective techniques do a rather poor job of measuring personality traits. Most of the traits measured by projective techniques require construct validation, but there is little evidence to support the construct validity for such measures. For example, there is no convincing evidence that any projective technique validly measures the trait of anxiety.

In applied settings, the evidence is clear that projective techniques have, at most, only a low level of validity in predicting particular criteria. They tend to correlate very little with criteria of vocational success. Also, they do a poor job of differentiating normal people from people who are diagnosed as neurotic, and they do a poor job of differentiating different types of mentally ill persons. There are scattered findings that particular techniques are valid for particular purposes, but the total evidence points to the fact that, as a group, projective techniques do not provide very valid measures of personality traits. The following sections will consider some of the reasons for this state of affairs.

**Reliability** Although there are some exceptions to the rule, projective techniques tend to have unacceptably low reliabilities. Although there are arguments about how the reliability of projective techniques should be measured, however it is measured, the typical finding is a reliability around .60, and very few reliabilities as high as .80 are found.

Logically, the most appropriate measure of reliability with projective techniques is the correlation of alternative forms administered and scored by different examiners, but very few studies of that kind have been done. With projective techniques, it is particularly important to develop alternative forms, because with most of the techniques, it is difficult to define the domain of content. For example, what is the domain of content for the Rorschach test? Is it all possible inkblots, all inkblots of particular kinds, or what? If an alternative form can be constructed and the two forms correlate highly, it gives one confidence that a definable domain of content is involved. With some of the projective techniques (e.g., the original Rorschach inkblots), there is no alternative form, and consequently the alternative-form reliability is unknown. Alternative forms also would be useful for practical purposes, such as in testing the amount of improvement during psychotherapy.

In addition to the need for alternative forms in studying the reliability of projective techniques, it is necessary to investigate the measurement error because of examiners. The interpretation of most projective techniques is highly subjective, and in such instances one is likely to find considerable measurement error because of differences in interpretations by different examiners.

**Standardization** As has been mentioned several times in this book, the essence of measurement in science is that the measurement procedures be *standardized*. If measures are standardized, their results are repeatable—repeatable by the same individual employing different forms of the same instrument and repeatable by different individuals. Because the results depend very much on the tester, most projective techniques are rather unstandardized. The tester influences the kinds of responses that the subject gives, and the interpretations of responses vary considerably with the tester. For example, studies with the Rorschach have found that different examiners tend to obtain different numbers of responses from subjects. Some examiners typically obtain only 20 responses, and others typically obtain 40 or more. Since many of the Rorschach scores correlate with the total number of responses given, those scores depend to some extent on the person administering the test. Male examiners tend to obtain different types of responses than female examiners, and different examiners tend to elicit different types of responses in particular categories (Masling 1960).

Examiners, in addition to their influence on the responses given to projective techniques, have an even more marked influence on the interpretation of results. With most projective techniques, the end result is not a set of trait scores, but a description of some aspects of the subject. On the Rorschach, for example, a semiobjective method is used for scoring individual responses, but those scores are only steppingstones to the interpretation; and the step from the scores to the interpretation is highly intuitive. Thus, after studying the responses given by a subject, the examiner might conclude, among other things, that the subject "is rigid, overintellectualizes, and has much free anxiety." There are, however, only rough guides as to how to make such interpretations, which is the major reason why some projective techniques are so unstandardized.

There is some evidence that projective techniques are projective for both the examiner and the subject (Masling 1960). For example, one study found that examiners who were rated by their colleagues as hostile tended to interpret the responses of psychiatric patients to a projective technique as being hostile. Aside from particular differences among examiners in the interpretation of responses, surely there are important differences among examiners in overall validity. One gets the impression that some examiners are very accurate in their interpretations and that others tend to miss the mark entirely. This would be much like the situation where some meteorologists were very accurate in measuring humidity and others were very poor in that regard. Then the accuracy of weather forecasting would differ greatly from locality to locality, and the data obtained from such observations would not aid the science of meteorology.

Since the validity of most projective techniques depends on the interaction of examiner, subject, technique, situation, and trait being measured, these techniques are unstandardized and thus should not be called tests. (Some exceptions will be discussed later.) Since obviously it is impossible to determine the validity of these myriad possible interactions of examiners and other factors, it is not possible to know the validity with which projective techniques are employed in particular instances. It is better to think of most projective techniques as "aids to interviewing." Although it is not clear that they actually aid interviewing, certainly they cannot.be classified as standardized measures of personality traits.

**Directions for research** In spite of the weaknesses of most projective techniques, the concept of projective testing still is promising. This is because there is so much everyday experience to support the notion that people tend to interpret unstructured stimuli in ways that relate to their personalities. The problem is that most projective techniques are psychometrically unsound vehicles for measuring anything. Projective testing might be advanced considerably by efforts to develop homogeneous scales for particular traits, e.g., gathering responses to inkblots that are thought to measure anxiety, standardization of procedures of administration and scoring, factor analysis of correlations among scales, and construct validation of the obtained factors. This would not necessarily be more difficult than the other approaches to the measurement of personality traits, but it is surprising how little work has been done in this regard.

The good things that can be done with projective techniques are exemplified by the work of Holtzman and his colleagues on inkblot tests. After careful psychometric work, they constructed alternative forms of an inkblot test, each test consisting of 45 blots. Homogeneous scales were developed for scoring particular types of responses, e.g., the tendency to see "good forms" and the tendency to respond to colors. Each subject makes only one response to each blot, and consequently there is no possibility of variation in that regard influencing results. Instructions and scoring are well standardized, and alternative-form reliabilities of most trait measures are acceptable. Norms were obtained from diverse groups across the country, and comparisons were made of average scores given by normal, neurotic, and psychotic populations. Although a great deal of research has been conducted with the Holtzman inkblot test (much of it rather informal), there is still little solid evidence about what, if anything, the instrument measures [see the summary of evidence in Klopfer and

Taulbee (1976) and in relevant sections of the Suggested Additional Readings]. Efforts also have been made to develop standardized versions of sentence-completion tests (discussed in Guilford 1959).

Projective techniques are founded on responses to unstructured stimuli, and that is good because it allows one to investigate interpretive responses. One can, however, push the concept of unstructuredness too far. Some projective testers apparently assume that *everything* in the situation should be unstructured. Consequently they do almost nothing to direct subjects' responses in one way or another, and they employ complex materials (e.g., TAT pictures of people in social situations) which permit subjects to go off in many different directions. A better approach is to have projective techniques entirely structured except for responses relating to a particular dimension, e.g., hostility. Materials should force all subjects to say something that relates to a single dimension. To do that requires simpler materials than sometimes are employed, materials that direct the subject toward responses related to the trait of interest, and/or instructions by the examiner that elicit relevant responses. For example, the subject can be shown a simple picture of two children fighting. It is obvious that they are fighting, and there are no other persons or objects in the picture to elicit nonrelevant responses. To ensure that the subject gives responses that relate to hostility, the examiner could ask, "Why do you think they are fighting?"

The success in the standardization of sentence-completion tests probably is because such tests structure responses up to the point where lack of structure is called for. For example, even though the following sentences do not entirely structure the subject's responses, they do ensure that the responses will relate to guilt feelings:

1. I wish that I had never _____
2. I feel guilty when _____
3. When I hurt others, _____

Because many projective techniques are so entirely unstructured, they do not obtain comparable information from subjects. One subject might give 10 responses that relate to anxiety, and another subject might not give any—but this may have nothing to do with the amount of that trait in the two subjects. If both subjects were required to give 20 responses structured so that they would provide information about anxiety, the latter person might prove to be more anxious. Also, because many of the techniques are so unstructured, the results must be influenced by incidental sets that subjects form. Most subjects, particularly adults, know that they are taking a personality test, and since the situation is so unstructured, they formulate hypotheses about how to respond. For example, on seeing an inkblot, an adult may think that it is a test of "childish imagination," since, after all, it is an inkblot and to call it anything else would be make-believe. Consequently the subject gives as few responses as possible, and the responses that are given concern physical resemblances between parts of the blot and objects in daily life. College students, being on their mettle in this regard, might react to the inkblot as being an intellectual task, and consequently they might try to give many clever interpretations.

Before progress can be made in the development of psychometrically sound projectives tests of personality, the cultism of many die-hard projective testers must be broken down. Some of them cling to the original, highly unstandardized procedures associated with the Rorschach test and the TAT, in which what the subject is doing and how the examiner arrives at an overall interpretation of personality is mainly a mystery. The basically good idea behind projective testing is too worthwhile to be wasted on such pseudoscience. It is hoped that in the future the same sound psychometric procedures which are discussed for developing all psychological measures will be used to develop valid projective tests.

## PHYSIOLOGICAL MEASURES OF PERSONALITY TRAITS

This is a short section because it does not take much space to summarize what is presently known about the possibilities of employing physiological variables as measures of personality traits. In spite of the fact that personality traits (if there are any general traits of personality) must have some type of physical representation inside the individual, to date there has been very little success in deriving measures of such traits from physiological processes. No physiological variable (or group of such variables) is known to correlate substantially with self-inventories, ratings, projective techniques, or other indications of personality traits; and there are no physiological variables that are known to sharply distinguish mentally ill people from normal people or different types of mentally ill persons from one another.

The generally discouraging results found from efforts to measure personality traits with physiological variables has led to diminution of research in that regard. Some of the earlier research is summarized by Guilford (1959) and by Stern and McDonald (1965). Efforts to differentiate schizophrenic mental patients from normals with physiological variables are summarized by Cromwell (1975). Reviewing many major works on personality measurement and personality research in general up to the time of writing this book, the author finds very little research being conducted on the measurement of personality with physiological traits. In some whole books devoted to personality measurement, the topic is not even mentioned; in other books on personality measurement, physiological variables are only briefly discussed.

**Physique** For centuries it has been thought that different types of body builds are related to different patterns of temperament; e.g., the fat person is jolly, the thin person is contemplative and morose, and the muscular person is extraversive and dominant. Factor analyses of body measurements have produced half a dozen factors (discussed in Guilford 1959), such as trunk length, trunk depth, and muscular thickness. There is little evidence that these factors relate to personality characteristics, and consequently the age-old assumption of relations between physique and personality is much in doubt.

**Blood chemistry** It is reasonable to hypothesize that some personality traits relate to some of the myriad chemical components of the blood stream. The numerous attempts to find such relations, however, have not yet met with success. Most of the efforts along these lines have been to find chemical differences between mentally ill persons and normal persons. Although there have been numerous suggestive findings (Stern and McDonald 1965), the evidence for the importance of any one chemical substance is rather weak so far. Very little is known about relations between blood chemistry and personality traits in normal people.

**Autonomic functioning** Potentially one of the richest sources of personality correlates is in the functioning of the autonomic nervous system. This system participates in the activation and deactivation of the organism. For example, it might be thought that anxious persons would show a pattern of autonomic responses typical of activation and that certain types of lethargic neurotic and psychotic persons would show a pattern of autonomic responses typical of deactivation. There are some small correlations between measures of autonomic functioning and self-inventories; otherwise, few relations have been found. Pupillary response has been found to be a very sensitive, easily measured index of autonomic activation (see the discussion in Nunnally et al. 1967). Some early findings suggested that pupillary response is a bidirectional indicator of emotion, with pupil enlargement related to viewing of pleasant objects and pupil constriction related to viewing of unpleasant objects. If that had been the case, then pupillary response potentially could have been very useful as an objective measure of personality traits as mirrored in emotional responses to different types of visual displays. It had been reported, for example, that the pupils of normal male heterosexual subjects dilated when viewing nude females but not nude males, and vice versa for homosexual subjects. However, these and other findings suggesting that pupillary response is a bipolar indicator of emotion were not borne out in subsequent, more carefully controlled investigations. Rather, it has been found that pupillary dilation occurs as a result of *any* type of activation—viewing pleasant pictures and unpleasant pictures, performing difficult mental tasks, lifting heavy weights, being threatened with the loud sound of a gunshot, and numerous other stimuli that tend to induce activation. Other measures of activation have been investigated as potential measures of personality, such as palmar sweat and the galvanic electrical skin response. With pupillary response and a number of other potential measures of activation, it has been possible to provide good measures of an overall state of autonomic activation or arousal, but individual differences in this regard have not led to known measures of personality traits.

**Regulatory processes** One might expect to find personality correlates in various regulatory processes, such as heart rate, blood pressure, breathing rate, typical amounts of sleep, fluid intake, etc. For example, one hears of the "hypertension syndrome," supposedly a type of individual whose psychological tension is manifested in heart rate, blood pressure, and other physiological variables. There is, however, very little evidence for these and other correlations between personality traits and regulatory processes. In an extensive review of the literature on studies relating blood pressure to personality traits (McGinn et al. 1964, for example,) few consistent correlations, if any, could be reported.

**Brain functioning** Since personality traits must be represented in some form in the brain, it is logical to hope that someday various aspects of brain functioning may be used as measures of personality traits. Of course, the problem is that it is so very hard to get at the brains of living people; consequently, until better techniques are available, little can be done to find measures of personality traits in terms of brain functioning. The most that has been done so far is to compare brain waves of normal people with those of groups of abnormal persons. Some suggestive small differences in that regard have been reported (Stern and McDonald 1965), but few correlations, if any, have been found between brain waves and personality characteristics in normal people. Brain waves are such gross indicators of brain functioning that it is unlikely they will be very useful for the measurement of personality traits.

**Reactions to stress** The studies of physiological variables discussed above concern measurements taken in normal states, for example, while the subject lies on a comfortable couch. Of equal interest are physiological reactions to stress. It has been hypothesized, for example, that anxious persons recover more slowly in their physiological reactions to stress than nonanxious persons. Typical stressful situations that have been employed in these studies involve electric shock, sudden loud noises, and highly speeded, difficult tests of ability. What has been found in such studies is that different persons respond in terms of *different* physiological indicators. For example, whereas one person typically responds to different stressful situations with increased blood pressure but not with increased rate of breathing, the reverse is true for another person. This tells us something interesting about physiological responses to stress, but it provides little encouragement for the measurement of personality traits in terms of physiological variables.

**Problems in measuring personality traits with physiological variables** One of the major problems in searching for physiological correlates of personality traits is that people's somatic complaints frequently are not matched by actual somatic responses (Stern and McDonald 1965). The person who complains of rapid heartbeat frequently does not have a rapid heart rate. The person who complains of being tense frequently does not show tenseness of muscles. The person who complains of difficulty in breathing may show no abnormality in actual breathing. Consequently it is necessary to make a careful distinction between the labels that people employ for conscious states (e.g., "tension") and physical states that go by the same names. Apparently this semantic confusion has led us to expect that it would be rather easy to find physiological correlates of some personality traits (e.g., anxiety), but that certainly has not been the case.

A second problem in the use of physiological variables as measures of personality traits is that many of the measures have very low reliabilities. In a study by Wenger (1948) of 19 physiological variables which were repeated after one day, only one variable had a reliability as high as .80, numerous were below .50, and one was only .11 (sublingual temperature). Repeated measures after three months tended to show even lower reliabilities. The reliabilities of individual variables were not so low, however, that it would not be possible to obtain highly reliable linear combinations of them.

A third problem in the use of physiological variables as measures of personality is that, at the present time, we are sorely lacking in techniques for measuring many physiological variables. Physiological psychology has burgeoned in recent years partly because of the development of ingenious measurement techniques, e.g., the techniques for measuring electrical activity in single cells of the brain. Many of these techniques, however, either kill or maim the organism. Until comparable measurements can be taken without hurting people, they cannot, of course, be used in the search for measures of personality traits. Some of the physiological variables that might relate to personality traits (e.g., chemical changes at the synapses of neurons in the brain) are so microscopic in locus and so "delicate" that it may be some time before adequate measurement techniques are developed.

The fourth, and major, problem concerns the basic logic of such investigations. It is hard to disagree with the statement that if general traits of personality exist, they are entirely represented within the physical structure of the person. It is quite another thing, however, to assume that personality traits are manifested in the same ways in different people or that they are manifested in ways that will lend themselves to measurement. Present evidence suggests that many physiological variables do not obey general laws (e.g., as in the studies of reactions to stress mentioned previously); rather, they tend to behave idiographically. It is as though people developed largely different "styles" of responding to the same types of conscious states. For this reason, the "visceral" variables (those outside the central nervous system) may not be usable as measures of personality traits. If that is true, it means that one must search for measures of personality traits in the central nervous system, particularly in the brain. At the present time, however, brain functions relating to even rather simple processes, such as memory, are in doubt, and it may be a long time before brain functions in general are fully understood. Also, personality may not be fully represented in gross structural or chemical differences among people, but rather may be represented in terms of what is "stored" as habits and memories in the brain. It is quite baffling to consider how one would ever recover those through measurements of brain processes in living humans. Even if that ever comes about, it may prove to be much more economical to measure personality traits in terms of overt behavior, as in the case of printed tests of personality. Obviously it is worthwhile to continue exploring the possibilities of measuring some personality traits with physiological variables, but at the same time, it also is obviously worthwhile to continue trying to develop measures of personality traits in terms of overt behavior (including verbal responses).

**Heredity** Most psychologists as well as most lay persons suspect that at least some types of personality characteristics may be partially inherited. For example, one hears an individual say "She inherited her temper from her mother" or "He got his stubbornness from his father's side of the family." If some tendencies toward certain personality traits exist, there is almost no hard evidence of it at present. Also, even if eventually it is found that some personality traits are influenced by heredity, simply having this information will not lead to the *measurement* of personality traits. If such inheritance acts like inheritance of most traits, then it will consist of a very complex throw of dice in which at best one can assess probabilities that a person will be influenced in one direction or another in personality characteristics because of hereditary factors. Obviously, the study of personality in terms of inheritance represents more of a potential arena for basic research than a viable approach to the direct measurement of personality characteristics.

## PERSONALITY TRAITS IN PERCEPTION AND JUDGMENT

One of the most hopeful places to find valid measures of personality traits is in individual differences in laboratory investigations of perception and judgment. Of course, such studies have a long tradition in experimental psychology, but only during the last 20 years have individual differences in those situations been related to personality. Whereas such studies ostensibly concern *abilities*, it may be that individual differences actually relate to personality traits.

Although so far the evidence for measuring personality traits in terms of perception and judgment is only suggestive, the approach has a number of attractive features. In contrast to rating methods and projective techniques, measures of judgment and perception are not dependent on the subjective processes of observers and test examiners. In contrast to self-inventories, measures of perception and judgment are not dependent on what individuals know about themselves and are willing to relate. In contrast to physiological measures, measures of perception and judgment are not fraught with technical difficulties.

**Suggestibility in judgment** In various tasks concerning judgment in experimental psychology the results are influenced by individual differences in suggestibility. In some cases this suggestibility comes from the influence of other individuals. For example, if a person is judging which of several lines cast on a screen is longest or which of several lights is brightest, that person might change opinion if the majority of the group designates a stimulus different from the one that appears to be highest with respect to the attribute in question. Another example of suggestibility is nonhuman contextual cues in making judgments. An example would be for an individual to be shown a spot of light on a white screen and asked to adjust a light focused on a black screen to the point where the two lights were of the same luminance. Individual differences might be found in the extent to which such contextual cues would influence judgments. There are hundreds of instances in which incidental cues of this kind might produce reliable individual differences; and if this were so, these and other aspects of suggestibility in forming judgments might relate to a general personality trait of suggestibility.

**Problem-solving styles** Numerous investigations have been undertaken of people's individual styles of solving problems. As a sample problem, the individual is given four blocks with sides colored red, white, green, or blue. The number of repeated colors and color placements on sides is varied complexly among the blocks. The subject is asked to stack the blocks so that each of the column sides is the same color. In testing individuals and having them verbalize their approaches, one frequently finds very different approaches to problem solving which seem to be typical of the personalities of the individuals involved. For example, one person will start on a trial-and-error basis, stacking the blocks in many different ways, apparently hoping to stumble onto a correct solution. A second individual will systematically formulate hypotheses one at a time and try them out. A third individual will spend much more time thinking about the problem, trying to mentally discover a principle whereby a solution can be obtained. A fourth individual will work back mentally from a picturization of the final solution to the kind of moves that would be required to solve the problem. Although most studies of such individual differences in problem-solving styles still are in an exploratory stage, eventually they might lead to important trait measures, ones which represent a bridge between personality and ability. The investigation of such problem-solving styles has been very important in the study of creativity.

**Field dependence** One of the most encouraging lines of evidence for the measurement of personality variables with tasks concerning perception and judgment comes from studies of field dependence (these studies are summarized by Holtzman 1965). The rod-and-frame test was first used as a measure of field dependence. In the test, a subject sits in a darkened room and looks at a luminous, square, wooden frame. The frame can be rotated to the left or to the right by the experimenter. In the center of the frame is a luminous rod which can be rotated with remote controls by the subject. With the frame tilted to the left or right at various angles, the subject tries to adjust the rod so that it is placed in a vertical position. This is difficult for the subject to do without being influences by the frame. The frame is spoken of as the *field,* and to the extent that the subject places the rod vertically with respect to the frame rather than the room, the subject is said to be *field-dependent.*

Field dependency scores on the rod-and-frame test correlate with other perceptual measures that also appear to concern field dependence. One of these is the embedded-figures test. On each item of the test, the subject tries to locate a simple geometric form embedded in a complex form. The total figure constitutes the perceptual field, from which the subject must differentiate the embedded figure. Numerous studies have found substantial correlations between the rod-and-frame test and the embedded-figures test, and both tests tend to correlate with other perceptual measures that apparently concern field dependence (Holtzman 1965). Suggestive correlations have been found between these measures and conventional measures of personality. The evidence is that the individual who appears "dependent" in tests of field dependence also tends to be dependent in social behavior.

**Categorizing behavior** Efforts have been made to develop personality measures from the ways in which people employ categories in tasks concerning judgment (this research is summarized in Holtzman 1965). The task used most frequently for that purpose is the object-sorting test. Typically the subject is presented with a miscellaneous collection of 50 or more objects (e.g., a spool, small rubber ball, paper clip, etc.) and told to sort them into groups of objects that "go together." It is left to the subject to judge how many categories should be used and what properties of objects should be used for forming categories. The measure which has been studied most often is simply the number of categories formed, which is thought to relate to *conceptual differentiation.* The person who employs many categories is thought to make fine conceptual differentiations, and the person who employs only a small number of categories is thought to make coarse conceptual differentiations.

Another example of a test concerning categorizing behavior is the Role Construct Repertory Test (see the discussion in Wiggins 1973). In a more recent form of the test, individuals are asked to describe themselves, family members (e.g., mother and spouse), and a variety of person concepts (e.g., a threatening person and a pitied person). Individuals are given a list of bipolar adjectives such as *kind-cruel, careless-careful, tense-relaxed,* etc. They are asked to indicate which of the adjective pairs applies to themselves and to the other person-concepts. Various statistical analyses can be obtained of the resulting data matrix that indicate to what extent individuals regard all the person-concepts as alike or different and to what extent they manifest a simple rather than a complex factor structure in dealing with the adjective pairs. This method is a rather complex approach to understanding the ways in which individuals categorize themselves and significant other persons in their environment. Presently it is being used rather extensively in studying personality traits.

The "REP test" also has been used extensively as a clinical instrument to help diagnose problems that individuals have in interacting with other people and in providing useful information for counseling.

**Eye movements** There is suggestive evidence that eye movements relate to personality variables. Gardner and his colleagues have investigated *scanning behavior* as measured by amount of eye movements of subjects when they are judging the size of one geometric form in the context of distracting forms (summarized in Messick and Ross 1962). Some subjects typically focus only on the relevant form, and the eyes of other subjects wander constantly about both the relevant form and irrelevant forms. There is suggestive evidence that extensive scanners tend to be obsessive or compulsive people, in contrast to restricted scanners, who tend to be the opposite.

There also has been a considerable amount of research to study scanning behavior in schizophrenic mental patients (summarized in Cromwell 1975). Scanning differences between schizophrenic patients and normal individuals have been proposed because of findings that the patients tend to be distracted in judging visual illusions when incidental visual cues are presented in the same context. The argument is that schizophrenics have difficulty "centrating," that is, holding their attention on relevant aspects of the visual judgment problem. Instead, they tend to continually scan around the incidental cues that are present.

**Looking time** A perceptual variable that might be useful for the measurement of personality traits is the amount of time that individuals take to look at different visual displays. A procedure that is employed for that purpose is as follows (Nunnally and Lemond 1973). Subjects sit about 6 feet from a movie screen, onto which pictures are shown from a Carousel slide projector. The subjects have a button which allows them to look at a picture as long as they choose and then move on to view each subsequent picture in turn. Usually the viewing of pictures is made part of an overall experimental session so that the subjects are free to spend as much time as they like in viewing each picture. In this way, an effort is made to study "natural" viewing time rather than viewing time when subjects are under pressure to make some specific type of response. Nunnally and his associates have investigated a wide variety of pictures in order to learn about some of the major determinants of voluntary visual attention. Although not a great deal has been done to date on the matter, the method potentially could be employed to investigate various personality characteristics, particularly various types of motives. Pictures could be purposefully constructed to concern various emotions such as aggression, love, achievement, and fear. Amounts of time spent looking at different pictures might indicate the concerns of individuals with the types of emotions portrayed in the pictures. There are numerous other ways in which measures of voluntary visual attention might be used to measure some types of personality traits; however, at present this is only an interesting possibility.

**Directions for research** So far the surface has been only scratched in the search for personality measures in situations involving perception and judgment. It would be best to summarize all the research to date in that regard as being only suggestive. The methods which have been discussed in this section are illustrative only of what might be done, not of what has actually been accomplished.

A principle that should be kept in mind is that it is not likely that strong correlations will be found between personality traits and *accuracy* of perception and judgment. Accuracy would be involved, for example, in estimating the size of illusory geometric forms or in the recognition threshold for emotionally toned words. In all psychophysical studies, individual differences in accuracy tend to be slight, and usually what reliable variance there is can be accounted for by factors other than personality traits. Richer ground for finding measures of personality traits is in selective attention and in the *style* with which an individual perceives and makes judgments. For example, scanning behavior, as discussed previously, concerns individual differences in style of inspecting visual displays rather than in accuracy of size estimation (although the two are not entirely unrelated). The previously discussed studies of looking time with respect to displays of emotion-related objects concerned selective attention to different objects, and accuracy of perception was not at issue.

The potential value of finding personality-like traits in traditional studies of judgment and perception is much the same as that discussed in the previous chapter with respect to traits of abilities. By tying in with carefully performed measurements of perception and judgment, the individual studying personality can profit from the theorizing and highly developed measurement procedures that are employed in much basic research in psychology. For example, in recent years a great deal of very careful work has been performed on the stages involved in studying the amount of time required to make various types of discriminations, e.g., amount of time to push one of two buttons to indicate whether a word shown on a screen was one of eight words shown previously. The various stages involved in these and many other carefully measured processes in experimental psychology potentially relate to very important psychological processes, and individual differences in those regards potentially relate to important dimensions of ability and personality. By forming a more close affiliation of studies of individual differences with typical laboratory investigations of perception and judgment, we might be able to advance the welfare of both aspects of the science.

## OTHER METHODS FOR THE MEASUREMENT OF PERSONALITY

In addition to the major approaches to the measurement of personality, there are numerous other approaches which do not fit any of the major classifications. A number of these will be illustrated here. More detailed accounts of the "other" approaches are given in the Suggested Additional Readings.

**Response styles**  Response styles are hypothesized to be reliable individual differences in test-taking habits. One of these is *acquiescence*, supposedly a tendency to say *yes* or to agree when an issue is ambiguous or very difficult. Another response style is *cautiousness*, which supposedly concerns the tendency to leave items on ability tests blank when the correct answer is in doubt. A third response style is *extremeness*, which supposedly relates to the tendency to mark the extremes of rating scales rather than point toward the middle.

More about response styles will be said in Chap. 16, but since they have been mentioned frequently as possible measures of personality, it is necessary to discuss them here. Unless one wants to call the social desirability factor in self-inventories a response style (the author prefers not to), there is very little evidence that measures of response style relate to personality. This is not because of a lack of studies in that regard, but because the many studies that have been done generally failed to find positive evidence. This work is critically evaluated by Rorer (1965) in an article which is aptly entitled "The Great Response-style Myth."

**Products of ability tests**  Tests that supposedly concern abilities also can be used to measure personality traits. Such tests frequently are spoken of as "objective" tests of personality. An example follows. One page of a test is filled with randomly ordered alphabetic letters. Subjects are told to circle each A and to mark an X through each B, and they are required to work quickly. On the next page of the test, subjects are told to reverse their method of operation, to mark an X through each A and circle each B. The extent to which the first task interferes with the second task is determined by subtracting the score on the first task from that on the second task. The amount of interference in that regard has been hypothesized as having relations with personality.

Another ability test that has been used as a personality test is the *color-word test*. The subject is given a stack of cards; on each is the name of a color. In each case the color name is printed in a different color, e.g., "blue" printed in red. The subject is required to say the words as rapidly as possible. Next the subject is asked to go back through the cards and state the color in which each word is printed. Supposedly the colors and names of colors will interfere with one another, and individual differences in the amount of this interference might be related to personality traits.

Products of ability tests have been used in the hope of measuring a trait of *rigidity*. A typical test is as follows. Subjects are given a list of reasoning problems, all the same basic type. The first 10 problems are solved rather easily by the application of a simple principle. The remaining items can be solved by the same principle, but they are much more easily solved by a second principle. To the extent that subjects fail to switch from employing the first principle to employing the second principle, they are said to be rigid.

The possibility of obtaining measures of personality from the products of ability tests is quite attractive, because such tests are not beset with some of the unfortunate features of other approaches to the measurement of personality;

e.g., logically they are not influenced by the social desirability factor. The results to date with such measures, however, have not been very successful (evidence is summarized by Holtzman 1965). Different tests intended to measure the same trait frequently do not correlate well with one another, and consequently the factor structures among such tests tend to be "weak." Also, personality measures obtained from ability tests correlate very little with other measures of personality, such as with ratings and self-inventories.

**Biographical inventories** Unlike self-inventories, biographical inventories ask the subject factual questions about personal history, e.g., about ages of parents and siblings, types of schools attended, hobbies, health problems, and membership in organizations. Inventories of this type have been rather successful in selecting personnel for particular vocations, but very little has been done to form general measures of personality traits from them. For two reasons, however, the possibility is attractive. First, to the extent that the questions concern factual matters, test scores are not likely to be strongly influenced by social desirability. Second, information about personal history logically should be rich in information about personality. If it were possible to learn enough about what has happened to a person and how the person has behaved in the past, it should be possible to make good predictions of future behavior.

A major problem in employing biographical inventories is that people frequently do not know the answers to many important questions about themselves, e.g., behavior in early childhood or the amount of body weight at different ages. Another problem is that it is difficult to find a standard list of questions that will get at the important background characteristics of people in general. To a large extent these may be particular to the person. The construction of biographical inventories has been dominated by "shotgun empiricism," with little theory being used to guide the work. More careful thought about the background characteristics that theoretically should relate to personality traits might lead to biographical inventories that validly measure some aspects of personality.

**Verbal behavior** Another possible approach to personality measurement involves words that individuals typically employ. It may prove to be the case that "words are the mark of a person," more so than clothes are. For example, by listening to the words that people employ, we frequently judge them to be either intellectuals, beatniks, psychotics, or a person in a particular profession. It may be that more subtle differences in word usage relate to personality characteristics.

One approach to investigating individual differences in word usage is with binary-choice measures of association (Nunnally and Hodges 1965). Typical items are as follows:

1. Snake: ＿＿＿ dangerous ＿＿＿ long
2. Orange: ＿＿＿ sweet ＿＿＿ round
3. Coal: ＿＿＿ burn ＿＿＿ dirty

In each item the subject picks one of the two response words as forming the best associate for the stimulus word. The responses of each subject are scored in terms of the tendency to give associations in different categories, some of these categories being (1) positive evaluations, e.g., orange-sweet and priest-kind, (2) negative evaluations, e.g., snake-dangerous and knife-hurt, and (3) antonyms, e.g., night-day and fast-slow. Factor analyses of associations have produced six factors (Nunnally and Hodges 1965). Some interesting differences have been found on the factors for different types of people (e.g., psychotic and normal persons), and some small correlations have been found with self-inventories. However, these and other individual differences in verbal behavior are mentioned only as possible measures of traits relating to human personality.

**Wastebasket approaches** Finally, in this section we should mention that there are many popular superstitions about ways to measure various personality characteristics which are not supported by fact. These include palmistry, astrology, facial features, hair coloring (redheads are not "hot-tempered"), handwriting, and dozens of other incidental features of people. Although some intelligent persons mistakenly place faith in these and other bits of information about people, scientifically these factors must be relegated to the wastebasket as potential measures of personality traits.

## THE FUTURE OF PERSONALITY-TRAIT MEASUREMENT

Although the art of producing adequate measures of personality measurement has developed slowly, and hindsight indicates that a vast amount of effort has been wasted on some approaches that proved ineffective, the prospects for future developments are far from dismal. We have learned that it will be necessary to rely heavily on reports by people of either their own characteristics or other people's characteristics. However, both self-inventories and observational methods can provide satisfactory approaches when they are carefully undertaken. Also there are many prospects for improving both approaches. Numerous other approaches mentioned in this chapter potentially could lead to valid measures of personality traits.

In the author's opinion, very fertile ground for developing future measures of personality traits lies in personal conceptions, as mentioned in the early pages of this chapter. Many examples of inventories to measure such personality characteristics have come on the scene [see mention of some of these in Sechrest (1976) as well as in relevant sections in the Suggested Additional Readings]. One example is the *locus-of-control scale,* which contains items concerning the extent to which the individual believes that getting ahead in life depends more on luck and help from others than on personal skill and hard work. This scale not only has correlated interestingly with a wide variety of other measures of personality but has proved to be very important in helping explain differences among subjects in many types of experiments on personality and psychotherapy. A second scale relating to personal conceptions is the *dogmatism scale* developed by Rokeach (1973), which contains items concerning the extent to which an individual takes fixed positions on social issues (e.g., abortion or trade with communist countries) or is flexible in changing opinions when new information is supplied. A third example of a scale to measure personal conceptions concerns the extent to which a person makes judgments about the world in terms of feelings and intuition or fact-finding and logic (see examples by Myers 1962). Apparently there are very reliable individual differences on items that concern the tendency to rely on intuition rather than logic, and such scores correlate interestingly with other measures of personality.

There are several reasons why the author thinks that inventories to measure various aspects of personal conceptions offer rich possibilities for the study of personality traits. First, many inventories can be constructed so that social desirability does not play an important part, and thus frankness of responding is not a major problem. Second, whereas it proves difficult to clearly express the meanings of many of the items on self-description inventories, frequently this is far less of a problem on inventories used to measure personal conceptions. Third, whereas on self-description inventories sometimes self-knowledge is a problem simply because individuals seldom think about themselves with respect to the trait being measured, many of the inventories used to measure personal conceptions concern issues with which individuals are confronted every day. Fourth, whereas there is a tendency for the numerous proposed measures in self-description inventories to collapse into no more than a handful of factors, apparently it is much easier to find relatively independent measures of personal conceptions, such as in the locus-of-control scale. Numerous important measures of personality might follow from a careful survey of potentially important dimensions of personal conceptions, the employment of proper methods of test construction, and the documentation of basic dimensions through factor analysis.

## SUGGESTED ADDITIONAL READINGS

Anastasi, A. *Psychological testing* (4th ed.). New York: Macmillan, 1976, chaps. 13 to 15.

Edwards, A. L. *The measurement of personality traits by scales and inventories.* New York: Holt, 1970.

Edwards, A. L., and Abbott, R. D. Measurement of personality traits: Theory and technique. In P. Mussen and M. Rosenzweig (eds.), *Annual review of psychology,* Vol. 24. Palo Alto, Calif.: Annual Reviews, 1973.

Guilford, J. P. *Personality.* New York: McGraw-Hill, 1959.

Kerlinger, F. N. *Foundations of behavioral research* (2d ed.), New York: Holg, 1973, chaps. 28 to 32.

Klopfer, W. G., and Taulbee, E. S. Projective tests. In M. Rosenzweig and L. Porter (eds.), *Annual review of psychology,* Vol. 27. Palo Alto, Calif.: Annual Reviews, 1976.

Molish, H. B. Projective methodologies. In P. Mussen and M. Rosenzweig (eds.), *Annual review of psychology,* Vol. 23. Palo Alto, Calif.: Annual Reviews, 1972.

Nunnally, J. C. *Introduction to psychological measurement.* New York: McGraw-Hill, 1970, chaps. 12 to 14.

Wiggins, J. S. *Personality and prediction: Principles of personality assessment.* Reading, Mass.: Addison-Wesley, 1973.

CHAPTER
# FIFTEEN

## MEASUREMENT OF SENTIMENTS

In Chap. 2 it was said that sentiment is a generic term for all forms of likes and dislikes, and a distinction was made between psychophysical methods concerning judgments and those concerning sentiments. In this chapter some methods for measuring various types of sentiments will be discussed, and since rating methods are most frequently employed for measuring sentiments, the major consideration will be given to rating methods. Measurement of sentiments will be discussed both for studies of individual differences and in controlled experiments. Two widely used rating methods, the semantic differential and the $Q$ sort, will be discussed in some detail.

## INTERESTS, VALUES, AND ATTITUDES

Many different types of sentiments are widely investigated in the behavioral sciences, including preferences, opinions, personal attractions, and so on. Rating methods will be discussed for studying all these types of sentiments, but in this section it will be useful to distinguish among three overlapping, widely investigated types of sentiments: interests, values, and attitudes.

*Interests* are preferences for particular activities. Examples of statements relating to interests are as follows:

1. I would rather repair a clock than write a letter.
2. I like to supervise the work of others.
3. I would enjoy keeping a stamp collection.
4. I prefer outdoor work to work in an office.

Athough investigations have been made of interests in many different types of activities, such as hobbies and reading habits, most frequently they are made of interests relating to vocational pursuits. Measures of vocational interests are used so widely for career planning in schools, industry, government agencies, and the armed forces that it is rare to find a person who has not taken at least one of the available inventories. [Interest inventories are discussed in detail in most introductory texts on psychological measurement, e.g., Cronbach (1970) and Nunnally (1970).]

The evidence is that measures of vocational interests are valuable aids to vocational counseling and educational guidance. Starting in the late teens, people's interests tend to stabilize and remain rather stable over periods of 10 or more years. Scores on interest scales are moderately predictive of what occupations people enter, satisfaction with occupations, and changes in occupations. Although interest inventories are primarily intended to predict how well people will like occupations rather than how well they will perform in them, positive correlations have been found between inventories and criteria of performance in some occupations. There is ample evidence that individuals can "fake" interest inventories if they choose to do so, e.g., respond in such a manner as to appear to be interested in sales. However, there is very little evidence that people generally do attempt to give misleading responses to interest inventories. This is because they are used mainly in career guidance for high school or college students, where the individual is usually in a testing atmosphere in which frankness of responding can reasonably be assumed. Also, interest inventories are very useful in many types of applied research concerning various training programs in schools at all levels, and in industry, government, and military establishments.

*Values* concern preferences for "life goals" and "ways of life," in contrast to interests, which concern preferences for particular activities. Examples of statements relating to values are as follows:

1. I consider it more important to have people respect me than to like me.
2. A person's duty to family comes before duty to society.
3. I do not think it is right for some people to have much more money than others.
4. Service to others is more important to me than personal ambition.

In contrast to measures of interests, measures of values are seldom employed in applied activities; instead, they usually are employed in basic research in sociology and social psychology. Also, in many cases the statements used in studies of values are similar to the statements employed in self-inventory measures of personality. Studies of values have been very diverse in content, ranging from simple studies of opinions regarding intellectual aspects of life to more abstract values regarding goals of self-attainment. Whereas interests concern preferences for particular activities and attitudes concern feelings toward target objects, values are broadly concerned with feelings about one's own participation and outlooks in life.

*Attitudes* concern feelings about particular social objects—physical objects, types of people, particular persons, social institutions, government policies, etc. Some statements relating to attitudes are as follows:

1. The United Nations is a constructive force in the world today.
2. Trade unions have too much effect on our economy.
3. All public schools should be fully integrated.
4. Fraternities and sororities do more harm than good.

The feature that distinguishes attitudes from interests and values is that attitudes always concern a particular "target" or object. In contrast, interests and values concern numerous activities—specific activities in measures of interests and very broad categories of activities in measures of values.

Whereas potentially there are many approaches to the measurement of sentiments (see discussions in the Suggested Additional Readings), by far the most widely used approach is through some type of self-report. Although there are many different particular ways of measuring self-report, generally these are referred to as *rating methods*. The rating methods which are used in the study of interests are usually quite simple. With measures of occupational interests, individuals usually are presented with a long list of statements and asked to either agree or disagree with each (on a two-point or multipoint scale); or subjects are presented with descriptions of three or more activities in a group and asked which they prefer most and which they prefer least (see discussions of these and other approaches in Kuder 1970). The measurement of interests has a technology of its own which is somewhat different from that found generally in the measurement of sentiments. This is particularly so with respect to one approach to the development of scales (e.g., for engineers or physicians) that concerns *criterion keying*. Essentially this technique consists of selecting items for the separate scales based on responses given by people in different occupations. Because this involves some of the problems discussed in Chap. 8 regarding the criterion-oriented approach to test construction, the use of criterion keying has been somewhat controversial. In addition to the use of criterion keying, most major vocational interest inventories have scales based on principles of homogeneity and factor analysis.

In contrast to the special technical issues involved in the development of interest inventories, measures of attitudes and values tend to be more straightforward. Since attitudes and values are measured in essentially the same way, the overall issues will be discussed under the rubric of attitude measurement.

**Approaches to the measurement of attitudes** The most direct approach to the measurement of attitudes is to ask people, in one manner or another, what their attitudes are. For example, subjects are presented with a list containing favorable and unfavorable statements toward the United Nations and asked to agree or disagree with each. Such self-report inventories are called *attitude scales*, and much of the literature on the measurement of attitudes concerns different methods for developing such scales. In addition to self-report, numerous other methods have been explored as measures of attitudes [these are discussed in Campbell (1950), Cook and Selltiz (1964), Kerlinger (1973), and Wiggins (1973)]. One approach uses physiological measures. For example, physiological processes, such as the galvanic skin response or pupillary response, can be measured while an individual reads statements relating to a particular national group or looks at a picture of blacks and whites in a social setting. Projective techniques have been employed for the measurement of attitudes, e.g., the use of TAT-type pictures showing blacks and whites in various social situations. Real, or near-real, behavior with respect to attitudinal objects has been explored in some cases as a measure of attitudes. For example, individuals have been asked to indicate the degree to which they would be willing to participate in activities relating to desegregation of the races.

Although some of the indirect approaches to the measurement of attitudes seem promising, a great deal more research must be done before such measures are actually usable. At present, most measures of attitudes are based on self-report, and from what evidence there is concerning the validity of different approaches to the measurement of attitudes, it is an easy conclusion that self-report offers the most valid approach currently available.

**Validity of self-report measures** Potentially, self-report measures of attitudes are susceptible to the same weaknesses as those that accompany self-description personality inventories. In particular, self-report measures of attitudes are limited to what individuals know about their attitudes and are willing to relate. Both these limitations, however, probably are not so severe in self-report measures of attitudes as they are in self-description inventories. On self-description inventories, some of the items require subjects to make fairly complex judgments about their social behavior, e.g., "Do you usually lead the discussion in group situations?" In contrast, most self-report measures of attitudes concern items relating to direct feelings about a particular object, e.g., "I would not mind having a Japanese immigrant as a neighbor." In comparison to self-description inventories, the items on self-report measures of attitudes usually are more understandable, and subjects feel more confident about their responses. (These assertions are based on informal experience with the two types of instruments, but not on any formal evidence.)

Self-report measures of attitudes probably have an advantage over self-description inventories in terms of the extent to which they are influenced by social desirability. Whereas all people tend to have the same concepts of social desirability of personality traits, people differ markedly in their concepts of social desirability of attitudes, e.g., regional differences in attitudes toward abortion or government programs of social welfare. Frankness of response on self-report measures of attitudes may be lessened by pressures from social groups, e.g., the prevalent attitudes in a college fraternity toward intercollegiate athletics or the prevalent attitudes in a factory toward a particular trade union. To the extent to which anonymity of responses can be ensured, however, self-report measures of attitudes logically should not be strongly influenced by lack of frankness on the part of subjects.

The validity of a self-report measure depends upon how results are interpreted. At one extreme, there is nothing wrong with the investigator having a direct interest in reported attitudes, regardless of whether such attitudes relate to attitudes measured in any other way. It has been noted on numerous occasions that verbalized attitudes usually do not correlate highly with behavior pertaining to the attitude. (Some evidence on this point is summarized by Guilford 1959.) This does not necessarily mean, however, that verbalized attitudes are invalid. In some cases they may be highly valid measures of *reported* attitudes, but not valid measures of attitudes measurable in other ways.

Actually, in many instances what people say is more predictive of the course of social action than what they may feel in any deeper sense. For example, if most people in a particular community *say* that they favor school integration, this might bring about rapid integration even if, "down deep," many of the people feel somewhat negative toward the idea. In some instances it is reasonable to believe that verbalized attitudes represent the "cutting edge" of changes in feelings. Thus people may start saying that they favor integration before their feelings catch up with their verbalized attitudes. Also, verbalized attitudes have powerful effects on courses of social action, as is evidenced by the extent to which government officials are strongly influenced by the results of opinion polls. So, then, one has a right to be directly interested in verbalized attitudes, without claiming that they have a high degree of correspondence with other attitude-related forms of behavior.

If one is mainly interested in verbalized attitudes for their own sake, *content validity* (Chap. 3) is the major issue. For that purpose, a broad sample of item content must be obtained, e.g., of statements relating to the United Nations or toward intercollegiate athletics. The broadness of the content must be judged by those involved in investigating the particular type of attitude. Next, the investigator must perform item analyses to determine the number and kinds of homogeneous scales that are implicit in the item pool. If a scale developed by this method is highly reliable and correlates highly with scales developed by other investigators using the same or different methods of scale construction, it can be said that the scale has a high degree of content validity for the measurement of verbalized attitudes.

Instead of being interested only in verbalized attitudes, one may be interested in explicating a particular type of attitude as a construct. Previously, an attitude was defined as a *feeling* toward a social object, but, of course, verbalized feelings provide only one indicant of such feelings. To explicate a particular attitude as a construct requires a multi-indicator approach (as discussed by Cook and Selltiz 1964). For example, in the course of explicating a construct concerning attitudes toward blacks, one might decide to investigate behavioral tests, projective techniques, and verbal report. If these correlate substantially, some combination of them could be said to have a measure of construct validity. Also, the construct validity of the combination of measures could be further evidenced in changes occurring in controlled experiments, e.g., in studies of attitude change involving persuasive communications or in structured group situations. To the extent that verbal report alone correlated highly with other measures related to the construct and faithfully mirrored changes in controlled experiments, it could be said to have a high degree of construct validity. Then it could be used alone, with some assurance that it was measuring more than verbal report. To the extent that a measure of verbal report had low correlations with other hypothesized indicants of the construct and only weakly differentiated differently treated groups in controlled experiments, it would not suffice as a sufficient measure of the construct.

Of course, it is far easier to talk about these complex approaches to explicating attitudes as constructs than it is to do anything about them. [For some attempts, see Campbell (1950) and Cook and Selltiz (1964).] At the present time, most investigations of attitudes in sociology and social psychology are undertaken with self-report measures, and although there is ample evidence that many of these validly measure verbalized attitudes, in most cases there is little or no evidence regarding the extent to which the instruments measure more than verbalized attitudes.

**Psychophysical methods** Many of the psychophysical methods discussed in Chap. 2 can be used to measure verbalized attitudes. Various kinds of comparative responses (as distinct from absolute responses) can be investigated for that purpose. For example, the order of preference for different national groups could be obtained by the method of rank-order or the method of pair comparisons. Since, however, the comparative-response methods provide no indication of overall level of response to the stimuli as a group, they are not used frequently in studies of attitudes. For example, no matter how much individuals liked or disliked foreigners as a group, this could not be told from their rank-ordering of the names of national groups. Comparative methods are more useful for scaling stimuli with respect to sentiments than for scaling individuals with respect to sentiments. Thus the method of rank-order would serve very well to develop a scale of preference for national groups, but it could not be directly employed to measure the attitude of one person toward, say, the Japanese. Since, as previously defined, an attitude concerns feelings about a particular social object rather than comparative differences in feelings among social objects, the comparative methods are not highly appropriate for the measurement of attitudes. Instead, it is more appropriate to use an absolute-response method. The numerous possible particular approaches to obtaining such absolute responses are said to constitute *rating scales*. Because of the importance of rating scales in the scaling of attitudes and the measurement of sentiments in general, the next section will discuss rating scales in some detail.

## PROPERTIES OF RATING SCALES

Rating scales are used very widely in almost all subareas of psychology and throughout the behavioral sciences. Particular technical problems and issues of scale construction arise in these many specific forms of research, but some characteristics of rating scales are quite general to their many uses. Now we will discuss some of the major psychometric properties of rating scales.

**Graphic and numerical scales** We usually think of rating scales as being presented graphically, e.g., as follows:

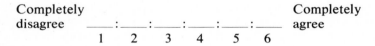

In some instances, however, the numbers are defined and written in spaces opposite the objects to be rated, instead of having the appropriate numbers marked on a graphic scale. It is customary to refer to these as *numerical scales* rather than graphic scales. The issue, however, usually concerns whether numbers will be employed with or without a graphic scale. Numbers are used as anchors in most rating scales. The numbers must first be defined:

1. Completely disagree
2. Mostly disagree
3. Slightly disagree
4. Slightly agree
5. Mostly agree
6. Completely agree

Employing the above scheme with a so-called numerical scale, the subject would be given a list of statements (say, concerning attitudes toward the United Nations). Opposite each statement would be a blank space, in which the subject would write the number corresponding to agreement or disagreement. In this instance a graphic scale would be employed as follows. First, as with the numerical scale, the numbers corresponding to the scale steps would be defined. Then, rather than write the number in a blank space, the subject would mark a graphic scale, as illustrated above, to indicate agreement or disagreement.

For several reasons, the graphic scale with numbers is preferable to the use of numbers without the graphic scale. First, because people frequently think of quantities as represented by degrees of physical extensions (e.g., the yardstick and the thermometer), the presence of a graphic scale probably helps to convey the idea of a rating continuum. Second, the graphic scale should lessen clerical errors in making ratings. If the meanings for numbers are defined only at the beginning of an inventory and subjects have to remember the meanings as they record the numbers in blank spaces, subjects are likely to forget the meanings of the numbers, e.g., to confuse ends of the scale or to assume that 4 means "mostly agree" when it was defined as "slightly agree." The presence of the graphic scale should lessen such errors, particularly if the ends of the scale are anchored by the extremes of the attribute being rated, e.g., "completely agree" and "completely disagree" as in the previous example. Third, if subjects write numbers in blank spaces, in some instances it will be difficult to decipher the numbers. For example, it might prove difficult to tell whether a particular number is 1, 7, or 9. Fewer errors in this regard are made in reading the points marked on graphic scales.

**Number of scale steps** In most cases the experimenter has a choice of the number of scale steps. He might decide to use a two-step (or dichotomous) scale, as follows:

Disagree    Agree

Or he might choose to employ many steps, as in the following example:

Strongly disagree \_\_\_:\_\_\_:\_\_\_:\_\_\_:\_\_\_:\_\_\_:\_\_\_:\_\_\_:\_\_\_:\_\_\_ Strongly agree
       1   2   3   4   5   6   7   8   9   10

In terms of psychometric theory, the advantage always is with using more rather than fewer steps. This is demonstrated by the numerous studies showing that the reliability of individual rating scales is a monotonically increasing function of the number of steps (Guilford 1954). Essentially the same principle is derivable from another body of evidence, that concerning relations between the number of scale steps and the *information* (or amount of discrimination) found in classical methods of psychophysical scaling (Garner 1960). The amount of discrimination provided by psychophysical scales (e.g., obtained from the average ratings by a group of subjects for 20 stimuli) increases with the number of scale steps up to at least 20 steps.

As the number of scale steps is increased from 2 up through 20, the increase in reliability is very rapid at first. It tends to level off at about 7, and after about 11 steps there is little gain in reliability from increasing the number of steps. To some extent, the monotonic relationship between scale reliability and number of scale steps may be at variance with common sense. For example, one might reason that, if there are numerous scale steps, subjects would have difficulty making up their minds and might mark a different point on a re-test. It is true that as the number of scale points increases, the error variance increases, but at the same time, the true-score variance increases at an even more rapid rate.

The only exception to the rule that reliability increases with the number of scale steps would occur in instances where a large number of steps confused subjects or irritated them to the point where they became careless. Then it would be possible to find the reliability decreasing with, say, as many as 20 steps. Isolated studies have reported such results (Guilford 1954), but such findings are rare. Also, in some rather unusual circumstances, little gain has been reported in employing multistep items over simple binary, agree-disagree responses (see discussion in Masters 1974). By far the bulk of the studies report increasing reliabilities up to 20 steps (although the increase from about 11 to 20 usually is small).

Another issue regarding the number of steps on rating scales concerns whether an even or an odd number of steps generally is preferable. The argument for an odd number is that it permits the use of a middle step meaning "neutral," "neither," or "neither agree nor disagree." This is thought to make subjects more "comfortable" in making ratings, and it can also be argued that subjects frequently have neutral reactions which should be measured. On the other hand, it can be argued that the use of a neutral step introduces response styles. Some subjects tend to use the neutral step more than others, and individual differences in that regard might not relate highly to the attitude in question. In looking through responses to attitude scales, frequently one sees the responses of subjects who made all their marks in the neutral step. This might represent a truly neutral attitude, but one has the suspicion that this is how the subjects said that they did not want to participate in the study. More to the point, in some studies it has been found that reliable differentiations can be made among persons who mark the neutral step. This can be done as follows. First, subjects are given five-step scales, each of which contains a neutral step. Later the scales are readministered to all subjects who marked the neutral step, except on the second occasion six steps are employed, with no neutral step present. The variance of ratings over subjects can then be shown to be reliable, indicating that there actually are reliable differences among subjects who marked the neutral step on the first administration of the scale. Actually, the issue of whether to have a neutral step apparently is not very important, particularly if scores are summed over a number of scales. Consequently, this decision is left largely to the judgment of the experimenter in the particular situation in which rating scales are employed.

**Summated scales** The question of the number of steps on a rating scale is very important if one is dealing with only one scale, but usually it is less important if scores are summed over a number of scales. The former would be the case, for example, if attitudes toward the United Nations were measured by only one scale, as follows:

United Nations

Unfavorable \_\_\_\_ : \_\_\_\_ : \_\_\_\_ : \_\_\_\_ : \_\_\_\_ : \_\_\_\_ Favorable

1　　2　　3　　4　　5　　6

When only one scale is used to measure attitudes, it is wise to have at least 10 steps. In the usual case, however, one obtains an overall measure of attitudes by summing the rating given to at least half a dozen scales. One could do this in the example above by having scales for the adjective pairs valuable-worthless, efficient-inefficient, effective-ineffective, and others. As another example of summated ratings, agree-disagree ratings would be summed over a number of positive and negative statements about the United Nations.

The reliability of summated ratings is directly related to the correlations among scales (which, as was discussed in previous chapters, is so in all uses of the summative model for constructing measures). The numbers of steps on rating scales tend to place limits on the sizes of correlations among scales. In the case of a two-step (or dichotomous) scale, the correlations are phi coefficients, and the sizes of phi coefficients are limited by the differences in $p$ values of items. Then, if there is a large standard deviation of $p$ values over items, the average correlation of items with one another will tend to be low; and according to the logic of coefficient alpha, the reliability will tend to be low. When there are three rather than two steps on the scale, the restriction on correlations is less, and it tends to become less and less as the number of scale steps is further increased.

In addition to the effect of the average correlation among items, the reliability of summated scales also depends directly on the number of items. If there are only half a dozen items in the scale, the reliability obtained from two-step scales might be markedly increased by an increase in the number of scale steps. If, on the other hand, there are over 20 items in the summated scale, it is seldom true that the reliability is materially increased by the addition of scale steps to the individual scales. Of course, in nearly all instances it is safer to have at least five or six steps than to hope that two-step scales will be sufficient. Also, seldom are there practical advantages in having only two steps unless binary responses are particularly appropriate for the collection of items (e.g., agree-disagree responses).

Reliabilities of summated attitude scales tend to be higher (holding numbers of items constant) than those of summated scales of abilities and self-inventory measures of personality. This is true even when two-step scales are used in the measurement of attitudes. Attitude scales tend to be highly reliable because the items tend to correlate rather highly with one another. This makes KR-20 high, which, for reasons discussed in previous chapters, usually is a good estimate of the alternative-form reliability measured over relatively short periods of time.

Individual scales on summated attitude scales tend to correlate substantially with one another because they obviously relate to the same object. For example, in a summated scale to measure attitudes toward the United Nations, the separate statements obviously relate to the same thing. It is easy for the experimenter to intuit items that will correlate highly with one another, and it is easy for the subject to see the common core of meaning in the items. For these reasons, one often finds reliabilities in the .90s for summated scales containing 30 statements rated on a two-step scale of agreement-disagreement. Also, one frequently finds, for example, that a summated scale consisting of six eight-step ratings has a reliability above .80. Reliability, then, usually is not a serious problem in the construction of summated attitude scales. At least this is so for the reliability over moderate periods of time (e.g., up to six months); but depending on the attitude being measured, systematic changes might be expected to occur in attitudes over longer periods, e.g., in attitudes toward the Russians or toward government practices.

**Physical appearance of scales** One of the *least* important considerations regarding rating scales is physical appearance. One choice, for example, is whether to place the scale horizontally or vertically on the page. Some have argued that the vertical scale is more familiar to the average person, as in reading a thermometer. Another choice concerns whether the steps are connected or separated, as in the following examples:

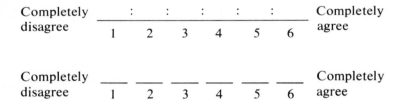

The argument for the separation of steps is that it lowers the probability that subjects will mark between steps, which sometimes occurs when there are no breaks between steps. The preference for a continuous line frequently is based on the experimenter's superstition that if ratings are made on a continuum, somehow this ensures that the scale numbers can be legitimately interpreted as forming an interval scale. Better arguments for making that assumption were given in Chap. 1.

Another consideration is whether steps will be "open," as shown in previous examples, or boxed, as follows:

These and other variations on the physical appearance of rating scales apparently make little difference in the important psychometric properties of ratings. Such differences usually are based more on esthetic preferences than on psychometric considerations.

**Object rated** Some important distinctions should be made among the different types of objects rated on rating scales. In the previous chapter were discussed some of the properties of ratings made of the personality characteristics of people. It was said that such ratings are strongly influenced by (1) the knowledge the observer (or rater) has of the ratee and (2) the rater's tendency to be "lenient" or "severe" in rating other people in general. Numerous other artifacts have been shown to influence the ratings of people (Guilford 1954). What is important to realize, however, is that, in many uses of rating scales, either ratings are not made of people or, if they are, they do not concern personality characteristics directly. In such cases many of the artifacts that plague ratings of personality characteristics of people either are logically not present at all or are present to a lesser extent.

In attitude scales, ratings frequently are made of agreement or disagreement with statements, e.g., "The United Nations is our best hope for permanent peace." In rating such statements, neither leniency nor lack of information influences ratings in the same way that they do in the ratings of the personality characteristics of people. Leniency in the case of attitude statements would be present only to the extent that the subject appeared to have either favorable or unfavorable attitudes regardless of the social object being considered. The extent to which that actually occurs is largely unknown. But if it occurred, either it would represent genuine individual differences in the tendency to have favorable rather than unfavorable attitudes, or it would represent social desirability. Lack of knowledge has a different effect in ratings of statements concerning attitudes than it does in ratings of people. In the latter, lack of information lowers the validity of ratings of people, but in the former, it may serve to explain *why* individuals have a particular attitude, although it does not necessarily lead to invalid measurements of what their attitudes actually are.

Instead of ratings being made of statements relating to attitudes, in some attitude scales ratings are made of the attitudinal object itself, as would be the case, for example, in having the United Nations rated on a seven-step scale bound by the adjectives *effective* and *ineffective*. Other attitudinal objects that could be rated directly are abortion, labor unions, Japan, educational television, and intercollegiate athletics. When attitudinal objects are rated directly, leniency (as the term applies in ratings of people) would spring from the same sources as it would in ratings of statements. Individual differences in that regard would represent either differences in favorable attitudes toward social objects or practices of all kinds (which is a rather farfetched notion) or differences in social desirability. Regarding the subjects' information about attitudinal objects, the caliber of their information might help explain why they have developed the particular attitude, but it would not influence the validity of measurements of their attitudes at one time. A person can, for example, hold genuinely negative or positive attitudes toward the United Nations or abortion while entertaining either very little information or much misinformation.

The major point to be made in this section is that the many factors that have been shown to influence ratings of people (Guilford 1954) do not necessarily have the same kinds and amounts of effects on ratings made for other purposes. The major factor limiting the validity of attitude ratings probably is social desirability, and as was mentioned previously, there are good logical grounds for thinking that social desirability plays less of a part in attitude scales than in self-inventory measures of personality.

**Types of anchors** Before subjects can employ rating scales, steps on the scales must be defined. The definitions of scale steps are referred to as *anchors*, and there are different types of anchors that can be employed. Usually numerical anchors are used in conjunction with other types of anchors. There is no harm in utilizing numbers on the scale, and they have several distinct advantages. If the meaning of each step on the scale is specified at the beginning of the rating form, as is usually the case, numbers provide an effective means of coordinating those definitions with the rating scales. A second advantage is that numbers on the rating scales constantly remind subjects of the meanings of scale steps. Another advantage of having numbers is that it facilitates the analysis of data, e.g., as in placing ratings on cards for computer analyses.

A special type of numerical anchor that is useful in many studies is found on *percentage scales*. On percentage scales, subjects rate themselves, or other people, on a continuum ranging from 0 to 100 percent, either in comparison to people in general or in comparison to some special reference group, e.g., other students in a particular college. The scale usually is divided into 10 steps, corresponding to intervals of 10 percentage points. However, it is sensible to employ more finely grained percentage scales, say, 20 steps of five percentage points each. Subjects can rate themselves, or someone else, in terms of attributes such as intelligence and energy, or the percentage scale can be used to measure sentiments. The latter would be the case, for example, if individuals were asked to rate how favorable they are toward labor unions in comparison to how people in general feel. Then, if they marked the step corresponding to the 70 to 80 percent level, this would mean that they consider themselves more favorable than 70 percent of people in general. Where they can be used, percentage scales usually are highly meaningful to subjects. Also, they make it very easy to formulate and communicate to the subject rating scales with many steps, which is frequently difficult with other forms of verbal anchors.

A second type of anchor which is widely used in rating scales concerns degrees of agreement and disagreement, as has been amply illustrated previously in this chapter. Where they can be applied, agreement scales are easy to work with, they are easily understood by subjects, and the results obtained from them are rather easily interpreted by researchers. Whereas, superficially, agreement scales might seem to concern judgments rather than sentiments, in attitude scales this is not the case. What individuals do in responding to agreement scales is to indicate their sentiments by agreeing or disagreeing with favorable and unfavorable statements.

Adjectives constitute a third type of anchor for rating scales, as was illustrated previously for scales anchored by valuable-worthless, effective-ineffective, and other pairs of bipolar adjectives. Attitude scales employing bipolar adjectives as anchors are easily constructed and applied to many types of attitudinal objects. Rating scales using bipolar adjectives as anchors are said to form a *semantic differential,* a matter that will be discussed in detail later.

A fourth type of anchor for rating scales is in terms of actual behavior, this type of anchor being more useful for the rating of people than for the rating of attitudes and other types of sentiments. A numerical scale for that purpose concerning the tendency of mental patients to have hallucinations is as follows:

1. Shows no signs of having hallucinations.
2. Gestures and talks to self as if having hallucinations on occasions, but does not verbalize hallucinations.
3. Verbalizes hallucinations only occasionally.
4. Actively hallucinates much of the time.

The rater would mark the one statement that best described each patient's tendency to hallucinate. There are three major difficulties with employing behavioral anchors. First, a different set of anchors is needed for each scale, which makes it difficult to construct inventories based on such scales. Second, in some cases it is not at all certain that the different behaviors used as anchors actually represent different levels of the trait in question. For example, in the four-step scale for hallucinatory behavior, one might argue that step 2 represents more involvement with hallucinations than step 3. Third, frequently it is difficult to find discrete, easily specified forms of behavior that relate to more general traits. This point was discussed in detail in the previous chapter.

A fifth type of anchor for rating scales concerns comparison stimuli, or *product scales*, as they are called. A classic example is a product scale for the legibility of handwriting. A six-step scale is employed, with each of the numbers 1 through 6 being illustrated with samples of handwriting at different levels of legibility. The handwriting samples appropriate for the different levels are obtained from prior research, in which experts are asked to make discriminations among samples of handwriting (with one or another of the psychophysical methods). Once the samples are chosen for each level of legibility, it is assumed that the samples (comparison stimuli) will be helpful in having ratings of handwriting made by people who are not highly expert in that regard. Usually verbal anchors are used in addition to comparison stimuli; e.g., in the six-step scale for handwriting, 6 equals "excellent" and 1 equals "very poor." In addition to scales for handwriting, product scales of this kind have been developed for artistic productions, but beyond that, few product scales are reported in the literature. Although they are attractive approaches to ratings when they can be developed, logically they are restricted to only a few types of ratings.

## MODELS FOR THE SCALING OF VERBALIZED ATTITUDES

Except in the unusual case where attitudes are measured with only one item, some model must be employed to specify how responses to a collection of items will be translated into an attitude scale. In Chap. 2 were discussed the various models that can be used for the scaling of people with respect to all kinds of psychological traits, attitudes included. What will be done in this section is to summarize the considerations that lead to an acceptance of one of the models over the others for the scaling of verbalized attitudes in most situations.

**Deterministic models** In deterministic models each item is assumed to have a perfect relationship, of one kind or another, with a hypothetical trait. In the scaling of attitudes, the trait in question is, of course, the set of true scores for subjects on the particular dimension of attitudes being investigated, e.g., verbalized attitudes toward the United Nations. The only deterministic model that has received wide attention for the scaling of verbalized attitudes is the monotone deterministic model, which is usually referred to as a *Guttman scale*. In this model, it is hypothesized that each dichotomous item has a perfect biserial (not point-biserial) correlation with the hypothetical trait.

A number of reasons were given in Chap. 2 why the monotone deterministic model is unrealistic for the measurement of most human traits, and this applies with particular force to the scaling of verbalized attitudes. The model does not take account of the amount of unique variance in each item, and consequently it is very difficult to find items that fit the model. The scales that partially fit the model nearly always have only a handful of items; thus only gross discriminations can be made among people. Also, the model leads only to an ordinal scaling of people with respect to attitudes. In Chap. 1 it was argued that psychology frequently has a legitimate claim to the measurement of human traits on at least interval scales, if not usually on ratio scales. Other reasons were given in Chap. 2 why the Guttman scale is an impractical approach to the measurement of most human traits. Aside from the few instances in which data fit the models well, the deterministic models mainly are useful as theoretical reference points for the development of practicable models for the actual scaling of attitudes.

**Nonmonotone probability models** A nonmonotone model logically underlies what is called the *Thurstone scale* for the measurement of attitudes. Like the Guttman scale, the Thurstone scale also deals with dichotomous responses to statements concerning attitudes, e.g., agreeing or disagreeing with the statement, "I feel a need for religion but do not find what I want in any one church." Each item is intended to represent, in a statistical sense, one point on an attitude continuum. Only persons in a narrow zone about that point are expected to agree with the item; persons having either more positive or more negative attitudes are expected to disagree with the item. In the ideal case, then, one would expect the item trace line for each item (the curve showing the probability of agreeing to the item as a function of the underlying trait) to be a normal distribution, with the mode corresponding to the true point on the attitude continuum.

The Thurstone scaling method employs judges to establish the scale points for items. In a typical study, 100 judges would rate the attitude implied by each of 100 statements. The judgments could be made on an 11-step continuum ranging from "strong positive attitude" to "strong negative attitude." The mean rating by judges is taken as the scale point for each item. About 20 items are selected for the final scale such that (1) each item has a small standard deviation of ratings over judges and (2) the mean ratings spread evenly from one end of the rating continuum to the other. When the scale is used in subsequent studies to measure the attitudes of people, subjects are instructed to mark only those statements with which they agree. (Some have advocated restricting subjects to marking the three statements with which they most agree.) The score for the subject is then the scale value of the median item endorsed or the average scale value of the items endorsed.

During the last 40 years, the Thurstone method of attitude scaling has been used very widely in psychology and sociology. As was said in Chap. 2, however, there are better methods for the scaling of attitudes. The original assumptions of the model are unrealistic for the scaling of attitude statements. It simply is very difficult to find items that have nonmonotone trace lines. One can find the approximate trace line by plotting the percentage of people who endorse an item as a function of scores on the total scale. In the effort to obtain nonmonotone items, the investigators frequently produce double-barreled statements, as was illustrated in Chap. 2. This is evidenced by the fact that so many of the items on such scales are populated by *and*'s, *but*'s, *or*'s, and other indicators of multiple ideas within statements.

Unless one assumes nonmonotone trace lines for items, it is rather difficult to see how the method of assigning scale scores makes much sense, e.g., taking the median scale point of three items marked as the attitude score for a person. In practice, however, few of the items on such scales have nonmonotone trace lines (Edwards 1957). Items on the extremes of the scale tend to have monotone trace lines, with the lines sloping downward for negative items and upward for positive items. Items near the middle of the scale tend to have flat trace lines, and thus they do a poor job of discriminating persons in terms of attitudes. The only items that might have distinctly nonmonotone trace lines would be moderately positive or moderately negative, and such items typically are double-barreled.

The major advantage assumed for Thurstone attitude scales over other types of scales is that they permit a direct interpretation of the attitude of an individual, or the average attitude of a group of people, without recourse to general norms for the attitude in question. In most studies in psychology and sociology, however, that is not really much of an advantage. In most studies, the researcher is interested in correlating individual differences in an attitude with other types of individual differences, or he or she is interested in the mean differences in attitudes of existing groups of people or of groups of people that are differently treated in controlled experiments. For those purposes, there is little need for a direct interpretation of the attitude of any one person, in an absolute sense. Also, in cases where such interpretations are important, they can be made with only modest precision from Thurstone scales. Even with the best of efforts to select items that judges agree on, the standard deviations of scale values over judges still are considerable. Also, it has been found that different types of judges give markedly different ratings to some of the statements employed in Thurstone scales (discussed in Edwards 1957). The rank-ordering of statements on the scale tends to remain the same, but the absolute scale values shift markedly. Then, if a direct interpretation is made of the responses of one person, we must ask the question, "In whose eyes?"

In the next section it will be argued that summative scales do, in general, constitute the best approach to the scaling of verbalized attitudes. Aside from the numerous logical arguments that favor summative scales, it has repeatedly been found that summative scales are somewhat more reliable than Thurstone scales.

**Summative models** As was said in Chap. 2, the summative model is the most generally useful in the scaling of people with respect to psychological traits. It assumes only that individual items are monotonically related to underlying traits and that a summation of item scores is approximately linearly related to the trait. One obtains a total score by adding scores on individual items (reversing the scoring for statements that imply negative attitudes). This same logic is applied to both dichotomous items and multipoint items.

Because summative scales for the measurement of attitudes were championed by Likert (1932), sometimes they are referred to as Likert scales. Summative scales have a number of attractive advantages over all other methods: they (1) follow from an appealing model, (2) are rather easy to construct, (3) usually are highly reliable, (4) can be adapted to the measurement of many different kinds of attitudes, and (5) have produced meaningful results in many studies to date.

## CONSTRUCTION OF SUMMATIVE SCALES FOR VERBALIZED ATTITUDES

The construction of summative attitude scales is only a special case of the general method for constructing nonspeeded (power) measures which was discussed in Chap. 8. In this section will be described a few of the particular features of constructing summative scales for attitudes. Aspects of scale construction will be illustrated with agree-disagree scales applied to statements concerning attitudes. The methods, however, are general to all summative scales. They apply, for example, to summative scales one obtains by adding responses to individual rating scales bounded by bipolar adjectives, and they apply to summative scales one obtains by adding responses to individual rating scales anchored by actual behaviors.

**Item pool** All the statements in the item pool should, of course, concern a particular attitudinal object, e.g., the United Nations or labor unions. Since it is usually easy to obtain a homogeneous scale for the measurement of attitudes, seldom are more than 40 items required in the item pool. Since the purpose of each item on a summative scale is to obtain reliable variance with respect to the attitude in question, most of the items should be either moderately positive or moderately negative. There is no place for truly neutral statements in summative scales. Statements that are very extreme in either direction tend to create less variance than statements that are less extreme. The pool of items should be about evenly divided between positive and negative statements.

**Data for item analysis** The item pool should be administered to a group of subjects that is similar to the groups with which the final instrument will be used, e.g., samples of college students for a scale to be used in research on college students or a broad sample of the general population for a scale that will be used in national surveys. Because it usually is rather easy to develop homogeneous scales of verbalized attitudes, the number of subjects need be no more than 10 times the number of items, but if larger numbers of subjects are easily obtained, the more subjects the better.

In the development of attitude scales, it is very important that the data for item analysis be obtained under circumstances very similar to those in which the final scale will be employed. For example, the data for an item analysis might be very misleading if they are obtained under conditions of anonymity for subjects but the final scale is intended for use in circumstances where responses of subjects will not be anonymous. Also, it is very important to think out carefully the instructions that will be used with the final instrument and use those instructions in obtaining data for item analysis.

**Item analysis** Before items are correlated with total scale scores, scoring should be reversed for negative statements. (The same result could be obtained by reversing the scoring for positive statements.) For dichotomous items, this would mean scoring 1 for agreement with positive statements and 0 for disagreement, and vice versa for negative statements. One reverses scales for negative statements when multipoint items are employed by subtracting each scale position from the number of scale steps plus 1. For example, if a seven-step scale is applied to each statement and 7 means "completely agree," the rating made of each negative statement would be subtracted from 8. This would then treat complete disagreement with a negative statement like complete agreement with a positive statement, and vice versa.

As was mentioned in Chap. 8, one of the difficulties in scoring responses in preparation for item analysis is that, with some item pools, the proper directions of scoring for many of the items are difficult to discern. This results in what was called *bipolar item pools*. Iterative procedures were mentioned in Chap. 8 for dealing with this situation. In the development of attitude scales (and for the measurement of sentiments in general), however, these procedures are seldom necessary. If, as advised earlier, all the statements are either moderately positive or moderately negative, the proper direction for scoring each item usually is very easy to discern. After the directions of scoring are established, it is very rare to find any item that has a substantial negative correlation with total scale scores.

After the directions for scoring are established, one obtains total scores over all items in the item pool by simply summing scores over items. At that point one could compute coefficient alpha (KR-20 for dichotomous items), or since that usually is very high when computed over the total item pool, one could proceed to the correlation of each item with total scores. Correlations would be regular PM coefficients of multipoint scales and point-biserial coefficients for dichotomous scales. Separate rank-orderings of the correlations should be made for both positive and negative statements. Then, working from the top of the rank-orders downward, one would choose an equal number of positive and negative items for the final scale. Say, for example, that out of a total item pool of 40 items, 10 positive and 10 negative statements are selected. The 20 items would then be combined to form a trial scale, and coefficient alpha would be computed for the 20 items. This would require computing the variance of each item and obtaining total scores summed over the 20 items (reversing directions of scoring negative items as before). If coefficient alpha is sufficiently high, the 20 items could be accepted as the final scale. In the construction of summative scales of attitudes, usually 20 statements selected in that way will have a reliability above .80. As was mentioned previously, the size of the reliability relates to the number of scale steps for the rating scale used with each statement.

**Weighting of individual scales** Numerous weighting scales have been proposed for the items on summative scales. For example, scores on each item could be weighted by the correlation of the item with total scale scores. Other approaches to weighting items were discussed in Chap. 8. For two reasons, it usually is not necessary to apply differential weights to the items on summative scales of attitudes (other than to reverse the scoring for negative statements). First, it is difficult to defend any particular method of weighting over the method of simply summing unweighted ratings. Second, and more to the point, weighted and unweighted summative scores usually correlate highly. A classic example was found in a study by Likert (1932), in which he compared unweighted scores with scores obtained by an elaborate method of weighting each item. The two sets of scores correlated .99.

**Factor analysis of items** In Chap. 8 it was advised that factor analysis of an item pool should be considered only as a last resort, after efforts to hypothesize homogeneous scales have led to naught. This is because the average correlation among items in the typical item pool is small, and the standard deviation of such correlations is small, this tending to be the case more with dichotomous items than with multipoint items. In these circumstances, the results of factor analyses tend to be very "messy." For two reasons, these conditions tend not to hold in item pools constructed for the measurement of attitudes. First, even if dichotomous items are employed for the measurement of attitudes, the correlations among them tend to be higher than for measures of ability and personality characteristics. Second, the fact that multipoint scales are employed more frequently than dichotomous scales to measure attitudes tends to further increase the size of the average correlation among items. In addition to the size of the average correlation among items, frequently there is enough variance in the sizes of correlations to document "strong" factors.

If one hypothesizes a number of factors relating to a particular attitude or, lacking hypotheses, one suspects that an item pool harbors a number of strong factors, there is nothing wrong with factor-analyzing the item pool initially rather than proceeding directly to the construction of a homogeneous scale, as was outlined previously. The factor structures obtained from multipoint ratings of attitudes frequently are as strong as those obtained from factor structures for whole tests of ability and personality characteristics.

An example of a domain of content in which a number of factors might be expected would be in relation to labor unions. A person might feel that labor unions are worthwhile in terms of the national economy but have a stifling influence on cultural values, or a person might think that labor unions are "bad" in both these respects but have a constructive influence politically. Factor analysis could be used to test hypotheses about the major factors of attitudes toward labor unions and to construct scales for the measurement of those factors. The use of factor analysis with item pools relating to attitudes is the major exception to the principle stated in Chap. 8 that it usually is unwise to start an item analysis with factor analysis.

## SEMANTIC-DIFFERENTIAL SCALES

A very useful type of scale is that which employs direct ratings of concepts with scales anchored on the extremes by bipolar adjectives:

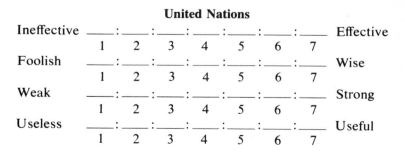

A collection of scales such as those above is referred to as a *semantic differential*. Although it will be convenient here to speak of *the* semantic differential, the term is used in a generic sense to refer to any collection of rating scales anchored by bipolar adjectives. Rather than the semantic differential being a particular instrument (or test, as some have called it), it is a very flexible approach to obtaining measures of attitudes and other sentiments. The flexibility of the approach is one of its appealing features. The object that is rated is referred to as a *concept*, and anything that can be named can be rated, e.g., Winston Churchill, peach ice cream, labor unions, birth control, my best friend, and automobiles. Not only are bipolar adjectives easily adapted to a multitude of concepts, but it is easy to apply a list of scales to a number of different concepts in the same rating form. For example, if one is interested in examining attitudes toward a number of different political figures, institutions, and forms of policy, these can all be investigated in the same instrument. Subjects have no trouble rating 20 concepts on 20 scales in an hour or less. The semantic differential is very flexible in another sense: it makes it easy to construct scales for the measurement of different facets of attitudes, a matter which will be discussed more fully later.

An impressive array of studies has been performed on semantic-differential scales by C. E. Osgood and his colleagues. Anyone who is interested in learning more about the semantic differential should consult the volume edited by Snider and Osgood (1969); described there in complete detail are the theoretical origins of the method, techniques of constructing scales, and application of the semantic differential in an extremely wide variety of investigations. Also see the discussion in Kerlinger (1973). The semantic differential was mainly developed in relation to a mediational theory of learning. Since in that theory the "meaning" of stimuli occupies a central role, some ways of measuring various facets of meaning are required to give the theory empirical implications. The semantic differential was developed as such a measure.

**Logic of the semantic differential** In spoken and written language, characteristics of ideas and real things are communicated largely by adjectives. Thus the characteristics of a particular person are communicated as being polite, urbane, timid, and intelligent; and a particular policy in foreign affairs is characterized as being outmoded, rigid, and discriminatory. If it is reasonable to assume that much of "meaning" can be, and usually is, communicated with adjectives, it is also reasonable to assume that adjectives can be used to measure various facets of meaning. To carry this line of reasoning a step further, to obtain anchors for the ends of rating scales, it is useful to work with pairs of bipolar adjectives. Most adjectives have logical opposites, such as is evidenced in the pairs sweet-sour, dark-light, and tall-short. Where an opposing adjective is not obviously available, one can easily be generated with "in-" or "un-," e.g., sufficient-insufficient and satisfactory-unsatisfactory. All that remains, then, is to (1) generate a wide sample of such pairs of adjectives, (2) use them as anchors on rating scales, as illustrated previously, and (3) search for common factors among the scales. If strong factors are found and the factors appear in ratings of many different kinds of concepts, the factors can be used as general measures of different factors of meaning.

**Factors in semantic-differential scales** Numerous factor analyses have been performed to date on semantic-differential scales (these are discussed in Snider and Osgood 1969). Different studies have employed different types of concepts, e.g., names of prominent persons, geometric forms, commercial products, persons with different types of physical or mental illness, different animals, and others. Studies have been performed of ratings made by people in different countries around the world and by different types of persons in this country. Also, many different adjective pairs have been used in one or more of the studies.

The numerous factor-analysis studies of semantic-differential scales lead to the conclusion that there are three major factors of meaning involved. The factors do not always have exactly the same content in different studies, and in some studies more than three prominent factors are found. The remarkable fact is, however, that three factors with similar content have occurred in so many analyses under such varied conditions. The most frequently found factor is *evaluation*, which is defined by pairs of adjectives like the following:

| | |
|---|---|
| good–bad | honest–dishonest |
| pleasant–unpleasant | positive–negative |
| fair–unfair | sweet–sour |
| wise–foolish | valuable–worthless |
| successful–unsuccessful | clean–dirty |

The evaluative factor is by far the strongest factor in semantic-differential scales. In some studies it is so strong that little common variance is left to define other factors. The evaluative factor is prominent because nearly all adjectives imply negative and positive characteristics. Actually it is difficult to think of bipolar pairs of adjectives that do not hint at evaluation. Even such pairs as wet-dry, long-short, and up-down hint of evaluation. The evaluative factor almost serves as a definition for the term *attitude*, and consequently scales on the evaluative factor should serve well as measures of verbalized attitudes.

The second strongest factor that frequently appears in factor analyses of semantic-differential scales is *potency*. Some of the pairs of adjectives that usually load on that factor are as follows:

| | |
|---|---|
| strong–weak | rugged–delicate |
| hard–soft | large–small |
| heavy–light | masculine–feminine |
| thick–thin | severe–lenient |

The third strongest factor that frequently appears is *activity*. Some pairs of adjectives relating to that factor are as follows:

| | |
|---|---|
| active–passive | quick–slow |
| tense–relaxed | hot–cold |
| excitable–calm | sharp–dull |
| impetuous–quiet | busy–lazy |

In comparison to the factor of evaluation, the factors of potency and activity are not as strong statistically; and whereas one can easily think of many adjective pairs that relate to evaluation, it is more difficult to find adjective pairs that clearly measure the other two factors. Typically it is found that even the best scales for measuring potency and activity also correlate with the factor of evaluation.

Less important than the correlations between scales used to measure the different factors are correlations between estimates of factor scores on the three factors. Typically half a dozen scales from each of the factors are used to determine factor scores. For this purpose, ratings simply are summed over the scales in each factor. When that is done, one typically finds positive correlations between the three factors; i.e., considering the extremes, some concepts tend to be rated as good, strong, and active, and at the other extreme some concepts tend to be rated as bad, weak, and inactive. Typically one finds an average correlation between measures of the three factors ranging from about .30 to about .50 in different studies, the size of the average correlation varying with the types of concepts being investigated.

In addition to these three factors that have appeared in numerous analyses, other prominent factors have been found in semantic-differential scales. Nunnally (1961) found a factor of *familiarity* (or *understandability,* as it was called), defined by scales like the following:

| | |
|---|---|
| familiar–unfamiliar | understandable–mysterious |
| usual–unusual | predictable–unpredictable |
| clear–confusing | simple–complex |

Potentially, the factor of familiarity is important for the scaling of stimuli to be used in controlled experiments. There are numerous instances in which actual familiarity and rated familiarity have proved to be important determiners of rate of verbal learning and rate of perceptual recognition.

Osgood (1962) reports a number of other factors that appear with particular types of scales and concepts. The factor structure tends to be more "diverse" when ratings are made of concepts relating to human personality, such as a good friend, a mother, and an athlete. With such concepts, one tends to find about eight factors, and partly because of the limited number of scales that can be employed in a study, only a few scales have substantial loadings on each factor. In several studies of concepts relating to personality, a factor of rationality has been found, which is defined by scales like logical-intuitive, objective-subjective, and rational-irrational. In the same studies, a factor of morality was found, with scales like moral-immoral, reputable-disreputable, and wholesome-unwholesome.

**Interactions of scales and concepts** One caution in employing semantic-differential scales is that the meanings of scales sometimes depend on the concept being rated. For example, whereas *sweet* is positively evaluative when applied to many concepts, it certainly is not positively evaluative when applied to the brand names for different beers. Whereas the scale tense-relaxed tends to measure the activity factor when applied to material objects, it tends to measure neurotic tendency when applied to persons. Whereas tough-tender would correlate positively with valuable-worthless in ratings of the photographs of men, the correlation obviously would be negative in rating the brand names of steaks, lamb chops, hams, and other meats. Many other examples could be given in which the meanings of scales differ with the concepts being studied and in which the size and directions of correlations among scales differ with the types of concepts.

The interaction of scales with concepts places a limit on the extent to which individual scales can be interpreted the same when applied to different concepts, and it also places a limit on the extent to which factors in semantic differential scales can be employed as general yardsticks (e.g., to measure evaluation) regardless of the concepts in a particular study. There are several lessons to be learned from these points. First, less scale-concept interaction is likely to occur when all the concepts in a particular study are from the same domain of discourse. For example, it would be better in most studies to have all the concepts be four-legged animals, all be types of persons, all be social institutions, rather than mix the three types of concepts in one study. There is no harm in having a mixed bag of concepts rated at the same time by the same people, but it usually makes more sense to perform separate analyses and make separate interpretations of the data for different types of concepts.

Second, it is wise to perform factor analyses for any type of concept which is to be investigated extensively. For example, if one intended to make extensive use of semantic-differential scales with many different types of geometric designs, it would be wise to investigate the factor structure of such scales with that particular type of concept rather than depend entirely on the factor structures found with other types of concepts. In that instance one would expect the three major factors to have much the same content (e.g., it would be surprising not to find good-bad and pleasant-unpleasant loading substantially on a factor of evaluation), but some of the factor content might be different from that typically found in other studies.

Third, instead of relying blindly on the scales that usually define factors in semantic-differential scales, it is wise to think carefully about possible interactions of scales and concepts in particular studies. For example, whereas the scale beautiful-ugly usually measures evaluation, anyone would be foolish to employ it for that purpose in ratings of famous political figures, e.g., Churchill, Napoleon, and Lincoln. In some instances a scale that usually does not load highly on a factor does have a high loading with a particular type of concept. This is the case for the scale effective-ineffective, which has only a moderate-sized loading on the evaluative factor with many types of concepts but has a high loading on that factor when the concepts concern professions, such as psychologist, psychiatrist, engineer, surgeon, and economist. Such concepts tend to "bunch" on the high end of most scales commonly used to measure the evaluative factor (e.g., good-bad and fair-unfair), but they are drawn apart on the scale effective-ineffective. Though the final test of the wisdom of selecting particular scales to be used with particular concepts is made by factor-analyzing the data, careful forethought can lead to a selection of scales that will manifest the desired factor structure.

**Use of semantic-differential scales** In previous sections some general suggestions were made about the employment of semantic-differential scales in research; here, some additional points will be made. When scores are summed over a number of scales, as is usually the case, the logic of constructing summative measures is the same as that discussed previously for the construction of summative scales of verbalized attitudes. That is, by methods of item analysis, one seeks a homogeneous group of scales that meets requirements of reliability. Usually it is not difficult to accomplish that goal. One frequently finds, for example, that half a dozen pairs of adjectives rated on seven-step scales have a coefficient alpha as high as .80.

It is well to employ numbers to designate the steps on semantic-differential scales, e.g., the numbers 1 through 7 to designate the steps of a seven-step scale. Also, the meanings of the numbers should be carefully defined and illustrated in the instructions to the inventory. For example, subjects can be told that, on the scale good-bad, 5 means "slightly good" rather than "bad," 3 means "slightly bad" rather than "good," and so on for the other steps on the scale.

There is nothing wrong with developing particular groups of scales for particular purposes rather than employing only the "standard" factors that have been found in studies of diverse concepts. For example, the following scales would be useful in studying subjective feelings of anxiety in experiments concerning the effects of different types of stressful circumstances:

| | |
|---|---|
| anxious–calm | afraid–unafraid |
| tense–relaxed | nervous–restful |
| disturbed–undisturbed | upset–quiet |

Of course, the advantage of summing scores over a number of scales rather than relying on one scale alone (e.g., anxious-calm) is that it permits finer differentiations among persons. Even though such scales in general usage may have somewhat different patterns of factor loadings with the "usual" factors, in such special uses as that illustrated above, the scales may correlate highly.

Numerous other special groups of scales can be employed in particular studies.

In addition to the summing of scores over groups of scales, in most studies it also is instructive to compare concepts on individual scales. Thus, as was mentioned previously, the scale effective-ineffective provides useful information about public attitudes toward professional groups, beyond that which is provided by other scales that typically have high loadings on the evaluative factor. As other examples, Nunnally (1961) found that the scale tense-relaxed served better than any other to differentiate public attitudes toward neurotic persons and normal persons, and that the scale predictable-unpredictable served better than any other scale to differentiate public attitudes toward psychotic persons and normal persons. Such differences between concepts on individual scales provide many hints for subsequent investigations.

As can be seen from the many investigations summarized by Snider and Osgood (1969), evidently the semantic differential has been very well received as a measurement method. It has become a very important workhorse in psychology for investigations of attitudes and other types of sentiments.

# THE *Q* SORT

The *Q* sort and the semantic differential gained their fame at about the same time, in the early 1950s. Beyond that similarity, however, they are very different types of rating tasks. The *Q* sort grew out of a more general methodology developed by Stephenson (1953) for the study of verbalized attitudes, self-description, preferences, and other issues in social psychology, clinical psychology, and the study of personality. A salient principle in that methodology is that, for the advancement of psychology, it is more important to make comparisons among different responses (e.g., statements regarding preferences) *within* persons than *between* persons. In other words, basic to Stephenson's methodology is a reliance on *comparative* rating methods and on an analysis of comparative data within persons even when absolute rating methods are employed. The *Q* sort is a handy comparative rating method that has proved useful for the type of study that Stephenson envisaged. Also, it has been used widely to study numerous issues ranging from psychotherapy to advertising. Wittenborn (1961) surveyed studies employing the *Q* sort up to 1961. Brown (1968) provided a comprehensive bibliography of studies employing the *Q* sort up to that time; some perspectives and examples are given by Kerlinger (1973).

Because the *Q* sort is a relative rating task which is used to study similarities among ratings of sentiments by different persons, it shares some of the same logical features and methods of analysis as profile analysis discussed in Chap. 12. For that reason, and because the *Q* sort is a very useful rating method in its own right, a detailed discussion follows.

**An illustrative study** Before the psychometric properties of the *Q* sort are discussed, a simple example will illustrate the nature of the rating method. The study concerns preferences for statues, each of 100 statues appearing separately in a photograph. The statues are from many different cultures around the world and from many different historical periods. Rather than rate each photograph separately, as with an absolute rating method such as the rating scale, the subject is asked to make comparative preferences by "sorting" the photographs into a specified number of piles. The end piles are designated "prefer least" and "prefer most," respectively. The particular feature of the $Q$ sort is that the subject is required to sort the stimuli in terms of a fixed distribution, usually an approximately normal distribution. A forced distribution that could be used for the study of 100 statues is as follows:

Number of photographs

| Prefer least | 2 | 4 | 8 | 12 | 14 | 20 | 14 | 12 | 8 | 4 | 2 | Prefer most |
|---|---|---|---|---|---|---|---|---|---|---|---|---|
| | 0 | 1 | 2 | 3 | 4 | 5 | 6 | 7 | 8 | 9 | 10 | |

Pile number

The number for each pile is written on a file card, and the cards are spread out in a line on a large table. To lessen order effects, the investigator shuffles the 100 photographs before giving them to the subject. Before sorting the photographs, the subject is instructed to look at them one at a time and then spread them out on the table to make comparisons among them. Preparatory to the actual sorting, the subject frequently is asked to place the photographs into three gross classes—definite likes, definite dislikes, and ambivalent. This is done only to facilitate the subsequent sorting, and responses made at that time can be changed later.

In the actual sorting of the photographs, the subject is instructed to work from both ends of the continuum toward the middle. The extreme likes and dislikes usually are spotted quicker than less extreme preferences. Also, since in correlational studies so much depends on the extreme scores, it is important that the subject pay particular attention to the placements in the two or three extreme piles on each end of the continuum. In a study of preferences, the subject usually would be instructed to work from the most-prefer end toward the middle and to find the 2 most preferred statues and place them in pile 10. From the remaining 98 photographs, the subject would pick the 4 that are next most preferred and place them in pile 9. From the remaining 94 photographs, the subject would pick 8 for pile 8; and from the remaining photographs, 12 to go in pile 7. Then the subject would be instructed to switch to the least-prefer end of the continuum, pick the 2 statues least preferred, and place these in pile 0, and work upward in that way through pile 3. The subject would then sort the remaining 48 photographs into piles 4, 5, and 6. Finally, the subject would be instructed to examine the entire ratings to make sure that photographs are not out of place, and if some are, to make rearrangements of positions of the photographs.

**Nature of the rating task** As was mentioned previously, the $Q$ sort obviously is a comparative rather than an absolute rating method. The task forces all subjects to have the same mean rating, and thus one learns nothing about level of response to the stimuli as a group. A subject could detest all the statues in the example above, or like them all very much, but no hint of that would be obtained from the $Q$ sort. All comparative rating tasks (e.g., the method of rank-order) force all subjects to have the same mean rating, and thus none of them are intended to provide information about absolute levels of response.

The $Q$ sort also requires subjects to distribute their responses in terms of a fixed distribution, usually an approximately normal distribution. This forces all subjects not only to have the same mean rating, but also to have the same standard deviation and the same curve shape of ratings. The $Q$ sort has been criticized on this score, because one could argue that subjects, if left to their own devices, would employ different shapes of distributions. For a number of reasons, such criticisms are not well justified.

If the intention is to obtain comparative ratings, as in the use of the $Q$ sort, it is necessary to stipulate the distribution mean, shape, and standard deviation in advance. This is exactly what is done in the method of rank-order, which is the logical paradigm for all comparative methods. With the $Q$ sort, if subjects are allowed to put as many stimuli as they like in a pile, the method begins to regress to the method of single stimuli, a method for studying absolute responses. For example, a photograph would be placed in the top pile not only because it was liked *more* than others, but also because it was liked very much in an absolute sense. If one wants to have comparative responses made with respect to all the stimuli in a set, rather than with respect to two at a time (as with the method of pair comparisons) or in other subsets, the mean, standard deviation, and curve form must be fixed.

Thus arguments about the use of a forced distribution in the $Q$ sort boil down to (1) whether a comparative rating method should be used in studies of the kinds where the $Q$ sort is used and (2) if so, whether the $Q$ sort should be used in preference to other comparative methods. The first point is well worth considering, and will be returned to later, but now let us consider the second point. The major reason for using the $Q$ sort rather than some other comparative rating method is that it greatly conserves the time taken to make ratings. For example, a $Q$ sort of 100 photographs would take no more than 30 minutes on the average, but a complete rank-ordering would probably take well over an hour and would prove very tedious to subjects. Because of the time other comparative rating methods take, they would be almost out of the question. For example, if the method of pair comparisons were used with 100 photographs and each subject judged each pair only once, the subject would have to make 4,950 comparisons. Obviously, most of the comparative rating methods are limited to rather small sets of stimuli. Even with the method of rank-order, it is difficult to employ more than 50 stimuli. The $Q$ sort, then, is a useful compromise between two needs: (1) the need to have precise differentiations made among the stimuli, as is done in the method of pair comparisons, and (2) the need to have comparisons made among the members of large sets of stimuli, which is the case in many studies in psychology.

It is best to regard the forced distribution in the $Q$ sort as an approximation to rank-order, a rank-ordering in which the number of tied ranks at each point is specified for the subject. The use of an approximately normal distribution rather than some other fixed distribution (e.g., a rectangular distribution) is justified in the general case, because (1) so many things in nature are distributed approximately that way and (2) it fits in with the statistical methods applied to the data.

Another reason why criticisms of the forced $Q$-sort distribution are largely unjustified is that the exact distribution form has little effect on the kinds of analyses which are made of the data. Correlation coefficients, and the factors obtained from them, are largely insensitive to changes in distribution shapes. Of course, they are not affected at all by changes in means and standard deviations of raw scores. To the extent that it is meaningful to apply inferential statistics to $Q$-sort ratings (e.g., a $t$ test of the mean preferences of one person for two types of statues), it is known that the results of such inferential statistics tend to be affected very little by changes in distribution form. For purposes of analysis, then, even if one allowed subjects to sort stimuli into any distribution form that they chose, differences in distribution forms among subjects would make little difference in the results of statistical analyses.

Actually, those who work extensively with $Q$ sorts recommend that a relatively large number of piles be employed and that the distribution be somewhat flatter than the normal distribution. This allows subjects to make rather fine discriminations among stimuli and tends to increase the reliability of ratings, the same as is done by increasing the number of steps on rating scales.

**Stimulus samples** It is to the credit of Stephenson and his colleagues that research with $Q$ sorts has emphasized the importance of stimulus (or content) sampling. As was mentioned in Chap. 1, psychology and other disciplines are faced with problems concerning two types of sampling—sampling of people and sampling of stimuli. While psychologists usually are careful to adequately sample people, at least to the point of obtaining sufficient numbers of subjects, and employ very elegant statistical methods for assessing the error associated with the sampling of people, usually less is done about the sampling of stimuli (or content). To take an oversimplified example, regardless of the type of rating method employed, one would not learn much about food preferences unless a representative list of food names were sampled. The sample would be inadequate if it left out all meats, included desserts of only certain kinds, or contained numerous foreign dishes unknown to the subjects. In more subtle ways, biased samples of content lead to poor measurements, e.g., a vocabulary test for the general population which is loaded with technical terms relating to particular occupations or a scale for verbalized attitudes toward the United Nations that contains statements about only restricted aspects of the organization.

The problem of sampling stimuli occurs in many types of ratings, but for good reasons it has had to be faced more squarely in the use of $Q$ sorts than in other rating methods. One reason is that the rating task makes sense only if all stimuli are from a specifiable domain of content. To understand why this is so, imagine that subjects are asked to rate the aesthetic quality of 100 photographs, of which 50 are pictures of statues and 50 are pictures of automobiles. In sorting the pictures the subject would have to decide not only which statues and which automobiles were more aesthetically pleasing, but also whether statues as a group were more aesthetically pleasing than automobiles as a group. Obviously, the results of such a study would be far more meaningful if separate $Q$ sorts were made of statues and automobiles. Although surely no one would mix such different types of stimuli in a $Q$ sort, to a lesser extent the use of $Q$ sorts is constantly plagued by the need to ensure that all stimuli are from some common frame of reference.

The problem with ensuring that all stimuli are from a common frame of reference is that it is hard to define a common frame of reference. The counterpart in the sampling of people is the problem of defining the population which the sample is intended to represent. There are some problems there, e.g., generalizing from studies of college students to people in general or deciding whether American Indians will be included in a national sample for obtaining norms for intelligence tests. The problems in defining populations of people are small, however, in comparison to the problems of defining "populations" of stimuli. These problems are particularly severe with one type of content that has been used frequently with $Q$ sorts—statements relating to personality traits, such as the following:

1. I have many friends.
2. Most people like me.
3. I am a nervous person.
4. I had an unhappy childhood.
5. I dread the future.
6. I enjoy physical exercise.

It is hard to see how a comparative rating method like the $Q$ sort makes sense with such diverse content as illustrated in the six statements above. Samples of statements concerning personality used with $Q$ sorts frequently fail to represent a common frame of reference because (1) they mix motives, social traits, and symptoms of maladjustment, (2) they contain statements relating to past, present, and future, (3) some statements concern self-description and others concern judgments about what other people think, and (4) some statements concern general traits (e.g., tendency to be anxious) and others concern rather specific habits (e.g., overeating). Even if none of these rather obvious failures to keep all stimuli in a common frame of reference occurs, frequently it is difficult to stipulate what domain of content is intended to be covered or to justify the method employed to sample the domain. Fortunately, these potential problems in formulating a reasonable stimulus sample are not large in studying many aspects of sentiments, such as in many studies of preferences, values, and opinions.

**Types of stimulus samples** Two types of content samples are employed with the $Q$ sort: *random* samples and *structured* samples. In both instances, it is important to realize that the so-called sampling is not done in the same way that one samples from populations of persons. Rather, in "sampling" materials for a $Q$ sort, one either constructs the materials or borrows them from some available source, e.g., a book containing many photographs of statues. The structured sample is one in which the experimenter stipulates the kinds of stimuli that will be included in the content sample in terms of an experimental design. An oversimplified example follows. In a study of photographs of statues, the experimenter decides to have some of the photographs be of oriental statues and others of occidental statues. Also, some of the photographs will concern abstract statues and others will be representational. The structured sample then could be summarized in terms of the following design:

|  | Oriental | Occidental |
|---|---|---|
| Representational | 25 | 25 |
| Abstract | 25 | 25 |

The experimenter would employ 25 photographs depicting statues that are both representational and oriental in origin, 25 that are both abstract and occidental in origin, and so on for the other two cells of the design. If there are no other facets of the design, the 25 photographs in each cell should be "random," which the experimenter best approximates simply by ensuring that they are diversely representative of sculptors and subject matters.

So that faith can be placed in a structured sample of content, two types of data must be obtained. First, prior to the use of the sample in $Q$ sorts, knowledgeable people should make judgments of the appropriateness of the classifications of stimuli. In the example above, one could have five artists independently judge the relevance of each photograph for its classification, e.g., by giving each artist the 100 photographs and having her or him place each photograph in the cell where it belongs. Only those photographs would be retained that received high agreement among judges. The second type of assurance for the correctness of cell placements comes from analyzing the responses of subjects who make $Q$ sorts of the stimuli. If the stimuli in a particular cell actually "hang together," it should be found that the variance of $Q$-sort ratings by each subject for the stimuli in any cell is considerably less than the variance of the $Q$-sort distribution. If that is not the case, it means that the stimuli that are assigned to a particular cell of the structured sample scatter all up and down the $Q$-sort continuum in the ratings made by each subject. Then, even if one could argue that there are good, logical reasons for the placements of stimuli in a structured sample, it would be obvious that the design did very little to explain the actual ratings made by subjects.

In some cases, it is very difficult to generate a sensible structured sample for the stimuli to be used in a $Q$ sort. This would be true, for example, in having psychotherapists make $Q$-sort ratings of the day-to-day progress of patients with statements like the following:

1. Spends much time expressing appreciation to me for my understanding
2. Avoids talking about painful issues
3. Seems more intent on the future than what the past was like
4. Seems discouraged about the possibility of solving major problems

With such statements, and with many other types of stimuli, the best that can be done is to "randomly sample" the desired number of "things" to be used in a $Q$ sort. What this means is that one tries to obtain a highly diverse collection of materials of the kind to be investigated, e.g., photographs of many different types of statues drawn from a number of different sources, statements about important things to observe in psychotherapy taken from a number of prominent books on the topic, or symptoms of mental illness taken from case histories in the files of a number of different types of psychiatric institutions.

Where it can be employed, the structured sample has obvious advantages over the so-called random sample. The facets of the structure help in communicating the nature of the content to other investigators. One of the problems with many "random" samples of content is that it is very difficult to specify the domain that has been "sampled." Also, the random sample typically attempts to cover too much ground, and consequently it is frequently learned from analysis of $Q$ sorts that insufficient numbers of stimuli of particular kinds were included in the sample. The structured sample serves to limit the content to manageable proportions, and it helps ensure that sufficient numbers of stimuli of the specified kinds are included. Also, as was mentioned previously, an analysis of the data obtained from investigating a structured sample will provide information about the adequacy of the placement of stimuli in the design. In sum, although the structured sample attempts to cover less ground than the random sample, it does a better job of specifying the ground to be covered, and it usually does a better job of covering that ground. In addition, the internal checks possible with the structured sample provide evidence regarding the original assignment of stimuli to cells.

When it is not possible to construct a structured sample of content initially, that frequently becomes possible after some investigations are made with a random sample. The results of statistical analyses may indicate that there are homogeneous groups of items, i.e., a number of items that tend to be given similar placements in $Q$ sorts, regardless of where they are placed as a group by different subjects. Results of these kinds could lead to asserting a structure for the sample. For the final structured sample, then, probably it would be necessary to discard some items that did not relate to the structured design and to add items in some cells to achieve equal numbers. Also, whether one achieves a structured sample initially or only after preliminary research, in continued research it frequently happens that additional facets are added to the design. This is because continued research teaches the investigator how to make important, new distinctions among the kinds of stimuli in the domain of interest.

**Analysis of Q-sort data** Many criticisms of research employing the $Q$ sort pertain not so much to the $Q$ sort itself but rather to methods of analysis that have been applied to $Q$-sort data. The most popular methods for concerned correlations, e.g., the correlation of two $Q$ sorts of the same material by the same subject under different conditions, or the correlation of $Q$ sorts by different persons. An example of the former would be to have one person make "sorts" under two sets of instructions, such as a set pertaining to the subject's aesthetic preferences for 100 statues and a set pertaining to the subject's estimate of what aesthetic preferences would be made by the average 10-year-old child. The PM correlation could then be computed between the two "sorts" by the same person. As an example of the latter approach to correlation, the PM correlation could be computed between the "sorts" made by two persons on a list of statements relating to personality traits. In addition to employing simple correlational methods with $Q$ sorts, many studies have used more complex methods of correlational analysis, including partial correlation, multiple correlation, and various methods of factor analysis.

In addition to correlational analysis, analysis of variance has also been employed with $Q$ sorts, with particular applicability to the data obtained from structured samples. For example, for the 2-by-2 factorial design mentioned previously for photographs of statues, one could employ the usual formulas for analysis of variance to examine the statistical significance of each of the two facets and of their interaction. To take an example at a simpler level of analysis, one could perform a $t$ test between the mean placements in the $Q$ sort for any two groups of items, regardless of whether those groups had been stipulated as part of a structured sample, e.g., a $t$ test between the mean ratings by one person for statues of humans and for statues of lower animals.

Although there is not sufficient space here to go into the many questions concerning various methods of analysis applied to $Q$-sort data, some of the major issues will be discussed. In this regard, it is important to take separate looks at *inferential statistics* applied to $Q$-sort data and *descriptive statistics* applied to $Q$-sort data. In considering the former, it is somewhat difficult to interpret inferential statistics applied in those instances where the sampling unit is the stimulus rather than the person and in which "degrees of freedom" are determined by the number of stimuli (e.g., photographs) rather than the number of persons. This is done when the usual "test for significance" is applied to a correlation between two "sorts" by the same or different persons. Let us say that the correlation is .40 between two sorts by one person, and there are 100 stimuli in the content sample. As has frequently been done, one can find a standard error for the correlation coefficient, inserting 100 as the sample size in the customary formulas.

To compute a standard error for a correlation coefficient in the above way assumes that it is legitimate to define the sample size as the number of stimuli employed in the $Q$ sort. Obviously, since the correlation is computed on the responses from only one subject, there is no basis at all for generalizing to other subjects. Logically, in such cases, inferential statistics concerns probability statements about relations between samples of content and a hypothetical "population"(universe or domain) of content. If, by considering the sample size to be the number of stimuli and a correlation of .40 reached acceptable levels of statistical significance, this would provide some statistical confidence that the domain correlation is different from zero. The domain correlation would be that obtained if the $Q$ sort contained every stimulus in a finite domain of stimuli, or in the case of an infinite domain of content, the hypothetical $Q$ sort made with an infinite number of stimuli.

In all other uses of inferential statistics where the sample size is considered to be the number of stimuli rather than the number of persons, probability statements necessarily relate only to stimulus sampling, and thus they have no direct implications for the generality of results over populations of persons. This is true, for example, in the use of analysis of variance with structured samples of stimuli. It was mentioned previously how one might employ the usual $F$ ratios to assess the main effects and interactions occurring in the placement of stimuli in one "sorting" by one person. If, then, one of the main effects proved to be "significant" in this way, what the experimenter would conclude is that the cell means would probably be different even if the $Q$ sort contained all the stimuli in a domain of stimuli.

As has been mentioned and illustrated at numerous points in this book, the theory of psychological measurement is more intimately related to principles concerning the sampling of content than to principles concerning the sampling of people. That does not mean, however, that it is necessary or wise to translate inferential statistics concerning the sampling of people into inferential statistics concerning the sampling of content. One can develop most of the necessary principles in the theory of psychological measurement without considering inferential statistics relating to content sampling.

If one employs inferential statistics with respect to problems of content sampling, as is frequently done with $Q$-sort data, one must be aware that the assumptions for using such statistics are much more difficult to justify than they are in sampling people. First, there must be a definable population (domain or universe), and it is difficult to define domains of content for $Q$ sorts. Second, the sampling unit must be defined. This is obviously the individual person in the usual sampling of people, but it is not so obvious what the sampling unit is with certain types of content, e.g., statements about psychotherapy or statements relating to personality traits. Third, the stimuli must be randomly sampled either overall (the so-called random sample for $Q$ sorts) or within specified categories (as in the structured sample for $Q$ sorts). As was mentioned previously, it is usually uncertain that one is sampling at all when one is obtaining or constructing material for a $Q$ sort, and it is even less certain that one is sampling randomly.

It is best not to make fine interpretations of the probability values found in applying inferential statistics to problems concerning the sampling of content. One does better to consider them as rough guides to the probable generality of findings over large collections of stimuli of the same general kinds. As an example, assume that the correlation of $Q$-sort self-descriptions by two persons is .80, and the correlation with the same stimuli for two other persons is 0. By applying the usual formulas for inferential statistics and using the number of stimuli as the sample size, one finds that the difference in the two correlations is accompanied by an extremely high level of statistical confidence. Then, even if it is usually difficult to justify the assumptions necessary to employ inferential statistics with problems concerning the sampling of content, the level of statistical confidence provides some assurance that the difference in the two correlations is "real" and not entirely due to the fortuitous circumstances that led to the selection of some materials rather than others for the $Q$ sort. In the same way, an informal use of analysis of variance and other inferential statistics with problems of content sampling is justified.

In most forms of analysis applied to $Q$-sort data, however, there is little need to make statistical inferences regarding the generality of results over hypothetical domains of content. Simple correlations, and more complex products of correlational analysis, can be used only as descriptive indices of degrees of relationship. Analysis of variance also can be used to provide descriptive indices, in contrast to the more customary probability statements. For example, the variance of means in any facet of a structured sample can be divided by the fixed variance of the $Q$-sort distribution, and that ratio would provide a direct index of the extent to which the facet has explanatory power for the variance of ratings. Other ratios of components of variance relating to the "sort" of one person for stimuli from a structured sample can be used as descriptive indices.

After descriptive indices are computed for each person, inferential statistics can be applied to the variabilities of such indices over a priori groups of persons (e.g., men versus women) or differences in differently treated groups in controlled experiments. An example of the former would be as follows. The purpose of the study is to compare the aesthetic preferences of college students with those of professional artists. The mean placement of 25 abstract oriental statues would be obtained for each person, resulting in a distribution of means for each of the two groups. The means and variances of those two distributions of means would be obtained, and this information would be used in a $t$ test of the differences in grand means of the two groups. Another example is as follows. Patients entering psychotherapy could be asked to make $Q$-sort descriptions of themselves and how they would like to be ideally. The two "sorts" are correlated for each patient, giving a distribution of such correlations over the number of patients in the study. All patients would be asked to repeat the two "sorts" on the completion of psychotherapy. The tendency for the "after" correlations to be higher than the "before" correlations could be assessed by any of the methods of inferential statistics relating to repeated observations, e.g., the sign test. In many other ways, the results from studies employing $Q$ sorts can be examined in terms of inferential statistics relating to the sampling of persons rather than to the sampling of stimuli.

**Summary remarks about the $Q$ sort** There are advantages and disadvantages to employing the $Q$ sort rather than other rating methods. The chief advantage is in those instances where one is seeking relatively precise comparative responses among a rather large number of stimuli. As was mentioned previously, highly precise comparative methods such as pair comparisons are almost out of the question with large numbers of stimuli. At the other extreme of the continuum of precision, one could make comparative analyses of absolute responses obtained from rating scales. An example concerning ratings of the physical attractiveness of men will illustrate the possibilities. If the stimuli were 100 photographs of men, it would be almost out of the question to employ pair comparisons and difficult to employ rank-order. Comparative ratings could be obtained quickly and easily with the $Q$ sort.

Another way to obtain comparative information about the rated attractiveness of the men would be as follows. Instead of having comparisons made among the men with regard to attractiveness, each photograph is rated on an eight-step scale, anchored on the extremes by "very attractive" and "very ugly." Then one could make comparative analyses among the absolute ratings given by each person. A first step would be to convert all distributions of ratings by different raters to a common distribution form. One could do this by standardizing the distribution of 100 ratings for each person. Then all subjects would have the same mean and standard deviation of ratings, and the standard scores would provide comparative information about the ratings made by each person. These scores could then be treated in all the ways that scores obtained from $Q$ sorts are treated.

If economy of time, effort, and money was the major consideration, it would pay to make comparative analyses of separate ratings rather than employ the $Q$ sort. Subjects can make 100 separate ratings in less than half the time that they can perform a $Q$ sort of 100 stimuli. In previous years, the $Q$ sort had a marked advantage in statistical analyses over comparative analyses of separate ratings. This is because in the $Q$ sort all sets of comparative ratings have a fixed distribution, and consequently there is no need to make conversions to a common distribution, as must be done in order to make comparative analyses of absolute responses. Also, with only a desk calculator, it is much faster to compute correlations between $Q$ sorts than between sets of absolute ratings (correlating over stimuli as is done in the $Q$ sort). Those were very important considerations years ago, but no longer. Most analyses these days are done on high-speed computers, and the difference in computer time to make analyses of $Q$ sorts and similar comparative analyses of absolute responses is trivial.

What, then, are the advantages of using $Q$ sorts over performing comparative analyses of absolute ratings? The major potential advantage is that one might obtain more precise comparative information from the $Q$ sort. The $Q$ sort explicitly requires the subject to make comparative responses, but this occurs only incidentally in making separate ratings. The various response styles that accompany absolute ratings (e.g., the tendency to make extreme ratings) could cloud the comparative information in such ratings. Also, the tendency of subjects to shift sets (e.g., to respond more favorably as they proceed from rating to rating) also would tend to cloud the comparative information in the ratings. Then, one would usually expect to find a higher reliability (e.g., retest) for comparative responses obtained from the $Q$ sort than from comparative analyses of absolute ratings.

Aside from questions of reliability, it is also possible that the factor composition of $Q$ sorts sometimes is somewhat different from comparatively analyzed ratings. In the latter, since the subject does not actually make comparative responses, it is an assumption on the part of the experimenter that a comparative analysis of those responses results in measurement of the same attributes that would be measured by actually obtaining comparative responses.

Even if the $Q$ sort has certain advantages as a method of eliciting comparative responses, a more basic question concerns whether it is wise to obtain comparative responses with sets of stimuli of the kinds that frequently are employed with the $Q$ sort. It can be strongly argued that comparative responses make sense only if all the stimuli in a set are from some common frame of reference. As was illustrated previously, it is hard to make a convincing case for this with some of the $Q$-sort samples that have been employed in studies to date.

In those cases where all stimuli are from a common frame of reference, whether one employs a comparative or an absolute rating method is largely independent of the methods of analyzing the data. One can employ an $R$-technique or $Q$-technique logic with either (the difference was discussed in Chap. 11). Data from the $Q$ sort usually have been analyzed in terms of the logic of its namesake, $Q$ technique. For example, one frequently correlates the "sorts" made by different persons and performs factor analyses of the correlations. In contrast, data obtained from absolute-response methods (e.g., rating scales) usually are analyzed in terms of the logic of $R$ technique. For example, in studying the factor structure of ratings of attitude statements, one usually would correlate scales over persons (instead of persons over scales) and factor-analyze the obtained correlations.

It is possible, however, to employ an $R$ technique logic in the analysis of $Q$-sort data and a $Q$-technique logic in the analysis of data obtained from methods that elicit absolute responses, although neither is frequently done. The latter has already been illustrated, as in the situation where comparative analyses are made of separate ratings of the members of a set of stimuli. Correlations between persons could be analyzed in all the ways typically employed with $Q$ sorts. To illustrate the other possibility, pairs of stimuli in $Q$ sorts could be correlated over persons, and correlations among stimuli could be treated as they are in $R$ technique.

The above considerations lead us to four major conclusions about the $Q$ sort and related methods of analysis. First, if one is seeking comparative responses, the $Q$ sort has certain advantages. Second, before the $Q$ sort is employed, it is important to ensure that sensible comparative responses can be made among the stimuli employed in a particular study. Third, if one elects to use the $Q$ sort as a rating method, one is not necessarily tied to the use of particular techniques of mathematical analysis rather than others. Fourth, choices among approaches to mathematical analysis (for example, $R$ technique versus $Q$ technique) are mainly matters of taste and hunch. In the long run we shall learn which approaches are generally more fruitful, but at this early stage in the growth of the science, it is good that all the research eggs are not being placed in the same methodological basket.

## SCALING OF STIMULI

Most of the discussion in this chapter has concerned the use of rating methods for the scaling of persons with respect to psychological traits. Summative scales based on statements concerning attitudinal objects are used to scale people in terms of their attitudes, e.g., toward the United Nations. Semantic-differential scales are used to measure individual differences in the connotative meanings of concepts. The $Q$ sort is used to measure individual differ-preferences for stimuli of different kinds.

In spite of the important place of rating methods in the scaling of people, it would be appropriate to close this chapter by reminding the reader that rating methods also are very useful for the scaling of stimuli. Numerous methods for scaling stimuli were discussed in Chap. 2, all of which, in essence are "rating methods." The particular rating methods discussed in this chapter frequently are used for the scaling of stimuli. Summative scales of agree-disagree ratings of statements can be used, for example, to scale typical reactions to different levels of dosage of a particular drug or to different types of psychotherapy. The semantic differential has many uses in the scaling of stimuli, as for the scaling of nonsense syllables in terms of degree of familiarity and the scaling of geometric designs in terms of pleasantness, complexity, and other characteristics. The $Q$ sort also has many applications to the scaling of stimuli. Words can be "sorted" in terms of emotionality; statements relating to personality traits can be "sorted" in terms of social desirability; and patches of gray paper can be "sorted" in terms of brightness.

When rating scales are used to scale stimuli rather than people, the major assumption is that individual differences are not important in judgments or preferences in relation to the particular set of stimuli. If that is a safe assumption, the experimenter can average over raters to obtain a scale for the stimuli. The assumption is safe with certain classes of stimuli (e.g., patches of gray paper) and not safe with other classes of stimuli (e.g., ratings of values). Whether or not the assumption seems safe a priori, the wisdom of making the assumption can be tested after the data are in hand. The extent to which subjects can be considered replicates of one another can be determined by an inspection of the correlations among subjects or, if necessary, by a factor analysis. Regardless of the details of constructing such scales, it is more important to keep in mind that the rating methods discussed in this chapter are important for the scaling of stimuli as well as for the scaling of people.

## SUGGESTED ADDITIONAL READINGS

Edwards, A. L. *Techniques of attitude scale construction.* New York: Appleton-Century-Crofts, 1957.

Edwards, A. L. *The measurement of personality traits by scales and inventories.* New York: Holt, 1970.

Guilford, J. P. Psychometric methods. New York: McGraw-Hill, 1954, chap. 11.

Kerlinger, F. N. *Foundations of behavioral research* (2d ed.). New York: Holt, 1973, chaps. 28 to 34.

Nunnally, J. C. *Introduction to psychological measurement.* New York: McGraw-Hill, 1970.

Snider, J. G., and Osgood, C. E. (eds.). *Semantic differential technique.* Chicago: Aldine, 1969.

Wiggins, J. S. *Personality and prediction: Principles of personality assessment.* Reading, Mass.: Addison-Wesley, 1973.

# SIXTEEN

## CONTINGENT VARIABLES—EFFECTS ON PSYCHOLOGICAL MEASUREMENTS

Potentially, measurements of all human traits are affected by many contingent variables, such as time limits, guessing, response styles, fatigue, motivation, etc. Although such contingent variables are present in any context in which measurements are undertaken, they represent potential problems for obtaining valid measurements. Thus, these contingent variables potentially can (1) reduce reliability, (2) introduce reliable sources of individual differences that lower overall validity, or (3) produce substantial correlations between tests or differences among means of experimental treatment groups which actually are spurious. This chapter will discuss ways of avoiding these problems through proper methods of test construction, administration, scoring, and statistical analysis of results.

There is no end to the contingent variables that potentially influence measures of psychological traits. Many of those variables have been almost entirely neglected, as is the case with the effects of motivation on test performance. Much of the evidence concerning some of the contingent variables has been incidentally obtained as part of studies performed for other purposes, which tends to be true of the evidence relating to the effects of time limits on tests of abilities.

## EFFECTS OF SPEED

Because of the theoretical and practical importance of the effects of speed on psychological measures, before about 1960 many investigations were made in this area. The most comprehensive single source for research results up to that time is a report of a symposium, "The effects of time limits on test scores," *Educational and Psychological Measurement*, 1960, *20*, 221–274. Surprisingly, there have been very few systematic investigations of test time limits during the intervening years. For example, in the very comprehensive and prestigious volume *Educational Measurement* edited by Thorndike (1971), various effects of speed are mentioned only in scattered places, there is no systematic overall review of the topic, and almost nothing in the way of empirical studies on the topic is reported. This is unfortunate because, as will be seen, there are some very large theoretical and practical problems regarding the effects of speed on psychological and educational tests.

There are two broad questions concerning speed, the first relating to psychological theories and the second relating to the methodology of measurement. The first question is, "Are speed of response and goodness of response interchangeable?" For example, would one expect a high correlation between the speed of solving very simple reasoning problems and the ability to solve difficult reasoning problems when no time limit is employed? Spearman (1927) claimed that speed of response and goodness of response are interchangeable concepts, and he mustered some evidence to support his point of view; but that point of view has been strongly challenged in the intervening years.

The second broad question is, "How do different time limits affect the psychometric properties of measurement methods?" For example, what would happen to the reliability of a particular test if the time limit were shortened from 50 to 30 minutes?

The problem with the two questions above is that they are far too broad to permit neat answers. In each case the answer is, "It depends." Each question must be broken down into a number of different questions relating to different types of instruments, different types of scoring, different methods of administration, different types of research designs, and different methods of analyzing the results. Some of the more important distinctions to be considered with respect to the effects of speed are discussed in this section.

**Types of instruments** Most of the practical and theoretical issues concerning speed relate only to measures of human ability rather than to measures of personality traits and sentiments. For example, almost no consideration has been given to the effects of speed on self-inventories, and most such instruments are administered under liberal time limits. In a test of ability, the hope is that the individual's ability will be directly manifested in the test score. Then, to the extent that individuals are made to hurry through the test, the score may represent somewhat different abilities than if they had been given all the time desired. In contrast, in a self-inventory, the score is not thought to represent a direct measure of personality in action. In that case the most that is hoped for is that the subjects will honestly relate how they usually behave in daily life, and thus measurement is indirect. To force subjects to speed through the inventory would not necessarily measure an interaction of speed with personality traits; rather, it would serve only to make the subjects describe themselves faster. Restrictive time limits may have small effects on the results of self-inventories and other nonability measures, but if they do, very little is known about such effects.

In a discussion of effects of speed, it is important to distinguish among tests of ability that are intended to serve basically different purposes, i.e., those requiring content validity, predictive validity, and construct validity, respectively. Accompanying these three types of instruments are different issues concerning speed—different degrees of practical importance, different theoretical concepts, and different approaches to investigating the effects of speed.

**Variables relating to speed** One reason why the two questions posed at the beginning of this section are not sufficiently specific is that they ask only about the effects of speed, without specifying the variables to be considered. One aspect of speed concerns *speed instructions.* For example, in measures of word association, subjects are usually instructed to work quickly and respond with the first word that comes to mind. With speed instructions, however, subjects frequently are not forced to perform at any set speed, item per item, or to stop responding after any particular amount of time. Also, in such cases no measurement is made of how rapidly subjects actually respond. As a variable, then, speed instructions serve only to encourage rapid responses. They do not ensure rapid responses by the average subject; they do not prevent individual differences in rate of response; and they do not necessarily lead to measures of individual differences in rate of response.

Another variable relating to speed is *preferred rate* of response, which concerns how rapidly subjects like to respond. Preferred rate can be purely measured only in the situation where (1) responses are very easy (i.e., not mentally difficult or physically exhausting) and (2) the experimenter does not provide incentives for responding either quickly or slowly. There are very few tasks that meet those standards. An example is when subjects are told to tap a stylus on a table at any rate that they choose, while the number of taps per unit of time is recorded. If a word-association test were given without speed instructions, the total time taken by each subject would be an almost pure measure of preferred rate in relation to that task. It would not be a completely pure measure of preferred rate, because there is a small amount of "mental strain" in forming associates, and individual differences in that regard would have different effects on preferred rate.

Preferred rate is the motivational component of the effects of speed on test scores. It concerns how rapidly the subject tries to work in a particular setting. Obviously, the purpose of speed instructions is to alter preferred rate, as in the example concerning the use of speed instructions with a test of word association. There are two important unsolved questions concerning preferred rate. First, is it a general trait of personality, or is it largely specific to the task at hand? Second, regardless of the generality of preferred rate, how does preferred rate interact with speed instructions? Even if the average person responds more quickly with speed instructions than without speed instructions, this still leaves open the question of whether changes in individual differences occur. If the correlation between scores in the two situations is 1.0 (after being corrected for attenuation), it means that speed instructions influence only the average rate of responding but do not alter individual differences in preferred rate. If the correlation is zero, it means that speed instructions erase individual differences in preferred rate.

One reason why we know so little about preferred rate is that it is very difficult to investigate preferred rate independently of other variables. In most tasks, the apparent preferred rate actually is a mixture of how quickly subjects would like to respond and how quickly they can respond. This is the case, for example, in a numerical computation test consisting of simple arithmetic problems. One person may take considerable time to complete the problems although that individual is making every effort to work quickly. Another person may feel no pressure to work quickly, but having superior ability for the type of problem, may complete the test in less time than the average person does.

Another distinction must be made between *response-time scores* and *time-limit accuracy scores*. With time-limit accuracy scores, the amount of time to complete a set of problems is held constant for all subjects, and the score for each subject consists of the number of problems correctly solved. This would be the case, for example, where subjects were given 20 minutes to solve as many arithmetic problems as they could out of a list of 30 problems. Response-time scores are used when each subject is required to work until a problem or a list of problems is solved, and the score consists of the amount of time used. In studies of individual differences, time-limit accuracy scores are employed more frequently than response-time scores, e.g., in measures of perceptual speed, verbal fluency, reading speed, and speed of numerical computation. Response-time scores are used very widely in controlled experiments, e.g., reaction time of humans and time rats take to traverse a maze. In studies of individual differences, time-limit accuracy scores are used more often than response-time scores because they have obvious practical advantages. The major advantage is that the former can be obtained easily in group testing, but the latter usually requires individual testing.

A final distinction in this section must be made between speed evidenced under two types of restrictive time limits. One type of time limit is that in which all subjects are given a set amount of time to respond to each item, which is referred to as a *paced* condition. This would be the case, for example, where subjects were given one minute to solve each of 20 arithmetic problems. After the time is up for one problem, subjects are required to hand their written answers to the experimenter. Next, another problem is handed to subjects, and they are given one minute to find the answer. The paced condition is seldom used in studies of individual differences, because obviously it has practical disadvantages. It has some important uses, however, in basic research concerning the effects of speed on test scores. In the more frequently employed time-limit method, subjects are given a set amount of time for completing a whole test. With the time-limit method, the subjects have to pace themselves. They might work slowly and strive for accuracy on the problems that they attempt, or they might work rapidly and sacrifice accuracy to attempt every item. They might work slowly on the first half of the problems but, seeing that the time is running out, make wild guesses on the remaining problems. Also, to the extent that there are individual differences in motivational characteristics relating to preferred rate, logically these should have a more pronounced influence on time-limit tests than on paced tests.

The major issues concerning speed relate to the psychometric characteristics of accuracy scores on time-limit tests. Such tests are used very widely, and it is in such tests that (1) special factors of ability concerning speed might occur and (2) individual differences in preferred rate and other response styles might strongly influence scores.

**Difficulty of items** It is important here to refresh the reader's memory about the types of items that are employed on pure speed tests and on pure power tests. On a *pure speed test*, the items are so easy that nearly all subjects would obtain perfect scores if they were allowed to take as much time as they liked. Such items are said to be of *trivial difficulty*. If one actually computed the difficulty levels for such items, by definition they would range upward from $p$ values of .90. With such items, the only way to obtain a reliable dispersion of scores is to employ highly restrictive time limits. There is no question, then, of whether restrictive time limits should be employed. Also, a good argument can be made that in most cases the ideal time limit is the one that produces the most reliable distribution of scores.

In contrast to a pure speed test, in a *pure power test* subjects are allowed to take as much time as they like. In such tests, the items cannot be of trivial difficulty, because that would not produce a desirable distribution of scores. A test composed of items having $p$ values of .90 or higher would probably not be highly reliable and the distribution of scores would be highly skewed. In Chap. 8 it was said that it is best to select test items not in terms of $p$ values, but rather in terms of item-test correlations. As was mentioned, however, the latter method tends to reject items with extreme $p$ values, e.g., those below .2 or above .8 on a free-response test.

The discussion of pure speed tests and pure power tests becomes somewhat complex when it must be considered that two types of combinations of these tests are frequently found in practice. The first occurs when restrictive time limits are placed on what was previously almost a pure power test, as in the following example. The power test is constructed from data obtained under very liberal time limits, and subsequently, the same liberal time limits are employed with the test. Later, someone decides to reduce the time limit, say, shortening it from 1 hour to 40 minutes. This type of mixture of speed and power will be referred to as a *time-power test*. A major question to be considered later is whether psychometric properties of timed-power tests usually are different from those of pure power tests.

A second type of mixture of speed and power occurs when the items are not completely trivial in difficulty when given under power conditions. Most of them are very easy—say, the $p$ values range from .8 to 1.0. To obtain a symmetrical, reliable distribution of scores, then, the experimenter investigates restrictive time limits for the test. This type of mixture of speed and power can be referred to as a speed and difficulty test, or more simply as a *speed-difficulty test*. It is important to distinguish between timed-power tests and speed-difficulty tests, because the issues are simpler with respect to the former and the practical problems are more severe with respect to the latter. These matters will be discussed in a later section.

**Types of time limits** Instead of speaking only of power conditions and restrictive time limits, one must make finer distinctions between these conditions. Because of the practical problems involved, it is very rare that a pure power condition is employed. There usually is a time limit, no matter how liberal it might be. Typically, when persons are allowed to take as much time as they like on tests of ability, the distribution of working times is highly skewed. For example, in a test that most persons complete in one hour, a small percentage of persons will remain for two hours, and one person will want to remain for four hours. In that case the experimenter natually considers the possibility of saving a great deal of time on the use of the test by requiring all subjects to finish in 90 minutes.

It is useful to think in terms of a *comfortable time limit*, which will be defined as the amount of time required for 90 percent of the persons to complete a test under power conditions. To determine the comfortable time limit in that way would, of course, require that the test be administered to an initial group of persons under power conditions. In some cases it is not feasible to make such a study, as in the case of classroom examinations that must be completed in 50 minutes. In these cases a check can be made of whether a comfortable time limit is being employed. At the end of the test, each person is asked to indicate whether she or he had sufficient time to complete the test. If at least 90 percent of the persons mark *yes*, it can be said that a comfortable time limit is being employed. Of course, the comfortable time limit is related to the type of person being tested. It might be markedly different, for example, for high school students and college students or for younger persons and older persons.

The comfortable time limit offers a basis for scaling all levels of restrictive time limits. Thus one could investigate the effects of employing only 75 percent of the comfortable time, 50 percent of the comfortable time, and so on. Also, the comfortable time offers a basis for comparing the effects of differences in restrictive time limits on different tests. For example, it would be meaningful to compare changes in mean scores on two tests as a function of varying fractions of the comfortable time limit, e.g., from 25 percent up to 200 percent of the comfortable time.

In most investigations of the effects of speed on test performance, no index comparable to the comfortable time has been obtained. Consequently one can only guess at the extent to which different time limits are actually restrictive. For example, cutting the usual time limit for a test in half might still provide more time than the comfortable time or might reduce the time to only a small fraction of the comfortable time. The lack of a uniform base for comparing the effects of different time limits (such as that provided by the comfortable time) is one of the major reasons it is so difficult to interpret the many, scattered studies that have been performed on the effects of different time limits on test performance.

**Potential effects of time limits**  Here we shall consider the potential effects of different time limits in relation to the comfortable time. The results from any measurement method are defined entirely in terms of a limited number of psychometric properties, these being the mean, standard deviation, distribution shape, reliability, and validity (including the factorial composition). Restrictive time limits potentially influence all these.

The potential effects of restrictive time limits on the mean score are obvious. If there are any effects at all, the expectation is that the mean will increase with increasing fractions of the comfortable time, with little increase being expected above 100 percent of the comfortable time. There is, however, no strict relationship between the mean and reliability or validity. A mean near the center of the usable score range (e.g., half of the number of items on a dichotomously scored free-response test) tends to favor high reliability, but the relationship holds in only a loose statistical way.

Effects of time limits on the standard deviation and distribution shape are important mainly in that they relate to reliability. The time limit that produces the largest standard deviation of scores usually produces the most reliable set of scores (as determined by separately timed halves or by alternative forms). Effects of time limits on the distribution shape are important because they relate to differences in reliability at different score levels. For example, if a particular time limit produces a distribution that is markedly skewed toward the high-score end of the continuum, this indicates that more reliable discriminations are made among persons of high ability than among persons of low ability. This is so regardless of the overall reliability, which, as was said above, is highly related to the standard deviation. The overall reliability is related to the distribution shape only indirectly through relations between shape and standard deviation.

All the above considerations still leave open the question of effects of restrictive time limits on validity. Later we shall consider effect of time limits on instruments that require different kinds of evidence for validity. There is, however, one standard that can be employed to determine effects of restrictive time limits on instruments of all kinds. This standard is the change in factor composition under different time limits. In any particular investigation, one might not know the factor composition of a test given under comfortable time limits, and one might not know whether changes in the factor composition under different time limits make the test more or less valid; but it is possible to tell whether the factor composition changes.

When the correlation between two sets of scores is corrected for attenuation, it is a direct index of the extent that the two instruments measure the same thing. The square of this is the common variance shared by the two measures. This leads to an approach for determining the effects of restrictive time limits on changes in the factor composition (and thus the validity) of different types of test materials. Alternative forms of a test can be constructed and administered to the same subjects on different days under different time limits. Assuming that previous studies have established the reliability of each test, the correlation between tests given under different time limits can be corrected for attenuation. The square of this result is then a measure of *shared common variance* *(SCV)*. A formula for obtaining this result is as follows:

$$SCV = \frac{r_{12}^2}{r_{11}r_{22}} \tag{16-1}$$

where $r_{12}$ = PM correlation between scores in time limits 1 and 2

$r_{11}r_{22}$ = reliabilities of scores in the two time-limit conditions

An example of the use of Eq. (16-1) is where the reliability of scores under one time limit is .8, the reliability under a shorter time limit is .6, and the squared correlation between the two sets of scores is .48. In that case the *SCV* equals 1.0. Thus scores obtained under more restrictive time limits have the same factor composition as scores obtained under more generous time limits, but the former are more reliable.

To investigate changes in *SCV* as discussed above, one must be careful to counterbalance testing sessions so as to control for practice effects, and one must investigate each alternative form in each time-limit condition. Because of the labors of performing studies of these kinds, very few have been done. One of the most thorough studies of this kind was by Morrison (1960).

**One-trial measures of the effects of time limits** Computation of the *SCV*, as described above, is based on correlations among alternative forms administered under different time limits. Consequently, all subjects have to be administered a number of alternative forms. Proposals have been made for examining changes in factor structure because of varying time limits in terms of item statistics rather than in terms of correlations between alternative forms [these are discussed in detail by Gulliksen (1950) and by Morrison (1960)]. One such index can be developed through the following line of reasoning. A pure speed test could be defined as one in which (1) no subject has time to attempt all items and (2) all attempted items are correct. In other words, subjects attempt each item as they work through the test, and they make correct responses on all items attempted up to the point that time is called. In this case there would be no attempted items that were not correct, and consequently the score for each person would equal the number of items attempted.

Logically, if a test is not a pure speed test, the above considerations will not hold exactly. If the test is a mixture of factors relating to power and speed, there will be some attempted items that are not correct. In this case the total number of incorrect responses given by each person can be decomposed in the following manner:

$$U = \text{number of unattempted items}$$

$$W = \text{number of incorrect attempted items}$$

$$X = \text{total number of errors, } U + W$$

A case in point would be where the individual attempts 30 items in a test containing 40 items. Of the 30 items attempted, three are responded to incorrectly; e.g., answers on three arithmetic problems are wrong. In this case $U = 10$, $W = 3$, and $X = 13$.

To the extent that the variance of $U$ is large with respect to variance of $X$, it could be argued that the test mainly concerns abilities relating to speed rather than abilities relating to power. Similarly, to the extent that the variance of $W$ is large relative to the variance of $X$, it could be argued that the test concerns abilities mainly relating to power rather than to speed. In considering the former possibility, the following index could be employed in experiments on the effects of different time limits on test performance:

$$\text{Degree of speeding} = \frac{\sigma_u^2}{\sigma_x^2} \qquad (16\text{-}2)$$

One could develop more refined formulas by considering possible correlations between $U$ and $W$, but Eq. (16-2) will illustrate the logic of one-trial measures of the effects of speed. Formulas such as Eq. (16-2) could be employed with respect to data obtained from the following type of study. One test is administered to different samples of subjects under different time limits, and the degree of speeding is determined separately for each time period. To the extent that shorter time limits result in a higher index than do longer time limits, it could be argued that changes in time limits tend to alter the factor composition of scores. Also, for any one time limit considered separately, the size of the index could be considered a measure of the extent that scores relate to abilities concerning speed rather than to abilities concerning power.

One-trial indices of the effects of speed will not be discussed here in greater detail because they have rightly fallen into disrepute. They are appealing for practical reasons: they do not require the construction of alternative forms, and they do not require each group of subjects to take more than one test. Beyond these practical advantages, however, the one-trial measures have little to recommend them. They are founded on a number of unreasonable assumptions, the first of which is that the degree of speeding is intimately related to the number of unattempted items $U$. In fact, the number of unattempted items is determined, in large measure, by the test instructions and the overall atmosphere in which the test is administered, regardless of the amount of time given to complete the test. Even if a very generous time limit is used for a power test, the experimenter can force the number of unattempted items to be large relative to the total number of errors simply by strongly warning the subjects to be sure to get all the answers correct as far as they go and not to guess when unsure. Conversely, even with a highly restrictive time limit applied to items of trivial difficulty, one can force a high ratio of incorrect attempted items $W$ to total errors by strongly urging all subjects to answer all items in the allotted time, even if this requires wild guesses on some of the items.

Even if the basic assumptions of the one-trial formulas for the effects of speed were not arguable, the one-trial indices would still fail to provide some important information. Administering the same test to different groups under different time limits can produce direct information about effects on the mean, distribution shape, standard deviation, and reliability, but it cannot provide direct information about effects of time limits on the factor composition of scores. Investigations of factor composition necessarily are based on correlations of alternative forms (or the same test) administered to the same subjects under different time limits, which is the case with the $SCV$ discussed previously.

**Timed-power tests**  Here we shall begin to review the evidence regarding effects of speed on performance, first by discussing the effects of employing restrictive time limits on tests that are constructed under power conditions. An outstanding example of a test that ordinarily would be given under power conditions is a vocabulary test. Although a "comfortable" amount of time is required for the subject to look over each item and to select the most appropriate answer, the intention is to measure knowledge of words rather than rapidity of response. Also, beyond the amount of time required to read and respond to the items, the allotting of additional time will not materially change scores. For example, if an individual does not know the meaning of the word *amalgamate*, an additional two minutes of staring at the word will not help select the correct alternative response. Conversely, however, it is an interesting question as to what extent one can reduce the comfortable time limit on such power tests and not adversely influence the distribution of obtained scores.

Essentially, the issues concern the effects on psychometric properties of tests when testing time is varied as a function of the comfortable time. As was mentioned previously, however, in most of the studies which have been conducted, no standard base (such as the comfortable time) was employed. Instead, in most studies the experimenters have simply varied the time and examined effects of different time limits on performance. The evidence, then, must be considered circumstantial rather than direct. There is, however, a wealth of circumstantial evidence to indicate that the *comfortable time can be decreased appreciably without seriously affecting any of the psychometric properties of tests.*

Examples of studies that support the above conclusion are reported by the following authors: Cronbach (1970), Kendall (1964), Lord (1956), Morrison (1960), Rimland (1960), Toops (1960), and Wesman (1960). Some studies have shown that doubling the usual time limit has little effect on performance, and other studies have shown that cutting the usual time limit in half has almost no effect. In some studies it has been found that even the mean performance is unaffected by cutting the usual time limit in half. Even in those cases where the mean was affected, the reliability tended to remain the same over broad ranges of time limits, e.g., time limits of 30, 40, and 50 minutes.

Obviously, there is a limit to the restrictive times that can be employed without affecting the reliability. For example, if the time limit were only one minute for a 40-item vocabulary test, the standard deviation of scores would be very small, and the reliability would be small also. The level at which time limits have a marked effect on the reliability has been surprisingly low in most studies, in comparison to the usual time limits employed for the tests and in comparison to the different time limits investigated.

Even in those studies where time limits were so restrictive as to materially influence the reliability, in most cases there was little evidence that the factor composition was materially influenced. An excellent study supporting this conclusion was performed by Morrison (1960). Even if restrictive time limits tend to increase or decrease the reliability, the reliable variance tends to relate to the same underlying factors; i.e., the $SCV$ is high.

Not all the evidence supports the above conclusions, as is shown in some of the studies summarized by Guilford (1954, pp. 366–370) and by Morrison (1960). In some cases the $SCV$ was sufficiently low to indicate that somewhat different factors were being measured by tests given under different time limits. In some studies this may have been because the investigations concerned speed-difficulty tests rather than timed-power tests; i.e., the average $p$ value of items under power conditions would be very high. Also, in many instances this may have been accounted for by the way items were ordered on the test. In many aptitude and achievement tests, there is a wide range of item difficulty, and the practice frequently is to order the items in terms of difficulty. Then the items at the beginning of the test are very easy, and the items near the end of the test are very difficult. By employing a very restrictive time limit for such a test, one could prevent most subjects from attempting more than half the items. Scores obtained under these conditions could then be compared with scores obtained from the same subjects on an alternative form of the test administered under a generous time limit. The $SCV$ might be considerably less than 1.0, but that might be entirely because of the way items were ordered on the test. The second half of the items on such tests not only are more difficult than those in the first half, but also tend to measure different factors.

Easy items and difficult items often measure somewhat different factors, even when one would guess that they measured the same thing. For example, in the typical "quantitative" test employed along with a verbal test for the selection of college students, the easy items at the beginning of the test tend to measure numerical skills, but the difficult items near the end of the test tend to measure reasoning abilities. On some tests of spatial relations, the easy items at the beginning of the test tend to measure somewhat different spatial factors than those measured by the difficult items near the end of the test. In such cases it is no wonder that restrictive time limits affect the factor composition of scores. But that does not mean that speed, per se, introduces new factors of ability. What it means is that restrictive time limits force the subject to take a somewhat *different* test than would be taken if a more generous time limit were employed.

The *SCV* tends to remain high where items are *randomly* ordered on tests. In this case, even if the time limit is very restrictive, subjects still are taking the *same kind* of test as they would if a generous time limit were employed.

A good working rule is that, on a timed-power test, the comfortable time can be cut by at least *one-third* without materially changing the standard deviation, reliability, or factor composition. It should be kept in mind that this rule applies to timed-power tests, ones that are constructed under power conditions. The definition of the comfortable time also should be kept in mind—the amount of time required for 90 percent of the subjects to say that they have had ample time to complete the test. The rule applies better when the mean score in the comfortable time is near the center of the effective range rather than near either extreme. That is the case in most tests constructed under power conditions (by methods discussed in Chap. 8).

The above rule tends to hold because most subjects can perform effectively at a faster rate than their preferred rate. In many instances subjects are annoyed by having to work faster, and they frequently claim that restrictive time limits hurt their performance when that is not actually the case.

Since power tests are not grossly affected by mildly restrictive time limits (e.g., employing the comfortable time rather than a more generous time limit), this offers an approach to a more efficient use of testing time. For example, this might permit one to give twice as many items on a multiple-choice achievement test, which in turn would permit a wider sampling of content. As another example, in basic research on human abilities, this might allow one to investigate more tests in a fixed amount of available testing time.

**Factors measured by speed and power tests** One question to raise regarding effects of speed on factors of ability is whether the factors measured by power tests tend to be the same as those measured by speed tests. Since it can be concluded that moderately restrictive time limits on power tests do not markedly alter their psychometric properties, the question also can be phrased in terms of the factors typically measured by timed-power tests and pure speed tests. Regarding the latter type of test, the discussion in this section will be concerned only with tests composed of items of trivial difficulty. A later section will consider the psychometric properties of speed-difficulty tests, on which restrictive time limits are employed with items that range in $p$ value from .8 to 1.0 when given under power conditions.

Although no general answer can be given to the question of differences in factor structure of power tests and speed tests, such tests tend to measure different factors. For example, speed tests concerning the production of simple words tend to measure a factor of verbal fluency, but power tests concerning the understanding of more difficult words tend to measure a factor of verbal comprehension. Simple items concerning perceptual judgment concern a factor of perceptual speed, but more difficult items concerning perceptual judgment tend to measure a factor of spatial visualization. And so it tends to be with the factors measured by the simple items on pure speed tests as contrasted with the factors measured by the moderately difficult items on pure power tests and timed-power tests. When the speed and power tests apparently concern the same types of mental operations (e.g., perceptual judgment), they typically correlate positively, but the *SCV* seldom is very high.

At the start of this section a question was raised regarding the interchangeability of speed of performance and goodness of performance. The question can now be rephrased as follows: Do items of trivial difficulty which are intended to measure the same thing as power items actually do so? The answer is that it depends on the type of ability being measured, but in general the two types of tests do not correlate highly. Thus the ability to perform quickly on very simple problems usually is quite different from the ability to perform at a high level on difficult problems.

**Speed-difficulty tests** The issues regarding the effects of speed on performance would be simpler if all tests were either pure speed tests or power tests (including those with only moderately restrictive time limits). The issues become somewhat blurred, however, when the speed-difficulty type of test must be considered. The items in such tests are so easy that, without highly restrictive time limits, it would not be possible to obtain a highly reliable distribution of scores. With such items, usually it is necessary to use a time limit that is only a small fraction of the comfortable time. The author does not know of any studies directly relating to this point, but it is probably true that many speed-difficulty tests are administered with less than one-quarter of the comfortable time. Although previously it was stated with some assurance that the comfortable time on timed-power tests can usually be cut by one-third without suffering important changes in psychometric properties, it would not be safe to say that the time can be cut below one-half without having major changes occur.

Whereas considerable research has been done to compare pure speed tests with power tests (including timed-power tests), very little has been done to compare speed-difficulty tests with the former two. Logically one would expect speed-difficulty tests to be mixtures of the factors defined by pure speed tests and those defined by power tests, but that is mainly an untested hypothesis. If the hypothesis is correct, it may be that the mixture of factors in the speed-difficulty test varies with different time limits.

Perhaps the easiest way to escape the confusion caused by speed-difficulty tests is to use them less frequently. Because they are neither pure speed tests nor power tests, it is difficult to develop adequate psychometric theory for them. Also, in many cases they probably are not doing a good job of what they are intended to do. For practical reasons, often they are used to measure abilities that logically concern power rather than speed. For example, one sees numerous reasoning tests of this kind, such as items concerning letter series and number series. The average item is rather easy, and consequently one increases the difficulty by employing highly restrictive time limits. Items of these types are used because it is very time-consuming to compose and administer large numbers of reasoning items that are moderately difficult when given in the comfortable time. In most cases, however, it is doubtful that the speed-difficulty test measures exactly what the experimenter is trying to measure.

**Implications for research** Whether or not one wants to employ pure speed tests or power tests depends on the type of test. In most instances it is not desirable to use speed tests for measures that require content validity, e.g., standardized achievement tests. Most measures that require content validity are supposedly related to abilities concerning power rather than speed. Of course, there are exceptions, such as in achievement examinations for reading speed, typing, and shorthand.

It is with measures that require content validity that the greatest danger arises in placing restrictive time limits on power tests. For example, restrictive time limits on a classroom examination might lower the mean score. Changes in the mean, per se, are of only incidental importance in most measures that require predictive validity or construct validity. In a classroom examination, however, grades are based to some extent on the absolute score obtained by each student, e.g., the number of correct answers given to multiple-choice questions. Before giving an examination, the instructor may decide that anyone who gets fewer than half the items correct will fail the course. Then, to the extent that the number of test items permits ample time or causes students to work quickly, the mean score may be influenced, which in turn would determine the number of students who fail. In such cases, and in many other instances where measures require content validity, the intention is not to test speed but level of performance.

As was said previously, on most power tests, moderately restrictive time limits seldom materially influence the psychometric properties of tests. If anything is affected, however, it is most likely to be the mean score. Consequently one should be very careful in applying highly restrictive time limits on many measures that require content validity, particularly with standardized achievement tests and classroom examinations. Even with such types of tests, however, it is safe to use the comfortable time, which frequently is less than half the total testing time required under pure power conditions.

With instruments used to predict specific criteria, the place of speed is a matter for research. In a particular instance, it may be that the abilities measured by pure speed tests are more predictive than the abilities measured by power tests, or vice versa. Also, with predictor instruments, it is an open question what effect there will be on validity of employing restrictive time limits on a power test. It might, for example, be found that a particular power test is more valid when the time limit is less than half the comfortable time.

With measures that require construct validity, there are no simple rules to guide the experimenter in the choice of pure speed tests or power tests. Logically, which of these should be used is determined by the theory being investigated if the theory is specific enough to make the choice clear. If the choice is to employ power tests, it is safe to administer those tests at two-thirds of the comfortable time. Testing time usually is at a premium in studies relating to construct validity, and consequently even if there is a slight effect of employing a moderately restrictive time limit, it usually is more than offset by the practical advantages.

## EFFECTS OF GUESSING

An issue that occurs in many types of experiments in psychology is that of the effects of "guessing" on the statistical and psychometric properties of score distributions. This issue arises in any investigation where the subjects are not free to respond in any way that they choose but rather are required to select one response from a number of specified responses. The most obvious instance in which this occurs is in a multiple-choice test of ability, particularly when subjects are required to attempt all items. Questions regarding the effects of guessing, however, are by no means restricted to multiple-choice tests of ability. Effects of guessing occur in many types of controlled experiments on learning, perception, and other topics. In a typical study of concept formation, the subject is shown a series of geometric designs, half of which represent instances of a concept and half of which do not represent instances of the concept. On each trial, then, the subject would have a 50-50 chance of being correct by guessing alone.

Another example involving a limited number of alternative responses occurs in certain types of studies of recognition thresholds. In the first phase of the study, one nonsense syllable is associated with a painful electric shock. Subjects are familiarized with a second nonsense syllable, but it is not associated with shock. In the visual recognition task, each syllable is shown for varying intervals of time, the intervals being gradually increased on each trial up to the point where the subjects are correct on every trial. On each trial, the nonsense syllable appears in one of the four corners of a screen rather than in the center of the screen. Instead of being asked to state what they see on each trial, the subjects are asked to state the corner in which a syllable appears, regardless of what the syllable is. In this type of experiment, the subjects have one chance in four of making the correct response on each trial by guessing alone.

Experimental procedures where guessing is a factor are employed in many different types of investigations, because often they allow one to investigate phenomena that would be difficult or impossible to investigate otherwise. Multiple-choice tests are used very widely, because they lend themselves to the measurement of many different traits and they have obvious practical advantages. In a study of concept formation, the subject must be asked to judge whether each stimulus does or does not fit the concept, and thus it is necessary to deal with only a limited number of alternative responses. In the study mentioned above concerning perception, the use of a multiple-choice procedure has some advantages over the use of a free-response procedure. For example, potentially it reduces response biases, such as the reluctance of subjects to verbalize a syllable that has been associated with shock, regardless of whether they actually see it.

Because of the obvious advantages of multiple-choice procedures in so many types of experiments, these procedures probably will continue to be used. Inherent in such procedures, however, is the problem of dealing with effects of chance success (guessing).

**A model for random responses** Here we shall discuss a simple model for predicting effects of random responses (guesses) on the psychometric properties of score distributions. The model is based on the primary assumption that, in multiple-choice tasks, the probability of making a correct response on each trial (or test item) is either 1.0 or the reciprocal of the number of available choices. On an intuitive level, this means that the subject either makes the correct response on each trial with perfect certainty or guesses blindly. In the latter case, the a priori probability of a correct response would equal $1/A$, where $A$ is the number of available choices. In a binary-choice test (e.g., a true-false test), the probability would be .5; in a test having four alternative answers for each question, the probability would be .25.

For reasons that will be discussed later, the above assumptions are seldom entirely realistic, and consequently predictions based on them seldom are precisely correct. Such predictions are, however, almost always correct with regard to the *direction* of effects on scores because of the use of multiple-choice procedures. For example, certain equations derivable from the above assumptions lead to predictions of the change in reliability expected if the number of alternative responses $A$ is increased or decreased by any particular amount. Although such predictions are not borne out exactly, the general trend of results is predicted.

The predictions discussed here follow from the above assumptions. Later we shall discuss how realistic the assumptions are in particular kinds of tests and experimental procedures.

A special set of symbols will prove useful in the discussion of the model for random responses:

$K$ = total number of test items
$R$ = number of correct or "right" responses
$W$ = number of incorrect or "wrong" responses
$T$ = number of items attempted, $R + W$
$A$ = number of alternatives for each item
$R_c$ = number of items for a person for which probability of correct response is 1.0 rather than $1/A$

All the terms in the list except the last one are obvious—some explanations are required regarding the meaning of $R_c$. It can be thought of as the score a subject would obtain on a particular test if guessing played no part. Although the analogy is somewhat misleading, one can also think of $R$ as the score a subject receives on a multiple-choice test, and $R_c$ can be thought of as the score that a subject would receive on the same items cast in a free-response (fill-in) format. It also is useful to think of $R_c$ as representing what the subject "really knows" and $R$ as the score obtained when some part is played by guessing.

Of course, it would be highly desirable to measure $R_c$ directly, but that is not possible. All that can be done is to estimate $R_c$ from the observable variables. The logic for that is as follows. It should be obvious that the number of observed correct scores $R$ can be constituted as follows:

$$R = R_c + p(T - R_c) \tag{16-3}$$

where $p = 1/A$. The meaning of Eq. (16-3) can be clarified by a hypothetical case. In working through a test, subjects mark the items that they "really know" ($R_c$). Then they attempt additional items ($T - R_c$). If all subjects attempt all items, the number of additional attempted items would be $K - R_c$. On each of those "guessed" items, the subject has a fixed probability $p$ of making a correct response, which is $1/A$. The probability of making an incorrect response $q$ equals $1 - p$, or $A - 1$ divided by $A$.

The following manipulations of Eq. (16-3) will show how an estimate of $R_c$ is obtained:

$$R = R_c + pT - pR_c$$
$$= R_c - pR_c + pT$$
$$= R_c(1 - p) + pT$$
$$= qR_c + pT \tag{16-4}$$
$$qR_c = R - pT$$
$$R_c = \frac{R - pT}{q}$$

Examination of the ratio of $p$ to $q$ in terms of the numbers of alternative responses shows that the above equation can be expressed as follows:

$$R_c = R - \frac{W}{A - 1} \tag{16-5}$$

Equation (16-5) is the well-known *correction for guessing*. The model has led to the conclusion that one obtains an estimate of $R_c$ by subtracting, from the actual number of correct $R$, a fraction of the number of the attempted but incorrect responses $W$. Thus the model leads to the conclusion that the particular fraction equals the reciprocal of the number of alternatives minus 1.

An example of how Eq. (16-5) is applied can be given in the situation where (1) there are four alternatives for each question, (2) the subject attempts 32 items out of, say, 40, and (3) 20 of the responses are correct and 12 are incorrect. The computations would be as follows:

$$R_c = 20 - \tfrac{12}{3}$$

$$R_c = 16$$

The estimate is that the subject "really knows" the answers to 16 items. Of course, it is something of a misnomer to refer to Eq. (16-5) as a "correction" for guessing, because all that it can do is *estimate* the effects of guessing. Whether or not it is an unbiased estimate depends on the correctness of the assumptions in the model.

**Effects of guessing on test parameters**  Here we shall continue to follow the logic of the model discussed above and examine some of the effects of guessing on the psychometric properties of score distributions. First, it is obvious that if subjects do guess when in doubt, or are forced to guess by the nature of the instructions, the estimate is that the mean score will increase. The expected amount of the increase is obtained by subtracting $R_c$ from $R$.

A reinspection of Eq. (16-5) makes it obvious that the difference between $R_c$ and $R$ for different people is directly related to $W$, the number of attempted but incorrect responses. In other words, Eq. (16-5) is based on the principle that the amount of guessing done by different people is directly related to the number of $W$ responses.

In the case where all subjects attempt all items, the expected gain from guessing is inversely related to $R_c$. People who know the least guess the most, and consequently they stand to gain most from guessing. Figure 16-1 shows the expected relationship between $R$ and $R_c$ for a test with 40 items and four alternatives for each item. People who "actually know" the answers to all 40 items are expected to obtain a score of 40. People who "actually know" the answers to none of the items are expected to obtain a score of 10, purely from guessing. The fact that $R_c$ and $R$ are linearly related is evidenced in Fig. 16-1 by the straight line of relationship between the end points of $R_c$.

Regardless of the estimated effects of guessing in the general case, there obviously are individual differences in the effects of guessing related to the amount of guessing. Also, for individuals who have the same $R$ and $W$ scores, the actual effects of guessing vary in terms of chance. If two people each guess at the answers for 10 true-false items, one person may get as many as 9 correct, and the other person may get only 1 correct. In a model for blind guessing, it is reasonable to assume that probabilities of correctly guessing on different items are independent, in which case the expected variance of the distribution of effects of guessing can be determined from the binomial theorem:

$$\sigma_{eg}^2 = npq \tag{16-6}$$

where $n$ = number of guesses made $(T - R_c)$

$p$ = probability of making correct response by guessing $1/A$

$q$ = probability of making incorrect response by guessing $(A - 1)/A$

$\sigma_{eg}^2$ = expected variance of $R - R_c$ for people who guess on $n$ items

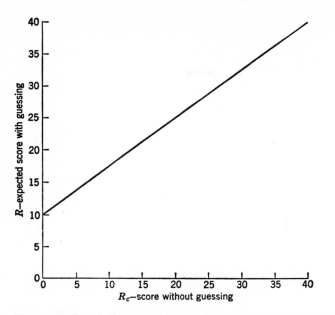

**Figure 16-1** Expected scores when guessing is a factor $(R)$ as a function of scores when guessing is not a factor $(R_c)$. The figure assumes that $R$ is based on a multiple-choice test with four alternatives for each item and that each subject attempts all items.

The meaning of Eq. (16-6) can be illustrated by the hypothetical case depicted in Fig. 16-1, in which there are 40 items, each item has four alternative answers, and $R_c$ ranges from 0 to 40. Also, in that example, each person is forced to respond to each item $(T = K)$. Persons who do not really know the answers to any of the items (for whom $R_c$ is zero) guess on all items. Then, in Eq. (16-6), $n$ is 40, $p$ is .25, and $q$ is .75. The expected variance of correct scores $R$ is then 7.5 for that particular group of people, and the expected standard deviation of $R$ for that group of people is the square root of 7.5 or 2.74.

Persons who know the answers to all items do not guess on any of them. Then $n$ is zero, the variance of actual scores $R$ because of guessing is zero, and all persons in that group have the same score on $R$ as on $R_c$. Since $\sigma^2_{eg}$ is a linear function of $n$ ($p$ and $q$ being constant in a particular type of test), the amount of variance because of guessing is a linear function of the number of items on which subjects guess. In the case where subjects are required to respond to all items, the variance of errors because of guessing decreases linearly with $R_c$. The effect expected in this situation is illustrated in Fig. 16-2.

What Fig. 16-2 illustrates is the fact that, when subjects are required to attempt all items, the variance of errors because of guessing is largest for persons who know the least, and it steadily decreases with increasing levels of $R_c$. It should be kept in mind that these results hold exactly only for those situations where subjects are required to attempt all items, as with most multiple-choice methods used in controlled experiments and most measures of individual dif-

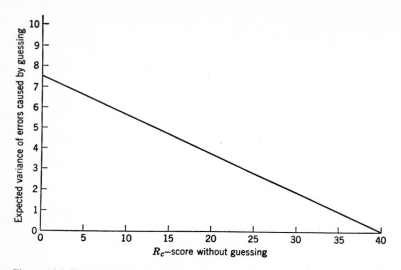

**Figure 16-2** Expected variance of errors because of guessing as a function of $R_c$. The figure assumes that there are four alternatives for each item on the multiple-choice test and that each subject attempts all items.

ferences used in basic research. In some applied uses of measures of human ability, however, subjects are urged not to guess when they are unsure of the correct answer. These cases will be discussed later.

The variance of errors because of guessing represents a component of measurement error in addition to that of the other types of measurement error inherent in the particular measurement tool. As is shown in Fig. 16-2, the amount of measurement error (unreliability) because of guessing is a decreasing function of actual ability. Then guessing not only increases the scores more for people of low ability as compared to people of high ability, but also makes the scores of the former type of people less reliable. Since Eq. (16-6) involves the number of items on which guesses are made $n$, it is only of theoretical interest. Estimates of the variance of scores because of guessing can be obtained, however, from actual data. Since $p$ and $q$ are known in any instance, all that is required is an estimate of $n$. By definition, $n$ equals the total number of attempted items $T$ minus the score that would be obtained if guessing were not involved $R_c$:

$$n = T - R_c \tag{16-7}$$

Equation (16-5) can be used to estimate $R_c$. Then it is permissible to write the following equation for $n$:

$$n = T - \left(R - \frac{W}{A-1}\right)$$

$$= T - R + \frac{W}{A-1}$$

Since by definition $T - R$ equals the number of attempted but incorrect responses, it is permissible to rewrite the above equation as follows:

$$n = W + \frac{W}{A - 1} \qquad (16\text{-}8)$$

Equation (16-8) is an estimate of the number of items on which the individual guesses ($n$). When that is multiplied by the product of $p$ and $q$, an estimate is obtained of the amount of measurement error because of guessing for people with the same number of attempted but incorrect responses $W$. This is stated in the form of an equation as follows:

$$\sigma_{eg}^2 = pq \left( W + \frac{W}{A - 1} \right) \qquad (16\text{-}9)$$

The use of Eq. (16-9) can be illustrated in the case where (1) a large number of people all have $W$ scores of 8, (2) there are five alternatives for each item, and (3) all subjects have the same $R_c$ score. The computations would be as follows:

$$\sigma_{eg}^2 = (.2)(.8)(8 + \tfrac{8}{4})$$

$$= (.16)(10)$$

$$\sigma_{eg}^2 = 1.6$$

Thus, in the above example, even though all subjects "know" the same amount, there is a variance of 1.6 in actual scores because of guessing.

**Use of corrections for guessing**  Although the model for random guessing leads to many important deductions about effects of guessing, it is proper to inquire about the accuracy of predictions from the model. Unfortunately, most of the evidence in this regard comes from a domain of data for which the model logically should be least accurate, that of achievement testing in education. Many of the items on such tests concern the recognition of facts or simple principles, as in the following item:

The speed of sound is affected by:

1. The loudness of the sound at its source
2. The medium in which it travels
3. The frequency, or pitch, of the sound
4. Phases of the moon

To illustrate the nature of guessing on educational tests, a poor alternative was purposely included in the above item. Even students who had no idea that 2 is the correct answer would be likely to recognize that alternative 4 is probably not the correct answer. In that case students would rule out alternative 4 and make a guess among the remaining alternatives if they chose to guess under instructions that discourage guessing. Then, in effect, there are not four alternatives, but only three. Another student may be slightly better acquainted with the particular issue and, in addition to ruling out alternative 4, knows enough to rule out alternative 3 also. Then, if the student guesses blindly, chances of getting a correct answer would be .5 rather than the probability of .25 which would follow from the model for blind guessing.

Because in most educational tests there is some opportunity for "narrowing" alternatives before guessing, this tends to make the correction for guessing [Eq. (16-5)] an *underestimate* of the actual effects of guessing (evidence summarized by Price 1964). One determines the amount of correction by dividing the number of attempted but incorrect responses $W$ by the number of alternative answers minus 1 ($A - 1$). Thus when $A$ is large, the amount of correction is small, and vice versa when $A$ is small. Because of the narrowing of alternatives before guessing, in effect the actual number of alternatives before guessing is smaller than that employed in the correction for guessing. Consequently there is a tendency in educational tests for the correction not to subtract enough.

In contrast to the effects of the narrowing of alternatives, the use of misleads as alternatives tends to make the correction for guessing [Eq. (16-5)] *overestimate* the effects of guessing. A *mislead* is a highly plausible but incorrect alternative. In some instances those misleads are so attractive that they "trap" even very knowledgeable students. An example of such a mislead would be in an item concerning a principle in physics that had been accepted as correct for many years but had recently been supplanted by a new principle. Then even some of the most knowledgeable students with regard to physics might be trapped by the mislead. If there are many such misleads on a test, the number of $W$ responses is not directly related to the actual amount of guessing. A student may make a strenuous effort not to guess when in doubt, but because of misleads make many $W$ responses. It can be argued that it is poor practice to include such highly plausible misleads, and good methods of test construction tend to weed them out. Rather than employ highly plausible misleads, it is better to compose the alternatives so that they all sound plausible to the student who knows very little about the particular issue; but only one of them is plausible to the student who is quite knowledgeable about the issue. To the extent that there are misleads, however, the correction for guessing tends to overcorrect.

The weight of the evidence (summarized by Price 1964) is that the correction for guessing generally tends to undercorrect rather than overcorrect. This is because most tests have few highly plausible misleads, but there are ample opportunities for narrowing alternatives before guessing.

Because of the above considerations, it is appropriate to ask whether the correction for guessing should be used in practice. The choice to use the formula or not depends, among other things, on the nature of the test instructions. If subjects are instructed to attempt every item and they do so, in most cases there is no reason to make the correction for guessing. In that case $W$ has a perfect negative correlation with $R$, and consequently corrected scores correlate perfectly with obtained scores. Then, for purposes of correlational analysis, obtained scores and corrected scores would produce identical results.

In most tests of ability employed in basic research and in most measures employed in controlled experiments, usually it is preferable to instruct all subjects to attempt all items even if that requires some blind guessing. On some types of educational tests, however, there are two major reasons for not instructing all subjects to attempt all items. First, this tends to introduce some unreliability into test scores. The difference in reliability under instructions to attempt all items and under instructions to not guess tends to be no more than about .03 or .04 in the typical study (evidence summarized by Price 1964). For reasons which were discussed in Chap. 7, such small differences in reliability might be important on educational tests, but they would not be important in most instruments used in basic research. Also, for practical purposes, often it is better to increase the reliability by adding items rather than to incur the side effects of not having students attempt all items (a matter which will be discussed later).

A second major reason for not instructing all students to attempt all items on educational tests is that it might lead to poor attitudes on the part of students. It can be argued that since students are not taught to guess blindly in daily schoolwork, but rather are taught to investigate facts and "think out" unsolved problems, forced guessing on multiple-choice tests would generate poor intellectual habits. The author personally considers it doubtful that multiple-choice tests have such far-reaching effects on the minds of students. Students may react somewhat negatively to guess-instructions *while taking a test*, but it is doubtful that study habits and thinking habits are materially influenced.

There are a number of major problems with employing instructions not to guess. First, it is hard to frame such instructions in a manner that students can understand in a way that does not actually penalize some students. The student frequently is told that it will not pay to guess when in doubt, but usually that is not true. Students may be told that they will be penalized for guessing (e.g., the correction for guessing will be employed), but since most students would find the nature of the penalty too difficult to understand, no explanation of the penalty usually is given. Thus the penalty stands only as a shadowy threat, which may do more to disturb students than if they were forced to attempt all items.

A second major problem with the use of instructions that discourage guessing is that different students respond differently to such instructions. There are reliable individual differences in amount of guessing even when all students are urged not to guess. Partly this is because there are degrees of guessing, ranging from blind guessing to answering a question on the basis of partial knowledge. Thus the meaning of "guessing" is open to differences in interpretation by different students. Individual differences in the tendency to guess relate more to personal idiosyncrasies than to intelligence and knowledge of the particular subject matter (Price 1964). Consequently individual differences in guessing usually serve to change the factor composition somewhat from that which would be obtained if all students were required to attempt all items. Thus, per unit of reliable variance, the latter type of instruction produces better results than instructions that discourage guessing.

If instructions that discourage guessing are used, a decision must be made about using corrections for guessing. For reasons discussed previously, the correction based on a model for blind guessing is not highly precise, but the alternative of making no correction at all also poses difficulties. A very conscientious student might lower her or his score appreciably by taking too seriously the instructions not to guess. Other formulas have been proposed to correct for guessing (summarized by Price 1964), but these tend to be no more precise in the general case than is the formula based on the model for blind guessing. Also, the models underlying these other corrections for guessing do not have the same power of explanation or practical advantages as afforded by the model for blind guessing.

The above considerations make it difficult to find an entirely satisfactory solution to the problem of correcting for guessing when instructions discourage blind guessing. Until a better solution is found, probably it is best to make the correction for guessing based on the model for blind guessing. The scores corrected for guessing typically have the same reliability as uncorrected scores on the same test, but there is considerable evidence that the predictive validity of the corrected scores is higher by about .03 (Guilford 1954; Lord 1963; Price 1964). Unless there is some good reason, however, to employ instructions that discourage guessing, it is better to require all subjects to attempt all items. This is feasible in nearly all measures used in basic research, and in the author's opinion, it also is feasible with most educational tests. In the written test instructions, it can be explained to students that, even when they think they are only guessing, they may have partial knowledge of a kind that will increase the chances of making a correct response. Also, to hammer home the point, a feasible approach is to tell students that even if they omit some items, they will automatically be given chance-level credit for such omitted items; e.g., one-fourth of the number of omitted items will be added to number-correct scores on the remaining items. This special instruction should make it obvious to students that it behooves them to guess, even if it is based on the sheerest of hints, rather than have the final score obtained partly by a purely random function of the number of omitted items.

**Use of the model for the estimation of test parameters** Even if the model for blind guessing leads to only moderately precise corrections for guessing, that does not necessarily destroy its general usefulness for predicting the effects of guessing on test reliability and other important psychometric properties of score distributions. We shall examine some of the evidence regarding how effectively the model for blind guessing is used for those purposes.

In a number of previous points in this book, it has been necessary to make a distinction between the possible score range and the *effective* score range. If the range is defined as the highest score minus the lowest score, the possible score range on a dichotomously scored test equals the number of test items. Of course, in any particular use of a test, it is not likely that scores will be so diverse as to fill up that range, but at least it is possible to have a range equal to the number of items. When guessing is a factor, however, it is necessary to think about an effective score range rather than a possible score range.

The effective score range is easily defined in the case where all subjects attempt all items. In that case the expected lower bound of the effective range equals the number of test items multiplied by the probability of guessing correctly by chance. Thus, on a 40-item test with four alternatives for each item, logically the effective score range is from scores of 10 to 40. If the model for blind guessing is correct, students who make scores of 10 "actually know" the answers to none of the questions, and consequently they guess on them all. Then it follows that scores of less than 10 occur only by chance. As a result of the variance of errors because of guessing ($\sigma_{eg}^2$), blind guessing would permit some scores to range below 10. If the model is accurate, however, the variance of scores below the chance level should be entirely because of chance, and consequently the scores should be totally unreliable. Although there is very little evidence to support the claim, this probably is the case with many types of measures that logically fit the model for blind guessing, e.g., in the use of multiple-choice procedures in studies of learning and perception. This is not always the case, however, in the use of educational tests. It has been found (Cliff 1958) that in some instances scores below the chance level actually are not entirely due to chance. In such instances scores below the chance level on one test correlate significantly with scores below chance level on an alternative form. Logically, this could only occur if the test contained items with many successful misleads which induced individuals with very low ability to perform worse than chance.

Previously some important deductions regarding the effects of guessing on test reliability were shown to follow from the model for blind guessing. Are those predictions accurate? Attempts have been made to answer the question by comparing the psychometric properties of multiple-choice tests with the psychometric properties of the same tests when presented in the form of completion (free-response) items. For example, subjects can be asked either to write in the correct solution to an algebraic problem or to select the correct answer from a number of alternative answers. If it is true that free-response tests are free from measurement error because of guessing, the model should lead to predictions of the increase in reliability in going from a multiple-choice test to a free-response test. An equation is available for that purpose (Nunnally 1967, p. 584). The evidence (Plumlee 1952) is that the equation leads to an overestimate of the gain in reliability in that case. In other words, the free-response test is not as reliable as predicted, or, to look at it the other way, the multiple-choice test is more reliable than predicted. The available evidence suggests that the actual gain in reliability is between one-half and two-thirds that predicted by Nunnally's equation.

The above type of evidence would seem to suggest that the model based on blind guessing leads to poor estimates of the effects of guessing on test reliability, but that is not necessarily the case. The flaw in that line of reasoning is a hidden premise that the multiple-choice test is only a less reliable cousin of the free-response test. Actually the model for blind guessing is not intended to estimate relations between a multiple-choice test and a free-response test of the same attribute. It is intended to estimate relations between a test with a particular number of alternatives for each item and a hypothetical test with an infinite number of alternatives for each item.

A free-response test is not the same as a test with an infinite number of alternative answers. Actually, free-response tests have some sources of measurement error that are not present in multiple-choice tests. Good multiple-choice items serve to "aim" knowledgeable students toward the correct answer. Items that are quite clear when presented in multiple-choice form sometimes are unclear when presented in free-response form. For example, the free-response form of an item is "An important product of Bolivia is _____." In the multiple-choice form, the "stem" of the item is followed by the names of four mining products—coal, tin, diamonds, and lead. When the question is presented in the multiple-choice form, all students will understand it, and knowledgeable students will know that the correct answer is "tin." If the same students were presented with the free-response item instead of the multiple-choice item, there would be some confusion regarding the meaning of the word *product*. Students would wonder whether the term referred to farm products, manufacturing products, mining products, or some other type of product. The confusion in that regard would introduce a source of measurement error in the free-response form that would be present to a lesser degree in the multiple-choice form. Then, even if there is some measurement error in the multiple-choice form because of guessing, there is a different type of measurement error in the free-response form because of confusion. For this reason, Nunnally's equation leads to an overestimate of the gain in reliability when going from one type of test to the other.

An actual test of the predictiveness of the above-mentioned equation relates to the concept of a test with an infinite number of alternatives. Of course, an infinite number of alternatives is only a handy fiction, but it is possible to investigate the extent to which the model for blind guessing predicts differences in reliability for different numbers of alternative answers to the same items. For example, if one of the incorrect alternatives is randomly removed from items having five alternatives, what would be the relative reliability of the four-alternative and five-alternative tests? Studies of this kind have been undertaken, and it has been found that reliability grows as a function of the number of alternative responses.

The influence on reliability of varying the number of alternative answers for items has been investigated with extensions of the model for blind guessing (see Nunnally 1967, chap. 15), other mathematical models (see Lord 1976), and in numerous empirical studies. There is an overwhelming conclusion coming from the separate forms of evidence: The overall reliability increases as the number of alternative answers increases, but by less than one might expect. Generally one finds a substantial increase in going from a two-choice (e.g., true-false) test to one with three alternative answers for each item, a worthwhile increase in going from three to four alternatives, a small increase in going from four to five alternatives, and negligible increases beyond that point. Typical findings are those by Ebel (1969) in a statistical simulation study regarding some plausible assumptions about the statistical characteristics of a 100-item test. In this case, his model indicated that the reliabilities would be, respectively, .74 for a two-item test, .83 for a three-item test, .86 for a four-item test, .87 for a five-item test, and .88 for a six-item test. The exact sizes of such increases would be complexly dependent upon the initial reliability of a two-alternative test, the correlations among the items, and other item characteristics. However, the results reported above are typical. It almost always pays to have more response alternatives than two, and it very seldom pays to have more than five. Consequently, either four or five alternatives are used on nearly all commercially distributed tests that are based on multiple-choice items. Interestingly enough, these magic numbers were derived from much intuition and practical experience more than from mathematical models or hard evidence. Rather than attempt to increase the overall reliability beyond that which can be obtained from four or five options for each item, it is best to use additional items.

Although the increase in reliability from raising the number of alternative answers frequently is not dramatic, it must be kept firmly in mind that this relates to the *overall reliability*. Modest gain in overall reliability in this regard may make for substantial gains in reliability for individuals at the lower end of the test continuum. The reader should refer back to Fig. 16-2, which shows that the unreliability because of guessing declines rapidly in going from the lower end of the ability continuum to the higher end. Consequently, the use of at least four or five alternative answers for each item mainly serves to reduce the measurement error in the lower sections of the trait continuum. Depending upon the testing problem, this might be a crucially important factor, i.e., in any circumstance where it was necessary to make discriminations among individuals of low ability. In that case, one might want to employ as many as seven or eight alternative answers for each item. Other than for the special circumstance in which the major purpose of the test is to make decisions about people in the lower regions of the trait continuum, the following general rule applies: Use either four or five alternative answers for each item and then employ enough items to reach the desired level of reliability.

**Speed tests** All the previous comments in this section regarding effects of guessing apply to power tests and power tests given under moderately restrictive time limits. On pure speed tests, the intention is for subjects to make correct responses as far as they can go until time is called. In that ideal situation, there would be no attempted but incorrect responses $W$, and according to the logic of the model for blind guessing, there would be no evidence of guessing and no correction to make. In many instances, however, there are appreciable numbers of $W$ responses, which raises questions about guessing.

On pure speed tests, the burden of preventing appreciable numbers of $W$ responses rests on the test instructions. Subjects must be warned that they will be penalized for guessing, but as was discussed previously, it is difficult to give a reasonable explanation of the nature of the penalty. Also, there are systematic individual differences in the way that subjects interpret and respond to such instructions.

In some instances it actually would behoove subjects to ignore instructions not to guess, particularly subjects who are very low in ability. This can be illustrated with speed items like the following:

$$
\begin{array}{ll}
\text{wH6¢le} \text{———} \text{wH6¢le} \\
\text{'r4ltY} \text{———} \text{'r4ltY} \\
\text{+glip?} \text{———} \text{+Glip?}
\end{array}
$$

The above items relate to the factor of *perceptual speed*, which is useful for, among other things, the selection of filing clerks. On each item, the subject makes a check mark to indicate whether each group is the same or different. Even under the usual instructions not to guess, it is obvious that some $W$ responses would be given. If a subject were very low in perceptual speed, it would probably benefit him or her to hurriedly mark every item. In this case, the subject could mark them all "same" or all "different"—it would not matter which. If there actually were no penalty for guessing (e.g., if the correction for guessing were not employed), in most cases that strategy would give the person a score near the mean of the distribution rather than on the bottom tail of the distribution.

One cannot handle problems arising from guessing on speed tests by having all subjects attempt all items, because speed tests are standardized so that the average subject has time to attempt only about half of the items. If many $W$ responses are given in a particular type of speed test, it is wise to make the correction for guessing [Eq. (16-5)]. Also, in that case, the model for blind guessing will specify the approximate effects of guessing on the psychometric properties of the instrument.

Whenever feasible, speed items should be in a free-response format or in some other form that discourages guessing. An example of a speed item in free-response form is an arithmetic item on a test concerning the factor of numerical computation. The subject fills in the correct answer rather than marking one of a number of alternative answers. If it is not practical to employ free-response items, one can discourage guessing by having a relatively large number of alternatives rather than only two alternatives such as illustrated previously for marking or not marking pairs of letter groupings. One could do this with pairs of letter groupings, for example, by making one of the letters in the second grouping different from that in the first. Then the subject would be required either to mark the letter in the second grouping that is different from that in the first grouping or to write the "different" letter in a space provided for the purpose.

If a type of item that greatly restricts $W$ responses is not employed, guessing can be a larger problem on speed tests than on power tests. In that case the reliability and factor composition of the scores depend too much on the test instructions and on individual differences in test-taking strategies.

## RESPONSE BIASES

Although the names frequently are used interchangeably in the literature, it is important to make a careful distinction between response styles and response bias. As will be explained more fully subsequently, a *response style* concerns reliable individual differences because of artifacts of measurement. As the term will be used here, a *response bias* does not necessarily concern reliable individual differences; rather, it concerns the effects of measurement artifacts on the *average responses* of a group of people—either on all subjects participating in the study or differently on different treatment groups.

An example of a response bias is the effect of guessing on the $p$ values of items when subjects are required to attempt all items. The bias in that case is toward making the $p$ values higher than would be the case if subjects were cautioned not to guess. As another example, there are numerous forms of semantic bias because of the wording of questions. For example, the use of extreme modifiers like *always* and *never* alters the average response from that which is obtained from the use of less extreme modifiers like *usually* and *seldom*. There are numerous examples of response bias that occur in psychophysical scaling. This occurs, for example, in the *method of limits*, where the subject makes same-different comparisons of different weights with a standard. One approach is to start the series of comparisons with a weight which is the same, or very nearly the same, as the standard and then gradually increase the size of the comparison weights until the subject is accurate in judgment 100 percent of the time. Another approach is to start the series of comparisons with a comparison weight which is clearly larger than the standard and then gradually decrease the size of the comparison weights until the subject is accurate in judgment only 50 percent of the time. Typically it is found that sensory thresholds derived from these two approaches are not quite the same, which points to sources of bias in the measurement methods.

Response biases are so legion in psychology and so diverse in type that there are not many general principles that apply. Rather, one can learn about the response biases in some methods of measurement only by having firsthand acquaintance with the methods. In most cases there are ways of dealing with the response bias that occurs in a particular measurement method. For example, either the effect of guessing on the $p$ value of items could be partly overcome with instructions not to guess or an approximate correction could be developed from the model for blind guessing. The bias that occurs in the method of limits, as illustrated above in a study of lifted weights, can be approximately offset if one averages the thresholds obtained from the ascending and descending series of judgments.

When a measurement artifact produces not only a change in the average response, but also reliable individual differences in that regard, it is referred to as a *response style*. Only some of the response biases produce reliable individual differences in response style. For example, there is little evidence of reliable individual differences in effects of ascending versus descending approaches to the measurement of threshold by the method of limits. Whereas there are known to be many, many forms of response bias, so far only a few types of reliable individual differences because of measurement artifacts (response style) are known to exist.

**Demand characteristics** The major class of response biases which has proved very troublesome in the behavioral sciences is referred to as *demand characteristics*. Essentially, a demand characteristic is any feature of the research project which induces subjects to respond "unnaturally." Such influences can be due to measuring instruments, instructions to subjects, apparatus, prior information that the subject obtains about the research, and even very subtle aspects of the interaction between subjects and experimenter. Before the term *demand characteristics* was developed, spurious effects of these kinds usually were referred to as *laboratory effects*, as in the following example.

One experiment concerns patterns of cooperation and competition in two-person games. Two subjects sit on opposite sides of a table. Each has a toy truck which can be moved on a semicircular track. If one subject can move a truck from the start zone to the goal zone, the reward will be a dime. However, the two subjects share a common portion of track. If both subjects enter that portion of track, neither can reach the goal, and the rules require that after a short period of time, both trucks be returned to their starting positions. What is typically found is that after a number of trials, the subjects take turns letting each other reach the goal. Manipulated in such experiments are magnitudes of rewards given the subjects, degrees to which subjects can penalize their partners for not cooperating, and numerous other variables of interest in the study of personality and social psychology.

It should be obvious that severe problems in terms of laboratory effects are encountered in experiments like that discussed above. For example, the subjects know that their behavior is being observed by the experimenter, and for that reason they may behave rather differently from the way they would in a cooperative situation in daily life. Also, the sheer artificiality of playing with toy trucks is likely to irritate, embarrass, or bore college students to the extent that any generalizable effects of the treatment parameters are obscured.

The most extreme example of a study dominated by laboratory effects is one that the author once heard proposed to measure the interest value of magazine advertisements. The plan was to tell each subject, "Just behave naturally and look through this magazine as you would in any other situation." An experimenter on the right of the subject was to use a stopwatch to measure the amount of time spent looking at each advertisement, and an experimenter on the left of the subject was to take notes regarding facial expressions and other indications of interest. The naive researchers were quickly dissuaded from undertaking the research because of laboratory effects that are too obvious for recitation here.

A less extreme example of an experiment in which potential laboratory effects are at issue is one in which the effects of relaxation therapy on test-taking anxiety are being investigated. Subjects are selected who rate themselves as having severe anxiety before and during course examinations. In a number of sessions, they are taught to relax many muscles of the body, which in turn results in a general mental relaxation; then they are gradually taught to relax when they form a mental image of going to and taking an examination. After the treatment is completed, subjects are asked to rate the amount of anxiety that they actually experience in taking examinations. A measure of improvement is obtained by comparing the ratings before treatment with the ratings after treatment.

The major source of laboratory effect in the aforementioned investigation is obvious. Subjects are under pressure to indicate that they have improved even if they actually have not. The experimenter has become their friend and has worked long hours trying to lower their anxiety. How can they say that all the efforts have been in vain? Few experimenters would be so naive as to take the results at face value. One precaution would be to use a number of control groups, such as (1) a group of nonanxious subjects who were given the same treatment, (2) a group of anxious subjects who were taught methods of relaxation but not in conjunction with mental images relating to the taking of examinations, (3) an anxious group that was tested at two points in time but given no treatment, and (4) a group of anxious subjects who received "discussion therapy" rather than relaxation therapy. Also, before the results could be trusted, experimenters would require the use of measures of improvement that were not so easily manipulated in such a way as to please the experimenter. It has been found, for example, that the grades of students given some forms of relaxation therapy tend to improve. Also, in some experiments it is possible to obtain rather objective indices of improvement. For example, in treating stage fright, judges can rate tremor of the voice, nervous movements, and other indications of fear.

**Control of response biases** It should be obvious that there are so many different types of potential response biases that only some general guidelines exist as to how to avoid them. Many of the particular techniques for avoiding such biases are specific to the particular kinds of investigations, e.g., studies of emotions, group processes, and psychotherapy. The most general caution is for experimenters to think carefully about how they themselves would respond in the experimental situation and avoid experimental procedures that would produce demand characteristics and other forms of bias. A second principle is to make experimental settings as free as possible from misunderstandings about the purposes and procedures of experimental activities. Often this can be done by having subjects go through all or part of the experimental procedures before the experiment is undertaken. Of course, this can be done only if there are no large "practice effects" or other ways in which a full demonstration of procedures can alter the subsequent data-gathering process. However, in many forms of basic research in learning, memory, perception, etc., there is no harm in giving subjects considerable practice on materials that are similar to those that they will deal with in the subsequent experiment.

A third principle is to perform naturalistic or seminaturalistic studies wherever possible, particularly if they involve live human interactions of people. So many of the small-group studies in social psychology have been shot through with demand characteristics and other forms of bias that they lack credibility to the scientific community.

A fourth principle is to divorce various segments of the experiment in time and place for subjects (and sometimes even for experimenters) such that one aspect of an investigation cannot have an effect on another aspect. For example, if a study is being undertaken of the influence of different types of psychotherapy on anxiety and other personality attributes measured by a self-inventory, there are numerous ways in which the self-inventory can be given in a different physical setting and by entirely different individuals from those that were associated with the therapy. Also, one can prevent the experimenters who participate in these two phases of the study from communicating about the status of particular patients. There are many other ways to isolate obtainable information from different parts of a study regarding both subjects and, in some cases, experimenters who participate in different phases of the investigation.

A fifth, and more general, admonition regarding the control of response biases is to place faith in a particular set of findings only if it is reproducible under a variety of social settings, experimenters, and measurement methods. Only in this way can one feel highly confident that results are not due to some type of laboratory effect, particularly in those areas such as the study of group processes where numerous forms of demand characteristics and other biases frequently hold sway.

## RESPONSE STYLES

In contrast to response biases, response styles concern systematic individual differences rather than effects only on overall group responses. Response styles are also frequently referred to as response sets and test-taking habits. As the term will be employed here, a *response style* is (1) a reliable source of variance in individual differences which (2) is an artifactual product of measurement methods and (3) is at least partially independent of the trait which the measurement methods are intended to measure. A careful look at the components of this definition will be necessary to clarify what is meant by response styles.

To illustrate the components of the definition above, an example of a simple type of response style will be used—the tendency to guess on multiple-choice tests when unsure. First, this tendency qualifies as a response style only if there are reliable individual differences in this respect. One could determine this, for example, by estimating the number of items on which subjects guess on alternative forms of tests [by Eq. (16-8)]. If the estimated guessing scores on the alternative forms correlate substantially, the tendency to guess is reliable, and thus it will fit the first component of the definition of a response style.

The second component of the definition of response styles states that they are artifactual products of measurement methods, and this is the most difficult component of the definition to express in operational terms. The idea is understandable, and it is easy to give numerous illustrations of such artifactual sources of variance, but it is difficult to say what is and what is not an artifactual source of variance. For an illustration, we can return to the example of reliable individual differences in amount of guessing. Such reliable individual differences occur only on certain types of measurement instruments employed in certain ways. Logically there are no reliable individual differences in the tendency to guess when in doubt on free-response tests. Also, there cannot be any reliable individual differences in this regard when all subjects are forced to respond to all items. In other words, then, reliable individual differences in the tendency to guess when in doubt are artifactually generated by the particular techniques of measurement.

Another example of an artifactual source of variance that qualifies as a response style is that of the reliable tendency to mark "true" rather than "false" when in doubt about the correct answer on a true-false test. Since reliable individual differences in this regard logically cannot occur on multiple-choice tests or on other types of tests, these reliable individual differences are artifactually generated by the particular technique of measurement.

The third component of the definition of response styles states that they are at least partly independent of the traits which instruments are intended to measure. Reliable individual differences in the tendency to guess when in doubt fit this requirement. As was mentioned previously, such individual differences have been found to have only negligible correlations with scores corrected for guessing. One makes the real test of the partial independence of the response style and the trait by computing the shared common variance (*SCV*), which was previously defined as the ratio of the squared correlation between two measures divided by the product of their respective reliabilities. If that is less than 1.0, the response style and the trait are not totally dependent; and to the extent that the *SCV* is near zero, the two are nearly independent (in the correlational sense of the term *independent*).

**Potential importance of response styles** There are three major reasons for investigating response styles. First, in some types of tests, they logically are correlated very little or even negatively with the trait in question. By definition stylistic variables are more like personality traits than like abilities. For example, the tendency to guess when unsure is not an ability in any obvious sense, and even though it might pay off in certain circumstances, it would serve only to cloud the measurement of a particular ability, e.g., spelling ability.

Even if stylistic variables usually lower the validity of instruments, this does not mean that they usually lower the reliability. In the oversimplified case where the reliable variance could be partitioned into additive components because of trait and style, the reliability of the sum could be estimated from the reliability of linear combinations (Chap. 7). The reliability of the sum might be either higher or lower than the reliability of the trait (with the stylistic variance removed), depending on the correlation between trait and style and on the reliability of each. If the reliability of variance because of the trait is only moderately high and the reliability because of stylistic variance is higher, the reliability of the sum (the obtained scores) could be much higher than the reliability of the trait (stylistic variance partialed from obtained scores). Potentially, this is one of the deceptive things about some response styles: they can add to the reliable variance and thus give the investigator a false sense of security with the measurement tool.

The second major reason for investigating response styles is that they might prove to be important measures of personality. Some of the response styles that have been cataloged sound like important personality traits, e.g., cautiousness, acquiescence, and extremeness. To the extent that such stylistic variables can be measured independently of content relating to nonstylistic variables or to the extent that they can somehow be separated from the variance of other traits, they might prove useful as measures of personality traits. For reasons which will be discussed later, mountains of research on the development of personality measures from response styles have met mainly with failure. Most of the supposed measures of personality that have been developed from scores concerning response styles falter on logical or empirical grounds, or both.

It should be obvious that the effort to measure response styles and validate them as measures of personality is at cross purposes with the effort to measure the nonstylistic variance in the same instruments. Thus, for example, it is illogical to expect the same instrument to be a good measure of both spelling ability and the willingness to gamble. Also, it is illogical to expect an inventory to be a good measure of both extraversion and the tendency to make extreme responses. Consequently, if one is interested in the trait supposedly measured by the instrument rather than in stylistic variance that creeps in the back door, one should do everything possible to rid the instrument of stylistic variance. If, on the other hand, the interest is in measuring the response style rather than the trait that supposedly is involved in the instrument, the experimenter should magnify the variance of the response style at the expense of the variance of the trait. For example, if one were interested in measuring the agreement tendency in agree-disagree dichotomous responses to attitude statements, one might promote the stylistic variance in that regard by making each item highly ambiguous, which is just the opposite of what one would do to obtain a reliable measurement of attitudes.

The third, final, and perhaps least important reason for investigating response styles is that some of them are scientifically interesting in their own right. For example, purely apart from any intention to develop a measure of personality, a researcher might be curious about the nature of people who tend to guess considerably when in doubt about correct answers on multiple-choice tests. Some small correlations have been found between this stylistic variable and measures of personality and ability, and the same is true for some of the other stylistic variables. Even though, as mentioned previously, this is far from sufficient evidence to show that any of the stylistic variables are adequate measures of personality traits, it does tell us something about the stylistic variables. Most stylistic variables, however, mainly are annoying things that are of scientific interest only for the first reason given in this section—to find ways of ridding instruments of their effects.

It is an understatement to say that the literature on response styles is voluminous up until about 1970 (but it has dwindled markedly since that time). There have been not only a number of major reviews of the literature, but even reviews of the reviews. A key to earlier literature is the incisive critical review by Rorer (1965), the temper of which is easily detected from the title: "The great response-style myth." The review by Damarin and Messick (1965) is particularly pertinent to one of the three reasons given previously for the investigation of response styles, that of the use of measures of response styles as measures of personality traits. Unless specifically referenced otherwise, statements here regarding empirical evidence relating to response styles are supported by findings summarized in these two reviews and at various places in the Suggested Additional Readings for this chapter—see in particular the relevant sections in Wiggins (1973). Following will be summarized in turn the issues and evidence relating to the types of response styles that have been investigated most extensively.

**Components of expressed self-desirability** In Chap. 14 the variable of social desirability was discussed, and it was said that much of the variance on all self-inventory measures of personality can be explained by a factor concerning the tendency to say good rather than bad things about oneself. (Evidence of the omnipresence and potency of this factor in self-inventories is summarized by Edwards 1964 and 1970.) This factor also is referred to as *social desirability,* and perhaps more appropriately, as *expressed self-desirability.* People who are high in the factor "say" many more good than bad things about themselves, and vice versa for people who are at the opposite extreme of the factor. The use of this terminology is not meant to prejudice the possibility that self-inventories measure personality, but it is intended to stick to known facts until more evidence is available. This is felt necessary because the general factor in self-inventories is given somewhat different names by different investigators, and these different names have different implications for psychological theories. For example, scales specifically intended to measure expressed self-desirability (called *social desirability scales,* or SD scales, by most persons who work with them) have very high positive correlations with scales intended to measure adjustment and very high negative correlations with scales intended to measure neuroticism and anxiety, respectively. The SD scales also have strong correlations with scales intended to measure the tendency to fake "good" on self-inventories.

As was mentioned in Chap. 14, it is meaningful to think of SD in terms of three hypothetical components: (1) the subjects' actual state of adjustment, (2) their knowledge of their own personal characteristics, and (3) their frankness in telling what they know. Some writers have gone to the extreme of interpreting SD only as conscious faking, or merely a response style, but this is a gross mistake. Only component 3 above, frankness, can be clearly classified either as faking or as a response style in self-inventories. No one would classify actual adjustment as a response style, for the term would be so global as to lose all meaning. In self-inventories, also it is not wise to think of component 2 above, self-knowledge, as a response style. Rather, it is best to think of self-knowledge as an inherent limitation to what can be learned about people from self-inventories. (As was mentioned in Chap. 14, in addition to these three systematic components of the variance in self-inventories, there is a considerable amount of measurement error introduced by a "communication barrier," in which subjects are limited by the fidelity of the verbal communication of the items to permit them to frankly relate what they know about their own personal characteristics.) Only component 3 above, frankness, clearly qualifies as a response style according to the definition given previously.

Evidence regarding the variance because of individual differences in frankness necessarily is indirect. Experiments have shown that to some extent people can make themselves appear more adjusted on self-inventories when they are instructed to fake "good," i.e., to be the opposite of frank. However, the fact that people can manipulate their scores somewhat by intentional faking does not mean that they actually do so in the usual testing situation. Further, mean differences under different instructions regarding frankness do not imply that the reliable variance because of frankness is large in any of the conditions. The mean score could shift without there being any reliable individual differences in frankness.

The fact that the rank-ordering of people is changed somewhat because of different test instructions, types of items, and situational variables does argue for the importance of variance because of frankness under some conditions. Changes in the rank-ordering of people under different experimental conditions relating to frankness, however, typically are not large, and consequently the correlations between scores in the different conditions tend to be high. If the correlation were low in that case, it could be argued that there is a large component of reliable variance because of frankness in one of the conditions. But if the correlations tend to be high, as is the case, the result could be interpreted with equal credibility as evidence either that frankness does not explain much of the variance on either occasion or that the effort to reduce variance because of frankness on one of the occasions was not successful. Thus, whereas this line of evidence provides little positive support for the contention that variance because of frankness plays a large part in self-inventories, it also does not rule out the possibility.

Efforts have been made to develop direct measures of individual differences in frankness, the products of which frequently have been referred to by the unfortunate term *lie* scales. Many of the scales to measure frankness are based on the same principle: if a person fails to admit common failings or lays claims to extraordinary virtues, the person is lying. Examples of such items follow:

1. I never say anything bad about anyone.
2. I am always honest in everything I do.
3. There have been occasions on which I felt jealous of other people.
4. I can remember times when I was embarrassed.

If a person answers *yes* to the first two items and *no* to the second two, this would be taken as evidence that the individual is lying, faking good, or, in the language being used here, not being frank in responding. Scales developed from items such as these are used to measure reliable individual differences in frankness.

The problem with scales to measure frankness developed in the manner described above is that they confound actual traits with frankness. It is entirely conceivable that some people have such sterling characteristics, or at least their self-knowledge leads them to think so, that they honestly respond in the direction taken to indicate conscious faking. Also, if there were no variance because of frankness, one would expect the probability of a person's responding in one way rather than another to be related to the trait itself. In that case, the person who actually is highly honest would have a higher probability of responding *yes* to item 2 above than would a person who actually is lower in honesty. For these reasons, the persons who obtain high scores on lie scales probably represent a mixture of people who actually are not being frank and people who either have sterling qualities or have misinformation about their own personal characteristics. To the extent that the variance in lie scales is caused by variance in self-knowledge rather than variance in frankness, it is inappropriate to refer to such scales as lie scales. Rather, insofar as such scales actually measure anything other than the trait in question, they measure a mixture of reliable sources of invalidity, including self-knowledge, frankness, and perhaps other variables not currently known.

Another approach to the independent measurement of individual differences in frankness is to key items empirically so as to differentiate groups that are given different instructions regarding frankness. One can do this, for example, by comparing the responses of subjects under instructions to be as frank as possible with the responses of the same subjects to the same items under instructions to fake good, i.e., to appear as well adjusted as possible. The items on which $p$ values shift the most are taken to be items that are sensitive to degrees of frankness. For example, if most people disagree with an item under instructions to be frank and agree with it under instructions to fake good, it is assumed that agreeing with that item under the usual instructions to be frank also is an indicator of the tendency to fake good. Not only is it unusual to find items that are so markedly affected by instructions, but the whole approach has a severe logical problem.

As was mentioned previously, a shift in mean response ($p$ value on individual items) is no guarantee that individual differences are affected or that such shifts point to ways to measure individual differences in the variables that produced the shift. It may be that different instructions relating to frankness result in large changes in $p$ values on some items, but that is only weak circumstantial evidence that individual differences in response to those items in any circumstance actually relate to degree of frankness.

Another severe logical problem with the above-mentioned method for deriving independent measures of individual differences in frankness is that it inevitably confounds measures of stylistic variables with measures of nonstylistic traits. If the scale for measuring frankness is derived from a scale intended to measure, say, dominance, the scoring key for the stylistic tendency probably will overlap the scoring key for the nonstylistic variable (which, as we shall see later, is a severe problem in all efforts to measure stylistic variables from items intended to measure nonstylistic traits). Then, even if the experimenter filled in at random the test responses on 100 test blanks, probably a substantial correlation between the two sets of "scores" would be found. Thus it is obvious that the so-called measure of the stylistic variable is confounded with the measurement of the trait. Even if one employs a hodgepodge of item content, this still does not overcome the difficulty. By this means it is possible to make the measure of stylistic tendency relatively pure of particular personality traits (e.g., dominance), but it is very difficult to prevent it from being confounded with expressed self-desirability. This is because almost all items usable for self-inventories tend to measure SD, even if items vary considerably in that regard. Unless the scale to measure a response style has equal amounts of variance from items keyed in a socially desirable and socially undesirable direction, which is a very difficult condition to obtain exactly, the measure of the stylistic tendency is artifactually confounded with actual adjustment. That logically follows if, as previously hypothesized, the major component of SD actually is adjustment.

From the above discussion it can be seen that the components of expressed self-desirability are complex, and presently there are no means for neatly unraveling them. Even if, on the average, people are not entirely frank in responding to self-inventories, it has not yet been convincingly demonstrated that *individual differences* in that regard explain a major portion of the variance of scores. It is more reasonable to think that a larger portion of the total variance is due to individual differences in self-knowledge, as such self-knowledge can be manifested through the "language barrier."

When discussing self-knowledge, one must consider not only the lack of knowledge, but also mistaken conceptions the subjects have of themselves. In addition, it is necessary to consider not only individual differences in overall amount of self-knowledge, but also differences in self-knowledge relating to different types of traits.

There are many ways in which people can lack knowledge about their own characteristics as mirrored in the items employed in self-inventories. They may have not been in many situations that permitted them to observe themselves in action or to observe the responses of other people to them; or when in such situations, they may have selectively attended to cues that supported an idealized self-concept. To some extent, we learn what we are like from important people in our lives, and in many cases these people are not correct about our actual characteristics. Also, there is some selective "forgetting" of our own actions and the ways in which other people have responded to us, and those memories that remain active frequently are reshaped in one way or another. To the extent that questionnaire items concern typical behavior over a long period of time or behavior in an earlier stage of life, individuals may be deficient in self-knowledge purely because they cannot accurately recall how they performed or how other people responded to them, e.g., as might be the case regarding the responses of adults to factual questions about forms of discipline in the home during childhood. Individuals might not understand exactly what information the item is seeking, they might have different meanings for some of the key words than those intended by the test constructor, or they might feel that the item "lumps together" traits that they had always considered separately. For these and other reasons, semantic problems tend to put a veil between self-knowledge and the picturing of that self-knowledge on self-inventories.

Although there are possible ways to investigate variance because of frankness and to reduce that variance in self-inventories, presently there are no hints as to how either could be done for the variable of self-knowledge. Individual differences in self-knowledge may be an inherent limitation to the validity of self-inventory measures of personality.

**Tendency to guess when in doubt** A response style which was considered previously in this chapter was the tendency to guess when in doubt about the correct answers on multiple-choice tests. There are reliable individual differences in that regard on particular types of tests (e.g., tests of word meaning and tests concerning history). Only a very small portion of the variance of scores, however, can be accounted for by that stylistic tendency. This was amply borne out in a thorough investigation by Waller (1974), who presented an excellent method for estimating scores on the stylistic trait relating to the tendency to guess and showed that the trait correlates zero with ability on vocabulary tests.

In early stages of research, the tendency to guess when in doubt was referred to as the *willingness to gamble*, and the opposite of it referred to as *cautiousness*. Continued research with the guessing tendency has shown that these broad trait names are entirely unjustified. The tendency is limited to true-false and multiple-choice tests of ability, particularly educational tests, and it is not even very consistent over tests in different subject matters. It does not correlate with the willingness to gamble in other types of situations, e.g., simulated betting situations in research on risk taking. There are some small correlations between the tendency to guess and personality variables (Price 1964). These correlations are so few, and so small in size, that there is little indication that the tendency to guess can be employed as an important measure of personality.

Most of the reliable variance of the tendency to guess when in doubt apparently relates to specific strategies for taking tests. Obviously it is desirable to limit the variance from this source as much as possible. To some extent that variance can be reduced by instructions that discourage blind guessing. In this case the correction for guessing also serves to further reduce the variance because of the guessing tendency. One can remove that variance altogether by requiring all subjects to attempt all items, in which case there cannot possibly be any variance in the tendency to guess when in doubt.

**Tendency to guess "true"** One of the findings that kindled the interest in response styles is that on true-false tests there are reliable individual differences in the tendency to guess "true" rather than "false." A measure of this tendency is simply the percentage of wrong answers marked "true." For example, if an individual has 10 incorrect answers, of which 3 are marked "false" and 7 are marked "true," the score on the stylistic variable would be 70. Not only is there modest reliability with respect to this tendency in particular tests, but also there are small correlations between this tendency on true-false tests in different subject areas.

The above finding led to the postulation of a very general personality trait, which has variously been referred to as the "agreement tendency," "acquiescence," and "yeasaying" as opposed to "naysaying." There are mountains of negative evidence now to show that these broad trait names are unjustified. The tendency to guess "true" on educational tests is not very general even over different types of educational tests, and there is no firm evidence at all that it correlates with the agreement tendency in measures of personality and sentiment. Also, there is no evidence that the tendency to guess "true" correlates with acquiescence, or yeasaying, in social situations.

The best solution to the problem of stylistic variance because of guessing "true" on true-false tests is to not use true-false tests unless there is some compelling reason to do so. Variance in that tendency obviously cannot occur on multiple-choice tests or free-response tests. Even if it were not for some variance because of guessing "true," most true-false tests suffer from other problems, such as the amount of measurement error from guessing and the difficulty in composing good item statements on some topics that are unambiguously true or false.

**The agreement tendency** Above it was said that the tendency to guess "true" is not a broad trait concerning the agreement tendency, but this does not rule out the possibility that such a trait exists in self-inventories and measures of sentiments. In the early stages of research on response styles, some investigators thought they had found evidence of the presence of such a trait in a measure of attitudes, the California *F* scale for the measurement of "authoritarian attitudes." A special form of the scale was constructed, in which each item was rewritten so as to make the meaning the reverse of that in the original scale. Ordinarily one would expect a high negative correlation between scores obtained from the customary scale and the reversed scale, but a substantial positive correlation was found instead. This led investigators to think that the scale mainly measured a tendency to agree rather than disagree, or *acquiescence* as it was called. This hypothesis led to volumes of research to measure a general trait of acquiescence, which so far has met mainly with failure [see evidence summarized by Bentler, Jackson, and Messick (1972) and Rorer (1965)].

The hypothesis behind the search for a general trait of acquiescence is that there are important individual differences in the extent to which people will agree with the opinions and decisions of other people rather than curry their disfavor. Logically, variance in such a trait should occur only when there is some room for doubt about the correctness of a point of view, because no matter how much an individual wants to please others, the person is not likely to agree that $2 + 2 = 13$ or that it is only 6 miles from New York to Chicago.

If there were some way to conclusively reverse the meaning of statements relating to attitudes, it would be possible to derive measures of the agreement tendency. One approach would be to subtract the number of unchanged "disagree" responses from the number of unchanged "agree" responses. The extreme of the agreement tendency would be represented by the person who agreed to all items on both the original statements and their reversals. The opposite extreme would be represented by the person who disagreed with all items on both forms. The difference between these two types of unchanged responses could serve as a measure of the agreement tendency for persons who are between the extremes of the trait.

Unfortunately it is very difficult to know when the meaning of an item actually has been reversed. Consequently the different reversed scales for the same trait correlate very little with one another, with most of the evidence in this regard coming from different efforts to reverse items on the $F$ scale. Also, correlations of those reversed scales with the original scale range all the way from high positive to as negative as the reliabilities of the scales will permit.

Rorer (1965) presents numerous examples of attempted reversals of items that, on close inspection, really are not reversals. An example is the following pair of statements, in which the second statement is intended to be a reversal of the meaning of the first statement:

*Item*  Obedience and respect for authority are the most important virtues that children should learn.

*Reversal*  A love of freedom and complete independence are the most important virtues children should learn.

Regardless of the agreement tendency, a person could realistically agree with both these statements or disagree with both. One might, for example, disagree with both because one is reluctant to say that one thing is most important for children to learn, or one might disagree with both because one thinks that something else is more important, e.g., religious devotion. Both the weight of the evidence and logical considerations indicate that it is not feasible to measure an agreement tendency with reversed scales.

Another approach to the measurement of the agreement tendency is with either highly ambiguous or very abstruse statements such as the following:

1. The International Monetary Fund should adopt a fiscal policy that fulfills a need for rapid balancing of reciprocal tariff obligations.
2. The orbit of the planet Saturn is more elliptical than that of Neptune.

The first statement is only a jumble of words that add up to nothing, and the second statement concerns matters with which very few persons are familiar. Logically, then, one might think that the tendency to agree rather than disagree with statements like these would represent acquiescence, this following from the notion that people agree with such statements because they are "pushed along" by the force of the statement itself. The evidence, however, is that such abstruse and ambiguous statements do not measure a trait of acquiescence. Scales based on such statements typically do not provide highly reliable individual differences among subjects. It is very rare, for example, to find persons who agree with as many as 90 percent of the statements on such scales or who disagree with 90 percent of the statements. Probably this is because subjects actually form opinions about such statements even when such statements are intended to be nonsense. For example, the statement above about the International Monetary Fund "sounds" like a good thing to do, because it speaks of "fulfilling a need." On the statement concerning orbits of two planets, the subject might not actually know the answer but might feel that he or she has a faint idea about the matter. For these and other reasons, scales composed of such statements are not entirely "contentless," and consequently the real or apparent content of the statements partly determines the responses of subjects. What little reliable variance there is on such scales is not related to other types of measures of acquiescence (e.g., measures derived from reversed scales), and such scales do not correlate with more behavioral measures of acquiescence (e.g., scores on conformity in group situations).

Another approach to the measurement of acquiescence is with "contentless" scales. For example, a method devised by Husek (1961) centers around a mock experiment in extrasensory perception. Subjects are asked to mark their agreement with each of 100 statements being read silently by the experimenter. Actually, the experimenter is not reading statements, and consequently subjects are agreeing and disagreeing with perfectly nothing. Another contentless measure is that developed by Nunnally and Husek (1958), which is posed as a test of ability to guess the meanings of German words. Randomly chosen abstruse German nouns are substituted for the subject and predicate of English sentences. Even if one spoke German fluently, the sentences would be nonsense. The subjects are agreeing or disagreeing with meaningless statements.

Both the contentless measures above have reliable variance, the reliability of the ESP testing being almost .90. The reliable variance in these and other contentless measures, however, apparently is not related to social acquiescence or any other personality trait, because the contentless instruments (1) correlate very little with one another, (2) correlate very little with measures of acquiescence derived from other approaches, and (3) do not correlate at all with behavioral indices of social acquiescence and other traits.

The overwhelming weight of the evidence now points to the fact that the agreement tendency is of very little importance either as a measure of personality or as a source of systematic invalidity in measures of personality and sentiments. What little stylistic variance there is because of that tendency, if any, can be mostly eliminated by ensuring that an instrument is constructed so that there is a balance of items keyed "agree" and "disagree" with respect to the trait in question.

**The extreme-response tendency** Another stylistic variable is the tendency to give extreme responses, which has been investigated mostly on rating scales used for the measurement of attitudes and other sentiments. The hypothesis is that, regardless of the content, people differ in the tendency to mark the extremes of rating scales rather than points near the middle of the scale. This hypothesis grew out of findings that there are small correlations between degrees of extremeness of ratings made by subjects on different rating tasks, e.g., on ratings of aesthetic preferences for pictures and ratings of attitudes toward minority groups.

The extremeness tendency logically should be evidenced in the sum of absolute differences of ratings from the midpoint of the scale. For example, on a seven-step scale of agreement and disagreement, a rating of 7 is scored 3, and a rating of 3 is scored 1. The sum of such deviations is taken as a score on the tendency to give extreme responses.

As is true of attempts to measure other stylistic variables, it is very difficult to prevent measures of extremeness from being confounded with actual attitudes or other sentiments. For example, if a person had either a strongly positive or a strongly negative attitude toward the United Nations, that individual would obtain a high sum of deviations from the center of the scale, but that could be entirely because of the attitude as validly reflected in his or her ratings rather than because of the tendency to give extreme responses.

Before concluding that there is reliable variance because of the extremeness tendency in a particular set of ratings, one must first score the responses in two ways: (1) as indicated above in terms of the sum of deviations and (2) in terms of the sum of dichotomized scores for the trait in question. For the latter, any rating to the left or to the right of the midpoint would be scored either as an "agree" or "disagree" response, regardless of how extreme the rating. This could then be considered a measure of the trait in which the extremeness logically is not present. The squared correlation between the two sets of scores should then be divided by the product of their internal-consistency reliabilities (coefficient alpha), the results being the shared common variance discussed previously. If that is considerably less than 1.0 (e.g., as low as .80), it can reasonably be concluded that the extremeness tendency is present to some degree. Then, by partialing the sum of dichotomous responses from the sum of midpoint deviations, one might obtain a relatively pure measure of the extremeness tendency.

What evidence there is suggests that a small amount of reliable variance on some instruments is due to the extremeness tendency, particularly on measures of attitudes. Also, some suggestive small correlations have been found between measures of the extremeness tendency and measures of intelligence (negative correlations) and measures of various personality attributes. Although the evidence does not point to extremeness tendency as being either very general across basically different types of instruments or an important measure of personality, it does suggest that stylistic variance because of the extremeness tendency may be a small source of systematic invalidity in some uses of rating scales. Of course, the usual way to score multipoint ratings is not dichotomously, but in terms of the sum of ratings (reversing scores of items that imply negative attitudes). When that is done, there is a danger of permitting stylistic variance because of the extremeness tendency to confound the actual measurement of attitudes. One can determine whether that occurs in particular instruments by computing the shared common variance between the dichotomously scored and continuously scored versions of the instrument. If that is not very high (e.g., less than .90), it might be wise to employ the dichotomous scoring rather than the continuous scoring in future uses of the instrument. This may result in a loss of reliability, but if it is feasible to increase the number of items, the reliability usually can be restored to satisfactory levels.

**Deviant-response tendency** The deviant-response tendency concerns individual differences in making uncommon responses. For example, if 80 percent of the people agree with a statement, anyone who disagrees with the statement is said to give a deviant response. It has been hypothesized (Berg 1961) that the deviant-response tendency is very general across many different types of instruments and that it is an important dimension of personality.

There is some evidence that the deviant-response tendency is rather general across self-inventories, but mainly this can be shown to be more parsimoniously explained in terms of conventional psychometric concepts rather than in terms of a new construct of deviant-response tendency. On inventories to measure adjustment, frequently most of the items indicative of maladjustment are keyed in terms of deviant responses. Following are two examples:

1. I feel that I am mentally healthy.
2. I sometimes think that someone is following me.

More than half the people will agree with the first statement, and far more than half the people will disagree with the second statement. Consequently anyone who gives different responses from those of the majority of the people certainly is, in one sense, giving deviant responses; but that does not mean that it is necessary to invoke a special construct concerning a dimension of personality to explain that behavior. It is more parsimonious to interpret such responses in terms of the traits which the instruments are intended to measure, including the components of expressed self-desirability.

Efforts have been made to develop scales of deviant responding by comparing the responses of normal persons with the responses of patients in mental hospitals. As might be expected, the responses of the hospital patients are deviant on the average with respect to the average responses of normal people. This is not very surprising, because highly deviant people are expected to give deviant responses in many different types of situations. Actually, it is hard to find a test of ability or measure of personality or sentiment on which the typical responses of hospitalized mental patients are not different on the average from those of normal people. Partly, however, that may be due to test-taking behavior rather than the traits supposedly measured by the particular instruments. For example, many mental patients are so confused and out of touch with reality that they give nearly random responses to tests and inventories. For reasons which will be discussed later, a person who gives random, or careless, responses will also give many deviant responses. This is evidenced, for example, in what would happen if a person flipped a coin to decide whether to agree or disagree with items in a list of statements like the following:

1. I sometimes think that I am God.
2. There is a squirrel in my head.
3. I am glass from the waist down.

It should be apparent that although the deviant-responding tendency has been discussed frequently as a response style, it is not a response style according to the definition given earlier. It is not an artifact of measurement; rather, it comes from a special way of analyzing the valid variance. Consequently it is neither desirable nor logically possible to construct instruments so that variance because of deviant responding will not be present.

The problem with the construct of deviant response is not so much that it is lacking in empirical support as that it is an overly global, nonanalytic construct that makes little contribution to psychological theories or programs of research. Just to say that people are deviant on the average in their responses does not tell whether they are deviantly "good" or deviantly "bad," e.g., deviantly wel. adjusted rather than maladjusted or deviantly high in intelligence rather than low in intelligence. Also, if one is to understand human traits, it is necessary to measure the particular ways in which some people are different from others rather than to lump deviant responses from instruments concerning many different factors of ability, personality characteristics, and sentiments. To understand human traits, one must employ concepts concerning measures of different traits and factors among those traits, and one adds very little to those concepts by postulating a deviant-response tendency. Doing so would be like abandoning techniques for diagnosing particular forms of illness in favor of a global technique that would determine only whether people are sick or well.

## SUMMARY OF RESEARCH ON RESPONSE STYLES

As can be seen from the preceding discussion, hindsight makes it clear that the research on response styles was mainly built on false hopes and methodological flaws. Unless one wants to speak of some of the components of expressed self-desirability as being response styles, there is little evidence that any of the response styles (1) explains more than a small fraction of the variance in any instrument intended to measure nonstylistic traits, (2) is highly general across basically different types of instruments, or (3) correlates substantially with experimentally independent measures of personality or ability. For these reasons, any variance attributable to response styles which occurs in using an instrument that is intended to measure a trait of ability or personality constitutes a systematic source of invalidity, and experimenters should do everything possible to get rid of such sources of variance.

## EFFECTS OF CARELESSNESS AND CONFUSION

Another important class of contingent variables concerns carelessness and confusion in relation to the purpose of the test, the test instructions, the item content, or other aspects of the testing situation. Carelessness and confusion are considered jointly because the expected effect is the same—they introduce a source of randomness into test responses. Of course, any particular person who is careless or confused might not act randomly, but that is the expected result for a group of persons who are either careless or confused. Since the effects of individual differences in motivation, fatigue, and physical health should relate to carelessness and confusion, what will be said in this section has some relevance for the former three variables also.

One sees ample evidence of the effects of carelessness and confusion in the responses to many different types of psychological measures. For example, on semantic-differential scales, frequently one sees the same concept rated as "highly useful" and "highly worthless." On a set of rating scales for the measurement of attitudes, one sometimes finds that the subject has marked both ends of all scales. One frequently sees "pattern" responding on rating scales, such as progressively marking the next higher step on each scale, marking all scales in the neutral category, or alternately marking the extreme ends of scales to form an illogical set of ratings. One sometimes finds other evidence regarding the effects of carelessness and confusion in comparing the responses of abnormal subjects with those of normal subjects. This would be the case, for example, if it were found that the mean evaluation scores for the concepts "devil" and "God" were not well separated in the abnormal group, because they always are well separated in normal groups.

The most danger from carelessness and confusion is when the purpose of the research is to compare mean responses by different types of people, e.g., children and adults. This is because carelessness and confusion can artifactually produce large apparent mean differences if one group is more careless or confused than the other. It is reasonable to expect that more carelessness or confusion will be found in some groups than in others when they are responding to particular kinds of testing materials. Thus one would expect more carelessness or confusion in hospitalized psychotics than in normal people, in children than in adults, and in deaf children than in normal children. When such groups are compared, there is a real danger that artifactual differences in mean scores may be only due to differences between groups in amount of carelessness or confusion. This actually may have been the case in many studies reported in the literature.

**Effects on test parameters** Carelessness and confusion are expected to have major effects: They introduce a source of measurement error in addition to that from guessing and other components of measurement error, and they serve to bias scores toward the *chance level.* The effects of carelessness and confusion are directly analogous to the effects of guessing on true-false and multiple-choice tests, but the effects of both are somewhat different from other sources of measurement error. To the extent that carelessness and confusion introduce some randomness into responses, it should be obvious that such randomness will introduce measurement error. The classical theory of measurement error (Chap. 6) assumes that measurement error results in a symmetric distribution of obtained (fallible) scores about the true score for each person. The errors because of carelessness and confusion, however, not only lower the precision of obtained scores, but also serve to *bias* obtained scores toward the chance level.

The *chance level* is the score that a person would be expected to obtain if she or he responded randomly to all items, a matter which was discussed previously with respect to guessing. If a person responds randomly to 20 agree-disagree statements concerning attitudes toward the United Nations, the best a priori estimate is that the individual will agree with 10 of the statements and disagree with 10. If agreement with each statement is keyed as a positive attitude and the total score equals the number of agreements on positive statements, the expected score is 10. If half the statements are keyed "agree" for a positive attitude and half are keyed "disagree," and the total score equals the number of agreements on the former plus the number of disagreements on the latter, again the expected score from complete confusion or carelessness will be 10.

On an instrument in which the total score consists of the sum of ratings on multipoint scales, complete confusion or carelessness would be expected to lead to a total score equaling the number of scales multiplied by the midpoint of the scales. For example, with a seven-step scale ranging from 1 to 7, the midpoint is 4. Thus, with 20 items, the expected score would be 80. With an eight-step scale, the midpoint would be 4.5 and the expected scores would be 90.

Whereas on tests of ability scores are not expected below the chance level, of course that is not the case on nonability measures such as measures of attitudes. For example, a person with a very negative attitude might disagree with 20 positive statements. If the scoring is in terms of the number of agreements to positive statements, that person will receive a score of 0 rather than the score of 10 expected by chance. Regardless of whether the person's true score is above or below the chance level, the effect of carelessness and confusion is to ref˜ess the score toward the chance level.

If all members of a group are careless or confused to the same extent, the rank-order of obtained scores is expected to be the rank-order of true scores, except for some random shifting about because of measurement error. Very high true scores and true scores far below the chance level would be expected to regress more than would true scores nearer the chance level, but the rank-order would be expected to remain the same. The net effect would be to shrink the distribution and shift the mean of true scores toward the chance level. In that case there would be some unreliability because of carelessness and confusion, but there would be no systematic source of invalidity.

If, however, there are individual differences in amount of carelessness or confusion, systematic sources of invalidity can be generated. Suppose, for example, that people with negative attitudes tend to be much more careless than people with mildly negative or positive attitudes. In this case the chance level might indicate a neutral attitude, and consequently the people with very negative attitudes would obtain less negative scores than would persons with mildly negative attitudes. Just what happens to scores when there are systematic individual differences in amount of carelessness or confusion is complexly interwoven with the type of item, the scoring key, and the correlation of the amount of carelessness and confusion with the trait in question. Whatever the specific effects, however, individual differences in amount of carelessness and confusion can be expected to add not only a component of measurement error, but also a component of systematic invalidity.

**Effects on different types of instruments** Effects of carelessness and confusion are interestingly different in terms of different types of instruments and different types of scoring keys. On tests of ability, the expectation is that scores will be lower, but that is not always the case on some tests of personality. If, as mentioned previously, the keyed responses on measures of maladjustment are deviant responses ($p$ values well removed from .5 in either direction for dichotomous items), carelessness and confusion will lead to scores indicative of a high level of maladjustment. On an interest inventory, carelessness and confusion could produce high interest scores on some scales (e.g., for engineers) and low scores on other scales, depending on the $p$ values of the items keyed for those scales.

Although it is expected that carelessness and confusion will regress scores toward the chance level, the relative standing of such scores depends on the mean and the standard deviation of responses of persons who are not careless or confused. If the mean of the total group were well above the chance level on a scale of attitudes, persons who were careless or confused would appear to have negative attitudes; but the reverse would be true if the mean of the total group were well below the chance level. For these reasons, the effects of carelessness or confusion will be interpreted quite differently depending on the way in which an instrument is keyed and the distribution of scores of persons who are not suffering from carelessness or confusion.

**Effects on correlations** If there is about the same amount of carelessness or confusion among the members of a group, the expectation is that correlations among different measures will be less than they would be otherwise. This is because of the measurement error introduced by carelessness and confusion. However, if there are systematic differences in carelessness or confusion, the effects on correlations among measures will depend on the correlation of amounts of carelessness and confusion with the traits in question. In rare instances the correlations could be inflated. That, however, is a result which is hardly to be expected, the more usual case being a lowering of correlations.

**Comparisons of groups** As was mentioned previously, the major danger from carelessness and confusion is comparing mean responses from different types of groups of people. An example will suffice to show how spurious results can be obtained in that case. In a hypothetical study, comparisons are made of the semantic-differential ratings by psychotics and normal persons of role concepts such as "father," "mother," "policeman," etc. Ratings are made on a seven-step scale, the midpoint being 4. It is found that normal subjects have an average evaluative rating for "father" of 6.1, and psychotic patients have an average rating for "father" of 4.8. It is found that the mean difference is highly significant statistically. It is tempting to interpret this finding as indicating that psychotic patients have less regard for their fathers than normal persons do. It is equally plausible, however, that the difference is due to much more confusion or carelessness on the part of the psychotic patients than on the part of normal subjects. It may be that the mean true score of psychotics is also 6.1, but because of carelessness or confusion, the mean obtained score is regressed to 4.8.

The possibility of obtaining statistically significant mean differences because of differences in amount of carelessness or confusion is an ever-present danger in research. The danger is most prominent when responses from different types of people are compared, but potentially it is also present when subjects are randomly assigned to different experimental treatments. To the extent that the different treatments incidentally lead to different amounts of carelessness or confusion, mean differences might be entirely due to those factors. For example, if one group of subjects makes self-ratings under constant threat of a painful electric shock, they might be more careless or confused than a group which makes ratings under less threatening conditions.

**Detection of carelessness and confusion**  As was mentioned previously, there are some forms of circumstantial evidence regarding the presence of carelessness and confusion, and such evidence can be sought when those factors seem to be important. On tests of ability, one form of evidence concerns the number of easy and difficult questions properly answered by the subjects. To take an extreme case, if a college student could not add $2 + 2$ in one part of a test, but could correctly solve a calculus problem in another part of the test, there would be some evidence of carelessness or confusion. In more subtle cases, a comparison of responses on rather easy items with those on rather difficult items will provide circumstantial evidence regarding carelessness or confusion.

On ratings of agreement and disagreement or on semantic-differential scales, circumstantial evidence regarding carelessness and confusion can be obtained from the number of incompatible responses, e.g., rating the same concept as "useful" and "worthless." These and other methods for detecting carelessness and confusion, however, provide only circumstantial evidence, because they are based on the assumption that, when people are not careless or confused, their behavior with respect to the items is perfectly uniform. Since the correlations among items usually are not large, many inconsistencies in responses from item to item are to be expected. Differences between groups in these regards, however, should provide useful suggestions about carelessness and confusion.

**Control of carelessness and confusion**  Of course, rather than looking for evidence of carelessness or confusion after it has occurred, it is far better to do everything possible to reduce those factors before data are gathered. One can do this by experimenting with the instructions to ensure that they are understandable, employing very simple language in items, using simpler types of items (e.g., binary-choice agree-disagree items rather than multipoint rating scales), and cross checking the results from one instrument with those from another instrument. After large amounts of measurement error and bias have been introduced because of carelessness or confusion, there are no sensible "correction procedures" that can be applied; attempting to do so would be as feasible as attempting to unscramble an egg.

## SUGGESTED ADDITIONAL READINGS

Edwards, A. L. Social desirability and performance on the MMPI. *Psychometrika,* 1964, *29,* 295–308.

Edwards, A. L. *The measurement of personality traits by scales and inventories.* New York: Holt, 1970.

Morrison, E. J. On test variance and the dimensions of the measurement situation. *Educational and Psychological Measurement,* 1960, *20,* 231–250.

Price, D. B. A group approach to the analysis of individual differences in the randomness of guessing behavior on multiple-choice tests and the development of scoring methods to take such differences into account. *Research Bulletin* No. 64–59. Princeton, N.J.: Educational Testing Service, 1964.

Rorer, L. G. The great response-style myth. *Psychological Bulletin,* 1965, *63,* 129–156.

Thorndike, R. L. (ed.). *Educational measurement* (2d ed.). Washington, D. C.: American Council on Education, 1971. (See the indexed discussions by various authors of effects of guessing, motivational variables, time limits, and other variables on test performance.)

Wiggins, J. S. *Personality and prediction: Principles of personality assessment.* Reading. Mass.: Addison-Wesley, 1973.

# BIBLIOGRAPHY

American Psychological Association. *Standards for educational and psychological tests.* Washington. D.C.: American Psychological Association, 1974.

Anastasi, A. *Psychological testing* (4th ed.). New York: Macmillan, 1976.

Angoff, W. H. Scales, norms, and equivalent scores. In R. L. Thorndike (ed.), *Educational measurement* (2d ed.). Washington, D.C.: American Council on Education, 1971.

Archer, C. O., and Jennrich, R. I. Standard errors for rotated factor loadings. *Psychometrika*, 1973, *38*, 581–592.

Baggley, A. R. *Intermediate correlational methods.* New York: Wiley, 1964.

Bechtoldt, H. P. Construct validity: A critique. *American Psychologist*, 1959, *14*, 619–629.

Bentler, P. M., Jackson, D. N., and Messick, S. J. A rose by any other name. *Psychological Bulletin*, 1972, *77*, 109–113.

Berg, I. A. Measuring deviant behavior by means of deviant response sets. In I. A. Berg and B. M. Bass (eds.), *Conformity and deviation.* New York: Harper & Row, 1961, pp. 328–379.

Binet, A., and Simon, T. Méthodes nouvelles pour le diagnostique du niveau intellectuel des anormaux. *Année Psychologie*, 1905, *11*, 191–244.

Bock, R. D., and Jones, L. V. *The measurement and prediction of judgment and choice.* San Francisco: Holden-Day, 1968.

Brown, S. R. Bibliography on *Q* technique and its methodology. *Perceptual and Motor Skills Monograph*, Supplement 4-V26, 1968.

Burt, C. *The factors of the mind: An introduction to factor analysis in psychology.* New York: Macmillan, 1941.

Campbell, D. T. The indirect assessment of social attitudes. *Psychological Bulletin*, 1950, *47*, 15–38.

Campbell, D. T. Recommendations for APA test standards regarding construct, trait, and discriminant validity. *American Psychologist*, 1960, *15*, 546–553.

Carroll, J. B. *Psychometric tests as cognitive tasks: A new "structure of intellect."* Technical Report #4, ONR RB 7416. Princeton, N.J.: Educational Testing Service, May 1974.

Cattell, R. B. The three basic factor-analytic research designs—their interrelations and derivatives. *Psychological Bulletin,* 1952, *49,* 499–520.

Cattell, R. B. *Personality and motivation structure and measurement.* Yonkers, N.Y.: World, 1957.

Cliff, R. The predictive value of chance-level scores. *Educational and Psychological Measurement,* 1958, *18,* 607–616.

Comrey, A. L. The minimum residual method of factor analysis. *Psychological Reports,* 1962, *11,* 15–18.

Comrey, A. L. *A first course in factor analysis.* New York: Academic, 1973.

Cook, S. W., and Selltiz, C. A multiple-indicator approach to attitude measurement. *Psychological Bulletin,* 1964, *62,* 36–55.

Cooley, W. W. Techniques for considering multiple measurements. In R. L. Thorndike (ed.), *Educational measurement* (2d ed.). Washington, D.C.: American Council on Education, 1971.

Coombs, C. H. *A theory of data.* New York: Wiley, 1964.

Coombs, C. H., Dawes, R. M., and Tversky, A. *Mathematical psychology: An elementary introduction.* Englewood Cliffs, N.J.: Prentice-Hall, 1970.

Cramer, E. M. On Browne's solution for oblique Procrustes rotation. *Psychometrika,* 1974, *29,* 159–163.

Cromwell, R. L. Assessment of schizophrenia. In M. Rosenzweig and L. Porter (eds.), *Annual review of psychology,* Vol. 26. Palo Alto, Calif.: Annual Reviews, 1975.

Cronbach, L. J. Coefficient alpha and the internal structure of tests. *Psychometrika,* 1951, *16,* 297–334.

Cronbach, L. J. *Essentials of psychological testing* (3d ed.). New York: Harper & Row, 1970.

Cronbach, L. J. Test validation. In R. L. Thorndike (ed.), *Educational measurement* (2d ed.). Washington, D.C.: American Council on Education, 1971.

Cronbach, L. J., Gleser, G. C., Nanda, H., and Rajaratnam, N. *The dependability of behav-*sampled single-factor tests: An empirical comparison. *Educational and Psychological Measurement,* 1962, *22,* 645–666.

Cronbach, L. J., and Gleser, G. C. Assessing similarity between profiles. *Psychological Bulletin,* 1953, *50,* 456–473.

Cronbach, L. J., and Gleser, G. C. *Psychological tests and personnel decisions* (2d ed.). Urbana, Ill.: University of Illinois Press, 1965.

Cronbach, L.J., Gleser, G.C., Nanda, H., and Rajaratnam, N. *The dependability of behavioral measurements.* New York: Wiley, 1971.

Cronbach, L. J., and Meehl, P. E. Construct validity in psychological tests. *Psychological Bulletin,* 1955, *52,* 281–302.

Damarin, F. L., and Messick, S. J. Response styles as personality variables: A theoretical integration of multivariate research. *Research Bulletin* No. 65-10. Princeton, N.J.: Educational Testing Service, 1965.

Ebel, R. L. Expected reliability as a function of choices per item. *Educational and Psychological Measurement,* 1969 *29,* 565–570.

Edwards, A. L. The relationship between the judged desirability of a trait and the probability that the trait will be endorsed. *Journal of Applied Psychology,* 1953, *37,* 90–93.

Edwards, A. L. *Techniques of attitude scale construction.* New York: Appleton-Century-Crofts, 1957.

Edwards, A. L. Social desirability and performance on the MMPI. *Psychometrika,* 1964, *29,* 295–308.

Edwards, A. L. *The measurement of personality traits by scales and inventories.* New York: Holt, 1970.

Edwards, A. L., and Abbott, R. D. Measurement of personality traits: Theory and technique. In P. Mussen and M. Rosenzweig (eds.), *Annual review of psychology,* Vol. 24. Palo Alto, Calif.: Annual Reviews, 1973.

Falmagne, J. C. Foundations of Fechnerian psychophysics. In D. H. Krantz, R. C. Atkinson, R. D. Luce, and P. Suppes (eds.), *Contemporary developments in mathematical psychology: Vol. 2. Measurement, psychophysics, and neural information processing.* San Francisco: Freeman, 1974.

Farina, A., Arenberg, D., and Guskin, S. L. A scale for measuring minimal social behavior. *Journal of Consulting Psychology,* 1957, *21,* 265–268.

Ferguson, G. A. On learning and human ability. *Canadian Journal of Psychology,* 1954, *8,* 95–112.

Fiedler, F. E. A comparison of the therapeutic relationships in psychoanalytic, non-directive, and Adlerian therapy. *Journal of Consulting Psychology,* 1950, *14,* 436–445.

Fisher, R. A. The use of multiple measurements in taxonomic problems. *Annals of Eugenics,* 1936, *7,* 179–188.

Fleishman, E. A. Toward a taxonomy of human performance. *American Psychologist,* December 1975, 1127–1149.

Fleishman, E. A., and Hempel, W. E. Changes in factor structure of a complex psychomotor test as a function of practice. *Psychometrika,* 1954, *19,* 239–252.

Foa, U. G. New developments in facet design and analysis. *Psychological Review,* 1965, *72,* 262–274.

French, J. W. The description of aptitude and achievement tests in terms of rotated factors. *Psychometric Monograph,* No. 5. Chicago: University of Chicago Press, 1951.

Garner, W. R. Rating scales, discriminability, and information transmission. *Psychological Review,* 1960, *67,* 343–352.

Gerberich, J. R. *Specimen objective test items: A guide to achievement test construction.* New York: Longmans, 1956.

Ghiselli, E. E. *Theory of psychological measurement.* New York: McGraw-Hill, 1964.

Ghiselli, E. E. *The validity of occupational aptitude tests.* New York: Wiley, 1966.

Girard, R. A., and Cliff, N. A Monte Carlo evaluation of interactive multidimensional scaling. *Psychometrika,* 1976, *41,* 43–64.

Glaser, R., and Nitko, A. J. Measurement in learning and instruction. In R. L. Thorndike (ed.), *Educational measurement* (2d ed.). Washington, D.C.: American Council on Education, 1971.

Goleman, D. A new computer test of the brain. *Psychology Today,* May 1976, 44–48.

Gorsuch, R. L. *Factor analysis.* Philadelphia: Saunders, 1974.

Grinker, R. R., Miller, J., Sabshin, M., Nunn, R., and Nunnally, J. C. *The phenomena of depressions.* New York: Hoeber-Harper & Row, 1961.

Guilford, J. P. *Psychometric methods.* New York: McGraw-Hill, 1954.

Guilford, J. P. *Personality.* New York: McGraw-Hill, 1959.

Guilford, J. P. Factorial angles to psychology. *Psychological Review,* 1961, *68,* 1–20.

Guilford, J. P. *The nature of human intelligence.* New York: McGraw-Hill, 1967.

Guilford, J. P., and Fruchter, B. *Fundamental statistics in psychology and education* (5th ed.). New York: McGraw-Hill, 1973.

Guilford, J. P., and Hoepfner, R. *The analysis of intelligence.* New York: McGraw-Hill, 1971.

Guion, R. M. *Personnel testing.* New York: McGraw-Hill, 1965.

Gulliksen, H. *Theory of mental tests.* New York: Wiley, 1950.

Gulliksen, H., and Messick, S. J. (eds.). *Psychological scaling: Theory and applications.* New York: Wiley, 1960.

Guttman, L. Image theory for the structure of quantitative variates. *Psychometrika,* 1953, *18,* 277–296.

Guttman, L. Best possible systematic estimates of communalities. *Psychometrika,* 1956, *21,* 273–285.

Hanson, G. R. Assessing the career interests of college youth: Summary of research and applications. *ACT Research Report,* December 1974, No. 67.

Harman, H. H. *Modern factor analysis* (3d ed.). Chicago: University of Chicago Press, 1976.

Harris, R. J. *A primer of multivariate statistics.* New York: Academic, 1975.

Hathaway, S. R., and McKinley, J. C. *Minnesota Multiphasic Personality Inventory: Manual for administration and scoring.* New York: Psychological Corporation, 1967.

Helmstadter, G. C. An empirical comparison of methods for estimating profile similarity. *Educational and Psychological Measurement*, 1957, *17*, 71–82.

Henryssen, S. Gathering, analyzing, and using data on test items. In R. L. Thorndike (ed.), *Educational measurement* (2d ed.). Washington, D.C.: American Council on Education, 1971.

Hills, J. R. Use of measurement in selection and placement. In R. L. Thorndike (ed.), *Educational measurement* (2d ed.). Washington, D.C.: American Council on Education, 1971.

Holtzman, W. H. Personality structure. In P. R. Farnsworth, O. McNemar, and Q. McNemar (eds.), *Annual review of psychology*. Palo Alto, Calif.: Annual Reviews, 1965, pp. 119–156.

Holzinger, K. J., and Harman, H. H. *Factor analysis*. Chicago: University of Chicago Press, 1941.

Holzinger, K. J., and Swineford, F. A study in factor analysis: The stability of a bi-factor solution. *Supplementary Educational Monographs*. No. 48. Chicago: University of Chicago Press, 1939.

Horn, J. L. Integration of concepts of reliability and standard error of measurement. *Educational and Psychological Measurement*, 1971, *31*, 57–74.

Horn, J. L. Human abilities: A review of research and theory in the early 1970's. In M. Rosenzweig and L. Porter (eds.), *Annual review of psychology*, Vol. 27. Palo Alto, Calif.: Annual Reviews, 1976.

Horn, J. L., and Knapp, J. R. On the subjective character of the empirical base of Guilford's structure-of-intellect model. *Psychological Bulletin*, 1973, *80*, 33–43.

Horst, P. *Psychological measurement and prediction*. Belmont, Calif.: Wadsworth, 1966.

Hotelling, H. Analysis of a complex of statistical variables into principal components. *Journal of Educational Psychology*, 1933, *24*, 417–441 and 498–520.

Huitema, B. E. *Analysis of covariance*. New York: Wiley-Interscience (in press).

Hull, C. L. *A behavior system*. New Haven, Conn.: Yale University Press, 1952.

Humphreys, L. G. The organization of human abilities. *American Psychologist*, 1962, *17*, 475–483.

Husek, T. R. Acquiescence as a response set and as a personality characteristic. *Educational and Psychological Measurement*, 1961, *21*, 295–307.

Jennrich, R. I. Standard errors for obliquely rotated factor loadings. *Psychometrika*, 1973, *38*, 593–604.

Jennrich, R. I., and Thayer, D. T. A note on Lawley's formulas for standard errors in maximum likelihood factor analysis. *Psychometrika*, 1973, *38, 571–580*.

Jones, L. V. The nature of measurement. In R. L. Thorndike (ed.), *Educational measurement* (2d ed.). Washington, D.C.: American Council on Education, 1971.

Jöreskog, K. G. Analyzing psychological data by structural analysis of covariance matrices. In D. H. Krantz, R. C. Atkinson, R. D. Luce, and P. Suppes (eds.), *Contemporary developments in mathematical psychology: Vol. 2. Measurement, psychophysics, and neural information processing*. San Francisco: Freeman, 1974.

Kaiser, H. F. The varimax criterion for analytic rotation in factor analysis. *Psychometrika*, 1958, *23*, 187–200.

Kaiser, H. F. A second-generation Little Jiffy. *Psychometrika*, 1970, *35*, 401–415.

Kaiser, H. F., and Rice, J. Little Jiffy Mark IV. *Educational and Psychological Measurement*, 1974, *34*, 111–117.

Kelly, E. L., and Fiske, D. W. *The prediction of performance in clinical psychology*. Ann Arbor, Mich.: University of Michigan Press, 1951.

Kendall, L. M. The effects of varying time limits on test validity. *Educational and Psychological Measurement*, 1964, *24*, 789–800.

Kendall, M. G. *Rank correlation methods*. London: Griffin, 1948.

Kennedy, J. J. The eta coefficient in complex ANOVA designs. *Educational and Psychological Measurement*, 1970, *30*, 885–889.

Kerlinger, F. N. *Foundations of behavioral research* (2d ed.). New York: Holt, 1973.

Kerlinger, F. N., and Pedhazur, E. J. *Multiple regression in behavioral research*. New York: Holt, 1973.

Klopfer, W. G., and Taulbee, E. S. Projective tests. In M. Rosenzweig and L. Porter (eds.), *Annual review of psychology*, Vol. 27. Palo Alto, Calif.: Annual Reviews, 1976.

Krantz, D. H., Atkinson, R. C., Luce, R. D., and Suppes, P. (eds.). *Contemporary developments in mathematical psychology:* Vol. 2. *Measurement, psychophysics, and neural information processing.* San Francisco: Freeman, 1974.

Krathwohl, D. R., and Payne, D. A. Defining and assessing educational objectives. In R. L. Thorndike (ed.), *Educational measurement* (2d ed.). Washington, D.C.: American Council on Education, 1971.

Kruskal, J. B. Multidimensional scaling by optimizing goodness of fit to a nonmetric hypothesis. *Psychometrika*, 1964, *29*, 1–27.

Kruskal, J. B., and Shepard, R. N. A nonmetric variety of linear factor analysis. *Psychometrika*, 1974, *39*, 123–157.

Kuder, F. Some principles of interest measurement. *Educational and Psychological Measurement*, 1970, *30*, 205–226.

Lewis, D. *Quantitative methods in psychology.* New York: McGraw-Hill, 1960.

Likert, R. A technique for the measurement of attitudes. *Archives of Psychology*, 1932, No. 140.

Lingoes, J. C., and Roskam, E. E. A mathematical and empirical analysis of two multidimensional scaling algorithms. *Psychometrika Monograph Supplement*, No. 19, 1973, *38* (Part 2).

Loevinger, J. Objective tests as instruments of psychological theory. *Psychological Reports* (Monograph No. 9), 1957, *3*, 635–694.

Lord, F. M. The relation of the reliability of multiple-choice tests to the distribution of item difficulties. *Psychometrika*, 1952, *17*, 181–194. (*a*)

Lord, F. M. A theory of test scores. *Psychometric Monograph*, 1952, No. 7. (*b*)

Lord, F. M. A study of speed factors in tests and academic grades. *Psychometrika*, 1956, *21*, 31–50.

Lord, F. M. Formula scoring and validity. *Educational and Psychological Measurement*, 1963, *23*, 663–672.

Lord, F. M. Individualized testing and item characteristic curve theory. In D. H. Krantz, R. C. Atkinson, R. D. Luce, and P. Suppes (eds.), *Contemporary developments in mathematical psychology:* Vol. 2. *Measurement, psychophysics, and neural information processing.* San Francisco: Freeman, 1974.

Lord, F. M. *Optimal number of choices per item—a comparison of four approaches,* Research Bulletin RB-76-4. Princeton, N.J.: Educational Testing Service, January 1976.

Lord, F. M., and Novick, M. R. *Statistical theories of mental tests.* Reading, Mass.: Addison-Wesley, 1968.

MacCallum, R. C. Relations between factor analysis and multidimensional scaling. *Psychological Bulletin*, 1974, *81*, 505–516.

Masling, J. The influences of situational and interpersonal variables in projective testing. *Psychological Bulletin*, 1960, *57*, 65–85.

Masters, J. R. The relationship between number of response categories and reliability of Likert-type questionnaires. *Journal of Educational Measurement*, 1974, *11*, 49–53.

Maxwell, A. E. Canonical variate analysis when the variables are dichotomous. *Educational and Psychological Measurement*, 1961, *21*, 259–272.

McClelland, G., and Coombs, C. H. ORDMET: A general algorithm for constructing all numerical solutions to ordered metric data. *Psychometrika*, 1975, *40*, 269–290.

McGinn, N. F., Harburg, E., Julius, S., and McLeod, J. M. Psychological correlates of blood pressure. *Psychological Bulletin*, 1964, *61*, 209–219.

McNemar, Q. *Psychological statistics.* New York: Wiley, 1962.

McQuitty, L. L., and Koch, V. L. Highest column entry hierarchial clustering: A redevelopment and elaboration of elementary linkage analysis. *Educational and Psychological Measurement*, 1976, *36*, 243–258.

Messick, S. J. Beyond structure: In search of functional models of psychological processes. *Psychometrika*, 1972, *37*, 357–375.

Messick, S. J., and Abelson, R. P. The additive constant problem in multidimensional scaling. *Psychometrika*, 1956, *21*, 1-17.

Messick, S. J., and Ross, J. (eds.). *Measurement in personality and cognition.* New York: Wiley, 1962.

Miller, T. W., and Weiss, D. J. *Effects of time limits on test-taking behavior,* Research Report 76-2. Minneapolis: University of Minnesota, April 1976.

Molish, H. B. Projective methodologies. In P. Mussen and M. Rosenzweig (eds.), *Annual review of psychology,* Vol. 23. Palo Alto, Calif.: Annual Reviews, 1972.

Morrison, E. J. On test variance and the dimensions of the measurement situation. *Educational and Psychological Measurement,* 1960, *20*, 231-250.

Mulaik, S. A. *The foundations of factor analysis.* New York: McGraw-Hill, 1972.

Muldoon, J. F., and Ray, O. S. A comparison of pattern similarity as measured by six statistical techniques and eleven clinicians. *Educational and Psychological Measurement,* 1958, *18*, 775-781.

Myers, I. B. *The Myers-Briggs Type Indicator: Manual.* Princeton, N.J.: Educational Testing Service, 1962.

Neuhaus, J. O., and Wrigley, C. The Quartimax method: An analytical approach to orthogonal simple structure. *British Journal of Statistical Psychology,* 1954, *7*, 81-91.

Nie, N. H., Hull, C. H., Jenkins, J. G., Steinbrenner, K., and Bent, D. H. *Statistical package for the social sciences* (2d ed.). New York: McGraw-Hill, 1975.

Nunnally, J. C. An investigation of some propositions of self-conception: The case of Miss Sun. *Journal of Abnormal and Social Psychology,* 1955, *50*, 87-92.

Nunnally, J. C. *Popular conceptions of mental health: Their development and change.* New York: Holt, 1961.

Nunnally, J. C. The analysis of profile data. *Psychological Bulletin,* 1962, *59*, 311-319.

Nunnally, J. C. *Psychometric theory.* New York: McGraw-Hill, 1967.

Nunnally, J. C. *Introduction to psychological measurement.* New York: McGraw-Hill, 1970.

Nunnally, J. C. *Educational measurement and evaluation* (2d ed.). New York: McGraw-Hill, 1972.

Nunnally, J. C. Vanishing individual differences—just stick your head in the sand and they will go away. *Journal of Instructional Psychology,* 1976, *3*, 28-40.

Nunnally, J. C., and Hodges, W. F. Some dimensions of individual differences in word association. *Journal of Verbal Learning and Verbal Behavior,* 1965, *4*, 82-88.

Nunnally, J. C., and Husek, T. R. The phony language examination: An approach to the measurement of response bias. *Educational and Psychological Measurement,* 1958, *18*, 275-282.

Nunnally, J. C., Knott, P. D., Duchnowski, A., and Parker, R. Pupillary response as a general measure of activation. *Perception and Psychophysics,* 1967, *2*, 149-155.

Nunnally, J. C., and Lemond, L. C. Exploratory behavior and human development. In H. W. Reese (ed.), *Advances in child development and behavior,* Vol. 8, New York: Academic, 1973.

Osgood, C. E. Studies on the generality of affective meaning systems. *American Psychologist,* 1962, *17*, 10-28.

Osgood, C. E., and Suci, G. J. A measure of relation determined by both mean differences and profile information. *Psychological Bulletin,* 1952, *49*, 251-262.

Osgood, C. E., and Tannenbaum, P. *The measurement of meaning.* Urbana, Ill.: University of Illinois Press, 1957.

Peterson, D. R. Scope and generality of verbally defined personality factors. *Psychological Review,* 1965, *72*, 48-59.

Plumlee, L. B. The effect of difficulty and chance success on item-test correlation and on test reliability. *Psychometrika,* 1952, *17*, 69-86.

Price, D. B. A group approach to the analysis of individual differences in the randomness of guessing behavior on multiple-choice tests and the development of scoring methods to take such differences into account. *Research Bulletin* No. 64-59. Princeton, N.J.: Educational Testing Service, 1964.

Rimland, B. The effects of varying time limits and of using "right answer not given" in experimental forms of the U.S. Navy Arithmetic Test. *Educational and Psychological Measurement*, 1960, *20*, 533-539.

Rokeach, M. *The nature of human values.* London: Cassell, Collier-Macmillan, 1973.

Romney, A. K., Shepard, R. N., and Nerlove, S. B. *Multidimensional scaling:* Vol. 2. *Theory and applications in the behavioral sciences.* New York: Seminar Press, 1972.

Rorer, L. G. The great response-style myth. *Psychological Bulletin*, 1965, *63*, 129-156.

Rotter, J. B., Rafferty, J. E., and Schachtitz, E. Validation of the Rotter Incomplete Sentences Blank for college screening. *Journal of Consulting Psychology*, 1949, *13*, 348-356.

Sawrey, W. L., Keller, L., and Conger, J. J. An objective method of grouping profiles by distance functions and its relation to factor analysis. *Educational and Psychological Measurement*, 1960, *20*, 651-673.

Sechrest, L. Personality. In M. Rosenzweig and L. Porter (eds.), *Annual review of psychology,* Vol. 27. Palo Alto, Calif.: Annual Reviews, 1976.

Shepard, R. N. The analysis of proximities: Multidimensional scaling with an unknown distance function. I. *Psychometrika*, 1962, *27*, 125-140. (*a*)

Shepard, R. N. The analysis of proximities: Multidimensional scaling with an unknown distance function. II. *Psychometrika*, 1962, *27*, 219-246. (*b*)

Shepard, R. N. Introduction to Volume I. In R. N. Shepard, A. K. Romney, and S. B. Nerlove (eds.), *Multidimensional scaling,* Vol. 1. New York: Seminar Press, 1972.

Shepard, R. N. Representation of structure in similarity data: Problems and prospects. *Psychometrika*, 1974, *39*, 373-421.

Shepard, R. N., Romney, A. K., and Nerlove, S. B. (eds.). *Multidimensional scaling.* Volume 1: *Theory.* New York: Seminar Press, 1972.

Shure, G. H., and Miles, R. S. Note of caution on the factor analysis of the MMPI. *Psychological Bulletin*, 1965, *63*, 14-18.

Snider, J. G., and Osgood, C. E. (eds.). *Semantic differential technique.* Chicago: Aldine, 1969.

Spearman, C. "General intelligence" objectively determined and measured. *American Journal of Psychology*, 1904, *15*, 201-293.

Spearman, C. *The abilities of man.* New York: Macmillan, 1927.

Stanley, J. C. Reliability. In R. L. Thorndike (ed.), *Educational measurement* (2d ed.). Washington, D.C.: American Council on Education, 1971.

Stanley, J. C., and Wang, M. D. Weighting test items and test-item options, an overview of the analytical and empirical literature. *Educational and Psychological Measurement*, 1970, *30*, 21-35.

Stephenson, W. The study of behavior. Chicago: University of Chicago Press, 1953.

Stern, J. A., and McDonald, D. G. Physiological correlates of mental disease. In P. R. Farnsworth, O. McNemar, and Q. McNemar (eds.), *Annual Review of Psychology,* Palo Alto, Calif.: Annual Reviews, 1965, p. 225-264.

Stevens, S. S. Problems and methods of psychophysics. *Psychological Bulletin*, 1958, *55*, 177-196.

Stevens, S. S. Ratio scales, partition scales, and confusion scales. In H. Gulliksen and S. Messick (eds.), *Psychological scaling: Theory and applications.* New York: Wiley, 1960.

Tatsuoka, M. M. *Multivariate analysis.* New York: Wiley, 1971.

Taylor, J. A. A personality scale of manifest anxiety. *Journal of Abnormal and Social Psychology*, 1953, *48*, 285-290.

Thorndike, R. L. (ed.). *Educational measurement* (2d ed.). Washington, D.C.: American Council on Education, 1971.

Thurstone, L. L. A law of comparative judgment. *Psychological Review*, 1927, *34*, 273-286.

Thurstone, L. L. A factorial study of perception. *Psychometric Monographs*, 1944, No. 4.

Thurstone, L. L. *Multiple-factor analysis.* Chicago: University of Chicago Press, 1947.

Thurstone, T. G. Primary mental abilities of children. *Educational and Psychological Measurement*, 1941, *1*, 105-116.

Tiedeman, D.V., Bryan, J. G., and Rulon, P. J. An application of the multiple discriminant function to data from the airman classification battery. *Research Bulletin* No. 52–37. San Antonio, Tex.: Lackland Air Force Base, 1952.

Timm, N. H. *Multivariate analysis.* Monterey, Calif.: Brooks/Cole, 1975.

Toops, H. A. A comparison, by work limit and time limit, of item analysis indices for practical test construction. *Educational and Psychological Measurement*, 1960, *20*, 251–266.

Torgerson, W. S. *Theory and methods of scaling.* New York: Wiley, 1958.

Tryon, R. C., and Bailey, D. E. *Cluster analysis.* New York: McGraw-Hill, 1970.

Tyler, L. E. Human abilities. In P. Mussen and M. Rosenzweig (eds.), *Annual review of psychology*, Vol. 23. Palo Alto, Calif.: Annual Reviews, 1972.

Ulrich, L., and Trumbo, D. The selection interview since 1949. *Psychological Bulletin*, 1965, *63*, 100–116.

Van de Geer, J. P. *Introduction to multivariate analysis for the social sciences.* San Francisco: Freeman, 1971.

Waller, M. I. Estimating guessing tendency. *Research Bulletin* 74–33. Princeton, N.J.: Educational Testing Service, August 1974.

Weiss, D. J. (ed.). *Computerized adaptive trait measurement: Problems and prospects.* Minneapolis: Department of Psychology, University of Minnesota, November 1975.

Weiss, D. J. *Final report: Computerized ability testing, 1972–1975.* Minneapolis: Department of Psychology, University of Minnesota, April 1976.

Wenger, M. A. Studies of autonomic balance in Army Air Forces personnel. *Comparative Psychology Monographs*, 1948, *19*, No. 101.

Wesman, A. G. Some effects of speed in test use. *Educational and Psychological Measurement*, 1960, *20*, 267–274.

Wesman, A. G. Writing the test item. In R. L. Thorndike (ed.), *Educational measurement* (2d ed.). Washington, D.C.: American Council on Education, 1971.

Wiggins, J. S. *Personality and prediction: Principles of personality assessment.* Reading, Mass.: Addison-Wesley, 1973.

Wish, M., Deutsch, M., and Biener, L. Differences in perceived similarity of nations. In A. K. Romney, R. N. Shepard, and S. R. Nerlove (eds.), *Multidimensional scaling*, Vol. 2. New York: Seminar Press, 1972.

Wittenborn, J. R. Contributions and current status of *Q*-methodology. *Psychological Bulletin*, 1961, *58*, 132–142.

Woodworth, R. S. *Personal data sheet.* Chicago: Stoelting, 1918.

Wright, B. D., and Douglas, G. A. Best test design and self-tailored testing. *Research Memo No. 19*. Chicago: University of Chicago, Statistical Laboratory, Department of Education, 1975.

Young, G., and Householder, A. S. Discussion of a set of points in terms of their mutual distances. *Psychometrika*, 1938, *3*, 19–22.

Zavala, A. Development of the forced-choice rating scale technique. *Psychological Bulletin*, 1965, *63*, 117–124.

# INDEXES

# NAME INDEX

Abbott, R. D., 587, 679
Abelson, R. P., 683
American Psychological Association, 113, 678
Anastasi, A., 526, 531, 543, 587, 678
Angoff, W. H., 264, 678
Archer, C. O., 422, 678
Arenberg, D., 568, 680
Atkinson, R. C., 85, 681, 682
Azuma, H., 209, 679

Baggley, A. R., 150, 678
Bailey, D. E., 429, 441, 442, 444, 467, 497, 685
Bechtoldt, H. P., 113, 678
Bent, D. H., 403, 683
Bentler, P. M., 667, 678
Berg, I. A., 670, 678
Biener, L., 491, 492, 685
Binet, A., 100, 504, 505, 507, 519, 549, 678
Bock, R. D., 54, 58, 60, 84, 678
Brown, S. R., 613, 678
Bryan, J. G., 460, 461, 685
Burt, C., 428, 508, 678

Campbell, D. T., 113, 591, 593, 678
Carroll, J. B., 526, 679
Cattell, R. B., 426, 549, 553, 679
Cliff, N., 488, 680
Cliff, R., 651, 679

Comrey, A. L., 404, 412, 413, 436, 679
Conger, J. J., 444, 684
Cook, S. W., 591, 593, 679
Cooley, W. W., 463, 464, 679
Coombs, C. H., 18, 34, 60, 61, 75, 85, 471, 488, 493–495, 679, 682
Cramer, E. M., 401, 679
Cromwell, R. L., 575, 582, 679
Cronbach, L. J., 89, 90, 113, 209, 222, 224, 227, 240, 255, 441, 442, 497, 589, 637, 679

Damarin, F. L., 661, 679
Darwin, C., 502, 503
Dawes, R. M., 18, 34, 61, 75, 85, 471, 493, 495, 679
Deutsch, M., 491, 492, 685
Douglas, G. A., 82, 323, 685
Duchnowski, A., 576, 683

Ebel, R. L., 653, 679
Edwards, A. L., 78, 553, 555, 557, 561, 587, 603, 604, 626, 661, 676, 679

Falmagne, J. C., 62, 680
Farina, A., 568, 680
Fechner, G., 62
Ferguson, G. A., 523, 680
Fiedler, F. E., 427, 680

# SUBJECT INDEX